W9-BHS-242

MARY AND JOHN GRAY LIBRARY
LAMAR UNIVERSITY

Purchased

with the

Student Library Use Fee

LTX
9-23-1
Gle

GLENCOE PHYSICAL SCIENCE

TEXAS

PHYSICAL SCIENCE REPORTS
and
TAAS PRACTICE EXAM

Superconductors

Stormy Weather Over Texas

BEC—A New Form of Matter

Anyone for a Game of Buckyball?

Down Under—In Texas

Some Calls of the Wild

The Wake Shield Facility

GLENCOE
McGraw-Hill

DISCARDED
LAMAR UNIVERSITY LIBRARY

SUPERCONDUCTORS

Basic Research—Texas Style

What do supermarkets, Superman, superstars, supersonic jets, and superconductors have in common? Nothing really except the prefix *super-*. *Super*, as you already know, means "over and above, more than, a higher degree than," and so on. Supermarkets are large stores that sell many different types of products. Superman, the man of steel, is a fictitious character who has extraordinary powers not possessed by other humans. Superstars are singers, actors and actresses, and athletes whose talents exceed those of their peers. A supersonic jet travels faster than the speed of sound. Now, what do you think the term *superconductor* means?

Electrifying!

A conductor is a material that allows electrons (electrical current) to move easily through it. Because no normal conductor is perfect, all of them tend to resist this flow of energy to varying degrees. As a result, normal conductors lose energy as heat because of friction. This characteristic is useful in hair dryers, toasters, and curling irons. A superconducting material, on the other hand, is a substance that allows electrons to flow through it with no resistance and therefore no loss of energy.

Chilled Out

Electrons are negatively charged and generally repel one another. At temperatures near absolute zero (−460°F or −273°C), though, electrons in superconducting materials tend to pair up. This attraction allows the pair to travel past any imperfections in a material without ever losing energy. That means that a wire made of a superconducting material could carry an electric current forever. The challenge is to find superconducting materials that can be made into wire. Since their discovery, superconductors have been formed by chilling alloys, elements, and even compounds with liquid helium or liquid nitrogen. Some superconductors, the low-temperature ones, can be cooled only with liquid helium. High-temperature superconductors operate at temperatures between 94 K (−290°F or −143°C) and 134 K. These materials can be cooled with inexpensive liquid nitrogen.

The Texas Center for Superconductivity

Among the forerunners in the research on superconductivity is Dr. Paul Chu at the University of Houston. Dr. Chu astounded the world in the late 1980s when he and a former graduate student, Dr. May-Kuen Wu, found superconductivity in copper oxide at 94 K. This discovery opened up the field of high-temperature superconductivity.

Dr. Chu's breakthrough led to the founding of the Texas Center for Superconductivity in 1992. It is the largest laboratory of its kind in the United States. At the Center, Dr. Chu and other scientists hope to develop new and better

Dr. Paul Chu

A maglev train rides on a cushion of air and does not touch the track. These nearly friction-less trains travel at speeds of 250 mph or more. Maglev trains are in use in Germany, England, and Japan.

superconductors and find practical uses for them. Many breakthroughs have already been made. In 1993, the Houston researchers discovered compounds that stayed superconductive at a temperature of 160 K. That is still extremely cold for human beings, but for a superconductor, it is almost toasty—"only" −171°F.

Super Uses for Superconductors

Much work remains to be done, however. One of the biggest problems researchers have to solve is how to make practical devices out of ceramics, which cannot be easily made into wire or film. Another problem is increasing the load of electrical current that superconductors can carry. But Dr. Chu believes that it is only a matter of time before the solutions to these and other problems are found.

He won't provide details, but Dr. Chu said the Center is studying an innovative way to use superconductors that would have tremendous market potential. "I'd like to see commercial projects come out of the Center . . . My interests are very broad," said the energetic physicist. "That's why I'm running around like a chicken without a head." If he's right about the potential of superconductivity, Dr. Chu is likely to be a busy man far into the future.

HERE TODAY, GONE TOMORROW?

Science is a process. The work of most scientists builds on the research of those before them. Sometimes, a scientist's work will disprove long-held ideas; sometimes the work expands on previous knowledge.

Use reference books to find out more about the work done on superconductivity during this century. Find out how maglev trains work. Based on your findings, do you think other applications of this research will become an everyday reality in your lifetime, or is high-temperature superconductivity a futuristic idea? Discuss your ideas with the class.

STORMY WEATHER OVER TEXAS

Stormy Energy

The ultimate source of Earth's energy is the sun. Some solar radiation is absorbed by the air and the planet's surface. Some of the energy is then reflected back into space; some is scattered by clouds in the atmosphere. Transfer of this energy occurs via radiation, convection, and conduction. A combination of these processes and interactive forces—gravity, friction, air pressure—produces the atmospheric phenomena known as weather.

Thunderstorms—How They Form

Thunderstorms are violent examples of convection caused by temperature imbalances in Earth's atmosphere. A thunderstorm occurs when relatively warm air at or near Earth's surface is forced rapidly upward through cooler, overlying air masses, resulting in an updraft. As the air pressure decreases, warm air expands and cools because some of its thermal energy is lost. As a result of this updraft, the air becomes saturated, condensation takes place, and a cumulus cloud begins to form.

As water vapor continues to condense, heat is released. This heat becomes the main source of energy for the cloud that forms. When water droplets within the cloud become large enough, gravity causes them to fall to Earth as rain. Although this rain usually lasts no more than 30 minutes, the amount that falls can be enormous. During 1995, a single thunderstorm dropped at least 10 inches of rain over some parts of Texas.

From your local newspaper or the nearest National Weather Station, find out the average number of thunderstorms your area in Texas experiences each year.

Lightning

During a thunderstorm, an intense electrical field is produced within the storm cloud. The lower part of the thundercloud has an overall negative charge. The upper portion of the cloud is positively charged. As the cloud passes over Earth, it causes a positive electrical field on the ground below. Lightning occurs when the difference between these opposite charges overcomes the air resistance. The potential difference between the ends of a flash of lightning can reach hundreds of millions of volts, making lightning dangerous. In fact, in a 25 year period, 130 people in Texas died after being struck by lightning.

Lightning over a city such as Dallas can be dramatic.

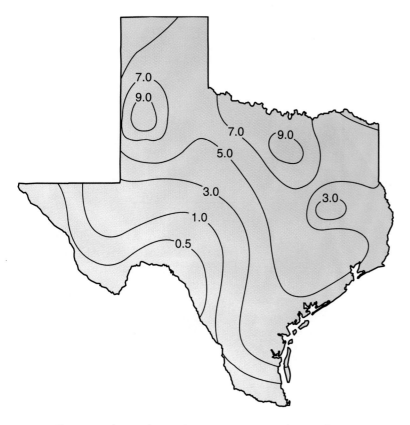

The map above shows the average annual tornado incidence per 10 000 square miles.

Texas Twisters

Tornadoes are violently rotating columns of air that move across land. A tornado is more short-lived than a thunderstorm. However, twisters are often more destructive than thunderstorms because of strong updrafts—high winds that can exceed 200 miles per hour—and great differences in air pressure. Rapid drops in air pressure have exceeded 200 pounds per square foot, which may cause buildings to literally explode as a tornado passes.

Look at the map above that shows average annual tornado incidence in Texas. How many tornadoes are likely to occur in your area in a given year?

HURRICANES

A hurricane is a third severe weather phenomenon that threatens residents of Texas—in particular, people who live along the Gulf coast. In fact, one of the most destructive hurricanes in Texas history occurred in 1900 and literally destroyed the city of Galveston. More than 15 feet of water washed away 3600 homes, killed 6000 people, and left another 10 000 homeless.

Find out how a hurricane forms, where its energy comes from, when such a storm is most likely to affect Texas, how to prepare for such a storm, and where to go in the event of an approaching hurricane.

Make a brochure that includes a detailed drawing of the stages of a hurricane, a thunderstorm, and a tornado. Label each with information about wind speed, air pressure, and precipitation. Include safety precautions. After receiving permission, distribute your brochure throughout your school.

BEC—A NEW FORM OF MATTER

Another State of Matter?

Scientists generally recognize four different states of matter—solids, liquids, gases, and plasma. You may already know that the atoms in each of these states of matter move in a different way. However, as temperature drops, atoms slow down. Is it possible to stop atoms completely? In 1924, Albert Einstein hypothesized that a fifth state of matter, now called a *condensate*, would form if a gas were cooled to absolute zero (about −460°F). He predicted that if a gas were cooled to such a low temperature, some of the atoms would slow down so much that they would condense and form a unique type of matter. It was further suggested that their motion would essentially be zero, and the atoms would form what might be called a super atom.

Rounding Up Rubidium, Linking Lithium

In 1995, two separate teams of researchers chilled different gases in an attempt to form the super atoms hypothesized in 1924. The first team, working at the Joint Institute for Laboratory Astrophysics in Boulder, Colorado, supercooled rubidium atoms. Rubidium atoms repel one another at low temperatures. The result was a super atom—a Bose-Einstein condensate, or BEC for short. It is named after Einstein and Indian scientist Satyendra Nath Bose, who collaborated with Einstein on a variety of scientific studies in the early 1900s.

The second team of physicists, led by Dr. Randy Hulet at Rice University in Houston, Texas, conducted a similar experiment using lithium atoms, which are attracted to each other at low temperatures. These researchers hypothesized that, when chilled, the atoms would condense to form a high-density liquid or gas.

Dr. Hulet's apparatus for producing BEC

Lasers were used to cool the lithium gas in a small container to about 100 billionth of a degree above absolute zero. Spinning magnets were used to trap some of the atoms in place long enough to form the condensate. The atoms merged, or came together, to form a blob-like cloud. Hulet hypothesized that because the super-cooled atoms apparently stopped moving, they were able to overcome the weak attraction they normally have for one another and they formed a condensate.

Now You See It, Now You Don't!

No one actually saw the condensate produced by either research team. So, you might ask, how did either team know they actually produced BEC? After the atoms had been chilled in the magnetic field, the magnets were allowed to spin on for several minutes. Then, the magnets were turned off and both teams passed a weak laser beam through the cloud of trapped atoms. A shadow produced by the tiny amount of condensate revealed its presence on a video screen.

Useful or Not?

The production of a small amount of a new form of matter is a step into new areas of science. Often it is years before a new idea or material becomes useful. Do all scientific ideas have to be useful? Be a scientifically literate person and watch for developments in BEC over your lifetime.

BACK TO THE DRAWING BOARD

Think about what you now know about this fifth state of matter. Use a paper punch to make 50 white disks. Use these disks, a piece of black construction paper, and some glue to illustrate the similarities and differences among a solid, a liquid, a gas, plasma, and a Bose-Einstein condensate. (Use ten disks for each model.) On separate squares of white paper, write three or four sentences explaining the arrangement and properties of atoms in each of your models. Attach each description next to the appropriate model.

ANYONE FOR A GAME OF BUCKYBALL?

A Different Kind of Ball Game

Unlike football, basketball, or baseball, buckyball isn't a game. The term is actually a nickname for an allotrope of carbon whose structure resembles a large, hollow soccer ball. Just what is this amazing buckyball? Read on to find out!

Carbon atom

A model of a molecule of buckminsterfullerene shows 60 carbon atoms.

Dr. Richard Smalley

Buckminsterfullerenes

Buckminsterfullerene, or the buckyball, was "discovered" in 1985 by Richard Smalley and a team of researchers at Rice University in Houston, Texas. The researchers placed carbon into a device that vaporized it with the help of a laser. The sample was then cooled in helium and ejected into a chamber. When the carbon gas condensed, it formed tiny spherical structures, each made of 60 carbon atoms. These carbon allotropes resembled the geodesic domes pioneered by R. Buckminster Fuller and were later named after Fuller.

What can you do with a buckyball?

Since buckyballs were isolated, scientists have worked to find applications for them. In one instance, they are trying to link buckyballs to form buckytubes, which might prove to be the strongest, thinnest fibers known. In addition, buckyballs might be used as conductors, semiconductors, and even superconductors. Perhaps the buckyball's unique structure could serve as a microelectronics substrate to which atoms could bond. The lubricating property of carbon gave other scientists the idea of using buckyballs as lubricants.

Still other scientists think the unique allotrope might act as an AIDS inhibitor. In fact, in 1993, researchers working independently in California and Georgia found that the size of a buckyball allows it to slip into certain areas on an HIV enzyme. Once in place, the carbon allotrope appeared to stop the production of new viruses in laboratory cultures. Work continues in this area.

Filling the Void

As you can see from the illustration on the opposite page, a buckyball is hollow. Since its discovery, many researchers have tried success-fully to "shoot" atoms into the center of the buckyball. One group of researchers was able to fill buckyballs with helium atoms. The researchers think that the resulting substance could be used as a chemical tracer. Because helium compounds are rare in nature, the unique helium-carbon compound could be used to track the spread of pollutants in a river and pinpoint the source of entry of the chemi-cals into the body of water. The same group of scientists was also able to incorporate neon into the buckyball structure. Other fullerene researchers found that the hollow space of a buckyball could be used as a package of sorts to store and protect delicate or unstable substances.

The Future of the Buckyball

Scientists in many laboratories around the world continue to experiment with buckyballs and their properties. The Texas team has focused its research with buckyballs to devel-oping and producing hollow car-bon fibers—only a molecule in diameter—into which metal atoms can be inserted. The Rice team predicts that these fibers will be extremely strong and be able to conduct electricity. These two properties alone will make buckytubes ex-tremely useful in many fields of study, particu-larly microelectronics.

BUILDING A BUCKYBALL

Carefully study the illus-tration of the buckyball on the opposite page. Work with two or three other students to build a three-dimensional model of a buckyball using clay and thin, flexible straws. Determine the number of straw pieces you will need. Compare your fig-ure to the numbers deter-mined by each member of your group. Cut the straws into the required number of pieces, making sure each piece is the same length. What do the straws represent? What does each piece of clay represent?

DOWN UNDER—IN TEXAS

Long Ago and Far Away

Have you or your family ever been spelunking? "What's spelunking?" you may be asking yourself. Spelunking is the sport of exploring caves. Some of the best spelunking spots in Texas lie in the Hill Country. How did these spectacular caverns form?

As you probably already know, Earth is a dynamic planet. You may have observed first-hand how beaches change with each wave that laps onto the shore or how heavy rains can quickly wash away soil from non-vegetated areas. These changes to our planet occur quickly. Other changes take place over hundreds, thousands, or even millions of years. Ocean basins open and close. Mountains are built up by forces deep within Earth and are weathered and eroded by processes at or near Earth's surface. Texas is no exception to these processes.

Several hundreds of millions of years ago, much of West Texas was covered by warm, shallow seas. The tropical waters were rich in two ions—Ca^{2+} (calcium ion) and CO_3^{2-} (carbonate ion), among many others. As CO_2 in the water evaporated or was lost to photosynthesis, the mineral calcite ($CaCO_3$) began to precipitate from the salty waters. As the calcite formed, it slowly built up on the ocean floor, where it gradually hardened to form a sedimentary rock called limestone.

Dissolution of Limestone

As the water receded over geologic time, thick beds of limestone became exposed at Earth's surface. Over a period of thousands of years, surface waters rich in carbon dioxide flowed over the limestone. The presence of CO_2 gas in the water caused the formation of a weak acid called carbonic acid. The slightly acidic waters washed over the rocks and trickled down into the tiny cracks etched by the acid. Over thousands of years, passages, pits, and chambers formed beneath Earth's surface.

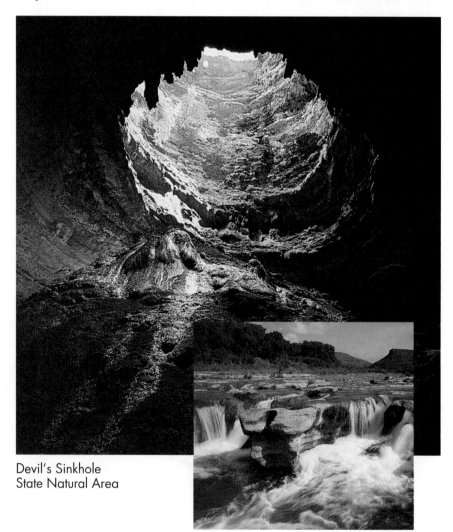

Devil's Sinkhole
State Natural Area

Devil's River cascades over limestone outcrops

Stalactites forming on cave ceiling

Stalactites and Stalagmites

The acidic water that shapes caves often continues to seep from the ceilings and floors of the caverns, forming stalactites and stalagmites. Icicle-like protrusions that hang from a cave's ceiling are called *stalactites*. Stalactites form as calcite precipitates from the acidic solution. *Stalagmites* form in much the same way. They build up from the cave's floor in pillar form. If these pillars become connected to overhanging stalactites, a cave column forms.

Some Texas Cave Dwellers

Most people think of caves as spectacular works of nature. While this perception is often true, few people realize that in addition to their aesthetic beauty, caves are habitats for many of Texas's unique fauna. Salamanders, lizards, and spiders are a few Texas cave residents. And the world's largest colony of bats—an estimated 20 million Mexican freetails—lives in Bracken Cave between Austin and San Antonio.

CREATING YOUR OWN CAVE

Obtain a piece of limestone and some acid from your teacher. Carefully use the dropper to apply the acid solution to your rock. What happens when the acid is placed on the limestone? Write an equation for this reaction. **CAUTION:** *Wear goggles and an apron and wash your hands.*

Fill two clean glass jars with very warm tap water. In each, make a saturated solution using baking soda. Twist two strands of wool yarn to form a single thread. Put one end of the thread into each of the jars. Between the jars, put a small piece of waxed paper. Observe what happens as the water evaporates. Explain how these formations are similar to cave formations.

SOME CALLS OF THE WILD

Dolphins Sound Off!

An estimated 35 000 Atlantic bottlenose dolphins live along the Texas coastline in the warm, salty waters of the Gulf of Mexico. These dolphins, along with seals and porpoises, belong to a group of marine mammals called *cetaceans*. Cetaceans have neither sound-producing vocal cords nor external ears—merely small, wax-filled holes on the sides of their heads. Yet these creatures rely strongly on their sense of sound to communicate and navigate. How have these animals become adapted to producing and sensing sounds in the deep blue sea?

Bottlenose dolphins emit a variety of groans, clicks, whistles, and squeals by pulsing air from a series of air sacs near the top of their nasal passages into a spongy organ in their foreheads called a melon. The melon focuses

Melon

the sound waves and projects them into a narrow beam near the front of the head. When this biological sonar strikes an object, it generates an echo. The echo is sensed by the dolphin's panbone, which is analogous to an ultrasensitive ear, in the animal's lower jaw. The bone transmits the message to the inner ear and finally to the dolphin's brain.

Animal, Vegetable, or Mineral?

The bottlenose dolphin's echolocation system is often used to locate objects. The time lapse between the dolphin's sending the signal and its return allows the animal to determine the distance between itself and a particular object. The intensity of the signal allows the cetacean to determine the position of the object.

Experiments with dolphins and porpoises have also shown that these cetaceans can use their echolocation systems to differentiate among objects of different sizes and compositions. In one study, dolphins were able to quickly locate a metal buckshot—only 1 mm in diameter—in a large pool of water. In another experiment, dolphins were able to differentiate between small metal discs of aluminum and copper. Even small pieces of fish that were located as far as 6 to 7 m (about 20 feet) from the mammals brought a response from the dolphins.

Dolphin Dialogues?

Not only can the bottlenose dolphins, which are common in Galveston Bay, locate objects such as food or mates with their sonar systems, but they also can use sounds in other ways. The sounds emitted by the Atlantic bottlenose dolphin can be used to communicate with other dolphins more than a mile away. Some researchers think that certain signals are used by the marine mammals to express the animal's emotional or physical state. A sound identified by scientists as a distress whistle is used to bring help. The bottlenose dolphins' biological sonar systems are also thought to be used by the animals to identify members of their pod (family group).

Do you hear what I hear?

The Atlantic bottlenose dolphin produces sounds with frequencies almost ten times higher than a human can produce (about 20 000 Hertz for a human vs. more than 160 000 Hz for a dolphin). Look at the graph below. Which group of animals produces sounds with the greatest range of frequencies? Which groups produce infrasonic sounds (those with frequencies below about 20 Hz)? Which groups are able to produce ultrasonic sounds (sounds emitted at frequencies greater than about 18 000 Hz)?

SOME MORE SOUNDS OF TEXAS

Find out about the sounds made and used by other animals in the Lone Star state. How did the state bird—the mockingbird—get its name? How do the hundreds of thousands of bats that live in the caves of Hill Country use sound? Is the screech owl misnamed? Does the chirping frog really chirp? Describe some of the calls made by a few of the songbirds of Texas.

Try to record some of the sounds made by various animals living in Texas.

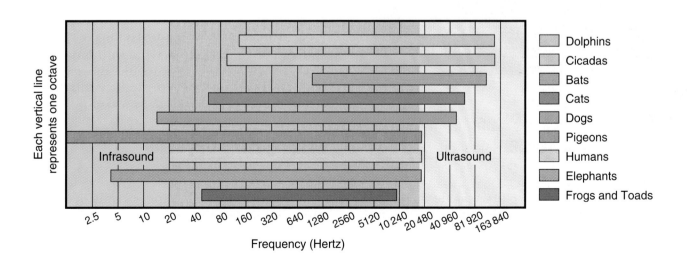

Each vertical line represents one octave

Infrasound   Ultrasound

Frequency (Hertz)

2.5 5 10 20 40 80 160 320 640 1280 2560 5120 10 240 20 480 40 960 81 920 163 840

Dolphins
Cicadas
Bats
Cats
Dogs
Pigeons
Humans
Elephants
Frogs and Toads

THE WAKE SHIELD FACILITY

Made in Space?

Take a look at the tag on your shirt or jacket. Were either of these pieces of clothing made in the United States? Check out your shoes—they were probably made in China, Brazil, or some other familiar country. Now, read the labels on some other objects or items you use every day. Where was each made?

Did any of the labels read "Made in Space"? Probably not. However, many experiments associated with the space program have allowed scientists to produce results or products not possible here on Earth. If successful, the Wake Shield Facility will allow significant advances in manufacturing in the field of microelectronics—specifically, cellular telephones, high-definition televisions, computers, and fiber-optics communications systems.

It's a Bird! It's a Plane! It's a Flying Saucer!

The Wake Shield Facility was designed and built by the Space Vacuum Epitaxy Center at the University of Houston. The Wake Shield Facility is a 3.6-meter diameter, 1.73 metric ton,

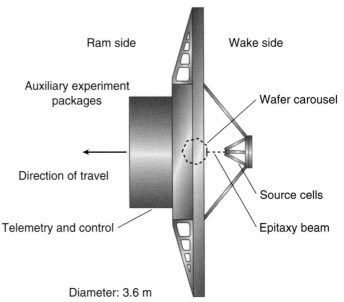

Wake Shield Facility

Ram side

Wake side

Auxiliary experiment packages

Wafer carousel

Direction of travel

Source cells

Telemetry and control

Epitaxy beam

Diameter: 3.6 m

25-million dollar, stainless steel, saucer-shaped satellite with two sides—a *ram* side and a *wake* side. Inside, experimental semiconductor chips and crystals are produced atom by atom, layer by layer. When deployed from the space shuttle, the Wake Shield Facility creates a vacuum wake that can push away any atoms that might contaminate the semiconducting materials being produced inside. The ram side of the satellite contains avionics equipment and an area for future space payloads.

Look at the sketch of the Wake Shield Facility shown above. Based on what you have just read, in which direction would the satellite have to travel in order to produce ultrapure semiconducting materials in its wake?

Making Pure Crystals

Producing semiconductor crystals involves preparing a surface with the desired atomic structure—making pits in it. Then, the pitted surface is bombarded with beams of molecules.

Atoms become attached to the pitted surface in the form of thin films. As the process continues, layer upon layer of atoms accumulate to form an ultrapure, semiconducting wafer or chip.

Two Down, Two to Go

In February of 1994, during its first of four planned missions into space, equipment aboard the Wake Shield Facility was to be used to produce nearly perfect crystals. However, water-vapor contamination from the space shuttle *Discovery* interfered with the production of ultrapure semiconducting materials.

In September of 1995, on its second mission, the Wake Shield Facility was deployed, and, in its three days of free flight, produced four hair-thin wafers as it hurtled through space at about 29 000 kilometers per hour. The 7 1/2-centimeter-wide semiconducting wafers took anywhere from three to eight hours to build. Scientists estimate that the ultrapure wafers should be 1000 to 10 000 times more contaminant free than similar semiconducting materials manufactured on Earth. Building chips in space is expensive. Discuss why science uses processes that may at first seem impractical.

SILICON SUBSTITUTES?

Today, the majority of semiconductors used in cellular telephones, computers, televisions, and the field of fiber optics are made of silicon. Find out what advantages and disadvantages this semiconducting material has over other semiconducting materials.

The Wake Shield Facility, shown here, is being retrieved in space after producing semiconducting chips.

PHYSIOGRAPHIC MAP OF TEXAS

Map Key

- High Plains
- Canadian Breaks
- Edwards Plateau
- Red Bed Plains
- Trans-Pecos Basin-Range
- Hill Country
- Lampasas Cut Plain
- Grand Prairie
- Cross Timbers
- Black Prairies

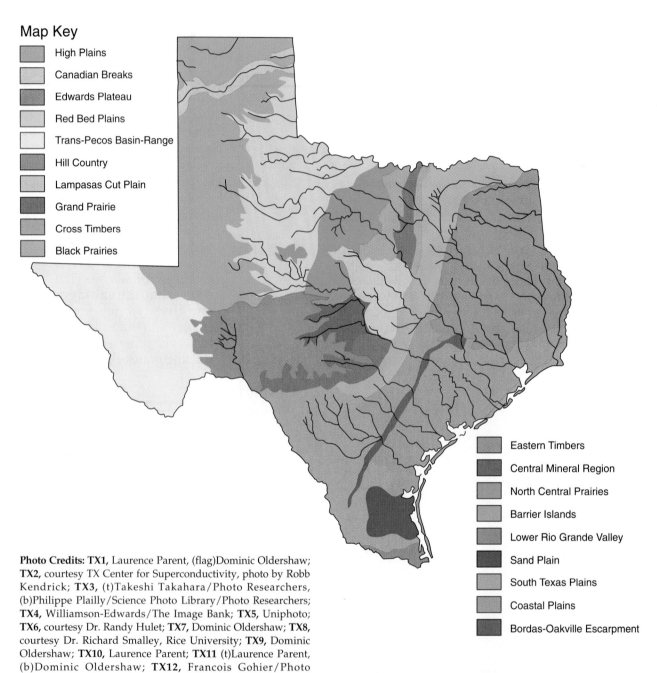

- Eastern Timbers
- Central Mineral Region
- North Central Prairies
- Barrier Islands
- Lower Rio Grande Valley
- Sand Plain
- South Texas Plains
- Coastal Plains
- Bordas-Oakville Escarpment

Photo Credits: TX1, Laurence Parent, (flag)Dominic Oldershaw; **TX2,** courtesy TX Center for Superconductivity, photo by Robb Kendrick; **TX3,** (t)Takeshi Takahara/Photo Researchers, (b)Philippe Plailly/Science Photo Library/Photo Researchers; **TX4,** Williamson-Edwards/The Image Bank; **TX5,** Uniphoto; **TX6,** courtesy Dr. Randy Hulet; **TX7,** Dominic Oldershaw; **TX8,** courtesy Dr. Richard Smalley, Rice University; **TX9,** Dominic Oldershaw; **TX10,** Laurence Parent; **TX11** (t)Laurence Parent, (b)Dominic Oldershaw; **TX12,** Francois Gohier/Photo Researchers; **TX13,** Robert and Linda Mitchell; **TX14,** Dominic Oldershaw; **TX15,** (t)Dominic Oldershaw, (b)NASA TV/AP/Wide World Photos; **TAAS 3,** NASA/FPG International; **TAAS 4, 5,** Thomas Veneklasen; **TAAS 8,** Doug Martin; **TAAS 11,** David Attie/PhotoTake NYC; **TAAS 13,** Timothy Fuller; **TAAS 14,** John Keating/Science Source/Photo Researchers; **TAAS 16,** Jose L. Palaez

Art Credits: TX5, Morgan-Cain and Associates; **TX7,** Morgan-Cain and Associates; **TX8,** Tom Kennedy/Romark Illustration; **TX13,** Morgan-Cain and Associates; **TX14,** Morgan-Cain and Associates; **TX16,** Tom Kennedy/Romark Illustration; **TAAS2,** Morgan-Cain and Associates; **TAAS 4,** S. Woodward; **TAAS 6,** Morgan-Cain and Associates; **TAAS 7,** Diphrent Strokes; **TAAS 8, 9, 10, 11, 12, 15,** Morgan-Cain and Associates

SC91189-3

Practice

■ Solving Problems

The forecast called for an unusually hot spring day for the start of San Antonio's Fiesta. Lorena didn't like heat, but she loved Fiesta and was planning on spending the whole day outside with friends. "I guess I'll just have to dress as comfortably as possible, and wear a hat for protection from the sun," she thought. "So, what'll it be—my midnight blue cowboy hat or the white one?"

Lorena remembered the last time she wore the dark blue hat on a sunny day—she had been pretty uncomfortable. But would she have been any cooler in a white hat? She decided to do a little experiment to find out. Answer the questions about Lorena's experiment.

1. Which procedure would best help Lorena decide which color hat would be coolest on a hot sunny day?
   A. Place the dark blue hat in the sunlight and the white hat in the shade; then measure the temperature of the air inside each hat to see which one is cooler after 15 minutes.
   B. Place the white hat in the sunlight and the blue hat in the shade; then measure the temperature of the air inside each hat to see which one is cooler after 15 minutes.
   C. Place both hats in the shade and measure the temperature of the air inside each hat to see which one is cooler after 15 minutes.
   D. Place both hats in the sun and measure the temperature of the air inside each hat to see which one is cooler after 15 minutes.

2. Before conducting the experiment, Lorena predicted the white hat would be cooler. This prediction was her _____.
   A. conclusion   C. scientific law
   B. hypothesis   D. theory

3. The temperature of the air inside the hats is called the _____.
   A. constant
   B. control
   C. dependent variable
   D. independent variable

Use the following graph to answer questions 4 and 5.

4. What was the temperature of the air inside the dark blue hat after 10 minutes?
   A. 25°C   B. 27°C   C. 30°C   D. 32°C

5. What can Lorena conclude from the data in this graph?
   A. The white hat stayed cooler than the dark blue hat did in the sunlight, and that's the one she should wear.
   B. The dark blue hat stayed cooler than the white hat in the sunlight, and that's the one she should wear.
   C. Both hats warm up the same amount in the sunlight so it doesn't matter which one she wears.
   D. The graph doesn't provide any meaningful information.

TAAS Practice

Forces and Motion

Read the following passage and answer the questions.

Newton's three laws of motion explain how a force will affect an object, including the swing of a bat on a ball.

Newton's first law is that a moving object will continue moving at the same speed and in the same direction unless a force acts on it. If the object is at rest, it remains that way unless a force acts on it to make it move. This first law is also called the law of inertia because inertia is the tendency for an object to resist any change in its motion (or lack of motion). Friction and gravity act on objects to change their inertia.

Newton's second law of motion is that a force acting on an object causes the object to accelerate in the direction of the force. The equation for this law is:

$$\text{Force} = \text{mass} \times \text{acceleration}$$

The mass and acceleration of an object and the force needed to move it are all related—they all depend upon each other.

According to Newton's third law of motion, for every action there is an equal and opposite reaction. When one object exerts a force on a second object, the second object exerts a force that is equal in size and opposite in direction. Now, think about a baseball pitch . . .

1. Newton's third law of motion explains that a batter swinging with the same force could hit a fast-pitched ball farther than a slow-pitched ball because the fast-pitched ball _____.
   A. curves
   B. exerts more force than the slow-pitched ball
   C. has more mass than the slow-pitched ball
   D. produces less friction

2. On a football kickoff, the fact that the running start of the kicker sends the ball farther than it would if he were standing still is best explained by Newton's _____.
   A. first law   C. third law
   B. second law   D. law of gravity

3. Which law of motion most fully explains what is happening in the photo of the space shuttle launch?
   A. first law
   B. second law
   C. third law
   D. law of gravity

4. An object moving through the vacuum of space will most likely _____.
   A. slow down because of friction
   B. continuously accelerate
   C. continue moving at the same speed and in the same direction
   D. continue moving at the same speed but change directions

5. It is important to wear safety belts in a vehicle because if a moving vehicle suddenly stops, the passengers _____.
   A. stop with it
   B. continue moving until a force stops them
   C. move backwards
   D. move faster than the vehicle was moving

⭐⭐⭐⭐ TAAS Practice

■ Machines at Work

Chances are that somehow, somewhere, you have used a machine today. In fact, you have probably used several machines today. They may not have been the noisy, high-powered kind, but you still probably used many devices that make work easier—machines.

A simple machine is a device that does work with only one movement. A simple machine makes work easier by changing the size or direction of the force exerted on it. Sometimes, both the size and direction of the force change. Simple machines usually have only one or two parts. Use the six simple machines shown here to answer the following questions.

1. Which machine is an inclined plane wrapped in a spiral around a cylinder?

2. Which machine is being demonstrated by the movement of the arm in the picture below?

3. Which of the following is another example of the simple machine shown in D?
   A. a winding staircase
   B. the front of a canoe moving through water
   C. a batter swinging a bat
   D. a faucet

4. Which machine is made of two wheels of different sizes that rotate together?

5. By pulling down on a rope, you cause a load at the other end of the rope to rise. Which machine is at work?

TAAS Practice

■ Bernoulli's Principle and Flight

Read the passage and decide which type of error, if any, appears in each underlined section. Mark the letter for your answer.

The girl in the photograph is demonstrating a (1) <u>property of fluids, that allows airplanes to fly.</u> As she blows across the top of the paper, she increases the velocity (2) <u>of the air, which is a fluid.</u> The velocity of the air over the paper is greater than the velocity of the air beneath the paper. (3) <u>According to bernoulli's principle,</u> the increased velocity of the air above the paper decreases the air pressure on top of the paper. (4) <u>The presure of the air</u> on the bottom of the paper is now greater than that on top of the paper. This greater air pressure pushes the paper upward.

The shape of an airplane wing causes these same changes in (5) <u>air velocity and air pressure. producing an upward force</u> for the plane.

1. **A.** Spelling error
   B. Capitalization error
   C. Punctuation error
   D. No error

2. **A.** Spelling error
   B. Capitalization error
   C. Punctuation error
   D. No error

3. **A.** Spelling error
   B. Capitalization error
   C. Punctuation error
   D. No error

4. **A.** Spelling error
   B. Capitalization error
   C. Punctuation error
   D. No error

5. **A.** Spelling error
   B. Capitalization error
   C. Punctuation error
   D. No error

TAAS Practice

Periodic Table

The periodic table of the elements is an arrangement of the known elements based on their properties and atomic numbers. It is an indispensable tool for most scientists, especially chemists, and is displayed on the walls of science offices and classrooms worldwide.

Part of the periodic table is shown below. Use the table to answer the questions.

1. Which element is a liquid at room temperature?
   A. carbon
   B. mercury
   C. palladium
   D. zinc

2. Of the elements shown, which has the highest atomic number?
   A. bismuth
   B. nickel
   C. nitrogen
   D. platinum

3. Based on the information available in the periodic table, which statement accurately describes silicon?
   A. Its symbol is Sn.
   B. It is the lightest of the elements shown.
   C. It is a gas.
   D. It has some properties of metals and non-metals.

4. What is the atomic number of silver?
   A. 14
   B. 47
   C. 50
   D. 81

5. What is the symbol for copper?
   A. Co
   B. Cp
   C. Cr
   D. Cu

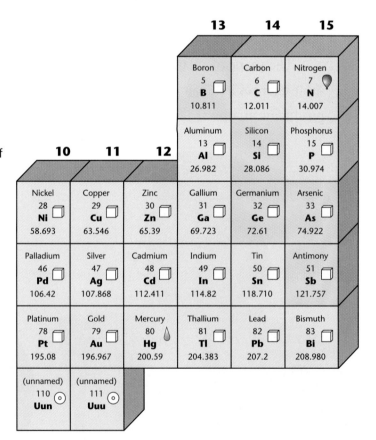

★★★★ TAAS Practice

■ Metals from Ores

Read the following passage and answer the questions.

What comes to mind when you hear the word metal? Perhaps you think about a hard, shiny solid; maybe it is silvery in color and cool to the touch, with a distinctive ringing sound when tapped with a hard object. Most of these images are fairly accurate. But if you were to apply these images to the way metals are found in nature, you could walk right over a metallic "gold mine" and not even know it.

Metals are usually not found in a form that is usable or in a form with which you are familiar. They usually occur in nature as ores—rock that contains useful metals or other elements that can be mined at a profit. An ore might just have bits of metal embedded in the rest of the rock. But more often than not, the metal is combined chemically with other elements as minerals. For example, iron is usually found in the form of the ore-minerals magnetite and hematite. Copper often comes from the mineral chalcopyrite, and aluminum from the ore bauxite.

In such cases, the metal cannot be separated simply by chiseling it out of the rock. For metal to be useful, it must be extracted from its ore and purified by smelting—a process of heating ore to remove oxygen and certain other impurities.

1. The main idea of this reading selection is that metals must be extracted from the ores in which they occur naturally. Which of the following details best supports this main idea?
   A. Metals are usually shiny, hard, and silvery.
   B. Smelting is one of the steps toward extracting metal from an ore.
   C. Iron is a useful metal.
   D. There are many copper mines in the United States.

2. Copper is a metal that is found in the ore called _____.
   A. bauxite   C. hematite
   B. chalcopyrite   D. magnetite

3. Most metals are _____.
   A. dull and yellowish
   B. liquids
   C. shiny, hard solids
   D. soft

4. Which statement is true about how metals are found and extracted?
   A. Most metals can be seen easily in nature.
   B. Most metals can be separated from the surrounding rock by breaking the metal from the rock.
   C. To extract most metals, the ore must be heated and treated in other ways.
   D. Metals usually are found lying on the bottom of riverbeds.

TAAS Practice

■ Alloys and Their Uses

Read the passage and choose the word or group of words that belongs in each space. Mark the letter for your answer.

In the Olympics, athletes who __1__ third place receive a bronze medal. What is bronze? You won't find it on the periodic table of elements as you will find silver or gold. Bronze __2__ an element; it is an alloy. An alloy is a mixture of a metal with one or more other elements. Bronze is an alloy of copper and tin, but bronze is __3__ than either copper or tin. That's the point of alloys—they have properties that are more __4__ than the properties of the component elements.

The gold jewelry shown here is actually an alloy of gold and copper. The alloy has the look of gold but the added strength and lower expense of copper. Adding strength is often a reason for making alloys. Titanium alloys are used in aircraft because __5__ offer considerable strength, resistance to corrosion, and the added benefit of light weight.

1. **A.** took
   B. take
   C. taked
   D. takes

2. **A.** is not
   B. isn't not
   C. not be
   D. would not be

3. **A.** strong
   B. stronger
   C. strongest
   D. most strong

4. **A.** use
   B. usefully
   C. usefulness
   D. useful

5. **A.** them
   B. they
   C. their
   D. they're

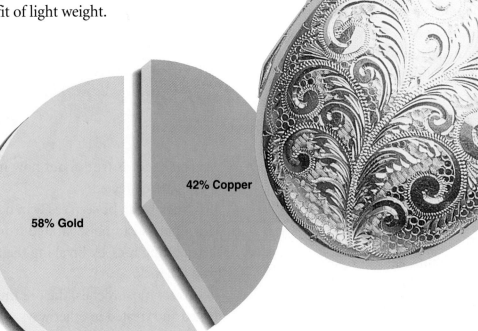

42% Copper

58% Gold

⭐⭐⭐⭐ TAAS Practice

■ Surface Area and Dissolving

When you make lemonade, you might begin by dissolving sugar in water. Would the sugar dissolve faster if it were one large lump or if it were broken up into granules? To answer this question, think of the surface area of the sugar. The more surface area of the sugar that is exposed to the water, the faster the sugar dissolves.

The diagram compares a large cube of sugar to one that is broken into smaller cubes. Refer to the diagram below to answer the following questions.

1. What is the surface area of the large cube?
   A. 24 cm^2
   B. 64 cm^2
   C. 384 cm^2
   D. 512 cm^2

2. What is the surface area of one of the smaller cubes?
   A. 12 cm^2
   B. 16 cm^2
   C. 64 cm^2
   D. 96 cm^2

3. The total surface area of the smaller cubes is
   A. 64 cm^2
   B. 384 cm^2
   C. 512 cm^2
   D. 768 cm^2

4. If you dissolved the large cube of sugar in water and the eight smaller cubes into the same size container of water, what would you expect to happen?
   A. The sugar would dissolve at the same rate in both containers.
   B. The large cube of sugar would dissolve faster than the smaller cubes.
   C. None of the sugar would dissolve in either container.
   D. The smaller cubes of sugar would dissolve faster than the large cube.

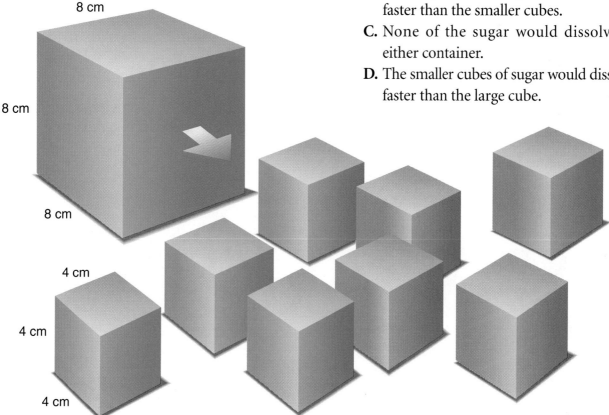

8 cm

8 cm

8 cm

4 cm

4 cm

4 cm

★★★★ TAAS Practice

■ Balancing Equations

A chemical reaction occurs when one or more substances are changed to new substances. A chemical equation uses formulas, numbers, and other symbols to describe a chemical reaction.

The illustration below shows a chemical reaction in which one unit of lead nitrate reacts with two units of potassium iodide to produce one unit of lead iodide and two units of potassium nitrate.

1. Which chemical equation correctly describes the reaction illustrated at the bottom of the page?
   A. $Pb(NO_3)_2 + KI \rightarrow PbI_2 + KNO_3$
   B. $Pb + NO_3 + KI \rightarrow Pb + I_2 + K + NO_3$
   C. $Pb(NO_3)_2KI \rightarrow PbI_2KNO_3$
   D. $Pb(NO_3)_2 + 2KI \rightarrow PbI_2 + 2KNO_3$

A chemical equation must always be balanced, showing the same number of atoms of each element on both sides of the equation. Because matter cannot be created or destroyed in a chemical reaction, a balanced equation shows a picture of what happens in the reaction.

Never change subscripts of a correct formula to balance an equation. Instead, place a whole-number coefficient to the left of the formula and multiply the number of elements in the formula of the reactants and products so that equal numbers of atoms are on both sides of the equation. If no number is given, the coefficient is 1.

2. How many atoms of oxygen are represented by the formula $3CO_2$?
   A. 1   B. 2   C. 3   D. 6

In questions 3 and 4, indicate which equation is balanced.

3. A. $Na + Cl_2 \rightarrow 2NaCl$
   B. $2Na + Cl_2 \rightarrow 2NaCl$
   C. $Na + Cl_2 \rightarrow NaCl$
   D. $3Na + Cl_2 \rightarrow 3NaCl$

4. A. $2H_2 + O_2 \rightarrow 2H_2O$
   B. $H_2 + O_2 \rightarrow H_2O$
   C. $4H_2 + O_2 \rightarrow 4H_2O$
   D. $H_2 + O_2 \rightarrow 2H_2O$

5. Choose the correct answer for balancing the following equation.
   $$BaCl_2 + Al_2O_3 \rightarrow BaO + AlCl_3$$
   A. $2BaCl_2 + Al_2O_3 \rightarrow 2BaO + 2AlCl_3$
   B. $3BaCl_2 + Al_2O_3 \rightarrow 3BaO + AlCl_3$
   C. $3BaCl_2 + Al_2O_3 \rightarrow 3BaO + 2AlCl_3$
   D. It is already balanced.

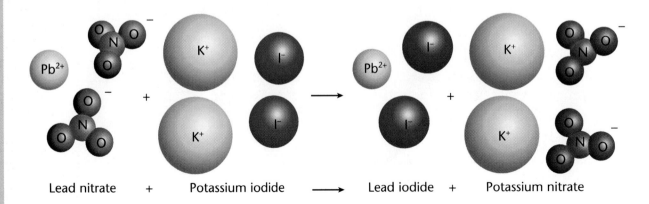

Lead nitrate   +   Potassium iodide   ⟶   Lead iodide   +   Potassium nitrate

TAAS Practice

A   Incoherent

Time

B   Coherent

Time

■ Lasers

Read the following passage and answer the questions.

The beams in this picture are produced by lasers. Notice that laser light stays in a narrow path rather than spreading out. Laser light is coherent light—it is energy of only one wavelength that travels with its troughs and crests together.

The drawings compare laser light and ordinary light. Notice how the light waves from ordinary light differ from each other. The troughs, crests, and wavelengths do not match. Furthermore, the waves travel in different directions. Ordinary light is incoherent.

The waves of laser light, on the other hand, are in step with each other. The wavelengths are the same, the troughs and crests are parallel, and the waves travel in the same direction so that the light remains a narrow, focused beam.

Laser light has many applications. It is used to read bar codes on packages, to carry phone signals through optical fibers, and to run compact discs. One of the most important uses of lasers is in medicine. Surgeons use narrow laser beams instead of scalpels to cut cleanly through body tissue.

1. A wavelength is the _____.
   A. height of a wave
   B. distance between a crest and a trough
   C. distance a wave travels
   D. distance between a crest and the next crest

2. In this passage, incoherent means _____.
   A. not understandable
   B. waves that do not align
   C. waves that travel in the same direction
   D. silent

3. If the troughs and crests of waves are parallel to each other, the waves _____.
   A. travel in all directions
   B. must be from ordinary light
   C. are the same distance from each other
   D. are incoherent

4. From this passage, you can tell that a scalpel is an instrument used to _____.
   A. stitch   C. clean
   B. cut   D. destroy

5. An application of an object is _____.
   A. its length
   B. its weight
   C. a way to make it
   D. a way to use it

★★★★
TAAS Practice

■ Producing Electric Current

Read the passage with underlined sections.

In the numbered questions that follow the reading, choose the best way to write each underlined section and mark the letter choice for your answer. If the underlined section needs no correction, mark the choice "Correct as is."

(1) <u>Most of the electricity you use each day was produced somewhere. This electricity is produced in a generator.</u> A generator, such as the one shown here, changes the mechanical energy of a moving wire coil or magnet into electrical energy. (2) <u>Spinning the wire coil or the magnet produces an electric current, it flows through the wire.</u>

The mechanical energy needed to spin the wire or magnet often comes from the steam produced in a power plant. (3) <u>The burning of fossil fuels or the splitting of nuclei heats water to produce steam, which turns the blades of a turbine to spin wire coils in a generator.</u> Moving water can also turn the blades of a turbine. (4) <u>For example, the force of falling water at dams. Turns the turbines of generators.</u>

1. **A.** Most electricity is produced in a generator, and you use electricity each day.
   B. Most of the electricity you use each day is produced in a generator.
   C. Each day you use electricity that is produced in a generator.
   D. Correct as is.

2. **A.** Spinning the coil or magnet produces an electric current it flows through the wire.

Magnet
Coil
Slip rings
Shaft
Brushes

B. Spinning the wire coil or the magnet produces an electric current, which flows through the wire.
C. An electric current flows through the wire after spinning the wire coil or the magnet.
D. Correct as is.

3. **A.** The burning of fossil fuels or the splitting of nuclei heat water to produce steam turns the blades of a turbine to spin wire coils in a generator.
   B. The burning of fossil fuels or the splitting of nuclei heat water to produce steam and turns the blades of a turbine to spin wire coils in a generator.
   C. The burning of fossil fuels or the splitting of nuclei heat water to produce steam. The steam turns the blades of a turbine, which spin wire coils in a generator.
   D. Correct as is.

4. **A.** For example, the force of falling water at dams that turns the turbines of generators.
   B. For example, the force of falling water at dams, which turns the turbines of generators.
   C. For example, the force of falling water at dams turns the turbines of generators.
   D. Correct as is.

TAAS Practice

■ Know Your Computer

Read the following passages and answer the questions.

What's the most important feature of a computer? A large screen? A color monitor? A CD drive? These are all nice extras, but the most important feature is the amount of memory the computer has. Information is collected, stored, and processed in the memory of the computer, and after all, storing and processing information is what computers do best.

Two major kinds of memory are RAM and ROM. RAM means random access memory. RAM stores information while it is being used. But once the computer is turned off, the information in RAM is lost. On the other hand, information in ROM is permanently stored in the computer. ROM means read only memory because the microprocessor can only read the information to operate the computer; new information cannot be added.

1. What is the main idea of this passage?
   A. Memory (RAM and ROM) is the most important feature of a computer.
   B. RAM means random access memory.
   C. ROM means read only memory.
   D. Information in RAM is lost when the computer is turned off.

2. A detail that supports the main idea is that _____.
   A. Some computers have CD drives.
   B. RAM means random access memory.
   C. Information in ROM is permanently stored in the computer.
   D. Information is collected, stored, and processed in the memory of a computer.

In order to permanently store new information in the computer, the information must be saved on a disk. Most personal computers have a large hard disk on which a lot of information can be stored. Most computers also have a disk drive so that information can be stored on a smaller floppy disk. With a floppy disk, you can transfer information from one computer to another.

3. The main idea of this passage is that _____.
   A. most computers have hard disks
   B. most computers have a disk drive
   C. information added to a computer must be saved on a disk
   D. floppy disks can be used to transfer information from one computer to another

4. A detail that supports the main idea is that _____.
   A. new information must be saved on a disk
   B. hard disks hold a lot of information
   C. floppy disks are small
   D. most computers have hard disks and a drive for floppy disks on which to save information

★★★★ TAAS Practice

■ Energy Debate

Read the following passage and answer the questions.

Speaker A: What do you think about the new equipment at the power plant? I read a report that says it will cut air pollution from the plant by 90 percent.

Speaker B: Well, I don't think it will cut it any more than ten percent, if we're lucky. If you ask me, the plant should be shut down.

Speaker A: What would you do for electricity?

Speaker B: We can all use solar energy and get as much electricity as we want. Solar cells convert sunlight directly into electricity.

Speaker A: Solar cells are too expensive for everyone to use. They work best only in places that get the most sunlight.

Speaker B: Then what about wind power? I could set up a windmill right here in the backyard.

Speaker A: Again, only a few places have enough wind consistently to provide for all the energy needs of that area. But every form of energy has some problems.

Speaker B: True, but I think there are enough alternatives that any community could try other things for at least some of their energy needs.

Speaker A: You may be right. I guess the best solution for

now might be a mixture of energy sources—whatever would work best for that area.

Speaker B: Right. And alternative sources should be as large a part of that mix as possible.

1. You can tell that Speaker A is _____.
   A. against the use of the new equipment at the power plant
   B. generally satisfied with the power plant
   C. doesn't understand energy sources
   D. isn't interested in discussing energy

2. Speaker B's statement about the new equipment cutting pollution by ten percent appears to be based on _____.
   A. one scientific study
   B. several scientific studies
   C. illogical reasoning
   D. opinion

For question 3, determine which statement is an opinion.

3. A. It will cut air pollution from the plant by 90 percent.
   B. Solar cells convert sunlight directly into electricity.
   C. I could set up a windmill right here . . . .
   D. Every form of energy has some problems.

4. By the end of the passage,
   A. Speaker A completely converts Speaker B to his or her way of thinking.
   B. Speaker B completely converts Speaker A to his or her way of thinking.
   C. Both speakers disagree with each other.
   D. Both speakers recognize the other's point of view.

TAAS Practice

■ What materials make the best insulators?

What keeps the temperature from getting too warm inside your home during the hot summer months? What keeps the temperature comfortable during cold winters? The answer is lots of things—open and closed windows, shades, heaters, air conditioners, and fans. Another part of the answer is the insulation between the walls of your home. Insulation slows the movement of heat through the walls of your home.

What materials make the best insulators? Do this activity to find out.

Objective

To find out what materials from a given list make the best insulators.

Materials

4 empty soup cans, 4 thermometers, watch or clock, newspaper, aluminum foil, several polystyrene cups, tape, clay, pitcher of hot water

Procedure

1. Make a table like the one shown.
2. Select three materials with which to thoroughly insulate three of the cans.
3. Wrap each of the three cans with one of the insulating materials. Cover the sides, the bottom, and the top of each can, leaving a flap that can be shut or taped, but through which you can pour hot water and insert a thermometer. Number each can.
4. Fill each can with hot water. Be careful not to spill water.
5. Quickly measure the temperature of the water in all four cans. Each temperature should be the same at this point. Record the temperatures in your data table.
6. Leave the fourth can as is.
7. In your table, record the temperature of each can every 2 minutes up to 20 minutes.
8. Clean up your lab station according to your teacher's directions.

Conclusions

1. Which can has the highest temperature at the end of 20 minutes?
2. Which material is the best insulator?
3. How might the results of the activity change if the amounts of insulating materials were doubled?
4. What was the purpose of can number 4?

Temperature at start and every 2 minutes (Time)										
	0	2	4	6	8	10	12	14	16	18	20
Can No. 1											
Can No. 2											
Can No. 3											
Can No. 4											

TAAS Practice

■ How do electric circuits differ?

Most circuits include a source of voltage, a conductor, and a device that uses the electricity. These parts form a complete path through which electrons can flow. This flow of electrons is electricity.

Most electrical items you use are probably wired in one of two ways—as series circuits or as parallel circuits. Both circuits have advantages and disadvantages. What is the difference between these two kinds of circuits?

Objective

To make a series circuit and a parallel circuit.

Materials

battery (6- or 9-volt), 2 lights with sockets, 4 pieces of insulated wire with ends stripped (about 20 cm each)

Procedure

1. Using some or all of the materials provided, make a series circuit.
2. Demonstrate whether or not a break in one part of the series circuit affects other parts of the circuit.
3. Make a drawing of your demonstration.
4. Using some or all of the materials provided, make a parallel circuit.
5. Demonstrate whether or not a break in one part of the parallel circuit affects other parts of the circuit.
6. Make a drawing of your demonstration.
7. Put away all equipment when you have finished this lab.

Conclusions

1. How did you determine whether or not a break in each circuit affected the rest of the circuit?
2. How do a series circuit and parallel circuit differ?
3. In which type of circuit does the same amount of electricity flow through every part of the circuit?
4. How do your demonstrations show that it is better to wire a building with parallel circuits rather than series circuits?

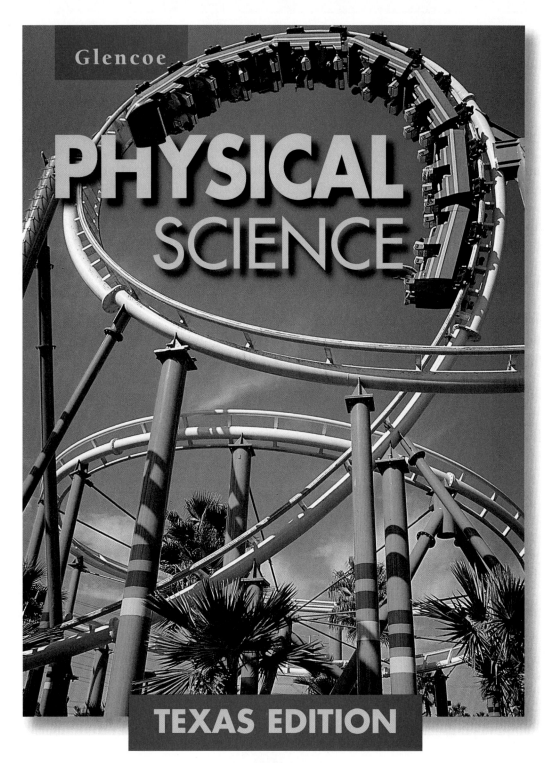

Glencoe

PHYSICAL SCIENCE

TEXAS EDITION

GLENCOE

McGraw-Hill

New York, New York   Columbus, Ohio   Mission Hills, California   Peoria, Illinois

A GLENCOE PROGRAM

Glencoe Physical Science

Texas Student Edition
Texas Teacher Wraparound Edition
Texas Lesson Plans
Practice Activities
Study Guide SE and TE
Reinforcement SE and TE
Enrichment SE and TE
Concept Mapping
Critical Thinking/Problem Solving
Activity Worksheets
Chapter Review
Chapter Review Software
Lab Manual SE and TE
Science Integration Activities

Cross-Curricular Integration
Science and Society Integration
Technology Integration
Multicultural Connection
Performance Assessment
Review and Assessment
Spanish Resources
MindJogger Videoquizzes and
  Teacher Guide
English/Spanish Audiocassettes
CD-ROM Multimedia System
Interactive Videodisc Program
Computer Testbank—
  DOS and Macintosh Versions

Transparency Packages:
  Teaching Transparencies
  Section Focus Transparencies
  Science Integration Transparencies

The Glencoe Science Professional Development Series
  Performance Assessment in the Science Classroom
  Lab and Safety Skills in the Science Classroom
  Cooperative Learning in the Science Classroom
  Alternate Assessment in the Science Classroom
  Exploring Environmental Issues

Cover Photograph: The roller coaster on the cover was photographed in Phoenix, Arizona by Ken Ross/FPG International.

Glencoe/McGraw-Hill

A Division of The **McGraw·Hill** Companies

Copyright © 1997 by the McGraw-Hill Companies, Inc. All rights reserved. Except as permitted under the United States Copyright Act, no part of this publication may be reproduced or distributed in any form or by any means, or stored in a database or retrieval system, without prior written permission of the publisher.

Send all inquiries to:
Glencoe/McGraw-Hill
936 Eastwind Drive
Westerville, OH 43081

ISBN 0-02-827931-X
Printed in the United States of America.
5 6 7 8 9 10 11 12   071/046   04 03 02 01 00 99 98 97

Authors

Charles W. McLaughlin has more than 25 years of experience as a high school chemistry teacher and is currently the coordinator of science education for the St. Joseph, Missouri school district. He holds a Ph.D. in chemistry from the University of Nebraska. The National Science Teachers Association has presented Dr. McLaughlin with three national awards for innovative science education, and he received a Presidential Award for Science Teaching.

Marilyn Thompson is currently teaching and pursuing graduate work in science education at the University of Kansas. Her career has included teaching physics, chemistry and physical science while serving as science department chair at Center High School in Kansas City, Missouri. Ms. Thompson received her B.A. degree in chemistry from Carleton College and her M.A. degree in science curriculum and instruction from the University of Kansas. She has conducted several summer workshops and courses in the physical sciences for K-12 teachers. Ms. Thompson is a member of NSTA and AAPT.

Contributing Writers

Linda Barr
Freelance Writer
Westerville, Ohio

Dan Blaustein
Science Teacher and Author
Evanston, Illinois

Pam Bliss
Freelance Science Writer
Grayslake, Illinois

Mary Dylewski
Freelance Science Writer
Houston, Texas

Nancy Ross-Flanigan
Syndicated Science Reporter
Detroit, Michigan

Helen Frensch
Freelance Writer
Santa Barbara, California

Steve Glazer
Freelance Writer
Champaign, Illinois

Rebecca Johnson
Freelance Science Writer
  and Author
Sioux Falls, South Dakota

Devi Mathieu
Freelance Science Writer
Sebastopol, California

Patricia West
Freelance Writer
Oakland, California

Consultants

Physics

Donald Bord, Ph.D.
Professor of Physics
University of Michigan-Dearborn
Dearborn, Michigan

Patrick Hamill, Ph.D.
Professor of Physics
San Jose State University
San Jose, California

Chemistry

Teresa Anne McCowen
Senior Lecturer
Butler University
Indianapolis, Indiana

Robert C. Smoot, M.S.
Rollins Teacher Fellow in Science
McDonough School
Owings Mills, Maryland

Multicultural

Karen Muir, Ph.D.
Lead Instructor
Department of Social and Behavioral Sciences
Columbus State Community College
Columbus, Ohio

Safety

Peggy W. Holliday
Science Education Specialist
NIOSH Certified Lab Trainer
Raleigh, North Carolina

Reviewers

Al Alvarez
Curriculum Consultant
San Antonio, TX

James E. Arnett III
South Doyle Middle School
Knoxville, Tennessee

Robert W. Avakian
Alamo Junior High School
Midland, Texas

D. Vance Baugher
Hannibal High School
Hannibal, Missouri

Anthony J. DiSipio, Jr.
Octorara Intermediate School
Atglen, Pennsylvania

Lorena R. Farrar
Westwood Junior High
Dallas, Texas

Elizabeth Hezel
St. Mary's School
Canandaigua, New York

Bettye Lou Jerrel
Evansville-Vanerburgh
   School Corporation
Evansville, Indiana

Ron Kinoshita
Gilroy Unified School District
Gilroy, California

Denise E. McCarthy
Ben Franklin Junior High
Fargo, North Dakota

Donna McLeish
Vigo County School District
Terre Haute, Indiana

Jim Nelson
Orange County Public Schools
Orlando, Florida

Jo Ann Pelkki
Saginaw City Schools
Saginaw, Michigan

Curtis A. Spenrath
Goose Creek Consolidated
   Independent School District
Baytown, Texas

Lisa Jean Wakeland
Chesterfield County
   Chester Middle School
Chester, Virginia

Raquél S. Williams
West End High School
Birmingham, Alabama

Contents

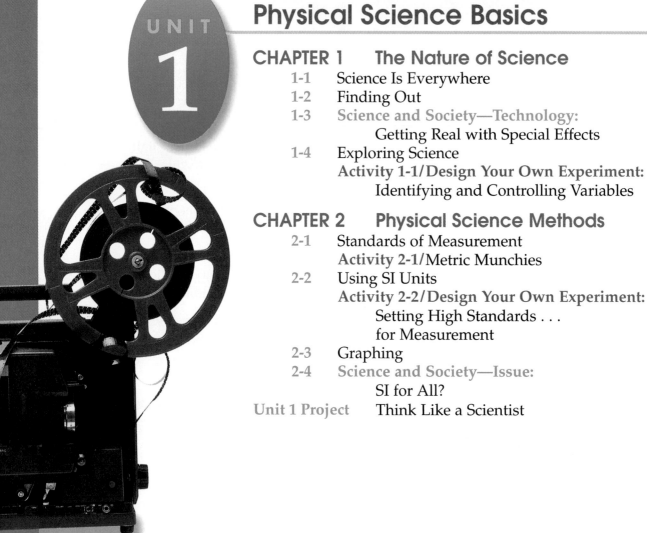

UNIT 1

UNIT 2

Contents

Contents

UNIT 3

The Nature of Matter   210

Contents

Kinds of Substances   326

UNIT 4

Contents

Contents

Contents

Contents

Electricity and Energy Resources   588

UNIT 7

Contents

Contents

Contents

Appendices

Skill Handbook

Activities

Activities

Explore Activities

MiniLABs

MiniLABs

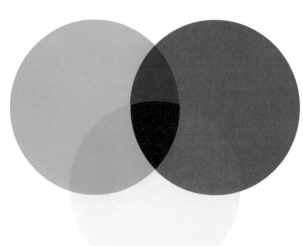

Problem Solving

Using Technology

Skill Builders

ORGANIZING INFORMATION
Sequencing: 36, 227, 579
Outlining: 17
Classifying: 717

THINKING CRITICALLY
Observing and Inferring: 9, 86, 261, 401,
    450, 473, 535, 550, 597, 688
Comparing and Contrasting: 69, 99, 131,
    250, 281, 379, 421, 504, 631, 663, 677, 703
Recognizing Cause and Effect: 82, 183, 445,
    521, 562

DESIGNING AN EXPERIMENT
Measuring in SI: 203, 239
Hypothesizing: 25, 116, 231, 453, 571, 611,
    627
Using Variables, Constants, and Controls:
    158, 320
Interpreting Data: 144, 344, 485

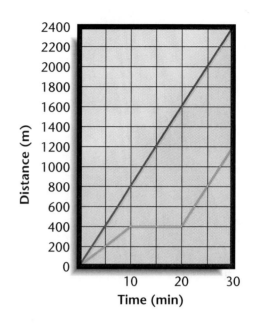

GRAPHICS
Concept Mapping: 45, 137, 170, 274, 308,
    351, 394, 434, 458, 476, 512, 541, 567,
    617, 637, 657, 691, 708
Making and Using Tables: 105, 165, 194,
    220, 302, 606
Making and Using Graphs: 51, 75, 291,
    365, 429
Interpreting Scientific Illustrations: 337,
    369, 653, 683

People and Science

Science Connections

Science and Art

Science and History

Science and Literature

Unit Contents

Physical Science Basics

What's Happening Here?

Anxiously waiting to see photographic images appear on developing film may seem to be far removed from learning science. Yet the chemical reactions, solutions, and techniques involved all depend on important scientific principles. Within this unit, you will observe that studying science allows you to find out about new ideas and to understand and measure what has been around you all your life. Begin this study, and see what develops.

Science Journal

The light in the photo developing lab looks mysterious, but it is used for an important reason. Find out the difference in the developing process for black-and-white and color photographs. Compare the two processes in your Science Journal.

Previewing the Chapter

The Nature of Science

Is science really everywhere you look? Something as common as videotaping a school event would not be possible without the application of many scientific principles and discoveries. From receiving, recording, and transmitting light and sound to the nerve impulses that tell your finger to press the *Record* button, you can notice many ways that science can be put to work for you.

EXPLORE ACTIVITY

Learn how developing skills and knowing how to apply them is necessary in both daily life and the study of science.

1. Obtain a video camera from your home or school. Be sure you have permission and know how to use the camera correctly.
2. Record several short school or class activities.
3. Watch your video with your classmates, and observe any problems with the taping. Were some events better taped than others?

Observe: In your Science Journal, record any problem present with the taping. Explain how developing certain skills could make taping more effective.

Previewing Science Skills

▶ In the Skill Builders, you will observe and infer, outline, and map concepts.

▶ In the Activity, you will observe, predict, and control variables.

▶ In the MiniLABs, you will measure in SI, control variables, and observe.

1•1 Science Is Everywhere

Science Words

technology
physical science

Objectives

* Compare and contrast pure science and technology.
* Define *physical science*.
* Discuss some of the topics covered in physical science.

Behind the Scenes

What was the best movie you saw last year? Was it an action/adventure film, a comedy, a thriller, or a romance? As you watched, did you ever wish you could sneak behind the scenes to see how the movie was made? You might be surprised to see that it isn't just the actors, producer, director, and crew that contribute to what you see on the screen. Science, too, plays a starring role, as shown in **Figure 1-1.**

Lights, Camera, Action!

Before a movie makes it to your local theater, every moment of every scene is captured on film through the lens of a motion picture camera. How do moviemakers use lenses to bring about the feeling of being close up or to produce panoramic shots of breathtaking scenery? The science of optics holds the answers.

An on-screen explosion, a lifelike robotic dinosaur, and heart-stopping sound effects all rely on scientific principles. None of these effects is possible without an understanding of chemical reactions, mechanics, hydraulics, electronics, and acoustics.

Science—Pure and Applied

It's not hard to see how a knowledge of chemical reactions would help someone figure out how to make a mock explosion in a movie, but not all connections between scientific knowledge and its practical uses are so obvious. For example, can you see any connection between moviemaking and the details of how human vision works? Read on!

Figure 1-1

See science in action behind the scenes on a movie set. *How do you think science is used on this set?*

INTEGRATION
Life Science

A Great Vision

The human eye receives images in the form of light waves, which are translated into nerve impulses. The impulses are sent to the brain, which converts the information back into images and then interprets those images. It takes the eye one-quarter of a second to receive and transmit the information for a single image. Now, here's where moviemaking comes in. Movie cameras take a series of still images at a rate of 24 per second. Projectors show the film at the same speed. But, because the human eye can't process more than four separate images per second, the images on the screen seem to blend together, creating the optical illusion of continuous motion.

Do you think the scientists who first studied human vision had motion pictures in mind? Certainly not. They just wanted to understand how the eye works. They were engaged in what is called *pure science*. But their pure science discoveries eventually made it possible for others to invent motion pictures, eyeglasses, contact lenses, and other visually related products we enjoy and depend on every day. These are examples of *applied science*.

Peel-and-stick notes

A Sticky Story

Visit any office where people pass paperwork back and forth, and you'll probably see notes written on colored slips of paper that can be stuck on and easily peeled off. The story of how those peel-and-stick notepads came to be invented could itself be the subject of a movie. The sound track would be supplied by the choir at the church where chemist Art Fry sang on Sundays. Fry always marked his place in the hymnbook with little scraps of paper. Sometimes the scraps fell out, and he couldn't find the right hymn when it came time to sing.

He remembered an adhesive developed a few years earlier by another scientist, Dr. Spencer Silver. Silver had thought the adhesive was useless because it wasn't strong enough to hold things together permanently. But sitting there in church, Fry suddenly saw thousands of uses for notepads with "temporarily permanent adhesive," as he called it. It took months of experimenting to get the formula just right, but when the sticky notepads finally were offered to the public, they were an instant hit.

Think Critically:

Use the above example to explain how pure science and applied science can be used together to solve problems.

Something New

Pure science is the gathering of new information or the discovery of a new relationship or fact. Pure science adds to the body of scientific knowledge but does not have to have practical uses. Not every scientific discovery will have common, everyday applications, but even those that do not may open up whole new fields of investigation.

Technology is the practical use of scientific information. Where does pure science leave off and technology begin? It's not always easy to tell. Scientific discoveries may lead to technical innovations which, in turn, may lead to further discoveries. Both pure science, for the advancement of knowledge, and applied science, or technology, are considered important parts of science as a whole.

A Guidance System

When you're looking for a specific movie at the video store, there is a logical system to guide you. New releases are in one section; action/adventure films, comedies, dramas, and musicals all have their own places. When you go to the grocery store with a shopping list, you know that certain foods are grouped together and that the aisles are arranged in a particular order. But suppose your mission was not to find a movie or a can of peaches, but to find out all you could about how cameras work. What sort of system would help you in your search through the vast world of science?

Major Categories

Your first step would be to narrow your search to one of the main categories of science: life science, which deals with living organisms; Earth science, which investigates Earth and space; or physical science, which deals with matter and energy. Physical science topics can be grouped into chemistry and physics. Each of these subdivisions also can be divided into more specific branches of science. How would you decide which branches of science would best help you understand how a camera works?

Physical Science

This textbook will be your guide through the major topics of physical science. **Physical science** is the study of matter and energy. Every measurable thing in the universe is either matter or energy. Plants and animals, rocks and

Figure 1-2

Lightning, thunder, and motion are examples of energy. Trees, rain, and clouds are all examples of matter.

8

clouds, eggs and elephants are all examples of matter. Lightning, thunder, and motion are all examples of energy, as shown in **Figure 1-2.**

In physical science, you'll study what makes up matter—its composition. You'll also learn about what matter is like and how it behaves. Hardness and taste are two examples of properties of matter that should already be familiar to you.

As you study physical science, you'll learn how matter and energy are related. You'll discover how energy is transferred through matter, as when the sound from the CD player in **Figure 1-3** reaches your ears. You'll find out how refrigerators stay cold and why an insulated jacket keeps you warmer than a thin shirt.

As you learn about sound and light, you'll discover the scientific side of music, photography, and other everyday activities. The study of electricity will help you understand what keeps your television and compact disc player running. In the study of force and motion, you'll learn why acorns fall to Earth and why satellites remain in orbit.

As you learn about physical science, notice how things and ideas are organized into systems and how different parts of a system interact. Your observations will lead you to ask questions. The rest of this chapter will help you learn how to go about answering those questions.

Figure 1-3

Everyday activities have scientific sides.

Section Wrap-up

Review

1. What is the difference between pure science and technology? Give an example of each.

2. Define *physical science.*

3. **Think Critically:** Pose three questions that you think could be answered by using physical science.

Skill Builder
Observing and Inferring
Bring in a newspaper or magazine article related to physical science. Summarize the article and explain whether it deals with a scientific discovery or a technological development. If you need help, refer to Observing and Inferring in the **Skill Handbook.**

Science Journal

Imagine that you are writing a screenplay about the invention of peel-and-stick notepads. Describe three scenes that would show audiences how pure science discoveries led to the invention.

1•2 Finding Out

Science Words

model
observation
hypothesis
theory
scientific law

Objectives

- Distinguish between problems and exercises.
- Evaluate approaches to solving problems.
- Compare and contrast hypothesis, theory, and scientific law.

Detecting Clues . . . Solving Problems

Science involves a lot more than collecting facts and sorting things into categories. The real business of science is solving problems—some that have everyday applications and others that are more abstract. In this section, you'll explore ways of solving problems.

At your after-school job at the local movie theater, the boss calls you aside and asks for some help. The projector shown in **Figure 1-4** isn't working right, and he can't figure out why. Could something be wrong with the lens that focuses the images on the screen? Is the film running too slowly or too quickly? What about the light source that shines through the film to project it onto the screen? Has the light burned out? Is there something wrong with the photoelectric cell that "reads" the sound track from the film and creates an electrical signal that is amplified and sent to speakers in the theater?

What is a problem?

Your boss has a *problem*. You've probably used that word many times without stopping to think exactly what it means. A problem is a situation in which something appears to be missing. A problem is not the same thing as an exercise. In an exercise, the steps required to find the solution are usually obvious. For example, finding the average weight of five classmates is an exercise if you know how to calculate averages. If you don't know how to find averages, then you do have a problem.

Figure 1-4

Most problems, such as what is wrong with this broken projector, can be solved by following a series of logical steps.

The broken projector is a problem, and because your boss asked you for help, it's now *your* problem. Simply observing that the projector isn't working won't help you find a solution. You must look for more clues before you can figure out what to do. Solving a problem involves finding missing information, but it's not always clear what kind of information is needed. Where would you start?

Patterns

As **Figure 1-5** shows, finding patterns can help solve problems. Does the projector work sometimes but not always? Does it stop working after it has been running for a while? To answer questions such as these, you need to observe the projector over time. You may need to take measurements. For example, you could use your watch to measure how long it takes from the time you turn on the projector until something goes wrong. Would one measurement be enough to show a pattern? No. You would need to make many identical measurements before you could detect a pattern.

Solving Problems

The problem of the broken projector has many possible solutions. An obvious one is to check that the projector is plugged in. Then, you might check to make sure the projector is turned on. After ruling out those easy solutions, how would you proceed?

Before you can solve a problem, you need to understand exactly what the problem is. That may sound obvious, but people often have trouble solving problems because they don't know where to start. Sometimes, that's because they haven't defined the problem clearly enough.

As you attack the movie-projector problem, you begin to look it over and ask the manager a lot of questions. Does it make any strange noises? Is a burning smell obvious when it runs? Your questions and observations will help you pinpoint the specific problem. You'll progress from knowing only that the projector isn't working to knowing, for example, that the mechanism that moves the film is broken. The more precisely you can define the problem, the less time you'll spend looking for solutions.

Figure 1-5

Searching for patterns is a good problem-solving strategy. *What patterns could help you solve this problem?*

Figure 1-6

Computer models are programs that predict how different designs behave under various conditions.

CONNECT TO

EARTH SCIENCE

The famous stone slabs in England called Stonehenge may represent an ancient calendar. *Research* how scientists used the four problem-solving strategies to decide possible meanings of Stonehenge.

Plan a Strategy

Once you've defined the problem, look for answers in a systematic way. Proceed in logical steps, starting with what you know. Keep track of your steps so that if an idea doesn't work, you can move on to something else instead of trying the same thing again. Here are some ways that will help you solve problems.

• *Use what you know about the problem to predict a solution, and try it.* If your effort fails, think about why it didn't work. Then make another prediction and try that. Keep eliminating possibilities until you find the one that works. You've probably used this method to search for something you've lost— such as last night's homework. Think about when you last saw the homework, and review where you've been since then. This process helps you to direct your search. Maybe you remember that you went to the kitchen for a snack after you finished your homework, so you look there. If you don't find it, you look in the next logical place—the chair where you sat to have your snack—and so on.

• *Look for patterns that will help you make predictions about the problem.* Suppose you occasionally break out in a rash. If you pay attention to what you eat, touch, and wear every day, you may find a pattern that helps you discover what's causing the rash. Putting information into a table or graph or making a drawing sometimes can help you find patterns.

• *Develop a model.* When your problem deals with something complicated or difficult to see, it may help to develop a model. A **model** is an idea, system, or structure that represents whatever you're trying to explain. The model is never exactly like the thing being explained, but it is similar enough to allow comparisons.

Before starting to shoot a movie, filmmakers sometimes build models to get an idea of how particular scenes will look. Models are used in scientific investigations, too. To find out how the shape of an airplane affects performance, scientists and engineers make model airplanes of different shapes. These models are based on theories that describe how moving air behaves. Engineers then test the different models under various conditions to find out which shape works best. They may also create different computer models, such as those shown in **Figure 1-6.**

• *Break the problem down into smaller, simpler problems.* Sometimes, it's hard to see what needs to be done when the problem is complicated. Look for ways to solve it step-by-step.

As you search for solutions, keep thinking about what you first knew about the problem and what you've learned from each problem-solving attempt. When you find a solution, think again about the problem and ask yourself whether your solution makes sense.

Thinking Critically

Imagine that you're in charge of sound effects for a school play. The script calls for a barking dog in one scene; a squawking bird in another; an alarm clock, a siren, a scream, and a car crash in others. You carefully tape-record each sound and splice them together on one tape, in the order the script calls for. But at dress rehearsal, everything goes wrong. When it's time for the alarm clock, you press the *Play* button on your tape recorder and get the sound of a squawking bird. Instead of the barking dog,

Problem Solving

Can you put that in writing?

Your report is due tomorrow morning and it has to be neat and readable. You enter the report into your computer and then give the command to print. Nothing happens. No, this is not a nightmare. It is really happening, and you need help. Can you apply problem-solving steps to analyze the problem and solve it?

Solve the Problem:

1. **As you gather information, look for any patterns. Has anyone else had problems with the printer? Have you had the same problem before?**
2. **Plan a strategy. What does a printer need to operate? How are those needs supplied to the printer? Can you check out each of those needs one at a time?**
3. **Once you think that you have enough information to solve the problem, make a prediction that you can test. The prediction can be simple. Is the printer plugged in? Is it turned on? If these predictions when tested don't solve your problem, you can still use them to guide you to another prediction.**

Think Critically:

If the printer is receiving power, what else could be causing the problem? Think about how the printer receives instructions to print. What might you predict about the computer and printer connection?

Figure 1-7

Critical thinking is an important problem-solving aid. *What is critical thinking?*

MiniLAB

How can still pictures appear to be moving?

Procedure

1. Obtain about a dozen small, unlined index cards. Place a rubber band tightly around one end of the stack of cards.
2. Using simple figures, draw a starting scene on the first card. On the next card, draw the same scene with a slight change in position to indicate motion. Repeat this step until all the cards are used.

Analysis

1. Grasp the end of the stack that has the rubber band on it, and flip the cards quickly. Record your observations in your Science Journal.
2. If you flip the cards more slowly, how does the smoothness of the apparent motion change?

you get a car crash. What's going on? Did you mix up the order of the sounds when you made the tape? Was there a script change that nobody told you about? Did someone play a prank on you and switch your tape for another one?

After thinking about it, you decide that you may have mixed up the order of sounds on your tape. How did you arrive at this conclusion? Without being aware of it, you probably used some aspect of critical thinking. Read on to find out more.

What is critical thinking?

Critical thinking is a process that uses certain skills to solve a problem. Let's see how you may have used critical thinking to solve the case of the scrambled sounds. First, you identified the problem—the wrong order of sounds—by comparing the sounds coming from your tape recorder to the sounds called for in the script. Next, you may have separated important information from unimportant information by deciding that it wasn't likely that the script had been changed at the last minute without your knowledge. Finally, you examined your assumption that you had spliced the sounds together in the correct order. You looked back at the script, thought about how rushed you were when you made the tape, and concluded that you made a mistake. You probably went one step further and analyzed your conclusion. You asked yourself if you had ever made similar mistakes when you were in a hurry. If the answer was yes, then you may have solved the problem.

Flex Your Brain, the series of steps outlined on the next page, is an activity that will help you to think about and examine how you think. Flex Your Brain is a way to keep your thinking on track when you are investigating a topic.

You start with what you know about a topic and move on to new conclusions and new awareness. You end by reviewing and discussing the steps you took.

Flex Your Brain

1 **Topic:** _____

2 **? What do I already know?**
1. _____
2. _____
3. _____
4. _____
5. _____

3 **Q:** Ask a question
_____

4 **A:** Guess an answer
_____

5 **How sure am I? (circle one)**

Not sure				Very sure
1	2	3	4	5

6 **? How can I find out?**
1. _____
2. _____
3. _____
4. _____
5. _____

7 **EXPLORE**

8 **Do I think differently?** → yes / no

9 **? What do I know now?**
1. _____
2. _____
3. _____
4. _____
5. _____

10 **SHARE**
1. _____
2. _____
3. _____

1 Fill in the topic.

2 Jot down what you already know about the topic.

3 Using what you already know (step 2), form a question about the topic. Are you unsure about one of the items you listed? Do you want to know more? Do you want to know what, how, or why? Write down your question.

4 Guess an answer to your question. In the next few steps, you will be exploring the reasonableness of your answer. Write down your guesses.

5 Circle the number in the box that matches how sure you are of your answer in step 4. This is your chance to rate your confidence in what you've done so far and, later, to see how your level of sureness affects your thinking.

6 How can you find out more about your topic? You might want to read a book, ask an expert, or do an experiment. Write down ways you can use to find out more.

7 Make a plan to explore your answer. Use the resources you listed in step 6. Then, carry out your plan.

8 Now that you've explored, go back to your answer in step 4. Would you answer differently?

9 Considering what you learned in your exploration, answer your question again, adding new things you've learned. You may completely change your answer.

10 It's important to be able to talk about thinking. Choose three people to tell about how you arrived at your response in every step. For example, don't just read what you wrote down in step 2. Try to share how you thought of those things.

Scientific Methods

As you puzzled over the broken movie projector or the scrambled sounds on the tape, you planned a strategy and went through a series of steps to solve the problem. That's how scientists have approached scientific problems since the time of the founders of modern science. The series of steps scientists use are called scientific methods. You'll be using these methods in investigations throughout this textbook.

The first step in a scientific method is **observation,** which is using your senses to gather information. Observations can be used to study what is happening in **Figure 1-8.** In science, tools such as microscopes, rulers, and clocks can help make your observations more precise.

Good observations lead to testable predictions about how to solve a problem or explain how something works. In science, a testable prediction is called a **hypothesis.** When studying falling bodies, you can observe repeatedly that objects fall with increasing speed. You could come up with a hypothesis that the farther something falls, the greater the speed it attains.

A hypothesis can be tested by conducting experiments and making further observations. If your first hypothesis is not supported, does that mean you are a failure as a scientist? No. Even today, in modern laboratories where top scientists use state-of-the-art equipment, science advances by trial and error.

Test the Hypothesis

If one hypothesis turns out to be unsupported, another one can be proposed and tested. It's never possible to prove that a hypothesis is absolutely right. However, you can keep ruling out possibilities until you settle on one you think is most supported. It may take many experiments and many different kinds of data to thoroughly test a hypothesis. The more results you obtain that support the hypothesis, the more confident you can be that it's supported.

Even when you're confident that your hypothesis is confirmed, other scientists may disagree with you. In science, differences of opinions and even conflicting results from similar experiments are normal. Scientists are trained to question everything and always to look for other possible explanations.

Figure 1-8

You can learn about gravity by observing how different objects fall.

Theories and Laws

Scientists use the information they gather during experiments to form a theory. A **theory** is an explanation based on many observations supported by experimental results. A theory is the most logical explanation of why things work the way they do. As new information is collected, a theory may need to be revised or discarded and replaced with another theory. An example of theory revision is shown in **Figure 1-9.**

Scientists also state scientific laws. A **scientific law** is a rule of nature that sums up related observations and experimental results to describe a pattern in nature. For example, scientists have observed for years that matter is never created or destroyed in chemical changes. This fact is stated as the law of conservation of mass. Generally, laws can be used to predict what will happen in a given situation, but they don't explain why. Theories can serve as explanations of laws. Like theories, laws can be changed or discarded if new observations show them to be incorrect.

Whether you're puzzling over a physical science mystery in the classroom or just trying to figure out where you left your homework, you can use what you've learned about problem solving to lead you to a solution.

Figure 1-9

Theories of the origin of the universe have changed over the years and will continue to change as new discoveries are made.

Section Wrap-up

Review

1. Explain the difference between an exercise and a problem. Give an example of each.

2. Compare and contrast these terms: *hypothesis, theory, scientific law.*

3. **Think Critically:** Develop a model to describe how you decide what to wear to school every day. Could someone who doesn't know you use the model to predict what you'll wear tomorrow?

Skill Builder
Outlining

Think of a problem you recently solved or tried to solve. Outline the steps you followed in searching for the solution. If you need help, refer to Outlining in the **Skill Handbook.**

Science Journal

In your Science Journal, describe exactly how you could solve the problem of making sure you are awake at a certain time each day. Then, describe how this problem can become an exercise.

TECHNOLOGY:
1•3 Getting Real with Special Effects

Objectives

- Discuss the ways technology has made movie special effects more realistic.
- List the areas of science that are drawn upon for movie special effects.

Figure 1-10

Technology has helped make movie special effects more realistic.

Technology Makes It Real

Have you ever watched an old horror movie and laughed at how unrealistic the monsters seemed? Maybe there were also scenes in which the cars, planes, ships, and even whole cities were obviously toys or poorly made models. In your mind, compare those scenes to a recent science fiction or horror film you've seen. Even though you knew that much of what you were seeing on the screen was achieved through special effects, didn't it all seem realistic?

Thanks to technological advances in everything from materials to computers, special effects in today's movies are more convincing than ever, as shown in **Figure 1-10.** Even the simplest props, such as fake rocks and windows that an actor can safely jump through, are improvements over the old versions. In old movies, rocks were made from papier mâché. Today, polyurethane foam can be molded, cut, or carved into realistic-looking boulders. In a method similar to that used to build surfboards and some automobile bodies, fiberglass is used to create lightweight imitation rocks. At one time, fake glass was made from hardened sugar water. This candy glass, as it was called, would melt under bright lights or when water was splashed on it. Now, most fake glass in the movies is made of plastic that snaps into pieces on impact.

Figure 1-11
Computers have improved the quality of movement in modern animation films.

Help by Computer

As you can see in **Figure 1-11,** computers have revolutionized special effects in all sorts of films—from cartoons to action adventures. You've probably seen animated films that use a process called claymation, in which figures are photographed one frame at a time and moved slightly between frames. Old attempts at claymation looked jerky and unnatural, but a technique called go-motion, in which computers move cameras and creatures at the same time, gives a much smoother effect.

Section Wrap-up

Review

1. Describe three ways that technological advances have made movie special effects more realistic.

2. Other than making movies more realistic, what are some advantages of using improved materials to make movie props?

Explore the Technology

The specialists who create lifelike mechanical creatures for motion pictures say they need to know as much about animal behavior and anatomy as they do about engineering. If you were trying to design a realistic, mechanical giant insect for a movie, what kinds of information would you gather, and how would you gather it, before you started working on your design?

CONNECT TO

LIFE SCIENCE

To create the sounds of dinosaurs for a movie, sound engineers may first study paleontologists' theories of how the extinct animals might have sounded. *Hypothesize* about how they combine sounds from an assortment of real-life animals to produce the dinosaur sounds.

SCIENCE & SOCIETY

1•4 Exploring Science

Science Words

experiment
control
constant
independent variable
dependent variable

Objectives

- Understand the importance of following guidelines in doing experiments.
- Define *constant, independent variable,* and *dependent variable.*
- Understand laboratory safety rules.

Scientifically Tested

Anyone who performs in a play or a film can be called an actor, whether or not that person makes a living by acting. A person who plays the piano doesn't have to sell out concert halls to be called a pianist. If you solve problems or find new facts by following the steps described in Section 1-2, are you a scientist?

What do scientists do? Scientists, such as the one shown in **Figure 1-12,** gather information from observations, look for patterns, form hypotheses, test their hypotheses with experiments, analyze the results, draw conclusions, and communicate results. The main work of scientists revolves around experiments—designing them, performing them, studying their outcomes, and deciding whether more experiments need to be done.

An **experiment** is an organized procedure for testing a hypothesis. When scientists conduct experiments, they usually are seeking new information. Classroom experiments often demonstrate and verify information that already is known but may be new to you. When doing an experiment, it is important to follow certain guidelines to reduce the chance of reaching wrong conclusions.

Popcorn on Ice

Look at **Figure 1-13.** Another problem has come up at the theater where you work. The popcorn just isn't popping as it should. Every batch has lots of unpopped kernels. You did so well solving the projector problem that the boss wants you to tackle this one. This time, you're going to approach the problem as a scientist would. You're going to experiment.

Figure 1-12

Scientists test their own hypotheses and check the work of other scientists.

20

Be in Control

You remember hearing somewhere that storing popcorn in a freezer makes it pop better. So, you try storing a package of popcorn in the theater's freezer for a day or two. Then, you pop the corn and count the unpopped kernels. Can you draw a meaningful conclusion from this experiment? No, because you don't have anything to compare your results with. Maybe you'd get the same number of unpopped kernels with corn stored at room temperature. You don't know because you didn't test any unfrozen popcorn.

To draw a conclusion, you often need a **control**—a standard for comparison. In an experiment, a control shows that your result is related to the condition you're testing and not to some other condition.

Figure 1-13

If there is a problem with popping this popcorn, an experiment can be conducted to help find out what's wrong. *What are some constants in such an experiment?*

Making Changes

To find out whether storing popcorn in the freezer makes a difference, you need to test popcorn stored at room temperature as a control. All other conditions should be the same for both batches of popcorn. The popcorn should be the same brand, equally fresh, stored for the same period of time, and popped in the same corn-popping machine. Only one factor, the place of storage, should differ between batches. By changing only one factor at a time, while keeping everything else the same, you can find out the effect of that factor. If you change more than one factor at a time, you will not be able to sort out the effects of each change. All of the other factors— brand of popcorn, freshness, storage period, and popping conditions—are constants. A **constant** is a factor that doesn't vary in an experiment.

Can you draw conclusions after popping just one bag of popcorn stored each way? What if one of the bags happened to be defective? To be sure of your conclusions, you should repeat the experiment several times with different bags of popcorn, storing half the bags in the freezer and half at room temperature.

USING MATH

In algebra, a variable is defined as a symbol that is used to represent an unspecified number. How is this definition similar to the definitions of independent and dependent variables?

Going Further

If your experiment shows that storing popcorn in the freezer makes it pop better, you may want to do another experiment to find out whether the length of time the popcorn is stored makes a difference. In the second experiment, all the popcorn would be stored in the freezer but for different lengths of time. Length of time would be the **independent variable,** the factor adjusted by the experimenter. The measure of popping success—the number of unpopped kernels—would be the dependent variable. A **dependent variable** is a factor whose value depends upon the value of the independent variable. What factors would be constants in this experiment?

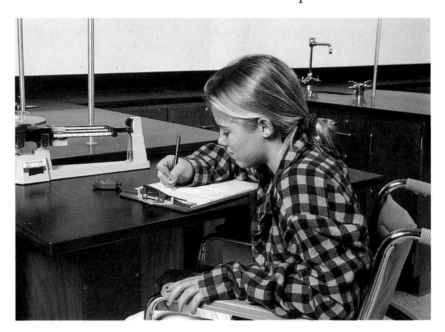

Figure 1-14

Keeping accurate records is an important part of scientific experimentation.

Watch Your Steps

As shown in **Figure 1-14,** keeping accurate records for an experiment will help you to draw conclusions and decide what to do next in your investigation. It will also allow others to duplicate your investigation. Although scientists agree that there is no one way to solve a problem, their scientific methods often include the following steps.

• *Determine the problem.* What do you want to find out?

• *Make a hypothesis.* What prediction do you want to test?

• *Test your hypothesis.* What steps can you take to reach a conclusion about your hypothesis? What measurements should you record?

• *Analyze the results.* What happens during your experiment?

• *Draw conclusions.* Do your observations and data suggest that your hypothesis is supported? If not, do you think your hypothesis should be changed, or does your experimental procedure need adjustment?

As you've seen, scientists use logical methods that can lead to new discoveries and solutions to many problems—just as you did with the popcorn problem. As you did, they record their results so that they can properly analyze them. And, they probably like good popcorn, too. So, are you a scientist? In the sense that you use the same methods that scientists use—yes, you are.

Play It Safe

In movies, the chase scenes, car crashes, and fiery explosions add to the excitement. Filming these scenes can be dangerous, but stunt people take many precautions to minimize their chances of getting hurt. They wear fireproof clothing and protective pads and use props that can be smashed over someone's head without hurting the person. The cars used in crash scenes are reinforced with steel bars to protect the drivers. Special seat belts, air bags, and padding also are used.

While doing science experiments, you'll be asked to follow safety rules, too. There are risks involved in handling glass, hot objects, sharp objects, and certain chemicals. Show proper respect for these new situations, and follow all safety rules, shown in **Figure 1-15,** below and on the next page.

Figure 1-15

The safety rules depicted here and on the next page are essential parts of working in a laboratory.

A First, know what you're supposed to do before you begin. Read and follow all directions carefully, and pay close attention to any caution statements.

B Dress appropriately to reduce the chance of accidents. Avoid clothing with large, floppy sleeves. Remove dangling jewelry, and tie back or cover long hair.

C Think about what you're doing. Handle glass carefully, and don't touch hot objects with your bare hands. To be on the safe side, treat all equipment as if it were hot. Wear safety glasses and a protective apron.

D Be sure you understand the safety symbols explained in Appendix B on page 731. They will be used throughout the textbook to alert you to possible laboratory dangers and precautions to take.

E Your workspace should contain only materials needed. Keep other objects out of the way. Arrange your equipment so that you won't have to reach over burners or across equipment that could be knocked over.

F Watch closely when your teacher demonstrates how to handle equipment, how to dispose of materials, how to clean up spills, and any other safety practices. Make sure you know the location and proper operation of safety equipment, such as fire extinguishers.

Exploring Your World

You've seen how scientists make observations, look for patterns, experiment, and draw conclusions. Every day, you can use the same methods to investigate what's going on around you and to safely solve problems for yourself, your friends, family, and community, as shown in **Figure 1-16.**

Figure 1-16

Safety precautions reduce the risk of injury whether on a movie set or in the lab.

Section Wrap-up

Review

1. What is the function of a control in an experiment?

2. You are doing an experiment to find out how the temperature of water affects the rate at which sugar dissolves. What factors should remain constant? What factors will vary?

3. **Think Critically:** Design an experiment to determine the fastest route from your home to school.

Skill Builder
Hypothesizing
A chemist made some observations about a new type of plastic that may biodegrade in acidic soils. State a possible hypothesis about these findings. How could your hypothesis be tested? If you need help, refer to Hypothesizing in the **Skill Handbook.**

USING MATH

Select one or more classmates to try the popcorn experiment described in this chapter at home. Use micro-wave popcorn, with at least five bags stored in the freezer and an equal number stored at room temperature. For pop-corn stored each way, calculate the average number of kernels left after popping.

Activity 1-1

Design Your Own Experiment
Identifying and Controlling Variables

When you have a problem to solve, a logical plan often works best. Suppose that at the theater concession stand, all the instructions for popping popcorn are followed, but the popcorn still burns. What might be the cause? Maybe not enough oil was used, the popcorn itself did not contain the right amount of moisture, the temperature was too high, or the popping time was too long. You have to be sure that you change only one variable at a time. Here's another problem to solve by controlling variables.

PREPARATION

Problem
In what way does one swinging weight influence another swinging weight?

Form a Hypothesis
Choose a variable and make a hypothesis about the relationship between the variable and how one swinging weight might affect another swinging weight.

Possible variables include string length, distance between weights, amount of weight, and distance of the swing.

Objectives
- Observe the movements of one swinging weight, and notice how these movements affect the movement of another swinging weight.
- Accurately measure changes of the variable.

Possible Materials
- string
- identical weights
- metric ruler
- ring stands
- scissors
- stopwatch or timer

Safety Precautions
Refer to Appendix B on page 731 for an explanation of safety symbols.

PLAN THE EXPERIMENT

1. As a group, agree upon and write out your hypothesis statement, clearly stating which variable you will be testing.
2. As a group, decide on the specific steps that you will use to test your hypothesis. Describe each step carefully.
3. Use the suggested materials to build a suspension setup similar to that shown. Your setup will differ according to the variable you have chosen to test. Remember to keep all other possible variables constant.
4. In your Science Journal, design a data table that can be used to record data and observations.

Check the Plan
1. Read over your steps to make sure that they are in a logical order, and test your hypothesis.
2. Will you want to test the variable more than once?
3. *Make sure your teacher approves your plan and that you have included any changes suggested in the plan.*

DO THE EXPERIMENT

1. With the suspended weights starting in a stationary position, pull one back a measured distance and release it. As it swings, observe the effect on the other weight that is attached to the string.
2. Be sure to make all time and distance measurements accurately and record them in your data table.

Analyze and Apply
1. **Compare** the findings about your variable with those of other groups that checked the same variable.
2. Was your hypothesis supported? Explain.
3. **Compare** your results with those of groups that tested different variables. Which variable seemed to have the most effect on the other weight? Explain.

Go Further

Make a hypothesis about how adding a third weight would affect the other two weights. Test your hypothesis.

People and Science

PRISCILLA KING, *Science Teacher*

On the Job

Q How do the science classes you teach on the Navajo reservation differ from those in an urban school?

A I try to build bridges between science and Navajo traditions. For example, when we're studying stars, I invite an elder from the tribe to present Navajo myths about the creation of the constellations. In a botany class, I help the students collect plants to dye wool for a Navajo rug. Instead of dissecting a frog, my class may butcher a sheep to study the muscles, organs, and bones. Then, in the Navajo way, we make a stew to eat in class and dry some meat to preserve it. Another project might be hunting a deer, studying its body, then tanning the hide. There are scientific principles to learn in every step of that process.

Q Is there a reason, besides the long Navajo tradition of sheep herding, for choosing a sheep over a frog for dissection?

A Yes. The Navajo believe that sheep are a part of our food source but that killing a frog, which is not a usual food source, requires a ceremony to reestablish harmony among living things.

Personal Insights

Q Does scientific problem solving also take a local twist in your classes?

A Yes. Because some of the students don't have running water in their homes, I show them how to test their water source and figure out how to improve its safety. Also, we do an experiment with yucca, a common plant in our area. Students make a shampoo from the yucca root and compare its cleansing properties with those of commercial shampoo.

Q How do you maintain your Navajo heritage?

A I continue to speak the language and keep my Navajo name, Nangisbah, which was given to me by my medicine-man grandfather when I was six years old. That name means "warrior." I guess it fits me because I stand up for what I think is right, even in small ways, like making sure the girls' volleyball team I coach has the same privileges as the football team.

Career Connection

Talk to several teachers in your school. Find out how they relate their subject to students' lives. Then make a poster to show what you learn.

- **Safety Consultant**
- **Curriculum Specialist**

Summary

1-1: Science Is Everywhere

1. Pure science involves gathering information or the discovery of a pattern. When that information is applied to some use, it becomes technology.
2. Physical science is the study of matter and energy.

1-2: Finding Out

1. A problem is a situation that seems to be missing some information. An exercise is a situation where known steps need to be taken to find a solution.
2. Solving problems involves looking for patterns, making predictions, and testing the predictions. Often, a model can be developed that helps to solve a problem.
3. A hypothesis is a testable prediction. A theory, based on many observations, is the most logical explanation of why things work. A scientific law is a summary of many experimental results that describes a pattern in nature.

1-3: Science and Society: Getting Real with Special Effects

1. New technology, new materials, and computer assistance have helped to make some events and objects in movies seem much more realistic than they have seemed in the past.

1-4: Exploring Science

1. An experiment is an organized procedure for testing a hypothesis.
2. Typically, an experiment will have a control, which is a standard for comparison, and two types of variables. Independent variables are adjusted to different values by the experimenter. Dependent variables have values that change with a change in an independent variable.
3. Tested experiments can be done safely when everyone is aware of and follows standard safety warnings.

Key Science Words

a. constant
b. control
c. dependent variable
d. experiment
e. hypothesis
f. independent variable
g. model
h. observation
i. physical science
j. scientific law
k. technology
l. theory

Reviewing Vocabulary

Match each phrase with the correct term from the list of Key Science Words.

1. the study of matter and energy
2. applying science to solve problems
3. an idea, system, or structure that can be used to solve a problem
4. a testable prediction
5. the use of human senses to gather information
6. an organized method of testing a hypothesis
7. describes but doesn't explain a pattern in nature
8. a factor that doesn't change in an experiment
9. a standard for comparison
10. factor in an experiment that is adjusted by the experimenter

Chapter 1 Review

Checking Concepts

Choose the word or phrase that completes the sentence or answers the question.

1. The study of science for the sole purpose of advancing our knowledge is called _____ science.
   a. experimental   c. hypothetical
   b. pure   d. technological
2. Physical science would involve the study of all of the following except _____ .
   a. the melting point of wax
   b. the composition of wax
   c. the behavior of bees producing wax
   d. energy released by burning wax
3. A(n) _____ is used as a standard for comparison in an experiment.
   a. control   c. independent variable
   b. theory   d. constant
4. A _____ is an explanation supported by experimental results.
   a. conclusion   c. scientific law
   b. theory   d. model
5. Advances in technology have helped to make modern movies _____ .
   a. unsafe to make   c. look jerky
   b. more realistic   d. appear unnatural
6. Which of these is not a safety rule to be followed in every laboratory?
   a. Follow all directions carefully.
   b. Clean up all spills immediately.
   c. Wear rubber-soled shoes at all times.
   d. Know the location of the fire extinguisher.
7. An experiment is used for testing a _____ .
   a. model   c. law
   b. theory   d. hypothesis
8. The _____ describe(s) the steps followed in conducting an experiment.
   a. problem   c. conclusion
   b. procedure   d. data
9. A scientific _____ is sometimes called a rule of nature.
   a. theory   c. model
   b. law   d. hypothesis

10. Which is the final step in an experiment?
    a. Reach a conclusion.
    b. State the problem.
    c. Set up a procedure.
    d. Record data.

Understanding Concepts

Answer the following questions in your Science Journal using complete sentences.

11. Why is it usually easier to find the solution to an exercise than it is to find the solution to a problem? Include examples in your answer.
12. Describe how a hypothesis, a theory, and a scientific law are related.
13. Discuss the importance of recording all observations and data when conducting a science experiment.
14. List four safety precautions to be followed in the science laboratory.
15. Describe a special effect that you remember from a movie, and explain how science may have been used to bring about the effect.

Thinking Critically

16. In a study of the sun, what questions might an applied scientist ask? A pure scientist? How might the two sets of questions be related?
17. What aspects of the following items would a physical scientist be interested in?
    a. an electric guitar
    b. a piece of coal

18. Which problem-solving approach would you use to solve the following problems? Explain your choice in each case.
    a. solving a complex word problem in math
    b. figuring out a secret code
    c. predicting how a skyscraper would be affected by an earthquake
19. Design an experiment to determine how the temperature of water affects the time it takes sugar to dissolve in it. Identify the variables, constants, and control, if any.
20. Explain this statement: Scientists often learn as much from an incorrect hypothesis as they do from one that is correct.

Developing Skills

If you need help, refer to the **Skill Handbook.**

21. **Comparing and Contrasting:** Compare and contrast the methods used to complete an exercise and to solve a problem.
22. **Hypothesizing:** Propose a hypothesis to explain why a balloon filled with air weighs more than a deflated balloon.
23. **Interpreting Scientific Illustrations:** The following are safety symbols used in two different experiments. Using Table B-2 on page 731 in Appendix B, write what safety precaution is indicated by each symbol.
    a.
    b.
24. **Using Variables, Constants, and Controls:** Do some objects fall faster than others? Design an experiment to find out. State your hypothesis and describe your procedure for testing it. Identify your variables, constants, and controls.

25. **Concept Mapping:** Fill in the following events chain concept map to show the steps in organizing a scientific experiment. Use the following terms: *draw conclusions, make a hypothesis, determine the problem, analyze the results,* and *test your hypothesis.*

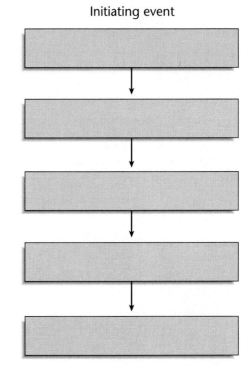

Initiating event

Performance Assessment

1. **Making and Using a Classification System:** One way to solve a problem is to look for patterns within a large system. When you enter a store that sells recorded music, what patterns can you see that help the overall organization of the music in the store? Explain.
2. **Designing an Experiment:** In Activity 1-1, you carefully controlled and identified variables to solve a problem. Assume you are testing two different ink pens to see which one writes for the longer time. What are some important constants to consider?
3. **Poster:** Make a poster that illustrates laboratory safety techniques.

Previewing the Chapter

2

Physical Science Methods

How are the winners in each event determined in the track meet pictured to the left? By carefully measuring and comparing quantities such as length and time, winners of sports events are decided. To be of value, the measurements must relate to a standard with which everyone agrees. Standard measurements are especially important in scientific experiments. In the chapter that follows, you will see how some of the measurement and graphing methods used in physical science are the same as those used to keep sports results consistent and fair.

EXPLORE ACTIVITY

Design your own measuring device.
1. Pick something in your classroom to use as a tool for measuring length. It might be a notebook, a pencil, a hand, or any other convenient device.
2. Working with a partner, measure a distance in the room with your measuring device. Record your measurement and make up a name for your measuring unit.
3. Now, have your partner measure the same distance, first using his or her own measuring device, then using yours. Record measures with proper unit names.

Observe: In your Science Journal, explain why you think it might be important to have standard, well-defined units to make measurements.

Previewing Science Skills

▶ In the Skill Builders, you will sequence, map concepts, and make and use graphs.

▶ In the Activities, you will observe, collect and organize data, and measure in SI.

▶ In the MiniLABs, you will measure in SI, make inferences, and make and use graphs.

2•1 Standards of Measurement

Science Words

standard
SI

Objectives

- Define standard of measurement.
- Identify the need for standards of measurement.
- Name the prefixes used in SI and indicate what multiple of ten each represents.

Units and Standards

Measuring is an important skill. In order for a measurement to be useful, a measurement standard must be used. A **standard** is an exact quantity that people agree to use for comparison. When all measurements are made using the same standard, the measurements can be compared to each other.

Look at **Figure 2-1.** Suppose you and a friend want to make some measurements to find out whether a desk will fit through a doorway. You have no ruler, so you decide to use your hands as measuring tools. Using the width of his or her hands, your friend measures the doorway and says it is 8 hands wide. Using the width of your hands, you measure the desk and find it is 7¾ hands wide. Will the desk fit through the doorway? You can't be sure. What if your hands are wider than your friend's hands? Then, the distance equal to 7¾ of your hands might be greater than the distance equal to 8 of your friend's hands.

What did you forget to do? Even though you both used hands to measure, you didn't check to see whether your hands are the same width as your friend's hands. In other words, you didn't use a measurement standard, so you can't compare the measurements.

Figure 2-1

Hands are a convenient measuring tool, but using them can lead to misunderstanding.

Measurement Systems

Suppose the label on a ball of string indicates that the length of the string in the ball is 150. Can you tell how much string is in the ball? No. It could be 150 feet, 150 meters, or 150 of some unit you've never heard of. In order for a measurement to make sense, it must include a number and a unit.

Your family may buy lumber by the foot, milk by the gallon, and potatoes by the pound. These measurement units are part of the English system of measurement, which is most commonly used in the United States. Most other nations use a system of measurement based on multiples of ten. The first such system of measurement, called the metric system, was devised by a group of scientists in the late 1700s.

Table 2-1

Common SI Prefixes		
Prefix	Symbol	Multiplying Factor
kilo-	k	1000
deci-	d	0.1
centi-	c	0.01
milli-	m	0.001
micro-	μ	0.000 001
nano-	n	0.000 000 001

Figure 2-2

The standard kilogram mass, composed of a platinum-iridium alloy, is kept at the International Bureau of Weights and Measures in Sèvres, France. *What is the purpose of a standard?*

International System of Units

In 1960, an improved version of the metric system was devised. Known as the International System of Units, this system is often abbreviated *SI,* from the French *Le Système Internationale d'Unités. SI* is the standard system of measurement used worldwide. All **SI** standards are universally accepted and understood by scientists. The standard kilogram is shown in **Figure 2-2.**

In SI, each type of measurement has a base unit, such as the meter, which is the base unit of length. In the next section, you will learn the base units in SI used to measure length, mass, time, temperature, volume, and density.

The SI system is easy to use because it is based on powers of ten. Prefixes are used with the names of the base units to indicate what power of ten should be used with the base unit. For example, the prefix *kilo-* means 1000, so a *kilometer* is 1000 meters. The most frequently used prefixes are shown in **Table 2-1.**

Measuring to the Moon

Even with dependable SI units for measurement standards, it is difficult to imagine measuring large distances such as that from Earth to the moon. Obviously, it would not be practical to use a meterstick or gigantic tape measure to find this distance. However, this distance has been measured. How was this done? Lasers produce extremely focused beams of light that are often used to measure both large and small distances. Scientists have determined that light travels a distance of 299 792 500 meters in every second through space. If you know how fast something travels and how long it travels, then the distance it travels can be calculated.

Mirrors on the Moon

U.S. astronauts set up light reflectors on the moon during an exploration trip in the 1970s. Pulses of laser light originating on Earth were aimed at these reflectors. The time for the light to travel from Earth to the moon and back was measured. Knowing this time and the speed of light, the distance from Earth to the moon was calculated to be 378 000 000 meters.

Astronomers have developed large units of measurement based on the speed of light for use in measuring vast distances between objects in space. A light-year is the distance light travels in one year. One light-year equals about 9.5 trillion kilometers. The nearest star is 4.2 light-years away.

CONNECT TO

EARTH SCIENCE

The standard measurement for the distance from Earth to the sun is called the *astronomical unit,* or AU. This distance is about 150 000 000 000 (1.5×10^{11}) m. In your Science Journal, *calculate* what one AU would equal in km.

Section Wrap-up

Review

1. In SI, the base unit of length is the meter. What would you call 0.1 meter? 1000 meters?

2. Why might it be desirable for scientists and manufacturers in the United States and other countries to use the same measurement standard?

3. **Think Critically:** Deimos is a small, natural satellite that orbits Mars. At one point, its diameter is 16 000 meters. How many kilometers is this?

Skill Builder
Sequencing
Using the information in **Table 2-1,** sequence the following units in order from largest to smallest: centigram, gram, milligram, kilogram, decigram. If you need help, refer to Sequencing in the **Skill Handbook.**

Science Journal

Examine the labels of at least five different food or drink products. In your Science Journal, report the metric and English equivalents of the weights or volumes of these products. Write a statement about how you feel about the use of SI units.

Activity 2-1

Metric Munchies

Look through a recipe book. Are any of the amounts of ingredients stated in metric units? Chances are, English measure is used. How could you convert English measurements to metric measurements?

Problem
How do kitchen measurements compare with metric measurements?

Materials
- balance
- graduated cylinder, 100-mL
- munchie ingredients
- measuring cup
- measuring teaspoon
- measuring tablespoon
- plastic container, 1-quart
- hot plate
- cooking pot
- oven mitt

Procedure
1. Copy the data table into your Science Journal.
2. Use the English-measure cup or spoon to measure out the amount of munchie ingredient assigned to your team.
3. Use the balance or graduated cylinder to determine the metric equivalent of the measured ingredient. Convert solid measurements to grams. Convert liquid measurements to milliliters.
4. Write the metric equivalent in your data table. Also write it on the metric ingredients list posted in the classroom.
5. At the direction of the teacher, place your ingredient in the cooking pot.
6. Watch as the teacher cooks the munchies, then write cooking instructions.

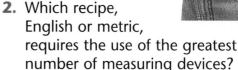

Analyze
1. The volume ratio of sugar to oatmeal is 2 to 3. What is the mass ratio?
2. Which recipe, English or metric, requires the use of the greatest number of measuring devices?
3. Which kind of measure tends to be more accurate, volume or mass?

Conclude and Apply
4. English-measured recipes tend to use whole numbers and simple fractions. **Explain** how you could simplify the metric recipe.
5. **Predict** how kitchen equipment would change if all recipes were metric.
6. **Explain** benefits and problems in changing all recipes to metric.

Data and Observations

Ingredient	English Measure	Metric
Margarine	1/2 cup	
Sugar	2 cups	
Cocoa	6 tablespoons	
Milk	1/2 cup	
Rolled oats	3 cups	
Vanilla	1 teaspoon	
Nuts	1/2 cup	

2•2 Using SI Units

Science Words

meter
volume
derived unit
liter
mass
kilogram
density
time
second
kelvin

Objectives

- Identify SI units and symbols for length, volume, mass, density, time, and temperature.
- Define *derived unit*.
- Convert a measurement among related SI units.

SI Units and Symbols

Every type of quantity measured in SI has a base unit and a symbol for that unit. These names and symbols are shown in **Table 2-2.** All other SI units can be derived from these seven base units.

Table 2-2

SI Base Units		
Quantity Measured	Unit	Symbol
Length	Meter	m
Mass	Kilogram	kg
Time	Second	s
Electric current	Ampere	A
Temperature	Kelvin	K
Amount of substance	Mole	mol
Intensity of light	Candela	cd

Length

The word *length* is used in many different ways. For example, the length of a novel is the number of pages or words it contains. In scientific measurement, length is the distance between two points. That distance may be the diameter of a period on this page or the distance from Earth to the moon. The SI base unit of length is the **meter** (m). A baseball bat is about 1 meter long. Metric rulers and metersticks are used to measure length.

Recall that measurement in SI is based on powers of ten. The prefix *deci-* means 1/10, so a decimeter is one-tenth of a meter. Similarly, a centimeter (cm) is one-hundredth of a meter. **Figure 2-3** shows how a meter and a yard compare. The diameter of a shirt button is about 1 cm.

$$100 \text{ cm} = 10 \text{ dm} = 1 \text{ m}$$

Centimeters can be divided into smaller units called millimeters (mm). A millimeter is 1/1000 of a meter. One tooth along the edge of a postage stamp is about 1 mm long.

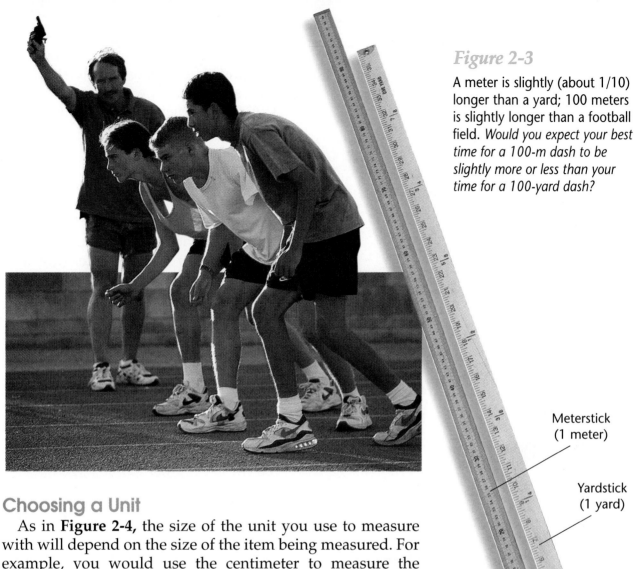

Figure 2-3

A meter is slightly (about 1/10) longer than a yard; 100 meters is slightly longer than a football field. *Would you expect your best time for a 100-m dash to be slightly more or less than your time for a 100-yard dash?*

Meterstick
(1 meter)

Yardstick
(1 yard)

Choosing a Unit

As in **Figure 2-4,** the size of the unit you use to measure with will depend on the size of the item being measured. For example, you would use the centimeter to measure the length of your pencil and the meter to measure the length of your classroom. What unit would you use to measure the distance from your home to school? You would probably want to use a unit larger than a meter. The kilometer (km), which is 1000 meters, is used to measure long distances. One kilometer is about ten football fields long.

Suppose you know the length of something in meters and want to change, or *convert*, the measurement to centimeters. Because 1 m = 100 cm, you can convert from meters to centimeters simply by multiplying by 100. Because SI is based on powers of ten, any unit can be converted to a related

1 cm

1 mm

Figure 2-4

The size of the object being measured determines which unit you should use. *What unit would you use to measure your height?*

Figure 2-5

One centimeter contains ten millimeters. *How many millimeters are in ten centimeters?*

unit by multiplying or dividing it by the appropriate power of ten. **Figure 2-5** shows units of length on a meterstick.

If you follow these rules, conversion will be easy.

- A measurement consists of two parts: a number and a unit label.
- To convert from larger to smaller units, multiply.
- To convert from smaller to larger units, divide.

For example, to convert 532 cm to meters, you divide because you're converting from smaller (cm) to larger (m) units. Because 100 cm = 1 m, divide 532 by 100. So, 532 cm = 5.32 m.

Another way to convert units is to multiply by a ratio that equals one. For example, 1 meter = 100 centimeters. Therefore,

$$\frac{1 \text{ meter}}{100 \text{ centimeters}} = \frac{100 \text{ centimeters}}{100 \text{ centimeters}} = 1$$

To convert 532 cm to meters, write

$$532 \text{ cm} \times \frac{1 \text{ m}}{100 \text{ cm}} = \frac{532 \text{ m}}{100} = 5.32 \text{ m}$$

The *cm* label is canceled because it appears in both the numerator and the denominator. Try the practice problems below.

USING MATH

Converting Meters to Centimeters

Example Problem:

How many centimeters are in 1.98 meters?

Problem-Solving Steps:

1. What is known?
   1 m = 100 cm
   You are converting from larger to smaller units.
2. When converting from larger to smaller units, multiply.
3. **Solution:** Multiply 1.98 by 100.   1.98 m = 198 cm

Practice Problems

1. How many centimeters are in 253.8 km?
Strategy Hint: First, change kilometers to meters; then, change meters to centimeters.
2. A bookshelf is 75 cm wide. How many decimeters is this? How many meters would this be?
Strategy Hint: Remember the meanings of the prefixes.

As you move ahead in this section, you will learn about several different types of measurements. Keep in mind that the conversion rules you have used here can be used with any base unit in SI because the system is based on powers of ten. The prefixes remain the same no matter what base unit you may be using.

Volume

The amount of space occupied by an object is called its **volume.** If you want to know the volume of a solid object, such as a building brick, you measure its length, width, and height, and multiply the three numbers together. For the brick, your measurements would be in centimeters, and the volume would be expressed in cubic centimeters (cm^3). For a larger object, such as a truck, your measurements might be in meters and the volume in cubic meters (m^3).

Width of sphere = 0.01 mm

USING TECHNOLOGY

Space Spheres ▽ △

The space shuttle *Challenger* served as the manufacturing site for one of the latest standard or reference materials produced by the National Bureau of Standards. The reference material is a polystyrene sphere that measures 10 micrometers across. The head of a pin could hold 18 000 of these spheres. The spheres will be packaged in a 5-mL vial containing about 30 million spheres in water. These spheres can be used as a reference for manufacturers and researchers who need to calibrate instruments to check particle size in products such as cosmetics, paint pigments, flour, toner used in photocopiers, and so on. The spheres can also be used to improve microscopic measurements made in areas such as medicine and electronics.

Weightless Manufacturing

The *Challenger* was chosen as the manufacturing site because of its weightless environment. Spheres produced by conventional processes on Earth float or sink during their formation. This results in spheres with a variation in diameter that is too great for use as a standard. Weightlessness allows the production of spheres that are uniform in size and shape.

Think Critically:

In your Science Journal, explain why particle size is important in the products listed.

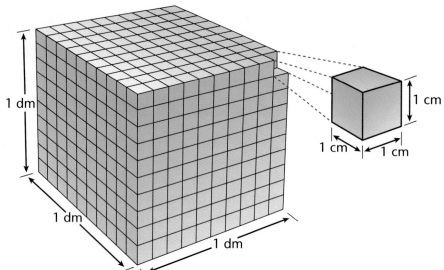

Figure 2-6

The large cube has a volume of 1 cubic decimeter (dm^3), which is equivalent to a liter. *How many cubic centimeters (cm^3) are in the large cube?*

Measuring Volume

No simple tool can be used to measure the volume of an object directly. As you saw in the example with the brick on the previous page, volume units are obtained by combining other SI units of length. Units obtained by combining SI units are called **derived units.**

How do you measure the volume of a liquid? A liquid has no sides to measure. In measuring a liquid's volume, you indicate the capacity of a container that holds that amount of liquid. Liquid volumes are sometimes expressed in cubic centimeters, as in doses of medicine. The most common units for expressing liquid volumes are liters and milliliters. A **liter** occupies the same volume as a cubic decimeter (dm^3). That is, a liter is the same volume as a cube that is 1 dm (10 cm) on each side, as in **Figure 2-6.** A liter is slightly larger than a quart. The

USING MATH

Converting Centimeters to Liters
Example Problem:
How many liters of gasoline are in 538 cm^3?

Problem-Solving Steps:
1. What is known?
    $1\ cm^3 = 1\ mL$ and $1\ L = 1000\ mL$;
    therefore, $1\ L = 1000\ cm^3$
    You are converting from smaller units to larger units.
2. When converting from smaller to larger units, divide.

3. **Solution:** Divide 538 by 1000. $538\ cm^3 = 0.538\ L$

Practice Problem
1. How many cubic centimeters are in 1.45 L of milk?

liter is not an SI unit, but it is used frequently with that system. Study the problems on page 42.

One liter (L) is equal to 1000 milliliters (mL). A cubic decimeter (dm^3) is equal to 1000 cubic centimeters (cm^3). So, because $1 L = 1 dm^3$, $1 mL = 1 cm^3$.

Suppose you wanted to convert a measurement in liters to cubic centimeters. The same rules you used for converting length can be used for any SI unit.

Mass

A table-tennis ball and a golf ball have about the same volume. But if you pick them up, you notice a difference. The golf ball has more mass. **Mass** is a measurement of the matter in an object. The SI unit of mass is the **kilogram** (kg). For measuring objects of small mass, grams (g) or milligrams are used. How many grams are in 1 kilogram?

In the laboratory, mass is measured with a balance. There are several different types of balances, but they all operate on the same principle. You use something of known mass to balance something else of unknown mass.

Density

If you were to take a cube of polished aluminum and a cube of silver the same size, they would look similar, and they would have the same volume. But the cube of silver would have more mass. The mass and volume of an object can be used to find the density of the material it is made of. **Density** is the mass per unit volume of a material.

Problem Solving

Verifying Volumes: Finding the Best Value

Suppose you are in charge of supplying a certain brand of soft drink for a large crowd at a picnic. At the store, you find two possible ways to buy the soft drink: 2-L bottles costing $1.30 each, and six-packs of 355-mL cans costing $2.50 per pack. Assuming cups are already provided, how will you decide which type of package is a more economical way to purchase the soft drink?

Solve the Problem:
1. **Determine how many milliliters of soft drink are in a 2-L bottle and how many are in a six-pack of soda cans. Also express each answer in liters.**
2. **Calculate the price per liter of soda for each type of packaging. Which is the best buy?**

Think Critically:
If you were buying the soft drinks for a large picnic, you would likely have a budget. If you have $40 to purchase this brand of soft drink, what is the maximum number of liters of soda you can purchase?

MiniLAB

What is the density of a pencil?

Procedure

1. Use a balance to measure the mass of a pencil in grams.
2. Put 90 mL of water into a 100-mL graduated cylinder. Lower the pencil, eraser end down, into the cylinder. Continue to push the pencil point down until it is completely underwater, but be sure your finger is not also submerged. Read the new volume to the nearest tenth of a milliliter.

Analysis

1. Calculate the pencil's density by dividing its mass by the change in volume of the water level when the pencil was completely underwater.
2. Is the density of the pencil greater or less than the density of water? How do you know?

Table 2-3

Material	Density (g/cm³)	Material	Density (g/cm³)
Hydrogen	0.000 09	Quartz	2.6
Oxygen	0.0013	Aluminum	2.7
Cork	0.24	Iron	7.9
Water	1.0	Copper	8.9
Glue	1.27	Lead	11.3
Sugar	1.6	Mercury	13.6
Table salt	2.2	Gold	19.3

Like volume, density is a derived unit. You can find the density of an object by dividing its mass by its volume. For example, the density of an object having a mass of 10 g and a volume of 2 cm³ is 5 g/cm³. This value is expressed as 5 grams per cubic centimeter. Notice that both the mass and volume units are used to express density. **Table 2-3** lists the densities of some familiar materials.

Time and Temperature

It is often necessary to keep track of how long it takes for something to happen, or whether something heats up or cools down. These measurements involve time and temperature. **Figure 2-7** shows some different kinds of clocks.

Time is the interval between two events. The SI unit for time is the **second.** In the laboratory, you will use a stopwatch or a clock with a second hand to measure time.

Figure 2-7

Water clocks, sundials, digital clocks, stopwatches, and atomic clocks are all devices that measure time. *Which clock is most accurate?*

What's Hot and What's Not

You will learn the scientific meaning of temperature in a later chapter. For now, you can think of temperature as a measure of how hot or how cold something is. The temperature of a material is measured with a thermometer.

Look at **Figure 2-8.** For most scientific work, temperature is measured on the Celsius (C) scale. On this scale, the freezing point of water is zero degrees (0°C), and the boiling point of water is one hundred degrees (100°C). Between these points, the scale is divided into 100 equal divisions. Each one represents 1 Celsius degree. On the Celsius scale, average human body temperature is 37°C, and a typical room temperature may be between 20°C and 25°C.

The SI unit of temperature is the **kelvin** (K). Zero on the Kelvin scale (0 K) is the coldest possible temperature, also known as *absolute zero*. That is −273°C, which is 273 degrees below the freezing point of water.

Most laboratory thermometers are marked only with the Celsius scale. Because the divisions on the two scales are the same size, the Kelvin temperature can be found by adding 273 to the Celsius reading. So, on the Kelvin scale, water freezes at 273 K and boils at 373 K. Notice that degree symbols are not used with the Kelvin scale.

Figure 2-8

These three thermometers illustrate the range of temperatures between the freezing point and boiling point of water. Although the numbers on the scales are different, they measure the same temperature range. *How do a Celsius and a Fahrenheit degree compare?*

Celsius   Fahrenheit   Kelvin

Section Wrap-up

Review

1. Make the following conversions.
   a. 100 cm to meters
   b. 2.3 dm³ to liters
   c. 27°C to K

2. Explain why density is a derived unit.

3. **Think Critically:** Chemists sometimes use density to identify a sample. What is the density of an unknown metal that has a mass of 178.0 g and a volume of 20.0 mL? Use **Table 2-3** to help you predict the possible identity of this metal.

USING MATH

You probably know how much you weigh in pounds. Calculate your mass in kilograms. HINT: At Earth's surface, an object weighing 1 pound has a mass of 0.45 kg.

Skill Builder
Concept Mapping

Make a network tree concept map to show the SI base units used to measure length, mass, time, and temperature. If you need help, refer to Concept Mapping in the **Skill Handbook.**

Setting High Standards. . . for Measurement

To develop the International System, people had to agree on set standards and basic definitions of scale. If you had to develop a new measurement system, people would have to agree with your new standards and definitions. In this activity, your team will use string to devise and test its own SI (String International) system for measuring length.

PREPARATION

Problem
What are the requirements for designing a new measurement system using string?

Form a Hypothesis
Based on your knowledge of measurement standards and systems, state a hypothesis about the relationship between measurement standards and consistency of measurements.

Objectives
- Design an experiment that involves devising and testing your own measurement system for length.
- Measure various objects with the string measurement system.

Possible Materials
- string
- scissors
- marking pen
- masking tape
- miscellaneous objects for standards

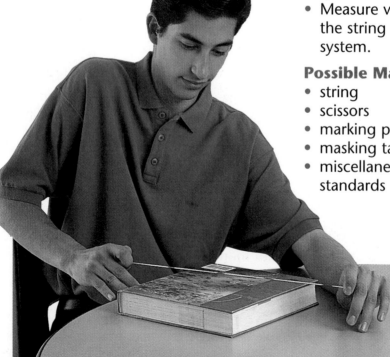

PLAN THE EXPERIMENT

1. As a group, agree upon and write out the hypothesis statement.
2. As a group, list the steps that you need to take to test your hypothesis. Be specific, describing exactly what you will do at each step.
3. Make a list of the materials that you will need to complete your experiment.
4. Design a data table in your Science Journal so it is ready to use as your group collects data.

Check the Plan

1. As you read over your experimental plan, be sure you have chosen an object in your classroom to serve as a standard. Keep in mind, it should be in the same size range as what you will measure.

2. Consider how you will mark scale divisions on your string. Plan to use different pieces of string to try different-sized scale divisions of the base unit.
3. What will your new unit of measurement be called? Come up with an abbreviation for your unit. Will you name the smaller scale divisions, too?
4. What objects will you measure with your new measuring unit? Be sure to include objects longer and shorter than your string. Will you measure each object more than once to test consistency?
5. *Make sure your teacher approves your plan and that you have included any changes suggested in the plan.*

DO THE EXPERIMENT

1. Carry out the experiment as planned.
2. Record observations that you make, and complete the data table in your Science Journal. Be sure to include a unit with your measurements.

Analyze and Apply

1. Which of your string scale systems will provide the most accurate measurement of small objects? **Explain.**

2. How did you record measurements that were between two whole numbers of your units? Are any of your scale divisions easy to report as decimal numbers? Why or why not?
3. When sharing your results with other groups, why is it important for them to know what you used as a standard?
4. **Infer** how it is possible for different numbers to represent the same length of an object.

Go Further

If you were to design a new measurement system for mass, what parts of your experimental plan would be the same as they were for this length-measuring system? What parts would be different?

2•3 Graphing

Science Words

graph

Objectives

- Identify three types of graphs and explain the correct use of each type.
- Distinguish between dependent and independent variables.
- Interpret graphs.

MiniLAB

How can a graph help you observe change?

Procedure

1. Place a thermometer in a plastic foam cup of hot, but not boiling, water.
2. Measure and record the temperature every 30 seconds for 5 minutes.
3. Repeat the experiment with freshly heated water. This time, cover the cup with a plastic lid.

Analysis

1. Make a line graph of the changing temperature from step 2, showing time on the *x*-axis and temperature on the *y*-axis. Then plot the changing temperature from step 3 on the same graph.
2. Use the graph to describe what happens during cooling in each cup.

Using Graphs

Often, it is helpful to be able to illustrate what happens during the course of an experiment. This can be done with a graph. A **graph** is a visual display of information or data. **Figure 2-9** is a graph that shows a girl walking her dog.

Graphs are useful for displaying information in business, sports, and many everyday situations. Different kinds of graphs—line, bar, and circle—are appropriate for displaying different types of information. It is important to use the correct kind of graph for the data you are presenting.

Figure 2-9

This graph tells the story of the motion that takes place when a girl takes her dog for an 8-minute walk. Study each segment of the graph. Use the drawings above each one to help you understand what the shape of that segment tells you about the motion of the girl and dog during that time interval. *Where are the girl and dog moving fastest?*

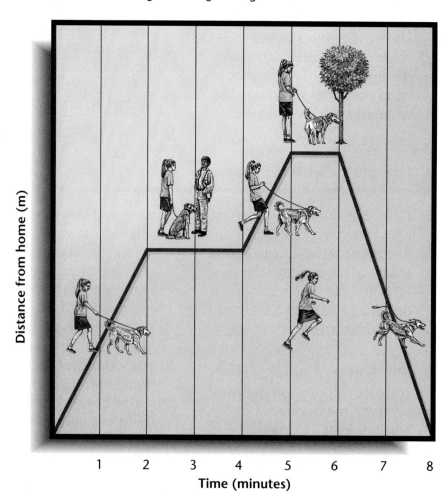

Distance from home (m)

Time (minutes)

Line Graphs

Line graphs are used to show trends or how the data change over time. Suppose you want to show how the temperature of a room changes after you switch on the heat one chilly morning. Taking temperature readings in the room every 5 minutes, you might collect information that looks like that shown in **Table 2-4.** If you look closely at the data, you can see how temperature changed over time. But the relationship is easier to see in the graphs shown in **Figure 2-10.** Both graphs show that temperature increased for the first 15 minutes, then stayed constant. Do the graphs tell you anything about what made the temperature change?

Table 2-4

Room Temperature	
Time* Temperature (°C)	
0	16
5	17
10	19
15	20
20	20
25	20
*minutes after turning on heat	

Figure 2-10

Both of the graphs below show the same information from **Table 2-4.** Notice, however, that the temperature scales along the vertical axes are different. *Which graph shows a bigger temperature change over the same 25-minute time period?*

A In this graph, each temperature interval represents 5°C. Because the temperatures measured were between 16 and 20°C, the portion of the graph below 16°C is not even used.

B In this graph, the break in the vertical axis between the 0 and the 15 means that numbers in this range have been left out to save space. Each temperature mark represents 1°C. The temperature range graphed covers about 5 degrees instead of the 20-degree range covered in **Figure 2-10A.** Because there is more space between the numbers on this vertical axis, the same change in temperature looks larger.

Graphs Show Change

In the example in **Figure 2-10,** two things are changing, or varying—time and temperature. Time is the independent variable. Its value does not depend on changes in the value of the other variable, temperature. Temperature is the dependent variable. Its value depends on changes in the time. In a line graph, the dependent variable always is plotted on the vertical *y*-axis, and the independent variable is plotted on the horizontal *x*-axis.

Bar Graphs

A bar graph is useful for comparing information collected by counting. For example, suppose you measured the temperature in every classroom in your school and organized your data in a table like **Table 2-5.** You could show these data in a bar graph like the one shown in **Figure 2-11.** The height of each bar corresponds to the number of rooms at a particular temperature.

In a line graph, adjacent points are related with a straight or curving line. In a bar graph, the bars are not connected.

Figure 2-11

The height of each bar corresponds to the number of rooms at a particular temperature.

Table 2-5

Temperature of Classrooms	
Temp. (°C)	Number of Classrooms
16	1
17	3
18	3
19	2
20	3
21	5
22	5
23	3

Circle Graphs

A circle graph, or pie graph, is used to show how some fixed quantity is broken down into parts. The circular pie represents the total. The slices represent the parts and usually are represented as percentages of the total.

Figure 2-12 illustrates how a circle graph could be used to show the percent of buildings in a neighborhood using each of a variety of heating fuels. You can easily see that more buildings use gas heat than any other kind of system. What else does the graph tell you?

When you use graphs, think carefully about the conclusions you can draw from them. Can you infer cause and effect from looking at a graph? How might the scale of the graph affect your conclusions? Is any information missing or improperly connected?

Figure 2-12

A circle graph shows the different parts of a whole quantity.

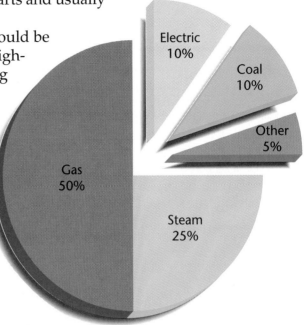

Section Wrap-up

Review

1. Your class does an experiment to show how the volume of a gas changes with changes in temperature. You are asked to make a line graph of the results. What are the dependent and independent variables?

2. Explain why points are connected in a line graph, but not in a bar graph.

3. **Think Critically:** A survey shows that, in your neighborhood, 75 people ride the bus; 45 drive their own cars; 15 carpool; 9 walk, ride bikes, or ride motorcycles; and the rest use different methods on different days to get to work. What kind of graph would be best for displaying these results at a neighborhood meeting? Draw it.

Skill Builder
Making and Using Graphs

Find a graph in a newspaper or magazine. Identify the kind of graph you found and write an explanation of what the graph shows. If you need help, refer to Making and Using Graphs in the **Skill Handbook.**

Using Computers

Spreadsheet Some computer programs make creating data tables and making graphs an easier task. Use a spreadsheet and a graphing program to make a data table and a line graph of the data you collected in the MiniLAB on page 48.

ISSUE:

2•4 SI for All?

SI Use in the United States

Can you think of any situations, other than in science classes, where you see SI units in use? Athletes compete on courses that are measured in meters, medicine is sold in milligrams and milliliters, and some soft drinks are sold in 2-L bottles. Imported equipment is manufactured to metric specifications, as shown in **Figure 2-13.** However, in the United States, other units of measure are still common. Carpenters still buy lumber measured in feet and inches, farmers measure their land in acres and their crops in bushels, fabric is sold by the yard, and highway signs give distances in miles and speed limits in miles per hour. Sometimes both systems are used, as shown in **Figure 2-14.**

A History of Conflict

For nearly 100 years, advocates of the metric system and the newer SI units have argued for widespread adoption of the system in the United States. Only a few countries in the world have not adopted SI as the official system of measurement. But opponents to changing the measurement system have argued just as vigorously against it.

Objectives

- Analyze the advantages and disadvantages of universal use of SI measurements.
- Give examples of SI units already commonly used in the United States.

Figure 2-13

The metric system is used universally, so when working on imported equipment, it is necessary to use metric tools.

2 Points of View

Drawbacks of Adopting SI

Many citizens resist the switch to SI units because they have grown up using such units as feet, pounds, and gallons, and they feel more comfortable using them. Some representatives of industry point out that such a changeover would require them to replace or convert their machinery and tools to the appropriate SI dimensions—a costly process.

Benefits of Adopting SI

Citizens in favor of adopting SI argue that because SI is based on powers of ten, conversions and calculations between different units are easier. For example, do you know how many cubic inches are in a fluid ounce? It is much easier to recall that one cubic centimeter is equivalent to one milliliter of fluid. Some business people also point out that one-time costs of making industrial machinery compatible with SI will easily be offset by the time and money saved by having products automatically ready for trade with other countries, nearly all of which use SI.

Figure 2-14

In order to acquaint people in the United States with metric measurements, many lengths and package net contents are given in both English and SI units.

Section Wrap-up

Review

1. Write a list of different units used to measure length in the United States. Then show the calculations necessary to convert from one unit to another. Do the same thing using SI units for length. Which is easier?

2. Write a one-paragraph essay summarizing your position on the adoption of SI in the United States.

Explore the Issue

Suppose that on the first day of the new year, the whole United States is to begin using only SI units. In your Science Journal, explain what changes would need to be made by that time. For whom would the change be most difficult or costly? Who would benefit most from this change? Explain your answers clearly.

Science Journal

In your Science Journal, explain your opinions about adopting SI in the United States.

SCIENCE & SOCIETY

Cubism

In this chapter, you learned about standard methods of measurement. What do you think might happen if some people decided to use different tools or units of measurement? Would their methods be understood and accepted by all? Probably not. In a similar vein, various artists in the early 1900s decided to challenge the Impressionist school of art that emphasized light, atmosphere, and perspective, and formed a new school of art called Cubism.

Cubists concerned themselves with the representation of form in their paintings and sculptures. They strove to use cylinders, spheres, and cones to create a three-dimensional perspective on a flat surface. This use of illusion gave the works an abstract look.

Some art critics link the Cubist movement to the physical world proposed by physicist Albert Einstein at the time. These critics interpret time as an actual dimension in the artwork. Objects in Cubist works, they argue, are not seen at one specific moment. Rather, the different views shown would have been seen by the artist at different times. The result is a piece of art as seen in both time and space.

Science Journal

Go to a nearby art museum and view some Cubist works on display. Or, browse through some art history books in the library to find some more examples of Cubism. Choose one or two pieces to describe, sketch, and discuss in your Science Journal.

Analytical Cubism

Analytical Cubism is the early phase of Cubism. It lasted only two years, from 1910 to 1912. Mentally, Analytical Cubists divided their subjects into numerous planes. When arranged on the canvas, these planes interlocked and overlapped to produce an abstract view of reality. Strong contrasts were made using only blacks, whites, grays, and sometimes browns.

Synthetic Cubism

The second phase of Cubism—Synthetic Cubism—gained popularity about 1912. The nearly one-color, abstract Analytical Cubist works of art gave way to more colorful works with a limited number of views of the subject. These Synthetic Cubist works of art also used a broader variety of textures and shapes.

Summary

2-1: Standards of Measurement

1. A standard of measurement is an exact quantity that people agree to use as a basis of comparison.
2. When a standard of measurement is established, all measurements are compared to the same exact quantity—the standard. Therefore, all measurements can be compared with one another.
3. In SI, prefixes are used to make the base units larger or smaller by powers of ten. The most common prefixes and their values are: *kilo-*, 1000; *deci-*, 0.1; *centi-*, 0.01; *milli-*, 0.001; *micro-*, 0.000 001; and *nano-*, 0.000 000 001.

2-2: Using SI Units

1. The most commonly used units in SI and their symbols include: length—meter, m; volume—cubic decimeter, dm^3; mass—kilogram, kg; time—second, s.
2. Any SI unit can be converted to any other related SI unit by multiplying or dividing by the appropriate multiple of ten.

2-3: Graphing

1. Line graphs show continuous changes between related variables. Bar graphs are used to show data collected by counting. Circle or pie graphs show how a fixed quantity can be broken into parts.
2. In a line graph, the independent variable is always plotted on the horizontal *x*-axis; the dependent variable is always plotted on the vertical *y*-axis.

2-4: Science and Society: SI for All?

1. There are many benefits and drawbacks to the adoption of SI.
2. SI units are already in wide use on consumer goods in the United States.

Key Science Words

a. density
b. derived unit
c. graph
d. kelvin
e. kilogram
f. liter
g. mass
h. meter
i. second
j. SI
k. standard
l. time
m. volume

Reviewing Vocabulary

Match each phrase with the correct term from the list of Key Science Words.

1. the modern version of the metric system
2. the amount of space occupied by an object
3. an agreed-upon quantity to be used for comparison
4. the amount of matter in an object
5. obtained by combining SI units
6. a visual display of data
7. the SI unit of mass
8. the SI unit of length
9. a metric unit of volume
10. mass per unit volume

Chapter 2 Review

Checking Concepts

Choose the word or phrase that completes the sentence or answers the question.

1. A meaningful measurement must have _____.
   a. a number only
   b. a unit only
   c. a number and a unit
   d. a prefix and a unit
2. The _____ is an example of an SI unit.
   a. foot   c. pound
   b. second   d. gallon
3. The system of measurement used by scientists around the world is the _____.
   a. SI   c. English system
   b. Standard system d. Kelvin system
4. SI is based on _____.
   a. inches   c. English units
   b. powers of five d. power of ten
5. The SI prefix that means 1/1000 is _____.
   a. kilo-   c. centi-
   b. nano-   d. milli-
6. The symbol for deciliter is _____.
   a. dL   c. dkL
   b. dcL   d. Ld
7. The symbol for _____ is µg.
   a. nanogram   c. microgram
   b. kilogram   d. milligram
8. _____ is the distance between two points.
   a. Volume   c. Mass
   b. Length   d. Density
9. Which of the following is not a derived unit?
   a. cubic decimeter c. cubic centimeter
   b. meter   d. grams per milliliter
10. 1000 mL is equal to all of the following except _____.
    a. 1 L   c. 1 dm^3
    b. 100 cL   d. 1 cm^3

Understanding Concepts

Answer the following questions in your Science Journal using complete sentences.

11. Why are SI measurements used in science classes?
12. Explain how to convert from one length measurement in SI to another. Can volume or mass measurements be converted in the same way? Why or why not?
13. Describe three different types of graphs and the types of data best displayed by each.
14. Suppose you set a glass of water in direct sunlight for two hours and measure its temperature every 10 minutes. What type of graph would you use to display your data? What would the dependent variable be? The independent variable?
15. What are some advantages and disadvantages of adopting SI for use in the United States?

Thinking Critically

16. Make the following conversions.
    a. 1500 mL to liters
    b. 2 km to cm
    c. 5.8 dg to mg
    d. 22°C to kelvin
17. Standards of measurement used during the Middle Ages were often based on such things as the length of the king's arm. What arguments would you use to convince people of the need for a different system of standard measurements?
18. List the SI units of length you would use to express the following. Refer to **Table 2-1** on page 35.
    a. the diameter of an atom
    b. the width of your classroom
    c. the width of a pencil lead
    d. the length of a sheet of paper
    e. the distance to the moon

19. Determine the density of each of the following objects.
a. mass = 15 g, volume = 2 cm^3
b. mass = 200 g, volume = 80 mL
c. mass = 1.8 kg, volume = 0.2 L

20. Suppose you measure the distance a go-cart travels every 5 seconds for a 60-second period. What kind of graph would you use to display your data? What would the dependent and independent variables be?

Developing Skills

If you need help, refer to the **Skill Handbook.**

21. Comparing and Contrasting: Consider the base units and conversion procedures in SI and the English system. Compare and contrast the ease with which conversions can be made among units within each system.

22. Hypothesizing: A metal sphere is found to have a density of 5.2 g/cm^3 at 25°C and a density of 5.1 g/cm^3 at 50°C. Propose a hypothesis to explain this observation. How could you easily test your hypothesis?

23. Concept Mapping: Complete the Concept Map for metric measurements using the following terms: *trends or change over time, bar, circle, information collected by counting, line, proportional parts of a whole.*

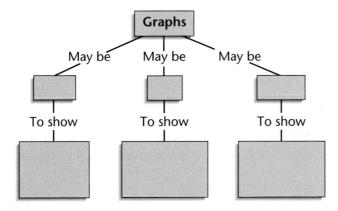

24. Making and Using Graphs: Using the data in **Table 2-3** on page 44, graph the densities of the following materials: water, sugar, salt, iron, copper, lead, and gold. Use the proper type of graph and let each unit on your graph represent 1.0 g/cm^3. Then, answer the following questions:
a. Why did you choose this type of graph?
b. What would be the mass of 5 cm^3 of sugar?
c. If you had a 1-g sample of each material shown in the graph, which sample would have the greatest volume?
d. How could your graph be made more accurate?

25. Measuring in SI: Determine the mass, volume, and density of your textbook, a container of milk, and an air-filled balloon. Make your measurements in SI units using the appropriate measuring tool and the quickest, most accurate method possible.

Performance Assessment

1. Making Observations and Inferences: In Activity 2-1, suppose you wanted to make five times that much food. Compare the difficulty of multiplying the English measurements five times with multiplying the metric measurements five times.

2. Designing an Experiment: Explain how you could improve the accuracy of the measuring system you used in Activity 2-2 for marking the scale divisions.

3. Using Math in Science: Find the SI equivalents of familiar measurements such as
a. your weight in newtons (1 lb = 4.5 N)
b. your mass in kilograms (1 kg = 2.2 lb)
c. volume of 1.5 gallons of milk in liters (1 gal = 3780 mL)

Think Like A Scientist

Your gym locker won't open. You can't decide what to eat for lunch. You need to explain to a friend how to get to your house. Every day you have problems that you need to solve and ideas that you need to communicate. Problem solving and communicating are not always easy to do. However, your ability to describe events or materials that you come in contact with can be improved by using measurements. In this project, begin to understand the importance of scientific processes by combining all three of these skills: problem solving, communication, and measurement.

Two Languages for Temperature

At the present time, the world uses primarily two systems for measuring temperature. The Fahrenheit and Celsius systems were both named after the scientists who developed these now-familiar temperature scales. Most countries around the world use the Celsius scale. Scientists also use the Celsius scale. In the United States, however, temperature is reported in degrees Fahrenheit. Because two temperature scales are commonly used, it is important to be able to convert, or translate, from one to the other.

Purpose
In this experiment, work with a partner to show the conversion of temperature measurements between the two systems.

Materials
- a Fahrenheit thermometer
- a Celsius thermometer
- a beaker of water
- a hot plate
- clamps for the thermometers

Procedure

1. Use the hot plate to heat a quantity of water in a beaker.

2. When the water begins to boil, turn off the power to the hot plate.

3. Carefully suspend both of your thermometers near each other in the hot water.

4. As the temperature begins to drop, record the temperature readings, taken at the same time, from each of the thermometers. Be sure to label each of your paired readings as either °C or °F.

5. Collect a total of ten separate paired temperature readings. You may place the beaker and thermometers in a refrigerator to make the water cool faster.

Using Your Research

To help you compare the two scales, use a technique scientists frequently use—prepare a graph. With your partner, set up a graph with °C on the vertical axis and °F on the horizontal axis.

Even though you may not have measured it, label your vertical axis so that it includes 0°C. Make a line graph that plots each of your pairs of temperature readings. What value on the Fahrenheit axis matches the 0°C reading? This value is the amount that each Celsius degree is offset from each Fahrenheit measurement.

Next, select any ten-degree change on the Celsius axis. Use the line that you made to determine how many degrees the Fahrenheit scale would change in that interval. Using these values, determine what ratio compares one Celsius degree to one Fahrenheit degree.

Use this information to show how to change a Fahrenheit measurement to a Celsius value. With your partner, make a large poster of your graph and use your poster to explain the differences in the two systems and how to convert from one system to the other.

Go Further

Find photographs of different scenes that show people or events that are in situations of obvious temperature ranges. Examples might include a sunny beach and a snow scene. Attach these to your graph with questions relating the temperature in each scene to the graph.

Another temperature scale used commonly by scientists is Kelvin. Find out how and why the Kelvin scale was developed and how it compares to the Celsius scale. Design a method to convert Celsius to Kelvin.

UNIT 2

Energy and Motion

What's Happening Here?

A bowling ball strikes the pins and scatters them in many directions. Some pins fall down, some fly through the air, and some may remain standing. What determines a pin's motion? You will discover that all motions are the result of forces. The forces acting on each bowling pin determine whether it will move and the direction of the movement. Forces may also be at work when an object is standing still, like the rock balanced in the small photo above. In this unit you will study the connections among force, motion, and energy.

Science Journal

The rock in the photograph above looks as if it will topple over any minute, but it has been there for thousands of years. In your Science Journal, describe how forces are involved in producing the formation. What force keeps it standing? What force will eventually make it fall?

Previewing the Chapter

Exploring Motion and Forces

Why is a water slide so exciting for many people? You may have enjoyed sliding down the slippery slope and splashing into the water at the bottom. What makes amusement park rides so much fun is their creative use of some basic laws of physics. In this chapter, you'll begin to explore the important connection between motion and forces that explains many familiar observations. The activity below illustrates this connection.

EXPLORE ACTIVITY

Find out about physics for one cent.

1. Use a plastic drink cup that is about two-thirds full of water or sand to anchor it. Lay a flat index card over the top of the cup.
2. Place a penny on the card, centered over the cup.
3. With a quick flick of your finger, give the card a horizontal push. What happens?
4. Crumple up a small piece of paper to about the size of a marble. Place it on the card and flick the card away. Record your observations.

Observe: In your Science Journal, explain why you think the penny and the crumpled paper behaved as they did.

Previewing Science Skills

▶ In the Skill Builders, you will **compare and contrast, make and use graphs,** and **observe and infer.**

▶ In the Activities, you will **measure, control variables,** and **experiment.**

▶ In the MiniLABs, you will **calculate, observe,** and **interpret.**

3•1 Motion and Speed

Science Words

speed
instantaneous speed
constant speed
average speed

Objectives

- Define *speed* as a rate.
- Perform calculations involving speed, time, and distance.
- Interpret distance-time graphs.

Understanding Speed

When something moves, it changes position. It travels from one place to another, even if only for a brief time. Think about an ice skater. If asked to describe the motion of speed skater Bonnie Blair in **Figure 3-1,** you could say something like "leaning forward with repetitive gliding strokes." How would you describe the motion of a person on a swing?

Motion and Position

You don't always have to see something move to know that motion has taken place. For example, suppose you look out a window and see a mail truck parked next to a mailbox. One minute later, you look out again and see the same truck parked down the street from the mailbox. Although you didn't observe the motion, you know the truck moved because its position relative to the mailbox has changed.

Thus, motion can be described as a change in position. To know whether the position of something has changed, you need a reference point. In the case of the mail truck, the mailbox was a reference point. You can also use a reference point to get a rough idea of how far the truck moved. However, you don't know how fast the truck moved to reach its new position.

Motion and Time

Descriptions of motion often include speed—how fast something moves. If you think of motion as a change in position, then speed is an expression of how much time it takes for that change in position to occur. Any change over time is called a rate. **Speed,** then, is the rate of change in position. Speed can also be described as simply a "rate of motion."

There are several useful measures of speed. The speedometer in a car shows instantaneous speed. **Instantaneous speed** is the rate of

Figure 3-1

Some speed skaters reach a speed of 56 km (35 mi)/h. Their uniforms help to maximize their speed.

motion at any given instant. At the moment the picture in **Figure 3-2** was taken, the car was traveling at a speed of 80 km/h. On a highway, a car may travel at the same speed for a fairly long period of time. A speed that does not vary is called a **constant speed.**

Figure 3-2
The speedometer of a car shows how fast the car is moving at any given instant. *Would the car's instantaneous speed remain the same or change if you measure it frequently during a rush-hour drive?*

Changing Speed

Much of the time, the speeds you deal with are not constant. Think about riding your bicycle for a distance of 5 km. As you start out, your speed increases from 0 km/h to, say, 20 km/h. You slow down to 12 km/h as you pedal up a steep hill and speed up to 35 km/h going down the other side of the hill. You stop for a red light, speed up again, and move at a constant speed for a while. As you near the end of the trip, you slow down and then stop. Checking your watch, you find that the trip took 15 minutes, or one-quarter of an hour. How would you express your speed on such a trip? Would you use your fastest speed, your slowest speed, or some speed in between the two?

In cases where rate of motion varies a great deal, the best way to describe speed is to use average speed. **Average speed** is the total distance traveled divided by total time of travel. On the trip just described, your average speed was 5 km divided by ¼ hour, or 20 km/h.

USING MATH

A line graph provides a "picture" of the bicyclist traveling 5 km in ¼ hour.

The *slope*, or steepness, of the line represents the average speed. Suppose another bicyclist traveled 5 km in ½ hour. Compared to the first graph, is this more steep or less steep? Is the average speed greater or less than the first speed?

Figure 3-3
A runner's speed can change from moment to moment during a race.

Calculating Speed

How could you find out who the fastest runner in your school is? One way would be to get all the students together to run in a giant race. However, this isn't very practical. A better way would be to have each student run a certain distance and to time each runner, as shown in **Figure 3-3** on page 65. The runner with the shortest time is the fastest student.

The relationship between distance, speed, and time is shown in the equation $d = v \times t$, where d = distance, v = speed, and t = time. If you know the distance and time, you can rewrite the equation as

$$v = \frac{d}{t}$$

to calculate the average speed.

The problems below will give you practice in calculating the average speed.

Graphing Speed

A distance-time graph makes it possible to "see" the motion of an object over a period of time. For example, the graph in **Figure 3-4** shows how two swimmers performed during a 30-minute workout. The smooth red line represents the

USING MATH

Calculating Speed

Example Problem:

Your neighbor says she can skate at a speed of 4 m/s. To see if you can skate faster, you have her time you as you skate as fast as you can for 100 m. Your time is 20 s. Who skates faster?

Problem-Solving Steps:

1. What is known?
distance, d = 100 m; time, t = 20 s
2. What is unknown? average speed, v
3. Use the equation $v = \frac{d}{t}$
4. Solution: $v = \frac{d}{t}$

$v = \frac{100 \text{ m}}{20 \text{ s}} = 5 \text{ m/s}$

Your neighbor's speed is 4 m/s; you skate faster.

Practice Problem

Florence Griffith Joyner set a world record by running 200 m in 21.34 s. What was her average speed?
Strategy Hint: In what units will your answer be given?

motion of a swimmer who swam 800 m during each 10-minute period. Her speed was constant at 80 m/min.

The blue line represents the motion of a second swimmer, who did not swim at a constant speed. She covered 400 m during the first 10 minutes of her workout. Then she rested for the next 10 minutes. During this time, her speed was 0 m/min. The slope of the graph over the next 10 minutes shows that she swam faster than before and covered 800 m. What total distance did she cover? What was her average speed for the 30-minute period? The problems below will give you practice in calculating the time during which a motion occurs.

Figure 3-4

The distance-time graph shown here makes it possible to visualize the motion of the swimmers. *Which person swam the farthest during the 30-minute workout?*

USING MATH

Calculating Time from Speed

Example Problem:

Sound travels at a speed of 330 m/s. If a lightning bolt strikes the ground 1 km away from you, how long will it take for the sound to reach you?

1. What is known?   distance, $d = 1$ km; speed, $v = 330$ m/s

2. Use the equation $d = v \times t$. Since you know d and v, rewrite the equation as $t = \dfrac{d}{v}$ to find the time t.

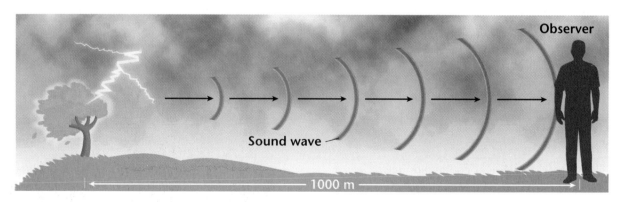

Observer

Sound wave

1000 m

3. Solution: $t = \dfrac{d}{v}$ $t = \dfrac{1 \text{ km}}{330 \text{ m/s}} = \dfrac{1000 \text{ m}}{330 \text{ m/s}} = 3.03$ s

Practice Problem

The world's fastest passenger elevator operates at an average speed of about 10 m/s. If the 60th floor is 219 m above the first floor, how long does it take the elevator to go from the first floor to the 60th floor?

Strategy Hint: Rearrange the equation.

Earth's Crust—Moving Right Along

Can you think of something that is moving so slowly you cannot watch its motion directly, yet you can see evidence of its motion over long periods of time? As you look around the surface of Earth from year to year, the basic structure of our planet seems the same. Yet, if you examined geological evidence of what Earth's surface looked like over hundreds of millions of years, you would see an ever-changing place, as shown in **Figure 3-5.**

250 million years ago

Figure 3-5

About 250 million years ago, the arrangement of the continents formed the supercontinent called Pangaea. *Are modern-day Europe, Asia and North America found in the northern or southern portion of Pangaea?*

180 million years ago

 About 180 million years ago, Pangaea began to separate into smaller pieces.

66 million years ago

 Continental movement continued. *In which direction is India moving in this diagram?*

Present

 Will the present arrangement of the continents change in the future? Explain.

How can continents move?

You may have studied about the theory of plate tectonics, which suggests that Earth's crust and solid upper mantle, shown in **Figure 3-6** as the lithosphere, form huge sections called plates. If you compare Earth to an egg, these plates are about as thick as the eggshell. The plates slide around slowly on a putty-like layer of partly molten mantle called the asthenosphere. A variety of geological changes, such as the formation of mountain ranges, earthquakes, and volcanic eruptions, can occur when these moving plates interact in different ways.

Measuring Speeds of Tectonic Movements

In most of the examples in this chapter, we were measuring speed based on traveling an easily measurable distance in a few seconds or minutes. The speeds of tectonic movements are best described in distance per year. In California, the movement along the San Andreas fault has an average drift speed of about 2 cm per year. The Australian plate's movement is one of the fastest, pushing Australia north at an average speed of about 17 cm per year. **Figure 3-5** illustrates the slow, long-term movement of the continents.

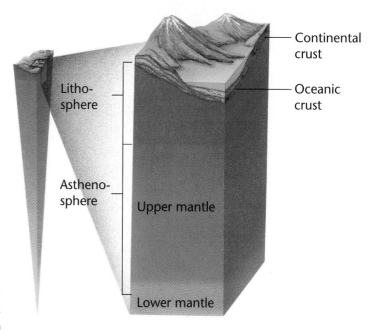

Figure 3-6

The diagram shows the different layers of Earth's crust and mantle.

Section Wrap-up

Review

1. What units would you use to describe the speed of a car? Would you use different units for the speeds of runners in a neighborhood race? Explain.

2. In a skateboarding marathon, the winner covered 435 km in 36.75 h. What was the winner's average speed?

3. **Think Critically:** Make a distance-time graph for a 2-hour car trip. The car covered 50 km in the first 30 minutes, stopped for 30 minutes, and covered 60 km in the final 60 minutes. Note the three graph segments. Which graph segment slopes the most? Which one does not slope? What was the car's average speed?

Skill Builder
Comparing and Contrasting
Compare and contrast the motions of a person on a swing and a person riding a merry-go-round. If you need help, refer to Comparing and Contrasting in the **Skill Handbook.**

Using Computers

Spreadsheet Given the information in the graph in **Figure 3-4,** use a computer to construct a data table listing the distance and time measurements from which the graph was made. Use a spreadsheet program to make your data table and use it, if possible, to re-create the graphs.

Design Your Own Experiment
Design a Slow Flyer

How do heavy jet planes fly high above Earth's surface? Their shape, wing design, and high thrust all contribute to their flying capabilities. Engineers use many physics principles to design flying machines to move fast, glide, or maneuver quickly.

PREPARATION

Problem

Can you design planes with specific flying behaviors from materials such as paper and tape? These behaviors can include speed and ability to glide for long distances.

Form a Hypothesis

Write a hypothesis about what types of design features will help a paper glider fly as slowly as possible. One important design feature will be the size and shape of the wings.

Objectives

• Design a paper glider to fly as slowly as possible.
• Measure distance and time and calculate your glider's speed.

Materials

• stopwatch or timer with second hand
• meterstick or metric tape measure
• goggles
• string
• paper sheets of various types
• transparent tape
• paper clips and stapler

Safety Precautions

Make sure you have a clear area to launch your glider; do not throw it toward another person.

PLAN THE EXPERIMENT

1. When you plan your experiment, decide how you can measure the speed of a paper glider.
2. In constructing your glider, be sure to consider its balance and stability.
3. Think about how the way you launch your glider will affect its speed.
4. If you need a data table, design one in your Science Journal so it is ready to use as your group collects data.

Check the Plan
1. Be sure you have considered all the factors that can affect glider speed.
2. Will you have more than one trial run with each design?
3. What measurements will you need to make to determine the speed of your glider? Who will make the measurements?
4. Will the data be summarized in a graph?
5. Be sure to make adjustments to your glider after your first trials to try to improve its performance. It will be best to adjust one factor at a time.
6. *Make sure your teacher approves your plan and that you have included any changes suggested in the plan.*

DO THE EXPERIMENT

1. Carry out the experiment as planned.
2. Be sure to enter all useful data in your Science Journal so you can make effective adjustments to your glider.

Analyze and Apply
1. **Compare** your results with those of other groups.
2. **Calculate** your glider's maximum, minimum, and average speeds.
3. If your glider travels a curved path, which distance measurement will give the slowest speed calculation— along the curved path or along the straight line between the starting and landing points?
4. What factors affected your glider's flight? **Predict** how you could change some of these factors.

Go Further

What types of contests exist for full-sized gliders piloted by people? Investigate and write a brief report that summarizes your findings.

3•2 Velocity and Acceleration

Science Words

velocity
acceleration

Objectives

• Compare and contrast speed, velocity, and acceleration.
• Calculate acceleration.

Velocity and Speed

You turn on the radio and hear the tail end of a news story about a tornado sighting in a storm, such as the one in **Figure 3-7.** The storm, moving at a speed of 60 km/h, has just left a town 10 km north of your location. Should you be worried? Unfortunately, you don't have enough information. Knowing only the speed of the storm isn't much help. Speed only describes how fast something is moving. You also need to know the direction the storm is moving. In other words, you need to know the velocity of the storm. **Velocity** describes both *speed* and *direction* of an object.

Picture a motorcycle racing down the highway at 100 km/h. It meets another motorcycle going 100 km/h in the opposite direction. The speeds of the motorcycles are the same, but their velocities are different because the motorcycles are not moving in the same direction.

You learned earlier that speed isn't always constant. Like speed, velocity may also change. Unlike speed, the velocity of an object can change even if the speed of the object remains constant! For example, if a car goes around a curve in the road, its direction changes. Even if the speed remains constant, the velocity changes because the direction changes.

Figure 3-7

Knowing the speed and direction of a tornado can be important for safety.

Acceleration

At the starting line of a drag strip, the driver idles the dragster's engine. When the starting signal flashes, the driver presses the gas pedal.

The car leaps forward, as shown in **Figure 3-8A,** moving faster and faster until it crosses the finish line. Then, in **Figure 3-8B,** the driver releases a drag chute and the car rapidly slows down and comes to a stop. While the car gains speed, it is accelerating. Strange as it may seem, the car is also accelerating as it slows down. How is this possible?

Figure 3-8

The dragster is accelerating in both of these photos.

 A The dragster accelerates continuously as it races down the track.

B The drag parachute is used to change the direction of the dragster's acceleration.

What is acceleration?

Acceleration is the rate of change of velocity. Because velocity includes both speed and direction, if either one changes, velocity will change. In other words, acceleration can occur through a change in speed or a change in direction.

If an object travels in a straight line and the directions of acceleration and velocity occur along the same line, as with the dragster, then acceleration is just the rate of change of speed. If the acceleration is in the same direction as the velocity, then the dragster *speeds up.* Its acceleration is positive. If they are in opposite directions, then the dragster *slows down.* Its acceleration is negative. These principles are illustrated in **Figure 3-9.**

The amount of acceleration depends on both the change in velocity and the time interval. The *time interval* is the amount of time that passed while the change in velocity was taking place. The acceleration will be large if the change in velocity is large; it will also be large if the change in velocity occurs in a small time interval.

Figure 3-9

The diagram indicates how positive and negative acceleration are defined. *Explain these two definitions.*

VELOCITY	ACCELERATION

Positive Acceleration

VELOCITY	ACCELERATION

Negative Acceleration

Procedure

1. Select a line or place a pencil on the floor to mark your starting point.
2. Beginning at the starting line, give your car a gentle push forward. At the same time, start your stopwatch.
3. Stop timing exactly when the car comes to a complete stop. Mark the spot at the front of the car with another pencil.
4. Record the time for the entire trip. Measure the distance to the nearest tenth of a centimeter and convert it to meters.

Analysis

1. Calculate the average speed during your car's trip. What was the car's average velocity?
2. How would the velocity reading differ if you repeated your experiment in exactly the same way in the opposite direction?
3. Describe any acceleration you observed the car undergo. How would you cause a greater acceleration?

Calculating Acceleration

To calculate average acceleration, divide the change in velocity by the time interval. To find the *change in velocity*, subtract the initial velocity (starting velocity), v_i, from the final velocity, v_f.

$$a = \frac{v_f - v_i}{t} = \frac{\Delta v}{t}$$

The symbol Δ is the Greek letter *delta* and stands for "change in."

When calculating acceleration, be sure to include all proper units and algebraic signs. The unit for velocity is meters/second (m/s) and the unit for time is seconds (s). Thus, the unit for acceleration is meters/second/second. This unit is usually written as m/s^2 and is read as "meters per second squared" or "meters per second per second."

You can see from the equation that acceleration will be positive if an object is speeding up and negative if an object is slowing down. In a horse race, for example, the outcome is often determined by whether a horse is speeding up or slowing down during the stretch run near the end of the race. When Secretariat set the speed record for the Kentucky Derby, **Figure 3-10,** he ran each quarter mile faster than the previous one. The graph in **Figure 3-10** illustrates Secretariat's motion.

When you work on acceleration problems, be careful to correctly identify the initial velocity and the final velocity. If

Figure 3-10

Horses often tire near the end of a race. *What shape would the graph have if Secretariat had slowed down near the finish line?*

you confuse them, the acceleration will have the wrong sign (positive or negative). The problems below provide practice in calculating acceleration.

USING MATH

Calculating Acceleration

Example Problem:

A car's velocity changes from 0 m/s to 30 m/s 10 seconds later. Calculate the car's average acceleration.

1. What is known?   initial velocity, $v_i = 0$ m/s; final velocity, $v_f = 30$ m/s; time, $t = 10$ s.

2. Use the equation $a = \dfrac{v_f - v_i}{t}$

3. **Solution:** $a = \dfrac{v_f - v_i}{t}$ $a = \dfrac{30 \text{ m/s} - 0 \text{ m/s}}{10 \text{ s}} = \dfrac{30 \text{ m/s}}{10 \text{ s}} = 3 \text{ m/s}^2$

The car's average acceleration is 3 m/s².

Practice Problem

As a roller coaster starts down a hill, its speed is 10 m/s. Three seconds later, its speed is 32 m/s at the bottom of the hill. What is the roller coaster's acceleration?
Strategy Hint: Find the change in velocity by subtracting initial velocity from final velocity.

Section Wrap-up

Review

1. One jet plane is flying east at 880 km/h, and another plane is traveling north at 880 km/h. Do they have the same velocities? The same speeds? Explain.

2. A swimmer speeds up from 1.1 m/s to 1.3 m/s during the last 20 s of the workout. What is the acceleration during this interval?

3. Think Critically: Describe three different ways to change your velocity when you're riding a bicycle.

Science Journal

In your Science Journal, explain why we have speed limits on streets and highways rather than velocity limits.

Skill Builder
Making and Using Graphs
Decide on a style of graph to show how velocity changes over time. Explain your choice. Show the graph. If you need help, refer to Making and Using Graphs in the **Skill Handbook.**

ISSUE:

3•3 A Crash Course in Safety

Objectives

- Analyze the motion that takes place in a car crash.
- Evaluate the effects of wearing seat belts during a car crash.
- State an informed opinion about whether laws should require people to wear seat belts.

Do you usually wear your seat belt when you travel in a car? Through experiments called crash tests, shown in **Figure 3-11,** and by studying actual car collisions, scientists have learned what happens to people in accidents. They have determined that many serious injuries and deaths can be prevented by the use of relatively inexpensive seat belts that cross a passenger's shoulder, chest, and lap. Many states have responded by requiring that drivers and front-seat passengers wear these restraining belts. Although the belts save lives, some citizens argue that seat-belt use should be a personal decision and not required by law.

What happens in a crash?

When a car traveling about 50 km/h collides head-on with something solid, the car crumples, slows down, and stops within approximately 0.1 second. Any passenger not wearing a seat belt continues to move forward at the same speed the car was traveling. Within about 0.02 second (one-fiftieth of a second) after the car stops, unbelted persons slam into the dashboard, steering wheel, windshield, or the backs of the front seats, as in **Figure 3-11.** They are traveling at the car's original speed of 50 km/h—about the same speed they would reach falling from a three-story building.

The person putting on a seat belt in **Figure 3-12** will be attached to the car and will slow down as the car slows down. The force needed to slow a person from 50 km/h to zero in 0.1 second is equal to 14 times that person's weight.

Figure 3-11

In crash tests, researchers put life-like dummies in cars and crash the cars into each other or into crash barriers.

The belt "gives" a little as it restrains the person, increasing the time it takes to slow him or her down and spreading out the force so it's not focused on only one part of the body.

2 Points of View

▶ Making Laws to Save Lives and Money

Car safety experts say that about half the people who die in car crashes would survive if they wore seat belts. Thousands of others would suffer fewer serious injuries. Those in favor of seat-belt laws maintain that it is a matter of public health and safety, similar to other laws aimed at preventing accidents and injuries. These preventable injuries and deaths are sad events for families involved and costly for individuals, insurance companies, and governmental agencies that must pay treatment bills.

▶ Making Our Own Choices

Some people resent laws that restrict individual choices. They think everyone should be free to decide whether or not to use seat belts. A person who violates other traffic laws, such as speed limits, endangers other innocent people. However, a person who chooses not to wear a seat belt endangers only himself or herself. Therefore, the individual should be free to make the choice without being penalized.

Figure 3-12

Drivers who are concerned about their personal safety wear seat belts.

Section Wrap-up

Review

1. Describe what happens to a person who's not wearing a seat belt during a car crash.

2. Describe how seat belts protect passengers and drivers during accidents.

Explore the Issue

Should states create laws that make seat-belt use mandatory? If you were a member of your state legislature, how would you vote? Support your position.

SCIENCE & SOCIETY

Connecting Motion with Forces

Science Words

force
balanced forces
net force
inertia
friction

Objectives

- Recognize different examples of forces.
- Identify cause-and-effect relationships between force and changes in velocity.
- Give examples of the effects of inertia.
- State Newton's first law of motion.

Figure 3-13

The force exerted by the bat sends the ball flying.

What is a force?

Push a door open. Stretch a rubber band. Squeeze a piece of clay. Slide a book across a table. In each case, you are applying a force. A **force** is a push or a pull one body exerts on another. Sometimes, the effects of a force are obvious, as when a moving car crashes into a stationary object, such as a tree. Other forces aren't as noticeable. Can you feel the force the floor exerts on your feet?

List all the forces you might exert or encounter in a typical day. Think about actions such as pushing, pulling, stretching, squeezing, bending, and falling.

Effects of Forces on Objects

In your list, what happens to the objects that have forces exerted on them? If an object is moving, does the force change the object's velocity? Think of a swinging bat hitting a softball, as in **Figure 3-13.** The ball's velocity certainly changes upon impact.

Balanced Forces

Force does not always change velocity. **Figure 3-14** illustrates a game of tug-of-war with a dog. You plant yourself firmly and lean back to push against the ground, causing the ground to push back on you. Your dog does the same. If you don't move forward or backward, the force of the dog pulling you forward must be balancing the force of the ground pushing you back. Forces on an object that are equal in size and opposite in direction are called **balanced forces.**

Unbalanced Forces

Now what happens if your feet hit a slippery spot on the ground? Your feet slip, and the ground can't exert as much force back on you. The forces of the dog pulling you forward and the ground pushing you back become unbalanced, and there is a net force on you. A **net force** on an object *always* changes the velocity of the object. When the dog pulls you forward with more force than the ground pushes back on you, you accelerate in the direction of the greater force.

Remember that velocity involves both speed and direction. A net force acting on an object will change its speed, direction, or both. In the tug-of-war, the net force on you causes both your speed and direction to change.

Figure 3-14

When the forces on the girl are balanced, she does not move. *What happens if the forces on her become unbalanced?*

Inertia and Mass

Picture a hockey puck sliding across the ice as in **Figure 3-15.** Its velocity hardly changes until it hits something, such as the wall, the net, or a player's stick. The velocity of the puck is constant, and its acceleration is zero until it hits something that alters its speed or direction.

The sliding puck demonstrates the property of inertia. **Inertia** is the tendency of an object to resist any change in its motion. If an object is moving, it will keep moving at the same speed and in the same direction unless an unbalanced force acts on it. In other words, the velocity of the object remains constant unless a force changes it. If an object is at rest, it tends to remain at rest. Its velocity is zero unless a force makes it move.

Would you expect that a bowling ball would have the same inertia as a table-tennis ball? Why would there be a difference? The more mass an object has, the greater its inertia is. Recall that mass is the

Figure 3-15

The velocity and acceleration of a hockey puck are constantly changing during a game.

Air Bags

Seat belts are designed to reduce the effect of inertia in a crash by holding the passengers in place. However, in a high-speed crash, belts provide limited protection to the head and upper body. These parts of the body can be protected by air bags, which provide an instantaneous cushion for the head and upper body at the time of impact.

Air bags are designed to be used in addition to seat belts. An air-bag system consists of one or more crash sensors, an ignitor and gas generator, and an inflatable nylon bag. The nylon bag for the driver is stored in the steering wheel, and the bag for the front-seat passenger is stored inside the dashboard. If a car hits something with sufficient force (speeds in excess of 15 to 20 km/h), impact sensors trigger the flow of electric current to an ignitor. The ignitor causes an explosive chemical reaction to occur, producing harmless nitrogen gas. The nitrogen gas propels the air bag from its storage compartment just in time to absorb the inertia of the occupants. The bag then immediately deflates so it will not interfere with the driver.

Think Critically:

Under what crash conditions would an air bag offer little or no protection?

Figure 3-16

Besides the paddle, what else changes the ball's velocity?

amount of matter in an object, and a bowling ball certainly contains more matter than a table-tennis ball. So the bowling ball would have greater inertia than the table-tennis ball. You wouldn't change the velocity of a bowling ball very much by swatting it with a paddle, but you could easily change the velocity of the table-tennis ball in **Figure 3-16.** Because the bowling ball has greater inertia, a much greater force would be needed to change its velocity.

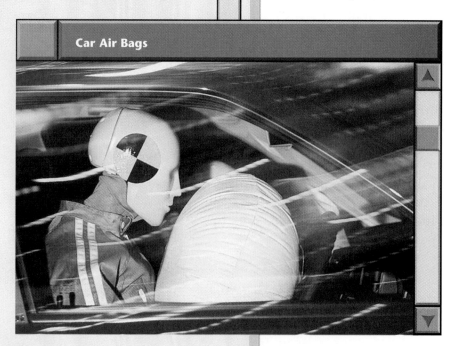

Car Air Bags

Newton's First Law

Forces change the motion of an object in very specific ways—so specific that Sir Isaac Newton (1642-1727) was able to state laws that describe the effects of forces.

Newton's first law of motion is that an object moving at a constant velocity keeps moving at that velocity unless a net force acts on it. If an object is at rest, it stays at rest unless a net force acts on it. Does this sound familiar? It is the same as the earlier discussion of inertia. Thus, you'll understand why this law is sometimes called the *law of inertia*. You've probably seen—and felt—this law at work without even knowing it. In **Figure 3-17,** you can see this law in action.

Figure 3-17

You can observe many common examples of Newton's first law in action.

A The young man is pushing the hand truck at a constant velocity. The boxes are also moving at the same constant velocity. There is no net force acting on either the hand truck or the boxes.

B The hand truck bumps into the curb and stops. However, the boxes keep moving forward even though no one has pushed them. Their inertia keeps them moving forward. The boxes also begin to fall because the force of gravity pulls them downward.

C The boxes finally come to rest on the ground. *Are the forces acting on them balanced or unbalanced?*

MiniLAB

How does friction act as a force?

Procedure

1. Place a sheet of plain white paper near the edge of a flat surface, then set a 100-g mass on the paper about 7 cm from the far end of the paper.
2. Grip the end of the paper near the table's edge and give it a quick, smooth, downward yank. What happens?
3. Replace the paper with a sheet of coarse sandpaper, rough side up, and repeat the procedure. Observe what happens to the mass.

Analysis

1. How do you interpret the different results?
2. How can Newton's first law help explain your observations?

Friction

You've just learned that inertia causes an object that is moving at constant velocity to keep moving at that velocity unless a net force acts on it. But you know that if you slide a book across a long table, it eventually slows down and stops. Why does it stop?

An unseen force is acting between the book and the table. The force is friction. **Friction** is the force that opposes motion between two surfaces that are touching each other. Would you expect more friction between an oily floor and a slick, leather shoe sole or between a rough sidewalk and the bottom of a tennis shoe? The amount of friction depends on two factors—the kinds of surfaces and the force pressing the surfaces together.

Life Without Friction

If there were no friction, your life would be much different. You wouldn't be able to walk or hold things between your fingers. Your shoes would fall off. Friction between the soles of your shoes and the floor makes it possible for you to walk. You can hold something with your fingers because of friction. Shoelaces remain tied because of friction. **Figure 3-18** shows the effect of friction on a soccer player.

As you complete this section, you should be more aware that force and motion are part of everything you do and everything that happens around you.

Figure 3-18

Soccer requires players to run, jump, pivot, and kick. *How is friction helping this soccer player?*

Section Wrap-up

Review

1. Before dancing on a smooth wooden floor, ballet dancers sometimes put a sticky powder called rosin on their shoe soles. Why? What force are they taking advantage of?

2. Explain which has greater inertia, a speeding car or a jet airplane sitting on a runway.

3. **Think Critically:** Think of and describe three examples from sports in which a force changes the velocity of an object or a person.

Science Journal

Inertia plays an important role in most sports. In your Science Journal, write a paragraph describing the role of inertia in your favorite sport.

Skill Builder

Recognizing Cause and Effect

Explain what happens to your body in terms of inertia, friction, and forces when you slip and fall on an icy sidewalk. If you need help, refer to Recognizing Cause and Effect in the **Skill Handbook.**

Gravity— A Familiar Force

Gravitational Force

A diver, poised high above the water in **Figure 3-19,** jumps up in the air and then hurtles toward the water. Why does the diver plunge downward instead of flying off into space? Seeing objects fall is a common experience. You may not have thought about it, but when you see something fall, you're watching the effects of the force of gravity.

Every object in the universe exerts a force on every other object. That force is **gravity.** Often, the force is too slight to notice. For example, there's a gravitational force of attraction between your hand and your pencil, but when you let go of your pencil, it doesn't stay in your hand. The gravitational force of Earth is much stronger than the gravitational force of your hand, so the pencil falls toward Earth.

What determines the force of gravity?

The amount of gravitational force between objects depends on two things— their masses and the distance between them. The masses of your hand and your pencil are small, so the force of attraction between them is weak. The mass of Earth is large, so the gravitational force between Earth and your pencil is strong.

The amount of Earth's gravitational force acting on an orbiting satellite depends on how close the satellite is to Earth. The closer it is to Earth, the stronger the pull of gravity. The farther away it is, the less effect gravity has on it. Thus, gravity will exert a stronger pull on a satellite in a lower orbit and a weaker pull on a satellite in a higher orbit.

Science Words

gravity
weight

Objectives

- Give examples of the effects of gravity.
- Relate gravitational force to mass and distance.
- Distinguish between mass and weight.

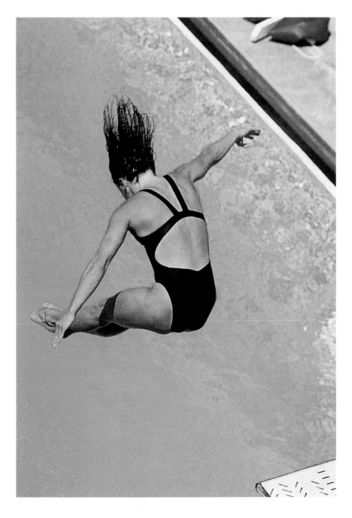

Figure 3-19

As the diver falls toward the water, she is under the influence of gravity and accelerates downward.

Problem Solving

An Experiment for the Shuttle

NASA was having a competition to select several student experiments for scientists to conduct while the space shuttle orbited Earth. Ellen decided to enter an experiment about how the time spent on a shuttle flight would affect the masses of the astronauts. The mass of each astronaut would be determined before and after the mission. During the flight, the astronauts would have to list the foods and liquids they consumed and eliminated, and the masses of each. Ellen's experiment required that the masses of the food and liquid packets be measured and labeled to the nearest 0.01 gram. It also required the astronauts to report on their daily activities.

Solve the Problem:

1. **Design a data table that can be used to record the required information for one astronaut for a period of five days.**
2. **How would the mass of any material on Earth compare with its mass during the shuttle mission?**

Think Critically:

What factors could cause changes in the astronauts' masses?

Weight

The measure of the force of gravity on an object is the object's **weight.** The term *weight* is most often used in reference to the gravitational force between Earth and a body at Earth's surface. Weight isn't the same as mass, but the two are related. Recall from Chapter 2 that mass is the amount of matter in an object. The greater an object's mass, the stronger the gravitational force on it. In other words, the more mass an object has, the more it weighs.

Mass is measured in grams (g) and kilograms (kg). Weight, which is a force, is measured in units called newtons (N). A kilogram of mass on Earth's surface weighs 9.8 N. On Earth, a cassette tape weighs about 0.5 N, a backpack full of books weighs about 40 N, and a wide-bodied jumbo jet weighs about 3.4 million N.

Table 3-1 shows how an object's weight depends upon the object's location.

Table 3-1

Weight Comparison Table					
Weight on Earth (lb)	Weight on Other Bodies in the Solar System (lb)				
	Moon	Venus	Mars	Jupiter	Saturn
75	12.5	67.5	28.5	190.5	87.0
100	16.7	90.0	38.0	254.0	116.0
125	20.8	112.5	47.5	317.5	145.0
150	25.0	135.0	57.0	381.0	174.0
2000	333.3	1800.0	760.0	5080.0	2320.0

Weight—It Depends on Where You Are

The gravitational force an object exerts on other objects is related to its mass. Earth exerts a stronger gravitational force on an object at its surface than the moon does on an object at its surface because Earth has more mass. Because of the moon's weaker gravitational force, a person weighing about 480 N on Earth would weigh only about 80 N on the moon. Does this mean that the person would have less mass on the moon than on Earth? No. Unlike weight, mass doesn't change with changes in gravity. Because mass remains constant, the astronaut in **Figure 3-20** would also have the same inertia on the moon as on Earth.

Figure 3-20

Astronauts jump higher on the moon than they can on Earth because of differences in gravity.

Measuring Forces

Scales use the principle of balanced forces to measure how much something weighs. To see the principle work, hang a rubber band from a hook or a nail. Then, attach something heavy to the lower end of the rubber band and see how much the band stretches. If you attach something even heavier, will the band stretch more? Yes, the band stretches until it is exerting an upward force equal to the weight of the object hung. Thus, the length of the rubber band is a measure of the force on it.

A scale works something like the rubber band. When you step on a bathroom scale, the force of your body stretches a spring inside the scale. The stretched spring pulls on levers,

CONNECT TO

LIFE SCIENCE

Research health problems encountered by astronauts after extended periods of reduced gravity.

Figure 3-21

A scale measures the force of gravity on the object or person being weighed.

B A system of levers and a spring are used to indicate the person's weight.

A When you stand on a bathroom scale, the downward force of gravity—your weight—is balanced by the upward force exerted by the spring inside the scale.

Main spring

Crank

Dial

Dial spring

Rack

Weight

Pinion

Calibrating plate

Fulcrum

as shown in **Figure 3-21,** until the upward force of the scale equals the downward force of your weight. The dial on the scale, which is marked off in units of weight, moves until the spring stops stretching. The number showing on the dial indicates your weight.

Section Wrap-up

Review

1. Arriving on a newly discovered Earth-sized planet, you find that you weigh one-third as much as on Earth. Is the planet's mass greater or less than Earth's?

2. Why don't you feel the gravitational force between your hand and a pencil? What do you feel?

3. **Think Critically:** Use Newton's first law and the concept of gravity to explain how a satellite orbits Earth.

Skill Builder
Observing and Inferring

Select three objects in the room and, without touching them, try to guess which weighs the most. What clues help you to make your guesses? How can you tell if you guessed right? If you need help, refer to Observing and Inferring in the **Skill Handbook.**

Science Journal

In your Science Journal, write a short story describing what a certain activity would be like if the gravitational force were half as strong. For example, you could write about playing sports, constructing a building, or riding a bicycle.

Activity 3-2

Balancing Forces Against Gravity

Imagine yourself hanging by your arms from a tree limb. Why do you eventually get tired and let go? When your arms get tired, they can't exert an upward force on your body to balance the force of gravity pulling your body down (your weight).

Problem
Determine the strengths of different types of paper.

Materials
- selection of different types of paper strips
- masking tape
- string
- beaker
- ring stand and ring
- sheets of newspaper
- scissors
- plastic cup
- sand, 250 mL
- balance

Procedure
1. Prepare a table with the headings *sample, mass of sand,* and *weight of sand.*
2. Place the ring stand as shown. Select a paper strip and record its identity in the data table. Cut the strip as shown. Tape one side of the strip to the ring and tape the other side to the cup.
3. Slowly pour sand into the cup until the paper strip begins to tear.
4. Use the balance to measure the combined mass of the cup and sand. Record this measurement and return the sand to its container.

5. Repeat steps 2, 3, and 4 using different types of paper strips.
6. Using the formula below, calculate and record the weights of the cup and sand for each paper strip tested.

   Weight = mass (in kg) × 9.80 N/kg

Data and Observations

Sample	Mass of Sand (g)	Weight of Sand (N)
a		
b		
c		

Analyze
1. The ability of a material to resist tearing is called shear strength. What did this investigation show about the shear strengths of different types of paper?
2. Why would it be incorrect to refer to shear strength in grams or kilograms?

Conclude and Apply
3. This investigation tests the shear strength in one direction only. How could you find out whether the shear strength depends on the direction in which the paper is torn?
4. **Predict** whether this investigation would work as well if water were used in place of sand.
5. Why is gravity a good choice of force to use for measuring the strength of different materials?

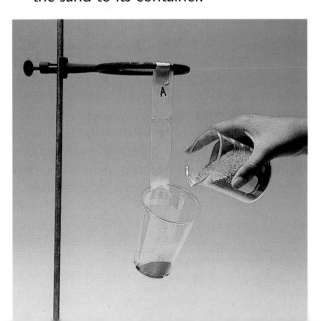

People and Science

DERIQUE, *Juggler*

On the Job

Q Can the principles of juggling be explained in words?

A You can think of a box with an X drawn inside it. A juggling pattern forms the X, with a ball going from a lower corner diagonally to an upper corner. Then the ball drops. The left hand throws from the left bottom corner of the box to the right side. The balls just miss one another.

Q What do you do when gravity, the juggler's "downfall," strikes?

A I accept that important law of physics and juggling: What goes up must come down. To overcome this, I trap the escaping juggling ball between my feet, jump up, release it and get it in the air again.

Q You sometimes juggle atop a unicycle. Does staying on a unicycle involve any other scientifically based skills?

A Yes, it's called counterbalancing. I have to keep shifting my weight from side to side and front to back.

Personal Insights

Q What made you want to become a juggler?

A In high school, I wasn't good enough for regular organized sports, but I wanted to be part of a group, so I took clown classes. When my group did shows for kids in hospitals, I discovered how great it feels to make people forget their troubles for a while. Overcoming gravity comes from the heart.

Career Connection

Performing arts and other occupations often require skills involving eye-hand coordination, spatial relationships, and overcoming forces through manipulation of objects. Choose an occupation that involves one of these skills and write a want ad for a newspaper for that job. Consider the following careers:

- Astronaut
- Physical Therapist

Chapter 3 Review

Summary

3-1: Motion and Speed
1. Motion is a change in position of a body. Speed is the rate at which a body changes position.
2. Average speed is the ratio of distance traveled to time and describes motion, even if speed varies.

3-2: Velocity and Acceleration
1. Velocity describes the speed and direction of a moving body.
2. Acceleration is the rate of change in velocity.

3-3: Science and Society: A Crash Course in Safety
1. Seat belts reduce injuries by limiting impacts and spreading out the force over more of the body.
2. Some people believe that seat belts should be required by law; others don't.

3-4: Connecting Motion with Forces
1. A force is a push or a pull one body exerts on another. Balanced forces acting on a body do not change the motion of the body. Unbalanced forces result in a net force, which always changes the motion of a body.
2. Inertia explains why a massive, fast-moving bowling ball is more difficult to stop than a table-tennis ball at the same speed.
3. Newton's first law says an object's motion will not change unless a net force acts on it.

3-5: Gravity—A Familiar Force
1. Gravity causes planets to orbit the sun and people to remain on Earth's surface.

2. The gravitational force between two objects depends on their masses and the distance between them.
3. Mass is the amount of matter in an object. Weight is the force of gravity on that mass.

Key Science Words

a. acceleration
b. average speed
c. balanced forces
d. constant speed
e. force
f. friction
g. gravity
h. inertia
i. instantaneous speed
j. net force
k. speed
l. velocity
m. weight

Reviewing Vocabulary

Match each phrase with the correct term from the list of Key Science Words.

1. rate of change in position
2. speed that does not change
3. rate of change in velocity
4. a push or pull exerted on an object
5. type of force that changes the motion of an object
6. tendency of an object to resist change in motion
7. a force that opposes motion between surfaces
8. force exerted by every object in the universe on every other object
9. measure of the force of gravity on an object
10. rate of motion at a given point in time

Chapter 3 Review

Checking Concepts

Choose the word or phrase that completes the sentence or answers the question.

1. The best way to describe the rate of motion of an object that changes speed several times is to calculate the object's _____.
   a. average speed   c. instantaneous speed
   b. constant speed   d. variable speed
2. Which of the following is a force?
   a. inertia   c. acceleration
   b. friction   d. velocity
3. The unit for _____ is m/s².
   a. weight   c. inertia
   b. acceleration   d. velocity
4. Which of the following is not used in calculating acceleration?
   a. initial velocity c. time interval
   b. average speed   d. final velocity
5. A body accelerates if it _____.
   a. speeds up   c. changes direction
   b. slows down   d. all of these
6. The gravitational force between two objects depends on their _____.
   a. masses   c. shapes
   b. velocities   d. volumes
7. _____ acts only between surfaces that are in contact.
   a. Inertia   c. Gravity
   b. Friction   d. A net force
8. An object's weight is directly related to its _____.
   a. volume   c. mass
   b. velocity   d. shape
9. An object of large mass has _____ than an object of small mass.
   a. less inertia   c. less weight
   b. more inertia   d. greater acceleration
10. A constant velocity means acceleration is _____.
   a. positive   c. increasing
   b. negative   d. zero

Understanding Concepts

Answer the following questions in your Science Journal using complete sentences.

11. Can you tell an object has moved if you do not see it move? What information would you need to calculate the object's speed? Its velocity?
12. Explain how it is possible for an automobile traveling at constant speed to be accelerating.
13. Friction and gravity are both forces. Describe at least two differences between them.
14. Compare and contrast mass and weight.
15. Describe some common effects of inertia.

Thinking Critically

16. Explain why a fast-moving freight train cannot be stopped quickly.
17. A cyclist must travel 800 km. How many days will the trip take if the cyclist travels 8 h per day at an average speed of 16 km/h?
18. A satellite's original velocity is 10 000 m/s. After one minute, it is 5000 m/s. What is the satellite's acceleration?
19. A cyclist leaves home and rides due east for a distance of 45 km. She returns home on the same bike path. If the entire trip takes 4 h, what is her average speed?
20. The return trip of the cyclist in question 19 took 30 min longer than her trip east, although her total time was still 4 h. What was her velocity in each direction?

Developing Skills

If you need help, refer to the **Skill Handbook.**

21. **Measuring in SI:** Which of the following represents the greatest speed: 20 m/s, 200 cm/s, or 0.2 km/s? HINT: Express all three in meters/second and then compare them.

22. **Observing and Inferring:** A car sits motionless on a hill. What forces are acting on the car? Are the forces balanced or unbalanced? Explain how you inferred your answers.

23. **Making and Using Tables:** The four cars shown in the table were traveling at the same speed, and the brakes were applied in all four cars at the same instant.

Car	Mass	Stopping Distance
A	1000 kg	80 m
B	1250 kg	100 m
C	1500 kg	120 m
D	2000 kg	160 m

What is the relationship between the mass of a car and its stopping distance? How do you account for this relationship?

24. **Making and Using Graphs:** The following data were obtained for two runners.

	Sally	Alonzo
Time	**Distance**	**Distance**
1 s	2 m	1 m
2 s	4 m	2 m
3 s	6 m	2 m
4 s	8 m	4 m

Make a distance-time graph that shows the motion of both runners. What is the average speed of each runner? What is the instantaneous speed of each runner 1 s after he or she starts? Which runner stops briefly? During what time interval do Sally and Alonzo run at the same speed?

25. **Concept Mapping:** Make a network tree concept map that defines the three kinds of speed described in this chapter.

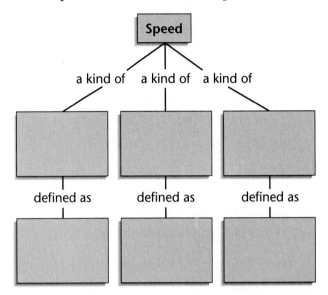

Performance Assessment

1. **Making Observations and Inferences:** In Activity 3-1 on page 70, you designed an experiment to find out how slowly you could make a glider fly. After observing the glider flights, you can make inferences about how glider design relates to glider speed. Redesign your glider to see how fast you can make it fly. What changes would you make? Try it and calculate your glider's speed.

2. **Data Table:** Use the procedure in Activity 3-2 on page 87 to test the shear strength of other materials such as aluminum foil, waxed paper, or human hair. Report your findings in a table.

3. **Formulating a Hypothesis:** Oils and waxes are lubricants, materials that are used to reduce the friction between surfaces. Form a hypothesis about which lubricant would work best on (a) a squeaky hinge and (b) a sticking dresser drawer.

Previewing the Chapter

92

Chapter 4

Acceleration and Momentum

When you watch a televised image of a rocket or space shuttle being launched, do you wonder how such a massive object is accelerated nearly straight up away from Earth? The exhaust gases escaping from the bottom of the rocket play a major role in this launch. Although advanced technology is used to control the motion of the rocket, a few basic physics principles can help you understand more about such events.

EXPLORE ACTIVITY

What propels a rocket upward?

1. Make a model rocket launcher by rolling and taping a piece of poster board into a cylinder with a diameter a few centimeters wider than a polystyrene cup. Cut a door large enough to insert an inflated balloon and your hand (as shown).
2. Inflate a long, slender balloon. Pinch the end closed and insert the top of the balloon into the launcher door. Place a polystyrene cup, open end down, over the top of the balloon as your rocket.
3. To launch your rocket, let the balloon go. Repeat steps 1 and 2. Record your observations and a sketch in your Science Journal.

Observe: What provides the force that pushes the rocket up? How is this like a real rocket?

Previewing Science Skills

▶ In the Skill Builders, you will **compare and contrast, make and use tables,** and **hypothesize.**

▶ In the Activities, you will **hypothesize, observe, collect and organize data,** and **analyze.**

▶ In the MiniLABs, you will **experiment, observe and infer,** and **hypothesize.**

4•1 Accelerated Motion

Science Words

Newton's second law of motion
air resistance
terminal velocity

Objectives

- Explain how force, mass, and acceleration are related.
- Compare the rates at which different objects fall.
- Observe the effects of air resistance.

Newton's Second Law

With Newton's first law, you learned how to describe the motion of a speeding sports car or a stationary hockey puck. You also learned that the motion of an object only changes if a net force acts on it, such as the brakes of a car or a fast-moving hockey stick. In the activity on page 93, you observed a net force acting on your balloon "rocket." As you study this chapter, you will find out some reasons why things move in the ways they do.

Study the photo of the tennis players in **Figure 4-1.** Each player can use a racket to produce an acceleration of the tennis ball. What effect would using a slightly heavier tennis ball have on the maximum accelerations?

You may not realize it, but in arriving at your answer, you have taken into account Newton's second law of motion. From experience, you know that mass, force, and acceleration are somehow related. **Newton's second law of motion** says that a net force acting on an object causes the object to accelerate in the direction of the force. The acceleration is determined by the size of the force and the mass of the object. A larger force acting on an object causes a greater acceleration. A larger mass requires a greater force than a smaller mass would require to achieve the same acceleration.

Figure 4-1

It is a definite advantage to be able to cause large accelerations of a tennis ball without losing placement control. *Which player is likely to apply the greater force on the ball? Why?*

The Force Equation

Newton's second law can be expressed in equation form as:

$$force = mass \times acceleration$$

$$F = ma$$

Mass is expressed in kilograms and acceleration is expressed in m/s². Thus, force is expressed in units of kg · m/s².

You learned in Chapter 3 that one newton is the standard unit for measuring force. A newton is the amount of force needed to accelerate an object with a mass of 1 kg at an acceleration of 1 m/s². In other words, $1 \text{ N} = 1 \text{ kg} \cdot \text{m/s}^2$.

Study the following Example Problem, then do the Practice Problems that follow.

CONNECT TO

LIFE SCIENCE

Many discus throwers lift weights to improve their performance. *Infer* how this might help them, using specific terms from Newton's second law.

USING MATH

Calculating Force

Example Problem:

How much force is needed to accelerate a 70-kg rider and her 200-kg motorcycle at 4 m/s²?

Problem-Solving Steps:

1. What is known?
   mass of rider, m_r = 70 kg
   mass of motorcycle, m_m = 200 kg
   acceleration, a = 4 m/s²

2. What is unknown?
   Force required, F

3. Choose the equation, $F = ma$.

4. Solution:
   The total mass, m, is 70 kg + 200 kg = 270 kg
   F = 270 kg × 4 m/s²
   = 1080 kg · m/s² = 1080 N
   A force of 1080 N is needed.

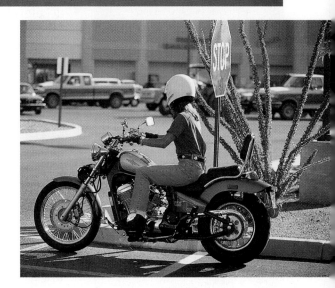

Practice Problems

1. It takes a force of 3000 N to accelerate an empty 1000-kg car at 3 m/s². If a 160-kg wrestler is inside the car, how much force will be needed to produce the same acceleration?

Strategy Hint: What units combine to make a newton?

2. A 63-kg skater pushes off from a wall with a force of 300 N. What is the skater's acceleration?

Strategy Hint: Rearrange the equation.

Falling Objects

It is hard to believe, but, if you dropped a bowling ball and a marble from a bridge at the same time, they'd both splash into the water at almost the same instant. (As you read further, you'll find out why they don't hit the water at exactly the same instant.) This means their accelerations would be just about the same. Would you have expected the bowling ball to hit the water sooner because it has more mass? It's true that the force of gravity would be greater on the bowling ball because of its larger mass. But the larger mass also gives the bowling ball more inertia, so more force is needed to change its velocity. The marble has a much smaller mass than the bowling ball, but its inertia also is much less. **Figure 4-2** shows the falling motion of two balls revealed by high-speed photography. The blue ball is more massive than the green one, but you can see that they fall at the same rate.

Acceleration Caused by Gravity

Near Earth's surface, gravity causes all falling objects to accelerate at 9.8 m/s². Does the number 9.8 seem familiar? When you studied the relationship between mass and weight, you learned that any object with a mass of 1 kg weighs 9.8 N on Earth. Now, you'll find out why.

Any force can be calculated using the equation:

$$F = m \times a.$$

The weight of an object, W, is the force of gravity acting on its mass. So, we can substitute and write:

$$W = m \times a.$$

Acceleration due to gravity is 9.8 m/s², therefore:

$$W = m \times 9.8 \text{ m/s}^2.$$

This means that a mass of 1 kg weighs 9.8 kg · m/s², or 9.8 N. You could calculate your weight in newtons if you knew your mass. For example, a person with a mass of 50 kg would have a weight of 490 N.

Remember that this discussion is concerned only with *falling* objects. This refers to an object that is dropped from some height and allowed to fall freely. As the object is released, the only downward force acting on it is gravity. The situation changes for an object that is *thrown* downward. In this case, the object is affected by gravity *and* the downward force of the throwing hand. Therefore, the object's downward acceleration would be greater than 9.8 m/s².

Figure 4-2

As the photograph shows, the rate of acceleration of a falling body is not affected by the mass of the body. *What effect does inertia have on the falling bodies?*

Air Resistance

Acceleration due to gravity (g) is the same for all objects, regardless of mass. This means that if no force other than gravity is present, all objects accelerate at 9.8 m/s^2. Think about that for a minute. Does a leaf accelerate as fast as an acorn? Does a feather fall as fast as a penny?

What would happen if you took two identical sheets of paper, crumpled one into a ball, and dropped both sheets at the same time, as shown in **Figure 4-3?** If your answer is that the crumpled ball would fall faster than the flat sheet, you are correct. But this behavior does not agree with what you've just learned. How can this disagreement be explained?

The only explanation for the behavior of the two sheets of paper is that some force is at work in addition to gravity. Anything that moves in Earth's atmosphere is affected by air resistance. **Air resistance** is the force air exerts on a moving object. This force acts in the opposite direction to that of the object's motion. In the case of a falling object, air resistance pushes up as gravity pulls down.

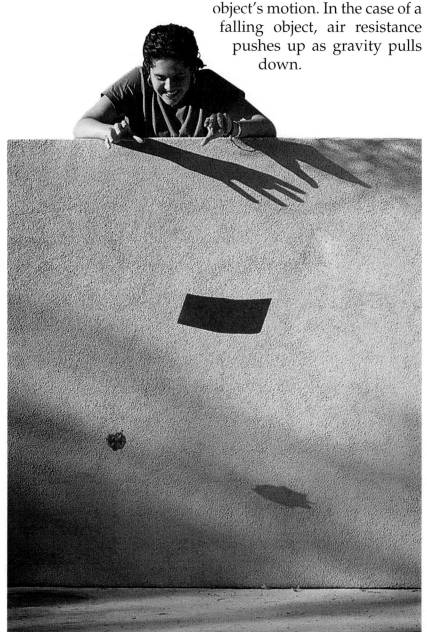

Mini LAB

How can air resistance change the acceleration of a falling object?

Procedure
1. Obtain a discarded book. Cut a piece of paper the same size as the cover of the book.
2. Predict whether the book or the paper will hit the floor first if you drop them the same way and at the same time.
3. Try dropping them side by side with the greatest surface area facing down. Which object has the greater acceleration?
4. Next, devise several methods to make the book and paper fall at nearly the same acceleration.

Analysis
1. If the acceleration of gravity is the same for all objects, how can you explain your results?
2. Describe the methods you discovered for making the book and paper fall at nearly the same acceleration. Analyze how they work.

Figure 4-3

Gravity and air resistance, the two forces acting on the paper, are invisible. *How do we know these forces exist?*

Air resistance

Figure 4-4

The Frisbee is designed to use air resistance to help it soar and maneuver as it moves through the air. *How does its shape produce different effects of horizontal and vertical air resistance?*

The amount of air resistance on an object depends on the speed, size, shape, and density of the object. It is air resistance that helps the Frisbee in **Figure 4-4** stay aloft for several seconds. The larger the surface area of the object, the greater the amount of air resistance on it. This is why feathers, leaves, and sheets of paper fall more slowly than pennies, acorns, and crumpled balls of paper. The snowflakes and hailstones shown in **Figure 4-5** fall at different speeds. A snowflake may follow a long and winding path to the ground. Once a hailstone is large enough, it falls straight down. Why do the shapes and masses of the snowflakes and hailstones cause them to have different accelerations?

Figure 4-5

The snowflakes (A) and the hailstones (B) are both solid forms of water.

Terminal Velocity

As an object falls through air, air resistance gradually increases until it balances the pull of gravity. According to the law of inertia, when the forces acting on an object are balanced, the motion of the object will not change. When this happens, the falling object will stop accelerating. It will continue to fall, but at a constant, final velocity like the parachutist in **Figure 4-6.** This **terminal velocity** is the highest velocity that will be reached by a falling object.

Think about the things you know about moving objects. You know that a leaf falls more slowly than an acorn. A rock that is dropped from a height of 10 m is traveling faster when it hits the ground than a rock dropped from 1 m. You will learn more about moving things as you continue reading this chapter.

Figure 4-6

Air resistance acts on the parachute, allowing the parachutist to fall at a terminal velocity that is slow enough to allow a safe landing.

Air resistance

Gravity

Section Wrap-up

Review

1. A weightlifter raises a 440-kg barbell with an acceleration of 2 m/s². How much force does the weightlifter exert on the barbell?

2. A softball is larger and more massive than a baseball. Use Newton's second law to explain why players can't throw or hit a softball as far as a baseball.

3. **Think Critically:** Use what you have learned about falling objects, air resistance, and terminal velocity to explain why a person can parachute safely to Earth from a high-flying airplane.

Skill Builder
Comparing and Contrasting

Use a balance to find the masses of an uninflated balloon and a balloon filled with air. Drop the two balloons from the same height at the same time, and compare and contrast the rates at which they fall. If you need help, refer to Comparing and Contrasting in the **Skill Handbook.**

USING MATH

You apply a force of 50 N to lift a package with a mass of 4 kg. Calculate the resulting rate of acceleration of the package.

Projectile and Circular Motion

Objectives

- Explain why things that are thrown or shot follow a curved path.
- Compare motion in a straight line with circular motion.
- Define *weightlessness.*

Projectiles

Have you noticed that nearly all the moving objects described in this unit so far have been moving in straight lines? But that's not the only kind of motion you know about. Skateboarders wheel around in circles, cars go around hairpin curves, and rockets shoot upward and curve back to Earth. How do the laws of motion account for these kinds of motion?

If you've ever played darts, thrown a ball, or shot an arrow from a bow, you have probably noticed that these objects didn't travel in straight lines. They start off straight, but they curve downward. That's why dart players and archers learn to aim above their targets.

Anything that's thrown or shot through the air is called a **projectile.** Because of Earth's gravitational pull and their own inertia, projectiles follow a curved path. They have both horizontal and vertical velocities. The basketball in **Figure 4-7** is a projectile.

Horizontal Motion

When you throw a ball, like the pitcher in **Figure 4-8,** the force from your hand makes the ball move forward. It gives the ball *horizontal motion*, that is, motion parallel to Earth's surface. Once you let go of the ball, no other force accelerates it forward, so its horizontal velocity is constant if you ignore air resistance.

Figure 4-7

A basketball becomes a projectile when it is shot toward the basket. *Describe the path the ball takes after it leaves the shooter's hands.*

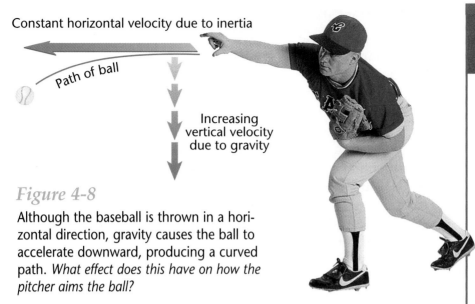

Constant horizontal velocity due to inertia

Path of ball

Increasing
vertical velocity
due to gravity

Figure 4-8

Although the baseball is thrown in a horizontal direction, gravity causes the ball to accelerate downward, producing a curved path. *What effect does this have on how the pitcher aims the ball?*

Vertical Motion

When you let go of the ball, something else happens, as well. Gravity starts pulling it downward, giving it *vertical motion*, or motion perpendicular to Earth's surface. Now the ball has constant horizontal velocity but increasing vertical velocity. Gravity exerts an unbalanced force on the ball, changing the direction of its path from forward only to forward and downward. The ball's horizontal and vertical motions are completely independent of each other.

If you throw a ball horizontally from shoulder height, will it take longer to hit the ground than a ball you simply drop from the same height? Surprisingly, both will hit the ground at the same time. If you have a hard time believing this, **Figure 4-9** may help. The two balls have the same acceleration due to gravity, 9.8 m/s^2 downward.

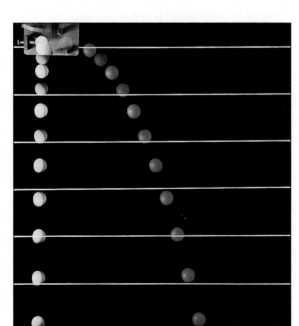

Figure 4-9

The two balls in the photograph were released at the same time. Although the red ball has horizontal velocity, gravity causes both balls to accelerate downward at the same rate.

MiniLAB

Do projectiles fall more slowly than dropped objects?

Procedure
1. Place a flat ruler near the edge of a table. Place a metal washer on the end of the ruler and extend that end of the ruler about 5 cm over the table's edge.
2. Place a second, identical washer on the corner of the table beside the ruler, as shown in the diagram below.
3. With a quick motion from the supported end of the ruler, slide the ruler out from under the first washer and knock the second washer forward so that it flies out from the table as a projectile.
4. Repeat the experiment several times, observing whether the washers hit the floor at the same time or different times by listening to the sound when they hit.

Analysis
1. Do the washers hit at the same time or at different times? Explain your answer, using your observations to support your conclusions.
2. Would the results be the same if you used two different masses, such as a washer and a small piece of tissue paper? Explain your prediction. Try it!

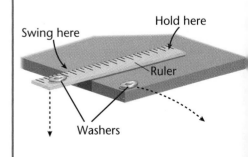

Hold here

Swing here

Ruler

Washers

Motion Along Curves

Recall that acceleration is a rate of change in velocity caused by a change in speed, in direction, or both. Now, picture a bicycle moving at a constant speed along the westbound straightaway of an oval track. Because its speed is constant in a straight line, the bicycle is not accelerating. However, when the bicycle enters a curve, even if its speed does not change, it is accelerating because its direction is changing. The change in the direction of the velocity is toward the center of the curve. Acceleration toward the center of a curved or circular path is called **centripetal acceleration.** The bicycles and their riders in **Figure 4-10** experience centripetal acceleration and lean toward the inside of the curve. The word *centripetal* means "toward the center."

Figure 4-10

These bicycle riders are experiencing centripetal acceleration.

A What is providing the centripetal force that helps these riders follow a circular path? In what direction are they accelerating?

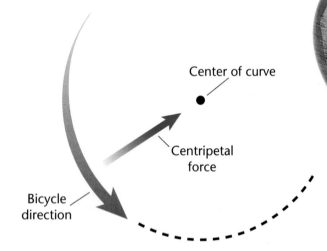

Center of curve

Centripetal force

Bicycle direction

B The direction of the riders' velocity is constantly changing because of the influence of centripetal force.

Centripetal Force

In order for the bicycle to be accelerating, some unbalanced force must be acting on it in a direction toward the center of the curve. That force is a centripetal force. **Centripetal force** is a force acting toward the center of a curved or circular path.

When a car rounds a sharp curve on a highway, the centripetal force is the friction between the tires and the road surface. But if the road is icy or wet and the tires lose their grip, the centripetal force may not be enough to overcome the car's inertia. The car would then keep moving in a straight line in the direction it was traveling at the spot where it lost traction.

Weightlessness in Orbit

Maybe you've seen pictures of astronauts floating inside the space shuttle with various pieces of equipment suspended in midair beside them. Any item that is not fastened down in the shuttle will float around and pose a possible hazard for the astronauts and their equipment. The astronauts and their belongings are experiencing the sensation of weightlessness.

But to be truly weightless, the astronauts would have to be free from the effects of gravity. Orbiting 400 km above Earth, the shuttle and everything inside it still respond to those effects. In fact, gravity keeps the shuttle in orbit.

Free-Falling

So what does it really mean to say that something is weightless in orbit? Think about how the weight of an object is measured. When you place an object on a scale, gravity causes the object to

USING TECHNOLOGY

Roller Coaster Physics

A roller coaster designer applies the laws of motion so that it will be the most exciting ride in the park. A ride begins when a chain pulls the cars to the top of the first hill. Once the cars are released, acceleration increases until all of the cars are headed downward.

The debate on which seat is the scariest continues to rage, and the answer is, "that depends." As the cars descend, their speed increases. The rear car starts down the slope at a much greater speed than the front car, thus giving the passengers the sense of being hurled over the edge. At the bottom of the hill, it is a different story. When the change in direction from down to up occurs, the front car will be going fastest and its passengers will experience the greater forces. As the cars pop over the top of the hill, the passengers in the rear car may experience a considerable force, resulting in the sensation of being thrown free.

As ride technology improves, roller coasters get larger and faster. The Magnum XL 200 at Cedar Point in Sandusky, Ohio, has a first hill 61 m (201 feet) high, reaches a speed of 112 km/h, and covers 1.6 km (5106 feet) of track in 2½ minutes.

Think Critically:

Describe the roller-coaster design that would result in the greatest sensations for the passengers.

Riders experience rapid acceleration

Figure 4-11

The space shuttle and everything in it are in free-fall around Earth, thus producing apparent weightlessness. *Are objects in orbit around Earth really weightless? Explain.*

push down on the scale. In turn, the scale pushes back on the object with the same force. The dial on the scale measures the amount of upward force needed to offset gravity.

Now suppose that the scale is falling, being pulled downward by gravity at the same rate as the object being weighed. The scale couldn't push back on the object, so its dial would read zero. The object would seem to be weightless. This is what is happening in a space shuttle orbiting Earth. The shuttle and everything in it, including the astronaut working in **Figure 4-11,** are all "falling" toward Earth at exactly the same rate of acceleration. When an object is influenced only by gravity, it is said to be in free-fall. An orbiting space shuttle and all its contents are in free-fall around Earth.

INTEGRATION
Life Science

Effects of Weightlessness

As you move about in your daily routines, the resistance provided by gravity helps you exercise your body. What happens to the physical condition of astronauts who experience the sensation of weightlessness for extended periods of time? When Russian cosmonauts experienced weightlessness for more than 200 consecutive days, they developed health problems. Health tests performed on American astronauts have also shown that some bone and muscle deterioration occurs during long periods of weightlessness.

Exercising in Space

Flight doctors have developed special exercise programs for astronauts to reduce the health problems related to weightlessness. Several activities, such as the one in **Figure 4-12,** are helpful. They include isometric exercises, in which muscles push against other muscles in the body. For example, you can feel some resistance if you place your left palm against your right palm and push your palms together for 10 seconds.

Aboard the space shuttle, astronauts also walk on a unique treadmill for 15 to 30 minutes each day. Special attachments to their arms and legs make their muscles work even harder. An air duct circulates air to help dry off their sweat. They can even listen to music or gaze out the window into space while they exercise.

Figure 4-12

Astronauts don't have much room to exercise inside the shuttle. Here astronaut Ellen Baker exercises aboard Columbia while in orbit.

Section Wrap-up

Review

1. Use a diagram similar to **Figure 4-8** to show why a dart player has to aim above the target to hit the bull's-eye. In your diagram, show the forces acting on the dart, the dart's path, and the two kinds of motion involved.

2. A child is swinging a yo-yo in a circle. What provides the force to keep the yo-yo going in a circle? What is the force called? What happens if the string breaks?

3. **Think Critically:** Does the mass of an astronaut change when he or she is in orbit around Earth? Does an astronaut's weight change?

Skill Builder
Making and Using Tables
Make a table showing important characteristics of projectile motion, circular motion, and free-fall. Table headings should include: *Kind of Motion, Shape of Path,* and *Laws or Forces Involved.* You may add other headings. If you need help, refer to Making and Using Tables in the **Skill Handbook.**

Science Journal

Write a paragraph describing a situation in which you experienced something close to free-fall or a feeling of weightlessness. Think about amusement park rides, elevators, athletic events, or even movie scenes.

Activity 4-1

Design Your Own Experiment
Ready...Set... Accelerate!

Imagine the changes in motion you would experience while riding a bicycle straight ahead and then going around a corner. As you started out, would you be accelerating forward? When you whip around a corner at constant speed, you are accelerating because your direction is changing. But in which direction is the acceleration?

PREPARATION

Problem
How can you use an accelerometer to determine the direction of acceleration in various types of motion?

Form a Hypothesis
Develop a hypothesis about the direction of acceleration in simple movements such as moving forward, backward, left, right, and in a circle.

Objectives
- Construct a simple accelerometer to use in determining the direction of acceleration in various movements.
- Observe the accelerometer as you accelerate in different directions.

Possible Materials
- clean, empty, 2-L plastic bottle with cap
- cork or other small object that floats in water
- thread
- water

Safety Precautions
Protect clothing and eyes. Provide enough floor space for students to safely spin around.

PLAN THE EXPERIMENT

1. Be sure your group has agreed upon a hypothesis statement.
2. Sketch the design for your accelerometer. See the photo and the list of suggested materials for some ideas.
3. As a group, make a detailed list of the steps you will take to test your hypothesis.
4. Gather the materials you will need to carry out your experiment.

Check the Plan

1. What will you use as your floating device in the accelerometer?
2. How long will your thread that anchors the floating device be?

3. What types of motion will you try to use your accelerometer to analyze? Be sure to include circular motion.
4. Be sure you observe the motion of your floating device when the accelerated motion begins.
5. *Make sure your teacher approves your plan and that you have included any changes suggested in the plan.*

DO THE EXPERIMENT

1. Carry out the experiment as planned.
2. Be sure to write down any observations that you make while doing your experiment. You might also include suggestions for improving your accelerometer.

Analyze and Apply

1. How did the floater act when you moved your accelerometer to the left, to the right, forward, and backward? What other motions did you try?

2. Did you try to **observe** any vertical motions with your accelerometer? If not, try it now. Was it effective? Why or why not?
3. What happened in the accelerometer when you held it while rotating in a circle? In what direction is this centripetal acceleration directed? What is providing the centripetal force?

Go Further

Think of a familiar carnival or amusement park ride. If you were carrying your accelerometer on this ride, what changes would you observe? Write a descriptive paragraph about your predictions. What industrial uses do you think more accurate accelerometers might have?

TECHNOLOGY:
4•3 Sending up Satellites

Science Words

artificial satellite

Objectives

- Explain how satellites are placed into orbit around Earth.
- Give examples of how satellites can be used.

What is an Earth satellite?

When watching a sports program, newscast, or weather report, have you heard the announcer state that a report was received "via satellite"? You may know that Earth's moon is a natural satellite, but the moon was not the source of these reports. What other satellites are orbiting Earth? **Artificial satellites** are human-made devices that orbit Earth for a specific purpose. Once in orbit, their motion and behavior are like those of natural satellites such as Earth's moon.

Launching Artificial Satellites

Newton's original idea of launching a satellite by blasting it horizontally from a mountaintop, illustrated in **Figure 4-13,** did not turn out to be practical, but in the 1950s, the developing field of rocketry did make launching satellites possible. A multistage rocket system typically boosts the satellite to the desired height of the orbit and then fires again to accelerate the satellite to the speed required to stay in orbit. This speed for circular orbits is around 8 km/s, or about 29 000 km/h.

In 1957, the former Soviet Union launched the first artificial Earth satellite. The satellite, called Sputnik, was a metallic instrument module having a mass of only 84 kg and a diameter of 60 cm. It orbited Earth about once every 90 minutes. Literally thousands of satellites have now been placed into orbit, including some that have orbited Mars, Venus, and Earth's moon.

Figure 4-13

Newton's idea of using cannons to launch satellites was based on the technology of the time. He proposed that if a cannonball were launched with large enough speed, the curve of its trajectory would match Earth's curve and the ball would orbit Earth at a constant height. *How is his idea similar to the way satellites are put into orbit today?*

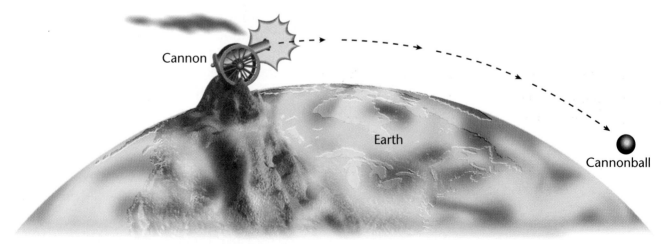

Cannon

Earth

Cannonball

How We Use Satellites

Artificial satellites, such as the one in **Figure 4-14,** serve a variety of different purposes. Communications and weather satellites are most familiar. These are usually geostationary satellites, which are put into orbit with a speed that matches the movement of Earth as it spins on its axis. Thus, as **Figure 4-15** shows, they appear to be stationary high above a given location on Earth. Communication satellites serve as receivers and transmitters to relay TV and radio signals around the world. Weather satellites use different photographic techniques to monitor weather patterns and ground temperatures.

Many satellites are used by the military to monitor actions in other countries—tiny details can be photographed from hundreds of kilometers above Earth.

Falling Satellites

Artificial satellites cannot orbit forever. Even in high orbits, small amounts of air resistance gradually cause a satellite to lose energy, allowing Earth's gravity to pull it lower. As a satellite is pulled downward into the denser part of Earth's atmosphere, it usually burns up in the extreme heat generated by atmospheric friction.

Figure 4-14

Satellites can remain in orbit performing their tasks for many years.

Figure 4-15

If you look up at a geostationary satellite, it appears to be hovering motionless overhead. *Why are communication satellites placed in geostationary orbits?*

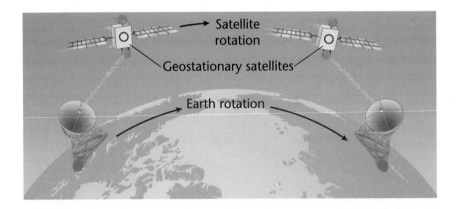

Satellite rotation

Geostationary satellites

Earth rotation

Section Wrap-up

Review

1. For what purposes are artificial satellites used?

2. Why are geostationary satellites often useful for communications and monitoring weather?

Explore the Technology

Rockets are used to launch satellites. Why do you think Newton's original idea has not been practical for launching satellites? Try to cite several problems.

SCIENCE & SOCIETY

4•4 Action and Reaction

Newton's third law of motion
momentum
law of conservation of momentum

Objectives

- Analyze action and reaction forces.
- Calculate momentum.
- Explain conservation of momentum.

Figure 4-16

The boy's leap will fall short of the dock. *What didn't he think about before he jumped?*

Newton's Third Law

A girl blows up a balloon and releases it, watching it dart away on a zigzag course. A young person enjoys bouncing on a trampoline. A boy leaping from a boat toward land falls in the water when the boat scoots away from the dock. As different as these examples of motion may seem, they all illustrate one point: forces always act in pairs, called action-reaction pairs.

Newton's third law of motion describes action-reaction pairs this way: When one object exerts a force on a second object, the second one exerts a force on the first that is equal in size and opposite in direction. A less formal way of saying the same thing is "to every action force there is an equal and opposite reaction force."

Action-Reaction Pairs

Let's look at two examples of the action-reaction pairs described earlier. When a person jumps on a trampoline, he or she exerts a downward force on the trampoline. The trampoline then exerts an equal force upward, sending the person high into the air.

In **Figure 4-16,** when the boy leaps from the boat, the boat exerts a force on his feet, moving him forward. His feet exert an equal and opposite force on the boat, sending it backward.

Figure 4-17

As the swimmer's hands and feet push against the water, the water pushes back, moving the swimmer forward.

Forces Acting on Different Objects

Newton's third law can be used to explain how the swimmer in **Figure 4-17** moves through the water. With each stroke, the swimmer's arm exerts a force on the water. The water pushes back on the swimmer with an equal force in the opposite direction. But if the forces are equal, how can the swimmer move forward? It's possible because the forces are acting on different things. The "action" force acts on the water; the "reaction" force acts on the swimmer. The swimmer, having less mass than the pool full of water, accelerates more than the water.

An important point to keep in mind when dealing with Newton's third law is that action-reaction forces always act on *different* objects. Thus, even though the forces may be equal, they are not balanced. In the case of the swimmer, water pushes her forward, overcoming the friction, or drag, she encounters. Thus, a net force, or unbalanced force, acts on the swimmer, and a change in motion can take place. The force pairs involved in passing a basketball will cause the wheelchair in **Figure 4-18** to roll backward.

Figure 4-18

The action of passing the basketball forward will propel the player slightly backward. *Would this be an advantage or disadvantage for the player?*

Rocket Propulsion

Rockets work on a principle similar to that which causes a balloon to move when air escapes. In the rocket, burning fuel produces hot gases that push against the inside of the rocket and escape out the bottom. The upward push of gases propels the rocket.

Figure 4-19

The "action force" of the expanding gases pushes the rocket upward. The "reaction force" of the rocket pushes the exhaust gases out.

Action Force
rocket accelerates

Reaction Force
escaping gases

Mini**LAB**

How can you deliver a payload with a balloon rocket?

Procedure
1. Make a guiding line for your balloon rocket by threading an 8-m string through a drinking straw. Tie each end to a chair and stretch it taut between the chairs.
2. Blow up a balloon and pinch the end. Tape a very small object to the balloon in a location that will interfere as little as possible with the rocket's flight.
3. With the straw at one end of the string, use tape to attach the inflated balloon to the straw.
4. Release the balloon. Measure to the nearest centimeter how far your rocket travels.

Analysis
1. What propels the balloon forward? How does this demonstrate Newton's third law?
2. Do you think your rocket would travel farther if it were not carrying the object? What changes could you make to allow your balloon to travel farther? Try it.

Momentum—Mass on the Move

If a toy truck rolls toward you, you can easily stop it with your hand. However, such a tactic would not work with a full-sized truck, even if it were moving at the same speed as the toy truck. It takes more force to stop the full-sized truck because it has more momentum than the toy truck has. **Momentum** is a property a moving object has because of its mass and velocity. Momentum can be calculated with this equation, in which p represents momentum.

$$momentum = mass \times velocity$$

$$p = mv$$

The unit for momentum is kg · m/s. Notice that momentum has a direction because velocity has a direction. Notice also that if an object is not moving, it has zero momentum.

Figure 4-20

Because of its much greater mass, the real truck has more momentum than the toy truck, even when the two trucks are moving at the same speed. *What would happen in a collision between a large truck and a small truck?*

The two trucks pictured in **Figure 4-20** may have the same velocity, but the full-sized truck has more momentum because of its greater mass. A speeding bullet has a large momentum because of its high velocity, even though its mass is small. A lumbering elephant may have a low velocity, but because of its large mass, it has a large momentum. The bumper cars shown in **Figure 4-21** are an example of how rapidly changing momentums can be fun.

Figure 4-21

Bumper cars are a favorite amusement-park ride for many people. *What factors could cause the momentum of one bumper car to be different from that of another bumper car?*

Conserving Total Momentum

The momentum of an object doesn't change unless its mass, or velocity, or both, change. But momentum can be transferred from one object to another. Consider the game of pool shown in **Figure 4-22.** Before the game starts, all the balls are motionless. Therefore, the total momentum of the balls is zero. There can be no momentum because none of the balls has a velocity.

What happens when a cue ball rolling across a pool table hits the group of balls that is standing still? At first, the rolling ball has momentum and the motionless balls do not. When the cue ball collides with the balls that were at rest, all the balls start moving. They gain momentum. The cue ball slows down and loses momentum. If you were to measure the total momentum of all the balls before and after the collision, it would be the same. The momentum the group of balls gains is equal to the momentum that the cue ball loses. Total momentum is conserved—it doesn't change.

Figure 4-22

The pool player is ready to start a game. *What is the total momentum of all the balls on the table?*

A The player strikes the cue ball and sends it hurtling toward the group of balls at the other end of the table. The cue ball is the only ball moving; thus, it is the only ball with momentum. It carries the total momentum of all the balls.

B After being struck by the cue ball, the other balls scatter around the table; some hit other balls, some hit the edge of the table, and others may hit nothing before stopping. At any instant, the total momentum of all the balls is equal to the momentum the cue ball had before it struck the rest of the balls.

The **law of conservation of momentum** states that the total amount of momentum of a group of objects does not change unless outside forces act on the objects. After the collision, the balls on the pool table eventually slow down and stop rolling. What outside force makes that happen?

With Newton's third law and conservation of momentum, you can explain many types of motion that may seem complicated at first. Bouncing on a trampoline, knocking down bowling pins with a ball, and tackling a football player are a few examples. Think about how you would explain these and other examples of motion.

All the balls have come to a stop and the player is ready to take the next shot. The total momentum of all the balls is zero again.

Problem Solving

An Icy Challenge

Suppose you are playing hockey on a frozen pond with some friends when one of them presents a challenge. From the middle of the frozen pond, you are challenged to find a way to get to the ground at the edge of the pond without pushing or walking with your legs or arms. Assume the pond is nearly frictionless. What do you have with you that will help you get off of the pond?

Solve the Problem:

1. **How does the statement that the pond is nearly frictionless affect your approach to solving this problem?**
2. **What is your momentum as you are standing in the middle of the frozen pond?**

Think Critically:

1. Describe your plan for getting to the edge of the pond. Be sure to describe any forces involved in your plan.
2. What motions would take place and why would they occur?
3. How would you change your plan if you almost made it to the edge?

Figure 4-23

A tackle being made in football is a good example of momentum being transferred and conserved. *If a football player wanted to increase his momentum, how could he do it?*

Most sports involve many rapid changes in momentum. The momentums of the ball carrier and the tacklers in **Figure 4-23** change when the tackle is made. Players who are moving have momentum, and the equipment they use—bats, balls, rackets, and pucks—also have their own momentum when they are put into play. In every case, the law of conservation of momentum is in effect.

Section Wrap-up

Review

1. A boater tries to jump a few feet from a boat to land. Instead, he lands in the water. Explain why.

2. Compare the momentums of a 50-kg dolphin swimming 16.4 m/s and a 6300-kg elephant walking 0.11 m/s.

3. **Think Critically:** Some ballet directors assign larger dancers to perform slow, graceful steps and smaller dancers to perform quick movements. Does this plan make sense? Why?

Skill Builder
Hypothesizing

You are a crane operator using a wrecking ball to demolish an old building. You can choose to use a 100-kg ball or a 150-kg ball. Which ball would knock the walls down faster? Which ball would be easier for you to control? Explain. If you need help, refer to Hypothesizing in the **Skill Handbook.**

Science Journal

In your Science Journal, use the law of conservation of momentum to explain the results of a particular collision you have witnessed. For example, think of games, sports, or amusement park rides or contests.

Activity 4-2

A Massive Problem

Some or all of the momentum of a billiard ball transfers to a second ball when they collide. What would happen if the second ball were a bowling ball?

Problem
How does mass affect momentum when two objects collide?

Materials
- dynamics carts (2)
- long rubber band
- building bricks (2)
- meterstick
- masking tape

Safety Precautions
Be sure that there is a clear path between the carts when they are released.

Procedure
1. Prepare a data table like the one shown.
2. Attach a long rubber band to the two dynamics carts. Move the carts apart until the rubber band is taut, but not stretched.
3. Mark the halfway point between the two carts with a piece of tape. Lay the meterstick on the table with the 50-cm mark beside the tape.
4. Pull the carts apart until the ends of the rubber band line up with the ends of the meterstick.
5. Release both carts at the same time so that they gain equal and opposite momentums. Observe and record the point along the meterstick where the carts collide and where the carts stop.

6. Place a brick on cart A and repeat steps 4 and 5.
7. Add a second brick to cart A and repeat steps 4 and 5.

Analyze
1. From the data, **conclude** which cart was moving faster.
2. How can both carts have equal and opposite momentums if they are traveling at different speeds?
3. How does the addition of mass to one cart affect the location of the collision point? How does it affect what happens to the carts after the collision?

Conclude and Apply
4. If one cart were released slightly before the other, how would the momentums of the two carts be affected?
5. Suppose momentum is said to be negative (−) in one direction and positive (+) in the opposite direction. If two carts with equal momentums are traveling in opposite directions, **predict** the total momentum of the two-cart system.

Data and Observations

	Collision Point	Distance Traveled		Location after Collision	
		Cart A	Cart B	Cart A	Cart B
Trial 1					
Trial 2					
Trial 3					

People and Science

SAMMY CHAN, *Pool Player*

On the Job

Q Mr. Chan, what scientific principles do you take into consideration as you plan shots?

A I often have to figure out angles and hit the ball a little off center. A difference of just millimeters in where I hit the ball will widen or narrow the angle and make all the difference in a shot. Often, I rehearse a shot in my mind, visualizing a clock face on the cue ball. This gives me a specific spot to aim for.

Q What does planning well result in?

A Sometimes, I set up three balls at the end of the table, one by each pocket and one in the middle. If I hit the cue ball just right, I can sink the left-hand ball, curve around the middle ball, and sink the right-hand ball.

Q Why is chalk put on the tip of a pool cue?

A Chalk roughens the tip of the cue and increases friction when the tip of the pool cue hits the shiny, smooth surface of the cue ball. Even weather affects a game. The felt on the table swells in hot, humid weather and becomes flatter and tighter in cold weather.

Personal Insights

Q Outside of the fun of the game of pool, why are you attracted to it?

A Pool is a game of discipline and planning. Actually, it's a lot like chess because you have to plan ahead. I never make a shot without planning my next several shots. I want to know exactly where the cue ball will end up after a shot.

Career Connection

Think about science-related careers that require good hand-and-eye coordination and planning. Investigate your choices in the *United States Government Handbook of Careers*, available in any public library.

Choose someone in your community to interview who is involved in one of these careers and present a summary of the interview in class. Some of these careers might be:

- **Hygienist**
- **Mechanical Engineer**
- **Civil Engineer**

Chapter 4 Review

Summary

4-1: Accelerated Motion

1. According to Newton's second law, a net force acting on an object causes the object to accelerate in the direction of the force. The size of the acceleration depends on the strength of the force and the mass of the object.
2. Near Earth's surface, gravity causes falling objects to accelerate at a rate of 9.8 m/s². Ignoring air resistance, all objects accelerate at this rate, regardless of mass.
3. Air resistance acts in the direction opposite to that in which the object is moving.

4-2: Projectile and Circular Motion

1. Objects thrown or shot through the air are called projectiles. All projectiles have both horizontal and vertical velocities. If air resistance is ignored, the horizontal velocity is constant; the vertical velocity, which is affected by gravity, increases.
2. When an object moves along a circular path, it is accelerated toward the center of the circle.
3. When an object is influenced only by gravity, it is said to be in free-fall. Objects in free-fall can be considered weightless.

4-3: Science and Society: Sending up Satellites

1. Artificial satellites are placed in Earth's orbit for communication, weather-monitoring, scientific, and military purposes.
2. Rockets are used to carry satellites up to the desired orbit height and to then give them the proper orbital velocity.

4-4: Action and Reaction

1. Forces always act in pairs. The forces in an action-reaction pair are always equal in size and opposite in direction.
2. All moving objects have momentum. The momentum of an object is the product of its mass and velocity.
3. The total momentum of a set of objects is conserved unless a net force acts on the set.

Key Science Words

a. air resistance
b. artificial satellite
c. centripetal acceleration
d. centripetal force
e. law of conservation of momentum
f. momentum
g. Newton's second law of motion
h. Newton's third law of motion
i. projectile
j. terminal velocity

Reviewing Vocabulary

Match each phrase with the correct term from the list of Key Science Words.

1. deals with action-reaction forces
2. force that opposes the motion of a falling object near Earth's surface
3. an object that is thrown through the air
4. acceleration toward the center of a circle
5. product of an object's mass and velocity
6. describes the effect of a net force on an object
7. causes circular motion
8. achieved when acceleration due to gravity is balanced by air resistance
9. describes the unchanging nature of the total momentum of a set of objects
10. human-made device that orbits Earth

Chapter 4 Review

Checking Concepts

Choose the word or phrase that completes the sentence or answers the question.

1. A net force acting on a moving object causes the object to _____.
   a. fall   c. stop
   b. accelerate   d. curve
2. _____ is the force of gravity on an object.
   a. Mass   c. Centripetal force
   b. Momentum   d. Weight
3. Which of these opposes acceleration due to gravity?
   a. momentum   c. reaction force
   b. air resistance d. terminal velocity
4. According to Newton's second law, _____ equals mass times acceleration.
   a. gravity   c. force
   b. momentum   d. weight
5. What force causes a leaf to fall more slowly than a penny?
   a. gravity   c. inertia
   b. momentum   d. air resistance
6. Which best illustrates Newton's third law?
   a. projectile motion   c. rocket propulsion
   b. circular motion   d. centripetal force
7. The _____ velocity of a projectile is considered to be constant.
   a. horizontal   c. accelerated
   b. circular   d. vertical
8. An object in free-fall can be considered _____.
   a. moving horizontally   c. motionless
   b. heavy   d. weightless
9. _____ is reached when air resistance and force due to gravity are equal.
   a. Negative acceleration
   b. Terminal velocity
   c. Centripetal acceleration
   d. Weightlessness
10. Which of the following does not affect the amount of air resistance that acts on an object?
    a. mass   c. shape
    b. size   d. speed

Understanding Concepts

Answer the following questions in your Science Journal using complete sentences.

11. On Earth, why does an object of large mass weigh more than an object of smaller mass?
12. Explain why gravity does not cause a falling object of large mass to accelerate at a faster rate than a falling object of smaller mass.
13. If the forces in an action-reaction pair are equal in size and opposite in direction, why aren't they balanced forces?
14. A spaceship orbiting Earth is held in its orbit by Earth's gravity. Yet, astronauts in the spaceship are said to be weightless. Explain.
15. Explain why a marble moves in a straight line as it rolls across the table but follows a curved path once it rolls off the table.

Thinking Critically

16. What force is exerted on a 1000-kg car accelerating at a rate of 15 m/s^2?
17. The motion of a 12-kg object is opposed by a 30-N force of friction. At what rate does friction slow the object down?
18. You are asked to design a winding mountain road. What force must you try to increase in designing this road? How might you do this?

19. A 4-kg bowling ball rolling at 6 m/s collides head-on with an identical, motionless bowling ball. If the first ball is moving forward at 2 m/s right after the collision, what is the speed and direction of the second ball?

20. The moon has no atmosphere and its gravity is about one-sixth as strong as that of Earth. Considering these factors, how would the motions of objects near the moon be different from the same motions near Earth?

Developing Skills

If you need help, refer to the **Skill Handbook.**

21. Interpreting Data: The table contains data about four objects dropped to the ground from the same height at the same time.
a. Which object falls fastest? Slowest?
b. On which object is the force of gravity greatest?
c. Is air resistance stronger on A or B?
d. Which object is probably largest in size? Explain your reasoning.

Time of Fall for Dropped Objects

Object	Mass	Time of Fall
A	5.0 g	2.0 s
B	5.0 g	1.0 s
C	30.0 g	0.5 s
D	35.0 g	1.5 s

22. Observing and Inferring: A girl weighing 360 N steps into a motionless elevator at the ground floor. She steps onto a scale and remains on the scale while the elevator accelerates, then moves at a constant speed, and finally slows to a stop at the 120th floor. During that time, the readings on the scale range from a high of 365 N to a low of 355 N. Infer what the reading was on the ground floor, on the way up, stopping, and stopped on the 120th floor. Why do these readings change?

23. Recognizing Cause and Effect: When using a high-pressure hose, why is it necessary for firefighters to grip the hose strongly and plant their feet firmly?

24. Concept Mapping: Make two events chains showing what happens when a rolling ball (Ball One) hits a resting ball (Ball Two). Use the phrases: *gains momentum, rests, rolls more slowly or stops, hits Ball Two, rolls, loses momentum, is hit by Ball One, starts rolling.*

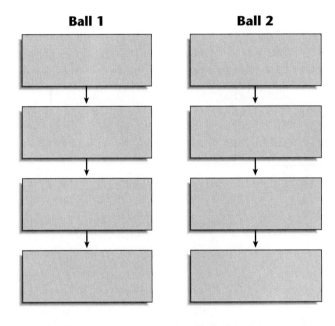

Performance Assessment

1. Designing an Experiment: Review the MiniLAB on page 112. Devise a way to make the rocket travel farther by using two balloons. Use physics terms to explain why this could be effective.

2. Analyzing the Data: Look back at your results from Activity 4-2 on page 117. Suppose you have cart A carrying a load that makes it twice as massive as cart B. Under what conditions could both carts have the same momentum?

3. Poster: Make a poster showing how a rocket engine works. Use Newton's third law to explain why a rocket lifts off.

Previewing the Chapter

Energy

ow many ways do you use your own energy every day? Every move you make requires the release of energy stored in your body. Some tasks, such as exercising on a stair climber, require more energy than others. In this chapter, find out about several different forms of energy and how they can be measured. In the activity below, observe how dependent you are on a ready source of energy.

EXPLORE ACTIVITY

Think about the energy involved as you try this workout.

1. Stand and hold your arms with your hands together, palms up, extended at waist level. Have a classmate stack books on your hands.
2. Raise the books to shoulder level, then lower them. Now try lifting them over your head.
3. Have your classmate add two more books to your pile. Repeat the lifting exercise.
4. Hold the books at shoulder level until your arms get tired.

Observe: Which activities require the most energy? Describe them in your Science Journal.

Previewing Science Skills

▶ In the Skill Builders, you will **compare and contrast, map concepts,** and **interpret data.**

▶ In the Activities, you will **measure in SI, observe and infer, collect and interpret data, make and use graphs,** and **hypothesize.**

▶ In the MiniLAB, you will **measure in SI, observe and infer,** and **hypothesize.**

5•1 Energy and Work

Science Words

energy
kinetic energy
potential energy
work
mechanical energy
law of conservation of
    energy

Objectives

- Distinguish between kinetic and potential energy.
- Recognize that energy is conserved when changing from one form to another.
- Compare the scientific meaning of *work* with its everyday meaning.

What is energy?

You have seen several examples of energy being used today. Just about everything you see or do involves energy. Energy is a bit mysterious. You can't smell it. In most cases, you can't even see it. Light is one form of energy you can see and without it, you wouldn't be able to see anything. You can't see electricity, but you can see its effects in a glowing lightbulb, and you can feel its effects in the heat produced by the coils of a toaster. You can't see the energy in the food in **Figure 5-1,** but you can see and feel its effects when your muscles use that energy to move.

Energy—An Agent of Change

If a baseball flies through the air and shatters a window, it certainly changes the window! When an object is able to change its environment, we say the object has energy. The baseball had energy and did work on the window by causing the window to move. In summary, the use of energy involves change.

Scientists have some difficulty defining energy because it exists in so many different forms. Some of these forms include radiant, electrical, chemical, thermal, and nuclear energy. Traditionally, energy has been defined as the ability to do work—to cause something to move. But when work is performed, there is always a change. This connection offers a useful general definition. **Energy** is the ability to cause change.

Figure 5-1

A nutritious, well-balanced lunch provides the body with "fuel." Energy stored in food is converted to a form that the body can use.

Kinetic Energy: On the Move

Usually, when you think of energy, you think of action—of some motion taking place. **Kinetic energy** is energy in the form of motion. A spinning bicycle wheel, the sprinting cross-country runners in **Figure 5-2,** and a flying plastic disk all have kinetic energy. How much? That depends on the mass and velocity of the moving object.

The greater the mass a moving object has, the more kinetic energy it has. Similarly, the greater an object's velocity, the more kinetic energy it has. The truck traveling at 100 km/h in **Figure 5-3** has more kinetic energy than the motorcycle traveling at the same speed. However, the motorcycle has more kinetic energy than an identical motorcycle moving at 80 km/h.

Potential Energy: Ready and Waiting

Energy doesn't have to involve motion. Even motionless, any sample of matter may have stored energy that gives it the potential to cause change if certain conditions are met. **Potential energy** is stored energy. The amount of potential energy a sample of matter has depends on its position or its condition.

A flowerpot sitting on a second-floor windowsill has potential energy due to its position. If something knocks it off the windowsill, gravity will cause it to fall toward the ground. As it falls, its potential energy changes to kinetic energy.

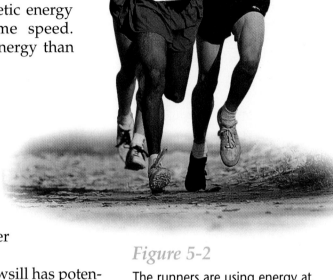

Figure 5-2

The runners are using energy at a high rate. *What types of activities require only a little energy?*

Greatest kinetic energy

100 km/hr

Least kinetic energy

80 km/hr

100 km/hr

Figure 5-3

The kinetic energy of each vehicle is different because kinetic energy depends on mass and velocity.

CONNECT TO

EARTH SCIENCE

Fast-flowing rivers and slow-moving glaciers both contain kinetic energy. A rock balanced high on a hill contains potential energy. *Hypothesize* other examples of kinetic and potential energy in nature.

The potential energy of the flowerpot in **Figure 5-4** is related to its distance above the ground. The greater its height, the greater its potential energy. A flowerpot sitting on a fifth-floor ledge has more potential energy than one sitting on a lower ledge.

If a flowerpot falls, the force of gravity accelerates it downward. The higher the flowerpot, the greater its final velocity will be. Thus, a flowerpot falling from a higher floor will have a higher velocity and more kinetic energy when it hits the ground than a similar pot falling from a lower floor.

You have learned about kinetic energy and some forms of potential energy. Other forms of potential energy will be discussed in later chapters of this book. In the following paragraphs, find out how the concepts of energy and work are related.

What is work?

To most people, the word *work* means something they do to earn money. In that sense, work can be anything from filling fast-food orders or loading trucks to teaching or doing office work at a desk. The scientific meaning of work is more specific. **Work** is the transfer of energy through motion. In order for work to take place, a force must be exerted through a distance.

Figure 5-4

Objects that can fall have one form of potential energy.

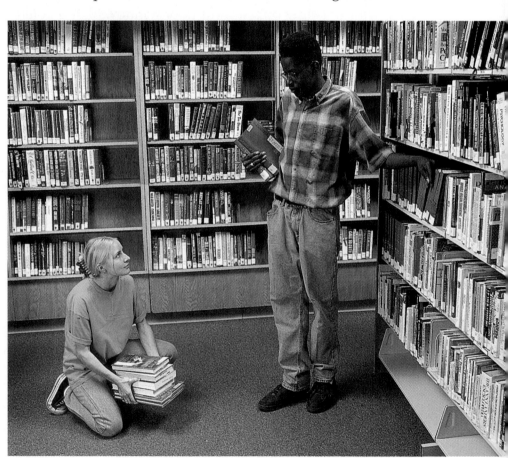

Figure 5-5

Work is done on the books when they are being lifted from the floor. The young man is not performing work on his books.

Calculating Work

In which case would you do more work—lifting a pack of gum from the floor to waist level or lifting a pile of books through the same distance? Would more work be done if the young woman in **Figure 5-5** lifted the books from the floor to her waist or if she raised them all the way over her head? The amount of work done depends on two things: the amount of force exerted and the distance over which the force is applied.

When a force acts over a distance *in the direction of an object's motion*, the work done can be calculated as

Work = force × distance

$$W = F \times d$$

Work, like energy, is measured in joules. The joule is named for the British scientist, James Prescott Joule. One joule is equal to a newton-meter (N · m), which is the amount of work done when a force of one newton acts through a distance of one meter. The stock-person in **Figure 5-6** is doing work. In the problems below, calculate the work done.

Figure 5-6
Stocking shelves is an important job in grocery stores. *How would you determine the amount of work done in stocking the shelves?*

USING MATH

Calculating Work

Example Problem:
A student's full backpack weighs 30 N. She lifts it from the floor to a shelf 1.5 m high. How much work is done on the pack full of books?

Problem-Solving Steps:
1. What is known?   Backpack weight, F = 30 N; distance, d = 1.5 m
2. What is unknown?   Work, W
3. Use the equation $W = F \times d$.
4. **Solution:** W = 30 N × 1.5 m
   = 45 N · m
   = 45 J

Practice Problems
1. A carpenter lifts a 45-kg beam 1.2 m. How much work is done on the beam?
Strategy Hint: The joule is a derived unit. What other units make it up?
2. A dancer lifts a 400-N ballerina overhead a distance of 1.4 m and holds her there for several seconds. How much work is done during the lift? During the time the ballerina is held overhead?
Strategy Hint: Work requires a force to be exerted over a distance.

There are two factors to keep in mind when deciding whether work is being done: something has to move, and the motion must be *in the same direction* as the applied force. If you pick up a pile of books from the floor, work is done on the books. They move upward, in the direction of the applied force. If you hold the books in your arms, no work is done on the books. Some upward force is still being applied (to keep the books from falling), but no movement is taking place. Even if you carry the books across the floor at a constant speed, no work is done on the books. The force being applied to the books is still upward, or vertical, but your motion across the floor is sideward, or horizontal. In the following paragraphs, you will examine the energy changes that result from the motion of a swing.

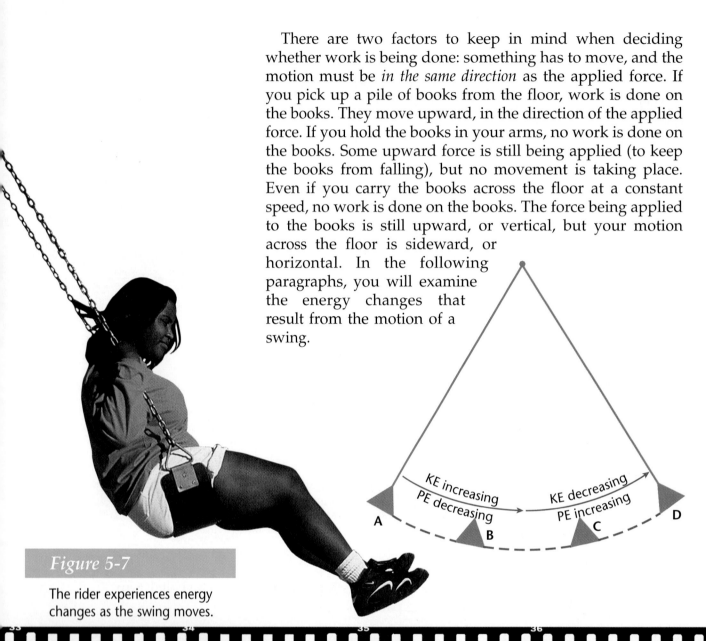

Figure 5-7

The rider experiences energy changes as the swing moves.

A At the rider's highest point, the mechanical energy is entirely potential.

B As she falls toward the bottom of the path, the rider accelerates and gains kinetic energy. Because the rider is not as high, her potential energy decreases by the same amount.

C As it rises toward the opposite side, the swing begins to slow down and lose kinetic energy. As it gains height, it also increases in potential energy.

D As the rider reaches the peak and prepares to fall again in the opposite direction, the mechanical energy of the swing is entirely potential.

Conservation of Energy

Perhaps you have ridden on a playground swing like the person in **Figure 5-7.** Try to remember what it was like swinging back and forth, high and low. Now think about the energy changes involved in such a ride.

The ride starts with a push to get you moving—to give you some kinetic energy. As the swing rises, kinetic energy changes to potential energy of position. At the top of each swing, potential energy is greatest. Then, as the swing moves downward, potential energy changes to kinetic energy. At the bottom of each swing, kinetic energy is greatest and potential energy is at its minimum.

As the swing continues to move back and forth, energy is converted from kinetic to potential to kinetic, over and over again. Taken together, the potential and kinetic energy of the swing make up its mechanical energy. **Mechanical energy** is the total amount of kinetic and potential energy in a system.

CONNECT TO

LIFE SCIENCE

A roller coaster lifts you high above the ground and also moves you at high speeds. Your body experiences many changes in kinetic and potential energy. *Hypothesize* the point at which your body has the most kinetic energy.

Conserving Energy—A Natural Law

Scientists have learned that in any given situation, energy may change from one form to another, but the total amount of energy remains constant. In other words, energy is conserved. This fact is recognized as a law of nature. According to the **law of conservation of energy,** energy may change form but it cannot be created or destroyed under ordinary conditions. This law applies to closed systems, in which energy cannot enter or leave the system.

Suppose the law of conservation of energy is applied to the swing. Would you expect the swing to continue moving back and forth forever? You know this doesn't happen. The swing slows down and comes to a stop. Where does the energy go?

If you think about it, friction and air resistance are constantly acting on the swing and rider just as they are also acting on the skateboarder in **Figure 5-8.** These unbalanced forces cause some of the mechanical energy of the swing to change to thermal energy—heat. With every pass of the swing, the temperatures of the swing, the rider, and the air around them go up a little bit. So the mechanical energy of the swing isn't lost, it is converted to thermal energy. Thermal energy is discussed in the next section.

Figure 5-8

Gravity provides the force to move the skateboarder down the ramp. *What energy changes are taking place?*

The Human Body—Balancing the Energy Equation

What forms of energy discussed in this chapter can you find in the human body? With your right hand, reach up and feel your left shoulder. Even with that simple action, you participate in the conversion of stored potential energy within your body to the kinetic energy of your moving arm as you do work on it. Did your shoulder feel warm to your hand? Some of the potential energy stored in your body is used to maintain a nearly constant internal temperature. Some of this energy is also converted to the excess heat that your body gives off to its surroundings. Even the person resting in **Figure 5-9** requires energy conversions.

The complex chemical and physical processes of your body also obey the laws of physics, including the law of conservation of energy. In your body, stored energy (such as that found in fat) is lost when work is done or heat is lost by your body to your surroundings. To maintain a healthy weight, you must have a proper balance between energy taken in and energy lost from your body as work or heat.

Figure 5-9
Even a person at rest is using energy. *Describe several ways that energy is being used in her body.*

Food—Our Chemical Potential Energy

What did you eat for breakfast this morning? Your body has been busy chemically changing your food into molecules that can combine with oxygen and be used as fuel. Even if you did not eat breakfast this morning, your body converts energy stored in fat for its immediate needs until you eat again. You are probably familiar with the food Calorie, a unit used by nutritionists to measure how much energy we get from specific foods. One Calorie is actually equivalent to a kilocalorie, or about 4180 joules. Every gram of fat a person consumes can supply nine Calories of energy. Carbohydrates and proteins each supply about four Calories of energy per gram.

Why does your body need such an energy supply? Food supplies the fuel used to maintain a nearly constant body temperature, to help your organs function, and to do work as you move your body. **Table 5-1** shows the amount of energy used in doing various activities. The energy needs of an individual are based upon factors such as body size, age,

USING MATH

A small bag of potato chips has about 270 Calories. Using **Table 5-1**, calculate how many minutes you would have to walk to "burn off" these Calories.

Table 5-1

Calories Used in 1 Hour			
Type of Activity	**Body Frames**		
	Small	**Medium**	**Large**
Sleeping	48	56	64
Sitting	72	84	96
Eating	84	98	112
Standing	96	112	123
Walking	180	210	240
Playing tennis	380	420	460
Bicycling fast	500	600	700
Running	700	850	1000

gender, heredity, and level of daily activity. In this section, you have learned about the sources and uses of energy and the different forms it takes.

Section Wrap-up

Review

1. Imagine that you're standing on a stepladder and you drop a basketball. The first bounce will be highest. Each bounce after that will be lower until the ball stops bouncing. Describe the energy changes that take place, starting with dropping the ball.

2. A game-show contestant won a prize by pushing a bowling ball 20 m using his nose. The amount of work done was 1470 J. How much force did the person exert on the ball?

3. **Think Critically:** Much discussion has focused on the need to drive more efficient cars and use less electricity. If the law of conservation of energy is true, why are people concerned about energy usage?

Skill Builder
Comparing and Contrasting
Compare and contrast the everyday meaning of work with the scientific definition of that term. Give examples of work in the everyday sense that would not be considered work in the scientific sense. If you need help, refer to Comparing and Contrasting in the **Skill Handbook.**

Science Journal
Your body used energy to move you into the room today. Where did this energy come from? In your Science Journal, write a paragraph describing where you acquired this energy. Trace it back through as many transformations as you can.

Design Your Own Experiment
Swinging Energy

Imagine yourself swinging in a swing. What would happen if a friend tried to stop you by grabbing the swing's chains halfway up as you passed the lowest point? Would you come to a complete stop or continue rising to your previous maximum height?

PREPARATION

Problem
How could you use a model to answer the questions in the swing situation described above?

Form a Hypothesis
Examine the pictured apparatus. How is it similar to the situation in the introductory paragraph? Hypothesize what will happen to the pendulum's motion and final height if its swing is interrupted by the crossarm.

Objectives
- Construct a pendulum to compare the exchange of potential and kinetic energy when a swing is interrupted.
- Measure starting and ending heights of the pendulum.

Possible Materials
- ring stand and ring
- support rod clamp, right angle
- support rod, 30 cm
- rubber stopper, 2-hole, medium
- string (1 m)
- metersticks
- graph paper

Safety Precautions
Be sure the base is heavy enough or well anchored so the apparatus will not tip over.

PLAN THE EXPERIMENT

1. As a group, write your hypothesis and list the steps that you will need to take to test your hypothesis. Be specific. Also, list the materials you will need.
2. If you need a data table, design one in your Science Journal.

Check the Plan

1. Set up the apparatus as shown in the diagrams. Be sure the crossarm intersects the pendulum string.
2. Devise a way to measure the starting and ending heights of the pendulum. Record your starting and ending heights in a data table.
3. Decide how you will release the stopper from the same height each time.
4. Be sure you try starting your swing both above and below the height of the crossarm.

How many times should you repeat each type of swing?

5. *Make sure your teacher approves your plan and that you have included any changes suggested in the plan.*

DO THE EXPERIMENT

1. Carry out the approved experiment as planned.
2. While the experiment is going on, write down any observations that you make and complete the data table in your Science Journal.

Analyze and Apply

1. When the stopper is released from the same height as the crossarm, is the ending height of the stopper exactly the same as its starting height? **Communicate** by explaining why or why not.
2. **Predict** what will happen when the starting height is higher than the crossarm.
3. **Analyze** the energy transfers. At what point along a single swing does the stopper have the greatest kinetic energy? The greatest potential energy?

Go Further

What happens if the mass of the stopper is increased? Try it. What effect would increased rider mass have on the person grabbing the swing?

5•2 Temperature and Heat

Science Words

temperature
thermal energy
heat

Objectives

- Recognize the difference between the motion of an object and the motion of the particles that make up the object.
- Contrast heat and temperature.
- Explain what determines the thermal energy of a sample of matter.

Figure 5-10

As the crucible is heated, the kinetic energy of the particles that make up the crucible increases. *How does the particle motion in (A) differ from that in (B)?*

Temperature

What do you know about temperature? When the air temperature outside is high, you probably describe the weather as hot. Ice cream, which has a lower temperature, feels cold. The words *hot* and *cold* are commonly used to describe the temperature of a material. Although not very scientific, these terms can be useful. Just about everyone understands that *hot* indicates high temperature and *cold* indicates low temperature.

When most people think of temperature, they automatically think of heat, also. This association makes sense, because heat and temperature are related. However, they are not the same. To understand the relationship between temperature and heat, you need to know about matter.

Matter in Motion

All matter is made up of particles so small that you can't see them, even with an ordinary microscope. The particles that make up any object are constantly moving, even if the object itself appears perfectly still. Everything you can think of—the book on your desk, the shoe on your foot, even the foot inside your shoe—is made up of moving particles.

You know that moving things have kinetic energy. Because the particles that make up matter are in constant motion, you can conclude that they have kinetic energy. The faster the particles move, the more kinetic energy they have. **Figure 5-10** illustrates particle movement in heated and unheated objects. **Temperature** is a measure of the average kinetic energy of the particles in a sample of matter. As the particles in an object move faster and their average kinetic energy becomes greater, the temperature of the object rises. Similarly, as the particles in an object move more slowly, their average kinetic energy decreases. Which particles are moving faster, those in a cup of hot tea or those in the same amount of iced tea?

Thermal Energy

If you place an ice-cold teaspoon on top of the scoop of ice cream in **Figure 5-11,** nothing will happen. But suppose you place a hot teaspoon on the ice cream. Now the ice cream under the spoon starts to melt. The hot spoon causes the ice cream to change because it transfers energy to the ice cream. Where does this energy come from? The spoon isn't moving, and its position is the same as that which the cold spoon had. So the energy is not due to the motion or the position of the spoon. Instead, it is related to the temperature of the spoon.

The change in the ice cream is caused by the flow of thermal energy from the spoon. Like temperature, thermal energy is related to the energy of the particles that make up matter. **Thermal energy** is the total energy of the particles in a material. This total includes both kinetic and potential energy. The kinetic energy is due to vibrations and movement within and between particles. The potential energy is determined by forces that act within or between the particles.

Suppose you stack two hot teaspoons at the same temperature on a scoop of ice cream. What will happen? The two spoons will melt more ice cream than the single spoon did in the same amount of time. The stacked spoons have twice as much mass and, therefore, twice as many moving particles. The more mass a material has at the same temperature, the more thermal energy it has.

Figure 5-11

The rate of melting depends on the amount of thermal energy present.

A   An ice-cold spoon has no effect on the ice cream.

B   One hot spoon causes some ice cream to melt.

C   Two hot spoons cause more ice cream to melt.

MiniLAB

Can shaking increase the temperature of sand?

Procedure
1. Pour sand into a plastic cup (with a well-fitting lid) until the sand is deep enough to just cover the bulb of a thermometer.
2. Measure and record the temperature of the sand to the nearest tenth of a degree. Remove the thermometer.
3. Place the lid snugly on the cup. While holding the lid firmly in place, shake the cup vigorously for several minutes.
4. Stop shaking, remove the lid, and immediately use the thermometer to measure the temperature of the sand.

Analysis
1. What effect did shaking have on the temperature of the sand?
2. Was energy created? Explain why or why not.

Problem Solving

A Cold Cup of Hot Chocolate . . . and a Warm Soft Drink

How can two liquids originally at very different temperatures become the same temperature? While working at a restaurant, Jonas was clearing the table where two customers had been sitting. One had been served a cup of hot chocolate and the other had been served a cold soft drink. When he picked up the remaining portions of their drinks, Jonas noticed that the hot chocolate and the cold soft drink were now both at the same temperature.

Solve the Problem:

1. **Assuming both drinks had the same mass, how did the thermal energy of the two drinks compare when the customers were first served the drinks?**
2. **Describe the heat transfer that took place to bring both drinks to room temperature.**

Think Critically:

Heat will flow between two objects only if they are not at the same temperature.

1. Where does the heat lost by the hot chocolate go?
2. If heat flows in only one direction, how can both hot and cold liquids reach room temperature as they sit on a table?

Different kinds of matter have different thermal energies, even when mass and temperature are the same. For example, a 5-g sample of sand has a different thermal energy than a 5-g sample of pudding at the same temperature. This difference is due mainly to the ways in which the particles of the materials are bound together.

It is important to remember that the thermal energy of a material depends on the *total energy of its particles*. The kinetic energy of the object itself has no effect on its thermal energy. For example, at 20°C, a golf ball has the same thermal energy whether it's sitting on the ground or speeding through the air.

Heat

What would happen if you pressed your left hand against a cool tile wall? Your hand would feel cooler. Its temperature would have decreased. If you then touched the same spot on the wall with your right hand, the spot wouldn't feel as cool as it did when you originally touched it. The temperature of the spot would have increased when you touched it with your left hand. Energy flowed from your warm left hand to the cool tile. **Heat** is the thermal (or internal) energy that flows from something with a higher temperature to something with a lower temperature. Remember that, in most cases, heat flows from warmer to cooler materials—

not from cooler to warmer. In **Figure 5-12,** the heat flows are making one hand warmer and one hand colder.

The next time you listen to a weather report, think about the difference between temperature and heat. And when you drop an ice cube into your drink, think about how the cooling occurs. Does the melting ice cause the liquid to cool? Or does heat flowing from the liquid to the ice cool the drink and cause the ice to melt?

Like work, heat is measured in joules and involves transfer of energy. Heat is energy transferred between objects at different temperatures. Work is energy transferred when a force acts over a distance.

Figure 5-12

Heat flows from hot chocolate to your hand, making your hand feel hot. Heat flows from your hand to a glass of iced tea, making your hand feel cold.
Why do people wear gloves in cold weather?

Section Wrap-up

Review

1. In terms of thermal energy, why does a bottle of soda left in the sun have a higher temperature than one left in an ice chest?

2. Which has more thermal energy, a 5-kg bowling ball that has been resting on a hot driveway for 4 hours on a 35°C day, or the same bowling ball rolling down a lane in an air-conditioned bowling alley?

3. **Think Critically:** Using your knowledge of heat, explain what happens when you heat a pan of soup on the stove, then put some leftover warm soup in the refrigerator.

Skill Builder
Concept Mapping
Create a network tree that shows how the following words and phrases are related: *energy, potential energy of particles, energy transfer (higher to lower temperature), heat, kinetic energy of particles,* and *thermal energy.* If you need help, refer to Concept Mapping in the **Skill Handbook.**

Science Journal

Use physics terms and concepts to explain why you take your temperature by placing a thermometer under your tongue and waiting several minutes. Write your explanation in your Science Journal.

ISSUE:

5•3 Thermal Pollution: Waste You Can't See

Science Words

thermal pollution

Objectives

* Identify some causes and effects of thermal pollution.
* Discuss possible solutions for thermal pollution problems.

Where does it come from?

If you have been in a city on a warm day, surrounded by cars, large buildings, and concrete, you may have noticed that it seemed to be hotter there than in the suburbs, where there's less traffic and less activity. Much of the energy used in everyday life—electrical, chemical, mechanical, radiant, or nuclear energy—ends up as waste thermal energy that is given off to the surroundings. The heat removed from air-conditioned buildings and vehicles is released to the outside air, just as heat is released into a kitchen by a refrigerator.

The level of waste heat can reach unhealthy levels. **Thermal pollution** occurs when waste heat significantly changes the temperature of the environment. It is a particular problem in areas where power plants and factories use water to cool their buildings and equipment, warming the water in the process. If the warmed water is dumped into a river, lake, or ocean, as in **Figure 5-13,** the added heat lowers the dissolved oxygen content and may cause serious problems for the plants and animals living there.

The added heat accelerates chemical-biological processes and can alter the reproductive processes of the water plants and animals. In extreme cases, major fish kills can result.

Figure 5-13

Hot wastewater is discharged into a river. *How might this affect the ecology of the river?*

2 Points of View

▶ Too many regulations for industry?

Thermal pollution can be reduced by releasing small amounts of warm water mixed with plenty of cooler water. But in order to cool the water, factories and power plants must build devices such as cooling towers. In these large structures, illustrated in **Figure 5-14,** water is cooled by fans or evaporation. Although the cooling towers are effective, they are also expensive. Businesses may be able to recover these costs by charging more for their products and services. However, if competition in the industry is so strong that a company can't raise prices, the company runs the risk of losing money and perhaps going out of business.

Some people argue that the government passes unnecessary laws and sets tight regulations that require businesses to build costly cooling mechanisms. They think that the effects of thermal pollution on the environment are not severe enough to justify raising the costs of operation, which then increases the prices paid by consumers. In their view, the government is creating regulations that are wasteful and unnecessary.

▶ Cooling Costs: It's Worth the Effort

Typically, the temperature of water discharged from an electric power plant ranges from 5 to 11 Celsius degrees above the temperature of the waterway that is receiving the discharge.

Because it is possible to cool water before releasing it back into a water system, some people argue that it is our responsibility to prevent damage to the environment from thermal pollution. They emphasize that the physical, chemical, and biological effects of a temperature rise can upset delicate aquatic ecosystems. They are concerned that if thermal pollution is not controlled, it will kill water plants and animals, destroy water-based ecosystems, and ruin recreational waterways for people who enjoy fishing, swimming, and boating.

Warm air outlet

Water distribution center

Hot water in

Cool air in

Figure 5-14

Cooling towers can cool large volumes of hot wastewater. *Why are they designed to be wide and open at the top?*

Figure 5-15

For healthy fish to exist in a waterway, the water temperature must not exceed harmful levels.

Many people argue that we can develop creative uses for the warm water. This would reduce or eliminate the need to dump the warm water into streams, rivers, or other waterways. Instead, the extra thermal energy in the water can be used to heat greenhouses or other buildings. These people argue that the costs associated with minimizing thermal pollution are a necessary part of an industrial society. In their view, we need to be willing to pay the costs so that people, such as the person fishing in **Figure 5-15,** can continue to enjoy the benefits.

Section Wrap-up

Review

1. Thermal pollution may encourage the growth of certain water plants and slow or destroy the growth of others. Why might this be a problem?

2. A company plans to build several greenhouses and to heat them using waste heat from cooling water. What factors should the company consider when making its plan?

Explore the Issue

A company wants to build a factory by a river that runs through your city, creating new jobs but also generating waste thermal energy. What steps would you take to find out whether the environment will be damaged? Should the company be allowed to build its factory?

Using Computers

Word Processing
Your representative in Congress will soon vote on a bill to require companies to reduce thermal pollution below specified levels. Write a two-paragraph letter to her explaining why she should or should not vote for the bill.

SCIENCE & SOCIETY

Measuring Thermal Energy

Specific Heat

If you have jumped into a swimming pool or lake on a hot summer day, did you find the water surprisingly cold? Even though lots of radiant energy has been transferred to the water from the sun, the temperature of the water is still cooler than that of the surroundings.

Different materials need different amounts of heat to produce similar changes in their temperatures. The materials have different specific heats. The **specific heat** (C) of a material is the amount of energy it takes to raise the temperature of 1 kg of the material 1 kelvin. Specific heat is measured in joules per kilogram per kelvin [J/(kg · K)]. **Table 5-2** shows the specific heats of some familiar materials. How does the specific heat of water compare with the specific heats of the other materials?

Heat Absorption

When you see how high the specific heat of water is compared to other materials, do you understand why one of the persons in **Figure 5-16** is testing the water before going in? The materials around the water heat up much faster than the water itself, so the water is cold compared with its surroundings.

Science Words

specific heat

Objectives

- Define *specific heat*.
- Calculate changes in thermal energy.

Table 5-2

Specific Heat of Some Common Materials (J/(kg · K))	
Water	4184
Alcohol	2450
Aluminum	920
Carbon (graphite)	710
Sand	664
Iron	450
Copper	380
Silver	235

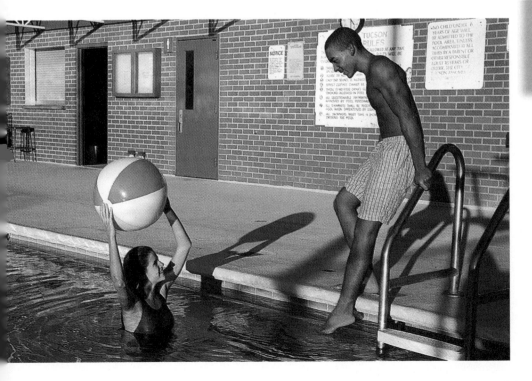

Figure 5-16

Because of its high specific heat, water warms up more slowly than its surroundings.

Infrared Weather Eyes ▼ ▲

The satellite picture you see on your TV weather show is usually an infrared image captured by a GOES (**G**eostationary **O**perational **E**nvironmental **S**atellite). A GOES remains in orbit directly above the same point on Earth's surface. Each satellite monitors a circular region of the surface 10 000 km across. Within this circle, clouds appear white and Earth's surface appears gray. A meteorologist can point out a line of clouds that indicates a weather front and run a sequence of images to demonstrate how that front is moving.

Warm objects give off more infrared radiation than cool objects. The satellite's sensors measure many bands of infrared radiation. One band indicates moisture in the air. Dry air appears black and moist air appears in varying shades of gray. Because bad weather often breaks out when dry air intrudes into moist air, these water-vapor images can be used to predict storms. Other bands of radiation reveal information about wind speed and direction, rainfall, fog, snow, and ice. Newer satellites may one day provide data for making accurate global weather forecasts 30 to 90 days in advance.

Think Critically:

In addition to weather information, what other kinds of data could an infrared-measuring satellite provide?

Water, alcohol, and other materials with a high specific heat can absorb a lot of energy with little change in temperature. The specific heats of different substances depend on the chemical makeup of the substances.

Calculating Thermal Changes

Changes in thermal energy cannot be measured directly, but they can be calculated. Specific heat can be used to determine changes in thermal energy. For example, you can place a heated mass or object in a calorimeter such as the one shown in **Figure 5-17**. By measuring the temperature increase in the water in the calorimeter, you can determine the change in thermal energy. Now, suppose you take a 32-g silver spoon from a pot of water at a temperature of 60°C and allow it to cool to room temperature, which is 20°C. You have enough information to find out the

Infrared Photograph of Weather Systems

change in the thermal energy of the spoon using the equation below.

$$\begin{matrix} \text{Change in} \\ \text{thermal energy} \end{matrix} = mass \times \begin{matrix} \text{Change in} \\ \text{temperature} \end{matrix} \times \text{specific heat}$$

$$Q = m \times \Delta T \times C$$

The symbol Δ (delta) means "change," so ΔT is the change in temperature. "Change" is included in Q, which is the variable for energy change.

$$\Delta T = T_{final} - T_{initial}$$

When ΔT is positive, Q is also positive; the object has increased in temperature and gained thermal energy. When ΔT is negative, Q is also negative; the object has lost thermal energy and decreased in temperature. The problems below will give you practice in calculating changes in thermal energy.

Thermometer

Stirrer

Cover

Inner chamber

Insulated flask (outer chamber)

Figure 5-17

Devices like this simple calorimeter are used to measure thermal energy transfer.

USING MATH

Calculating Changes in Thermal Energy

Example Problem:
A 32-g silver spoon cools from 60°C to 20°C. What is the change in its thermal energy?

Problem-Solving Steps:
1. What is known?
   Mass of spoon, m = 32.0 g = 0.0320 kg
   The spoon is made of silver.
   The specific heat, C, of silver is 235 J/(kg · K).
   Initial temperature, $T_{initial}$ = 60.0°C
   Final temperature, T_{final} = 20.0°C
2. What is unknown?
   Change in thermal energy, Q
3. Use the equation $Q = m \times \Delta T \times C$.
4. **Solution:** $Q = m \times (T_{final} - T_{initial}) \times C$
   $= 0.0320 \text{ kg} \times (20.0°C - 60.0°C) \times 235 \text{ J/(kg · K)}$
   $= -301 \text{ J}$
   The spoon loses 301 J of thermal energy as it cools.

Practice Problems
1. Calculate the change in thermal energy when 230 g of water warms from 12°C to 90°C.
Strategy Hint: Will your answer be a positive or negative number?
2. A 45-kg brass sculpture gains 180 480 J of thermal energy as its temperature increases from 28°C to 40°C. What is the approximate specific heat of brass?
Strategy Hint: What is the unknown information?

CONNECT TO

CHEMISTRY

While Karen was blow-drying her hair, she noticed that her silver earring had become uncomfortably hot. If her earring was about the same mass as her earlobe, *infer* which of the two had the higher specific heat.

Figure 5-18
Different animals use different methods to cool themselves. *Why are elephants' ears so large?*

The thermal energy characteristics of complex systems depend on the specific heats of the substances involved and the masses and shapes of the systems. For example, as shown in **Figure 5-18,** elephants fan their ears to dissipate heat and lower their body temperature. Without this ability, the large mass, shape, and high specific heat of the materials in an elephant's body would keep its temperature too high.

With your new understanding of specific heat, think about temperature changes you've observed in objects around you. Now you have an idea about why a kettle of water takes so long to boil and why a sandy beach heats up quickly on a sunny day.

Section Wrap-up

Review

1. A bucket of sand and a bucket of water are side by side in direct sunlight. Which warms faster? Why?

2. Use **Table 5-2** on page 141 to calculate the change in thermal energy when a 55-g iron nail cools from 90°C to 25°C.

3. **Think Critically:** Water and a liquid called ethylene glycol are used in automobile radiators to keep the engine from overheating. Explain whether you would rather have a coolant with a high or a low specific heat.

Skill Builder
Interpreting Data
Equal amounts of iron, water, and sand, all at the same initial temperature, were placed in an oven and heated briefly. Use the data in **Table 5-2** on page 141 to match each final temperature with the appropriate material: 31°C, 5°C, and 46°C. If you need help, refer to Interpreting Data in the **Skill Handbook.**

USING MATH

Suppose you are on a diet that recommends intake of 9 000 000 J (more than 2000 Calories) each day. If you add this amount of heat to 50 kg of water, how much would the water's temperature rise?

Activity 5-2

A Hot Topic

Heat can often be used to change the shape of something. If you have ironed clothes or curled your hair, you have used heat to help you accomplish the task. How much heat is required to do these things? In this activity, you will use your understanding of specific heat to find out how much heat is released from an electric hair curler.

Problem
How much thermal energy is transferred by an electric hair curler?

Materials

- set of electric hair curlers
- thermometers, Celsius (2)
- plastic foam cup
- graph paper
- balance
- graduated cylinder

Procedure

1. Prepare a data table like the one shown.
2. Measure the mass of the plastic cup. Fill the cup about halfway with cool water and measure its mass again. Find the mass of the water in kilograms.
3. Carefully remove a heated curler from its heating unit. Stand the curler, open end up, on the table and pour in 2 mL of cool water. **CAUTION:** *Don't touch any hot metal parts when handling heated curlers—wear gloves if they are available.*
4. Using two thermometers, measure and record the temperature of the water in the cup and the temperature of the water in the curler.
5. Carefully lower the curler into the cup of water. Measure and record the water temperature every minute for 5 minutes. **CAUTION:** *Turn the heating unit off immediately after completing the activity.*
6. Prepare a time-temperature graph, with time along the *x*-axis and temperature along the *y*-axis. Plot both the heating and cooling curves.

Data and Observations

Time in Minutes	Water Temperature (°C)	
	in curler	in cup
0		
1		
2		
3		
4		
5		

Analyze

1. What happened to the water in the cup? Explain in terms of heat.
2. What was the change in temperature of the water in the cup over the 5-minute interval?
3. Using the formula below, find the change in thermal energy (*Q*), in joules, of the water in the cup.
   $$Q = m \times \Delta T \times C$$

Conclude and Apply

4. Does the curler still have thermal energy available to continue heating the water after 5 minutes? How do you know?
5. **Compare** your results with those of your classmates. Do some curlers provide more heat than others? Which curlers provide the most heat?
6. How do the starting temperatures of all the curlers **compare?**
7. Which statement is more accurate: "Some curlers are hotter than others," or "Some curlers contain more thermal energy than others"? **Communicate** your answer in a brief oral explanation.

Inuit Clothing: Life on Top of the World

Anyone who has ever experienced the stinging cold of sub-zero weather knows this fact well: The trick to winter survival is to prevent your body's thermal energy from being lost to the environment. For the Inuit people of Greenland and the northernmost parts of North America, surviving in bitterly cold weather for a large part of the year is a way of life.

Insulating with Clothing

With its frigid, sub-zero temperatures and its icy, snow-covered landscape, the Arctic is one of the harshest places on Earth. Perhaps more than anything else, Inuit clothing and the way it is worn allows its wearers to survive comfortably in the far north.

Although technology and other cultural influences have changed the basic way of life of the Inuit, many of their historical practices still exist. This is particularly true in their clothing. Traditionally, skins and furs from seal, caribou, fox, and polar bear were used to fashion all articles of clothing, including coats, hats, mittens, shirts, boots, pants, and socks.

In cold winter weather, the Inuit wear two suits of clothing. The inner layer of clothing is worn with the fur against the skin, and the outer layer is worn with the fur facing out. The use of fur and two layers of clothing illustrates a knowledge of how to conserve thermal energy and stay warm in cold weather. Animal fur is excellent for preventing thermal energy loss. It acts as an insulator, which is a material that prevents heat transfer. The long, thick hairs trap pockets of air that are warmed when placed close to the body. Also, the hairs themselves are hollow, so the air inside them is another barrier to the flow of heat away from the body. An additional layer of insulation is also formed between the two layers of clothing.

Science Journal

Write a short story or a non-fiction piece about either the coldest or warmest weather you've experienced in your life. Describe the temperature and other environmental conditions you observed. How were you able to adapt to the weather conditions? Explain how your clothing choices allowed you to remain comfortable.

Summary

5-1: Energy and Work

1. Energy is the ability to cause change. Energy may be in the form of motion (kinetic energy) or it may be stored (potential energy).
2. Energy exists in many different forms, and it can change from one form to other forms with no loss of total energy.
3. Work is the transfer of energy through motion. Work is done only when force produces motion in the direction of the force.

5-2: Temperature and Heat

1. All matter is made up of tiny particles that are in constant motion. This motion is not related to or dependent on the motion of the object.
2. Heat and temperature are related, but they are not the same. The temperature of a material is a measure of the average kinetic energy of the particles that make up the material. Heat is the energy that flows from a warmer to a cooler material.
3. The thermal energy of a material is the total energy—both kinetic and potential—of the particles that make up the material.

5-3: Science and Society: Thermal Pollution: Waste You Can't See

1. When waste heat finds its way into rivers, lakes, and oceans, it can damage or destroy the plants and animals living there.
2. Government and industry continue to debate whether the benefits of regulating thermal pollution are worth the costs to society.

5-4: Measuring Thermal Energy

1. Different materials have different heat capacities, or specific heats.
2. The specific heat of a material can be used to calculate changes in the thermal energy of the material.

Key Science Words

a. energy
b. heat
c. kinetic energy
d. law of conservation of energy
e. mechanical energy
f. potential energy
g. specific heat
h. temperature
i. thermal energy
j. thermal pollution
k. work

Reviewing Vocabulary

Match each phrase with the correct term from the list of Key Science Words.

1. the ability to cause change
2. energy of motion
3. Under normal conditions, energy cannot be created or destroyed.
4. energy required to raise the temperature of 1 kg of a material 1 K
5. total energy of the particles in a material
6. the transfer of energy through motion
7. transfer of energy from warmer to cooler materials
8. stored energy
9. measure of the average kinetic energy of the particles in a material
10. the total amount of kinetic and potential energy of an object

Chapter 5 Review

Checking Concepts

Choose the word or phrase that completes the sentence or answers the question.

1. The basic SI unit of energy is the _____.
   a. kilogram
   c. newton
   b. joule
   d. kelvin
2. If the velocity of an object increases, the _____ of the object will also increase.
   a. kinetic energy
   c. specific heat
   b. mass
   d. potential energy
3. Which of these is not used to calculate change in thermal energy?
   a. volume
   c. specific heat
   b. temperature change
   d. mass
4. The _____ of a material is a measure of the average kinetic energy of its particles.
   a. potential energy
   c. temperature
   b. thermal energy
   d. specific heat
5. Which of these does not represent work done on a rock in the scientific sense?
   a. lifting a rock
   c. holding a rock
   b. throwing a rock
   d. dropping a rock
6. The total amount of kinetic and potential energy in a closed system is called _____.
   a. specific heat
   c. stored energy
   b. mechanical energy
   d. temperature
7. As the temperature of a material increases, the average _____ of its particles increases.
   a. kinetic energy
   c. specific heat
   b. potential energy
   d. mass
8. Kinetic energy is directly related to _____.
   a. volume
   c. mass
   b. force
   d. position
9. The _____ of an object depends upon its position.
   a. kinetic energy
   c. potential energy
   b. thermal energy
   d. temperature
10. Materials with a high _____ absorb a lot of energy with little change in temperature.
    a. potential energy
    b. kinetic energy
    c. velocity
    d. specific heat

Understanding Concepts

Answer the following questions in your Science Journal using complete sentences.

11. Describe two types of potential energy. How does this energy differ from kinetic energy?
12. Describe the energy changes in a swinging pendulum. Explain how energy is conserved, even as a pendulum slows down.
13. Compare and contrast heat, temperature, and thermal energy.
14. A copper bowl and a silver bowl of equal mass were heated from 27°C to 100°C. Which required more heat? Explain.
15. Describe some possible benefits and drawbacks of building large cooling towers to reduce thermal pollution from a power plant.

Thinking Critically

16. While performing a chin-up, Carlos raises himself 0.8 m. How much work does Carlos, who weighs 600 N, accomplish doing a chin-up?
17. A football player picks up a football, runs with it, and then throws it to a teammate. Describe the work done on the ball.
18. Why does air feel cold on a windy winter day and hot on a calm summer day?
19. How much thermal energy does 420 g of liquid water gain when it is heated from its freezing point to its boiling point?
20. If 50 g of water and 50 g of sand each absorb 200 J of solar energy, what will be the temperature change of each material?

Developing Skills

If you need help, refer to the **Skill Handbook.**

21. **Comparing and Contrasting:** Compare and contrast heat and work.
22. **Hypothesizing:** Suppose you are sitting beside an outdoor swimming pool when someone dives into the pool and splashes water on you. Your body jumps or tenses in reaction to the cold water. Propose a hypothesis to explain why, after a few seconds, the water on your skin no longer feels cold.
23. **Concept Mapping:** Below is a concept map of the energy changes of a gymnast bouncing on a trampoline. Complete the map by indicating the type of energy— kinetic, potential, or both—the gymnast has at each of the following stages in his or her path:
    a. halfway up;
    b. the highest point;
    c. halfway down;
    d. the lowest point, just before hitting the trampoline.

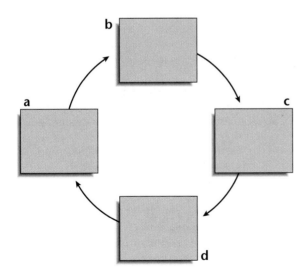

24. **Interpreting Data:** A young man with a medium-size body frame wants to burn at least 400 Calories by exercising for an hour. Using **Table 5-1** on page 131, decide which activities will enable him to reach his goal.
25. **Using Numbers:** A non-SI unit often used to measure thermal energy is the Calorie, which is equal to 4.18 J. The numbers of Calories needed to raise the temperatures of 1-kg samples of three different materials 1°C are given below. Convert each value to joules.

Specific Heats (Non-SI Units)	
Material	**Calories**
wood	550
glass	120
mercury	33

Performance Assessment

1. **Making a Graph:** Choose a playground activity or amusement park ride that you enjoy. Placing time on the horizontal axis, sketch a graph that shows how your kinetic and potential energies change during the activity or ride.
2. **Designing an Experiment:** In Activity 5-2 on page 145, you determined the amount of thermal energy stored in a heated hair curler. Design an experiment to reheat the rollers to their original temperature without using the base of the hair curler apparatus.
3. **Poster:** Make a poster showing sources of energy other than burning fossil fuels (gas and oil). List the advantages and disadvantages of each. Indicate the resource that you think is the best and explain why.

Previewing the Chapter

Using Thermal Energy

Is the process of keeping something warm similar to the process of keeping something cool? The hot-dog vendor and the ice-cream vendor shown in this photograph are both making use of methods that block the transfer of thermal energy. In the activity below, measure the effects of thermal-energy flows.

Explore Activity

Measure the effects of thermal energy on the move.

1. Turn on a lamp with a bare lightbulb. Do not touch the bulb with your hand or any other object.
2. For one minute, hold a thermometer steadily 5 cm from the lightbulb, at the level of the filament. Record the temperature.
3. Repeat step 2 at distances of 10 cm, 15 cm, and 20 cm. At what distance is there no measurable temperature change after one minute?
4. With the thermometer at the 10-cm position, place a book between the thermometer and the lamp and repeat the measurement. Also, try this with a piece of paper instead of a book.

Observe: How does distance affect the temperature change caused by thermal energy on the move? How effective were the barriers? Explain your answers in your Science Journal.

Previewing Science Skills

▶ In the Skill Builders, you will **use variables, constants, and controls; make and use tables;** and **map concepts.**

▶ In the Activities, you will **observe, collect** and **organize data, model, analyze,** and **infer.**

▶ In the MiniLABs, you will **analyze** and **hypothesize.**

6•1 Thermal Energy on the Move

Science Words

conduction
fluid
convection
radiation
insulator

Objectives

- Compare and contrast the transfer of thermal energy by conduction, convection, and radiation.
- Differentiate between conductors and insulators.
- Explain how insulation affects the transfer of energy.

Conduction

Thermal energy travels as heat from a material at higher temperature to a material at lower temperature. If you pick up an ice cube, heat from your hand transfers to the ice, causing the ice to melt. If you pick up a hot spoon, the heat from the spoon moves to your hand, perhaps causing you to drop the spoon. How does thermal energy move from place to place?

One way is by conduction. **Conduction** is the transfer of energy through matter by direct contact of particles. Recall that all matter is made up of tiny particles that are in constant motion. The temperature of a material is a measure of the average kinetic energy of its particles.

Transfer by Collisions

Energy is transferred when particles moving at different speeds bump into each other. When faster-moving particles collide with slower-moving particles, some of the momentum of the faster-moving particles passes along to the slower-moving particles. The faster particles slow down and the slower particles speed up.

Heat may be transferred by conduction through a given material or from one material to another. Think about what happens when one end of a metal spoon is placed in boiling water. Heat from the water is transferred to the spoon. The end of the spoon in the water becomes hotter than the other end of the spoon. But, eventually, the entire spoon becomes hot, as in **Figure 6-1.**

Figure 6-1

Part of the spoon is heated by contact with the hot water (A). Heat is transferred through the metal spoon, particle by particle, until the entire spoon is hot (B). *What would happen if you used a wooden spoon? What if the spoon were bent?*

Figure 6-2

Use of these kitchen items is related to their heat-conducting properties. *Which items conduct heat well? Which ones block it?*

Conduction takes place in solids, liquids, and gases. Because their particles are packed closer together, solids usually conduct heat better than liquids or gases. However, some solids, such as the pots in **Figure 6-2,** conduct heat better than others. Many metals have loosely held electrons that move around easily and transfer kinetic energy to nearby particles more efficiently. Silver, copper, and aluminum are good heat conductors, while wood, plastic, glass, and fiberglass are poor conductors of heat. Why do you think cooking pots are made of metal? What are the handles usually made of?

Convection

Liquids and gases differ from solids because they flow. Any material that flows is a **fluid.** The most important way thermal energy is transferred in fluids is by convection. **Convection** is the transfer of energy by the bulk movement of matter. How does this differ from conduction? In conduction, energy moves from particle to particle, but the particles themselves remain approximately in place. In convection, fluid particles move from one location to another, carrying energy with them.

When heat is added to a fluid, the particles begin to move faster, just as the particles of a solid do. However, the particles of a fluid have more freedom to move. Therefore, they move farther apart, or expand. The hot-air balloon in **Figure 6-3** shows the expansion of a heated fluid.

MiniLAB

How is heat transferred by conduction?

Procedure

1. Dip the heads of five small thumbtacks into melted wax and attach them with soft wax at 5-cm intervals along the shaft of a long, metal spatula or fork used for outdoor grilling. **CAUTION:** *Be sure it has an insulated handle, or use an oven mitt.*
2. Hold the far end of the spatula or fork in the flame of a lab burner. Measure and record how long it takes for each thumbtack to fall.
3. Repeat the activity using a heat-resistant, glass stirring rod of similar size. Use an oven mitt to hold the rod.

Analysis

1. How is the order in which the thumbtacks fell related to conduction?
2. How did the results with the glass rod differ? Explain.

Figure 6-3

Heat from the flame causes the air inside the balloon to expand.

153

Figure 6-4

Only the radiant energy that is absorbed is converted to thermal energy.

Sun

Outer space

Radiation

Reflected by atmosphere

Atmosphere

Reflected by surface

Absorbed by atmosphere

Absorbed by Earth

Earth

Transfer by Currents

Now think about what happens when a pot of water is heated. The stove burner heats the bottom of the pot by conduction. Water touching the bottom of the pot is also heated by conduction. As this water is heated, it expands and becomes less dense. Cooler, denser water at the top of the pot sinks and pushes the hot water upward. As the hot water rises, it cools by conduction, becomes more dense, and sinks, forcing warmer water to rise. This movement creates convection currents. These currents transfer thermal energy from warmer to cooler parts of the fluid.

Winds are examples of convection currents. The air above the equator is warmer than the air at any other place on Earth, and therefore it is pushed upward. However, air at the poles is much cooler than it is anywhere else. This cold, dense air sinks and moves along Earth's surface away from the poles. Some ocean currents are also convection currents.

Radiation

There are 150 million kilometers of empty space between Earth and the sun. How does thermal energy reach Earth? In order for conduction or convection to take place, matter must be present. But there is almost no matter in outer space. There is a third type of heat transfer that does not require matter. **Radiation** is the transfer of energy in the form of waves. Energy that travels by radiation is often called radiant energy. As **Figure 6-4** illustrates, once radiant energy from the sun reaches Earth, some of it is reflected, or bounced back, toward space, and some is absorbed. Only radiant energy that is absorbed changes to thermal energy.

Different materials absorb radiant energy differently. Shiny materials reflect radiant energy; dull materials absorb it. Dark-colored materials absorb more radiant energy than light-colored materials. This explains why summer clothing is usually made of lighter-colored materials, and winter clothing is darker colored.

Any object warmer than 0 K emits radiation. If you hold your hand near a lighted electric bulb, your hand feels the heat. The bulb's radiation is converted to thermal energy as it is absorbed by your hand.

Reducing Thermal-Energy Flow

When the weather is cold, doesn't it feel good to wrap yourself up in a thick sweater or curl up under a thick quilt? And in hot weather, wouldn't you rather have juice from a bottle that has been inside a picnic cooler than one that has been sitting out on a table?

What do these situations have in common? In each case, some method is used to reduce the flow of heat by conduction, convection, or radiation. In the first case, the material of the sweater or quilt traps your body heat and keeps it from escaping to the open air. In the second case, the material of the picnic cooler keeps heat from flowing to the juice. Similarly, the feathers of the birds in **Figure 6-5A** help to restrict heat flow away from the bird's body.

Insulators

Good **insulators** do not allow heat to move easily through them. Some insulators, such as wood, plastic, glass, and fiberglass, have already been identified as being poor conductors.

Gases, such as air, are excellent insulators. Several types of insulating material contain many tiny pockets of trapped air. These pockets restrict the formation of convection currents, and the trapped air is a good insulator. Plastic foam is a type of insulation commonly used in beverage cups and picnic coolers. This foam is mostly tiny pockets of trapped air. Down jackets, such as the one shown in **Figure 6-5B,** and quilts are stuffed with tiny feathers or fibers that trap air.

Buildings are insulated to keep warm air inside in cold weather and outside in hot weather. In the United States, about ten percent of all energy produced is used to heat buildings, so you can see why it is important to prevent as much heat loss as possible. Later in this chapter, you will learn how air conditioners are used to remove heat from building interiors. Insulation reduces the amount of heat that flows into a cooled building from the outside, keeping the inside of the building cooler.

Building insulation is usually made of some fluffy material, such as fiberglass, cellulose, or treated paper. The insulation is packed into outer walls and attics, where it reduces heat flow.

Figure 6-5

Although people use coats and birds have feathers, the effect is the same—to reduce thermal transfer.

A Feathers protect ducks by insulating them against loss of body heat.

Down filling and air spaces

Cold air

Body heat

Outer shell blocks heat from leaving

B Many small air pockets trap body heat and keep it from escaping.

Problem Solving

The Warm House

Mary and a group of her friends volunteered to help build a house with the Habitat for Humanity organization.

One day, the group went to the new house to install insulation. They wanted to make sure that the house was properly constructed to withstand the cold winters in the area.

The group worked on all the exterior walls to see that they were properly insulated. They used 1"-thick foam insulation backed with aluminum foil. During the next week, they went up to the attic to install two layers of 12"-thick fiberglass insulation between the rafters. Afterward, they checked to see that all the windows had stickers indicating that they were double-paned thermal windows.

Solve the Problem:

1. **Why did the Habitat group install more insulation in the attic than in the walls?**
2. **What do the foam insulation, the fiberglass insulation, and the thermal windows have in common that helps them to prevent the loss of heat?**

Think Critically:

The insulation in the home that the group worked on was expensive. Why might they think that it was a good investment or not?

Insulation Ratings

To help consumers understand the energy-transfer qualities of the many materials used in building construction, a rating system has been established in which each material is given an *R*-value. The *R* indicates resistance to heat flow. **Table 6-1** shows the *R*-values for some common building materials. The *R*-value of a material is a measure of the resistance that a 1 m x 1 m square slab of the material has to heat flow per centimeter of the material's thickness.

To have a well-insulated house, materials with a total *R*-value of at least 19 should be used in the outer walls and those with total *R*-values of 30-44 should be used in the roof or ceilings. Higher *R*-values are needed for roofs and ceilings because the warmest air inside the house is carried upward by convection currents. The *R*-values needed for comfort also depend on the local climate.

Even though glass is a good insulator, windows do transfer thermal energy. A single pane of glass has an *R*-value of only 1, but using double-pane windows, such as the one in **Figure 6-6,** reduces heat loss considerably because a thin sandwich of air is trapped between two panes of glass. The air is an excellent insulator, and the narrow space restricts the formation of convection currents.

Some double-pane windows have a higher *R*-value because air is replaced with a harmless, colorless gas that is a better insulator. Argon is the gas most frequently used in windows because it is nonreactive and inexpensive. These windows are especially useful in cold climates or where temperature extremes can be uncomfortable or even dangerous.

Adding insulation and specially equipped windows are not the only ways to reduce heat loss from buildings. Many buildings, especially older ones, have cracks and gaps around windows and doors through which heat escapes. These heat leaks can be filled with caulking, putty, or weather stripping to reduce energy loss and to lower fuel bills.

Glass

Dead-air space

Figure 6-6

The air trapped in this double-pane window serves as a layer of insulation.

Table 6-1

R-Values of Various Materials*	
Material	**R-Value**
Brick	0.08/cm
Plasterboard (drywall)	0.35/cm
Stucco	0.08/cm
Wood siding	0.60/cm
Air space	1.82-3.56/cm
Fiberglass	1.22/cm
Loose cellulose	1.46/cm
Aluminum siding	0.01/cm
Loose foam	1.89/cm
Loose vermiculite	1.09/cm

*The total *R*-value is the product of the *R*-value and the thickness of the layer in centimeters.

Figure 6-7

The plastic container, vacuum layer, and reflecting surfaces all add to the insulating properties of vacuum bottles. *How does each of these features block the transfer of heat?*

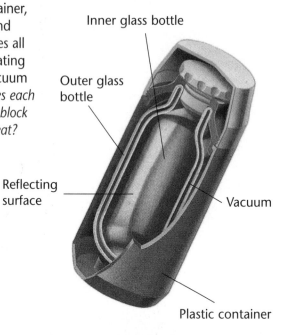

Inner glass bottle

Outer glass bottle

Reflecting surface

Vacuum

Plastic container

You may have used a vacuum bottle, like the one in **Figure 6-7,** to carry cold or hot liquids for lunch. This bottle is similar to a double-pane window. It has a double glass wall with a vacuum between the layers to prevent heat transfer by convection. One side of each layer is coated with aluminum to reduce heat transfer by radiation.

Now that you know about how thermal energy is transferred, think about things you can do to stay cooler or warmer. You can sit under a shady umbrella or put on a sweater. You can wear light-colored clothing or close a window. You can weatherproof your home by adding insulation and eliminating heat leaks around windows and doors. What other ways can you think of?

Section Wrap-up

Review

1. Name and describe three methods of thermal energy transfer.

2. Explain why poor conductors of heat are good insulators of heat.

3. Why do many cooking pots and pans have wooden or plastic handles?

4. **Think Critically:** For many years, many fast-food restaurants served their hot sandwiches in plastic foam containers instead of wrapping them in less expensive paper. Why was plastic foam used?

Skill Builder

Using Variables, Constants, and Controls
Design an experiment to find out which material makes the best insulation: plastic foam pellets, shredded newspaper, or crumpled plastic bags. Remember to state your hypothesis and indicate what factors must be held constant. If you need help, refer to Using Variables, Constants, and Controls in the **Skill Handbook.**

USING MATH

Suppose you were planning to use fiberglass insulation to achieve a total *R*-value of 30. Use the information in **Table 6-1** to calculate how thick (cm) the fiberglass layer must be.

People and Science

MAGALI REGIS, *Architect and Solar Cooking Expert*

On the Job

Personal Insights

Q Ms. Regis, you teach people in Haiti how to build and use solar cookers. Why is this important?

A One of the reasons we're trying to introduce solar cooking is because of the terrible deforestation problems Haiti faces. The Haitian people cook with charcoal, which is made from wood. And people have to pay for charcoal. It's not cheap. Sunlight is free. So solar cookers save them money. That means they can eat better food, or maybe send an extra child to school.

Q How does a solar box cooker work?

A You have a box with a glass cover on top that lets in sunlight. The box is well sealed, so heat cannot escape. You put your food in a thin-walled black pot in the center of the box. The inside of the box is lined with a reflecting material like aluminum foil. The box becomes an oven that can be used to bake bread, or cook cornmeal, rice, and vegetables.

Q Are there other solar cookers?

A Another type is the parabolic cooker, which is more like the burner on a stove. It has the shape of a satellite dish and is lined with reflective material. It focuses sunlight on a point just above the center of the dish, where you place your pot. It produces temperatures high enough for boiling and frying.

Q How did you become involved in teaching solar cooking?

A To me, solar technology is the way to go to help reduce the need to burn fuels. I first saw a solar cooker during a visit to an organic farm in Oregon—we cooked on it almost every day during the summer.

Career Connection

Architects design buildings and supervise their construction. Use the yellow pages of the phone book to find an architect in your area. Interview him or her to find out how architects are trained and what their work is like. Ask how the need for heating and air conditioning influences building design.

- **Architect**   - **Building Contractor**

Design Your Own Experiment
Creating Convection Currents

What happens when you use ice cubes to cool a drink? After a while, the drink feels cooler than before you added the ice. What actually happens to the particles that make up the ice cube when it melts?

PREPARATION

Problem
How does convection aid in the cooling of a drink when ice is added?

Form a Hypothesis
Write a hypothesis describing what you think will happen when a colored ice cube melts in a sample of warm fresh water and in a sample of warm salt water.

Objectives
- Design an experiment to explore the relationships between convection currents and fluid density.
- Observe what happens when a colored ice cube melts in warm fresh water and salt water.

Possible Materials
- colored ice cubes
- warm, fresh water
- salt
- tongs
- a ruler
- thermometer
- beaker, 250-mL
- stirring rod

Safety Precautions
Be sure to keep thermometers away from the table's edge. Stir with stirring rods only, not thermometers.

SALT WATER

FRESH WATER

PLAN THE EXPERIMENT

1. Remember that the temperature will vary with the depth of the water.
2. Avoid creating convection currents by physically disturbing the water.
3. If you need a data table, design one in your Science Journal.

Check the Plan

1. Be sure your data table has space to record the water temperature in salt water and in fresh water at the surface, the bottom, and at one (or more) measured depth(s) in between. Will you measure these temperatures before adding ice, after the ice has been melting for a few minutes, or both?
2. The photo at the right shows a way to place the colored ice cube into the water samples while keeping the water as still as possible.

3. How will you make a saturated solution of warm salt water? Will you do the experiment the same way with the fresh water and salt water?
4. Do you have to run any tests more than one time?
5. In addition to your temperature measurements, how will you record your observations of what is happening?
6. *Make sure your teacher approves your plan and that you have included any changes suggested in the plan.*

DO THE EXPERIMENT

1. Carry out the approved experiment as planned.
2. During the experiment, write down any observations that you make and complete the data table in your Science Journal.

Analyze and Apply

1. As the ice melts, **compare** what happens to the colored

meltwater in the samples of fresh water and salt water.
2. Do you observe convection currents in this activity? Explain.
3. Of the three liquids involved in this activity (warm fresh water; warm salt water; and cold colored meltwater), **predict** which is the most dense.

Go Further

Predict what would happen to the coloring and temperature of the liquid if you left the beaker containing fresh water and a colored ice cube untouched for 30 minutes. Test your prediction.

Science Words

radiator
solar energy
solar collector

Objectives

- Describe three types of conventional heating systems.
- Explain how solar energy can be used to heat buildings.
- Explain the differences between passive and active solar heating systems.

Figure 6-8

The design of this radiator permits large quantities of air to be heated by contact with its surface. *How does the warm air near the radiator get to other parts of the room?*

Conventional Heating Systems

What is the climate like where you live? Is it cold part of the year or is it warm all year-round? Sometimes, even in warm climates, the weather can be cold enough that buildings need to be heated. For this reason, most buildings have some kind of heating system.

All heating systems must have a source of energy, such as fuel or electricity. The simplest type of heating system is one in which fuel, such as wood, coal, or gas, is burned right in the area to be heated. The energy released by the burning fuel is transferred to the surrounding air by conduction, convection, and radiation.

Radiator Systems

Many heating systems use radiators to transfer energy. The **radiator** shown in **Figure 6-8** is a device with a large surface area designed to heat the air near it by conduction. Convection currents then circulate the heat to all parts of the room.

In some heating systems, radiators are heated by electricity. However, most systems are designed so that fuel is burned in a furnace, and the heat is transported to radiators throughout the building. In the system shown in

Figure 6-9

In this heating system, water is heated by a furnace. The hot water is pumped to the radiators to heat the rooms of the house.

Baseboard radiator
Pump
Expansion tank
Hot water heater
Burner
Smoke outlet

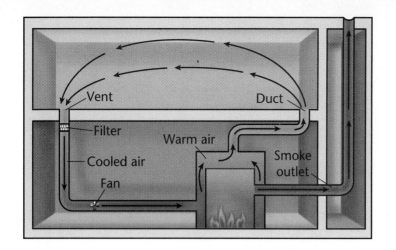

Figure 6-10

In a forced-air heating system, air heated by the furnace is used to heat the rooms of the house.

Figure 6-9, the furnace uses the energy to heat water, which is then pumped through pipes to the radiators. The cooler water is returned to the furnace to be heated again.

In a similar type of heating system, the furnace heats water to its boiling point, producing steam. The steam travels through insulated pipes to the radiators. As it cools, the steam condenses to water, which returns to the furnace. Steam-heating systems use about one-fiftieth as much water as hot-water systems, but the pipes and furnace need special insulation to keep the steam from condensing before it reaches the radiators.

Forced-Air Systems

In the forced-air system shown in **Figure 6-10,** energy released in the furnace heats air. A blower forces the heated air through a system of large pipes, called ducts, to openings, called vents, in each room. In the rooms, the warm air circulates by convection. Cooler air returns through other vents and ducts to the furnace to be reheated.

Electrical Heating Systems

Some buildings are heated entirely by electricity. Heating coils are enclosed within floors or ceilings and are heated by electrical energy. Nearby air is heated by conduction, and people and materials in the room are also warmed by radiation. Such systems, sometimes called radiant electric heating systems, provide even heating but may be too expensive to operate because of the cost of electricity in some areas.

Solar Heating

If you have ever gotten into a car that has been sitting in direct sunlight for any length of time, you know that energy from the sun can be changed to thermal energy. Energy from the sun is known as **solar energy.** Because solar energy is free, the idea of using it to heat buildings is especially appealing.

CONNECT TO

LIFE SCIENCE

People devised numerous ways to heat their homes before electricity and gas services were available. This allowed them to live in more places on Earth. *List* some of the methods human beings have used to stay warm.

Procedure
1. Make a solar cooker by gluing aluminum foil to a large piece of poster board.
2. Bend the board into a U-shape so that the ends of the board are nearly parallel, but about 30 cm apart. Use string stretched between its corners to hold the board in this shape.
3. Use wire coat hangers to make a mount that will hold the board with the center of the U pointing directly at the sun.
4. Predict where the hottest region of your solar cooker is. From another string bridge connecting the edges of the board, dangle a piece of chocolate into the hottest area.
5. Check the chocolate every few minutes to see if it begins to melt. You might wish to try other spots, as well.

Analysis
1. Which energy-transfer process is heating your chocolate the most? Explain.
2. How might you make the cooker more effective?

String holding poster board in curved shape

Foil

Suspended chocolate

Curved poster board

Figure 6-11

This passive solar heating system changes the sun's energy to thermal energy.

Passive Solar Heating

Two basic types of systems are used to capture solar energy and convert it to thermal energy to heat buildings. The first type is passive solar heating. Passive systems use no fans or mechanical devices to transfer heat from one area to another. Some materials in the system absorb radiant energy during the day, convert it to thermal energy, and radiate the thermal energy after dark.

As shown in **Figure 6-11,** a home with a passive solar heating system usually has a wall of large windows on the south side to receive maximum sunlight. The other exterior walls are heavily insulated and have few windows. During the day, sunlight passes through the windows and is absorbed by materials such as water or concrete. The radiant energy is converted to thermal energy, which is stored in the absorbing material. Later, when the house begins to cool, the stored energy warms the rooms.

Active Solar Heating

As you may have guessed, the second type is called an active solar heating system. Most active solar heating systems include **solar collectors,** devices that absorb radiant energy from the sun. The collectors are usually installed on the roof or south side of a building. The radiant energy is used to heat water or air that is then pumped throughout the house.

Figure 6-12 shows a home with one type of active solar collector. The metal plate absorbs radiant energy from the sun. Why do you think it's painted black? The glass or plastic sheets reduce energy loss due to convection. Water-filled pipes are located just beneath the metal plate. Radiant energy is absorbed and converted to thermal energy to heat the water in the pipes. A pump circulates the heated water to radiators in the system. Cooled water is returned to the collector to be reheated. Some systems have large, insulated tanks for storing heated water to be used as needed.

Figure 6-12

The house below is heated by an active solar heating system. Metal plates on the roof absorb heat from the sun. The operation of the system is illustrated in B.

A

Pipes for liquid

Glass sheets

Black metal plate

Insulation

Solar energy collector

Energy from the sun

Cooled liquid

Heated liquid

Warm air

Pump

Water storage tank

Fan

Heat exchanger

B

Section Wrap-up

Review

1. What are the main differences among electrical, radiator, and forced-air heating systems?

2. Compare and contrast active and passive solar heating systems.

3. **Think Critically:** Suppose you are an architect from a cold climate who has been asked to design a building for Tucson, Arizona, where the temperature averages 22°C and can reach 50°C in summer. What do you know about keeping buildings warm that will help a building stay cool in hot weather?

Skill Builder
Making and Using Tables
In a table, organize information about the kinds of heating systems discussed in this section. Include any type of information you think is important. If you need help, refer to Making and Using Tables in the **Skill Handbook.**

Science Journal

In your Science Journal, describe and diagram the heating system in your home, apartment, or school. Explain how conduction, convection, and radiation are involved.

Using Heat to Do Work

Science Words

heat engine
combustion
internal combustion
    engine
external combustion
    engine
heat mover

Objectives

* Describe how internal combustion engines and external combustion engines work.
* Explain how a heat mover can transfer thermal energy in a direction opposite to that of its natural movement.

Heat Engines

Heat engines are devices that convert thermal energy into mechanical energy. Heat engines burn fuel in a process called **combustion,** which means rapid burning. The two main classes of heat engines are based on where combustion happens—inside the engine or outside the engine.

Internal Combustion Engines

In an **internal combustion engine,** fuel burns inside the engine in chambers called cylinders. Gasoline and diesel engines such as those used in cars and trucks are examples of internal combustion engines.

Figure 6-13A shows what the cylinders look like inside the gasoline engine of a car. Each cylinder has at least two openings that open or close with valves. A piston inside each cylinder moves up and down, turning a crankshaft. The motion of the crankshaft is transferred to the wheels of the car through a series of moving parts. The wheels exert a force on the road through the tires. The equal and opposite force of the road on the tires pushes the car forward.

Each up or down movement of the piston is called a stroke. An automobile engine is called a four-stroke engine because the piston makes four strokes in each cycle. Follow the steps of the four-stroke cycle in **Figure 6-13B–E.**

Some engines have fuel injectors instead of carburetors. In fuel-injected engines, only air enters the cylinder during the intake stroke. During the compression stroke, fine droplets of fuel are injected directly into the compressed air in the cylinder. The other steps are the same as in an engine with a carburetor.

Figure 6-13

Most car engines have either four or six cylinders. *List at least one advantage and one disadvantage of one of these engine types.*

Cylinder

Valve

Piston

Crankshaft

To wheels

 A typical arrangement of cylinders and pistons in a gasoline engine is shown.

In a diesel engine, fuel also is injected into compressed air in the cylinder. But the engine has no spark plugs. The fuel-air mixture is compressed so much that it becomes hot enough to ignite without a spark.

In an internal combustion engine, only part of the thermal energy produced by burning fuel is converted to mechanical energy. The rest is left over as waste thermal energy due to friction and the heating of engine parts. Gasoline engines convert only about 12 percent of the chemical potential energy in the fuel to mechanical energy. Diesel engines convert up to 25 percent of the fuel's potential energy to mechanical energy.

External Combustion Engines

In an **external combustion engine,** fuel is burned outside the engine. In old-fashioned steam engines such as those used to power early locomotives, fuel was burned to boil water in a chamber outside the engine. The resulting steam passed through a valve in the engine, where it pushed a piston. The motion of the piston was transferred to the wheels of the locomotive.

Intake valve   Cylinder   Fuel-air mixture   Piston   Spark plug   Exhaust valve

Crankshaft   Exhaust gases

B *Intake stroke.* In another part of the engine called the carburetor, gasoline is broken up into fine droplets and mixed with air. In the cylinder, the intake valve opens and the piston moves downward, drawing the fuel-air mixture into the cylinder.

C *Compression stroke.* The intake valve closes, and the piston moves up. The fuel-air mixture is squeezed, or compressed, into a smaller space.

D *Power stroke.* When the piston is almost at the top of the cylinder, a spark plug produces a hot spark that ignites the fuel-air mixture. As the mixture burns, hot gases expand, forcing the piston down. Energy is transferred from the piston to the wheels of the car through the crankshaft and other moving parts.

E *Exhaust stroke.* The piston moves up again, forcing the waste products from burning the fuel-air mixture out the exhaust valve.

Modern steam engines, such as those used in electrical power stations, don't have pistons. Instead, steam is directed onto huge, fanlike devices called turbines. The steam pushes against the turbine blades, which then rotate rapidly to turn a cylindrical shaft, thus producing mechanical energy.

Heat Movers

When you put warm food into a refrigerator, the food gets cooler. Where does the thermal energy in the food go? Feel the back of the refrigerator, and you'll notice that it's warm. But you know that heat always flows from warmer to cooler areas. So how can heat flow from the cool refrigerator to the warm room? It can't unless work is done. The energy to do the work comes from the electricity that powers the refrigerator.

A refrigerator is an example of a heat mover. A **heat mover** is a device that removes thermal energy from one location and transfers it to another location at a different temperature. As shown in **Figure 6-14,** refrigerators use the process of evaporation to remove heat from the food inside. A liquid is pumped through coils inside the refrigerator. In most cooling systems, liquid Freon is used because it evaporates at low temperatures. As the liquid evaporates, it absorbs heat, cooling the inside of the refrigerator. The Freon gas is then pumped to a compressor on the outside of the refrigerator. Compressing the Freon causes its temperature to rise above room temperature. So, the Freon loses heat to the air around it and condenses again. The excess heat is transferred into the room, sometimes with the help of fans.

An air conditioner is another kind of heat mover. It removes thermal energy from a warm house and transfers it to the even warmer outdoor surroundings. Refrigerators and air conditioners are heat engines working in reverse —they use mechanical energy to move thermal energy from cooler to warmer areas.

A heat pump is a special two-way heat mover. In warm weather, it operates like an air conditioner. In cold weather, it removes thermal energy from cool outside air and transfers it to the inside of the house.

Figure 6-14

In a heat mover such as a refrigerator, thermal energy is removed from one location and is released in another location. *Where does the heat that is removed from food in a refrigerator go?*

Freezer unit

Liquid Freon

Heat from warm air

Freon vapor

Storage tank

Compressor

Heat into room   Condenser coils

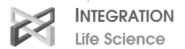

Sweat—The Human Coolant

After exercising on a warm day, you may feel hot and be drenched with sweat. But if you were to take your temperature, you would probably find it close to your normal body temperature of 37°C. How does your body stay cool in hot weather?

In reading about refrigerators, you learned that a refrigerant such as Freon removes heat from food as it changes from a liquid to a gas. This process, called evaporation, is also important in maintaining a healthy internal body temperature. When a liquid changes to a gas, energy is absorbed from the liquid's surroundings. Heat is removed from your body as your perspiration evaporates, making you cooler.

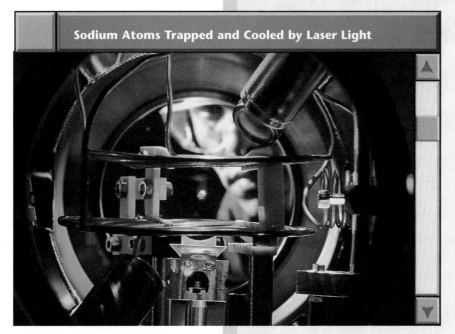

Sodium Atoms Trapped and Cooled by Laser Light

USING TECHNOLOGY

Cooling Crystals

Do you know the coldest temperature something could actually become? Recall that zero on the Kelvin scale is called absolute zero, the point at which all particle motion stops. Physicists are trying to bring small samples of matter to the coldest temperature possible. Some samples have been chilled to 180 billionths of a degree above absolute zero (−273.15°C).

Physicists think about extremely low temperatures in terms of slowness of particle vibrations rather than as chilliness. They can bring matter to such low temperatures by using magnetic fields or special lasers to decrease the particle vibrations.

Property Changes

Many properties of matter change at temperatures near absolute zero. Studying materials at extremely cold temperatures may better explain magnetism and the behavior of the particles in atoms.

Researchers at the National Institute of Standards and Technology hope that reaching such temperatures will improve the accuracy of atomic clocks, which depend upon natural vibrations of atoms to keep time.

Think Critically:

Do you think super-cold freezers could be used to bring matter to a temperature of absolute zero? Why or why not?

CONNECT TO

EARTH SCIENCE

Freon is a type of chlorofluorocarbon (CFC). *Describe* the main environmental effect that may result when Freon is released in the atmosphere.

The energy lost by your body becomes part of the thermal energy of your evaporated sweat.

Why do humid days feel hotter than dry days?

Have you ever wondered why humid days feel warmer than dry days at the same temperature? On humid days, more water vapor is in the air around you. Your sweat doesn't evaporate as quickly. In fact, some of this water vapor actually condenses and releases energy to your skin. Condensation, the change from a gas to a liquid, is the opposite of evaporation. Evaporation is a cooling process, and condensation is a warming process.

The dog in **Figure 6-15** is cooling herself by panting. Because dogs only sweat between their toes, they pant to cause evaporation from their respiratory systems to stay cool.

Figure 6-15

Evaporation is helping to keep this dog cool. *Would there be more evaporation on a hot, dry day or a hot, humid day?*

Section Wrap-up

Review

1. How do diesel and gasoline engines differ?

2. In a heat engine, what happens to the thermal energy that is converted from chemical energy?

3. **Think Critically:** Explain whether it is a good idea to cool your house by leaving the refrigerator door open.

Skill Builder
Concept Mapping
Make a cycle concept map to show the steps in one cycle of a four-stroke internal combustion engine. If you need help, refer to Concept Mapping in the **Skill Handbook.**

Science Journal

Only a small percentage of the chemical potential energy of gasoline is actually used to move your car. In your Science Journal, describe the evidence that much of the energy is wasted.

Activity 6-2

The Four-Stroke Engine

As you examine the piston movements in a four-stroke engine, can you identify and detect changes in kinetic and potential energy?

Problem
How do the kinetic and potential energies change during a four-stroke cycle?

Materials 🔫 👋 🥽
- matches
- flask, 250-mL
- large syringe, plastic
- rubber tubing (3 pieces)
- small piece of cloth or yarn
- rubber stopper, 2-hole, with glass tubing
- glass or plastic "T"
- pinch clamps (2)

Procedure
1. Set up a model four-stroke engine as shown.
2. Prepare a data table like the one below.
3. With all clamps closed, ignite a small piece of cloth or yarn and drop it into the flask. **CAUTION:** *Exercise caution when using open flames.* Allow the flask, representing the carburetor, to fill with smoke.
4. With the piston inside the syringe, open the intake clamp and pull the piston down.
5. Close the intake clamp and push the piston up into the syringe.
6. Release the piston and observe what happens.
7. Open the exhaust clamp and push the piston up into the syringe.
8. Close the exhaust clamp and repeat steps 4-7.

Analyze
1. What happens to the smoke particles when the intake clamp is closed and the piston moves into the syringe?
2. What happens when the piston is released?
3. What happens to the smoke particles when the exhaust clamp is opened and the piston moves into the syringe?

Conclude and Apply
4. In this model, **explain** what the smoke represents in steps 4, 5, and 7.
5. **Infer** the best instant to explode a fuel-air mixture.
6. **Identify** in which stroke kinetic energy is changed to potential energy.

Data and Observations

Step	Stroke	Observations
4		
5		
6		
7		

TECHNOLOGY:
6•4 Energy from the Oceans

Science Words

ocean thermal energy conversion

Objectives

- Explain how differences in ocean temperatures can be used to operate a heat engine that changes thermal energy to mechanical energy.
- Discuss the advantages and disadvantages of ocean thermal energy conversion.

Figure 6-16

Ocean waves and tides carry large amounts of energy. *Explain the effects they have on the rocks and sand along the shoreline.*

Oceans—Natural Reservoirs of Energy

Earth's dwindling supply of fossil fuels is making it necessary for researchers to develop ways to make use of natural, renewable energy sources. One of the largest energy sources covers nearly three-fourths of Earth's surface—the oceans. With such a large surface area and depths up to 11 000 m, the oceans have the ability to absorb radiant energy from the sun and store it as thermal energy. In addition to thermal energy, the oceans also contain a vast amount of mechanical energy. You can see the effects of this energy in **Figure 6-16.**

Ocean waters are in constant motion. The mechanical energy of moving water can be used to rotate turbines and generate electricity, as in hydroelectric plants in rivers. Several plants already make use of moving water resulting from tides, and scientists are working on ways to use the energy in ocean currents and waves.

Ocean Thermal Energy Conversion

Where do you think ocean temperatures are the highest and the lowest? In tropical or subtropical regions, there can be a more than 20°C difference between warm surface waters and cold bottom waters. Energy researchers are trying to improve methods of extracting and using energy stored in warm surface waters.

Ocean thermal energy conversion (OTEC) is a process that uses heat engines to convert differences in ocean water temperature into mechanical energy to drive turbines. An OTEC heat engine uses heat from warm surface water to vaporize a working fluid with a low boiling point, such as ammonia. **Figure 6-17** illustrates how an OTEC heat engine works. How is this similar to the refrigeration process described in the last section?

Figure 6-17

This OTEC heat engine uses ammonia as a working fluid. The turbine is driven by the ammonia vapor and is connected to a generator to produce electricity. The warm water is drawn from the ocean surface; the cold water from a depth of 1000 m.

Electric power generator

Turbine

Ammonia vapor

Ammonia condenses

Condenser

Cold water outlet

Cold water intake (5°C) from deep water

Pump

Ammonia liquid

Warm water outlet

Evaporator

Ammonia evaporates

Warm water intake (25°C) from surface water

Is OTEC practical?

The construction and operation of several small plant designs have shown that OTEC is possible. Improved designs will likely increase the efficiency of such plants. They require a lot of energy to operate because large amounts of water must be pumped from ocean depths.

Additional study must be done to determine possible environmental effects of pumping so much cold water to the surface in warm-water regions. The environment marine organisms are accustomed to, especially with respect to dissolved oxygen and nutrient levels, could be altered by temperature changes. The main attraction of OTEC lies in the fact that radiant energy supplied by the sun to heat the surface water is a dependable and free source of energy. OTEC plants may be land-based or built on floating ocean platforms.

Figure 6-18

This land-based OTEC plant uses a system of pipes and pumps to transport water from the nearby ocean.

Section Wrap-up

Review

1. Explain how temperature differences at different depths of the ocean provide a possible energy source.

2. What do you think are the possible advantages and disadvantages of developing OTEC as an energy source?

Explore the Technology

Energy researchers must anticipate world energy demands and available resources years in advance. What circumstances might make OTEC plants difficult and costly to build? What areas of the world do you think would benefit most from developing OTEC processes? Be sure to explain your answers.

SCIENCE & SOCIETY

Chapter 6 Review

Summary

6-1: Thermal Energy on the Move

1. Thermal energy can be transferred by conduction, convection, and radiation. Unlike radiation, conduction and convection can occur only when matter is present.
2. Conductors allow heat to flow easily. Insulators resist heat flows.

6-2: Using Heat to Stay Warm

1. Heating systems are generally identified by the medium that transfers the thermal energy. The three most common media are hot water, steam, and air.
2. A solar heating system converts radiant energy from the sun to thermal energy.
3. Passive solar systems do not have devices to transfer heat from one part of the system to another. Active solar systems use fans or pumps to serve this purpose.

6-3: Using Heat to Do Work

1. Heat engines are devices that convert thermal energy produced by burning fuel into mechanical energy. In an internal combustion engine, fuel is burned inside the engine. In an external combustion engine, fuel is burned outside the engine.
2. Heat movers move thermal energy from one place and release it in another place.
3. Sweating helps humans cool their bodies through evaporation.

6-4: Science and Society: Energy from the Oceans

1. Differences in ocean temperatures can be used to operate a heat engine.

2. Additional research needs to be done to improve the efficiency and evaluate the environmental effects of OTEC.

Key Science Words

a. combustion
b. conduction
c. convection
d. external combustion engine
e. fluid
f. heat engine
g. heat mover
h. insulator
i. internal combustion engine
j. ocean thermal energy conversion
k. radiation
l. radiator
m. solar collector
n. solar energy

Reviewing Vocabulary

Match each phrase with the correct term from the list of Key Science Words.

1. energy transfer by direct contact of particles
2. energy transfer by movement of particles from place to place
3. energy transfer by electromagnetic waves
4. material that resists the flow of heat
5. device that absorbs the sun's radiant energy
6. device that converts thermal energy into mechanical energy
7. rapid burning
8. a device that transfers thermal energy from one place to another
9. type of engine in which fuel is burned inside the engine
10. a process that uses a difference in water temperatures to operate a heat engine

Chapter 6 Review

Checking Concepts

Choose the word or phrase that completes the sentence or answers the question.

1. Which is not a method of heat transfer?
   a. conduction   c. radiation
   b. insulation   d. convection
2. In _____, fuel is burned inside chambers called cylinders.
   a. internal combustion engines
   b. external combustion engines
   c. heat pumps
   d. steam engines
3. Waste gases are removed during the _____ of a four-stroke engine.
   a. power stroke   c. compression stroke
   b. intake stroke   d. exhaust stroke
4. Which material is a poor insulator of heat?
   a. aluminum   c. air
   b. feathers   d. plastic
5. A _____ is an example of a heat mover.
   a. refrigerator   c. combustion engine
   b. steam engine   d. four-stroke engine
6. In which of these forms is water not a fluid?
   a. liquid water   c. water vapor
   b. ice   d. steam
7. Heat can move easily through a good _____.
   a. insulator   c. conductor
   b. carburetor   d. collector
8. Which of these does not require the presence of particles of matter?
   a. radiation   c. convection
   b. conduction   d. combustion
9. In order for radiant energy to change to thermal energy, it must be _____.
   a. reflected   c. convected
   b. conducted   d. absorbed
10. A _____ changes thermal energy into mechanical energy.
    a. heat engine   c. solar collector
    b. refrigerator   d. conductor

Understanding Concepts

Answer the following questions in your Science Journal using complete sentences.

11. Describe all of the ways in which energy is transferred while a pot of soup is heated on an electric stove. Indicate how each type of energy transfer takes place.
12. Explain how convection currents are created. Describe two examples of convection currents that occur in nature.
13. Why is winter clothing generally darker in color than summer clothing? Explain why wearing two or three layers of clothing helps to keep you warmer in cold weather than does one thick layer.
14. Compare and contrast passive and active solar heating. On what basic principle are both systems based?
15. Describe at least two ways the oceans can be used as a source of energy.

Thinking Critically

16. The energy transfer shown in **Figure 6-1** on page 152 takes place at the particle level of matter. Thus, the transfer of energy cannot be observed directly. Think of an analogy or model using visible objects that you could use to demonstrate the process of conduction.
17. Explain why the inside of an automobile left sitting in direct sunlight for several hours becomes warm.
18. Design a line of clothing to be used on an Arctic expedition. Describe the articles of clothing and explain why each will keep the wearer warm in extremely cold conditions.
19. The engines of many high-performance cars have four valves per cylinder rather than the usual two-valve arrangement. These engines also have fuel injectors at each cylinder rather than a single carburetor. How do these differences improve the performance of the engine?

20. Describe how an automobile air conditioner using Freon gas works. Explain why the engine must be running in order for the air conditioner to work.

Developing Skills

If you need help, refer to the **Skill Handbook.**

21. **Interpreting Data:** Using the *R*-values given in **Table 6-1** on page 157, design an energy-efficient house. Indicate the type and thickness of the different materials to be used to construct the walls and ceilings.

22. **Sequencing:** Order the events that occur in the removal of heat from an object by a refrigerator. Start with the placing of a warm object in the refrigerator and finish with the change in Freon from a gas to a liquid.

23. **Concept Mapping:** Complete the following events chain to show how an active solar heating system works.

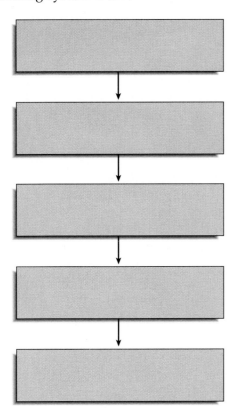

24. **Recognizing Cause and Effect:** Describe the problems that might occur if the following events happened in a fuel-injected gasoline engine. Indicate the engine stroke that will be affected: (a) exhaust valve stuck closed, (b) clogged fuel injector, (c) bad spark plug, (d) intake valve will not close.

25. **Using Variables, Constants, and Controls:** Design an experiment to test the effects of surface area and length of a material on heat conduction. Indicate your hypothesis, variables, and constants. How will you organize and interpret your data?

Performance Assessment

1. **Formulating a Hypothesis:** Review Activity 6-1 on page 160. What do you think would happen if you were to use a funnel to add warm water (colored red) to the bottom of a beaker of cold water? Explain your answer.

2. **Oral Presentation:** Study the four-stroke engine model in Activity 6-2 on page 171. Explain how this model differs from an actual engine.

3. **Making Observations and Inferences:** Identify the building materials used in or on the walls, ceilings, or attic space in your home and school. Which ones are good heat insulators?

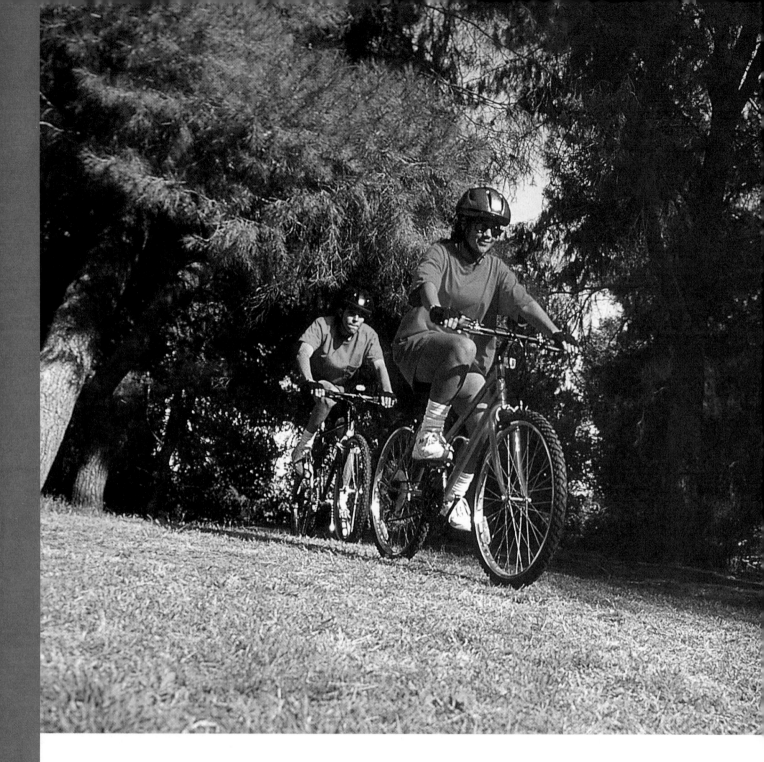

Previewing the Chapter

Chapter 7

Machines— Making Work Easier

People use machines to make jobs easier. What comes to mind when you think of machines? You might list computers, washing machines, and electric drills as examples. Many machines are simple and do not need electricity to operate. What kinds of machines are in a bicycle?

EXPLORE ACTIVITY

How can a machine make it easier to move an object?

1. Try to lift a stack of two or three books off a table using only your fingertips.
2. Then place the stack of books on the end (at the 5-cm mark) of a meterstick so the entire width of the bottom book is resting on the stick.
3. Push up on the meterstick at the 40-cm mark to lift the books.
4. Repeat the experiment twice, lifting at the 70-cm mark and then at the 100-cm mark (the opposite end).

Observe: Which time did you need the most force to lift the books? The least? In your Science Journal, describe which setup gives you the greatest lifting advantage and try to explain why.

Previewing Science Skills

► In the Skill Builders, you will recognize cause and effect, make and use tables, and map concepts.

► In the Activities, you will analyze, communicate, measure in SI, and experiment.

► In the MiniLABs, you will observe and measure in SI.

7•1 Why We Use Machines

Science Words

machine
simple machine
effort force
resistance force
ideal machine
mechanical advantage

Objectives

- Explain how machines make work easier.
- Calculate mechanical advantage.

What are machines?

Have you used any machines today? You probably know that a bicycle is a machine. Pencil sharpeners and can openers are also machines. If you have turned a doorknob or twisted off a bottle cap, you have used a machine. A **machine** is a device that makes work easier.

Keeping It Simple

Some machines are powered by engines or electric motors; others are people-powered. Some machines are complex; others are simple. A **simple machine** is a device that does work with only one movement. There are six types of simple machines, examples of which are shown in **Figure 7-1.** You'll learn more about each type in a later section of this chapter.

Figure 7-1

Familiar examples of simple machines can be found in the following places.

A in the kitchen

C in construction

B in sports

Advantages of Simple Machines

Suppose you wanted to pry the lid off a wooden crate with a crowbar. You'd slip the end of the crowbar blade under the edge of the crate lid and push down on the handle. You would do work on the crowbar, and the crowbar would do work on the lid.

Machines make work easier by changing the force you exert in size, direction, or both. **Figure 7-2** shows how the crowbar changes the size and direction of your force as you attempt to lift the lid.

Overcoming Gravity and Friction

When you use a simple machine, you are trying to move something that resists being moved. For example, when you use a crowbar to move a large rock, you are working against gravity—the weight of the rock. When you use a crowbar to remove a lid, you are working against friction—the friction between the nails in the lid and the crate.

Applying Force and Doing Work

Two forces are involved when a machine is used to do work. The force applied *to* the machine is called the **effort force (F_e)**. The force applied *by* the machine to overcome resistance is called the **resistance force (F_r)**. In the crate lid example, you apply the effort force to the crowbar handle. The resistance force is the force the crowbar applies to the lid.

There are also two kinds of work to be considered when a machine is used—the work done *on* the machine and the work done *by* the machine. The work done on the machine is called work input (W_{in}); the work done by the machine is called work output (W_{out}). Recall that work is the product of force and distance: $W = F \times d$. Work input is the product of the effort force and the distance that force is exerted: $W_{in} = F_e \times d_e$. Work output is the product of the resistance force and the distance that force moves: $W_{out} = F_r \times d_r$.

Remember that energy is always conserved. So, you can never get more work out of a machine than you put into it. In other words, W_{out} can never be greater than W_{in}. In fact, whenever a machine is used, some energy is changed to heat due to friction. So, W_{out} is always smaller than W_{in}.

Although a perfect machine has never been built, it helps to imagine a frictionless machine in which no energy is converted to heat. Such an **ideal machine** is one in which work input equals work output. For an ideal machine,

$$W_{in} = W_{out}$$

$$F_e \times d_e = F_r \times d_r$$

Figure 7-2

The crowbar is used to multiply the effort force and open the crate. However, to gain force, the effort must push through a greater distance than the resistance distance.

CONNECT TO

LIFE SCIENCE

Birds fly using their wings to move them through the air. *Identify* the resistance and effort forces for this simple machine by making a labeled drawing.

In most cases, a machine multiplies the force applied to it—F_r is greater than F_e. So, in order for W_{in} to equal W_{out}, the effort force must travel farther than the resistance force—d_e must be greater than d_r.

Mechanical Advantage

Think again about the crate lid example. The distance you move the crowbar handle (d_e) is greater than the distance the crowbar moves the lid (d_r). So, the end of the crowbar must exert more force on the lid (F_r) than you exert on the handle (F_e). The machine multiplies your effort, but you must move the handle a greater distance.

The number of times a machine multiplies the effort force is the **mechanical advantage (MA)** of the machine. To calculate mechanical advantage, you divide the resistance force by the effort force.

$$MA = \frac{\text{resistance force}}{\text{effort force}} = \frac{F_r}{F_e}$$

Work the problems below to see how mechanical advantage is related to effort force and resistance force.

Some machines don't multiply force. They simply change the direction of the effort force. For example, when you pull

USING MATH

Calculating Mechanical Advantage

Example Problem:

A worker applies an effort force of 20 N to pry open a window that has a resistance force of 500 N. What is the mechanical advantage of the crowbar?

Problem-Solving Steps:

1. What is known?
      resistance force, F_r = 500 N
      effort force, F_e = 20 N
2. What is unknown?
      mechanical advantage, MA
3. Choose the equation.

   $$MA = \frac{F_r}{F_e}$$

4. **Solution:** $MA = \dfrac{500 \text{ N}}{20 \text{ N}} = 25$

Practice Problem

Find the effort force needed to lift a 2000-N rock, using a jack with a mechanical advantage of 10.

Top of blind

Slats

Pullcord

Figure 7-3

Miniblinds are a familiar example of a simple machine that changes the direction of a force.

down on the cord of window blinds, such as those in **Figure 7-3,** the blinds go up. Only the direction of the force changes; the effort force and resistance force are equal, so the mechanical advantage is 1.

Other machines, such as third-class levers, have mechanical advantages that are less than 1. Such machines are used to increase the distance an object moves or the speed at which it moves.

Section Wrap-up

Review

1. Explain how simple machines can make work easier without violating the law of conservation of energy.

2. A carpenter uses a claw hammer to pull a nail from a board. The nail has a resistance of 2500 N. The carpenter applies an effort force of 125 N. What is the mechanical advantage of the hammer?

3. **Think Critically:** Give an example of a simple machine you've used recently. How did you apply effort force? How did the machine apply resistance force?

Skill Builder
Recognizing Cause and Effect
When you operate a machine, it's often easy to observe cause and effect. For example, when you turn a doorknob, the latch in the door moves. Give five examples of machines and describe one cause-and-effect pair in the action of each machine. If you need help, refer to Recognizing Cause and Effect in the **Skill Handbook.**

USING MATH

Suppose you want to use a simple machine to lift a 6000-N log from a fallen tree. What effort force will you need if your machine has a mechanical advantage of 25? Of 15? Of 1? Show your calculations.

Design Your Own Experiment
Access for Everyone

If you were in a wheelchair or unable to climb stairs, would you be able to get into your home or school and move around? It is now law that public buildings must be accessible to people who are wheelchair-bound. What are some features you have seen that make this possible? In this experiment, you will use simple machines to design a house, school, or other public building that is wheelchair-accessible.

PREPARATION

Problem
How can you use simple machines to make a building accessible to people in wheelchairs?

Form a Hypothesis
Brainstorm ideas with your group and generate a hypothesis statement about how you could solve the problem stated above.

Objectives
- Apply simple machines in designing a building plan.
- Explain the purpose of each

simple machine used in the plan, including how it provides a mechanical advantage.

Possible Materials
- poster-sized paper
- ruler or meterstick
- pencils
- markers

PLAN THE EXPERIMENT

1. Agree on the type of building your group wishes to design, and sketch a rough diagram of it in pencil on one side of your paper.
2. Determine at least three features that will help make your building accessible and easy to use for people in wheelchairs. At least two must relate directly to simple machines.
3. Preview the details about these simple machines in Section 7-2.
4. On your rough diagram, sketch how and where your features will be used.

Check the Plan

1. Before you draw your final plan, make sure your group has reached agreement on the features and design.

2. Why would your building be difficult to access without these special features? Think about a non-accessible building as your control.
3. Explain how you can get the greatest advantage out of each simple machine feature. For example, if you are using an inclined plane for a ramp, would a long, gradual ramp or a short, steep ramp be more effective? Why?
4. *Make sure your teacher approves your plan and that you have included any changes suggested in the plan.*

DO THE EXPERIMENT

1. Draw your final plan as clearly as possible on large paper or poster board.
2. Be sure to label your features. Discuss what function the simple machines perform in each case. Prepare to present your plan to the class.

Analyze and Apply

1. Briefly **communicate** your plan to the class and **analyze** the designs of other groups.

Which features are most commonly used?
2. Identify at least two simple machines found in a wheelchair and **discuss** where they are found.
3. You designed a new wheelchair-accessible building. **Infer** what methods might be feasible to make an old building wheelchair-accessible.

Go Further

Organize and conduct a survey of handicap accessibility of buildings in your neighborhood. What things should you check for? You might investigate four categories of buildings: homes, schools, private buildings, and other public buildings.

Science Words

lever
fulcrum
effort arm
resistance arm
pulley
wheel and axle
inclined plane
screw
wedge

Objectives

- Describe the six types of simple machines.
- Calculate the ideal mechanical advantage for different types of simple machines.

Levers

If you've ever ridden a seesaw, pried the cap from a bottle of soda pop, or swung a tennis racket, you have used a lever. A **lever** is a bar that is free to pivot, or turn, about a fixed point. The fixed point of a lever is called the **fulcrum.** The part of the lever on which the effort force is applied is called the **effort arm.** The part of the lever that exerts the resistance force is called the **resistance arm.**

Suppose you are using a tire tool to pry the tire from a bicycle wheel before you change the tire. You can see in **Figure 7-4** that the rim of the wheel acts as the fulcrum. You push down on the effort arm of the tire tool. The tool pivots about the fulcrum, and the resistance arm exerts a force on the tire, lifting it upward.

Figure 7-4

The tire tool is used as a lever to pop the bicycle tire out of the rim. *What acts as the fulcrum?*

Finding the Ideal Mechanical Advantage

The type of lever shown in **Figure 7-4** makes work easier by multiplying your effort force and changing the direction of your force. You've learned that the mechanical advantage of any machine can be calculated by dividing the resistance force by the effort force. You can also use the lengths of the arms of a lever to find the *ideal mechanical advantage* of the lever. The length of the effort arm is the distance from the fulcrum to the point where effort force is applied. The length of the resistance arm is the distance from the fulcrum to the point where the resistance force is applied. The following equation, which assumes no friction, can be used to find the ideal mechanical advantage (IMA) of any lever.

$$IMA = \frac{\text{length of effort arm}}{\text{length of resistance arm}} = \frac{L_e}{L_r}$$

Practice calculating ideal mechanical advantage by working the following problems.

USING MATH

Ideal Mechanical Advantage of a Lever

Example Problem:

A worker uses an iron bar to raise a manhole cover weighing 65 N. The effort arm of the lever is 60 cm long. The resistance arm is 10 cm long. What is the ideal mechanical advantage of the bar?

Problem-Solving Steps:

1. What is known?   effort arm, L_e = 60 cm
                                     resistance arm, L_r = 10 cm

2. What is unknown?   ideal mechanical advantage, *IMA*

3. Choose the equation. $IMA = \dfrac{L_e}{L_r}$

4. **Solution:** $IMA = \dfrac{60 \text{ cm}}{10 \text{ cm}} = 6.0$

Practice Problems

1. You use a crowbar 140 cm long as a lever to lift a large rock. The rock is 20 cm from the fulcrum. What is the *IMA* of the lever?
2. An oar used to row a boat has the handle 50 cm from the fulcrum and the blade 125 cm from the fulcrum. What is the ideal mechanical advantage of the oar?

Figure 7-5

The classes of levers differ in the positions of the effort force, the resistance force, and the fulcrum. Their purposes also differ.

Types of Levers

There are three different types, or classes, of levers. These classes are based on the positions of the effort force, resistance force, and fulcrum. **Figure 7-5** shows the three classes of levers.

First class

A First Class: These levers, with the fulcrum located between the effort and resistance forces, are usually used to multiply force. If a large effort force is used on the shorter arm of the lever, it can also be used to multiply distance.

B Second Class: The resistance is located between the effort force and the fulcrum in second-class levers. These levers always multiply force.

Second class

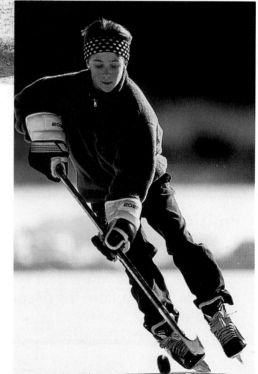

C Third Class: The effort force is located between the resistance force and the fulcrum in third-class levers. The effort arm is always shorter than the resistance arm, so it cannot multiply force and its *MA* is always less than one. *What is the purpose of a third-class lever?*

Third class

Levers with a Human Touch

Try holding a book or other object at your side with your arm straight down and palm facing forward. Keeping your upper arm at your side, bend your elbow and raise the book to chest height. Weightlifters call this lift a curl. What is supplying the effort force? Think about the mechanics of such a simple lifting task. You have many natural levers in your body composed of bone and muscle systems that give your body its form and ability to function.

Locating Levers

Although all lever classes are found in your body, the majority are third-class levers such as using your arm in the curl. Recall that third-class levers cannot multiply force. What advantage do they provide? As in a hockey stick or fishing rod, third-class levers provide a greater range of distance and speed of motion than the effort force itself can provide. Your biceps muscles used in the curl have a limited length, but they can supply more effort force to increase the range and speed of motion of the resistance force (your forearm). In this case, your elbow serves as the fulcrum. You would also use your arm as a third-class lever to pitch a baseball.

Can you find any first- or second-class levers in your body? Try sitting in an upright position and completely relaxing your neck. Your head tips forward because your neck muscles support the effort force to hold up the resistance weight of your head, acting as a first-class lever. Your foot becomes a second-class lever when you stand on your toes. Examine **Figure 7-6** to find out how you can identify the effort and resistance forces in these levers. What other levers can you identify in your body?

INTEGRATION
Life Science

Figure 7-6

Your body's structural system of muscles and bones contains natural examples of first-, second-, and third-class levers.

A First-class lever

B Second-class lever

C Third-class lever

MiniLAB

How do pulleys make work easier?

Procedure

1. Working in groups of three, tie one end of a rope to a piece of PVC pipe or a broomstick handle. Wrap the other end around another piece of pipe once (see Figure A below).
2. Two of the group members should each hold one pipe horizontally in their hands, with the pipes about 30 cm apart. The third person should grasp the free end of the rope and slowly try to pull the pipes together while the others try to hold the pipes firmly in place.
3. Wrap the rope again around the first pipe (B). What happens now when the third person tries to pull the pipes together?
4. Wrap the rope one or two more times across the pipes (C) and repeat the experiment.

Analysis

1. How is this similar to a pulley system? What increases the mechanical advantage of these pipe pulleys?
2. Does this machine multiply the energy of the person pulling? Why or why not?

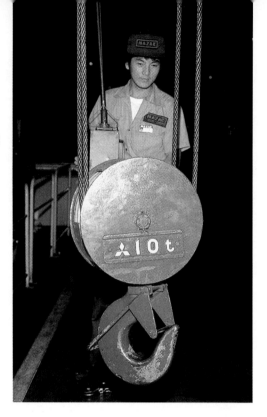

Figure 7-7

Construction workers rely on simple machines for safety. *What type of pulley is shown in this photograph?*

Pulling with Pulleys

Have you ever seen someone raise a flag on a flagpole? A pulley is used to help get the flag to the top of the pole. A **pulley** is a grooved wheel with a rope or a chain running along the groove.

A pulley works something like a first-class lever. Instead of a bar, a pulley has a rope. The axle of the pulley acts like the fulcrum. The two sides of the pulley are the effort arm and the resistance arm.

Positioning Pulleys

Pulleys can be fixed or movable. A *fixed* pulley is attached to something that doesn't move, such as a ceiling, wall, or tree. A fixed pulley, such as the one used at the top of a flagpole, can change the direction of an effort force. When you pull down on the effort arm with the rope, the pulley raises the object attached to the resistance arm. The *IMA* of a single fixed pulley is 1. Thus, a single fixed pulley does not multiply the effort force.

A *movable* pulley is attached to a construction crane, as shown in **Figure 7-7**. The difference between a fixed pulley and a movable pulley is shown in **Figure 7-8.** Unlike the fixed pulley, a movable pulley does multiply the effort force. Because a movable pulley multiplies force, its MA is greater than 1. In fact, the *IMA* of a single movable pulley is 2. This means that, assuming no friction, an effort force of 1 N will lift a weight (resistance) of 2 N. In order to conserve energy, the effort distance must be twice as large as the resistance distance.

IMA = 1
Single Fixed Pulley

IMA = 2
Single Movable Pulley

IMA = 4
Block and Tackle

The Block and Tackle

Fixed and movable pulleys can be combined to make a system of pulleys called a block and tackle. Depending on the number of pulleys used, a block and tackle can have a large mechanical advantage. The ideal mechanical advantage of any ideal pulley or pulley system is equal to the number of ropes that support the resistance weight. As **Figure 7-8** shows, the only rope that does not support the resistance weight is the rope leading from the pulley system down to the effort force.

Figure 7-8

The ideal mechanical advantage of each type of pulley can be found by counting every rope supplying an upward support force on the resistance.

Wheel and Axle

Look closely at a doorknob or the handle of a water faucet. Do you recognize these as simple machines? Do they seem to make work easier? If you don't think so, remove the knob or handle from its narrow shaft. Now, try opening the door or turning on the water by rotating that shaft with your fingers. After a few minutes, you'll appreciate the fact that the knob and handle, together with their shafts, are machines. They do make work easier.

Figure 7-9

A water faucet is an example of a wheel and axle. Without the faucet handle (wheel), the shaft of the faucet (axle) is difficult to turn.

Doorknobs, Faucets, and Ice-Cream Makers

Doorknobs, faucet handles, and ice-cream makers are examples of a wheel and axle. A **wheel and axle** is a simple machine consisting of two wheels of different sizes that rotate together. An effort force is usually applied to the larger wheel. The smaller wheel, called the axle, exerts the resistance force. In many cases, the larger wheel doesn't look like a typical circular wheel. It may be a crank handle, like that of the ice-cream freezer on the next page, or a faucet, as in **Figure 7-9.** But it always travels in a circle.

Figure 7-10

The length of the crank handle represents the radius of the wheel. The axle radius is represented by the turning paddle inside the ice-cream maker.

It might help to think of a wheel and axle as being a lever attached to a shaft. The radius of the wheel is the effort arm, and the radius of the axle is the resistance arm. The center of the axle is the fulcrum. As with the lever, the ideal mechanical advantage of a wheel and axle can be calculated by dividing the radius of the wheel (effort arm) by the radius of the axle (resistance arm).

$$IMA = \frac{\text{radius of wheel}}{\text{radius of axle}} = \frac{r_w}{r_a}$$

USING MATH

Calculating *IMA* of a Wheel and Axle

Example Problem:

In the ice-cream freezer shown in **Figure 7-10**, the wheel has a radius of 20 cm. The axle has a radius of 15 cm. What is the ideal mechanical advantage of the wheel and axle?

Problem-Solving Steps:

1. What is known?   radius of wheel, r_w = 20 cm
                        radius of axle, r_a = 15 cm

2. What is unknown?   ideal mechanical advantage, *IMA*

3. Choose the equation. $IMA = \frac{r_w}{r_a}$

4. Solution: $IMA = \frac{20 \text{ cm}}{15 \text{ cm}} = 1.3$

Practice Problem

An automobile steering wheel with a diameter of 48 cm is used to turn the steering column with a radius of 4 cm. What is the *IMA* of this wheel and axle?

Figure 7-11

Gears are a form of wheel and axle. *What causes the rear wheel of the bicycle to turn?*

Gearing Up

Gears are modified wheel-and-axle machines. A gear is a wheel with teeth along its circumference. **Figure 7-11** shows two ways gears work. Effort is exerted on one of the gears, causing the other gear to turn. In most gear systems, the larger gear is the effort gear. The ideal mechanical advantage of a pair of gears is found by dividing the radius of the effort gear by the radius of the resistance gear. This is known as the gear ratio of the pair.

Inclined Plane

Suppose you had to move a heavy box from the ground up onto a porch. Would you rather lift the box straight up or slide it up a ramp like the one in **Figure 7-12?** The ramp would make your job easier. A ramp is a type of **inclined plane,** which is a sloping surface used to raise objects.

The amount of work done on the box is the same whether you lift it straight up or slide it up the ramp. But remember that work has two parts—force and distance. When you lift the box straight up, the distance is small, but the force is large. Using the ramp, you cover more distance, but you exert less force.

You can calculate ideal mechanical advantage of an inclined plane using distances.

$$IMA = \frac{\text{effort distance}}{\text{resistance distance}} = \frac{\text{length of slope}}{\text{height of slope}} = \frac{l}{h}$$

Figure 7-12

The ramp is an example of an inclined plane.

The Screw

The screw and the wedge, **Figure 7-13,** are examples of inclined planes that move. A **screw** is an inclined plane wrapped in a spiral around a cylindrical post. If you look closely at a screw, you'll see that the threads form a tiny ramp that runs from its tip to near its top. As you turn the screw, the threads seem to pull the screw into the wood. The wood seems to slide up the inclined plane. Actually, the plane slides through the wood.

The Wedge

A **wedge** is an inclined plane with one or two sloping sides. Chisels, knives, and ax blades are examples. A typical inclined plane stays in one place while materials move along its surface. A wedge is a moving inclined plane. The material remains in one place while the wedge moves through it.

Perhaps you've noticed that the six types of simple machines are all variations of two basic machines—the lever and the inclined plane. As you go about your daily activities, look for examples of each type of simple machine. See if you can tell how each makes work easier.

Figure 7-13

The blade of the knife and the threads of the screw are special types of inclined planes.

Section Wrap-up

Review

1. Give one example of each kind of simple machine. Use examples different from the ones in the text.

2. Explain why the six kinds of simple machines are really variations on just two basic machines.

3. **Think Critically:** When would the friction of an inclined plane be useful?

Skill Builder
Making and Using Tables
Organize information about the six kinds of simple machines into a table. Include the type of machine, an example of each type, and a brief description of how it works. You may include other information if you wish. If you need help, refer to Making and Using Tables in the **Skill Handbook.**

Using Computers

Word Processor Using a word processor, write a separate paragraph about each class of lever. Describe at least two examples of each class, identifying the effort force, resistance force, and fulcrum for each. Use **Figure 7-5** to help you.

Activity 7-2

Levers

Did you ever play on a seesaw when you were younger? Wasn't it much easier to balance your friend on the other end if both of you weighed about the same? If your friend was lighter, you probably moved toward the fulcrum to balance the seesaw. How did this help? Moving toward the fulcrum shortened the effort arm. In this activity, you will balance a lever to determine the mass of a coin.

Problem
How can a lever measure mass?

Materials
- sheet of paper, 20 cm × 28 cm (8½″ × 11″)
- coins, 3 (quarter, dime, nickel)
- balance
- metric ruler

Procedure
1. Make a lever by folding the paper into a strip 3 cm wide by 28 cm long.
2. Mark a line 2 cm from one end of the paper strip. Label this line *Resistance.*
3. Slide the other end of the paper strip over the edge of a table until the strip begins to teeter on the edge. Mark a line across the paper at the table edge and label this line *Effort.*
4. Measure the mass of the paper to the nearest 0.1 g. Write this mass on the *Effort* line.
5. Center a dime on the *Resistance* line.
6. Locate the fulcrum by sliding the paper strip until it begins to teeter on the edge. Mark the balance line. Label it *Fulcrum #1.*
7. Measure the lengths of the resistance and effort arms to the nearest 0.1 cm.

8. Calculate the *IMA* of the lever.
9. Multiply the *IMA* times the mass of the lever to find the approximate mass of the coin.
10. Repeat steps 5 through 9 with the nickel and then with the quarter. Mark the fulcrum line #2 for the nickel and #3 for the quarter.

Analyze
1. In this activity, is the effective total length of the lever a constant or a variable?
2. Are the lengths of the resistance and effort arms constants or variables?
3. What provides the effort force?
4. What does it mean if the *IMA* is less than 1.0?

Conclude and Apply
5. Is it necessary to have the resistance line 2.0 cm from the end of the paper? Explain.
6. The calculations are done as if the entire weight of the paper is located at what point?
7. **Infer** why mass units can be used in place of force units in this kind of problem.

TECHNOLOGY:
7•3 Mending with Machines

Science Words

bionics

Objectives

- Explain what the science of bionics involves.
- Contrast two methods of using electrical signals to trigger motion of a limb or other bodily process.

The Human Body as a Machine

You have learned that some parts of the body work like machines. Some, such as your arms and legs, act as simple machines and are controlled by nerve impulses from your brain. What happens when a part of the human body no longer functions correctly or has to be removed?

Bionics—Making New Parts

Some organs, such as kidneys, eyes, and hearts, can be transplanted from another person. But many times, an appropriate technique or donor does not exist. Some of the most common replacement procedures involve artificial parts, such as a hip or knee joint. **Bionics** is the science of designing artificial replacements for parts of the human body. Artificial replacements are also called prostheses. Specialized prostheses made of new shock-absorbing material can even make it possible for a leg amputee to ski competitively, as in **Figure 7-14,** or complete a lengthy triathlon.

Making Electrical Connections

In the 1700s, a scientist named Alessandro Volta observed that muscles can be affected by small electric shocks. This observation is used in a technique called functional neuromuscular stimulation (FNS). These FNS systems have allowed people with paralyzed legs to walk again and maintain muscle tone. To cause a walking motion, FNS systems use a control unit to cause the proper amount of electric current to be emitted from small electrodes on the thighs of patients whose leg muscles are inactive due to spinal injury.

Figure 7-14

A special prosthesis helps this skier perform well in competition.

Currently, rehabilitation researchers are working on developing an arm prosthesis as shown in **Figure 7-15,** which will be capable of helping an amputee feel sensations such as pressure and texture. To feel these sensations, the brain must receive appropriate neural impulses from the limb. Sensors and a power source capable of generating artificial neural signals would be placed in the prosthesis, and the sensors would be connected to the remaining healthy portion of the natural arm's nerve.

Just Think About It

An exciting new technology may hold possibilities for helping people regain some use of a dis-functional organ or limb. Scientists are experimenting with brain-to-computer interfaces. Electrodes are used to stimulate or collect signals from neurons in the brain. This type of neural prosthesis may allow people to control motors, computers, and even artificial limbs with natural electrical impulses originating in their brains. Some research even suggests that a tiny camera could be linked to these electrodes to provide sight to a person without directly using the eyes. How else might this technology be useful?

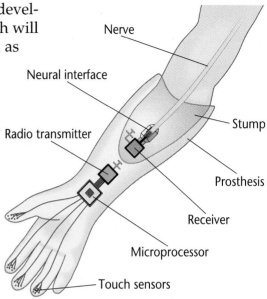

Figure 7-15

Prostheses like this one may soon help amputees experience sensations such as pressure and partially regain their sense of touch.

Section Wrap-up

Review

1. What is the purpose of the study of bionics? Explain at least two helpful inventions that have resulted from bionics research.

2. FNS systems and brain-to-computer interface systems both make use of electrical signals to move muscles. In what ways do these systems differ?

Explore the Technology

Imagine that you are a doctor working with a patient who has recently had his arm amputated below the elbow. If you were trying to advise the patient about what options are available for regaining some practical use of the arm, what would you point out as the strong points of the techniques discussed above? What are the drawbacks of each technique? Write up your arguments in the form of a report.

Science Journal

Knee joint replacements are made of modern materials. In your Science Journal, make a diagram of a replacement joint and label the material each part is made of. Write a paragraph explaining the use of each material.

SCIENCE & SOCIETY

Objectives

- Recognize the simple machines that make up a compound machine.
- Calculate the efficiency of a machine.
- Describe the relationship among work, power, and time.

Compound Machines

Many machines you use, such as a lawn mower or a pencil sharpener, are made up of several simple machines. A combination of two or more simple machines is a **compound machine.** Even a tool as simple as an ax is a compound machine made up of a wedge and a lever.

Often, the simple machines that make up a compound machine are concealed. However, in one familiar compound machine—the bicycle—many of the simple machines are visible and easily recognized.

Pedal Power

Look at the bicycle in **Figure 7-16.** The pedal mechanism is a wheel-and-axle system made up of two wheels attached to the same axle. Each pedal moves in a circle, like a wheel. The axle is a gear. The effort force exerted on the pedals by the rider turns this pedal gear. The bicycle chain transfers the force to a smaller gear attached to the rear wheel. This wheel gear is actually the effort wheel of the rear wheel-and-axle system. As the wheel gear turns, it causes the rear wheel to turn, and the wheel exerts the resistance force on the road. Because the wheel gear is smaller than the pedal gear that drives it, the rear wheel turns faster than the pedals do.

Figure 7-16

A racing bike uses wheels and axles in the form of gears to produce an *MA* of less than 1. Force is sacrificed to gain speed.

Finding the Mechanical Advantage of a Bicycle

The overall mechanical advantage of a bicycle is the ratio of the resistance force exerted by the tires on the road to the effort force exerted by the rider on the pedals. A one-speed bicycle has only two gears. Its gear ratio is fixed, so its mechanical advantage cannot be changed. This makes it a one-speed bike. A ten-speed bike has two pedal gears and five wheel gears. By shifting gears, the rider can change gear ratios, which changes the mechanical advantage and helps the rider maintain a steadier rate of pedaling over different terrains.

A bicycle has many other simple machines. Some of these machines are shown in **Figure 7-16.** See if you can tell what each does. Can you think of any others?

Problem Solving

Frivolous Machines

Creating machines for various tasks has long been a favorite pastime of inventors and even cartoonists. In the mid-1900s, Rube Goldberg published syndicated cartoons that often featured bizarre devices or machines to tackle simple, everyday tasks. These sketches became popular, so cumbersome, elaborate, or ridiculous machines are frequently called "Rube Goldberg devices."

These creative and wacky devices are often designed from a combination of simple machines made of ordinary materials. This sketch suggests a device to turn off a ringing alarm clock. It begins with the person in bed nudging the cat off his feet and onto a lever to drink some milk. Can you figure out how the device depicted in this cartoon works?

Solve the Problem:

1. **What simple machines can you identify in this cartoon?**
2. **Describe, step by step, what happens as this device functions. What step do you think might be the most likely to malfunction? Why?**

Think Critically:

Design your own Rube Goldberg device to blow out a candle, shut off an alarm, open a window, or do some other ordinary task. Be sure your device uses at least four distinct steps. What simple machines are used in your device?

Science book

Pulley

Physical Science

Ruler

Milk

Shoe

Baseball

Ramp

Ball hits alarm button

CONNECT TO

CHEMISTRY

A material called graphite is sometimes used as a lubricant to increase the efficiency of machines. Find out what element graphite is made of and *infer* why it eases the movement of machines.

Efficiency

You learned earlier that some of the energy put into a machine is lost as thermal energy produced as a result of friction. The work put out by a machine is always less than the work put into the machine.

Efficiency is a measure of how much of the work put into a machine is changed to useful work put out by a machine. The higher the efficiency of a machine, the greater the amount of work input that is changed to useful work output. Efficiency is calculated by dividing work output by work input and is usually expressed as a percentage.

$$\text{efficiency} = \frac{W_{\text{out}}}{W_{\text{in}}} \times 100\% = \frac{F_r \times d_r}{F_e \times d_e} \times 100\%$$

Why must the efficiency of a machine always be less than 100 percent? Can you think of ways to increase the efficiency of a machine?

Many machines can be made more efficient by reducing friction. This is usually done by adding a lubricant, such as oil or grease, to surfaces that rub together, as shown in **Figure 7-17**. After a time, dirt will build up on the grease or oil, and the lubricant will lose its effectiveness. The dirty lubricant should be wiped off and replaced with clean grease or oil. What other ways can increase the efficiency of a machine?

USING MATH

Calculating Efficiency

Example Problem:

A sofa weighing 1500 N must be placed in a truck bed 1.0 m off the ground. A worker uses a force of 500 N to push the sofa up an inclined plane that has a slope length of 4.0 m. What is the efficiency of the inclined plane?

Problem-Solving Steps:

1. What is known?

   resistance force, F_r = 1500 N
   effort force, F_e = 500 N
   resistance distance, d_r = 1.0 m
   effort distance, d_e = 4.0 m

2. What is unknown?   efficiency

3. Choose the equation. $\text{efficiency} = \dfrac{F_r \times d_r}{F_e \times d_e} \times 100\%$

4. **Solution:** $\text{efficiency} = \dfrac{1500 \text{ N} \times 1.0 \text{ m}}{500 \text{ N} \times 4.0 \text{ m}} \times 100\% = 75\%$

 Calculator Hint: Combine all math into one calculator operation. Enter:
1500 × 1.0 ÷ 500 ÷ 4.0 × 100 = and your calculator will read **75.**

Power

Suppose you and a friend are pushing boxes of books up a ramp to load them into a truck. The boxes weigh the same, but your friend is able to push a box a little faster than you can. Your friend moves a box up the ramp in 30 seconds. It takes you 45 seconds. Do you both do the same amount of work on the books? Yes. This is true because the boxes weighed the same and were moved the same distance. The only difference is in the time it takes you and your friend to do the work.

Figure 7-17

Oiling machines reduces friction and makes them operate more efficiently. Dirty oil should be replaced periodically with clean oil.

MiniLAB

Can you measure the power of a toy car?

Procedure
1. Wind up a toy car and place it at the bottom of an inclined plane.
2. Experiment to adjust the angle of the inclined plane (using books to stack under a board) so the car will reach the top at the slowest speed possible.
3. Measure the time in seconds for the car to travel to the top of the plane.
4. Measure the weight of the car in newtons using a spring scale.
5. Measure the height of the inclined plane in meters. Be sure to measure from the floor or the tabletop straight up to the top of the inclined plane.

Analysis
1. Use weight and height (as force and distance) to calculate the work done in joules.
2. What is the power of your toy car? Divide your work in joules by the time in seconds to get power in watts.
3. What could you do to increase the power of the car as it travels up the same inclined plane?

Nanomachines ▽ △

Can you imagine tiny machines one-thousandth the diameter of a human hair? A new branch of science—called nanotechnology—is aimed at producing chemical clusters of less than 50 atoms, electronic components, and even machines or robots by constructing them molecule by molecule. These will be measured in nanometers, a unit representing one-billionth of a meter.

Scientists have already succeeded at building switches out of single atoms and constructing clusters of small numbers of atoms or molecules. This is made possible by the scanning tunneling microscope, which allows individual atoms to be manipulated. This technology is being used in efforts to develop nanomachines.

Nanomachines may be engineered that could be injected into the body to clean out arteries or clean up hazardous materials in the environment. The potential benefits could drastically change industry.

Think Critically:

What are some of the problems currently encountered by mechanical engineers that would likely be helped by constructing machines at the micro or nano level?

Your friend has more power than you have. **Power** is the rate at which work is done. In other words, power is a measure of the amount of work done in a certain amount of time. To calculate power, divide the work done by the time required to do the work.

$$\text{power} = \frac{\text{work}}{\text{time}}$$

$$P = \frac{W}{t}$$

Power is measured in watts, named for James Watt, who worked on the steam engine. A watt (W) is one joule per second. A watt is pretty small—about equal to the power used to raise a glass of water from your knees to your mouth in one second. Because the watt is such a small unit, large amounts of power often are expressed in kilowatts. One kilowatt (kW) equals 1000 watts.

The power ratings for appliances are listed in watts. Power ratings can be used to compare the rate at which machines do work. Where the same amount of work

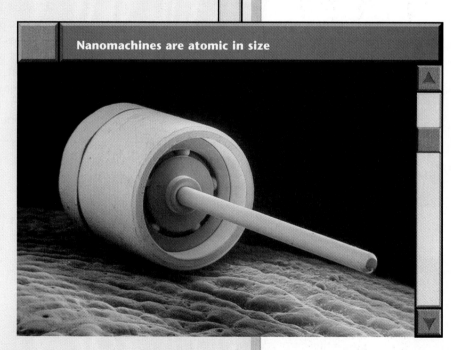
Nanomachines are atomic in size

is done at different rates, different amounts of power are required. Study the Example Problem below to see how work and power are related.

USING MATH

Calculating Power

Example Problem:

A figure skater lifts his partner, who weighs 450 N, 1.0 m in 3.0 s. How much power is required?

Problem-Solving Steps:

1. What is known?   force, F = 450 N
                     distance, d = 1.0 m
                     time, t = 3.0 s

2. What is unknown?   power, P

3. Choose the equation. $P = \dfrac{W}{t} = \dfrac{F \times d}{t}$

4. **Solution:**

$$P = \frac{450 \text{ N} \times 1.0 \text{ m}}{3.0 \text{ s}} = 150 \text{ W}$$

Section Wrap-up

Review

1. Give an example of a compound machine. What are the simple machines that make it up?

2. How are power, work, and time related?

3. **Think Critically:** You buy a secondhand lawn mower with an efficiency of 30 percent. By repairing and lubricating it, you increase its efficiency to 40 percent. How does this affect the work put out by the lawn mower for a given amount of work put in?

Skill Builder
Measuring in SI

A 500-N passenger is inside a 24 500-N elevator that rises 30 m in exactly 1 minute. How much power is needed for the elevator's trip? If you need help, refer to Measuring in SI in the **Skill Handbook.**

Science Journal

A pair of scissors is a compound machine. In your Science Journal, draw a diagram of a pair of scissors and label the simple machines you can identify. Explain the purpose of each simple machine in this device.

Building the Pyramids

The ancient Egyptians had to rely on simple machines for building the great pyramids. Somehow they managed to raise, and precisely place, huge building stones weighing as much as 50 tons. How they did it is still largely a mystery.

For many years, the accepted theory has been based on the use of the inclined plane in the form of ramps made of mud and stone.

Beginning with the Lever

Some historians have begun to believe that this theory is wrong. These historians believe that the primary machine was not the inclined plane, but the lever. According to this theory, instead of ramps, there were relatively narrow sets of long stone stairs built perpendicular to each face of the pyramid. Workers would use levers to raise each stone slowly from one level to the next.

Because they couldn't raise the gigantic stones all at once, they did it a little at a time. They'd lever one end up a small distance and slide a piece of wood underneath. Then they would do the same to the other end. Then they would raise the first side a little farther and place a second block of wood on top of the first, and so on until they could slide the stone onto the next level and start again.

This theory was first proposed by the Greek historian Herodotus in the fifth century B.C. While it's finding new popularity among some scholars, it remains controversial.

The truth is, we may never know for certain how the pyramids were built. But these giant monuments do prove that hard work can be accomplished with simple machines.

Science Journal

What if you had to lift something too heavy for you, without anybody around to help? In your Science Journal, write about how you would solve the problem, and what simple or compound machine(s) you would use.

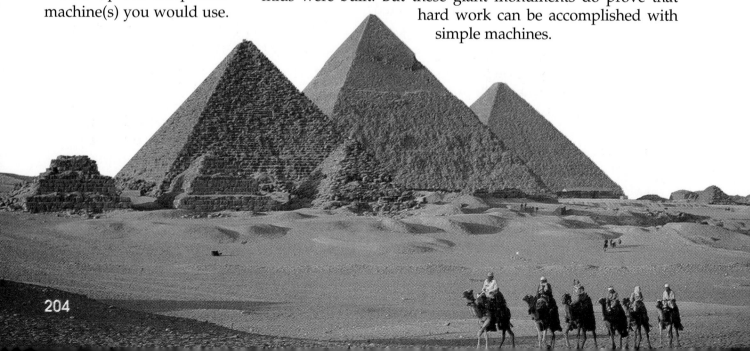

Chapter 7 Review

Summary

7-1: Why We Use Machines

1. A machine makes work easier by changing the size of the force applied to it, the direction of that force, or both.
2. The number of times a machine multiplies the force applied to it is the mechanical advantage of the machine.

7-2: The Simple Machines

1. A lever is a bar that is free to pivot about a fixed point called a fulcrum. A pulley is a grooved wheel with a rope running along the groove. A wheel and axle consists of two different-sized wheels that rotate together. An inclined plane is a sloping surface used to raise objects. The screw and the wedge are special types of inclined planes.
2. Each type of simple machine has a specific equation for calculating its ideal mechanical advantage. Each equation is related to the distance the effort force moves divided by the distance the resistance force moves.

7-3: Science and Society: Mending with Machines

1. The science of bionics is the creation of artificial replacements for parts of the body that are not functioning properly.
2. Electronic stimulation can be used to move paralyzed muscles or provide sensations for prosthetic limbs.

7-4: Using Machines

1. A combination of two or more simple machines is called a compound machine.
2. The efficiency of any machine is a ratio of the useful work put out by the machine to the work put into the machine.

3. Power is a measure of the amount of work done in a certain amount of time. The SI unit of power is the watt.

Key Science Words

a. bionics
b. compound machine
c. efficiency
d. effort arm
e. effort force
f. fulcrum
g. ideal machine
h. inclined plane
i. lever
j. machine
k. mechanical advantage
l. power
m. pulley
n. resistance arm
o. resistance force
p. screw
q. simple machine
r. wedge
s. wheel and axle

Reviewing Vocabulary

Match each phrase with the correct term from the list of Key Science Words.

1. any device that accomplishes work with only one movement
2. force applied by a machine
3. a device in which work output equals work input
4. a bar that pivots about a fixed point
5. two different-sized wheels that rotate together
6. a combination of simple machines
7. the work output of a machine divided by the work input
8. the rate at which work is done
9. the fixed point of a lever
10. an inclined plane wrapped around a cylinder

Chapter 7 Review

Checking Concepts

Choose the word or phrase that completes the sentence or answers the question.

1. There are _____ types of simple machines.
   a. three   b. six   c. eight   d. ten
2. Which of these cannot be done by a machine?
   a. multiply force
   b. multiply energy
   c. change direction of a force
   d. work
3. In an ideal machine, the work input _____ work output.
   a. is equal to   c. is less than
   b. is greater than   d. is independent of
4. The _____ of a machine is the number of times it multiplies the effort force.
   a. efficiency   c. mechanical advantage
   b. power   d. resistance
5. To raise a resistance 4 m, the effort rope of a single fixed pulley must move _____.
   a. 2 m   b. 8 m   c. 1 m   d. 4 m
6. The ideal mechanical advantage of a pulley system in which five ropes support an object is _____.
   a. 2.5   b. 5   c. 10   d. 25
7. In a wheel and axle, the resistance force is usually exerted by the _____.
   a. axle   c. gear ratio
   b. larger wheel   d. pedals
8. The *IMA* of an inclined plane 8 m long and 2 m high is _____.
   a. 2   b. 4   c. 16   d. 8
9. As the efficiency of a machine increases, the _____ of the machine increases.
   a. work input   c. friction
   b. work output   d. *IMA*
10. The *IMA* of an inclined plane can be increased by _____.
    a. increasing the length
    b. increasing the height
    c. decreasing the length
    d. making its surface smoother

Understanding Concepts

Answer the following questions in your Science Journal using complete sentences.

11. Describe and give examples of three ways that a simple machine can make work easier.
12. If machines make work easier, explain why most machines actually increase the amount of work you do in accomplishing a task.
13. Distinguish between a single fixed pulley and a single movable pulley, and describe the advantages of using each. Compare each type of pulley to its corresponding class of lever.
14. Explain how sharpening a knife changes its *MA*.
15. The efficiency of an automobile is usually expressed in terms of gas mileage. How can changing the engine oil increase the gas mileage of the automobile?

Thinking Critically

16. A cyclist applies a force of 250 N to the pedals of a bicycle. If the rear wheel applies a force of 200 N to the road surface, what is the *MA* of the bicycle?
17. An adult and a small child get on a seesaw that has a movable fulcrum. When the fulcrum is in the middle, the child can't lift the adult. How should the fulcrum be moved so that the two can seesaw? Explain.
18. You have two screwdrivers. One is long with a thin handle, and the other is short with a fat handle. Which would you use to drive a screw into a board? Explain your choice.
19. Using a ramp 4 m long, workers apply an effort force of 1250 N to move a 2000-N crate onto a platform 2 m high. What is the efficiency of the ramp?
20. How much power does a person weighing 500 N need to climb a 3-m ladder in 5 seconds?

Developing Skills

If you need help, refer to the **Skill Handbook.**

21. **Sequencing:** Make an ordered list to show how some of the simple machines in a bicycle work to make the bicycle move. Start with the feet applying force to the pedals.

22. **Making and Using Graphs:** An ideal lever has a fixed effort arm length of 40 cm. Calculate the effort force needed to raise a 10-N object with these resistance arm lengths: 80 cm, 40 cm, 20 cm, and 10 cm. Construct a line graph relating these resistance arm lengths to effort force. Describe the relationship between these two variables.

23. **Interpreting Scientific Illustrations:** Study the diagram of a garden hoe and answer the questions.
    a. What type of machine does the diagram represent? (Be specific.)
    b. What does the longer, red arrow represent?
    c. What does point A represent?
    d. What is represented by segment AC? Segment AB?
    e. What is the *IMA* of this machine?
    f. How does this machine make work easier?

24. **Concept Mapping:** Complete the concept map for simple machines using the following terms: *inclined plane, lever, lever types, pulley, screw, wedge,* and *wheel and axle.*

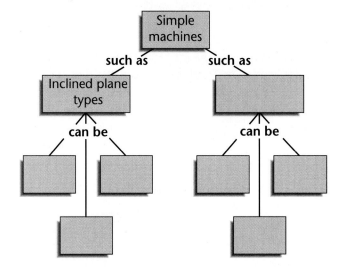

Performance Assessment

1. **Measuring in SI:** The SI unit of power, the watt, is a derived unit. Using the definition of *power*, develop the formula for calculating power and determine the fundamental SI units for expressing power.

2. **Designing an Experiment:** You measured the power of a toy car in the MiniLAB on page 201. Design a procedure to determine your own power as you walk up an incline. Conduct your experiment.

3. **Invention:** Design a human-powered machine of some kind. Describe the simple machines used in your design, and tell what each of these machines does.

Physics In Sports

In some sports, such as swimming and cross-country running, the winner of a competition is determined by who can move at the fastest average speed. Other sports, such as basketball, figure skating, and ultimate Frisbee, depend on accuracy, technique, and teamwork. You have learned that forces are used to control motion by changing the speed or the direction of an object's motion. These same forces are used to accelerate equipment or human bodies in sports.

Analyze a Sport

Select a sport or physical activity that your group would like to study. Choose a sport you can actually play or observe. Use direct observations and measurements to explore the dynamics, or the motion and forces, involved in this sport. Suggestions for sports are listed below.

* soccer
* swimming
* volleyball
* handball
* wrestling

* basketball
* biking
* gymnastics
* running
* football

* tennis
* softball
* baseball
* table tennis
* weightlifting

For the sport of your choice, research the following information.

1. What is the history of your sport? When and by whom was it invented? How much has it changed since it was invented?

2. Describe the objects in motion in your sport. Do people move around a lot? Do they move in straight lines or do they change directions? Is a ball or other object the focal point of the game?

3. What two things must be measured to determine the average speed of an object? Design a way to measure the average speed of a moving person or object in this sport, such as the speed of a served tennis ball. Try it! Describe how this speed is controlled by the athlete.

4. Review the definition of *work*. Try to identify and describe at least two examples of an action in which work is done in your sport. Remember, the force and the distance moved must be in the same direction. What information would you need to calculate the amount of work done?

5. Find at least one example of each of Newton's laws of motion in your sport. Describe each example as clearly as possible.

Using Your Research

After you have investigated the questions, design a presentation for the class about the physics of your sport. Your presentation should answer the questions you investigate. Use actual demonstrations of the sport as much as possible to help make your explanations clear. You might consider videotaping some motions involved in your sport if the sport itself cannot be easily demonstrated in the classroom. If possible, dress as a person would dress to participate in the sport.

Go Further

Each and every movement in each and every sport contains a great deal of physics. Make a poster that includes at least one diagram or picture of a specific action. Show an analysis of all forces and motion existing in this action by pointing to specific parts of the body or equipment that are in use. Consider the role friction plays in your sport. In what circumstances is friction desirable? Undesirable? Using your understanding of the physics involved, describe several specific things that an athlete could use to improve performance in this sport.

UNIT

3

Unit Contents

The Nature of Matter

What's Happening Here?

The interior of a chambered nautilus shell shows how nature uses a pattern to create a useful and beautiful design. You make use of patterns when sorting and organizing things. When sorting coins, you don't have to look at every one, because their properties enable you to feel the differences among them. Atoms also have properties that allow you to predict what they will do. Organizing atoms and the matter that they make up may not be as simple as sorting coins, but the patterns and properties discussed in the next four chapters will help you sort out many of the things you see in nature.

Science Journal

For many years scientists have believed in the existence of atoms. Only in the last few years, however, have their distinctive patterns become visible. Write in your Science Journal about how the scanning tunneling microscope helps scientists to see atoms. Include a drawing if possible.

Previewing the Chapter

Solids, Liquids, and Gases

You have likely had the experience of eating a rapidly melting ice cream cone. When changing from solid to liquid, all substances absorb energy. The large photo shows liquid ingredients being poured into an ice-cream maker. How does energy play a role in this process? What is the purpose of the ice? You will find the answers to these questions in this chapter as you study the states of matter and ways to change from one state to another.

EXPLORE ACTIVITY

Observe what happens during a change of state.

1. Obtain a small scented candle and place it on a flat, non-flammable surface. In your Science Journal, list the properties of the candle that allow you to classify it as a solid.
2. Under your teacher's direction, light the candle. List observations about changes the candle undergoes. **CAUTION:** *Keep hair and clothing away from the open flame.*
3. As the candle burns, what observations can you make about the three states of matter—solid, liquid, and gas?

Observe: In your Science Journal, describe what role energy played in bringing about the changes of state in the matter making up the candle.

Previewing Science Skills

▶ In the Skill Builders, you will **make and use a table, map concepts, hypothesize,** and **measure in SI.**

▶ In the Activities, you will **observe, organize** and **collect data, infer, communicate, measure,** and **classify.**

▶ In the MiniLABs, you will **observe** and **hypothesize.**

8•1 Matter and Temperature

Science Words

states of matter
kinetic theory of matter
crystal
plasma
thermal expansion

Objectives

- Describe the four states of matter.
- Use the kinetic theory of matter to explain the characteristics of solids, liquids, and gases.
- Explain the thermal expansion of matter.

States of Matter

After swimming on a hot day, Eli was having a refreshing glass of ice water. As he rested by the pool, the water on his arm evaporated and the ice cubes melted in his glass. In how many different forms does water exist in this example? Ice, liquid water, and water vapor are examples of the three most familiar states of matter—solid, liquid, and gas. **Figure 8-1** shows water as it can be found in nature.

All matter takes up space and has mass, yet matter can exist in different states. There are four **states of matter**—solid, liquid, gas, and plasma. The state of a sample of matter depends on its temperature. For example, water ordinarily exists as ice at low temperatures and as liquid water at moderate temperatures. At higher temperatures, water changes to the gas state as water vapor. At still higher temperatures, the matter in water becomes plasma. Each state has characteristics that are used to identify it, as you'll see.

Figure 8-1

Water can exist in nature as a solid, a liquid, or a gas. *What states do you see in this photo?*

Solids

A metal spoon, a cube of sugar, and a piece of cement are classified as solids. Every solid has a definite shape and a definite volume. For example, a metal spoon stays spoon-shaped whether it's in your hand or in a glass of water. And, because no ordinary amount of force can squeeze the spoon into a smaller space, it has a definite volume.

Figure 8-2

Although the particles in a solid, such as this crystal of table salt, vibrate, they do not move out of position. *What other kitchen solid can you think of that has crystals you can see?*

— Chlorine

— Sodium

What accounts for the characteristics of solids? Tiny particles in constant motion make up all matter. This idea is called the **kinetic theory of matter.** The particles in solid matter are held close together by forces between them. This is why a solid can't be squeezed into a smaller space. The particles can vibrate close to their neighbors, but they lack enough energy to move out of position. Thus, they lack enough energy to move over or around each other. This explains why a solid holds its shape.

Crystalline Solids

In most solids, the particles are arranged in repeating geometric patterns. These arrangements are **crystals.** Different kinds of solids have crystals of different shapes. In the magnified view of **Figure 8-2,** you can see that crystals of table salt are little cubes. A snowflake is a crystal of water that has the shape of a hexagon.

Noncrystalline Solids

Some materials, such as glass, many plastics, and some kinds of wax, appear to be solids but are not made of crystals. They are often called amorphous solids. The word *amorphous* means "having no form." Many scientists think some of these noncrystalline materials should be classified as thick liquids.

USING MATH

A hexagon is a six-sided figure that occurs in ice crystals and honeycombs. It is an efficient shape that *tessellates* a surface; that is, it covers the surface with no overlapping or gaps. Name another shape that tessellates a surface. What shape that you see in the salt crystals will also tessellate a surface?

Liquids

If you don't eat it quickly enough, a solid scoop of ice cream will turn into a liquid, taking the same shape as your bowl or cup. A liquid flows and takes the shape of its container. However, like solids, liquids can't normally be squeezed to a smaller volume. If you push down on a liter of water with a moderate amount of force, its volume remains a liter.

Figure 8-3

The particles in a liquid are close together, but they have enough energy to move over and around one another.

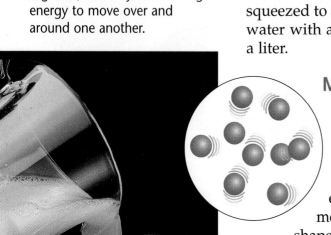

More Motion

Just as the kinetic theory explains the properties of solids, it also explains the properties of liquids. Because a liquid can't be squeezed, its particles must also be close together, like those of a solid. However, they have enough kinetic energy to move over and around each other. This movement of particles lets a liquid flow and take the shape of its container. Thus, the orange juice poured into a glass in **Figure 8-3** will take the shape of the glass.

Because its particles are held close together, almost as close as those of a solid, liquid matter does have a definite volume. If you pour 1 L of orange juice into a 2-L bottle, it will not spread out to fill the bottle. Likewise, you couldn't force the liter of juice into a half-liter container. The two containers in **Figure 8-4** contain the same volume of liquid.

Science Journal

In your Science Journal, explain how the motion of particles changes when matter changes from one state to another.

Figure 8-4

Although its volume does not change, the shape of a liquid depends on the shape of its container.

Gases

You may have pumped air into a basketball, tire, or balloon and noticed that the air takes the shape of the object. Gases are "springy"—they expand or contract to fill the space available to them and can be squeezed into a smaller space. A gas has neither a definite shape nor a definite volume.

According to the kinetic theory of matter, the particles of a gas have enough energy to separate completely from one another. Therefore, the particles are free to move in all directions until they have spread evenly throughout their container. **Figure 8-5** shows a test for a gas that has filled a room as its particles spread. Because the particles of a gas are not close together, they can also be squeezed into a smaller space. When you pump up a bicycle tire, you are forcing more and more air particles into the same space.

Figure 8-6 explains the relationship between particles and energy in a solid, in a liquid, and in a gas.

Figure 8-5

This test disk is used to detect released carbon monoxide in all parts of a building. *Why would a detector be effective even if it were not right next to the gas leak?*

Figure 8-6

The energy of particles is different for each state of matter.

Gas	Liquid	Solid

A In gas samples, the particles have enough energy to overcome attractive forces that would hold them together.

B The particles composing a liquid don't have enough energy to overcome all attractive forces, but they do have enough energy to move around each other.

C Solids are made up of particles that do not have enough energy to move from one place to another. *How does that affect the shape of a solid?*

CONNECT TO

LIFE SCIENCE

The word *plasma* is from a Greek word that means "something that can be formed or molded." In your Science Journal, *compare and contrast* the term *plasma* as it is used in life science to the way it is used in physical science.

Plasma

So far, you've learned about the three familiar states of matter. But none of these is the most common state of matter in the universe. For example, 99 percent of the mass of our solar system is contained in the sun. The most common form of matter in the universe is the type found in stars like the sun and the nebula shown in **Figure 8-7.** Such matter is called plasma.

Plasma is a gaslike mixture of positively and negatively charged particles. You know that particles of matter move faster as the matter is heated to higher temperatures. The faster they move, the greater the force with which they bump into other particles, or collide. As matter is heated to very high temperatures, the particles begin to collide violently. As a result, the particles break up into the smaller particles they are made of. These particles are electrically charged.

Besides light from the sun, you can observe the effects of plasma in your home or school. When a fluorescent light is switched on, electricity causes particles of mercury gas inside the tube to form plasma.

Figure 8-7

These photos show examples of matter in the plasma state.

A The sun

B The Eta Carinae Nebula

Thermal Expansion

You have learned how the kinetic theory accounts for characteristics of different states of matter you see and touch every day. The kinetic theory also explains other things you may have observed. For example, have you ever noticed the strips of metal that run across the floors and up the walls in long hallways of concrete and steel buildings? Maybe you've seen these strips in your school. These strips usually cover gaps in the building structure called expansion joints. Expansion joints allow the building to expand in hot weather and shrink in cold weather without cracking the concrete. As you drive onto or off a bridge, you will usually pass over a large steel expansion joint.

The Heat and Motion Connection

Almost all matter expands as it gets hotter and contracts when it cools. This characteristic of matter is called **thermal expansion.** You can compare thermal expansion to a crowd of people. When the people are quiet and still, they are able to stand close

Problem Solving

Mind over Matter

Martin, Rita, and L.J. were working on fixing up an old car and they needed some nuts and bolts to make their repairs. L.J. found a jar of assorted nuts and bolts in the garage, but they had trouble removing the metal lid. After struggling for a few minutes, Rita suggested that running hot water over the metal lid might make it easier to open.

Solve the Problem:

1. **Think about the effect of energy on the motion of particles. How would you describe the effect of heat energy on the metal?**
2. **After the hot-water treatment, the jar easily opened. Why did this work better than just forcing the lid off the jar?**

Think Critically:

Sealing containers is important in preserving freshness and preventing spoilage. Explain two reasons why a food container that was closed when it was warm might become tight as it cooled.

together. As the people become restless, they jostle one another and the crowd spreads out.

How does the kinetic theory of matter explain thermal expansion? In a solid, forces between the particles hold them together. As the solid is heated, these particles move faster and faster and vibrate against each other with more force. As a result, the particles spread apart slightly in all directions, and the solid expands. This explains why expansion joints are needed in buildings and on bridges. The same effect also occurs in liquids and gases. A common example of this is shown in the thermometers in **Figure 8-8.**

As the liquid in a bulb is heated, the energy causes more movement of the particles. This energy is transferred to other parts of the liquid. The liquid in the narrow part has to expand only slightly to show a large change on the temperature scale.

Figure 8-8

An important example of thermal expansion is found when liquid that is heated, even slightly, expands and moves up through a narrow tube in a thermometer.

Section Wrap-up

Review

1. Compare the characteristics of solids and liquids.

2. You pour 500 mL of a green material into a 1-L flask and stopper it. The material completely fills the flask. What state of matter is the material? Explain how you know.

3. In terms of particle motion, explain why copper shrinks when it cools.

4. **Think Critically:** In old houses, the window glass is thicker at the bottom of the panes than at the top. What accounts for this thickening?

Skill Builder
Making and Using Tables
Make a table to classify several materials as a solid, liquid, gas, or plasma. Include columns for properties and a description of particles for each state. If you need help, refer to Making and Using Tables in the **Skill Handbook.**

USING MATH

The density of a sample of water vapor is 0.0031 g/mL. The density of a second sample of liquid water is 1.0 g/mL. How many times more dense is the liquid than the vapor? How does this relate to the spacing of the water molecules?

Activity 8-1

Properties of Liquids

Why is a soft drink considered a liquid? Why is a hamburger considered a solid? Each state of matter has its own characteristics that allow us to classify it as that state.

Problem
How can the properties of a material be used to classify it as a solid, a liquid, or a gas?

Materials
- dropper
- food coloring
- wooden stick
- graduated cylinder
- 4% solution of powdered borax in water
- 4% solution of polyvinyl alcohol (PVA) in water
- paper cup
- goggles
- apron

Procedure
1. Copy the data table and use it to record your observations.
2. Using a graduated cylinder, measure 30 mL of PVA solution into a paper cup. Add 2 drops of food coloring.
3. Using a dropper, add about 3 mL of borax solution to the PVA in the cup, and begin to stir vigorously with a wooden stick.
4. After it has been stirred for 2 minutes, what is the consistency of the material?
5. Transfer the material to your hand. **CAUTION:** *Do not taste or eat the material, and be sure to wash your hands after the activity.* Rate the ease with which the material flows.
6. Form the material into a ball and then place it in the cup to test its ability to take the shape of its container.
7. Compare the volume of the new material with the volume of the original material before stirring.

Analyze
1. Is the new material most like a gas, a liquid, or a solid?
2. What other materials have you seen that have similar properties to this one?
3. Considering the flow of the new material, how would you rate the strength of the attraction among its particles?

Conclude and Apply
4. Using the kinetic theory of matter, describe the closeness of the particles of matter in the new material.
5. How can properties of this material be used to **classify** it?

Data and Observations

Property	Observation	Interpretation
Ability to flow		
Shape change		
Volume change		

ISSUE:

8•2 Fresh Water—Will there be enough?

Science Words

polluted water
thermal pollution

Objectives

- Describe how people use and pollute water.
- Discuss how people can save water and stop pollution.

Fresh Water

For living things, like yourself, the most important liquid on Earth is fresh water. It is not as abundant as you might think. Fresh water, which is water that is not salty, makes up only 0.75 percent of the water available on Earth in the liquid state.

How much water do you think you use in a day? Take a guess. Did you say 1700 gallons? For the average person in the United States, that's the correct answer! Each person uses about 200 gallons a day for cooking, bathing, toilet use, and heating and cooling homes. Add to this the 750 gallons per person a day used to produce materials and energy, and another 750 gallons per person a day used to water crops. **Table 8-1** lists only a few ways you use water.

Water Pollution

Not only do humans use huge amounts of fresh water, humans also pollute their natural supplies of this liquid. **Polluted water** refers to water that contains such high levels of unwanted materials that it is unacceptable for drinking or other specific purposes. Sometimes, the pollution is visible, as in **Figure 8-9.**

Water that runs off land after rain falls and snow melts may wash animal and plant wastes into our water supplies. Human activities in cities may contaminate rivers with raw sewage. Fertilizers, pesticides, and herbicides used on farms

Table 8-1

Ways Water Is Used			
Estimated Gallons of Water Used to:			
Make 1 gallon of milk	5	Produce 1 gallon of gasoline	10
Brush teeth with water running	1-2	Do one load of laundry	32-59
Flush a toilet	5-7	Burn a 100-watt lightbulb for	
Shower for 1 minute	3-5	10 hours	80
Make enough steel for a table knife	6	Wash a car at home with	
Wash car at self-service car wash	5-10	a hose	up to 150

may enter the groundwater. Toxic chemicals from home use may end up in our water supply if they are not disposed of properly.

Another form of water pollution can occur when electrical generating plants or industries release large amounts of heated water into rivers. The excess heat in the water is called **thermal pollution.** If water temperature is changed too much, some organisms that live in the water will die.

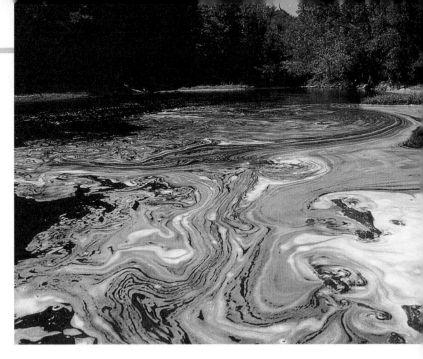

Figure 8-9

Many sources are possible for this pollution.

Points of View

Regulating Pollution

Scientists are trying to develop better ways to contain and dispose of industrial and farming by-products to reduce water pollution. Congress also passes laws governing the release of and the levels of various materials in water supplies.

Cost of Regulation

New methods for stricter control of industrial and farming by-products disposal will raise costs of these processes. Improving water-treatment facilities will also increase our costs for fresh water.

Section Wrap-up

Review

1. What are two main reasons that there could be a shortage of clean water?

2. List five sources of water pollution.

Explore the Issue

Are the benefits of regulation worth the costs? What problems are likely to happen if costs of industrial and farming by-product disposal become more expensive? What problems are likely if we don't regulate what is allowed in our fresh water?

MiniLAB

Can dissolved chemicals be filtered out of a solution?

Procedure
1. Test 50 mL of water with litmus paper.
2. Add 50 mL of vinegar to the water.
3. Test with litmus paper.
4. Pour solution through filter paper, and retest with litmus paper.

Analysis
1. Was there any visible residue on the filter?
2. Did the filter remove the acid?
3. What other method could you try to make the water pure?

SCIENCE & SOCIETY

8•3 Changes in State

Science Words

evaporation
condensation
heat of fusion
heat of vaporization

Objectives

- Interpret state changes in terms of the kinetic theory of matter.
- Account for the energy of the heats of fusion and vaporization in state changes.

Identifying Changes in State

If you've ever seen ice cream melt before you could eat it, you have seen matter change state. Solid ice crystals in the ice cream melt when they change from the solid state to the liquid state. When melting, a solid changes into a liquid. You put water in the freezer to make ice cubes. When freezing, matter changes from the liquid state to the solid state.

When you boil water, you observe another change of state, called vaporization. When boiling, you add heat to a liquid until it reaches a temperature at which it changes to bubbles of gas below its surface. Many liquids don't need to boil to change to a gas. During **evaporation,** a liquid changes to a gas gradually at temperatures below the boiling point. When you come out of a pool into warm air, water on your skin soon evaporates. You'll see later how this drying helps cool you. In **Figure 8-10,** evaporation helped dry, or solidify, the concrete.

Figure 8-10

Freshly poured concrete includes liquid water spread into a thin layer over a large surface area. As the water particles gain energy, they can overcome attractions to other particles and evaporate, leaving behind a dry, solid surface.

Figure 8-11

Condensation appears on many
surfaces.

A The dew on this car is
condensed water.

B *Why does water condense
on a mirror after a shower?*

Have you noticed that ice cubes seem to shrink when
they've been in the freezer for a long time? This shrinkage
happens because of another change of state called sublimation. In sublimation, a solid changes directly to a gas without
going through the liquid state.

You see another change of state when your glass of ice-cold
soft drink "sweats." The drops of water on your glass appear
when gaseous water condenses on the cold surface.

Condensation takes place when a gas changes to a liquid.
Generally, a gas will condense when cooled to or below its
boiling point. Two examples of this are seen in **Figure 8-11.**

MiniLAB

**Can you detect energy
changes during evap-
oration?**

Procedure
1. Use a dropper to place
   5 drops of rubbing alcohol
   on the back of your hand.
2. Wait for 2 minutes.

Analysis
1. During the 2 minutes, what
   sensation involving energy
   did you notice?
2. What changes in appearance of the rubbing alcohol
   did you notice?
3. In your Science Journal,
   explain how you know
   that evaporation requires
   an input of energy.
4. From where did that energy
   input come in this example?

Heat and State Changes

The kinetic theory of matter explains changes of state. The amount of energy needed to change a material from the solid state to the liquid state is the **heat of fusion.** For water, the heat of fusion is 334 kJ/kg. The amount of energy needed to change a material from a liquid to a gas is the **heat of vaporization.** For water, this value is 2260 kJ/kg. **Figure 8-12** details the energy changes involved in state changes.

Figure 8-12

In this example, watch how temperature, energy supplied, and the motion of particles are related.

A As a sample of ice is warmed and the temperature is measured every 30 seconds, the particles of solid water absorb the applied heat energy. *What effect does this energy have on the motion of the particles?*

B As heat energy continues to be supplied, you may notice that the solid water now begins to appear as a liquid, but the temperature is not rising. To change a solid to a liquid, many forces must be overcome. For each kilogram of ice you want to melt, 334 kJ must be supplied.

C Once the work of melting is accomplished, the applied heat energy causes the water particles making up the liquid to move faster. As you can see on the graph, the temperature begins to rise.

D Once the boiling point has been reached, the liquid becomes a gas, and the temperature again remains constant. At the heat of vaporization, the forces of attraction between particles are totally overcome. This requires 2260 kJ of energy. *Why do you think this value is so much higher than the heat of fusion?*

Look at **Figure 8-13.** You can also use the kinetic theory to explain how water evaporates from your skin and how it cools you. When a liquid evaporates, the particles do not all have the same kinetic energy. Many fast-moving particles break away from the liquid and become a gas. As these fast-moving water particles leave, the average kinetic energy of the remaining particles becomes less. As a result, the temperature of the remaining water goes down. Because the water is now cooler than your skin, it takes heat from your skin and cools you.

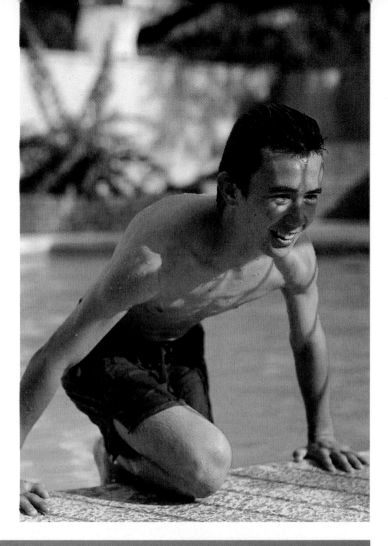

Figure 8-13

The water spread over your skin after swimming absorbs energy from your body and the air and evaporates. *How does the temperature of the air affect the speed of evaporation?*

Section Wrap-up

Review

1. Name and describe the state changes in which solids and liquids become gases.

2. Use the kinetic theory to explain melting.

3. What happens to the energy put into a liquid during boiling?

4. **Think Critically:** Steam must lose its heat of vaporization in order to condense. How does this fact help explain why steam can cause more severe skin burns than liquid water at its boiling point?

Skill Builder

Sequencing

Sequence the processes that occur when ice is heated until it becomes steam and then the steam is cooled until it is ice again. If you need help, refer to Sequencing in the **Skill Handbook.**

Science Journal

A glass of water and a puddle of water, both containing the same volume of water at the same temperature, are left to evaporate. Which do you think will evaporate sooner? In your Science Journal, write and explain your answer.

8•4 Behavior of Gases

Science Words

pressure
pascal
Boyle's law
Charles's law

Objectives

- Explain how a gas exerts pressure on its container.
- State and explain how the pressure of a container of gas is affected when the volume is changed.
- Explain the relationship between the temperature and volume of a gas.

Pressure

Every time you feel the wind on your face, you observe the behavior of a gas—rather, the mixture of gases that is Earth's air, or atmosphere. Even when the wind is calm, the air exerts a force called pressure.

What causes the pressure of a gas? Particles of matter are small—many billions of particles of air fill an inflated toy balloon. When riding on a bike, you're riding on pockets of colliding air particles inside your tires. You have learned that the particles of air, like those in all gases, are constantly moving. They're free to fly about and collide with anything in their way. The collisions with the inside walls keep the balloons or tires inflated and cause the force that you feel when you squeeze them. The motion of the particles in air is illustrated in **Figure 8-14.**

The total amount of force exerted by a gas depends on the size of its container. **Pressure** is the amount of force exerted per unit of area.

$$P = \frac{F}{A}$$

Measuring Pressure

The **pascal** (Pa) is the SI unit of pressure. One pascal of pressure is a force of one newton per square meter. This is a small pressure unit, so most pressures are given in kilopascals (kPa).

Earth's atmosphere exerts pressure on everything within it. At sea level, atmospheric pressure is 101.3 kPa. This means that at Earth's surface, the atmosphere exerts a force of about 100 000 N on every square meter. This amount of force is equal to a weight of 100 000 N—about the weight of a large truck.

Figure 8-14

The force of particles of air in constant motion colliding with the inside walls of the tire keeps a tire inflated.

Our Atmosphere—A Sea of Air

You can see right through it, and most of the time you can't even feel it. But the air we breathe and live in contains many gas particles that cause the air pressure you have just been reading about. The atmosphere closest to Earth's surface, up to approximately 16 to 17 km, is called the troposphere. In the troposphere, you come into direct contact with nitrogen, oxygen, argon, carbon dioxide, and water vapor. These particles are moving incredibly fast, approaching 1610 km per hour. At these speeds, one particle may collide with another, or you, as often as every billionth of a second. Millions of fast-moving, colliding particles create air pressure in every square meter of the troposphere.

Higher Altitudes Mean Less Pressure

Above the troposphere, there are fewer gas particles and fewer collisions, which means less pressure. The stratosphere continues to about 50 km above Earth's surface. At higher distances, the mesosphere and thermosphere continue. If the air pressure is measured at 5 km above Earth, the pressure will have dropped from 101 kPa at Earth's surface to approximately 54 kPa. At 50 km, the pressure may be only 0.15 kPa. An example of the effect of altitude on pressure is shown in **Figure 8-15.**

Boyle's Law

Suppose you have some gas in a sealed flexible container, such as a balloon. You can squeeze or stretch the container without changing the amount of gas trapped inside.

The pressure of a gas depends on how often its particles strike the walls of the container. If you squeeze some gas into a smaller space, its particles will strike the walls more often, giving an increased pressure. This behavior explains why when you squeeze a balloon into a smaller space, it causes the balloon to push back with more force. The reverse happens, too. If you give the gas particles more space, they will hit the walls less often and the gas pressure will be reduced. Robert Boyle (1627-1691), a British scientist, described this property of gases. According to **Boyle's law,** if you decrease the volume of a container of gas, the pressure of the gas will increase, provided the temperature does not change. Increasing the volume causes pressure to drop. As you'll see, it is important that the temperature remains constant.

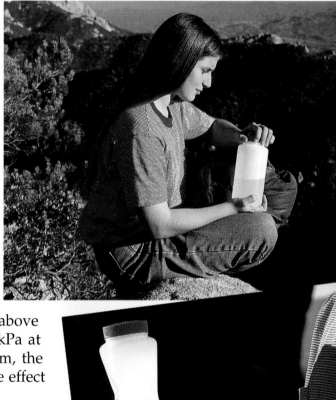

Figure 8-15

At lower altitudes (bottom), air pressure increases. The air trapped inside the bottle during a high-altitude biking trip (top) exerts less pressure than the air back home. *Why does the bottle have less volume in the bottom photo?*

Gaseous Giants

Imagine a balloon so immense that, when fully inflated, it will hold a volume of gas equivalent to 168 Goodyear blimps! Scientists are sending such balloons into the stratosphere, the layer of the atmosphere that is above 99 percent of Earth's air. These giant balloons are filled with helium gas, which gives them their lift. One of these balloons may hoist a load higher than a cruising jumbo jet, but lower than an orbiting satellite in space. The initial volume of helium required to lift the load might be the size of a small house. In the stratosphere, the volume may reach the size of 283 of the houses!

Scientists use the balloons for research. For example, a load of sensing equipment may gather data on how ozone gas is formed in the upper atmosphere. Ozone helps protect life by absorbing a dangerous form of energy given off by the sun. Because the sky is clear in the stratosphere, another load may be a telescope for studying the energy given off by the sun and other stars. Such studies help scientists understand the makeup and behavior of matter.

Think Critically:
Using the kinetic theory and Boyle's law, explain why the balloon gets so much larger as it rises through the atmosphere.

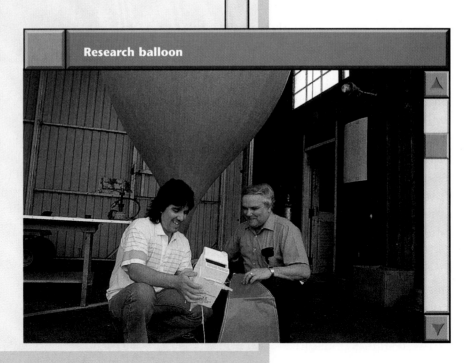

Research balloon

Charles's Law

If you've seen a hot-air balloon being inflated, you know gases expand when heated. Jacques Charles (1742-1823) was a French scientist who studied gases. According to **Charles's law,** the volume of a gas increases with increasing temperature, provided the pressure does not change. As with Boyle's law, the reverse is true, also. The volume of a gas shrinks with decreasing temperature. **Figure 8-16** demonstrates Charles's law.

Using his law, Charles was able to calculate the temperature at which a gas would have a volume of zero. The kinetic theory would say that this is the temperature at which all particle motion of matter should stop. Charles found this temperature to be –273°C, or 0 K, also called absolute zero. In reality, gases cannot be cooled to zero volume. Instead, they condense to liquids when cooled below their boiling points.

Figure 8-16

Hot-air balloonists use Charles's law with every launch. As the temperature of the trapped air is increased, the volume of the balloon also increases.

You can explain Charles's law by using the kinetic theory of matter. As a gas is heated, its particles move faster and faster and its temperature increases. Because the gas particles move faster, they begin to strike the walls of their container more often and with more force. If the walls are free to move, the gas pushes the walls out and expands.

Section Wrap-up

Review

1. When you bounce a basketball on the floor, the air pressure inside the ball increases for a moment. Explain why this increase occurs.

2. Why does a closed, empty, 2-L, plastic soft-drink bottle cave in when placed in a freezer?

3. **Think Critically:** Labels on cylinders of compressed gases state the highest temperature to which the cylinder may be exposed. Give a reason for this warning.

Skill Builder

Hypothesizing

A bottle of ammonia begins to leak. An hour later, you can smell ammonia almost everywhere, especially near the bottle. State a hypothesis to explain your observations. If you need help, refer to Hypothesizing in the **Skill Handbook.**

> **Using Computers**
>
> **Spreadsheet** Once you have completed Activity 8-2 on pages 232 and 233, use the temperature and volume in a spreadsheet. Generate a graph from the spreadsheet data.

Design Your Own Experiment
More Than Just Hot Air

The rapidly moving, small particles in a sample of a gas, such as air, respond easily to changes in temperature. In this activity, you will investigate the nature of that response. Does the volume expand or contract when the temperature of a gas is raised? Can you find a regular pattern when you examine several measurements?

PREPARATION

Problem
How does changing the temperature of a gas sample change its volume?

Form a Hypothesis
State your hypothesis about how the volume of a gas changes when its temperature changes.

Objectives
- Observe the changes in the volume of a gas as the temperature of the gas is changed.
- Design an experiment that tests the effects of changing temperature on the volume of a gas in a balloon.

Possible Materials
- string
- marking pen
- meterstick
- bucket of ice
- tongs
- heat-proof gloves
- beaker of boiling water
- thermometer
- safety goggles
- 2 medium, round balloons
- hot plate

Safety Precautions

Wear goggles and use heat-proof gloves or tongs to handle the balloons near heated air or steam.

PLAN THE EXPERIMENT

1. As a group, agree upon and write out your hypothesis statement.
2. As a group, list the steps that you need to take to test your hypothesis. Be specific, describing exactly how you will treat the balloon with various temperatures and how long you will use each treatment.
3. Make a list of the materials that you will need to complete your experiment.
4. Before you begin, make a table to record your data in your Science Journal.

Check the Plan

1. Read over your entire experiment to make sure that all steps are in logical order. Identify how and when you will check temperatures and changes in the size of the balloon.

2. Identify any constants and the variables of the experiment.
3. Have you allowed for a control? How will the control be treated?
4. Do you have to run any tests more than one time?
5. Will the data be summarized in a graph?
6. *Make sure your teacher approves your plan and that you have included any changes in the plan.*

DO THE EXPERIMENT

1. Carry out the approved experiment as planned.
2. While the experiment is going on, write down any observations that you make and complete the data table in your Science Journal.

Analyze and Apply

1. **Compare** your volume and temperature results with those of other groups.

2. How did the balloon's volume change when temperature changed?
3. Use a line **graph** to display your results and those of other groups.
4. From the graph, what can you **conclude** about the relationship between temperature and gas volume?

Go Further

If you extended your graph line to "zero volume," what temperature value would you find?

8•5 Uses of Fluids

Science Words

buoyant force
Archimedes' principle
Pascal's principle
Bernoulli's principle
Venturi effect

Objectives

- State Archimedes' principle and predict whether an object will sink or float in water.
- State Pascal's principle and describe the operation of a machine that uses Pascal's principle.
- State Bernoulli's principle and describe a way that Bernoulli's principle is applied.

Archimedes' Principle

Have you ever relaxed by floating quietly on your back in a swimming pool? You seem weightless as the water supports you. If you climb slowly out of the pool, you feel as if you gain weight. The farther out you climb, the more you have to use your muscles to support yourself. When you were in the pool, you experienced buoyancy. Buoyancy is the ability of a fluid—a liquid or a gas—to exert an upward force on an object immersed in it. This force is called **buoyant force.**

The amount of buoyant force determines whether an object will sink or float in a fluid. If the buoyant force is less than the object's weight, the object will sink. If the buoyant force equals the object's weight, as in **Figure 8-17,** the object floats. Sometimes, the buoyant force on an object is greater than its weight. This force is what seems to pull a helium-filled balloon upward in the air. When the balloon is released, the unbalanced buoyant force causes the balloon to accelerate upward.

Figure 8-17

There are different forces acting on a person lying on the ground beside a pool and in water.

Steel ship hull

Weight

Buoyant force

Steel block

Weight

Buoyant force

Weight

Wood block

Buoyant force

Figure 8-18

Notice that the weight and buoyant forces balance for floating objects.
Which of these objects have balanced forces?

How do ships float?

Archimedes, a Greek mathematician who lived in the third century B.C., made a discovery about buoyancy. According to **Archimedes' principle,** the buoyant force on an object in a fluid is equal to the weight of the fluid displaced by the object. If you place a block of pine wood in water, it will push water out of the way as it begins to sink—but only until the weight of the water it displaces equals the block's weight. The block floats at this level, as shown in **Figure 8-18.**

Suppose you drop a solid steel block the same size as the wood block into water. When the steel block is placed into the water, the steel block begins to push aside water as it sinks. Buoyant force begins to push up on the block. However, the density of steel is much greater than that of wood. As a result, the buoyant force never becomes great enough to equal the weight of the steel block, and it sinks to the bottom.

How, then, does a steel ship float? Suppose you formed the steel block into a large, hollowed-out bowl shape. As this shape sinks into water, it displaces much more water than the solid block. Soon, it displaces enough water to equal the weight of the steel, and it floats.

Pascal's Principle

If you dive underwater, you can feel the pressure of the water all around you. You live at the bottom of Earth's atmosphere, which also is a fluid that exerts a pressure.

MiniLAB

How does applied pressure affect different areas of a fluid?

Procedure
1. Draw water into a small medicine dropper and place it into a 2-L, clear, soft-drink bottle that is filled to within 1 cm of the top.
2. Draw in or expel water from the dropper until it just barely floats.
3. Place the soft-drink bottle lid tightly back on the bottle.

Analysis
1. How does adding water inside the dropper affect its overall density?
2. When you squeeze the sides of the soft-drink bottle, what effect do you notice on the water level inside the dropper?
3. In your Science Journal, describe how Pascal's principle explains the movement of water inside the contained dropper.

Figure 8-19

The convenience of squeezable toothpaste is based on Pascal's principle.

CONNECT TO

PHYSICS

Applied pressure on a small piston can be transferred to a large piston. Hydraulic lifts based on this principle are used on rides in amusement parks. *Calculate* the pressure applied in each piston.

Area = 5 cm²   Area = 50 cm²
500 N   5000 N

Small piston

Large piston

This pressure is also all around you, even though you aren't aware of it. Blaise Pascal (1623-1662), a French scientist, discovered a useful property of fluids. **Pascal's principle** states that pressure applied to a fluid is transmitted unchanged throughout the fluid. For example, when you squeeze one end of a balloon, the balloon pops out on the other end. When you squeeze one end of a toothpaste tube, as in **Figure 8-19,** toothpaste emerges from the other end.

Applying the Principle

Hydraulic machines that move heavy loads use Pascal's principle. Maybe you've seen a car raised using a hydraulic lift. Look at the hydraulic machine to the left to see how a machine of this type works. A small cylinder and a large cylinder are connected by a pipe. The cross section of the small cylinder has an area of 5 cm². The cross section of the large cylinder is 50 cm². Each cylinder is filled with a hydraulic fluid, usually oil, and has a piston that rests on the oil's surface.

Suppose you apply 500 N of force to the small piston. The pressure on the small piston is expressed in this equation.

$$P = \frac{F}{A} = \frac{500 \text{ N}}{5 \text{ cm}^2} = \frac{100 \text{ N}}{\text{cm}^2}$$

Pascal's principle says that this pressure is transferred unchanged throughout the liquid. Therefore, the large piston will also have a pressure of 100 N/cm² applied to it. But the area of the large piston is 50 cm². So, the total force on the large piston is 100 N/cm² × 50 cm² = 5000 N. With this hydraulic machine, you could use your weight to lift something ten times as heavy as you are.

Bernoulli's Principle

It took humans thousands of years to learn to do what birds do naturally—fly, glide, and soar. Obviously, it was no simple task to build a machine that could lift itself off the ground and fly with people aboard. The ability of an airplane to rise into the air is an example of another property of fluids stated in Bernoulli's principle. Daniel Bernoulli (1700-1782) was a Swiss scientist who studied the properties of moving fluids such as water and air. He published his discovery in 1738. According to **Bernoulli's principle,** as the velocity of a fluid increases, the pressure exerted by the fluid decreases.

Figure 8-20 shows Bernoulli's principle at work. Another way to demonstrate Bernoulli's principle is to blow across the surface of a sheet of paper. The paper will rise. The velocity of the air you blew over the top surface of the paper is greater than that of the quiet air below it. As a result, the downward air pressure above the paper decreases. The higher air pressure below the paper exerts a net force that pushes the paper upward.

Figure 8-20

Blowing between two empty aluminum cans can cause them to be forced together.

A The moving air between the cans exerts less pressure than the air on either side of each can at that moment.

B As a result, the cans move together because of the increased pressure of the air around the cans.

Now, look at the curvature of the airplane wing in **Figure 8-21.** As the plane moves forward, the air passing over the wing must travel farther than air passing below it. To take the same time to get to the rear of the wing, air must travel faster over the top of the wing than below it. Thus, the pressure above the wing is less than the pressure below it. The result is a net upward force on the wing, lifting the airplane in flight.

Figure 8-21

The design of airplane wings is an application of Bernoulli's principle. Note the curvature of the upper portion. *Which side has more pressure exerted on it?*

Did you know that baseball pitchers use science? If the pitcher puts a spin on the ball, air moves faster along the side of the ball that is spinning away from the direction of the throw. Look at **Figure 8-22.** The ball's spin results in a net force that pushes the ball toward the low-pressure direction. The force gives the ball a curve.

Windy Cities

Fluids flow faster when forced to flow through narrow spaces. As a result of this speed increase, the pressure of the fluid drops. This reduction in pressure in these spaces is a special case of Bernoulli's principle called the **Venturi effect.**

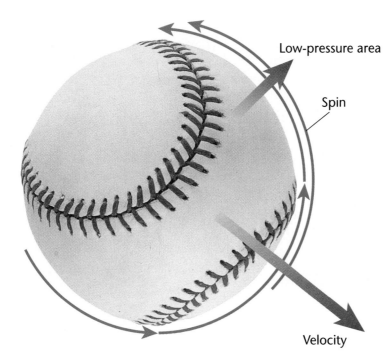

Low-pressure area

Spin

Velocity

Figure 8-22

Air moves faster along the side of a spinning ball that is moving away from the direction of the throw.

A dramatic demonstration of the Venturi effect has occurred in cities where the wind is forced to blow between rows of skyscrapers. The reduced air pressure outside of buildings during strong winds has caused windows to be forced out by the higher air pressure inside the buildings.

Section Wrap-up

Review

1. How is it possible that a boat made of concrete can float?

2. State Bernoulli's principle and tell how it explains the lift on an airplane.

3. **Think Critically:** If you fill up a balloon with air, tie it off, and release it, it will fall to the floor. Why does it fall instead of float?

Skill Builder
Measuring in SI
The density of water is 1.0 g/cm³. How many kilograms of water does a submerged 120-cm³ block displace? One kilogram weighs 9.8 N. What is the buoyant force on the block? If you need help, refer to Chapter 2 and to Measuring in SI in the **Skill Handbook.**

USING MATH

If you wanted to lift an object weighing 20 000 N, how much force would you have to apply to the small piston on page 236?

DEBRA MOORE, *Glass Artist*

On the Job

Q Besides transforming materials from solid to liquid and back to solid, what scientific principles are involved in working with glass?

A When I spin glass as I heat it, centrifugal force creates a round shape. Also, as I tell my students, gravity is the glassblower's best friend. If you want your molten glass in a stretched-out shape, you just hold it up until it's as long as you want.

Q Do you teach glassblowing to young people?

A I'm currently working with a group of 13- to 18-year-olds. They are turning old bottles they collect in their community into a beautiful chandelier. The young people are divided into teams of three. One team takes the solid blue water bottles we find, uses high heat to open them up, and then creates a fluted shape on the rim of the cups while the glass is in the liquid state. The glass is liquefied by breaking up one bottle and melting it on a long, flat shovel in the glory hole. The glory hole is a large, round oven heated to about 1000°F. Meanwhile, another team shapes glass leaves and flowers for decorations. Young people find the glassblowing studio an exciting place.

Personal Insights

Q What fascinates you about glass?

A I love the way glass looks in its glowing, molten form. It's like honey. Then, when it's blown and cooled, it has the appearance of a frozen liquid. I also love the colors glass comes in. Even the color names can inspire me—smoky topaz, opal lilac, reddish aurora.

Career Connection

Glass now can be made to have different specifications for different purposes. Chemists and engineers develop the processes used to make different kinds of glass. Investigate a few of the different types of glass and make a chart comparing and contrasting them. Research the following careers to find out how a knowledge of glassmaking is important.

- **Ceramic Engineer**
- **Industrial Designer**

Chapter 8 Review

Summary

8-1: Matter and Temperature

1. There are four states of matter: solid, liquid, gas, and plasma.
2. According to the kinetic theory, all matter is made of constantly moving particles.
3. Most matter expands when heated and contracts when cooled.

8-2: Science and Society: Fresh Water—Will there be enough?

1. Fresh water on Earth is scarce, and this water is often wasted or polluted.
2. There are many ways in which people can save water, and laws can be passed to regulate pollution.

8-3: Changes in State

1. Changes of state can be interpreted in terms of the kinetic theory of matter.
2. The energy of the heat of fusion and vaporization overcomes attractive forces between particles of matter.

8-4: Behavior of Gases

1. Gas pressure is caused by moving particles colliding with the inside walls of its container.
2. Boyle's law states that the volume of a gas decreases when the pressure increases, at constant temperature.
3. Charles's law states that the volume of a gas increases when the temperature increases, at constant pressure.

8-5: Uses of Fluids

1. Archimedes' principle states that the buoyant force on an object in a fluid is equal to the weight of the fluid displaced.
2. Pascal's principle states that pressure applied to a fluid is transmitted unchanged throughout the fluid.
3. Bernoulli's principle states that the pressure exerted by a fluid decreases as its velocity increases.

Key Science Words

a. Archimedes' principle
b. Bernoulli's principle
c. Boyle's law
d. buoyant force
e. Charles's law
f. condensation
g. crystal
h. evaporation
i. heat of fusion
j. heat of vaporization
k. kinetic theory of matter
l. pascal
m. Pascal's principle
n. plasma
o. polluted water
p. pressure
q. states of matter
r. thermal expansion
s. thermal pollution
t. Venturi effect

Reviewing Vocabulary

Match each phrase with the correct term from the list of Key Science Words.

1. The volume of a gas is reduced when the temperature is decreased.
2. water that exceeds government limits for impurities
3. liquid changes to gas below the boiling point
4. amount of force exerted per unit of area

5. The buoyant force on an object in a fluid equals the weight of the displaced fluid.
6. the SI unit of pressure
7. particles are arranged in regular patterns
8. a gaslike mixture of charged particles
9. Matter is made of tiny, moving particles.
10. energy needed for a liquid to boil

Checking Concepts

Choose the word or phrase that completes the sentence.

1. The temperature at which all particle motion of matter would stop is _____.
a. absolute zero   c. 0°C
b. its melting point   d. 273°C
2. The state of matter that has a definite volume and a definite shape is _____.
a. gas   c. plasma
b. liquid   d. solid
3. The most common state of matter is

_____.

a. gas   c. plasma
b. liquid   d. solid
4. Most pressure is measured in _____.
a. grams   c. newtons
b. kilopascals   d. kilograms
5. Pascal's principle is the basis for _____.
a. aerodynamics   c. hydraulics
b. buoyancy   d. changes of state
6. Bernoulli's principle explains why _____.
a. airplanes fly   c. pistons work
b. boats float   d. ice melts
7. Particles separate completely from each other in a(n) _____.
a. gas   c. solid
b. liquid   d. amorphous material
8. The state of the matter in the sun and other stars is primarily _____.
a. amorphous   c. liquid
b. plasma   d. gas
9. In general, as a solid is heated, it _____.
a. becomes a gas   c. contracts
b. condenses   d. expands

10. A material's heat of fusion gives the amount of energy needed to _____.
a. condense a gas   c. melt a solid
b. boil a liquid   d. evaporate a liquid

Understanding Concepts

Answer the following questions in your Science Journal using complete sentences.

11. How might wastewater in the home be recycled instead of being poured into the sewer system?
12. Why would it be incorrect to say, "This room is full of air"?
13. What energy changes occur when hot tea is poured over ice?
14. Use the kinetic theory to explain why liquid water forms on the outside of a glass of cold lemonade.
15. Why might rocks in a creek hurt your feet more than the same rocks would in deeper water?

Thinking Critically

16. Use Charles's and Boyle's laws to explain why you should check your tire pressure when the temperature changes.
17. Explain how food might get freezer burn. How might you prevent it?
18. Alcohol evaporates more quickly than does water. What can you tell about the forces between the alcohol particles?

use and until all vapors are gone. DO NOT SM(
– Extinguish all flames, pilot lights and heate
Turn off stoves, electric tools and appliances,
any other sources of ignition. CONTENTS UN
PRESSURE. Avoid prolonged exposure to sun
or heat from radiators, stoves, hot water
other heat sources that may cause bursting.
not puncture, incinerate, burn or store ab
120°F. Do not discard empty can in home garb
compactor.
**CONTAINS XYLENE AND TOLUENE
VAPOR HARMFUL.** Use with adequ
ventilation. Avoid continuous breathing of va

19. Why do aerosol cans have a "do not incinerate" warning such as the one in the photo on page 242?

20. Applying pressure lowers the melting point of ice. Why might an icy road at –1°C be more dangerous than an icy road at –10°C?

Developing Skills

If you need help, refer to the **Skill Handbook.**

21. Observing and Inferring: Infer the air pressure effect on a small car when a tractor-trailer passes it.

22. Making and Using Graphs: A group of students heated ice until it melted and then turned to steam. They measured the temperature each minute and graphed the results. Their graph is provided below. In terms of the energy involved, explain what is happening at each letter (a, b, c, d) in the graph.

23. Concept Mapping: Use a cycle map to show the changes in particles as cool water boils, changes to steam, and then changes back to cool water.

24. Interpreting Data: As elevation increases, boiling point decreases. List each of the following locations as *at sea level, above sea level,* or *below sea level.* (Boiling point of water in °C is given.)
Death Valley (100.3), Denver (94), Madison (99), Mt. Everest (76.5), Mt. McKinley (79), New York City (100), Salt Lake City (95.6)

25. Recognizing Cause and Effect: List possible effects for each of the following causes.
a. Perspiration evaporates.
b. Pressure on a balloon decreases.
c. Your buoyant force equals your weight.

Performance Assessment

1. Graph from Data: Using your data from Activity 8-2, convert the temperature readings from Celsius to Kelvin and replot the data. Is the volume-temperature relationship the same?

2. Report: Research the effects of pressure changes on the human body and write a report. Include in your report any precautions that must be taken in dealing with pressure changes in space and when deep-sea diving.

3. Display: Research crystal growing and the conditions needed to grow a perfect crystal. Grow crystals of several different materials and display them.

Cool water

Hot water

Hot water

Steam

Previewing the Chapter

Classification of Matter

Did you ever watch a construction crew pour concrete for a building? What is concrete? Actually, you can't classify fresh concrete as only one of the states of matter. Rather, it is a mixture of solids—portland cement, sand, rocks—and a liquid, water. Do the following activity to make some classroom concrete and observe its properties. As you study the chapter, you'll find out more about this and other matter around you.

EXPLORE ACTIVITY

Making Concrete

1. Measure 10 g crushed calcium carbonate; 20 g fine sand; 30 g clean, small pebbles; and 5 g water into a plastic cup.
2. Stir the materials together thoroughly.
3. Allow the combined materials to dry in the cup overnight.

Observe: In your Science Journal, describe any changes you noticed in the stirred materials after they dried. Discuss whether your product still would be concrete if you changed the amounts of the materials.

Previewing Science Skills

► In the **Skill Builders**, you will **compare and contrast** and **observe and infer**.

► In the **Activities**, you will **classify, make and use tables, observe**, and **hypothesize**.

► In the **MiniLABs**, you will **observe, infer**, and **compare**.

9•1 Composition of Matter

Science Words

element
compound
substance
heterogeneous mixture
homogeneous mixture
solution
colloid
Tyndall effect
suspension

Objectives

- Distinguish between substances and mixtures.
- Compare and contrast solutions, colloids, and suspensions.

Substances

You can easily tell whether a line is drawn in ink or pencil. The lines look different because they are made of different materials. Look at **Figure 9-1.** Notice that a pencil is made of several kinds of materials. You could classify the materials of the pencil according to the four states of matter. Another way to classify materials is by the units they are made of.

Elements

The units that make up all matter are called atoms. If all the atoms in a sample of matter have the same identity, that kind of matter is an **element.** The carbon used in a pencil point contains only carbon atoms. Carbon is an element. The copper in a penny is an example of another element. In a pure copper sample, all the atoms have the same identity. Altogether, there are 111 recognized elements. The names of most of the elements are in a table on pages 732-733.

Compounds

Materials called **compounds** are made from atoms of two or more elements that are combined. The ratio of the different atoms in a compound is always the same. For example, the elements hydrogen and oxygen can combine to form the compound water. The atoms of elements in water are present in the ratio of two hydrogen atoms to one oxygen atom.

When was the last time you ate a compound whose elements

Figure 9-1

A pencil is made up of several different materials. *Which of these materials can you identify as elements?*

Figure 9-2

Sugar is a compound of carbon, oxygen, and hydrogen.

are a black solid and two invisible gases? One compound that fits this description is sugar. You can recognize sugar by its white crystals and sweet taste. But the elements that form sugar—carbon, hydrogen, and oxygen—are neither white nor sweet, as shown in **Figure 9-2.** Like sugar, compounds usually have a different appearance from the elements that make them up.

Oxygen, carbon, water, sugar, baking soda, and salt are examples of materials classified as substances. A **substance** is either an element or a compound. Elements and compounds cannot be reduced to more basic components by physical processes.

Mixtures

When you have a sore throat, do you gargle with salt water? Salt water is classified as a mixture. A mixture such as salt water is a material made up of two or more substances that can be separated by physical means.

Unlike compounds, mixtures do not always contain the same amounts of the different substances that make them up. You may be wearing clothing made of permanent-press fabric. This fabric is a mixture of fibers of two materials—polyester and cotton. The fabric may contain varying amounts of polyester and cotton, as shown by the labels in **Figure 9-3.** Fabric with more polyester is more resistant to wrinkling than is fabric with less polyester.

Figure 9-3

Permanent-press fabrics are mixtures that have variable composition.

How can mixtures be separated?

Find out about the nature of a heterogeneous mixture.

Procedure

1. Put equal amounts of soil, clay, sand, gravel, and pebbles in a clear plastic gallon jar. Add water until the jar is almost full.
2. Stir or shake the mixture thoroughly. Predict the order in which the materials will settle.
3. Observe what happens and compare your observations to your predictions.

Analysis

1. In what order did the materials settle?
2. Explain why the materials settled in the order they did.
3. How could the individual materials in such a mixture be separated?

USING MATH

The concentration of a solution can be expressed using percentages. For example, a 5 percent solution of sodium hydroxide contains 5 g of NaOH in each 100 g of solution. Calculate the number of grams of NaOH in 250 g of a 10 percent solution.

A mixture in which different materials can be easily distinguished is called a **heterogeneous mixture.** Permanent-press fabrics are heterogeneous mixtures, and you can detect the different materials by sight or with a microscope. Granite, concrete, pizza, and dry soup mixes are examples of other heterogeneous mixtures.

Solutions

The salt water you gargle with looks like water and tastes salty. Like a polyester-cotton fabric, salt water is in some ways similar to the substances it contains. But you can't see the particles in salt water even with a microscope. A material, such as salt water, in which two or more substances are uniformly spread out is a **homogeneous mixture.**

For example, rubbing alcohol is a common disinfectant. It appears clear, even though it is made up of particles of alcohol in water. A **solution** is another name for a homogeneous mixture. Particles in solutions are so small that they cannot be seen even with a microscope. The particles have diameters of about 0.000 000 001 m (1 nm). These particles will never settle to the bottom of their container. Solutions remain constantly and uniformly mixed. Substances and mixtures are summarized in **Figure 9-4.**

Figure 9-4

Every sample of matter is an element, a compound, or a mixture. *Which of these types of matter are substances?*

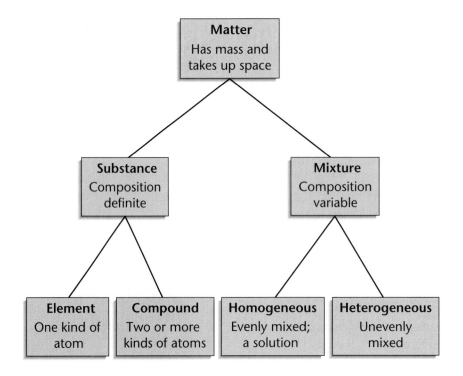

Figure 9-5

Unlike the particles in a solution, the particles in a colloid are large enough to scatter light.

 A beam of light goes straight through a solution.

B Gelatin is a colloid that may seem to be clear until you shine a light on it. Then you see that its particles scatter light.

Colloids and Suspensions

When you drink a glass of whole or low-fat milk, you are drinking a mixture of water, fats, proteins, and other substances. Milk is a colloid. A **colloid** is a heterogeneous mixture that, like a solution, never settles. One way to tell a colloid from a solution is shown in **Figure 9-5.** Milk appears white because its particles scatter light. The scattering of light by particles in a mixture is called the **Tyndall effect.** You can see the Tyndall effect in all colloids.

Problem Solving

Cooking a Colloid

The term *colloid* comes from the Greek word for glue. Gelatin, which is used to make some types of glue, was one of the first colloids studied. Gelatin consists of large strands of small units that are twisted and held together by weak attractions. Heat from boiling water is sufficient to break these attractions and uncoil the strands. When the strands are cooled, the attractions re-form, but the strands are tangled into new positions with water trapped in the spaces between the strands. This creates a semisolid colloid.

Presweetened gelatin desserts have a sweetener, such as sugar or aspartame, added to the dry gelatin. This sweetener helps disperse the dry gelatin in the hot water to which it is added. But unsweetened gelatin is first added to cold water, and then the water is heated. Why is unsweetened gelatin added to cold water instead of hot water?

Think Critically:

1. What role does boiling water play in the formation of the colloid?
2. The strands of most of the collagen in gelatin must be separated and dispersed in order to avoid clumps in the final product. How does cold water assist this process?
3. Could presweetened gelatin desserts be added to cold water and then heated? Explain.

Table 9-1

Comparing Solutions, Colloids, and Suspensions			
Description	**Solutions**	**Colloids**	**Suspensions**
Settle upon standing	No	No	Yes
Can be separated using filter paper	No	No	Yes
Sizes of particles	0.1-1 nm	1-100 nm	Greater than 100 nm
Scatter light	No	Yes	Yes

CONNECT TO

LIFE SCIENCE

Most milk containers carry the label *Homogenized.* Find out what part of the milk is homogenized and *describe* the process in your Science Journal.

Some mixtures are neither solutions nor colloids. If you fill a glass with pond water, you may notice that the water is slightly muddy. If you let it stand long enough, the silt will fall to the bottom of the glass and the water will clear. River deltas are examples of what happens when muddy water slows down and suspended soil particles settle out. Muddy water is a suspension. A **suspension** is a heterogeneous mixture containing a liquid in which visible particles settle. Another example of a suspension is glacial meltwater, which has a milky appearance. Particles carried by the meltwater settle out, forming glacial deposits such as alluvial fans.

Table 9-1 summarizes how the different types of mixtures vary in characteristics. You can use the information in this table to classify different kinds of mixtures.

Section Wrap-up

Review

1. How is a container of hydrogen gas and oxygen gas different from a container of water vapor?

2. Distinguish between a substance and a mixture.

3. **Think Critically:** Why do the words "Shake well before using" on a bottle of fruit juice indicate that the juice is a suspension?

Skill Builder
Comparing and Contrasting
In terms of suspensions and colloids, compare and contrast a glass of milk and a glass of grapefruit juice. If you need help, refer to Comparing and Contrasting in the **Skill Handbook.**

Science Journal

In your Science Journal, make a list of the liquids you consumed yesterday. Classify each as a solution, a colloid, or a suspension.

Activity 9-1

Elements, Compounds, and Mixtures

Elements, compounds, and mixtures all contain atoms. In elements, the atoms all have the same identity. In compounds, two or more elements have been combined in a fixed ratio. In a mixture, the ratio of substances present can vary.

Problem
What are some differences among elements, compounds, and mixtures?

Materials
- plastic freezer bag containing the following labeled items
- copper foil
- small package of salt
- piece of solder
- aluminum foil
- chalk (calcium carbonate) or baking soda (sodium hydrogen carbonate)
- piece of granite
- sugar water in a vial

Procedure
1. Copy the data table into your Science Journal and use it to record your observations.
2. Obtain a prepared bag of numbered objects.
3. Use the data table to identify each object and classify it as either an element, a compound, a heterogeneous mixture, or a homogeneous mixture. The names of all the elements appear in the periodic table on pages 732-733. Any of the

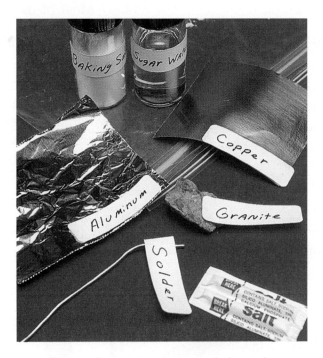

objects that are compounds have been named as examples in Section 9-1.

Analyze
1. If you know the name of a substance, how can you find out whether it is an element?
2. How is a compound different from a mixture?
3. Were the mixtures you identified homogeneous or heterogeneous?

Conclude and Apply
4. Examine the contents of your refrigerator at home. **Classify** what you find as elements, compounds, or mixtures.
5. If they are described, all materials can be classified. **Compare and contrast** elements, compounds, and mixtures.

Data and Observations

Object	Identity	Classification
1		
2		
3		
4		
5		
6		
7		

TECHNOLOGY:
9•2 The Colloid Connection

A Water-Purifying Colloid

Most of us just turn a tap for a drink of fresh water. Did you realize that a useful colloid may help make this possible?

In most municipal water-treatment plants, water is first taken from a river and quickly filtered. Then it is allowed to settle to remove some of the clays and other suspended materials. However, many fine particles still remain in the water, and they need to be removed. Water sanitation engineers have developed techniques that use colloids to remove these fine particles.

Figure 9-6 shows how such a colloid is formed and used. The newly formed colloid has a fluffy, gel-like appearance. It is capable of trapping microorganisms and many of the finely dispersed particles that escaped filtering because some of the particles stick to the gel.

Figure 9-6

A A colloid can be used to remove impurities in water. To make this colloid, measured amounts of lime and alum are added to the water. These compounds form a colloid of the compound aluminum hydroxide.

C From this point, the water may be sprayed through air to add oxygen to the water. It can then be treated with chlorine for further purification.

B Later, the gel can be filtered out through beds of fine sand. *Why can the gel be filtered out but the microorganisms can't be removed by this method?*

Breaking up a Colloid

Colloids are not always helpful. Some colloids may cause pollution rather than ridding the environment of pollutants. For example, a familiar sight around some factories is large smokestacks with columns of dense smoke billowing skyward. In addition to materials that can't be seen, smoke may contain significant amounts of carbon and uncombusted coal fragments. These particles make up soot, which is suspended in the air. To avoid polluting the air, this colloid must be broken up before it is released into the atmosphere. The colloid structure is destroyed in a process called **coagulation.** In coagulation, small, suspended particles are attracted to each other. They clump together, forming a particle that is too large to remain suspended.

Engineers have designed a way to remove most of the soot in smokestack exhaust in industrial locations, as shown in **Figure 9-7.** The particles can be collected later for further disposal.

Figure 9-7

The soot colloid is vented into a chamber where it is subjected to a high voltage. At this point, the soot particles become negatively charged. They attract uncharged soot particles, and these larger particles are then attracted to a positive part of the chamber, where they accumulate. If soot is effectively removed, the products from a smokestack appear much cleaner.

Section Wrap-up

Review

1. Even though water is settled and filtered, it still is often treated with a colloid before it is used for drinking. Explain what advantage colloid treatment has for purifying water.

2. How does smoke fit the definition of a colloid?

Explore the Technology

Heating a colloid often causes the velocities of the particles to increase to a level at which high-impact collisions cause them to coagulate. In your Science Journal, explain why it is necessary to use some other technique when coagulating soot in smoke.

SCIENCE & SOCIETY

9•3 Describing Matter

Science Words

physical property
physical change
chemical change
chemical property
law of conservation of
    mass

Objectives

* Give examples of physical properties.
* Distinguish between physical and chemical changes.
* Distinguish between chemical and physical properties.
* State and explain the law of conservation of mass.

Physical Properties

You can bend an empty aluminum can, but you can't bend a piece of chalk. Chalk doesn't bend—it breaks. Brittleness is a characteristic that describes chalk. Its color and shape also describe the chalk. Any such characteristic of a material that you can observe without changing the substances that make up the material is a **physical property.** Examples of physical properties you have learned about are color, shape, size, density, melting point, and boiling point. You can describe matter using physical properties. Look at **Figure 9-8.** Does all matter have physical properties?

Some physical properties describe the appearance of an object. For example, you might describe an iron nail as a pointy-ended cylinder made of a dull, gray-colored solid. By describing the shape, color, and state of the nail, you have listed several of its physical properties. Some physical properties can be measured. For instance, you could use a metric ruler to measure one property of the nail—its length. What physical property of the nail is measured with a balance?

USING MATH

Is the length of a nail most likely to be 3 mm, 3 cm, or 3 km?

Figure 9-8

Each of the items pictured has its own properties. *What are the physical properties of the CD cases?*

If you had a soft drink in a cup, you could measure its volume and temperature and describe its odor. Each of these characteristics is a physical property of the soft drink. Some physical properties describe the behavior of a material or a substance. As you may know, all objects made of iron are attracted by a magnet. Attraction by a magnet is a property of the substance iron. Every substance has physical properties that distinguish it from other substances.

Identification by Properties

Do you pick out the grapes in a fruit salad and eat them first, last, or maybe not at all? If you do, you are using physical properties to identify the grapes and separate them from the other fruits in the mixture. **Figure 9-9** shows a mixture of pebbles and sand. You can identify the pebbles and grains of sand by differences in color, shape, and size. By sifting the mixture, you can quickly separate the pebbles from the grains of sand because they are different sizes.

Now look at the mixture of iron filings and sand shown in **Figure 9-10B.** It would be impossible to separate this mixture with a sieve because the filings and grains of sand are the same size. A more efficient way is to pass a magnet through the mixture. When you pass a magnet through the mixture, the magnet attracts the iron filings and pulls them from the sand. In this way, the difference in a physical property, such as attraction to a magnet, can be used to separate substances in a mixture. A practical example of using the physical property of magnetism is shown in **Figure 9-10A.**

Figure 9-9

This mixture of pebbles and sand can be separated by physical means, such as using different sizes of filters.

Figure 9-10

Iron can be separated from other materials because it has the physical property of magnetism.

A The iron in these materials to be recycled can be separated by a magnet.

B A mixture of sand and iron filings can be separated with a magnet. The iron filings are magnetic. The sand is not.

Figure 9-11

When iron melts and then re-cools, physical changes occur. *Does the identity of the iron change?*

CONNECT TO

EARTH SCIENCE

Recycling conserves natural resources. In some large recycling projects, it is difficult to separate aluminum metal from scrap iron. *Investigate* the physical properties of the two metals that would help you separate them.

Physical Changes

If you break a piece of chalk, its original size and shape change. You have caused a change in some of its physical properties. But you have not changed the identity of the substance that makes up the chalk.

The changes in state that you studied in Chapter 8 are all examples of physical changes. When a substance freezes, boils, evaporates, sublimes, or condenses, it undergoes physical changes such as those shown in **Figure 9-11.** Energy changes occur during these changes in state, but the kind of substance—the identity of the element or compound—does not change.

The Identity Remains the Same

As shown in the picture above, iron will change states if it absorbs or loses enough energy. In each state, it will have physical properties that identify it as the substance iron. A change in size, shape, or state of matter is called a **physical change.** Sometimes, a color change indicates a physical change. Physical changes do not change the identities of the substances in a material.

Just as physical properties can be used to separate mixtures, so can physical changes. For example, if you let a cup of salt water stand for a week, you'll find that the water has evaporated, leaving salt crystals inside the cup. The process of evaporating water from salty seawater is used to produce drinking water.

Chemical Changes

From observations of what happens around you, you know that changes do occur in which substances change their identities. Fireworks explode, matches burn, eggs rot, and bikes and car bodies rust. What do changes in these materials have in common?

Burned toast, burned soup, and burned steak all smell burned. The smell is different from the smell of bread, soup, or steak. The odor is a clue that a new substance has been produced. A change of one substance in a material to a different substance is a **chemical change.** Many signs can tell you when a chemical change has taken place. For example, the foaming of an antacid tablet in a glass of water and the smell in the air after

Aerogels

Imagine a block of gelatin dessert in which all of the liquid has been replaced with air. It might look like a frozen cloud and would be called an aerogel.

Light passing through the tiny pores and microscopic framework of an aerogel is bent, giving the aerogel a bluish color against a dark background and a yellowish color in the light. The framework is so weakly connected that the aerogel is a poor conductor of heat and an excellent insulator.

The insulating property of aerogels has caught the interest of industry. Aerogels can be used to replace the current foam insulation used in refrigerators. A one-inch thick aerogel in a double-pane window insulates as well as 30 layers of glass. They block sound so well that the Navy may use them to reduce noise levels in submarines. They are ideal for cameras that focus by response to sound waves.

A black, pure-carbon aerogel has also been made that is an excellent conductor of electricity. Using this aerogel, it would be possible to create a car part that would hold enough electrical charge to accelerate an electric vehicle from a standstill without draining the battery.

Think Critically:

What property of aerogels might limit their use as an insulator in double-pane windows?

Aerogel

a thunderstorm indicate that new substances have been produced. In some chemical changes, a rapid production of energy, such as the light and sound of an exploding firecracker, is a clue.

A Change in Identity

When iron is exposed to the oxygen and water in the air, the iron and oxygen slowly form a new substance, rust. When hydrogen gas is burned in a rocket engine, the elements hydrogen and oxygen combine to form water. Burning and rusting are chemical changes because different substances are produced.

INTEGRATION
Earth Science

Figure 9-12

Calcium carbonate is found in cave formations and on Earth's surface in formations such as the White Cliffs of Dover, England.

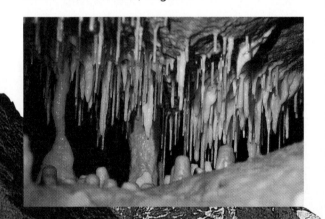

Weathering: Chemical or Physical Change?

The effects of nature's forces on Earth's surface provide many opportunities to observe dramatic changes. Steep canyon walls, shifting sand dunes, and unusual limestone formations are easily observed at various global locations. Would you classify the changes that caused these formations as physical changes or chemical changes? Geologists, using the same criteria that you have learned in this chapter, would classify some weathering changes as physical and some as chemical.

Large rocks can split when water seeps into small cracks, freezes, and expands. However, the smaller pieces of newly exposed rock still have the same properties as the original sample. This change is a physical change.

Limestone, shown in **Figure 9-12,** may be washed away by rain and moving rivers, which is another physical change. Sometimes, however, the water is acidic. If this is the case, the changes may produce new products. Solid calcium carbonate, a compound found in limestone, does not easily dissolve in water. But when calcium carbonate reacts with an acid, it changes into a new substance, calcium hydrogen carbonate, that can dissolve in water. This change in limestone would be classed as a chemical change because the identity of the calcium carbonate changes. The mineral feldspar is also susceptible to acid attack.

Figure 9-13

Flammability or combustibility is a chemical property of some materials used in the home. *How do flammability and combustibility differ?*

NET WT. 10 OZ. (283.75 grams)

DANGER! EXTREMELY FLAMMABLE CONTENTS UNDER PRESSURE. KEEP FROM HEAT OR FLAME.

BEFORE USING, CAREFULLY READ CAUTIONS AND HEALTH HAZARDS INFORMATION ON BACK PANEL.

Cleans carbs and injectors
Reduces intake valve deposits
Removes water
Fights gas line freeze
Saves gas

DANGER: HARMFUL OR FATAL IF SWALLOWED OR INHALED. SKIN IRRITANT. COMBUSTIBLE.
Read cautions on back panel.
8 FL. OZ. 236 mL

Chemical Properties

Look at **Figure 9-13.** You have probably seen these warnings on cans of paint thinners and lighter fluids for charcoal grills. The warnings indicate that these liquids burn quickly. The tendency of a substance to burn is an example of a chemical property. A **chemical property** is a characteristic of a substance that indicates whether it can undergo a certain chemical change. Many substances are flammable or combustible. Knowing which materials contain substances that have this chemical property allows you to use them safely.

If you look around a drugstore, you might notice that many medicines are stored in dark bottles. These medicines contain compounds with a similar chemical property. Chemical changes will take place in the compounds if they are exposed to light. What physical property do these bottles have in common?

Even though there are thousands of substances and billions of mixtures, they do share a few common physical and chemical properties. You can use these properties to study matter further.

Science Journal

Over the past couple of days, you have observed or been part of many chemical and physical changes. In your Science Journal, describe five chemical changes and five physical changes that you have noticed in the past two days.

Discover some clues that indicate that a physical or a chemical change has occurred.

Procedure

1. Add water to a 250-mL beaker until it is half-full.
2. Add a crystal of potassium permanganate to the water and observe what happens.
3. Add 1 g of sodium hydrogen sulfite to the solution and stir until the solution becomes colorless.

Analysis

1. Is dissolving a chemical or a physical change?
2. What evidence of a chemical change did you see?

The Conservation of Mass

Wood is combustible, or burnable, which is a chemical property. Suppose you burn a large log on a campfire until nothing is left but a small pile of ashes. During the burning, smoke, heat, and light are given off. It's easy to see that a chemical change occurs. At first, you might also think that matter was lost during this change because the pile of ashes looks much smaller than the log. In fact, if you could measure both the mass of the log and the mass of the ashes, the mass of the ashes would be less than that of the log. But suppose that during the burning, you could collect all the oxygen in the air that was combined with the log during the burning. And suppose you could also collect all the smoke and gases that escape from the burning log and measure their masses, too. Then you would find that there is no loss of mass during the burning, as shown in **Figure 9-14.**

Not only is there no loss of mass during burning, there is no loss or gain of mass during any chemical change. In other words, matter is neither created nor destroyed during a chemical change. This statement is known as the **law of conservation of mass.** According to this law, the mass of all substances present before a chemical change equals the mass of all the substances remaining after the change. How does **Figure 9-15** illustrate the law of conservation of mass?

Figure 9-14

Although you can't see the gases used or formed when a log burns, there is no loss or gain of mass. *What gas is necessary for burning to take place?*

Figure 9-15

A chemical change between two compounds demonstrates the law of conservation of mass.

Why do substances have physical and chemical properties and undergo physical and chemical changes? These properties and changes are the result of what atoms are present and how they are arranged. The composition and arrangement are different for each substance.

Section Wrap-up

Review

1. In terms of substances, explain why evaporation of water is a physical change and not a chemical change.

2. Give an example of a chemical change that occurs when you prepare a meal.

3. Why is being flammable a chemical property rather than a physical property?

4. **Think Critically:** The law of conservation of mass applies to physical changes as well as to chemical changes. How might you demonstrate this law for melting ice?

Skill Builder
Observing and Inferring
Observe a burning candle. What evidence do you have that there are chemical and physical changes in the candle as it burns? If you need help, refer to Observing and Inferring in the **Skill Handbook.**

USING MATH

Two chemicals with a combined mass of 25.48 g react in a flask that has a mass of 142.05 g. A gas is produced that totally escapes into a flask that has an empty mass of 141.65 g. After the reaction, the first flask and its contents have a mass of 167.16 g. Calculate the total mass of the second flask and gas.

Activity 9-2

Design Your Own Experiment
Checking Out Chemical Changes

Mixing materials together does not always produce a chemical change. You must find evidence of a new substance with new properties being produced before you can conclude that a chemical change has taken place. Try this activity and use your observation skills to make careful deductions about changes.

PREPARATION

Problem
What evidence indicates a chemical change within a mixture?

Form a Hypothesis
Think about what happens when small pieces of limestone are mixed with sand. Now think what happens when limestone is mixed with an acid. Based on these thoughts, form a hypothesis about the relationship between mixing substances together and chemical changes.

Objectives
- Observe the results of adding dilute hydrochloric acid to baking soda.
- Infer that the production of new substances indicates a chemical change.
- Design an experiment that allows you to compare the activity of baking soda and the activity of the resulting product.

Possible Materials
- goggles
- baking soda
- small evaporating dish
- hand lens
- dilute hydrochloric acid, HCl
- 10-mL graduated cylinder
- electric hot plate
- apron

Safety Precautions
Wear safety goggles during any laboratory work. Use care when pouring the dilute acid. Quickly wash any spills with water, and notify your teacher.

PLAN THE EXPERIMENT

1. As a group, agree upon and write out the hypothesis statement.
2. To test your hypothesis, devise a plan to compare two different mixtures. The first mixture consists of 3 mL of hydrochloric acid and 0.5 g of baking soda. The second mixture is 3 mL of hydrochloric acid and the solid product of the first mixture. Describe exactly what you will do at each step.
3. Make a list of the materials that you will need to complete your experiment.
4. Design a data and observations table in your Science Journal so that it is ready to use as your group observes what happens.

Check the Plan
1. Read over your entire experiment to make sure that all steps are in logical order.

2. Identify any constants and the variables of the experiment.
3. Should you run any test more than one time?
4. How will observations be summarized?
5. *Make sure your teacher approves your entire plan before you begin and that you have included any changes in the plan.*

DO THE EXPERIMENT

1. Carry out the experiment as approved.
2. While the experiment is going on, write down any observations that you make and complete the data and observations table in your Science Journal.

Analyze and Apply
1. **Compare** your results with those of other groups.
2. What different properties of any new substances did you **observe** after adding hydrochloric acid to the baking soda?

Go Further

If you had used vinegar, which contains acetic acid, as the acid, do you think your results would be different? Explain.

Copper Art

If you wanted a small copper statue for your room, you'd probably be thinking about something the color of a penny. But if you were a sculptor planning a copper statue for a park, you might be thinking about something green.

Just as iron rusts when it combines with oxygen in the air, copper combines with other substances in the atmosphere to form a green coating of copper carbonates, copper sulfates, and copper chlorides. Artists call this coating a patina. They may decide to make a sculpture out of copper because they want the look of the patina rather than the look of the pure copper.

Patinas do more than merely look nice. They also protect the sculpture. Once the patina forms, air can no longer get to the metal underneath. Therefore, the layer of oxidized copper stops further corrosion.

Working with Copper

There are other reasons some artists like working with copper. It's a soft metal and easy to mold, but it becomes stiffer when hammered or bent. This is known as work-hardening.

Copper also has some disadvantages. It can be too soft for some projects. It also conducts heat so well that it can be difficult to weld. The heat from the welding torch can quickly spread throughout the copper. Then the metal may melt all over—not just around the weld.

To get slightly different properties, artists may decide to work with copper alloys instead of pure copper. An alloy is a homogeneous mixture of a metal with different metals or other elements. Different copper alloys have different degrees of hardness, are more suitable for welding, and develop patinas of various colors.

Science Journal

Copper was the first metal used for tools and ornaments by some ancient cultures. Write a few paragraphs in your Science Journal hypothesizing why much early metalwork was done with copper.

Summary

9-1: Composition of Matter

1. Elements and compounds are substances; a mixture is composed of two or more substances.
2. A solution is a homogeneous mixture. Colloids and suspensions are two kinds of heterogeneous mixtures.

9-2: Science and Society: The Colloid Connection

1. Lime and alum form an aluminum hydroxide colloid that is used to help remove finely suspended particles from water supplies.
2. Exhaust from some industries may be a soot-containing colloid, which can be coagulated by using electricity in the smokestacks.

9-3: Describing Matter

1. Physical properties are characteristics of materials that you can observe without changing the identities of the substances themselves.
2. In physical changes, the identities of substances in materials do not change. In chemical changes, substances in materials change to different substances.
3. Physical properties can be observed without changing the identities of substances; chemical properties indicate chemical changes substances can undergo.
4. The law of conservation of mass states that during any chemical change, matter is neither created nor destroyed.

Key Science Words

a. chemical change
b. chemical property
c. coagulation
d. colloid
e. compound
f. element
g. heterogeneous mixture
h. homogeneous mixture
i. law of conservation of mass
j. physical change
k. physical property
l. solution
m. substance
n. suspension
o. Tyndall effect

Reviewing Vocabulary

Match each phrase with the correct term from the list of Key Science Words.

1. process used to reduce a colloidal form of air pollution
2. mixture of parts that can be easily distinguished
3. all atoms in a sample have the same identity
4. change in size, shape, or state
5. change of substance to a different substance
6. combined atoms of two or more elements
7. either an element or a compound
8. mixture that scatters light and never settles
9. an indication of whether a chemical change can occur in a substance
10. In a chemical change, matter is neither created nor destroyed.

Chapter 9 Review

Checking Concepts

Choose the word or phrase that completes the sentence or answers the question.

1. A copper wire will bend. This is an example of _____.
   a. a chemical property
   c. conservation
   b. a physical property
   d. an element
2. Which of the following is not an element?
   a. water
   c. oxygen
   b. carbon
   d. hydrogen
3. An example of a chemical change is _____.
   a. boiling
   c. evaporation
   b. burning
   d. melting
4. Gelatin is an example of a _____.
   a. colloid
   c. substance
   b. solution
   d. suspension
5. A sunbeam is an example of _____.
   a. an element
   c. a suspension
   b. a solution
   d. the Tyndall effect
6. One way to destroy a colloid is called _____.
   a. combustion
   c. coagulation
   b. filtration
   d. technology
7. The red color of a rose is a _____.
   a. chemical change
   c. physical change
   b. chemical property
   d. physical property
8. The process of evaporating water from seawater for drinking is a _____.
   a. chemical change
   c. physical change
   b. chemical property
   d. physical property
9. Which warning label indicates a chemical property of the material being labeled?
   a. "Fragile"
   c. "Handle with Care"
   b. "Flammable"
   d. "Shake Well"
10. Which of the following is a substance?
    a. colloid
    c. mixture
    b. element
    d. solution

Understanding Concepts

Answer the following questions in your Science Journal using complete sentences.

11. Describe a carton of milk using its physical properties.
12. The soft metal sodium and the greenish gas chlorine combine to form table salt, sodium chloride. How do you know table salt is a compound?
13. The word *colloid* means "gluelike." Why was *colloid* chosen to name certain mixtures?
14. Use a nail rusting in air to explain the law of conservation of mass.
15. Mai says that ocean water is a solution. Ed says that ocean water is a suspension. Are they both correct? Explain.

Thinking Critically

16. Rust is formed from oxygen and iron. How might you keep an iron pipe from rusting?
17. By mistake, scrap iron was put in with the glass at a recycling center. How might you separate the mixture?
18. Not all solutions are liquid. Why is a metal alloy, such as brass, considered a solution?
19. Use what you know about suspensions to explain why deltas form at the mouths of large rivers.
20. Why do many medications, such as the one in the photo, have instructions to shake well before using?

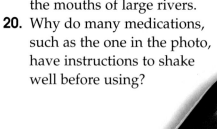

Developing Skills

If you need help, refer to the **Skill Handbook.**

21. **Recognizing Cause and Effect:** List at least two causes and two effects of industrial colloids.
22. **Making and Using Tables:** Different colloids may involve different states. For example, gelatin is formed from solid particles in a liquid. Complete the following table, using these common colloids: smoke, marshmallow, fog, paint.

Types of Colloids

Colloid	Example
Gas in solid	
Solid in liquid	
Solid in gas	
Liquid in gas	

23. **Using Variables, Constants, and Controls:** Marcos took a 100-cm^3 sample of a suspension, shook it well, and poured equal amounts into four different test tubes. He placed one test tube in a rack, one in very hot water, one in warm water, and the fourth in ice water. He then observed the time it took for each suspension to settle. What was the variable in the experiment? What was one constant?
24. **Interpreting Data:** Starting with a 25-cm^3 sample of pond water, Hannah poured 5 cm^3 through a piece of filter paper. She repeated this with four more pieces of filter paper. She dried each piece of filter paper and measured the mass of the sediment. Why did the last sample have a higher mass than did the first sample?

25. **Concept Mapping:** Make a network tree to show types of liquid mixtures. Include these terms: *homogeneous mixtures, heterogeneous mixtures, solutions, colloids,* and *suspensions.*

Performance Assessment

1. **Designing an Experiment:** Assume that some sugar was put into some rice by mistake. Design an experiment to separate the mixture. In your Science Journal, list your hypothesis and your experimental steps. Perform the experiment and summarize the results.
2. **Making and Using a Classification System:** Design a system for classifying different heterogeneous mixtures. State what the system is based on, and give several examples of using the system.
3. **Investigating the Issue Controversy:** Research the air pollution problem in Los Angeles. What causes the problem? What health and other problems are caused by the pollution? Could solutions such as those used to remove soot from smoke in industrial smokestacks be used to clear up the Los Angeles pollution? Why or why not? Present your results in an oral presentation.

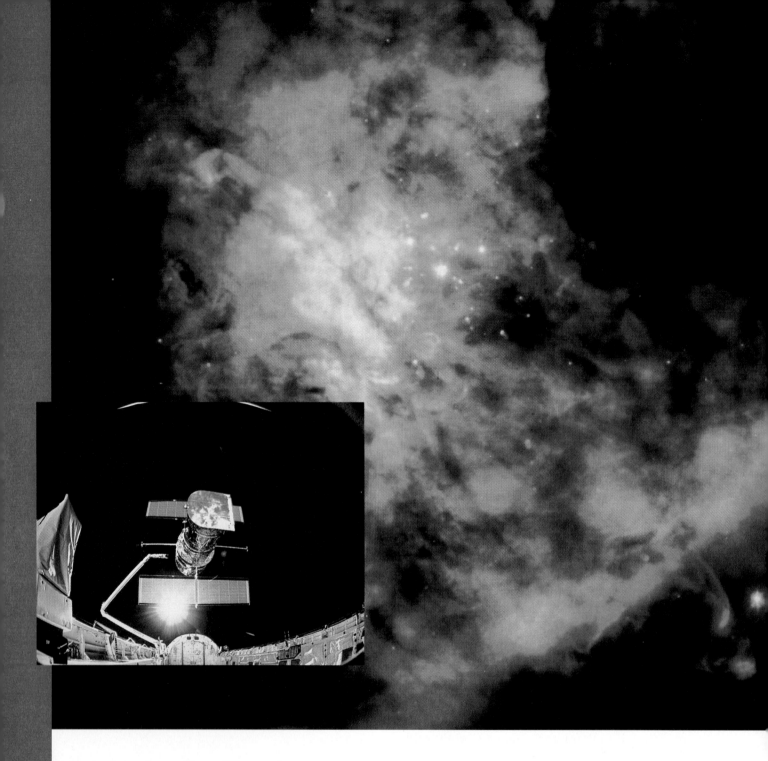

Previewing the Chapter

Chapter 10

Atomic Structure and the Periodic Table

The launch and alignment of the Hubble space telescope shown here has allowed us to have unusually clear views of objects in distant space. The collection of stars shown in this photo could represent a model for the structure of atoms. In the pages that follow, you will learn about scientists' models of atoms.

EXPLORE ACTIVITY

Make a model of an atom using pieces of hardware.

1. Count the number of different pieces of hardware your group was given.
2. Bury these pieces in a ball of modeling clay.
3. Trade balls of clay with another group.
4. Without pulling apart the clay, use toothpicks to find out how many pieces of each kind of hardware are in the ball. Keep track in your Science Journal, and sketch the shapes as they develop.

Observe: How many of each kind of hardware did you determine? Were you right? Now you have experienced using indirect evidence, as scientists do, to infer the identity and quantity of the hidden parts of a model.

Previewing Science Skills

▶ In the Skill Builders, you will **map concepts, make and use a table,** and **make and use a graph.**

▶ In the Activities, you will build **models, infer, compare and contrast,** and **interpret data.**

▶ In the MiniLABs, you will **observe** and **infer.**

10•1 Structure of the Atom

Science Words

chemical symbol
nucleus
electron
proton
neutron
atomic number
electron cloud

Objectives

- List the names and symbols of common elements.
- Describe the present model of the atom.
- Describe how electrons are arranged in an atom.

Chemical Symbols

Do the letters C, Al, Ne, and Ag mean anything to you? Each letter or pair of letters is a **chemical symbol,** which is an abbreviated way to write the name of an element. The black material on a burned match is carbon—C. You may wrap food in foil made of aluminum—Al. Have you noticed the bright glow of electrical signs? Many are filled with neon—Ne. You often use coins that contain copper—Cu.

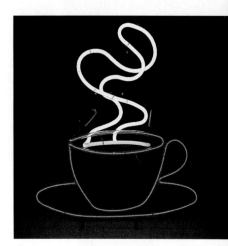

Chemical symbols consist of one capital letter or a capital letter plus one or two small letters. For some elements, the symbol is the first letter of the element's name. For other elements, the symbol is the first letter of the name plus another letter from its name. Some symbols, such as Ag, are derived from Latin. *Argentum* is Latin for "silver." Which symbols in **Table 10-1** might come from Latin?

Table 10-1

Symbols of Some Elements			
Element	**Symbol**	**Element**	**Symbol**
Aluminum	Al	Iodine	I
Calcium	Ca	Iron	Fe
Carbon	C	Magnesium	Mg
Chlorine	Cl	Mercury	Hg
Copper	Cu	Nitrogen	N
Fluorine	F	Oxygen	O
Gold	Au	Potassium	K
Helium	He	Silver	Ag
Hydrogen	H	Sodium	Na

Matter and Atoms

The idea of atoms began more than 2400 years ago with Greek thinkers, who defined atoms as the smallest parts of matter. Atoms consist of a positively charged center, or **nucleus,** surrounded by negatively charged particles called **electrons.** The two major kinds of particles in the nucleus are

Table 10-2

Comparison of Particles in an Atom			
Particle	Relative Mass	Charge	Location in the Atom
Proton	1	1+	Part of nucleus
Neutron	1	none	Part of nucleus
Electron	0	1−	Moves around nucleus

protons and **neutrons.** Together, these are referred to as nucleons. The nucleus contains most of the mass of the atom. The mass of a proton is about the same as that of a neutron. The mass of an electron is about 1/2000 the mass of a proton. The electron's mass is so small that it is considered negligible when finding the mass of an atom.

A neutron is neutral, which means it has no charge. A proton has a positive charge. As a result, the net charge on the nucleus is positive. The amount of positive charge on a proton is equal to the amount of negative charge on an electron. **Table 10-2** summarizes this information. Although atoms are composed of smaller particles, scientists still consider atoms to be the basic building blocks of matter.

Counting in Atoms

The **atomic number** of an atom is the number of protons in its nucleus. Every atom of the same element has the same number of protons. For example, every carbon atom has six protons. Therefore, it has the atomic number six. Atoms of different elements have different numbers of protons. For example, every carbon atom has six protons, but every oxygen atom has eight protons.

The number of electrons in a neutral atom is equal to the number of protons. A neutral carbon atom, then, has six electrons because it has six protons. Because the numbers of positively charged protons and negatively charged electrons in an atom are equal, the atom as a whole is electrically neutral.

USING MATH

You can use the integers +6 and −6 to represent the charge of 6 protons and 6 electrons in a carbon atom. The addition problem +6 + (−6) = 0 shows that the charge is neutral. Write an addition problem that shows that an oxygen atom with 8 protons and 8 electrons is neutral.

Models of the Atom

As scientists continued to study matter and atoms, they tried to form a mental picture or model of what an atom might look like. A model helps us understand something we cannot see directly, usually because it is too large or too small. A good model of the atom must explain all the information about matter and atoms. As more information was collected, scientists changed their models. Therefore, the model of the atom we use today is the result of the work of many scientists.

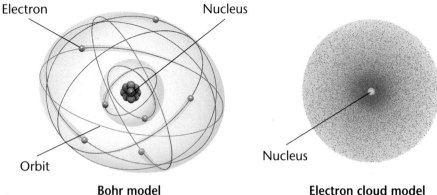

Bohr model

Electron cloud model

One of the early models of an atom looked like the one on the left in **Figure 10-1.** It was developed by the Danish scientist Niels Bohr in 1913. Bohr pictured the atom as having a central nucleus with electrons moving around it in well-defined paths, or orbits.

Figure 10-1

The left illustration is an early model of an atom with defined paths for electrons. The right illustration is a later model showing a region where electrons are likely to be. *Why is the later model more accurate?*

The Atom: A Cloudy View

In 1926, scientists developed a better model of the atom. In this model, the electrons moved about in a region called an **electron cloud** as in **Figure 10-1.** This cloud surrounds the nucleus of the atom. It describes the region where an electron is likely to be at any time. The diameter of the nucleus is about 1/100 000 the diameter of the electron cloud. Look at **Figure 10-2.** Suppose you built a model of an atom with an electron cloud as wide as a football field. The atom's nucleus would be about the thickness of the wire in a paper clip!

Because an electron's mass is so small, it is impossible for you—or anyone—to describe exactly where it is as it moves in the atom. All anyone can give is its probable location. Describing an electron's location around a nucleus is like trying to describe your location in your science class at any given moment. Your most probable location during the class is at your desk. Other possible, though less probable, locations are at the pencil sharpener and at the teacher's desk.

Figure 10-2

In this example, the paper clip wire represents the width of a nucleus. The outer seats of the stadium represent the outer electrons. *What makes up most of the atom?*

A Probability Model

You may have heard the expression, "you can't be everywhere at once." The multiple-exposure photo in **Figure 10-3** shows what it might be like if you could. The electron cloud model of the atom is based on the same idea. Scientists make calculations of the electron's most probable locations around the nucleus. If each location were marked with a dot, the closer spacing of the dots would indicate the most probable area for an electron. This is called an electron cloud because the dots give a cloudlike appearance when taken altogether.

Figure 10-3

If you could combine photos taken of a person in a room, you would not know exactly where that person was, but you could predict the most likely places. *In what area of this classroom would you most likely find the student?* Our best understanding of electron locations is similar to this.

Energy Levels and Electrons

Figure 10-4 illustrates another way to look at the placement of electrons. The electrons in an atom make up the electron cloud. Within the electron cloud, electrons are at various distances from the nucleus. Electrons closest to the nucleus have low energy. Electrons farther away from the nucleus

Figure 10-4

Sulfur's atomic number is 16. It has 16 protons and 16 electrons. The electron arrangement of sulfur is shown here.

 A The first level is filled with only two electrons.

B The second energy level has one spherical area and three pairs of lobes. This level can accommodate eight electrons. *How many of the electrons in sulfur remain?*

C The third level has areas of probability shaped like the second, only larger.

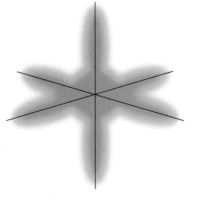

D If all of these levels were superimposed upon each other, you would have an electron cloud model for a sulfur atom with its 16 electrons.

CONNECT TO

PHYSICS

When a glass rod is rubbed with silk, the rod becomes positively charged. *Infer* what type of particle in the atoms in the rod has been removed?

have higher energy. You can represent the energy differences of the electrons by picturing the atom as having energy levels.

Energy levels are somewhat like shelves of a refrigerator door. A carton on the lowest shelf represents an electron in the lowest energy level. The difference in spacing of the shelves could indicate the differences in the amount of energy the electrons in that level can have. Shelves of a refrigerator door can usually hold the same number of cartons. Unlike refrigerator shelves, each energy level of an atom has a different maximum number of electrons it can hold. The lowest energy level can hold just two electrons. The second energy level can hold eight electrons, and the third energy level, a maximum of 18 electrons.

Table 10-3

Electrons in Energy Levels	
Energy Level in Atom	Maximum Number of Electrons
1	2
2	8
3	18
4	32

Section Wrap-up

Review

1. Write the chemical symbols for the elements carbon, aluminum, hydrogen, oxygen, and sodium.

2. List the names, charges, and locations of three kinds of particles that make up an atom.

3. What does an electron cloud represent?

4. Think Critically: How might an electric fan that is turned on be a model of an atom? How is the fan unlike an atom?

Skill Builder
Concept Mapping

Make a concept map for the parts of an atom. Include the following terms: *electron cloud, nucleus, electrons, protons,* and *neutrons.* Also provide the charge of each part. If you need help, refer to Concept Mapping in the **Skill Handbook.**

USING MATH

Scientists often refer to the probability areas for electrons as orbitals. Each orbital, regardless of shape or level, can hold a maximum of two electrons. Using **Table 10-3,** determine how many electron orbitals would exist in each of the first four energy levels.

Activity 10-1

Models of Atomic Structure

Building a model can help you understand how a complex system operates. Something as simple as a paper and magnet model can give you information about the relationship between the parts of an atom.

Problem
How can you build a model to help you understand how the main parts of an atom are related?

Materials
- magnetic board about 20 cm × 27 cm
- one 0.5-cm piece and 20 1-cm pieces of rubber magnetic tape
- circles of white paper 4 cm wide
- circles of red paper 1 cm wide
- marker

Procedure
1. Choose an element with an atomic number of 1 through 20. Determine the number of each kind of particle needed to make up an atom of that element.
2. Use a marker to write the number of protons and neutrons on a paper circle. This represents the nucleus of the atom.
3. Use a 0.5-cm magnetic strip to attach the model nucleus to one side of a magnetic board.
4. Attach the red paper circles to the 1-cm magnetic strips. Arrange these model electrons in energy levels around the nucleus. Use as many of these electrons as you need for your element.
5. Remove either the model nucleus or the model electrons from the magnetic board and ask classmates to identify the element.
6. Repeat steps 1 through 5 for another element.

Analyze
1. In a neutral atom, which particles will always be present in equal numbers?
2. Hypothesize what you think would happen to the charge of an atom if one of the electrons were removed from the atom.
3. Except for hydrogen, how many first-level electrons did each selected atom contain?

Conclude and Apply
4. How is this **model** of an atom similar to an actual atom?
5. Name two differences, other than size, between your model and an actual atom.
6. **Predict** what happens to the atom if one proton is removed from the nucleus and one electron is also removed.

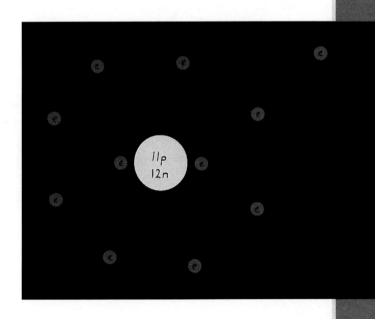

TECHNOLOGY:
10•2 Smaller Particles of Matter

Science Words

quark

Objectives

- Identify quarks as particles of matter that make up protons and neutrons.
- Explain how particle accelerators are used to study particles within atoms.

Looking for Quarks

You know that protons, electrons, and neutrons make up atoms. Are these particles made up of even smaller particles? Scientists hypothesize that electrons are not made of any smaller particles. Protons and neutrons, however, are made up of smaller particles called **quarks.** At present, scientists have confirmed the existence of six uniquely different quarks. A particular arrangement of three quarks held together with strong nuclear force produces a proton. Another arrangement of three quarks produces a neutron. A breakdown of an atom and its parts is shown in **Figure 10-5.**

Studying Collisions

Fermilab, in Batavia, Illinois, houses a machine that can generate the tremendous forces that are required to study quarks. This machine, the Tevatron, shown in **Figure 10-6,** is approximately 6.4 km in circumference. Electric and magnetic fields are used to accelerate, focus, then collide fast-moving protons. Studying the collisions reveals information about the inner structure of the atom.

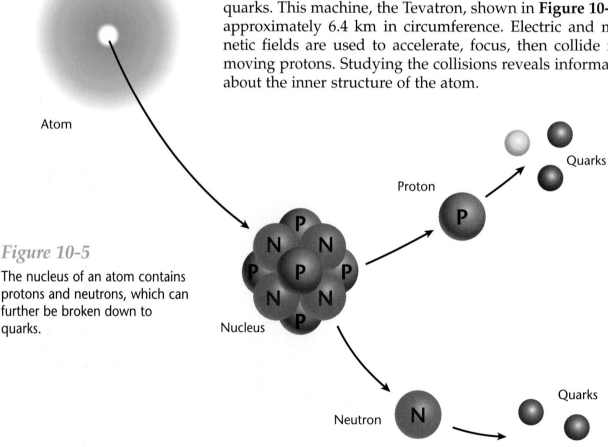

Figure 10-5

The nucleus of an atom contains protons and neutrons, which can further be broken down to quarks.

Atom

Nucleus

Proton

Quarks

Neutron

Quarks

Figure 10-6

This view of the Tevatron tunnel gives you an idea of its immense size. *Why is such a long tunnel needed?*

Tevatron

The Last Quark?

Finding the sixth quark took a team of nearly 450 scientists several years. The collisions of protons with oppositely charged particles at high energies were necessary to produce the sixth quark—typically referred to as the "top" quark.

Just as police investigators can reconstruct traffic accidents from clues at the scene, trained scientists are able to examine tracks left after proton collisions. The tracks of the sixth quark were hard to detect. Only about one-billionth of a percent of the proton collisions yielded evidence of a sixth quark.

Section Wrap-up

Review

1. What are quarks?

2. How does the Tevatron help scientists study the atom?

Explore the Technology

It may seem odd that tremendous amounts of energy are needed to effectively break open such small bits of matter as protons. Think about cracking open a peanut between your finger and thumb. Now consider breaking open a walnut or Brazil nut. This usually requires some impact beyond your own fingers. Which nut is held together with the greater force? What do you conclude about the forces holding quarks together in protons?

Mini LAB

How can indirect evidence be used to identify known objects?

Procedure

1. In your two-member team, have one person make an imprint or track of two objects in a pan of shallow flour or sand.
2. The other partner must now identify which objects were used to make the tracks.
3. Smooth the surface, trade roles, and repeat the process.

Analysis

1. What made some objects easy to identify?
2. How does the force involved in making the imprints affect the observed tracks? How does the same reasoning apply to detecting quarks?

SCIENCE & SOCIETY

10•3 Masses of Atoms

Science Words

mass number
isotope
average atomic mass

Objectives

- Compute the atomic mass and mass number of an atom.
- Identify and describe isotopes of common elements.
- Interpret the average atomic mass of an element.

Atomic Mass

If asked to estimate the height of your school building, you would not give an answer in miles. Realizing the scale of the building, you would more likely think about the height in feet. When thinking about the small masses of atoms, scientists found that even grams were not small enough. The unit of measurement of those particles is the atomic mass unit (u). In fact, the mass of a proton or a neutron is almost equal to 1 u. This is not a coincidence—the unit was defined that way. The atomic mass unit is defined as one-twelfth the mass of a carbon atom containing six protons and six neutrons. Remember that the mass of a carbon atom is in its nucleus because the atom's six electrons have a negligible mass. Therefore, each of the 12 particles in the nucleus must have a mass nearly equal to one-twelfth the mass of the carbon atom. Thus, a proton or a neutron has a mass of about 1 u. To help you understand this concept, look at **Figure 10-7.**

Figure 10-7

You can compare a carton of eggs to a carbon atom. *What number do they have in common?*

A A carton of eggs contains six brown eggs and six white eggs.

B You could define a mass unit as one-twelfth the mass of the entire dozen.

C The mass of each egg, brown or white, would be equal to your defined unit.

Mass Number

The **mass number** of an atom is the sum of the number of protons and the number of neutrons in the nucleus of an atom. As you can see in **Table 10-4,** the mass number of an atom is almost equal to the mass of its most common form, expressed in atomic mass units.

If you know the mass number and the atomic number of an atom, you can then calculate the number of neutrons. The number of neutrons is equal to the atomic number subtracted from the mass number.

number of neutrons = mass number − atomic number

Isotopes

Not all the atoms of an element have the same number of neutrons. Atoms of the same element that have different numbers of neutrons are called **isotopes.**

Suppose you have a sample of the element boron like the powder shown in **Figure 10-8.** Naturally occurring atoms of boron have mass numbers of 10 or 11. How many neutrons are there in a boron atom? It depends upon the boron to which you are referring. Obtain the number of protons from **Table 10-4** and use the formula above to calculate that a boron isotope may contain five or six neutrons. Use the example above to help you.

Figure 10-8

Boron has two naturally occurring isotopes.

B

Boron Isotopes

Mass number	11
# of protons	-5
# of neutrons	6
Mass number	10
# of protons	-5
# of neutrons	5

Table 10-4

Mass Numbers of Some Atoms					
Element	Symbol	Protons	Neutrons	Mass Number	Average Atomic Mass*
Boron	B	5	6	11	10.81
Carbon	C	6	6	12	12.01
Oxygen	O	8	8	16	16.00
Sodium	Na	11	12	23	22.99
Copper	Cu	29	34	63	63.55
* to two decimal places					

Problem Solving

An Unstable Isotope: Providing Medical Help

A common treatment for cancer tumors is intense, high-energy radiation. Where can doctors find such focused high energy? Understanding the makeup of some isotopes helps solve this problem.

The clustering of protons and neutrons in a nucleus of some isotopes does not produce a stable, low-energy situation. On some occasions, the number of protons and neutrons in a nucleus produces a high-energy, unstable nucleus. In this situation, the nucleus spontaneously changes to become more stable. To do this, the nucleus must give off excess energy in the form of radiation.

A particular application of this situation is found in the treatments of thyroid gland tumors. In order to function properly, the thyroid gland must absorb iodine.

Solve the Problem:

1. If an unstable isotope of iodine were carefully administered to a thyroid tumor patient, why might it cure the person?
2. Why is it important to use iodine isotopes in this particular situation instead of carbon isotopes?

Think Critically:

Iodine typically can be found as one of two isotopes: iodine-131 and iodine-130. How many neutrons are present in each? In this case, the isotope that spontaneously gives off radiation is the one with the most neutrons. Which one is the unstable isotope?

Identifying Isotopes

Figure 10-9 shows models of the two isotopes of boron. Because the numbers of neutrons in the isotopes are different, the mass numbers are also different. You use the name of the element followed by the mass number of the isotope to identify each isotope: boron-10 and boron-11. Because most elements have more than one isotope, each element is given an average atomic mass. The **average atomic mass** of an element is the average mass of the mixture of its isotopes.

For example, four out of five atoms of boron are boron-11, and one out of five is boron-10. Thus, in an average sample of five atoms of boron, four atoms are likely to have a mass of 11 u. One atom will have a mass of 10 u. If you measured the mass of the five atoms, you would find it to be 54 u. The average atomic mass of the boron mixture is 54 u divided by 5, or 10.8 u. That is, the average atomic mass of the element boron is 10.8 u. Note that

Figure 10-9

The two isotopes of boron have different numbers of neutrons and different mass numbers. *How many neutrons are in each isotope?*

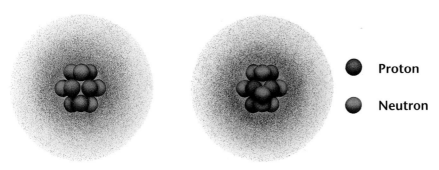

● Proton

● Neutron

CONNECT TO

LIFE SCIENCE

Living organisms on Earth contain carbon. Carbon-12 makes up 99 percent of this carbon. Carbon-13 and carbon-14 make up the other one percent. Which isotopes are archaeologists most interested in when they determine the age of carbon-containing remains? *Explain* your answer in your Science Journal.

the average atomic mass of boron, given in **Table 10-4,** is close to the mass of its most abundant isotope, boron-11.

For another example, hydrogen has three isotopes—hydrogen-1, hydrogen-2, and hydrogen-3. Each has one proton. How many neutrons does each have? The most abundant isotope is hydrogen-1, and the element's average atomic mass is 1.008. The average atomic mass of each element can be found in the periodic table of elements.

Section Wrap-up

Review

1. A chlorine atom has 17 protons and 18 neutrons. What is its mass number? What is its atomic number?

2. How are the isotopes of an element alike and how are they different?

3. **Think Critically:** Chlorine is used to treat most city water systems. The atomic number of chlorine is 17. The two naturally occurring isotopes of chlorine are chlorine-35 and chlorine-37. The average atomic mass of chlorine is 35.45 u. Why does this indicate that most chlorine atoms contain 18 neutrons?

Skill Builder
Comparing and Contrasting
How does the average atomic mass relate to the mass number of an atom? If you need help, refer to Comparing and Contrasting in the **Skill Handbook.**

Using Computers

Spreadsheet Use a spreadsheet to construct a table organizing information about the atomic numbers; atomic mass numbers; and the number of protons, neutrons, and electrons in atoms of oxygen-16 and oxygen-17.

Design Your Own Experiment

Candy-Covered Isotopes

The extremely small size of atoms makes it impossible to count them or determine their individual atomic masses using direct means. An instrument called a mass spectrometer allows for such determinations. As demonstrated earlier in this section, average atomic masses depend on the number and masses of the isotopes of an element.

In this activity, find out how you can use colored candy to represent the atoms in an average mass calculation.

PREPARATION

Problem
How can you calculate the average mass of a mixture of objects?

Form a Hypothesis
Based on the calculations and information in this section, state a hypothesis about samples of isotopes regarding number of objects, their individual masses, and average masses.

Objectives
- Using two types of coated candy, make a model to represent the average atomic mass calculations of isotopes.

- Calculate the average mass of candy samples.

Possible Materials
- container of red chocolate-center candy
- container of red peanut-center candy
- container of green chocolate-center candy
- container of green peanut-center candy

Safety Precautions 🚫
Do not eat candy samples used in this activity.

Data and Observations

	Peanut candy × mass	Chocolate candy × mass	Average $\dfrac{\text{total mass}}{\text{total candies}}$
Red			
Green			

PLAN THE EXPERIMENT

1. Within your group, for purposes of this activity, make a basic assumption that a red peanut candy is twice as massive as the red chocolate candy. Use the ratio of four times more massive for the green peanut candies and three times more massive for green chocolate candies.

2. Decide on a plan to test your hypothesis. Be sure to design a data table in your Science Journal to use with your plans.

Check the Plan

1. If you assume that the mass of one red chocolate candy is 1 and that the mass of the red peanut candy is 2, can you now calculate the total mass of any mixture of red candy?

2. Using your total mixture, can you now calculate the mass, in terms of red candy units, of the mixture?

3. Using the number of candies, design a plan to calculate the average mass of red candy.

4. Use your plan and other assumptions about green candy to deduce the average mass of green candy.

5. *Make sure your teacher approves your plan and that you have indicated any changes suggested in the plan.*

DO THE EXPERIMENT

1. When you count candy pieces, make sure to record the number of each type you use.

2. Show all of your calculations and label your answers in an orderly data table.

Analyze and Apply

1. **Compare** your results of the average mass of red candy with those of your classmates. Do the same for the average mass of green candy.

2. Did you find that regardless of the number of candies used in your groups, the average masses for each type of candy were the same? **Explain** why or why not.

Go Further

If a bag of red peanut candies contains eight pieces, how many red chocolate pieces would you have to add to the same bag to produce an average mass equal to your answer in this activity?

10•4 The Periodic Table

Science Words

periodic table
group
dot diagram
period
metal
nonmetal
metalloid

Objectives

- Describe the periodic table of elements and use it to find information about an element.
- Distinguish between a group and a period.
- Use the periodic table to classify an element as a metal, nonmetal, or metalloid.

Structure of the Periodic Table

On clear evenings, you can see the phases of the moon. Each month, the moon seems to grow larger, then smaller, in a repeating pattern. This type of change is periodic. *Periodic* means "repeated in a pattern." Look at a calendar. The days of the week are periodic because they repeat themselves every seven days. The calendar is a periodic table of days. You use calendars to organize your activities.

In the late 1800s, Dimitri Mendeleev, a Russian chemist, searched for a way to organize the elements. When he arranged all the elements known at that time in order of increasing atomic masses, he discovered that there was a pattern. Chemical properties found in lighter elements could be shown to repeat in heavier elements. Because the pattern repeated, it could be considered periodic. Today, we call this arrangement a **periodic table** of elements. An early periodic table is shown in **Figure 10-10**.

Figure 10-10

Among his contributions to science, Mendeleev is best known for his periodic chart of the elements. *Why do you think there are question marks in some places on his chart?*

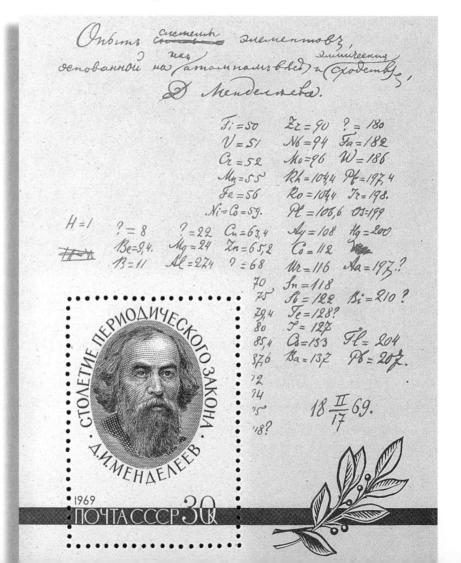

284

Mendeleev's periodic table had blank spaces. He looked at the properties and atomic masses of the elements surrounding these blank spaces. From this information, he predicted the properties and the mass numbers of new elements that had not yet been discovered. Sometimes, you make predictions like this. Suppose someone crossed out a date on a calendar, as shown. You could predict the missing date by looking at the surrounding dates. Mendeleev's predictions proved to be quite accurate. Scientists later discovered elements, such as germanium, having the properties that he had predicted **(Table 10-5).**

Counting Protons: An Improved Table

Although Mendeleev's arrangement of elements was successful, it did need some changes. On Mendeleev's table, the atomic mass gradually increased from left to right in each row. If you look at the modern periodic table as shown on pages 286 and 287, you will see several examples, such as cobalt and nickel, where the mass decreases from left to right. However, you may notice that the atomic number always increases from left to right. The work of Henry G.J. Moseley, a young English scientist, in 1913 led to the arrangement of elements based on their properties and atomic numbers instead of an arrangement based on atomic masses.

Each box in the periodic table contains information about the elements that you studied earlier in this chapter. Look at **Figure 10-11.** This box represents the element boron. The atomic number, chemical symbol, name, and average atomic mass are included in this box. The boxes for all of the elements are arranged in order of their atomic numbers.

Figure 10-11

The periodic table shows the symbol, name, atomic number, and atomic mass of each element.

Table 10-5

"Ekasilicon" (Germanium)		
Properties	**Predicted**	**Actual**
Atomic mass	72	72.6
Density	5.5 g/cm³	5.35 g/cm³
Color	dark gray	gray-white
Effect of water	none	none
Effect of acid	slight	HCl: no effect
Effect of base	slight	KOH: no effect

Table 10-6

PERIODIC TABLE OF THE ELEMENTS
Based on Carbon 12 = 12.0000

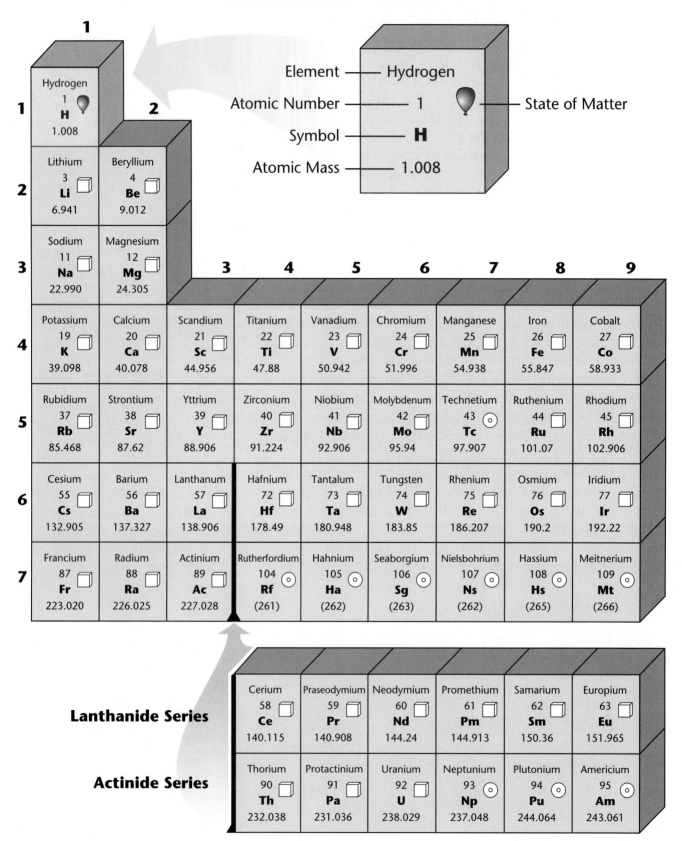

Element —— Hydrogen
Atomic Number —— 1 —— State of Matter
Symbol —— **H**
Atomic Mass —— 1.008

Lanthanide Series

Actinide Series

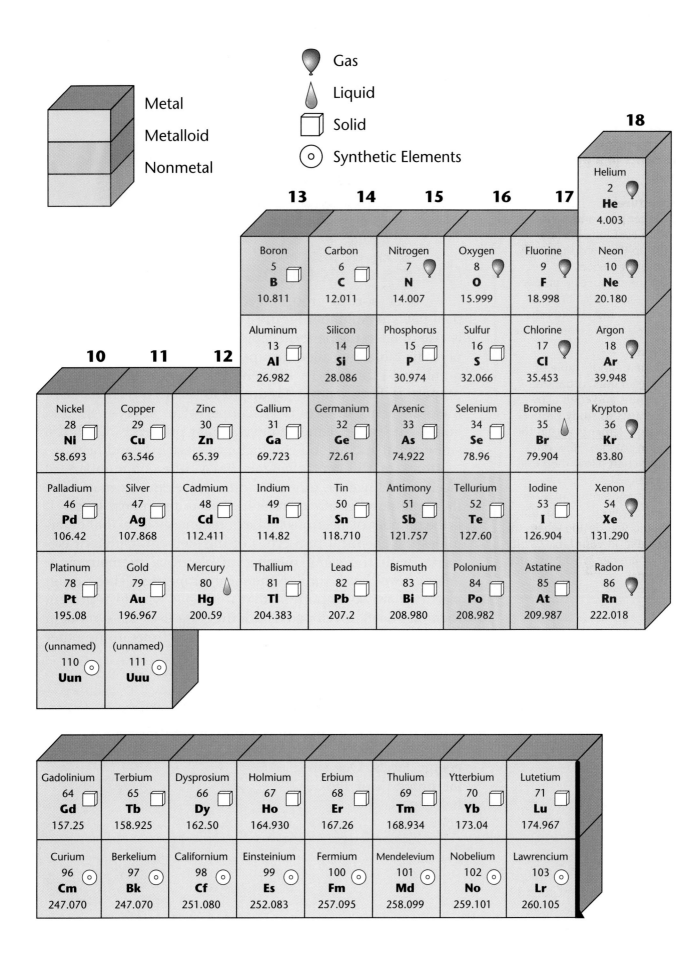

Metal
Metalloid
Nonmetal

Gas
Liquid
Solid
Synthetic Elements

		18
		Helium 2 He 4.003

13	14	15	16	17	
Boron 5 B 10.811	Carbon 6 C 12.011	Nitrogen 7 N 14.007	Oxygen 8 O 15.999	Fluorine 9 F 18.998	Neon 10 Ne 20.180
Aluminum 13 Al 26.982	Silicon 14 Si 28.086	Phosphorus 15 P 30.974	Sulfur 16 S 32.066	Chlorine 17 Cl 35.453	Argon 18 Ar 39.948

10	11	12						
Nickel 28 Ni 58.693	Copper 29 Cu 63.546	Zinc 30 Zn 65.39	Gallium 31 Ga 69.723	Germanium 32 Ge 72.61	Arsenic 33 As 74.922	Selenium 34 Se 78.96	Bromine 35 Br 79.904	Krypton 36 Kr 83.80
Palladium 46 Pd 106.42	Silver 47 Ag 107.868	Cadmium 48 Cd 112.411	Indium 49 In 114.82	Tin 50 Sn 118.710	Antimony 51 Sb 121.757	Tellurium 52 Te 127.60	Iodine 53 I 126.904	Xenon 54 Xe 131.290
Platinum 78 Pt 195.08	Gold 79 Au 196.967	Mercury 80 Hg 200.59	Thallium 81 Tl 204.383	Lead 82 Pb 207.2	Bismuth 83 Bi 208.980	Polonium 84 Po 208.982	Astatine 85 At 209.987	Radon 86 Rn 222.018
(unnamed) 110 Uun	(unnamed) 111 Uuu							

Gadolinium 64 Gd 157.25	Terbium 65 Tb 158.925	Dysprosium 66 Dy 162.50	Holmium 67 Ho 164.930	Erbium 68 Er 167.26	Thulium 69 Tm 168.934	Ytterbium 70 Yb 173.04	Lutetium 71 Lu 174.967
Curium 96 Cm 247.070	Berkelium 97 Bk 247.070	Californium 98 Cf 251.080	Einsteinium 99 Es 252.083	Fermium 100 Fm 257.095	Mendelevium 101 Md 258.099	Nobelium 102 No 259.101	Lawrencium 103 Lr 260.105

Procedure
1. Gather pens and pencils from everyone in class.
2. Group the pens separately from the pencils.
3. Decide on specific properties—such as color, mass, or size—and arrange the writing utensils into a table.

Analysis
1. In the periodic table of the elements, organized columns and rows allow scientists to study properties of elements within the same column. How does your chart allow the same practice?
2. If someone brought a new pen or pencil to class, how would you decide where to place it on your table? Write your answer in your Science Journal.

Figure 10-12

These objects can be classified as sports balls. *What similar properties do they have?*

Groups of Elements

We often sort or group objects because of the properties they have in common. **Figure 10-12** shows an example. This is also done in the periodic table. The vertical columns in the periodic table are called **groups,** or families. The groups are numbered 1 through 18. Elements in each group have similar properties. For example, **Figure 10-13** shows objects made of three elements in Group 11: copper—Cu, silver—Ag, and gold—Au. These elements have similar properties. Each is a shiny metal and a good conductor of electricity and heat.

Atoms of different elements have different numbers of electrons. However, atoms of different elements may have the same number of electrons in their outer energy levels. It is the number of electrons in the outer energy level that determines the chemical properties of the element. Different elements with the same number of electrons in their outer energy level have similar chemical properties. These outer electrons are so important that a special way to represent them has been developed. A **dot diagram** uses the symbol of the element and dots to represent the electrons in the outer energy level.

Family Traits

The dot diagrams of the atoms of the elements in Group 17, called the halogens, are shown in **Figure 10-14.** They all have seven electrons in their outer energy levels. One similar property of the halogens is the ability to

Figure 10-13

The elements copper, silver, and gold are all found in Group 11 on the periodic table. *What similar properties do they possess?*

Figure 10-14

In each of these dot diagrams, the seven dots represent seven outer electrons. *What group do these elements belong to?*

form compounds with elements in Group 1. The elements in Group 18 are known as noble gases. Noble gases do not usually form compounds. We say they are stable, or unreactive. The atoms of all the noble gases except helium have outer energy levels that contain eight electrons, as shown in **Figure 10-15.** You will learn more about the significance of electron arrangement of elements in later chapters.

Identifying a New Element

You have now learned that each element can be specifically identified by its atomic number—the number of protons in the nucleus of an atom. The number of neutrons may vary, as with isotopes. The number of electrons also may vary if some outer ones are removed or added. However, if the number of protons in an atom changes, then the atom has a new identity.

Recipe for an Element

As you will find in later chapters, chemical elements that you commonly encounter only change their number of protons through nuclear reactions. Were there ever more elements than we can now identify? Many scientists believe that the stable elements that we now have may at one time have been part of heavier elements that split apart. If you wanted to test part of that theory, you would have to bring existing elements together with a lot of energy to form superheavy atoms. For example, element 103, lawrencium, can be formed in a particle accelerator by colliding boron with an isotope of californium. How many total protons are found in californium and boron?

A New Member of the Family

Scientists in Berkeley, California; Dubna, Russia; and Darmstatdt, Germany, have been colliding particles to attempt to form elements 110 and 111. The German team has succeeded in showing evidence of creating isotopes of element 110. Although the synthesized element fell apart in

Figure 10-15

In each of these dot diagrams, the eight dots represent eight outer electrons. *What group do these elements belong to?*

INTEGRATION
Physics

Seeing Atoms ▽ △

For more than 50 years, scientists have been able to see extremely tiny things with electron microscopes. But it was less than 20 years ago that scientists first saw atoms with scanning probe microscopes. These microscopes are the result of a new approach to how we see objects. Instead of shining light or a beam of electrons on an object, these new microscopes drag a probe across the surface of an object. The position of the probe is then changed, and it is dragged across the surface again. This process, called scanning, is repeated many times to build an image of the peaks and valleys on the surface of the object. Scanning is like going into a dark room and using your hand as a probe to feel a chair to determine its shape, instead of shining a light on it.

The key development in the invention of the scanning probe microscope was a system that moves the probe in precise steps smaller than the width of an atom. In addition to seeing atoms, these probes enable scientists to move single atoms.

Think Critically:

Atoms range in radius from 0.053 nm to 0.27 nm. What everyday objects, like two kinds of balls, would represent this range in size?

approximately 270 microseconds, there was enough evidence of its presence to claim production of the heaviest known element. The German physicists used lead and nickel atoms to add the newest member to the family of the chemical elements. Look on the periodic table on pages 286-287 to see where element 110 now resides.

Periods of Elements

The horizontal rows of elements in the periodic table are called **periods.** Notice the stair-step line on the right side of the periodic table. All the elements to the left of this line, except hydrogen, are metals. Iron, zinc, and copper are examples of metals. Most **metals** have the common properties of existing as solids at room temperature and being shiny and good conductors of heat and electricity. **Figure 10-16** shows the metal gallium and its use in a semiconductor.

Scan of gallium arsenide

Those elements to the right of the stair-step line on the periodic table are classified as **nonmetals.** Oxygen, nitrogen, and carbon are examples of nonmetals. At room temperature, most nonmetals are gases and some are brittle solids. Most nonmetals do not conduct heat and electricity well.

The elements next to the stair-step line are **metalloids** because they have properties of both metals and nonmetals. Boron and silicon are examples of metalloids.

Elements in Groups 3 through 12 are called the transition elements. They are metals but have properties not found in elements of other groups. Copper and iron are examples of common transition elements.

Figure 10-16

Gallium is a metal that has a low melting point. It is used in the form of gallium arsenide in the semiconductor shown above.

Section Wrap-up

Review

1. Use the periodic table to find the name, atomic number, and average atomic mass of the following elements: N, Ca, Kr, and W.

2. Give the period and group in which each of these elements is found: nitrogen, sodium, iodine, and mercury.

3. Write the name of each of these elements and classify it as a metal, a nonmetal, or a metalloid: K, Si, Ba, and S.

4. **Think Critically:** Both the Mendeleev and Mosely periodic charts have gaps for as-then-undiscovered elements. Why do you think the chart used by Mosely could be more accurate at predicting where new elements would be placed?

Skill Builder
Making and Using Graphs
Construct a circle graph showing the elements classified as metals, metalloids, and nonmetals. If you need help, refer to Making and Using Graphs in the **Skill Handbook.**

Science Journal
From the periodic table on pages 286-287, choose a synthetic element and write a brief biography of the element in your Science Journal. Include information about the element's name, location of the synthesis research, and the people responsible.

People and Science

DR. BRENNA FLAUGHER, *Particle Physicist*

On the Job

Q Dr. Flaugher, is particle physics the same as atomic physics?

A Atomic physicists study the atom as a whole. Particle physicists work on a smaller scale, inside the atomic nucleus. They are interested in the particles and forces that make up protons and neutrons.

Q You are on a team of physicists who found the sixth quark. How did you know it was there to find?

A Particle physicists have a theory, called the Standard Model, that explains how particles fit together to form protons and neutrons. According to this model, quarks come in pairs. After the bottom quark was found in 1977, physicists began looking for its partner, which was named *top*. We finally found it in 1995.

Q Why did it take so long to find the top quark?

A It turns out to be much bigger than we thought. When physicists first began looking for the top quark, they were searching for a particle with twice the mass of the bottom quark. The top quark is actually about 35 times more massive than its partner.

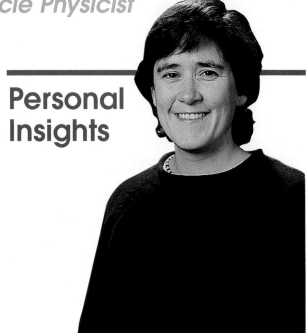

Personal Insights

Q Why did you choose a career in particle physics?

A It's a real frontier. This is a very exciting field—we are doing things that have never been done before. The collider is like a powerful microscope that lets us look deeper and deeper into the workings of nature. The particles we study are very, very small, but they can help us understand very big things, like why matter has mass, why gravity works the way it does, what happens inside stars, and how the universe was formed.

Career Connection

Physicists, electronics engineers, mechanical engineers, civil engineers, computer specialists, science writers, and repair technicians all worked together to discover the top quark. Talk with a career counselor at a local high school or college to find out what kinds of education and training these careers require.

- **Physics Teacher**
- **Nuclear Technician**

Summary

10-1: Structure of the Atom

1. A chemical symbol is a shorthand way of writing the name of an element.
2. An atom consists of a nucleus made of protons and neutrons surrounded by an electron cloud.
3. The electrons in an atom are arranged in several energy levels, each of which is able to hold a certain number of electrons.

10-2: Science and Society: Smaller Particles of Matter

1. Quarks are particles of matter that make up protons and neutrons.
2. Protons can be broken into quarks by having them collide while traveling near the speed of light.

10-3: Masses of Atoms

1. The number of neutrons in an atom can be computed by subtracting the atomic number from the mass number.
2. The isotopes of an element are atoms of that same element that have different numbers of neutrons.
3. The average atomic mass of an element is the average mass of the mixture of its isotopes.

10-4: The Periodic Table

1. The periodic table of elements is an arrangement of elements according to repeated changes in properties.
2. In the periodic table, the 111 elements are arranged in 18 vertical columns, or groups, and seven horizontal rows, or periods.
3. Metals are found at the left of the periodic table, nonmetals at the right, and metalloids along the line that separates the metals from the nonmetals.

Key Science Words

a. atomic number
b. average atomic mass
c. chemical symbol
d. dot diagram
e. electron
f. electron cloud
g. group
h. isotope
i. mass number
j. metal
k. metalloid
l. neutron
m. nonmetal
n. nucleus
o. period
p. periodic table
q. proton
r. quark

Reviewing Vocabulary

Match each phrase with the correct term from the list of Key Science Words.

1. an abbreviated way to write the name of an element
2. an atomic particle with no charge
3. any of two or more atoms of the same element with a different number of neutrons
4. average mass of the mixture of isotopes
5. positively charged center of an atom
6. particle that makes up protons and neutrons
7. the region formed by electrons
8. the number of protons in the nucleus
9. total number of protons and neutrons in the nucleus
10. a horizontal row in the periodic table

Chapter 10 Review

Checking Concepts

Choose the word or phrase that completes the sentence or answers the question.

1. The state of matter of most of the elements to the left of the stair-step line in the periodic table is _____.
   a. gas   c. plasma
   b. liquid   d. solid
2. If a pattern repeats itself, it is _____.
   a. isotopic   c. periodic
   b. metallic   d. transition
3. _____ is an element that would have similar properties to those of neon.
   a. Aluminum   c. Arsenic
   b. Argon   d. Silver
4. Boron is a _____.
   a. metal   c. noble gas
   b. metalloid   d. nonmetal
5. The element potassium is a _____.
   a. metal   c. nonmetal
   b. metalloid   d. transition element
6. The element bromine is a _____.
   a. metal   c. nonmetal
   b. metalloid   d. transition element
7. The halogens are those elements in Group _____.
   a. 1   c. 15
   b. 11   d. 17
8. In its group, nitrogen is the only element that is a _____.
   a. gas   c. metal
   b. metalloid   d. liquid
9. _____ is a shiny element that conducts electricity and heat well.
   a. Chlorine   c. Hydrogen
   b. Sulfur   d. Magnesium
10. The atomic number of Re is 75. The atomic mass of one of its isotopes is 186. How many neutrons are in an atom of this isotope?
    a. 75   c. 186
    b. 111   d. 261

Understanding Concepts

Answer the following questions in your Science Journal using complete sentences.

11. Why do electrons keep moving around the nucleus and not away from the atom?
12. Why do some chemical symbols have one letter and some have two or three letters?
13. A silver sample contains 52 atoms, each having 60 neutrons, and 48 atoms, each having 62 neutrons. What is the sample's average atomic mass?
14. According to currently accepted ideas, how do protons and electrons differ in structure?
15. Why are protons and neutrons also known as nucleons?

Thinking Critically

16. We know that properties of elements are periodic. List at least two other things in nature that are periodic.
17. Lead and mercury are two pollutants in the environment. From information about them in the periodic table, why are they called *heavy metals?*
18. Ge and Si are used in making semiconductors. Are these two elements in the same group or the same period?
19. U and Pu are named for objects in nature. What are these objects, and what other element is named after a similar object?
20. Ca is used by the body to make bones and teeth. Radioactive Sr is in nuclear waste. These two elements are in the same group. Yet one is safe for people and the other is hazardous. Why is this Sr hazardous to people?

Developing Skills

If you need help, refer to the **Skill Handbook.**

21. **Making and Using Tables:** Use the periodic table to list a metal, a metalloid, and a nonmetal each with five outer-level electrons.

22. **Comparing and Contrasting:** From the information found in the periodic table and reference books, compare and contrast the properties of chlorine and bromine.

23. **Interpreting Data:** If scientists have determined that a neutral atom of rubidium has an atomic number of 37 and a mass number of 85, how many protons, neutrons, and electrons does the atom have?

24. **Concept Mapping:** As a star dies, it becomes more dense. Its temperature rises to a point where He nuclei are combined with other nuclei. When this happens, the atomic numbers of the other nuclei are increased by 2 because each gains the two protons contained in the He nucleus. For example, Cr fused with He becomes Fe. Complete the concept map below showing the first four steps in He fusion.

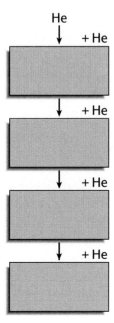

25. **Sequencing:** What changes in the periodic table would occur in periods 1 through 4 if the elements were arranged according to increasing average atomic mass instead of atomic number? How do we know that arrangement by atomic number is correct?

Performance Assessment

1. **Asking Questions:** Research the attempts made by Johann Döbereiner and John Newlands to classify the elements. Research the background and work of these scientists and write your findings in the form of an interview.

2. **Display:** Make a display of samples or pictures of several elements, such as the application of neon in the photograph below. List the name, symbol, atomic number, average atomic mass, and several uses for each element.

3. **Research and Report:** Research and report on models of the atom from the time of the ancient Greeks until the present.

Previewing the Chapter

Chemical Bonds

Whenever you see a brilliant display of fireworks, like the one over the Tower Bridge in London, you observe a chemical change in which chemical bonds break and others form. Forming a chemical bond is usually an energy-releasing process, as is shown by the energy given off when fireworks explode. Evidence of a chemical change provides evidence of a chemical bond. The materials in fireworks combine, or bond, with oxygen from the air to make new substances. Can you think of other changes that involve combining with oxygen?

EXPLORE ACTIVITY

Find evidence of the formation of a chemical bond.

1. Obtain two identical test tubes.
2. Insert some steel wool into the bottom of one test tube.
3. Invert both tubes and place them into a beaker of water.
4. Adjust the water level in both to be approximately 1 cm into the openings.

Observe: After a few days, what differences do you notice that indicate a chemical change? Summarize your observations in your Science Journal.

Previewing Science Skills

▶ In the **Skill Builders,** you will **make and use a table; map concepts;** and **use variables, constants, and controls.**

▶ In the **Activities,** you will **observe, compare, classify,** and **hypothesize.**

▶ In the **MiniLAB,** you will **observe and infer.**

11•1 Why Atoms Combine

Objectives

- Describe how a compound differs from the elements that compose it.
- Explain what a chemical formula represents.
- State a reason why chemical bonding occurs.

Compounds

Most of the matter around you is in the form of compounds or mixtures of compounds. The water you drink, the carbon dioxide you exhale, and the salt contained in some foods are examples of compounds.

Some of the matter around you is in the form of uncombined elements, such as iron and oxygen. But, like many other pairs of elements, iron and oxygen tend to unite chemically to form a compound when the conditions are right. You know how iron exposed to oxygen and water forms rust, a compound. Rusting is a chemical change because a new substance, as shown in **Figure 11-1,** is produced.

Figure 11-1

When iron and oxygen combine, a new substance, rust, forms. The properties of rust differ from those of iron and oxygen.

Compounds have properties unlike those of their elements. Table salt, for example, is made up of the elements sodium and chlorine. Sodium is a shiny, soft, silvery metal that reacts violently with water. Chlorine is a greenish-yellow gas that can kill an animal that inhales a few deep breaths of the gas. These elements combine to form table salt, or sodium chloride, as shown in **Figure 11-2.**

Formulas

Do you recall that the chemical symbols Na and Cl represent sodium and chlorine? When written as NaCl, the symbols make up a formula, or chemical shorthand, for the compound sodium chloride. Another formula you may recognize is H_2O, for water. The formula is a combination of the symbols H and O and the subscript number 2. *Subscript* means "written below." A subscript number written after a symbol tells how many atoms of that element are in a unit of the compound. If a symbol has no subscript, the unit contains only one atom of that element.

Look at the formula for iron(III) oxide: Fe_2O_3. The symbol for iron, Fe, is followed by the subscript 2, and the symbol for oxygen, O, is followed by the subscript 3. Other examples of formulas are shown in **Figure 11-3.**

Figure 11-2

Sodium, a soft, silvery metal, combines with chlorine, a greenish-yellow gas, to form sodium chloride, a white crystalline solid. *How are the properties of table salt different from those of sodium and chlorine?*

Figure 11-3

These models show the ratios and the arrangements of atoms in water and carbon dioxide.

Water

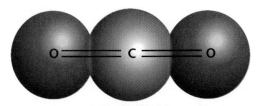

Carbon dioxide

A The formula H_2O shows there are two atoms of hydrogen for one atom of oxygen in one unit of the compound water. Put another way, the ratio of hydrogen atoms to oxygen atoms in water is 2 to 1.

B For one atom of carbon, there are two atoms of oxygen in carbon dioxide.

Table 11-1

Some Familiar Compounds		
Familiar Name	**Chemical Name**	**Formula**
Lye	Sodium hydroxide	NaOH
Vinegar	Acetic acid	$HC_2H_3O_2$
Ammonia	Ammonia	NH_3
Grain alcohol	Ethanol	C_2H_5OH
Sand	Silicon dioxide	SiO_2
Battery acid	Sulfuric acid	H_2SO_4
Stomach acid	Hydrochloric acid	HCl
Milk of magnesia	Magnesium hydroxide	$Mg(OH)_2$
Cane sugar	Sucrose	$C_{12}H_{22}O_{11}$

The **chemical formula** for any compound tells what elements it contains and the ratio of the atoms of those elements. What elements are in each compound listed in **Table 11-1?** What is the ratio of atoms in each compound?

Chemically Stable Atoms

What causes elements to form compounds? Look at the periodic table on pages 732 and 733. It lists 111 elements, most of which can, and often do, combine with other elements. But the six noble gases in Group 18 seldom combine with other elements. Why do the noble gases so infrequently form compounds? The reason is that the arrangement of electrons in their atoms makes them chemically stable, or resistant to change.

Outer Levels: Getting Their Fill

What electron arrangements make atoms stable? An atom is **chemically stable** if its outer energy level is completely filled with electrons. For the atoms of most elements, the outer energy level is filled when it contains eight electrons. Atoms of the noble gases neon, argon, krypton, xenon, and radon all contain eight electrons in the outermost energy level. For atoms of helium, the outermost energy level is filled when it has two electrons.

Figure 11-4 shows dot diagrams of some of the noble gases. Remember from Chapter 10 that a dot diagram of an atom shows the number of electrons in its outer energy level. Notice that each of these elements has eight outer electrons.

USING MATH

The formula H_2O represents one molecule of water. To represent two molecules of water, use a coefficient as you would in algebra—$2H_2O$. The formula for carbon dioxide is CO_2. How would you represent three molecules of CO_2?

Figure 11-4

Dot diagrams of noble gases show that they all have a stable, filled outer level.

Because each noble gas has an outer level that is filled with electrons, each of these elements is chemically stable. Thus, the noble gases don't form compounds naturally. A few compounds of xenon, krypton, and radon have been prepared in the laboratory under special conditions. Each atom of all the elements *except* the noble gases has from one to seven electrons in its outer energy level. These atoms tend to lose, gain, or share electrons with other atoms. When gaining, losing, or sharing electrons, attractions form between atoms, and compounds form. In one of these ways, an atom may have its outer energy level filled, resulting in an outer energy level similar to that of a noble gas.

Losing, gaining, and sharing electrons are the means by which atoms become stable and form chemical bonds. A **chemical bond** is a force that holds together the atoms in a substance. As sodium and chlorine become bonded, each sodium atom loses one electron and each chlorine atom gains one. As a result, each atom in sodium chloride, NaCl, has eight electrons in its newly formed outer energy level. **Figure 11-5** illustrates this process.

USING MATH

You can use integers to represent positive and negative charges of atoms. If a neutral atom gains an electron, the new charge is $0 + (1-) = 1-$. The atom has a net charge of $1-$. What equation shows a neutral atom losing an electron? What is the net charge?

Figure 11-5

When sodium combines with chlorine, each sodium atom loses an electron and each chlorine atom gains an electron. *Why is the compound sodium chloride stable?*

$$\text{Na}\cdot + \cdot\text{Cl} \longrightarrow [\text{Na}]^+ + [:\text{Cl}:]^-$$

Sodium atom   Chlorine atom   Sodium chloride

In chlorine gas, two chlorine atoms share electrons, as shown in **Figure 11-6.** In its formula, Cl_2, the subscript 2 shows that two atoms are bonded together.

As you have read, compounds make up most of the matter around you. Why is this so? The answer is that the arrangements of electrons in most atoms make them chemically unstable. By sharing or transferring electrons, atoms achieve more stable arrangements of electrons.

Figure 11-6

This dot diagram shows the formation of chlorine gas, Cl_2, from two atoms of chlorine. *How is the bond in Cl_2 different from the bond in NaCl?*

| Chlorine atom | Chlorine atom | Chlorine molecule |

Section Wrap-up

Review

1. What happens to the properties of elements when atoms form compounds?

2. Write formulas for (a) a compound with one calcium atom and two fluorine atoms and (b) a compound with two aluminum atoms and three sulfur atoms.

3. Why do most elements tend to form compounds?

4. **Think Critically:** The label on a box of washing soda states that it contains Na_2CO_3. Name the elements in this compound. In what ratio are they present?

Skill Builder
Making and Using Tables
The compounds in **Table 11-1** on page 300 that contain carbon are classified as organic, and the others are classified as inorganic. Reorganize the contents of the table using these groups. If you need help, refer to Making and Using Tables in the **Skill Handbook.**

Science Journal

A chemical bond is not a thing that can be touched. Using electron arrangements, energy, and stability, write in your Science Journal a paragraph describing a chemical bond.

Activity 11-1

Eggshell Electrons

You know how important electrons are in chemical bonding and how this bonding is based on the arrangement of electrons. Show how electrons control bonding by forming some model bonds.

Problem
How can a visible model show how energy levels fill when atoms combine?

Materials
- modified egg carton
- marbles

Procedure
1. Obtain a modified egg carton and marbles from your teacher. The carton represents the first and second energy levels of an atom. The marbles represent electrons.
2. Place one marble in each depression of the carton. Start with the pair of depressions that represents the first energy level of the atom.
3. Place the remaining marbles in receptacles representing the second energy level. In which column would your element appear on the periodic chart?
4. Compare your model with those of your classmates. Find one or more other cartons that, when combined with yours, will make it possible for each of the two cartons to have eight marbles in its second energy level.
5. In your Science Journal, make a list of the combinations you were able to make with your classmates' models.

Analyze
1. Generally, do elements in metal groups on the periodic table have more or fewer electrons in their outer energy levels than do nonmetals?
2. The combinations you found could represent chemical formulas. Why did some formulas require more than one atom of an element?

Conclude and Apply
3. Would your **model** be more likely to represent a metal or a nonmetal atom? Explain.
4. **Predict** what group of elements your **model** would be in if you received eight marbles. Explain.

Kinds of
Chemical Bonds

Science Words

ion
ionic bond
covalent bond
polar molecule
nonpolar molecule

Objectives

- Describe ionic bonds and covalent bonds.
- Identify the particles produced by ionic bonding and by covalent bonding.
- Distinguish between a nonpolar covalent bond and a polar covalent bond.

Ions and Ionic Bonds

The brilliant flash of a camera and a bright white explosion in a fireworks display both show what happens when magnesium metal combines with oxygen, as shown in **Figure 11-7.** Recall how the atoms of these elements bond chemically when mixed. An atom of magnesium has two electrons in its outer level, as shown below. When that atom loses two electrons from its third level, the second level becomes a complete outer level because it contains eight electrons. But the atom now contains 12 protons, with a total positive charge of $12+$, and ten electrons, with a total charge of $10-$. Because $(12+) + (10-) = 2+$, the atom now has a net charge of $2+$. Atoms that have a charge are called **ions.** Magnesium with a $2+$ charge is called a magnesium ion. The charge would be shown as a superscript adjacent to the element's symbol, Mg^{2+}, to indicate its charge. *Superscript* means "written above."

An oxygen atom has six electrons in its outer energy level. When the atom gains two electrons, its outermost energy level contains eight electrons. The atom now has eight protons, with a total charge of $8+$, and ten electrons, with a total charge of $10-$. Because $(8+) + (10-) = 2-$, the atom has a net negative charge of $2-$. In other words, it is now an oxygen ion, which you write with a superscript minus sign, O^{2-}, to indicate its charge. However, the compound

Figure 11-7

When burned, magnesium combines with oxygen.

Mg: — : ⟶ [Mg]²⁺

Magnesium atom   **Electrons**   **Magnesium ion**

:Ö· + : ⟶ [:Ö:]²⁻

Oxygen atom   **Electrons**   **Oxygen ion**

Magnesium oxide

Figure 11-8
This dot diagram for magnesium oxide, MgO, shows that both ions are stable.

MgO as a whole is neutral because the total net positive charge equals the total net negative charge. The dot diagram for MgO is shown in **Figure 11-8.**

Opposites Attract

An ion is an atom that is either positively or negatively charged. Compounds made up of ions are ionic compounds, and the bonds that hold them together are ionic bonds. An **ionic bond** is the force of attraction between the opposite charges of the ions in an ionic compound.

Figure 11-9 shows another example of ionic bonding—the formation of magnesium chloride, $MgCl_2$. When magnesium reacts with chlorine, a magnesium atom loses two electrons and becomes a positively charged ion, Mg^{2+}. Notice that you write $2+$ on the symbol for magnesium to indicate the ion's net charge. At the same time, each of the two chlorine atoms gains one electron and becomes a negatively charged chloride ion, Cl^-. The compound as a whole is neutral. Why? Because the sum of the net charges on all three ions is zero.

CONNECT TO
EARTH SCIENCE

Farmers must sometimes add lime, calcium oxide, to their soil. What is the formula of calcium oxide? *Predict* whether calcium oxide is likely to be an ionic compound.

Figure 11-9

Magnesium chloride can be extracted from seawater and used as a source of magnesium metal.

Magnesium atom + Chlorine atoms → Chloride ion   Magnesium ion   Chloride ion

Nervous Ions

Ions are not just something you read about in a science book. Every movement you make—from the slight eye movements needed to read this sentence to the larger movement of turning the page—depends on ions and their relationship to the actions of muscles. How do muscles receive the signal to move? You may be surprised to find out that muscle movements depend on the movement of ions into and out of nerve cells. Nerve cells are surrounded by sodium, potassium, and chloride ions.

INTEGRATION
Life Science

Figure 11-10

As these ions move in and out of the nerve fibers, through the cell membrane, they set up an electrical pulse that results in a signal moving along a nerve. For example, many sodium ions, which are positively charged, are outside of a normal nerve cell membrane, while negative ions stay on the inside, which makes a slight charge build up in that area of the nerve.

The typical speed for signals moving along nerve cells is between 40 and 60 m/s. As you think about gaining and losing electrons to make ions, remember how important they are to many functions of your body.

Molecules and Covalent Bonds

Most atoms become more chemically stable by sharing electrons, rather than by losing or gaining electrons. In **Figure 11-6** on page 302, you saw how two chlorine atoms share electrons. Notice that the chlorine particle, Cl_2, is not charged—it is neutral. The chlorine is not in the form of ions, but rather molecules. Neutral particles formed as a result of electron sharing are called **molecules.**

The attraction that forms between atoms when they share electrons is known as a **covalent bond.** In the case of chlorine, a covalent bond is formed between two atoms of the same element. Covalent bonds also form between atoms of nitrogen, the gas that makes up most of the air. As you can see in **Figure 11-10,** two atoms in a molecule of nitrogen share six electrons, forming three covalent bonds between the atoms.

Polar and Nonpolar Molecules

Atoms in molecules do not always share electrons equally. An example is a molecule of hydrogen chloride, HCl. A water solution of HCl is hydrochloric acid, which is used in laboratories, to clean metal, and in your stomach to digest food.

Hydrogen chloride molecule (polar)

MiniLAB

What type of molecule is water?

Find out what type of bonding is present in a water molecule.

Procedure
1. Turn on the faucet to produce a thin stream of water.
2. Rub an inflated balloon with wool or fur.
3. Bring the balloon near the stream of water, and describe your observations.

Analysis
1. Explain your observations.
2. In terms of the observations, explain what type of bonding is in a water molecule.

Figure 11-11

A dot diagram and model for a molecule of hydrogen chloride show the sharing of electrons.

Chlorine atoms have a stronger attraction for electrons than hydrogen atoms do. As a result, the electrons shared in hydrogen chloride will spend more time near the chlorine atom than near the hydrogen atom. Look at **Figure 11-11.** This unequal sharing of electrons gives each chlorine atom a slight negative charge and each hydrogen atom a slight positive charge. This type of molecule is called polar. *Polar* means "having opposite ends." A **polar molecule** is one that has a positive end and a negative end. Water is another example of a compound with polar molecules, as shown in **Figure 11-12** on page 308, as is sugar.

Some molecules, such as those of nitrogen, are nonpolar because the two nitrogen atoms share their electrons equally. A **nonpolar molecule** is one that does not have oppositely charged ends. Look again at the diagram of a nitrogen molecule in **Figure 11-10.**

Bond Busters

Human activities generate toxic compounds in huge amounts. One way to get rid of toxic compounds is to change them chemically into other harmless compounds; that is, their chemical bonds must be broken. Then the atoms could bond into different molecules of less harmful substances.

From oil spills on water to toxic solvents at hazardous waste sites, scientists are using microbes as bond busters. The microbes eat the compounds, which change chemically as they are digested. To create a strain of pollutant-eating microbes, scientists first add a pollutant to a population of microbes. Most of the microbes die, leaving only the hardiest ones to reproduce. Scientists then seed polluted areas with these microbes and add fertilizer and oxygen to promote their growth. The microbes break down the toxic compounds and then, with the food source gone, the microbes die. At least 1000 different strains of bacteria and fungi are now helping to get rid of pollutants. The biggest advantage of the microbial approach is that instead of relocating the pollutants, the microbes destroy them.

Think Critically:

What would be the disadvantages of using microbes compared to removing or burning contaminated soil?

Bacteria

Figure 11-12

The combination of hydrogen atoms and an oxygen atom forms a polar molecule.

A As hydrogen atoms approach an oxygen atom, their electrons are attracted to the oxygen atom.

B Although the pull of oxygen is strong, hydrogen does not lose its electrons. It shares them with the oxygen atom. Because the electrons are more attracted to the oxygen atom than to the hydrogen atoms, the sharing is unequal.

C Unequal sharing of electrons produces an area of negative charge and an area of positive charge on the molecule. Because the electrons spend more time around the oxygen atom, this atom has a slightly negative charge. The hydrogen atoms have a slightly positive charge.

You have read about two main ways chemical bonding takes place, producing two kinds of compounds—ionic and covalent. These groups of compounds have contrasting properties. Ionic compounds are usually formed by bonding between a metal and a nonmetal. Bonds between nonmetal atoms are covalent. Most ionic compounds are crystalline solids with high melting points. Many covalent compounds are liquids or gases at room temperature. In later chapters, you will learn more about compounds of each type.

Section Wrap-up

Review

1. Compare ionic and covalent bonds.

2. What type of particle is formed by the following bonds: (a) ionic, (b) polar covalent, (c) nonpolar covalent?

3. **Think Critically:** From the following list of symbols, choose two elements that are likely to form an ionic bond. Select two elements that would likely form a covalent bond. Explain your choices.

Cl, Ne, S, Ca, K

Skill Builder

Concept Mapping

Using the following terms, make a network tree concept map of chemical bonding: *ionic, covalent, ions, positive ions, negative ions, molecules, polar, nonpolar*. If you need help, refer to Concept Mapping in the **Skill Handbook.**

USING MATH

Aluminum oxide, Al_2O_3, can be produced during space shuttle launches. Show that the sum of the positive and negative charges in a unit of Al_2O_3 equals zero.

People and Science

DR. ALVARO GARZA, *Physician*

On the Job

Q What are the sources of lead poisoning?

A It results from someone ingesting or inhaling something that contains lead. Years ago, gasoline had a high lead content. Now the source is primarily lead-based paints in older homes.

Q How does lead poisoning affect young children?

A At high levels, it can be deadly. Even at lower levels, it may affect behavioral and brain development.

Q What treatments are available to children with high levels of lead in their blood?

A At the extreme, a child may need hospitalization and chelation therapy. That's the injection of a substance that chelates, or forms bonds, to the lead so that it can be excreted through the kidneys. It is most important to stress preventive measures, such as frequent washing of children's hands and toys. Nutrition is important, too, especially adequate iron and calcium in the intestine to decrease the body's absorption of lead.

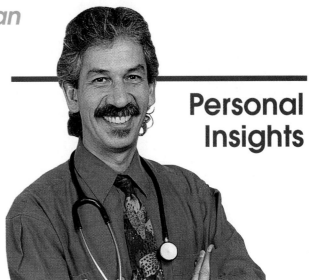

Personal Insights

Q Childhood lead poisoning occurs mostly in low-income inner-city neighborhoods. How do you feel about this?

A Environmental and social justice is very important to me. I often work with community-based organizations. It's vital to educate neighborhood activists so they can be leaders in health education in their own communities.

Q When you give talks at schools, how do you hope students perceive you?

A I'd like them to think of me as an activist, someone who works for a better world and healthier lives for kids.

Career Connection

Working in the public health sector involves educating people to take care of their own families' health. Use the information given about childhood lead poisoning to make a poster that could be displayed in your community.

- **Public health worker**
- **Pharmacist**

Activity 11-2

Become a Bond Breaker

The basic structural units of ionic compounds are ions. For covalent substances, molecules make up the basic units. By using controlled heat to melt substances, you can test various compounds to rate the attractive forces between their basic units. Would a substance that is difficult to melt have strong forces or weak forces holding its basic units to each other?

PREPARATION

Problem
How do the attractive forces between ions compare to the attractive forces between molecules?

Form a Hypothesis
Based on what you know about ions and molecules, state a hypothesis about which would generally have stronger attractions between their structural units.

Objectives
- Observe the effect of heat on melting points of selected substances.
- Design an experiment that allows you to make some inferences that relate ease of melting and forces of attraction between particles of a substance.

Possible Materials
- small samples of crushed ice, table salt, sugar
- wire test-tube holder
- test tubes
- goggles
- laboratory burner
- timer

Safety Precautions
Keep a safe distance from the open flame of the lab burner. Wear proper eye protection. Do not continue heating beyond 5 minutes.

PLAN THE EXPERIMENT

1. As a group, agree upon and write a hypothesis statement.
2. As a group, write a detailed list of steps needed to test your hypothesis.
3. Make a list of materials that you will need to complete your experiment.
4. Design a data table in your Science Journal to record your observations.

Check the Plan
1. As you heat materials in a test tube, what variables are you controlling?
2. How are you timing the heating of substances?
3. Will you run any tests more than one time?
4. *Make sure your teacher approves your plan and that you have included any changes suggested in the plan.*

DO THE EXPERIMENT

1. Carry out the experiment as planned.
2. While you are observing the heating of each substance, think about the movements of the particles. Which particles are held together by ionic bonds? Which are made up of covalent molecules?

3. Be sure to write down how long it takes to melt the tested substances.

Analyze and Apply
1. **Compare** your results with those of other groups.
2. **Classify** your tested substances as more likely ionic or covalent.
3. Which substances are generally more difficult to melt?
4. Sugar is known as a polar covalent compound. **Infer** how polarity affects melting point.

Go Further

Because you tested a limited number of samples, you can't make conclusions about all ionic and covalent substances. But if you had to make a prediction, which do you think would be easier to melt, KBr or candle wax? Candle wax is made up of many of the same types of atoms that make up sugar.

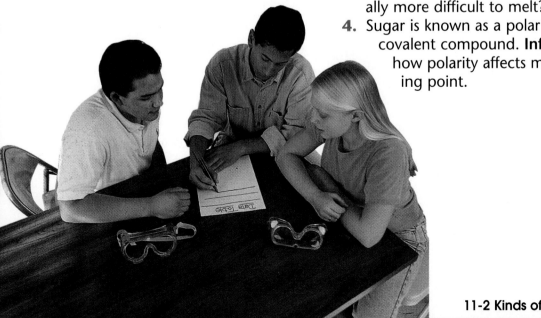

ISSUE:

11•3 Chemical Risks in the Home

Science Words

toxic
corrosive

Objectives

- Describe the dangers posed by hazardous compounds in the home.
- Demonstrate a knowledge of safer alternative compounds to use.

Chemicals—Not Just in the Lab

Professional chemists regularly work with chemicals that may be hazardous. They have learned to follow safety precautions and minimize risks. Do you realize that you, too, often work around hazardous chemicals? A hazardous chemical is one that can affect the health and safety of people or harm the environment. If you read the labels on household materials, you will often see strong health warnings.

Classifying the Problems

Hazardous chemicals usually fit one of three categories. **Toxic** compounds are poisonous. The compounds that help disinfectants work and repel insects are often toxic. The term **corrosive** comes from Latin roots meaning "to tear up." This type of compound is useful for unclogging drains and cleaning ovens and can be found in car batteries. However, corrosives cause problems when they come in contact with human skin or some metals. The third overall class of hazardous compounds is made up of compounds that burn easily. They are said to be flammable. Gasoline, paint thinners, and some aerosols are common examples of flammable materials.

The type of bonding in a compound helps determine how hazardous a material is. For example, the bonding in acetone, found in some paint removers, is covalent. Many covalently bonded compounds readily evaporate, which makes them easily inhaled and probably flammable. Ionic compounds are not likely to evaporate. Drain cleaners often contain NaOH, an ionically bonded compound.

Is there any way to control what hazardous compounds are used and how they are used? What can you do to minimize risk to yourself, your family, and the environment?

Table 11-2

Tips to Prevent Pollution from Hazardous Materials

1. Use safer alternatives.
2. Recycle oil, antifreeze, and used batteries.
3. If you must buy a hazardous product, buy only the amount you need.
4. Store hazardous materials in their original containers, away from children.
5. Keep hazardous materials that easily evaporate in tightly closed containers.
6. Share your knowledge of the problem of hazardous household compounds with others.

2 Points of View

Laws to Regulate Sale, Use, and Disposal of Hazardous Household Materials

Some people think that laws should be enacted that control hazardous materials. They believe that without any restrictions, it is inevitable that potentially hazardous materials will be released to harm the environment. Laws have been enacted that require an additional disposal fee for proper handling of discarded oil from automobiles, old batteries, and tires. These added fees help pay for recycling and proper disposal of some hazardous products. By paying small fees now for proper handling and recycling efforts, we can avoid more costly water and environmental cleanup costs and possibly even increased health costs. Do you think the fees are worth the cost?

Individual Responsibility

Some consumers resent being told how they must deal with potentially hazardous materials. How can an individual handle such materials in a responsible manner?

One solution is to use less harmful compounds as substitutes for potentially hazardous materials. Other possible solutions are shown in **Table 11-2.**

Figure 11-13

Warning labels on these home chemicals advise consumers about how to use the products safely.

Section Wrap-up

Review

1. What are the three main categories of hazardous household compounds?

2. Freon from air-conditioning systems is almost certainly responsible for some destruction of Earth's protective ozone layer. Improper handling of Freon can expose it to air, where it evaporates easily. Do you think Freon is more likely a covalently bonded or ionically bonded compound?

Explore the Issue

If you were a member of your state legislature and a law concerning fees for proper disposal of old lead and acid from car batteries were being considered, what would you want to do? Do you think present laws are adequate? Should the laws be more strict? Who would possibly benefit? Who would complain? Answer these questions in your Science Journal.

SCIENCE & SOCIETY

Formulas and Names of Compounds

Science Words

oxidation number
binary compound
polyatomic ion
hydrate

Objectives

• Explain how to deter-mine oxidation numbers.
• Write formulas for compounds from their names.
• Name compounds from their formulas.
• Describe hydrates and their formulas.

Oxidation Numbers

The people in **Figure 11-14** seem to have little in common. If the alchemist knew the composition of silver tarnish, how might he write its formula? The modern chemist does know its composition; it is Ag_2S. When you get to the end of this section, you, too, will know how to write formulas of compounds.

Assigning Oxidation Numbers

You can figure out formulas with the help of oxidation numbers. What are these numbers? An **oxidation number** is a positive or negative number assigned to an element to show its combining ability in a compound. In other words, an oxi-dation number indicates how many electrons an atom has gained, lost, or shared when bonding with other atoms. For example, when sodium forms an ion, it loses an electron and

Figure 11-14

The medieval alchemist and the modern chemist are shown at work investigating matter. Notice how each would write symbols for the elements silver and sulfur. Silver tarnish is silver sulfide, a compound of silver and sulfur.

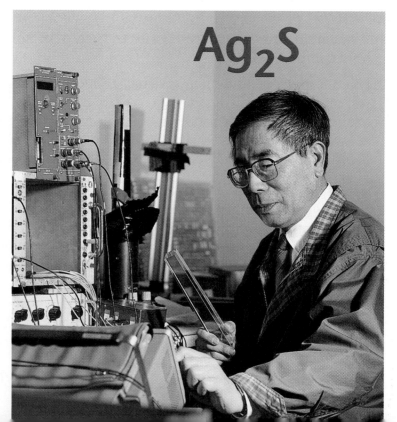

1+
1

2+
2

3+ 4+ 3− 2− 1−
13 14 15 16 17

0
18

Variable oxidation states

3 4 5 6 7 8 9 10 11 12

1																		
1 **H**																		2 **He**
2 3 **Li**	4 **Be**											5 **B**	6 **C**	7 **N**	8 **O**	9 **F**	10 **Ne**
3 11 **Na**	12 **Mg**											13 **Al**	14 **Si**	15 **P**	16 **S**	17 **Cl**	18 **Ar**
4 19 **K**	20 **Ca**	21 **Sc**	22 **Ti**	23 **V**	24 **Cr**	25 **Mn**	26 **Fe**	27 **Co**	28 **Ni**	29 **Cu**	30 **Zn**	31 **Ga**	32 **Ge**	33 **As**	34 **Se**	35 **Br**	36 **Kr**
5 37 **Rb**	38 **Sr**	39 **Y**	40 **Zr**	41 **Nb**	42 **Mo**	43 **Tc**	44 **Ru**	45 **Rh**	46 **Pd**	47 **Ag**	48 **Cd**	49 **In**	50 **Sn***	51 **Sb**	52 **Te**	53 **I**	54 **Xe**
6 55 **Cs**	56 **Ba**	57 **La**	72 **Hf**	73 **Ta**	74 **W**	75 **Re**	76 **Os**	77 **Ir**	78 **Pt**	79 **Au**	80 **Hg**	81 **Tl**	82 **Pb***	83 **Bi**	84 **Po**	85 **At**	86 **Rn**
7 87 **Fr**	88 **Ra**	89 **Ac**	104 **Rf**	105 **Ha**	106 **Sg**	107 **Ns**	108 **Hs**	109 **Mt**	110 **Uun**	111 **Uuu**							

*In Group 14, Sn and Pb also exhibit 2+ oxidation states.

The lanthanide and actinide elements are not shown in this table.

has a charge of 1+. Therefore, the oxidation number of sodium is 1+. When chlorine forms an ion, it gains an electron and has a charge of 1−. Therefore, the oxidation number of chlorine is 1−.

Binary Compounds

Oxidation numbers are often a periodic property of elements. The numbers with signs printed on the periodic table shown in **Figure 11-15** are the oxidation numbers for these elements in many of their binary compounds. *Bi-* means "two," and a **binary compound** is one that is composed of two elements. Sodium chloride is an example of a binary compound.

Like sodium, each metal in Group 1 loses its one outer electron in bonding, so each of these elements has an oxidation number of 1+. Remember, losing electrons produces a positive oxidation number in an element. Each metal in Group 2 loses both its outer electrons in bonding, so each has an oxidation number of 2+.

Like chlorine, each of the nonmetals in Group 17 gains one electron in bonding, so each of these elements has an oxidation number of 1−. Remember, gaining electrons produces a negative oxidation number in an element. Each nonmetal in Group 16 typically gains two electrons in bonding, so each has an oxidation number of 2−.

Some elements have more than one oxidation number. Copper, as you can see in **Figure 11-16**, can be either Cu⁺ or

Figure 11-15
This part of the periodic table shows oxidation numbers for elements in Groups 1, 2, 13, 14, 15, 16, 17, and 18.

Figure 11-16
Here are some elements that have variable oxidation numbers. Not all possible oxidation numbers are shown.

Copper(I)	Cu^+
Copper(II)	Cu^{2+}
Iron(II)	Fe^{2+}
Iron(III)	Fe^{3+}
Chromium(II)	Cr^{2+}
Chromium(III)	Cr^{3+}
Lead(II)	Pb^{2+}
Lead(IV)	Pb^{4+}

Cu^{2+}. In the name of a compound of copper, the Roman numeral equals the oxidation number of copper in that compound. Thus, the oxidation number of copper in copper(II) oxide is 2+. Iron may be Fe^{2+} or Fe^{3+}. Thus, the oxidation number of iron in iron(III) oxide is 3+.

Formulas for Binary Compounds

Once you know how to find the oxidation numbers of elements in binary compounds, you can write formulas by using the following rules: (1) Write first the symbol of the element that has the positive oxidation number. Hydrogen and all metals have positive oxidation numbers. (2) Then write the symbol of the element with the negative oxidation number. (3) Add subscripts so that the sum of the oxidation numbers of all the atoms in the formula is zero. Study the following example of how to write the formula of a specific compound.

USING MATH

Writing Formulas for Binary Compounds

Example Problem:
What is the formula of a compound composed of only sulfur and aluminum?

Problem-Solving Steps:

1. Write the symbol of the positive element followed by the symbol of the negative element.   Al   S

2. Look up oxidation numbers for each element. Write oxidation numbers above the symbols.

$$\overset{3+}{Al} \quad \overset{2-}{S}$$

3. Determine how many atoms of each element you need so that the sum of the oxidation numbers is zero.

Hint: The least common multiple of 2 and 3 is 6.

$$\overset{3+}{Al_2} \quad \overset{2-}{S_3}$$
$$2(3+) + 3(2-) = (6+) + (6-) = 0$$

4. **Solution:** Write the subscripts.
    Final Formula: Al_2S_3

Practice Problems

1. Write the formula for the binary compound of calcium and oxygen.
Strategy Hint: Be sure to use the smallest possible subscript numbers to make the sum zero.
2. Write the formula of the binary compound of copper(II) and sulfur.
Strategy Hint: The Roman numeral II tells you the oxidation number of copper.

Table 11-3

Elements in Binary Compounds			
Element	***-ide* Naming**	**Element**	***-ide* Naming**
Chlorine	Chloride	Oxygen	Oxide
Fluorine	Fluoride	Phosphorus	Phosphide
Nitrogen	Nitride	Sulfur	Sulfide

Naming Binary Compounds

You can name a binary compound from its formula by using these rules: (1) Write the name of the first element. (2) Write the root of the name of the second element. (3) Add the ending *-ide* to the root. **Table 11-3** lists several elements and their *-ide* counterparts. For example, $CaCl_2$ is named calcium chloride.

To name compounds of elements having two or more oxidation numbers, first figure out the oxidation numbers of the elements. Study the next example problem and then do the practice problem.

USING MATH

Naming Some Binary Compounds

Example Problem:

What is the name of CrO?

Problem-Solving Steps:

1. Write the name of the positive element.   (ANS: chromium)
2. If this element has more than one oxidation number, use the oxidation number of the negative element to figure out the oxidation number of the positive element. Write this number as a Roman numeral after the name of the element.

    $? + (2-) = 0; ? = 2+$
    Cr   O
    chromium(II)

3. Add the root of the name of the second element, followed by -ide. (ANS: oxide)
4. **Solution:**   chromium(II) oxide

Practice Problem

Name the following compounds.

   Li_2S, MgF_2, FeO, CuCl

Strategy Hint: For names of elements with more than one oxidation number, remember to include the Roman numeral. For names of nonmetals in binary compounds, use **Table 11-3.**

Compounds with Polyatomic Ions

Table 11-4

Polyatomic Ions

Charge	Name	Formula
1+	Ammonium	NH_4^+
1–	Acetate	$C_2H_3O_2^-$
	Chlorate	ClO_3^-
	Hydroxide	OH^-
	Nitrate	NO_3^-
2–	Carbonate	CO_3^{2-}
	Sulfate	SO_4^{2-}
3–	Phosphate	PO_4^{3-}

Not all compounds are binary. Have you ever used baking soda in cooking, as a medicine, or to brush your teeth? Baking soda, which has the formula $NaHCO_3$, is an example of a compound that is not binary. What four elements does it contain? Some compounds, including baking soda, are composed of more than two elements because they contain polyatomic ions. The prefix *poly-* means "many," so *polyatomic* means "having many atoms." A **polyatomic ion** is a positively or negatively charged, covalently bonded group of atoms. So, the compound as a whole contains three or more elements.

Table 11-4 lists several polyatomic ions. To name a compound that contains one of these ions, first write the name of the positive element. For a compound of the ammonium ion, NH_4^+, write ammonium first. Then, use **Table 11-4** to find the name of the polyatomic ion. For example, K_2SO_4 is potassium sulfate. What is the name of $Sr(OH)_2$?

To write formulas for compounds containing polyatomic ions, follow the rules for writing formulas for binary compounds, with one addition. Write parentheses around the group representing the polyatomic ion when more than one of that ion is needed.

USING MATH

Writing Formulas with Polyatomic Ions

Example Problem:

What is the formula for calcium nitrate?

Problem-Solving Steps:

1. Write symbols and oxidation numbers for calcium and the nitrate ion.

$$\overset{2+}{Ca} \quad \overset{1-}{NO_3}$$

2. Write in subscripts so that the sum of the oxidation numbers is zero. Enclose the NO_3 in parentheses.

$$\overset{2+}{Ca} \quad \overset{1-}{(NO_3)_2}$$

3. Solution: Final formula: $Ca(NO_3)_2$

Practice Problems

1. What is the formula for sodium sulfate?

Strategy Hint: When only one polyatomic ion is needed in a formula, do not enclose the ion in parentheses.

2. What is the formula for magnesium chlorate?

Strategy Hint: Because the subscript 3 in ClO_3^- is part of the ion, it should not be changed when written as part of a formula.

Hydrates

Some ionic compounds may have water molecules as part of their structure. These compounds are called hydrates. A **hydrate** is a compound that has water chemically attached to its ions. *Hydrate* comes from a word that means "water." For example, when a water solution of cobalt chloride evaporates, pink crystals that contain six water molecules for each unit of cobalt chloride are formed. The formula for this compound is $CoCl_2 \cdot 6H_2O$ and its name is cobalt chloride hexahydrate. *Hexa-* means "six." You can remove water from these crystals by heating them. The resulting blue compound is called *anhydrous,* which means "without water." The blue paper in **Figure 11-17** on page 320 has been soaked in cobalt chloride solution and heated.

Like many anhydrous compounds, cobalt chloride gains water molecules easily. You may have seen weather predictors made from blue paper that turns pink in humid air. The paper contains cobalt chloride. How does it react to the presence of water vapor?

Problem Solving

The Packet of Mystery Crystals

When a new videocassette recorder (VCR) was delivered to Peter's home, he was eager to start using it to tape programs. He asked for and got the job of unpacking the VCR. When he lifted the equipment from the carton, a small flat packet fell out. A label on the packet read "Contains silica gel. Do not eat." What is silica gel, and why was it in the VCR carton?

Solve the Problem:

1. Use a reference book to find out what silica gel is.
2. Explain what silica gel would do if water molecules were in the air.
3. Why was the packet of silica gel placed in the carton with the VCR?

Think Critically:

1. The chemical formula for silica gel is SiO_2. How does this formula differ from the formula of what is present in the packet after it has been in moist air for several days?

Just Add Water

Have you ever made a mold or cast with plaster of paris? If so, you have made a hydrate. When you mix plaster of paris with water, it absorbs water and changes into a hydrated form of calcium sulfate known as gypsum.

Water in a hydrate has lost its properties because it is chemically attached. Not all crystals are hydrates. The only way to detect the presence of water in crystals is to heat the solid material and see whether it gives off steam and changes to powder. For example, if you heat hardened plaster of paris, it will give off steam, crumble, and become powdery. How would you write the formula for this powder?

You have learned how to write formulas of binary ionic compounds and of compounds containing polyatomic ions. Using oxidation numbers to write formulas, you can predict the ratio in which atoms of elements may combine to form compounds. You have also seen how hydrates have water molecules as part of their structures and formulas. As you study the chapters that follow, you will see many uses of formulas.

Figure 11-17

The blue cobalt chloride on these paper strips is anhydrous. A hydrate forms when water is added to anhydrous cobalt chloride.

Section Wrap-up

Review

1. Name the following: NaI, FeBr$_3$, K$_2$SO$_4$, NH$_4$Br.

2. Write formulas for (a) lithium sulfide, (b) calcium acetate, and (c) barium oxide.

3. Write formulas for the following: (a) the anhydrous form of CoCl$_2$ · 6H$_2$O and (b) calcium sulfate dihydrate.

4. **Think Critically:** Plant food may list potassium nitrate as one ingredient. What is the formula for this compound?

USING MATH

The charge on the phosphate ion, found in some detergents, is 3−. Using **Table 11-4**, find the oxidation number of P.

Skill Builder
Using Variables, Constants, and Controls
Design an experiment to distinguish between crystals that are hydrates and those that are not. Include crystals of iron(II) chloride, copper(II) nitrate, and crystals of sucrose. If you need help, refer to Using Variables, Constants, and Controls in the **Skill Handbook.**

Summary

11-1: Why Atoms Combine

1. The properties of compounds are generally different from those of the elements they contain.
2. A chemical formula for a compound indicates the composition of a unit of the compound.
3. Chemical bonding occurs because atoms of most elements become more stable by gaining, losing, or sharing electrons.

11-2: Kinds of Chemical Bonds

1. Ionic bonds between atoms are formed by the attraction between ions. Covalent bonds are formed by the sharing of electrons.
2. Ionic bonding produces charged particles called ions. Covalent bonding produces units called molecules.
3. The unequal sharing of electrons produces compounds that contain polar bonds, and the equal sharing of electrons produces nonpolar compounds.

11-3: Science and Society: Chemical Risks in the Home

1. Compounds that are toxic, corrosive, or flammable are hazardous.
2. People can protect their health and the environment from hazardous compounds in the home.

11-4: Formulas and Names of Compounds

1. An oxidation number indicates how many electrons an atom has gained, lost, or shared when bonding with other atoms.
2. In the formula of an ionic compound, the element or ion with the positive oxidation number is written first, followed by the one with the negative oxidation number.
3. The name of a binary compound is derived from the names of the two elements that compose the compound.
4. A hydrate is a compound that has water chemically attached to its ions and written into its formula.

Key Science Words

a. binary compound
b. chemical bond
c. chemical formula
d. chemically stable
e. corrosive
f. covalent bond
g. hydrate
h. ion
i. ionic bond
j. nonpolar molecule
k. oxidation number
l. polar molecule
m. polyatomic ion
n. toxic

Reviewing Vocabulary

Match each phrase with the correct term from the list of Key Science Words.

1. a charged group of atoms
2. a compound composed of two elements
3. a molecule with opposite charges on each end
4. a positively or negatively charged atom
5. a chemical bond between oppositely charged ions
6. chemical bond formed from shared electrons
7. crystalline substance that contains water
8. outer energy level is filled with electrons
9. shows an element's combining ability
10. tells which elements are in a compound and their ratios

Checking Concepts

Choose the word or phrase that completes the sentence or answers the question.

1. The elements that are least likely to react with other elements are the _____.
   a. metals
   b. noble gases
   c. nonmetals
   d. transition elements

2. The oxidation number of Fe in Fe_2S_3 is _____.
   a. 1^+
   b. 2^+
   c. 3^+
   d. 4^+

3. The name of CuO is _____.
   a. copper oxide
   b. copper(I) oxide
   c. copper(II) oxide
   d. copper(III) oxide

4. The formula for copper(II) chlorate is _____.
   a. $CuClO_3$
   b. $CuCl$
   c. $Cu(ClO_3)_2$
   d. $CuCl_2$

5. Which of the following is a nonpolar molecule?
   a. N_2
   b. H_2O
   c. $NaCl$
   d. HCl

6. The number of electrons in the outer energy level of Group 17 elements is _____.
   a. 1
   b. 2
   c. 17
   d. 7

7. An example of a binary compound is _____.
   a. O_2
   b. NaF
   c. H_2SO_4
   d. $Cu(NO_3)_2$

8. An example of an anhydrous compound is _____.
   a. H_2O
   b. $CaSO_4$
   c. $CuSO_4 \cdot 5H_2O$
   d. $CaSO_4 \cdot 2H_2O$

9. An atom that has gained an electron is a _____.
   a. negative ion
   b. positive ion
   c. polar molecule
   d. nonpolar molecule

10. An example of a covalent compound is _____.
    a. sodium chloride
    b. calcium fluoride
    c. calcium chloride
    d. water

Understanding Concepts

Answer the following questions in your Science Journal using complete sentences.

11. What does the formula CO_2 tell you about a molecule of carbon dioxide?

12. By what three ways can atoms become chemically stable?

13. How can chromium form two different compounds with oxygen?

14. Why is the formula for milk of magnesia written $Mg(OH)_2$ instead of MgO_2H_2?

15. What compounds can be formed from element X, with oxidation numbers 3+ and 5+, and element Z, with oxidation numbers 2− and 3−? Write their formulas.

Thinking Critically

16. Anhydrous magnesium chloride is used to fireproof wood. Draw a dot diagram of magnesium chloride.

17. Baking soda, which is sodium hydrogen carbonate, and vinegar, which contains hydrogen acetate, can be used as household cleaners. Write the chemical formulas for these two compounds.

18. Artificial diamonds are made using thallium carbonate. If thallium has an oxidation number of 1+, what is the formula for the compound?

19. The formula for a compound that composes kidney stones is $Ca_3(PO_4)_2$. What is the chemical name of this compound?

20. Ammonium sulfate is used as a fertilizer. What is its chemical formula?

Developing Skills

If you need help, refer to the **Skill Handbook.**

21. **Comparing and Contrasting:** Compare and contrast polar and nonpolar molecules.
22. **Interpreting Scientific Illustrations:** Write the name and formula for the compound illustrated below.

23. **Hypothesizing:** Several uses of HCl were given to you in Section 11-2. HF is another acid, and it is used to etch glass. If HCl is hydrochloric acid, what is the name of HF?
24. **Observing and Inferring:** Ammonia gas and water react to form household ammonia, which contains NH_4^+ and OH^- ions. If the formula for water is H_2O, what is the formula for ammonia gas?
25. **Concept Mapping:** In photosynthesis, green plants that are in sunlight convert carbon dioxide and water to glucose, $C_6H_{12}O_6$, and oxygen, O_2. In respiration, glucose and oxygen react to produce carbon dioxide and water and release energy. In the map below, write in the formulas of the molecules and the names of the processes.

Performance Assessment

1. **Formulating a Hypothesis:** Calcium chloride is sometimes used in winter to help melt ice. Lard is mostly made from carbon and hydrogen and may be used in cooking. Using the same techniques that you used in Activity 11-2 on pages 310-311, what would you hypothesize about the bonding types and melting points of these two materials?
2. **Designing an Experiment:** Cobalt chloride hydrate changes color as the water part of the molecule is attached or removed. Devise a way that this could be used to determine the humidity in your classroom.
3. **Model:** One common form of phosphorus, white phosphorus, has the formula P_4 and is formed by four covalently bonded phosphorus atoms. Make a model of this molecule, showing that all four atoms are now chemically stable.

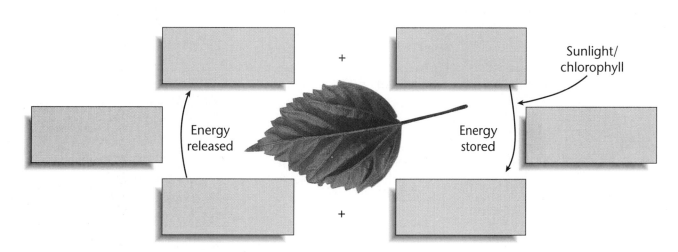

A View of the Atom

Throughout history, we have records of people who wondered what made up matter. Although it is difficult for many people to visualize, all matter is made up of small pieces of material called atoms. If you asked several people to describe or diagram the general appearance of an atom, you would get many different responses. In fact, some scientists would also have varying opinions. How do we describe something we cannot see? What do you think an atom looks like?

Annie Jump Cannon

Atomic Sleuth

Our current view of the atom is the result of historical investigations and modern experimental results. From the following list, work with other class members and choose two scientists to research. It would be best if all of the following scientists could be researched by the class.

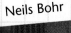
Neils Bohr

- Democritus
- John Dalton
- J.J. Thomson
- Ernst Rutherford
- Marie Curie
- Annie Jump Cannon
- Neils Bohr
- Louis de Broglie
- Werner Heisenberg
- Murray Gell-Mann
- Lise Meitner

Werner Heisenberg

Procedure

For each of your chosen scientists, answer the following questions.

1. In what country or countries did the scientist live and work?

2. When was the scientist born? If no longer living, when did he or she die?

3. What area or areas of science did the scientist study?

4. Summarize the scientist's contributions to atomic structure. How did his or her findings help our modern view of the atom?

5. What are some important or interesting facts about the scientist?

Using Your Research

With the information that you now have, make a presentation to your class. You could dress in costume to give the report. You could work with other students to make a panel of Distinguished Scientists, each student presenting and debating his or her contributions to our view of the atom. Another alternative would be to present the information as if it were a television special. Whether you use one of these suggestions or another type of presentation, be creative.

Scientist:
1. What country?
2. When born, date of death?
3. What area of science?
4. Contributions to atomic structure:
5. Important or interesting facts:

Go Further

Even today, we still have much to learn about the structure of atoms. Investigate two of the following questions.

1. Why do many scientists believe that protons and neutrons are made of quarks?

2. How small are atoms? If placed end to end, how many oxygen atoms would form a line one centimeter long?

3. How heavy are atoms? If you had 28 g of gold, how many gold atoms would you have?

4. How does probability relate to our modern view of the atom?

5. How has the scanning tunneling microscope helped us to understand the structure of atoms?

Unit Contents

Kinds of Substances

What's Happening Here?

Even after you think *you're* done with a piece of chewing gum, look again—it still has plenty of stretch and give for the shoe of the next passerby. Chewing gum gets its stretch from its structure—a special arrangement of atoms called a polymer. A model of the chewing gum polymer is shown above. In this unit you'll learn about polymers and many other kinds of substances—metal, non-metal, organic, biological—and the special properties of each. So the next time you get rid of your gum, remember its properties and throw it in the trash.

Science Journal

There are many materials besides gum and tennis shoes that have the characteristics of stretchiness and elasticity. In your Science Journal, write a report on other products and materials with these characteristics and explain why these characteristics are important.

Al	Si	P	S
.982	28.086	30.974	32.066
allium	Germanium		ium
31	32		
Ga	Ge		
.723	72.61		
dium	Tin		ium
49	50		2
In	Sn	Sb	Te
4.82	118.710	121.757	127.60
allium	Lead	Bismuth	Polonium
81	82	83	84
Tl	Pb	Bi	Po

Previewing the Chapter

Elements and Their Properties

his beautiful diamond is made up of atoms of the element carbon. Most matter can be described by the elements of which it is made. Each element has distinct properties. Elements arranged together on the periodic table have similar properties. Knowing the properties of elements allows us to use them in a variety of practical ways. This chapter will describe groups of elements and help you to learn how they are related.

EXPLORE ACTIVITY

Some clues are in color.

1. Using tongs, carefully hold a clean paper clip in the hottest part of a lab burner flame until no additional color is observed.
2. Dip the hot paper clip into a solution of copper(II) sulfate.
3. Using the tongs, repeat step 1, observing any color change.
4. Repeat these steps using solutions of strontium chloride and sodium chloride.

Observe: How can observation of color be used to identify elements in solutions? Based on your observations, devise a plan in your Science Journal to determine whether chlorine or strontium was giving the color you observed in a particular test.

Previewing Science Skills

▶ In the **Skill Builders**, you will **interpret scientific illustrations, make and use a graph,** and **map concepts.**

▶ In the **Activities,** you will **observe, compare, predict, infer,** and **build a model.**

▶ In the **MiniLABs,** you will **observe** and **draw conclusions**

12•1 Metals

Science Words

malleable
ductile
metallic bonding
radioactive element
transition element

Objectives

* Describe the properties of a typical metal.
* Identify the alkali and alkaline earth metals.
* Differentiate among three groups of transition elements.

Figure 12-1

Gold can be hammered into thin sheets. The sheets, called gold leaf, can be applied to many types of surfaces. *What is this property of metals called?*

Properties of Metals

Have you ever seen very old jewelry or statues made of gold and copper? These were two of the first metals used thousands of years ago. The use of silver and tin soon followed. Then came iron. But aluminum—the metal used in thousands of soft-drink cans—wasn't discovered until a little more than 100 years ago.

Gold, copper, silver, tin, iron, and aluminum are typical metals. What do these and other metals have in common? Most metals are hard, shiny solids. Metals are also good conductors of both heat and electricity. These properties make metals suitable for uses ranging from kitchen pots and pans to wires for electric appliances. Because metals reflect light well, they are also used in mirrors. Metals are **malleable,** which means they can be hammered or rolled into sheets. The gold leaf shown in **Figure 12-1** is used for elaborate decoration. Metals are also **ductile,** which means they can be drawn into wires like the ones shown in **Figure 12-2.**

The atoms of metals generally have from one to three electrons in their outer energy levels. Metals tend to give up electrons easily. Remember from Chapter 11 what happens when metals combine with nonmetals? The atoms of the metals tend to lose electrons to the atoms of nonmetals, and form ionic bonds. The second type of bond you studied is the covalent bond, which generally forms between atoms of nonmetals.

Figure 12-2

Metals can be drawn into wires. This property is called ductility. The gauge of a wire is related to its thickness. A large number indicates a thinner wire.

Bonding in Metals

A third type of bonding, neither ionic nor covalent, occurs among the atoms in a metal. In **metallic bonding,** positively charged metallic ions are surrounded by a "sea of electrons." Outer-level electrons are not held tightly to their particular nucleus. Rather, the electrons move freely among many positively charged ions. The electrons form a cloud around the ions of the metal as shown in **Figure 12-3.**

Figure 12-3

In metallic bonding, the moving outer electrons, depicted by the cloud, cover the rest of the atoms no matter where the electrons are in the metal. *How does this differ from covalent bonding?*

Metallic bonding explains many of the properties of metals. For example, when a metal is hammered into a sheet or drawn into a wire, it does not break because the ions are in layers that slide past one another. And because the outer-level electrons are weakly held, metals are good conductors of electricity.

Look at the periodic table on pages 286-287. How many of the elements in the table are classified as metals? Except for hydrogen, all the elements in Groups 1 through 12 are metals. You will learn about metals in some of these groups and others throughout this chapter.

MiniLAB

How can metallic bonding explain the flexibility of metals?

Procedure

1. Using tongs, carefully hold two pieces of metal wire in a lab burner flame until they are glowing red-hot.
2. Quickly drop one of the hot wires into a beaker of cold water. Allow it to cool.
3. Allow the other hot wire to cool slowly.
4. Hold the ends of each piece of cooled wire and bend them.

Analysis

1. What do you observe about the flexibility of the two cooled wires?
2. How can metallic bonding be used to help explain your observations?

The Alkali Metals

The elements in Group 1 of the periodic table are the alkali metals. Like other metals, Group 1 metals are shiny, malleable, and ductile. They are good conductors of both heat and electricity. The alkali metals are highly reactive metals. **Figure 12-4** shows how reactive they are with water. As a result of their reactivity, why would you expect to find the alkali metals in nature only in the form of compounds?

Each atom of an alkali metal has one electron in its outer energy level. This electron is given up when an alkali metal combines with another atom. The result is a positively charged ion in a compound such as sodium chloride, NaCl, or potassium bromide, KBr.

Alkali metals and their compounds have many uses. You and other living things need potassium and sodium compounds—such as table salt, NaCl—to stay healthy. Doctors use lithium compounds to treat bipolar disorder. The operation of some photocells depends upon rubidium or cesium compounds.

Francium, the last element in Group 1, is extremely rare and also radioactive. The nucleus of a **radioactive element** breaks down and gives off particles and energy. You will study radioactive elements later.

1

| Lithium |
| 3 |
| **Li** |
| 6.941 |

| Sodium |
| 11 |
| **Na** |
| 22.990 |

| Potassium |
| 19 |
| **K** |
| 39.098 |

| Rubidium |
| 37 |
| **Rb** |
| 85.468 |

| Cesium |
| 55 |
| **Cs** |
| 132.905 |

| Francium |
| 87 |
| **Fr** |
| 223.020 |

Sodium (Na)

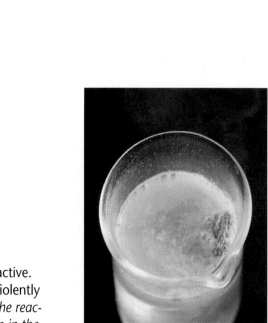

Lithium (Li)

Potassium (K)

Figure 12-4

Alkali metals are very reactive. Li, Na, K, and Cs react violently in water. *Why wouldn't the reaction of francium be shown in the photo?*

The Alkaline Earth Metals

The alkaline earth metals make up Group 2 of the periodic table. Like the alkali metals, these metals are shiny, malleable, ductile, and so reactive that they are not found free in nature. Each atom of an alkaline earth metal has two electrons in its outer energy level. These electrons are given up when an alkaline earth metal combines with another element. The result is a positively charged ion in a compound such as calcium fluoride, CaF_2.

Bats, Batteries, and Beryls

Emeralds and aquamarines are gemstone forms of beryl, a mineral that contains beryllium. Do you watch fireworks on the Fourth of July? The brilliant red in fireworks is produced by compounds of strontium.

Magnesium can be made into a fine wire that burns so brightly that it is used in some photographic flashbulbs. Magnesium metal is also used in fireworks to produce brilliant white. Magnesium's lightness and strength account for its use in cars, planes, and spacecraft. Magnesium is also used to make such things as household ladders and baseball and softball bats, such as the one shown in **Figure 12-5.** Most life on Earth depends upon chlorophyll, a magnesium compound that enables plants to make food.

Calcium is seldom used as a free metal, but its compounds are needed for life. Calcium phosphate in your bones helps make them strong. Marble and limestone are calcium carbonate.

2

| Beryllium |
| 4 |
| **Be** |
| 9.012 |

| Magnesium |
| 12 |
| **Mg** |
| 24.305 |

| Calcium |
| 20 |
| **Ca** |
| 40.078 |

| Strontium |
| 38 |
| **Sr** |
| 87.62 |

| Barium |
| 56 |
| **Ba** |
| 137.327 |

| Radium |
| 88 |
| **Ra** |
| 226.025 |

Some barium compounds are used to diagnose digestive disorders. The patient swallows a barium compound, which can absorb X rays. As the barium compound goes through the digestive tract, a doctor can study the X rays. Radium, the last element in Group 2, is radioactive. It was once used to treat cancers. Today, other radioactive substances are replacing radium in cancer therapy.

Transition Elements

Figure 12-6

The colors of these gems are due to compounds of transition elements.

An iron nail, a copper wire, and a silver dime are examples of objects made from transition elements. The **transition elements** are those elements in Groups 3 through 12 of the periodic table. Typical transition elements are metals and have one or two electrons in the outer energy level. These metals are less active than those in Groups 1 and 2.

The gems in **Figure 12-6** contain brightly colored compounds of transition elements. Brilliant cadmium yellow and cobalt blue paint pigments are made from compounds of transition elements. But cadmium and cobalt paints are so toxic that their use is now limited.

Iron, Cobalt, and Nickel

Iron, cobalt, and nickel form a unique cluster of transition elements. The first elements in Groups 8, 9, and 10, respectively, are known as the iron triad. The elements of the triad are the only ones known to create a magnetic field.

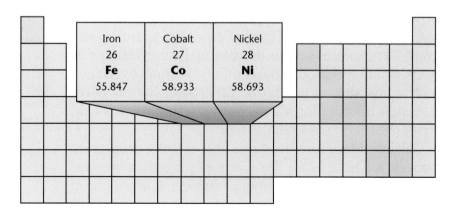

Iron	Cobalt	Nickel
26	27	28
Fe	**Co**	**Ni**
55.847	58.933	58.693

Iron is second only to aluminum among the metals in abundance in Earth's crust. As the main component of steel, iron is the most widely used of all metals. Some steels also contain cobalt. Nickel is added to other metals to give them strength. Nickel is also often used to give a shiny, protective coating to other metals.

Copper, Silver, and Gold

Can you name the main metals in the coins in **Figure 12-7** on page 336? They are copper, silver, and gold—the three elements in Group 11. They are so unreactive that they can be found as elements in nature. For centuries, these metals have been widely used as coins. For this reason, they are known as the coinage metals.

Copper is often used in electric wiring because of its superior ability to conduct electricity and

USING TECHNOLOGY

Metals with Memory

What would a radio antenna in space have in common with your smile? They both benefit from nitinol. Nitinol is a metal alloy with a memory.

Nitinol is the name given to the metal mixture, or alloy, made from the transition elements nickel and titanium. The alloy, which is made into a preset shape, can later be deformed into a new shape.

Practical Uses

So how is this used on teeth? The wire connecting brackets in braces is nitinol. If the teeth are not properly aligned, the wire will be deformed from its preset shape. Soon, the wire will attempt to return to its original shape, putting pressure on the bracketed teeth and moving them.

Engineers also made use of nitinol when a large radio antenna was compactly folded during launch into space. Once in orbit, the metal with a memory absorbed heat and began to unfold into its original shape. This property of nitinol is also useful in eyeglass frames.

Think Critically:

Elements that can form shape-memory alloys, SMAs, are found in Groups 3 through 12 on the periodic table. List other properties of these elements in your Science Journal.

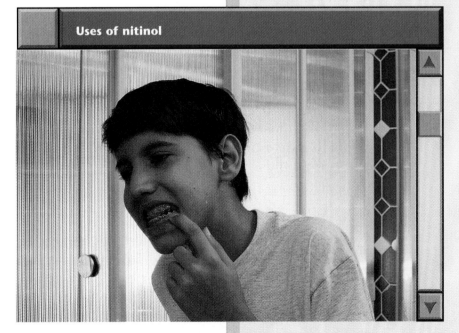

Uses of nitinol

its relatively low cost. Can you imagine a world without photographs and movies? Because silver iodide and silver bromide break down when exposed to light, these compounds are used to make photographic film and paper. Much silver is also used in jewelry. The yellow color, relative softness, and rarity of gold account for its use in jewelry.

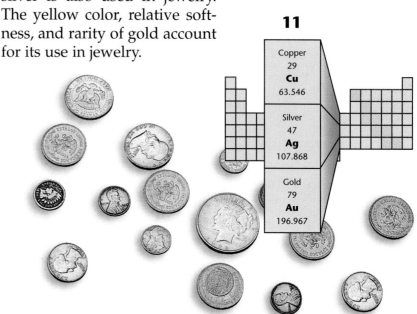

11

| Copper |
| 29 |
| **Cu** |
| 63.546 |

| Silver |
| 47 |
| **Ag** |
| 107.868 |

| Gold |
| 79 |
| **Au** |
| 196.967 |

Figure 12-7

Some Group 11 elements are used to make coins.

12

| Zinc |
| 30 |
| **Zn** |
| 65.39 |

| Cadmium |
| 48 |
| **Cd** |
| 112.411 |

| Mercury |
| 80 |
| **Hg** |
| 200.59 |

Zinc, Cadmium, and Mercury

Zinc, cadmium, and mercury make up Group 12 of the periodic table. Zinc combines with oxygen in the air to form a thin protective coating of zinc oxide on the surface of the metal. Zinc is often used to coat, or plate, other metals, such as iron. Cadmium is also used in plating and in rechargeable batteries.

Mercury is a silvery, liquid metal used in thermometers, thermostats, switches, and batteries. Mercury is poisonous, and mercury compounds can accumulate in the body. People have died of mercury poisoning that resulted from eating fish from mercury-contaminated water.

Look at the periodic table on pages 286-287. Which elements do you think of as being typical metals? Transition elements are the most familiar because they occur in nature as elements. Group 1 and Group 2 metals are found in nature only in compounds.

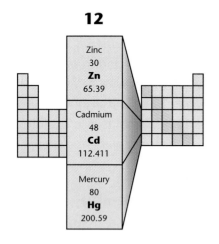

INTEGRATION
Earth Science

Metals in the Crust

When we examine pictures of metals and their compounds, we are really seeing only half the story. Where are metals found? How do we obtain them? Earth's crust contains many compounds and a few examples of uncombined metals such as gold and copper. Metals must be dug, or mined, from Earth's hardened outer layer.

Due to varying conditions in different areas, some metals are deposited more in one place than in another. For example, most of the world's platinum is found in South Africa. Large amounts of cobalt can be found in Morocco, Zaire, and Canada. Chromium is important to the United States, but we must import most of it from South Africa, the Philippines, and Turkey.

Ores: Minerals and Mixtures

Metals in Earth's crust that are in a combined form are found in ores. Typically, an ore consists of a metal compound, or mineral, within a mixture of clay or rock. Lead metal is usually found combined with sulfur in the form of galena, or lead sulfide. After an ore is mined and brought from Earth's surface, minerals must be separated from the rock. Then the mineral is often converted to another chemical form. Galena is converted to lead oxide. This step involves heat and is called roasting. Finally, the metal is refined into a pure form. It may later be alloyed with other metals. Removing the waste rock can be very expensive. If the cost of removing the waste rock gets higher than the value of the desired material, the mineral will no longer be classified as an ore.

USING MATH

Several elements are present in Earth's crust. The approximate percentage of each element is as follows:
Oxygen, 46.6
Silicon, 27.7
Aluminum, 8.1
Iron, 5.0
Calcium, 3.6
Sodium, 2.8
Potassium, 2.6
Magnesium, 2.1
Other elements include titanium, hydrogen, phosphorus, and manganese, which account for 1.5 percent. Make a circle graph of these data.

Section Wrap-up

Review

1. You are given a piece of the element palladium. How would you test it to see if it is a metal?

2. On the periodic table, how does the arrangement of the iron triad differ from the arrangements of the coinage metals and of the zinc group?

3. **Think Critically:** If X stands for a metal, how can you tell from the formulas XCl and XCl_2 which compound contains an alkali metal and which contains an alkaline earth metal?

Skill Builder

Interpreting Scientific Illustrations
Draw dot diagrams to show the similarity among chlorides of three alkali metals: lithium chloride, sodium chloride, and potassium chloride. If you need help, refer to Interpreting Scientific Illustrations in the **Skill Handbook.**

Science Journal

We encounter examples of metals nearly everywhere. In your Science Journal, write a paragraph describing how a specific metallic element has an effect in your life. Which group is that metal in on the periodic table?

TECHNOLOGY:
12•2 New Elements, New Properties

transuranium element

Objectives

- Distinguish among elements classified as lanthanides, actinides, and transuranium elements.
- Determine the uses of transuranium elements.
- Compare the pros and cons of making new elements.

Figure 12-8

These control rods contain plutonium, element 84. *How would plutonium be classified?*

Elements Beyond 92

What if you made something that always fell apart? You might think you were not successful. Yet nuclear scientists are learning to do just that. By combining existing elements with fast-moving particles, they have been successful at creating elements not typically found on Earth. Except for one, the short-lived elements have more than 92 protons. All of these synthetic elements are unstable and fall apart quickly. Elements having more than 92 protons, the atomic number of uranium, are called **transuranium elements.**

| 104 Rf | 105 Ha | 106 Sg | 107 Ns | 108 Hs | 109 Mt | 110 Uun | 111 Uuu |

| 93 Np | 94 Pu | 95 Am | 96 Cm | 97 Bk | 98 Cf | 99 Es | 100 Fm | 101 Md | 102 No | 103 Lr |

Additions to the Family

If you look at the periodic table on pages 286-287, you will see breaks in periods 6 and 7. The first break includes a series of 14 elements with atomic numbers of 58-71. The elements in this series are known as the lanthanides. The second break includes elements with atomic numbers ranging from 90-103. These elements are known as actinides. Ten synthetic elements are found in the actinide series. Where are the others placed on the periodic table? Technetium is element number 43. The newest synthetic elements are placed in period 7.

Synthesis: A Smashing Success

If atoms and other particles are smashed together with sufficient force, they will fuse to form a new identity. For example, neptunium, element 93, can be made by bombarding uranium with neutrons. Atoms of neptunium do not stay together for long. Half of the synthesized atoms disintegrate in about two days. This may not sound useful, but when neptunium atoms fall apart, they form plutonium. This highly toxic element has been used in control rods of nuclear reactors, such as those shown in **Figure 12-8**, and in bombs. Plutonium can also be changed to americium, element 95. This transuranium element is used in some home smoke detectors such as the one in **Figure 12-9**.

58 Ce	59 Pr	60 Nd	61 Pm	62 Sm	63 Eu	64 Gd	65 Tb	66 Dy	67 Ho	68 Er	69 Tm	70 Yb	71 Lu
90 Th	91 Pa	92 U	93 Np	94 Pu	95 Am	96 Cm	97 Bk	98 Cf	99 Es	100 Fm	101 Md	102 No	103 Lr

Figure 12-9

Synthesis of elements has resulted in life-saving smoke detectors.

Why make elements?

Bringing atoms and particles together through collision requires advanced technology and is expensive. Why do we need new elements? By studying how the synthesized elements form and fall apart, we can gain an understanding of the forces holding other elements together. When these atoms fall apart, they are said to be radioactive. Technetium's radioactivity makes it ideal for many medical applications. At this time, many of the synthetic elements are so unstable that, once made, they last only small fractions of seconds. In addition, some can be made only in small amounts. However, further advances in technology may bring production up to larger amounts. The as-yet-undiscovered applications could prove to be more valuable than their costs.

Section Wrap-up

Review

1. How is an element classified as a transuranium element?

2. Where are the actinides located on the periodic table?

Explore the Technology

Explain why making unstable elements can be useful.

SCIENCE & SOCIETY

12•3 Nonmetals

Science Words

diatomic molecule
sublimation

Objectives

• Recognize hydrogen as a nonmetal.
• Compare and contrast properties of the halogens.
• Describe properties and uses of the noble gases.

Properties of Nonmetals

Figure 12-10 shows that you're mostly made of oxygen, carbon, hydrogen, and nitrogen. Calcium, a metal, and other elements make up the remaining four percent of your body's weight. Phosphorus, sulfur, and chlorine are among other elements found in your body. These elements are classified as nonmetals.

Look at the periodic table on pages 286 and 287. How many elements are nonmetals? Notice that most nonmetals are gases at room temperature. Several nonmetals are solids, and one nonmetal is a liquid.

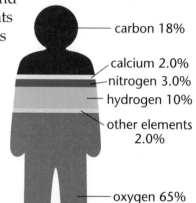

carbon 18%
calcium 2.0%
nitrogen 3.0%
hydrogen 10%
other elements 2.0%
oxygen 65%

Figure 12-10

Humans are made up of mostly nonmetals.

Attracting Electrons

In contrast to metals, solid nonmetals are dull. Because they are brittle and powdery, they are neither malleable nor ductile. The electrons in most nonmetals are tightly attracted and are restricted to one atom. So, as a group, nonmetals are poor conductors of heat and electricity.

Most nonmetals form both ionic and covalent compounds. Examples of these two kinds of compounds are shown in **Figure 12-11.** When nonmetals gain electrons from metals, the nonmetals become negative ions in ionic compounds. An example of such an ionic compound is potassium iodide, KI,

potassium iodide

ammonia

Figure 12-11

Nonmetals form both ionic and covalent compounds. *Which picture depicts which kind of bonding?*

which is often added to table salt. KI is formed from the non-metal iodine and the metal potassium. On the other hand, when bonded with other nonmetals, atoms of nonmetals usually share electrons and form covalent compounds. An example is ammonia, NH_3, the gas you can smell when you open a bottle of household ammonia.

The noble gases, Group 18, make up the only group of elements that are all nonmetals. Group 17 elements, except for astatine, are also nonmetals. Several other nonmetals, found in Groups 13 through 16, will be discussed later. Except for hydrogen, all of the nonmetals are located on the right side of the periodic table.

Hydrogen

Do you know that approximately 90 percent of all the atoms in the universe are hydrogen? Most hydrogen on Earth is found in the compound water. When water is broken down into its elements, hydrogen forms as a gas made up of diatomic molecules. A **diatomic molecule** consists of two atoms of the same element. Thus, the formula for hydrogen gas is H_2, shown in **Figure 12-12.**

Small, But Active

Hydrogen is highly reactive. A hydrogen atom has a single electron, which the atom shares when it combines with other nonmetals. Hydrogen burns in oxygen to form water, H_2O. In forming water, hydrogen shares electrons with oxygen. Hydrogen also shares electrons with chlorine to produce hydrogen chloride, HCl.

Hydrogen may gain an electron when it combines with alkali and alkaline earth metals. The compounds formed are hydrides, such as sodium hydride, NaH.

hydrogen molecule gas

Figure 12-12

Hydrogen gas, which consists of diatomic molecules, combines with oxygen in an oxyhydrogen torch.

MiniLAB

Can you detect chlorine in your drinking water?

Procedure

1. In separate test tubes, obtain 2 mL of chloride standard solution, distilled water, and drinking water.
2. Carefully add five drops of silver nitrate solution to each and stir. **CAUTION:** *Avoid contact with the silver nitrate solution.*

Analysis

1. Which solution will definitely show a presence of chloride? How did this result compare to the result with distilled water?
2. Which result most resembled your drinking water?

Figure 12-13

The halogens bromine and iodine are used in the bulbs of halogen lamps.

17

| Fluorine 9 **F** 18.998 |
| Chlorine 17 **Cl** 35.453 |
| Bromine 35 **Br** 79.904 |
| Iodine 53 **I** 126.904 |
| Astatine 85 **At** 209.987 |

The Halogens

Look how bright the high-tech lamp is in **Figure 12-13.** Its light and that of the headlights of some cars are supplied by halogen lightbulbs. These bulbs contain small amounts of bromine or iodine. These elements, as well as fluorine, chlorine, and astatine, are called halogens and are found in Group 17.

Because an atom of a halogen has seven electrons in its outer energy level, only one electron is needed to complete this energy level. If a halogen gains an electron from a metal, an ionic compound, called a salt, is formed. The word *halogen* means "salt former." In the gaseous state, the halogens form very reactive diatomic covalent molecules and can be identified by their distinctive colors, as shown in **Figure 12-14.**

Fluorine is the most chemically active of all the elements. Hydrofluoric acid, a mixture of hydrogen fluoride and water, is used to etch glass and to frost the inner surfaces of lightbulbs. Other fluorides are added to toothpastes and to city water systems to prevent tooth decay. Does your community add fluorides to its water?

CONNECT TO

EARTH SCIENCE

Compounds called chlorofluorocarbons are used in refrigeration systems. If released, these compounds destroy ozone in the atmosphere. *Draw* the electron dot diagram for CF_2Cl_2 in your Science Journal.

Figure 12-14

These are the gaseous halogens chlorine, bromine, and iodine.

Uses of Halogens

The odor near swimming pools is the odor of chlorine. Chlorine compounds are used to disinfect water. Chlorine, the most abundant halogen, is obtained from seawater. Household and industrial bleaches used to whiten flour and paper also contain chlorine compounds.

Bromine, the only nonmetal that is liquid at room temperature, is extracted from compounds in seawater. Other bromine compounds are used as dyes in cosmetics, such as the lipsticks shown in **Figure 12-15.**

Iodine, a shiny gray solid at room temperature, is obtained from seawater. When heated, iodine changes directly to a purple vapor. The process of a solid changing directly to a vapor without forming a liquid is called **sublimation.** Recall that sublimation accounts for ice cubes shrinking in freezers. Iodine is essential in your diet for the production of the hormone thyroxin and to prevent goiter, an enlarging of the thyroid gland in the neck.

Astatine, the last member of Group 17, is radioactive and rare. But it has many properties similar to those of the other halogens.

Figure 12-15

Dyes in some cosmetics contain bromine compounds. *What unique physical property does bromine have?*

Figure 12-16

Neon signs contain several noble gases.

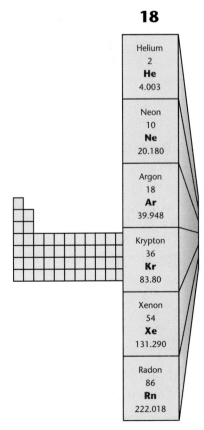

The Noble Gases

Why are the noble gases called noble? It was known that these gases did not naturally form compounds. Thus, they were thought of as the nobility of elements because nobles did not mix with common folk. However, in the early 1960s, scientists were able to prepare some compounds of noble gases.

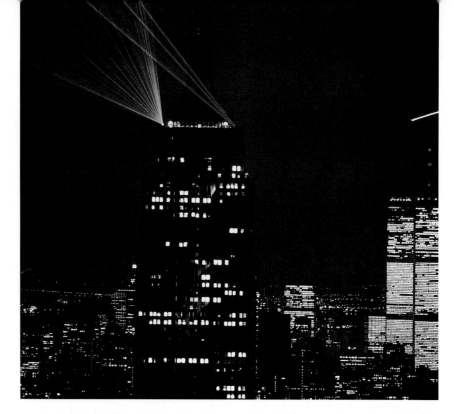

Figure 12-17

Noble gases are used to produce laser light shows.

As you recall, each element in Group 18 is stable because its outer energy level is full. The stability of the noble gases plays an important role in their uses, such as those shown in **Figures 12-16** and **12-17**.

Both the halogens and the noble gases illustrate that each element in a group has some similar properties but also has unique properties and uses.

Section Wrap-up

Review

1. What are two ways in which hydrogen combines with other elements?

2. Rank the following nonmetals from lowest number of electrons in the outer level to highest: Cl^-, H^+, He, H.

3. What property of noble gases makes them useful?

4. **Think Critically:** Why must hydrofluoric acid always be stored in plastic bottles?

Using Computers

Graphing Prepare a bar graph comparing nonmetals and metals as solids, liquids, and gases at room temperature.

Skill Builder

Interpreting Data

Within the following compounds, identify the nonmetal and list its oxidation number: MgO, NaH, $AlBr_3$, FeS. If you need help, refer to Interpreting Data in your **Skill Handbook.**

Activity 12-1

Nonmetal Reaction

If you examine the label on some common household bleach, you will likely find that the active ingredient is NaClO, sodium hypochlorite. In this activity, you will remove the oxygen from this compound in order to identify its presence.

Problem

How can you use the properties of oxygen to identify its presence?

Materials

- large test tube
- large wooden match
- 20 mL liquid laundry bleach (5 percent sodium hypochlorite)
- 0.5 g cobalt chloride
- goggles

Procedure

1. Put on safety goggles.
2. Carefully pour about 20 mL of liquid laundry bleach into a large test tube.
3. Add about 0.5 g of cobalt chloride to the bleach.
4. A gas will start to form in the liquid. Place your thumb loosely over the opening of the tube until you feel some slight pressure, but do not attempt to prevent the escape of the gas from the tube.
5. Have a classmate carefully bring a lighted match near the opening of the tube.
6. Blow out the flame of the match and insert the glowing end of the match into the upper half of the tube.

Analyze

1. An increase in the amount of oxygen in a container can cause a glowing match to burst into flame. Were the bubbles given off in your tube oxygen? Explain your answer.
2. Look at the formula for sodium hypochlorite present in bleach, NaClO. What two nonmetals does this compound contain?

Conclude and Apply

3. Liquid bleach is sometimes used as a disinfectant in kitchens. As the sodium hypochlorite in bleach decomposes, or breaks down, what product do you **predict** might appear?
4. Sunlight can also decompose hypochlorite. **Observe** the materials used to make containers of different sizes and brands of bleach. In what way are the containers all alike? **Infer** a reason for this similarity.

12•4 Mixed Groups

Science Words

semiconductor
allotrope

Objectives

- Distinguish among metals, nonmetals, and metalloids in Groups 13 through 16 of the periodic table.
- Describe the nature of allotropes.
- Recognize the significance of differences in crystal structure in carbon.

Locating the Mixed Groups

Can an element be both a metal and a nonmetal? In a sense, some elements are. They are the metalloids, and they have both metallic and nonmetallic properties. A metalloid may conduct electricity better than many nonmetals but not as well as some metals. In the periodic table, the metalloids are the elements located along the stair-step line. The mixed groups—13, 14, 15, and 16—contain metals, nonmetals, and metalloids.

The Boron Group

Boron, a metalloid, is the first element in Group 13. If you look around your home, you may find two compounds of boron. One of these is boric acid, a mild antiseptic. The other is borax, which is used in laundry products to soften water. Less familiar are the boranes, which are compounds of boron used in fuels for rockets and jet airplanes.

Aluminum, a metal, is also in Group 13. Aluminum is the most abundant metal in Earth's crust. Aluminum is used in soft-drink cans, foil wrap, and cooking pans. You may also see aluminum on the sides of buildings. And because aluminum is both strong and light, it is used to build airplanes.

When you operate electronic equipment, such as the calculator shown in **Figure 12-18,** you may be using one of the other metals in Group 13. These metals are gallium, indium, and thallium, used to produce semiconductors. **Semiconductors** conduct an electric current under certain conditions. You will learn more about semiconductors in Chapter 23.

Figure 12-18

Calculators contain semiconductors. *What metals from Group 13 are used to produce semiconductors?*

13

| Boron 5 **B** 10.811 |
| Aluminum 13 **Al** 26.982 |
| Gallium 31 **Ga** 69.723 |
| Indium 49 **In** 114.82 |
| Thallium 81 **Tl** 204.383 |

Figure 12-19

Two allotropes of carbon are graphite (A) and diamond (B). *What geometric shapes make up each allotrope?*

The Carbon Group

Each element in Group 14, the carbon family, has four electrons in its outer energy level. But this is where much of the similarity ends. Carbon is a nonmetal; silicon and germanium are metalloids; tin and lead are metals.

What do the diamond in a diamond ring and the graphite in your pencil have in common? It may surprise you to learn that they are both carbon. How can this be? Diamond and graphite are examples of allotropes. **Allotropes** are different forms of the same element having different molecular structures. Look at **Figure 12-19**. Graphite is a black powder that consists of hexagonal layers of carbon atoms. In the hexagons, each carbon atom is bonded to three other carbon atoms. The fourth electron of each atom is bonded weakly to the layer next to it. This structure allows the layers to slide easily past one another, making graphite an excellent lubricant.

14

| Carbon |
| 6 |
| **C** |
| 12.011 |

| Silicon |
| 14 |
| **Si** |
| 28.086 |

| Germanium |
| 32 |
| **Ge** |
| 72.61 |

| Tin |
| 50 |
| **Sn** |
| 118.710 |

| Lead |
| 82 |
| **Pb** |
| 207.2 |

Problem Solving

Waiting to Be Discovered

In sports, the "Rookie of the Year" award typically designates a player who had an outstanding first year and shows great potential for continued achievement. Most of the selections live up to that expectation, but not all. At the beginning of the 1990s, *Science* magazine selected Buckminsterfullerene as the "Molecule of the Year." This allotrope of carbon was isolated by R.E. Smalley when some carbon materials were subjected to laser bursts. Later, the carbon condensed into unusual spherical elements. The tiny spheres were later shown to be made of 60 carbon atoms arranged in an open cage that could resemble a hollow soccer ball.

Many new uses of this third allotrope were thought possible. Interesting medical applications were proposed to attach special disease-attacking components to the outside of the molecule. Another idea was to insert radioactive atoms inside the cage. They could then be injected inside a patient to arrive at a specific site. Another problem the new molecule could solve is the separation of mixtures. Buckminsterfullerene molecules, also called Buckyballs, can be packed into containers and used as separating sieves.

Solve the Problem:

1. **Use a tall cylinder of glass marbles to represent Buckminsterfullerene molecules, and a mixture of sand or salt and small BB pellets to represent a mixture of chemical compounds.**
2. **Pour the sand and BB mixture over the marbles.**

Think Critically:

1. How did the packing and spacing of the spherical marbles enhance the separation of your mixture?
2. How could Buckyballs be used to separate compounds?
3. Can you think of other potential uses for this molecule?

Buckminsterfullerene

A tetrahedron is a polyhedron with four congruent faces, each of which is an equilateral triangle. Use the figure below as a pattern and make a tetrahedron out of paper.

Fold lines

Tough Tetrahedrons

A diamond is clear and extremely hard. In a diamond, each carbon atom is bonded to four other carbon atoms at the vertices, or corner points, of a tetrahedron. In turn, many tetrahedrons join together to form a giant molecule in which the atoms are held tightly in a strong crystal structure. This structure accounts for the hardness of diamond.

Carbon occurs as an element in coal and in compounds in oil, natural gas, and foods. Carbon in these materials may combine with oxygen to produce carbon dioxide, CO_2. In the presence of sunlight, plants utilize CO_2 to make food. In Chapter 13, you will study other carbon compounds—many essential to life.

Unleaded Plus 87

THIS SALE

GALLONS

87

Unleaded Plus 87

Gasoline

THE GASOLINE DISPENSED FROM THIS PUMP IS OXYGENATED AND WILL REDUCE CARBON MONOXIDE POLLUTION FROM MOTOR VEHICLES. THIS GASOLINE CONTAINS UP TO 10% ETHANOL BY VOLUME. THE REQUIRED REGULATORY COMPLIANCE PERIOD IS: SEPTEMBER 30 THROUGH MARCH 31.

Figure 12-20

The carbon group includes lead and tin.

A Most gasolines are no longer leaded.

B Pewter contains tin and other metals. *Why would dishes made of lead be dangerous?*

Silicon is second only to oxygen in abundance in Earth's crust. Most silicon is found in sand, silicon dioxide, SiO_2, and in almost all rocks and soil. The crystal structure of silicon dioxide is similar to the tetrahedrons in diamond. Silicon occurs as two allotropes. One of these is a hard, gray substance, and the other is a brown powder.

Both silicon and germanium, the other metalloid in the carbon group, are used in making semiconductors, which you'll learn about in Chapter 23. Tin and lead are typical metals. Tin is used to coat other metals to prevent corrosion. Tin is also combined with other metals to produce bronze and pewter. Lead was once used widely in paints and antiknock gasoline. However, lead is poisonous, so it has been replaced in these materials.

The Nitrogen Group

The nitrogen family makes up Group 15. Each element has five electrons in its outer energy level. These elements tend to share electrons and to form covalent compounds with other elements.

Each breath you take is about 80 percent gaseous nitrogen, in the form of diatomic molecules, N_2. If you look again at **Figure 12-10** on page 340, you'll see that nitrogen is the element fourth in abundance in your body. Yet you and other animals and plants can't use nitrogen as N_2. The nitrogen must be combined into compounds, such as nitrates—compounds that contain the nitrate ion, NO_3^-. Much nitrogen is used to make nitrates and ammonia, NH_3, both of which are used in fertilizers.

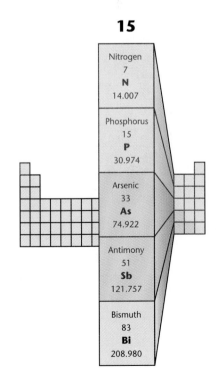

15

| Nitrogen |
| 7 |
| **N** |
| 14.007 |

| Phosphorus |
| 15 |
| **P** |
| 30.974 |

| Arsenic |
| 33 |
| **As** |
| 74.922 |

| Antimony |
| 51 |
| **Sb** |
| 121.757 |

| Bismuth |
| 83 |
| **Bi** |
| 208.980 |

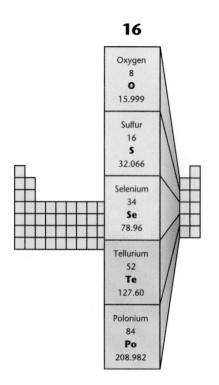

16

| Oxygen |
| 8 |
| **O** |
| 15.999 |

| Sulfur |
| 16 |
| **S** |
| 32.066 |

| Selenium |
| 34 |
| **Se** |
| 78.96 |

| Tellurium |
| 52 |
| **Te** |
| 127.60 |

| Polonium |
| 84 |
| **Po** |
| 208.982 |

Figure 12-21

Sulfur is typically a bright yellow nonmetal. One allotrope of sulfur has eight-sided crystals. The other allotrope has a needlelike crystal. *What is an eight-sided object called?*

Phosphorus is a nonmetal that has three allotropes. Uses of phosphorus compounds range from water softeners to fertilizers to match heads. Antimony is a metalloid, and bismuth is a metal. Both elements are used with other metals to lower their melting points. It is because of this property that the metal in automatic fire-sprinkler heads contains bismuth.

The Oxygen Group

The oxygen group makes up Group 16 on the periodic table. You can live for only a short time without the nonmetal oxygen, which makes up about 20 percent of air. Oxygen exists in the air as diatomic molecules, O_2. During electrical storms, some oxygen molecules, O_2, change into ozone molecules, O_3. Do you notice that O_2 and O_3 are allotropes?

Nearly all living things on Earth need free oxygen, as O_2, for respiration. Living things also depend on a layer of ozone, O_3, around Earth for protection from some of the sun's radiation, as you will learn in later chapters.

The second element in the oxygen group is sulfur. Sulfur is a nonmetal that can exist in allotropes as different-shaped crystals and as a noncrystalline solid. In **Figure 12-21,** you see a magnified view of two different crystalline allotropes of sulfur. Sulfur combines with metals to form sulfides of such distinctive colors that they are used as pigments in paints.

The nonmetal selenium and two metalloids, tellurium and polonium, are the other Group 16 elements. Selenium is the most common of these. This element is one of several that you need in trace amounts in your diet. Many multivitamins contain this nonmetal as one of their ingredients. In **Figure 12-22,** you can read the label and find other elements present in vitamins. Selenium can be toxic if there is too much in your system.

Figure 12-22

Selenium is one of several elements needed by the body in trace amounts.

Section Wrap-up

Review

1. Why are Groups 14 and 15 better representatives of mixed groups than are Group 13 or Group 16?

2. How do the allotropes of sulfur differ?

3. **Think Critically:** Why is graphite a lubricant while a diamond is the hardest gem known?

Skill Builder
Concept Mapping
Make a concept map for allotropes of carbon, using the terms *graphite, diamond, buckminster-fullerene, sphere, hexagon,* and *tetrahedron*. If you need help, refer to Concept Mapping in the **Skill Handbook.**

Science Journal

In your Science Journal, write a paragraph in which you discuss the term *valuable* when applied to an element. Consider rarity, usefulness, and durability.

Design Your Own Experiment
Slippery Carbon

Often, a lubricant is needed when two metals touch each other. For example, a sticky lock can sometimes work better with the addition of a small amount of graphite. What gives this allotrope of carbon the slippery property of a lubricant?

PREPARATION

Problem
Why do certain arrangements of atoms in a material cause the material to feel slippery?

Form a Hypothesis
Based on your understanding about how carbon atoms bond, form a hypothesis about the relationship of graphite's molecular structure to its physical properties.

Objectives
- Make a model that will demonstrate the molecular structure of graphite.
- Compare and contrast the strength of types of bonding in graphite.
- Infer the relationship between bonding and physical properties.

Possible Materials
- thin spaghetti
- toothpicks
- small gumdrops
- thin polystyrene sheets
- flat cardboard
- scissors

Safety Precautions
Use care when working with scissors, sharp toothpicks, and spaghetti.

PLAN THE EXPERIMENT

1. As a group, agree upon a logical hypothesis statement.
2. As a group, sequence and list the steps you need to test your hypothesis. Be specific, describing exactly what you will do at each step to make a model of the types of bonding present in graphite.
3. Remember that graphite consists of rings of six carbons in a flat hexagon. These rings are interconnected. In addition, the flat rings in one layer are weakly attached to other flat layers.

4. Make a list of possible materials you plan to use.

Check the Plan
1. Read over the entire experiment to make sure that all steps are in logical order.
2. Will your model be constructed with materials that show both weak and strong attractions?
3. *Make sure your teacher approves your plan and that you have included any changes suggested.*

DO THE EXPERIMENT

1. Have you selected materials to use in your model that demonstrate both weak and strong attractions?
2. Once your model has been constructed, write down any observations that you make and include a sketch for your Science Journal.

Analyze and Apply
1. **Compare** your model with designs and results of other groups.

2. How does your model illustrate two types of attractions found in the graphite structure?
3. How does the bonding in graphite explain graphite's lubricating properties? Write your answer in your Science Journal.

Go Further

Oils are used on bike chains, engine parts, and other areas where metals touch. Find out how these lubricants work.

Science & ART

Pottery and Clay

In this chapter, you found out that the element hydrogen makes up nearly 90 percent of the universe. However, 82 percent of Earth is made up of oxygen, silicon, and aluminum. The clays formed by these three elements have been used by people for nearly 7000 years.

Pottery clay is approximately 40 percent aluminum oxide, 46 percent silicon oxide, and about 14 percent water. The presence or absence of impurities in clay creates the wide variety of pottery from delicate, porcelain Chinese teacups to Hopi earthenware pots.

Stains and Glazes

Prehistoric potters did little to change or enhance the colors of their works of art. Glazes, or glassy coatings, appeared about 2700-2100 B.C., when Persian and Egyptian potters made pastes of quartz and sand mixed with either copper or manganese. Copper glazes left the ceramics turquoise, and manganese glazes made them violet or purple.

Today, many artists use metal oxides to enhance or even alter the basic color of the clay. Wedgwood jasperware gets its blue color from an oxide of cobalt. Iron oxides, often present in clay, provide the earthy red and brown tones common among Native American pottery.

Firing

Firing is the application of heat to a piece of pottery. In oxidized firing, a kiln, or oven, rich in oxygen allows the combination of metals within the clays and the glazes through combustion. This results in clean, unspotted pottery. Reduction firing—firing with no oxygen present—takes place in a kiln fueled by natural gas, wood, or oil, and leaves a characteristic speckled look.

Different colors can be obtained from the same glazes. Reduction firing of copper oxide glazes will produce a deep, blood-red color. When the same glazes undergo oxidized firing, various shades of green are produced.

Science Journal

Design a simple piece of pottery and describe in your Science Journal the methods and glazes you would use to produce your finished look.

Summary

12-1: Metals

1. A typical metal is a hard, shiny solid that—due to metallic bonding—is malleable, ductile, and a good conductor.
2. Groups 1 and 2 are the alkali and alkaline earth metals, which have some similar and some contrasting properties.
3. The iron triad; the coinage metals; and the zinc, cadmium, and mercury group are among the transition elements, which make up Groups 3-12 on the periodic table.

12-2: Science and Society: New Elements, New Properties

1. The lanthanides and actinides have atomic numbers 58-71 and 90-103, respectively, whereas transuranium elements have atomic numbers greater than 92.
2. The making of synthetic elements with no immediate practical use is controversial.

12-3: Nonmetals

1. As a typical nonmetal, hydrogen is a gas that forms compounds by sharing electrons with other nonmetals and also with metals.
2. All the halogens, Group 17, have seven outer electrons and form both covalent and ionic compounds, but each halogen has some properties unlike the others.
3. The noble gases, Group 18, are elements whose properties and uses are related to their chemical stability.

12-4: Mixed Groups

1. Groups 13 through 16 of the periodic table include metals, nonmetals, and metalloids.
2. Allotropes are forms of the same element having different molecular structures.

3. The properties of three forms of carbon—graphite, diamond, and buckminster-fullerene—depend upon the differences in their crystal structures.

Key Science Words

a. allotrope
b. diatomic molecule
c. ductile
d. malleable
e. metallic bonding
f. radioactive element
g. semiconductor
h. sublimation
i. transition element
j. transuranium element

Reviewing Vocabulary

Match each phrase with the correct term from the list of Key Science Words.

1. can be drawn out into a wire
2. after uranium on the periodic table
3. can be hammered into a thin sheet
4. process of changing directly from a solid to a gas
5. will conduct an electric current under certain conditions
6. different structural forms of the same element
7. composed of two atoms
8. breaks down and gives off particles, radiation, and energy
9. in Groups 3-12 on the periodic table
10. Positively charged ions are surrounded by freely moving electrons.

Checking Concepts

Choose the word or phrase that completes the sentence or answers the question.

1. When magnesium and fluorine react, what type of bond is formed?
   a. metallic
   b. ionic
   c. covalent
   d. diatomic
2. What type of bond is found in a piece of pure gold?
   a. metallic
   b. ionic
   c. covalent
   d. diatomic
3. Because electrons move freely in metals, metals are _____.
   a. brittle
   b. hard
   c. dull
   d. conductors
4. The _____ make up the most reactive group of all metals.
   a. iron triad
   b. coinage metals
   c. alkali metals
   d. alkaline earth metals
5. The most reactive of all nonmetals is _____.
   a. fluorine
   b. uranium
   c. hydrogen
   d. oxygen
6. The element _____ is always found in nature combined with other elements.
   a. copper
   b. gold
   c. magnesium
   d. silver
7. The least magnetic of these metals is _____.
   a. cobalt
   b. iron
   c. nickel
   d. titanium
8. When neptunium atoms fall apart, they form _____.
   a. ytterbium
   b. promethium
   c. americium
   d. plutonium
9. An example of a radioactive element is _____.
   a. astatine
   b. bromine
   c. chlorine
   d. fluorine
10. The only group that is completely nonmetallic is Group _____.
    a. 1
    b. 2
    c. 17
    d. 18

Understanding Concepts

Answer the following questions in your Science Journal using complete sentences.

11. Reading from top to bottom on the periodic table, metallic properties of elements increase; reading from left to right, metallic properties decrease. Which element is the most metallic of all? Explain your answer.
12. The most abundant elements in Earth's crust are a nonmetal, a metalloid, and two metals. List the four elements.
13. Why do oxygen and nitrogen occur in the air as diatomic molecules, but argon, neon, krypton, and xenon occur as single atoms?
14. Explain why hydrogen, a nonmetal, is on the metal side of the periodic table.
15. Name three metals used to coat other metals. Why is one metal used to coat another?

Thinking Critically

16. Why was mercury used in clinical thermometers, and why is it no longer used for that purpose?
17. The density of hydrogen is so low that it can be used to fill balloons to make them lighter than air. Why is helium used more frequently?
18. Why is aluminum used instead of steel in building airplanes?
19. Why are silver compounds used in photography? Name two nonmetals extracted from seawater that are also part of these compounds.
20. Like selenium, chromium is poisonous but is needed in trace amounts in your diet. How does this information apply to the safe use of vitamin-mineral pills?

Developing Skills

If you need help, refer to the **Skill Handbook.**

21. **Making and Using Tables:** Use the periodic table to classify each of the following as a lanthanide or actinide: californium, europium, cerium, nobelium.

22. **Comparing and Contrasting:** Aluminum is close to carbon on the periodic table. Explain why aluminum is a metal and carbon is not.

23. **Observing and Inferring:** You are shown two samples of phosphorus. One is white and burns if exposed to air. The other is red and burns if lit. Infer why the properties of two samples of the same element differ.

24. **Recognizing Cause and Effect:** Plants need nitrogen compounds. Nitrogen fixing changes free nitrogen into nitrates. Lightning and legumes are both nitrogen fixing. What are the cause and effect of nitrogen fixing in this example?

25. **Concept Mapping:** Complete the concept map below for some common metals. You may use symbols for the elements.

Performance Assessment

1. **Analyzing the Data:** The model you made in Activity 12-2 on pages 352-353 helps explain the lubricating ability of graphite. Use that same model to explain how the graphite in a pencil is able to leave a mark on a piece of paper.

2. **Investigating an Issue Controversy:** Research the pros and cons of using nuclear energy to produce electricity. Prepare a report that includes data as well as your informed opinion on the subject. If several class members do research, conduct a debate on the issue.

3. **Newspaper Article:** Research the source, composition, and properties of asbestos. What properties made it suitable for use in construction in the past? How did these same properties cause asbestos to become a health hazard, and what is being done now to eliminate the hazard? Write a newspaper article that shares your findings with the public.

Previewing the Chapter

Organic and Biological Compounds

Many of the objects in the photo have one main element in common. The food, the plastic bags and containers, the wool sweater, and even the person contain many molecules based on the element carbon. Why does carbon form so many compounds? Why are the compounds so different? In this chapter, find out about this unique and important element.

EXPLORE ACTIVITY

What element forms from the breakdown of bread and paper?

1. Place a small piece of bread in a test tube.
2. Using a test-tube holder, hold the tube over the flame of a laboratory burner until you observe changes in the bread.
3. Using a clean test tube and a small amount of paper instead of bread, repeat the procedure.

Observe: In your Science Journal, compare the changes that occurred in the two test tubes.

Previewing Science Skills

▶ In the **Skill Builders**, you will **make and use a graph, interpret scientific illustrations**, and **compare and contrast**.

▶ In the **Activities**, you will **observe, predict**, and **make a model**.

▶ In the **MiniLABs**, you will **make a model, observe, predict**, and **compare and contrast**.

Science Words

organic compound
hydrocarbon
saturated hydrocarbon
isomers
unsaturated
   hydrocarbon

Objectives

* Describe structures of organic compounds and explain why carbon forms so many compounds.
* Distinguish between saturated and unsaturated hydrocarbons.
* Identify isomers of organic compounds.

Organic Compounds

What do cassette tapes and CDs, you, and your athletic shoes have in common? Each is made up mostly of substances called organic compounds. Most compounds that contain the element carbon are **organic compounds.** There are several exceptions, such as carbon monoxide, carbon dioxide, and carbonates. Overall, more than 90 percent of all compounds are organic compounds.

You probably recognize that the word *organic* is similar to the word *organism.* At one time, scientists assumed that only living organisms could produce organic compounds. However, by 1830, scientists were making organic compounds artificially in laboratories. But scientists didn't change the name of these carbon-containing compounds. Today, most of the millions of different organic compounds that exist are synthetic, and the manufacturing of organic compounds is one of the world's largest industries.

Bonding—Carbon Connections

You may wonder why there are so many organic compounds. There are several reasons, and they are related to the element carbon. First, a carbon atom has four electrons in its outer energy level. Recall that this electron arrangement means that each atom can form four covalent bonds with atoms of carbon or with other elements. Four is a large number of bonds compared to the number of bonds that atoms of other elements can form. **Figure 13-1** shows the results of some of the ways carbon can bond in an organic compound.

Figure 13-1

Many items used every day are made from organic compounds.

Figure 13-2

Carbon atoms bond to form chains, branched chains, or closed rings.

A Heptane, found in gasoline mixtures, is an example of carbon atoms bonding in a chain. Each dashed line represents a single covalent bond.

B Isoprene, a molecule that can connect to itself to form natural rubber, has one branch in its carbon chain. In addition, some of the carbon atoms have formed double bonds, shown by the double lines. *How many total bonds do you notice for each carbon atom?*

C Vanillin, the compound responsible for the flavor of vanilla beans, shows carbon atoms bonded in a closed ring. Notice that atoms of other elements may be attached to the ring.

Second, many different arrangements of single, double, and triple bonds can exist between carbon atoms. Each arrangement forms a molecule of a different organic compound. A carbon atom can also bond with atoms of many other elements, such as hydrogen and oxygen, as shown in **Figure 13-2.**

Hydrocarbons

Carbon forms an enormous number of compounds with hydrogen alone. A compound made up of only carbon and hydrogen atoms is called a **hydrocarbon.** You can learn a lot about other organic compounds by studying hydrocarbons. Does the furnace, stove, or water heater in your home burn natural gas? Almost all the natural gas used for these purposes is the hydrocarbon methane. The chemical formula of methane is CH_4. There are other ways to represent methane. The structural formula in **Figure 13-3** shows that four hydrogen atoms are bonded to one carbon atom in a methane mol-

USING MATH

The melting point of methane (CH_4) is −183°C, of ethane (C_2H_6) is −172°C, of propane (C_3H_8) is −188°C, and of butane (C_4H_{10}) is −138°C. Use these data to make a scatter plot in which the number of carbon atoms is the independent variable and the melting point is the dependent variable. Use the graph to predict the melting point of octane (C_8H_{18}).

Figure 13-3

Natural gas is mostly methane, CH_4.

Methane
CH_4

When engineers separate the hydrocarbons found in crude oil, they use the different boiling points of the hydrocarbons. Using **Figure 13-5,** what would you *predict* for the number of carbon atoms in the hydrocarbons that make up kerosene, which has a boiling point of approximately 175°C?

Table 13-1

Some Hydrocarbons		
Name	**Chemical Formula**	**Structural Formula**
Methane	CH_4	H–C–H (with H above and below)
Ethane	C_2H_6	H–C–C–H (with H above and below each C)
Propane	C_3H_8	H–C–C–C–H (with H above and below each C)
Butane	C_4H_{10}	H–C–C–C–C–H (with H above and below each C)
Pentane	C_5H_{12}	H–C–C–C–C–C–H (with H above and below each C)

$$H-\underset{\underset{H}{|}}{\overset{\overset{H}{|}}{C}}-\underset{\underset{H}{|}}{\overset{\overset{H}{|}}{C}}-\underset{\underset{H}{|}}{\overset{\overset{H}{|}}{C}}-H$$

Propane
C_3H_8

Figure 13-4

Bottled gas is mostly propane, C_3H_8.

ecule. Each line between atoms represents a single covalent bond. As you recall, a covalent bond is formed when two atoms share a pair of electrons. The space-filling model in **Figure 13-3** on page 361 shows the relative volumes of the electron clouds in the molecule.

Methane and other hydrocarbons account for more than 90 percent of the energy sources used in homes, schools, industry, and transportation. Hydrocarbons are also important in manufacturing almost all the organic compounds used in products ranging from fertilizers to skateboards.

Some stoves, most outdoor grills, and hot-air balloons burn the bottled gas propane, another hydrocarbon. Its chemical formula is C_3H_8, as shown in **Figure 13-4.**

Single Bonds

In some hydrocarbons, the carbon atoms are joined by single covalent bonds. Hydrocarbons containing only single-bonded carbon atoms are called **saturated hydrocarbons.** The carbon atoms in a molecule of propane are bonded by single covalent bonds. Propane is a saturated hydrocarbon. As you can see, the carbon atoms in propane seem to form a short chain. Propane is a member of a group of saturated hydrocarbons in which the carbon atoms form chains. **Table 13-1** lists

Figure 13-5

Boiling points of hydrocarbons in natural gas are shown here. *What happens to the boiling point as the number of carbon atoms in the chain increases?*

methane, propane, and three other similar hydrocarbons. Notice how each carbon atom appears to be a link in the chain within the molecule. **Figure 13-5** shows a graph of the boiling points of these hydrocarbons.

Isomers

Perhaps you have seen or know about butane, which is a gas sometimes burned in camping stoves and lighters. The chemical formula of butane is C_4H_{10}. Another hydrocarbon also has the same chemical formula as butane. How can this be? The answer lies in the arrangement of the four carbon atoms. Look at **Figure 13-6.** In a molecule of butane, the carbon atoms form

Table 13-2

Properties of Butane Isomers		
	Butane	**Isobutane**
Description	Colorless gas	Colorless gas
Density	0.60 kg/L	0.62 kg/L
Melting point	–138°C	–160°C
Boiling point	–0.5°C	–12°C

Butane C_4H_{10}

MiniLAB

How many structures can be shown for octane?

Octane, C_8H_{18}, is a hydrocarbon used in fuels. Remembering that each carbon atom can form four bonds and each hydrogen one, make models of the possible structures of octane.

Procedure
1. Use soft gumdrops to represent carbon atoms.
2. Use raisins to represent hydrogen atoms.
3. Use toothpicks for chemical bonds.

Analysis
1. How do you distinguish one structure from another?
2. Do you think the different shapes cause different properties?
3. What was the total of different molecules found in your class?

Figure 13-6

Two isomers of butane are shown.

Isobutane
C_4H_{10}

Problem Solving

The Case of the Overripe Tomatoes

Marc helped out at home by preparing dinner on Mondays and Thursdays. He was also responsible for buying any groceries needed to prepare the meals. One Monday, Marc bought an overripe avocado to use for guacamole that evening and some green tomatoes to use for a salad on Thursday. He thought the tomatoes would be juicy but still firm by Thursday evening. The grocery clerk put the avocado and tomatoes in a brown paper bag.

When Marc arrived at home, his father decided to take the family out to dinner, so he didn't have to prepare dinner that evening.

On Thursday, Marc opened the paper bag. The avocado was rotten, and the tomatoes were overripe—not firm as he had expected. Marc knew that fruits give off ethylene gas as they ripen. But the tomatoes ripened more quickly than Marc expected.

Think Critically:
Why did the avocado rot? What caused the tomatoes to ripen more rapidly than expected?

a continuous chain. The carbon chain of isobutane is branched. The arrangement of carbon atoms in each compound changes the shape of the molecule. Isobutane and butane are isomers.

Isomers are compounds that have identical chemical formulas but different molecular structures and shapes. There are thousands of isomers among the hydrocarbons. **Table 13-2** on page 363 summarizes several properties of the two isomers of butane.

Multiple Bonds

Do you like bananas? They are among the many fruits and vegetables that ripen with the help of ethylene. Ethylene is the common name of the hydrocarbon ethene, C_2H_4. Did you ever watch a welder using an acetylene torch? The common name of the hydrocarbon ethyne, C_2H_2, which is fuel for this torch, is acetylene. Compare the structural formulas for ethene and ethyne, which are shown in **Figure 13-7**.

Hydrocarbons that contain at least one double or triple bond between carbon atoms, such as ethene and ethyne, are called **unsaturated hydrocarbons**. Remember that *saturated* hydrocarbons contain only single bonds between carbon atoms. Fats and oils can also be classified as unsaturated or saturated because parts of their molecules are similar to saturated and unsaturated hydrocarbon molecules.

Figure 13-7

Hydrocarbons may contain double or triple bonds between carbon atoms.

$$H-C\equiv C-H$$
Ethyne C_2H_2

A Ethene gas ripens fruit. The double lines between the carbon atoms in ethene represent a double covalent bond. A double covalent bond is the sharing of two pairs of electrons—in other words, four electrons.

B Ethyne, also called acetylene is used in welding. The three lines in ethyne represent a triple covalent bond.

Ethene C_2H_4

Section Wrap-up

Review

1. Why can carbon form so many organic compounds?

2. Compare and contrast ethane, ethene, and ethyne.

3. How is an unsaturated hydrocarbon different from a saturated hydrocarbon?

4. **Think Critically:** Cyclopropane is a saturated hydrocarbon containing three carbon atoms. In this compound, each carbon atom is bonded to two other carbon atoms. Draw its structural formula. Are cyclopropane and propane isomers? Explain.

Skill Builder
Making and Using Graphs

Make a graph of **Table 13-1.** For each compound, plot the number of carbon atoms on one axis and the number of hydrogen atoms on the other axis. Use the graph to predict the formula of hexane, which has six carbon atoms. If you need help, refer to Making and Using Graphs in the **Skill Handbook.**

USING MATH

Compare the formulas of three saturated hydrocarbons: C_2H_6, C_3H_8, and C_4H_{10}. What relationship do you see between the number of carbon atoms and the number of hydrogen atoms in each? Compare the number of carbon and the number of hydrogen atoms in the unsaturated hydrocarbons C_2H_4, C_3H_6, and C_4H_8.

13•2 Other Organic Compounds

Science Words

aromatic compound
substituted hydrocarbon
alcohol

Objectives

- Describe characteristics of aromatic compounds.
- Classify groups of organic compounds as substituted hydrocarbons.

Aromatic Compounds

Chewing flavored gum or dissolving a candy mint in your mouth releases pleasant flavors and aromas. Many chemical compounds produce pleasant odors. Other compounds have unpleasant smells. The compound that produces the fragrance of wintergreen is depicted in **Figure 13-8.**

Figure 13-8

Wintergreen is an example of an aromatic compound.

You might guess that aromatic compounds are smelly—and most of them are. An **aromatic compound** is a compound that contains the benzene ring structure. Look at a model of benzene, C_6H_6, and its structural formula in **Figure 13-9.** As you can see, the benzene molecule has six carbon atoms bonded into a ring. The electrons shown as three double bonds and

Figure 13-9

Benzene, C_6H_6, can be represented by (A) a space-filling model, (B) a structural formula, or (C) the benzene ring symbol.

Benzene C_6H_6

three single bonds that form the ring are actually shared by all six carbon atoms in the ring. This equal sharing of electrons is represented by the special symbol shown in **Figure 13-9C.** The sharing of these electrons causes the benzene molecule to be very stable. Many compounds contain this stable ring structure. Knowing the structure of benzene can help you to picture hundreds of different aromatic organic compounds.

Can you recognize the odor of moth crystals? One example of an aromatic compound is naphthalene. One type of moth crystal is made of naphthalene, as shown in **Figure 13-10.** Notice that naphthalene is made up of two ring structures.

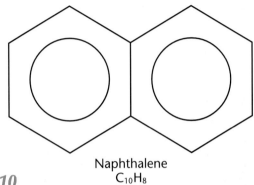

Figure 13-10

Naphthalene
$C_{10}H_8$

Moth crystals are naphthalene.

Substituted Hydrocarbons

Usually, a cheeseburger is a hamburger covered with melted American cheese and served on a bun. However, you can make a cheeseburger with Swiss cheese and serve it on slices of bread. If you ate this cheeseburger, you would notice that the substitutions affect the taste.

Chemists make similar changes to hydrocarbons. These changes produce compounds called substituted hydrocarbons. A **substituted hydrocarbon** has one or more of its hydrogen atoms replaced by atoms of other elements. Examples of substituted hydrocarbons are shown in **Figure 13-11** on page 368.

MiniLAB

Are esters aromatic compounds?

Organic compounds known as acids and alcohols react to form another type of organic compound called an ester. Esters frequently produce a recognizable aroma.

Procedure

1. Use a hot plate to heat a beaker of water to approximately 70°C.
2. In a medium-sized test tube, place approximately 0.2 g of salicylic acid.
3. Add 2 mL of methyl alcohol to the test tube.
4. Your teacher will use a dropper to carefully add three to five drops of concentrated sulfuric acid. **CAUTION:** *Sulfuric acid is caustic. Avoid all contact.* Mix all the contents together.
5. Place the test tube in the hot water for 12 to 15 minutes.
6. After removing the tube from the hot water and allowing it to cool, carefully wave your hand over the top of the tube to detect any new aroma.

Analysis
1. What did you smell?
2. Esters typically evaporate easily. What evidence did you notice that showed this statement to be true?

Alcohols and Acids

Have you ever used rubbing alcohol to soothe aching muscles after too much exercise? Did you know you were using a substituted hydrocarbon? Alcohols are an important group of organic compounds. An **alcohol** is formed when $-OH$ groups replace one or more hydrogen atoms in a hydrocarbon, as shown in **Figure 13-11B. Table 13-3** lists several alcohols.

Organic acids form when a carboxyl group, $-COOH$, is substituted for three hydrogen atoms attached to the same carbon atom. Look at **Figure 13-11C.** The structures of ethane, ethanol, and acetic acid are similar. Do you see that acetic acid is a substituted hydrocarbon?

Figure 13-11

Several types of compounds are substituted hydrocarbons.

A A compound used in dry cleaning, tetrachloroethene, C_2Cl_4, is a substituted hydrocarbon. The prefix *tetra-* means "four," and *chloro-* refers to chlorine. C_2Cl_4 is formed when four chlorine atoms replace the hydrogen atoms in ethene, C_2H_4.

Tetrachloroethene
C_2Cl_4

C Recall that vinegar contains acetic acid. Acetic acid is an example of an organic acid. Many fruit juices contain similar organic acids.

Acetic acid CH_3COOH

B Ethanol, C_2H_5OH, is an alcohol produced by the fermentation of sugar in corn and other grains and in many fruits. Alcoholic beverages contain ethanol. As you will learn in the next section, this alcohol is sometimes added to gasoline. Ethanol is also a good cleaning fluid because it can dissolve substances that don't dissolve in water.

Ethanol C_2H_5OH

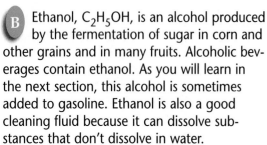

Table 13-3

Common Alcohols				
	Methanol	**Ethanol**	**Isopropyl alcohol** **(rubbing alcohol)**	**Phenol**
	H | H–C–OH | H	H H | | H–C–C–OH | | H H	H OH H | | | H–C–C–C–H | | | H H H	⬡–OH
Uses **Fuel**	✓	✓		
Cleaner	✓	✓	✓	
Disinfectant			✓	
Manufacturing chemicals	✓		✓	✓

You have learned about a wide range of organic compounds and have seen how they affect you individually. In the next section, investigate how organic compounds affect all of society.

Section Wrap-up

Review

1. What do the structures of all aromatic compounds have in common?

2. How is each of the following a substituted hydrocarbon: (a) tetrachloroethene, (b) ethanol, (c) acetic acid?

3. **Think Critically:** Chloroethane, C_2H_5Cl, can be used as a spray-on anesthetic for localized injuries. How does chloroethane fit the definition of a substituted hydrocarbon? Diagram its structure.

Skill Builder
Interpreting Scientific Illustrations
Formic acid, HCOOH, is the simplest organic acid. Draw its structural formula by referring to the structure of acetic acid in **Figure 13-11C.** If you need help, refer to Interpreting Scientific Illustrations in the **Skill Handbook.**

Science Journal

Examine the different ways a benzene molecule can be represented, as shown in **Figure 13-9.** In your Science Journal, write a paragraph that explains how benzene can be represented by a six-sided figure with a circle in it.

ISSUE:

13•3 Growing Energy on the Farm

Science Words

biomass
biogas
energy farming
gasohol

Objectives

- Describe the role of biomass and biogas in increasing our energy supply.
- Analyze the positive and negative aspects of raising crops to be harvested for their energy value.

Energy Production: A Global Problem

Transportation, heating, cooling, and making electricity all require energy. In most cases in the United States, fossil fuels—which consist of natural gas, coal, or petroleum—are the primary sources of energy. Fossil fuels are convenient energy sources. Coal, the most abundant energy source in the United States, and other fossil fuels are considered to be nonrenewable because they require millions of years to be replaced. Conservation will help us prolong our supplies of fossil fuels, but we will eventually deplete them.

Energy Farming

Approximately half of the world's population does not have access to fossil fuel energy sources. Instead, they use biomass and biogas as an energy source. **Biomass,** as shown in **Figure 13-12,** is organic material from wood, sugarcane, corn, crop, and animal wastes. Many people burn biomass such as wood and peat on a regular basis, but so far, in some areas, it has been impractical to use as a major source of energy for such things as electricity. Biomass is being burned in the power plant shown in **Figure 13-13.** Brazil has done studies also and is well on the way to having a large wood biomass power plant. If biomass is allowed to rot in the absence of air, bacteria break down the wastes to produce biogas. **Biogas** is a mixture of gases, mostly methane, produced from biomass.

Controlled planting and usage can make these energy sources renewable. Can enough plants be grown and harvested to provide biomass and biogas for realistic energy supplies? Growing plants for this purpose is called **energy farming.**

Figure 13-12

Sources of energy include biomass, such as animal wastes. Here, cow manure is collected to be used as an energy source.

2 Points of View

Harvesting Energy—The Good News

Burning biomass or biogas to make heat to produce steam to generate electricity may produce less air pollution than the burning of fossil fuels. Fermenting corn to make alcohol to mix with gasoline, a mixture called **gasohol,** will allow current gasoline supplies to last longer. Because most of these techniques make use of existing technology or technology similar to what exists, they can be used readily.

Figure 13-13

This biomass power plant provides energy for hundreds of homes in California.

Hidden Problems

While advantages exist, biomass production on a larger scale could result in problems. Using scarce agricultural land and diverting water to energy farms make growing food crops more difficult. Heating, fermenting, and extracting alcohol from plant material may require more energy than it produces. Combustion of biomass may create air pollution problems. For example, a form of bromine has been detected in the smoke from burning trees in forest fires. Bromine is capable of destroying more ozone than chlorine destroys.

The advantages and disadvantages of energy farming should be evaluated. Can solutions be found for the problems associated with energy farming? Will it provide a major source of energy in the future?

Section Wrap-up

Review

1. What compound can be found in biogas mixtures?

2. What reasons can be given for developing energy farms?

Explore the Issue

Although it is difficult to estimate, some forecasters predict that the world's oil reserves could be down to less than ten percent of the current level within the next 50 years. How could well-managed energy farms provide some worldwide answers to this problem?

SCIENCE & SOCIETY

Alcohols and Organic Acids

Have you ever wondered how chemists change one substance into another? You have learned that changing the bonding among atoms holds the key to that process.

Problem

How can the bonding in an alcohol change in a way that changes the alcohol into an acid?

Materials

- test tube and stopper
- 1 mL 0.01M potassium permanganate solution
- 1 mL 6M sodium hydroxide solution
- 3 drops of ethanol
- goggles
- apron
- 10-mL graduated cylinder

Procedure

1. Pour 1 mL of 0.01M potassium permanganate solution and 1 mL of 6M sodium hydroxide solution into a test tube. **CAUTION:** *Handle both of these chemicals with care; immediately flush any spill with water.*
2. Add 3 drops of ethanol to the test tube.
3. Stopper the test tube and gently shake it for 1 minute. Observe and record any changes you notice in the tube for the next 5 minutes.

Analyze

1. What is the structural formula for ethanol?
2. What part of a molecule identifies a compound as an alcohol?
3. What part of a molecule identifies a compound as an organic acid?

Conclude and Apply

4. What evidence did you **observe** of a chemical change taking place in the test tube?
5. In the presence of potassium permanganate, an alcohol may undergo a chemical change into an acid. If the alcohol used is ethanol, what would you **predict** to be the formula of the acid produced?
6. The acid from ethanol is found in a common household product—vinegar. What is the acid's common name?

Data and Observations

Changes in Mixture

Biological Compounds

Proteins

Did you ever loop together strips of paper to make paper chains for decorations? Have you ever strung paper clips together? Both a paper chain and a string of paper clips can represent the structure of polymers. **Polymers** are huge molecules made of many smaller organic molecules that have formed new bonds and linked together. The smaller molecules are called monomers. Monomers within a certain polymer are usually very similar in size and structure. You can picture a monomer as an individual loop of paper or an individual paper clip. **Figure 13-14** shows this model of a polymer. As you will learn in Chapter 14, plastics are polymers. Many of the important biological compounds in your body also are polymers. Among them are the proteins.

Proteins are polymers formed from organic compounds called amino acids. Even though there are millions of different proteins, there are only 20 common amino acids.

Versatile Molecules

Different types of proteins make up many of the tissues in your body, such as muscles and tendons, as well as your hair and fingernails. A protein in your blood called hemoglobin carries oxygen, **Figure 13-14.**

Science Words

polymer
protein
nucleic acid
carbohydrate
lipid

Objectives

- Describe the formation of polymers and discuss their importance as biological compounds.
- Compare and contrast proteins, nucleic acids, carbohydrates, and lipids.

Hemoglobin

Figure 13-14

This paper chain is similar to a polymer because smaller units are linked to form a larger unit. Blood contains a complex protein, which is a polymer called hemoglobin.

Red blood cells

Figure 13-15

Some high-protein foods are shown. *Why is it important to eat foods that contain protein?*

The enzymes that regulate chemical reactions in your body are proteins. In fact, proteins account for 15 percent of your weight. That's about half the weight of all materials other than water in your body. Several high-protein foods are shown in **Figure 13-15.**

Two amino acids are shown in **Figure 13-16A.** The –COOH group is the carboxylic acid group. If you look again at **Figure 13-11C** on page 368, you'll see that the structure of this group appears also in acetic acid. The $-NH_2$ group is called the amine group. Both groups appear in every amino acid.

Peptide bonds form when the amine group of one amino acid combines with the organic acid group of another amino acid. Look at **Figures 13-16B** and **C.**

Your body makes proteins from amino acids. The amino acids come from eating and digesting foods that contain proteins. Digestion breaks the protein polymers into monomers of amino acids, which your body uses to make new proteins.

Figure 13-16

In a protein polymer, peptide bonds link together molecules of amino acids.

B When amino acids react to form a protein, water is formed from the –OH from a carboxylic acid group of one amino acid and a –H from an amine group in the other amino acid.

A Notice that each of these amino acids contains a –COOH group and a $-NH_2$ group.

Glycine

Cysteine

C The remaining parts of the molecules form a peptide bond.

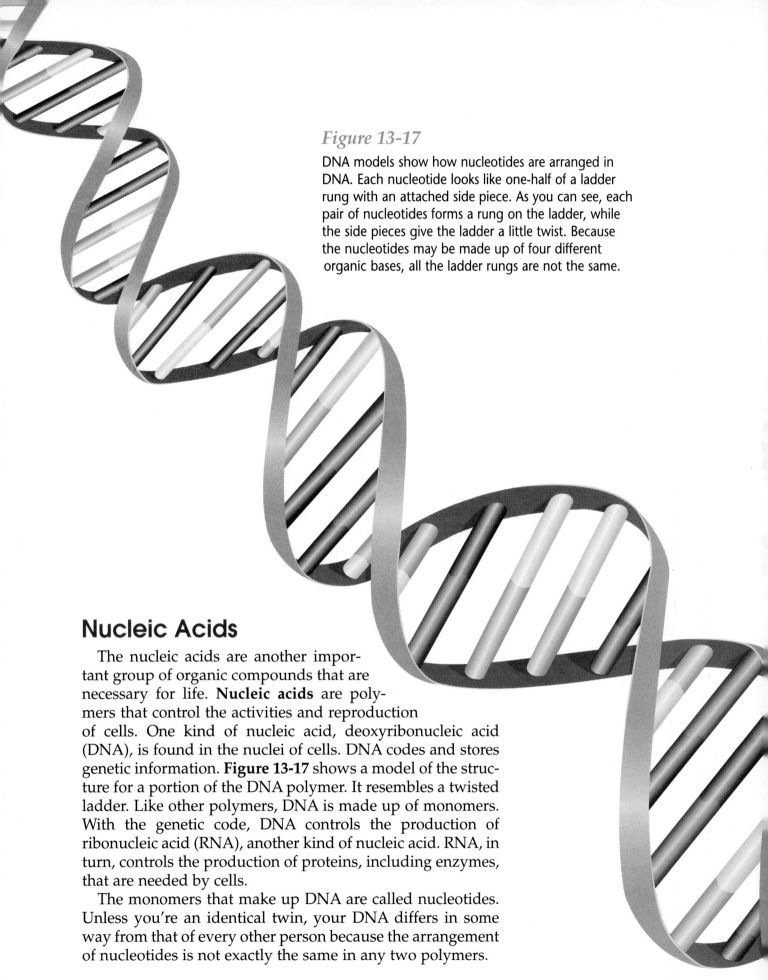

Figure 13-17

DNA models show how nucleotides are arranged in DNA. Each nucleotide looks like one-half of a ladder rung with an attached side piece. As you can see, each pair of nucleotides forms a rung on the ladder, while the side pieces give the ladder a little twist. Because the nucleotides may be made up of four different organic bases, all the ladder rungs are not the same.

Nucleic Acids

The nucleic acids are another important group of organic compounds that are necessary for life. **Nucleic acids** are polymers that control the activities and reproduction of cells. One kind of nucleic acid, deoxyribonucleic acid (DNA), is found in the nuclei of cells. DNA codes and stores genetic information. **Figure 13-17** shows a model of the structure for a portion of the DNA polymer. It resembles a twisted ladder. Like other polymers, DNA is made up of monomers. With the genetic code, DNA controls the production of ribonucleic acid (RNA), another kind of nucleic acid. RNA, in turn, controls the production of proteins, including enzymes, that are needed by cells.

The monomers that make up DNA are called nucleotides. Unless you're an identical twin, your DNA differs in some way from that of every other person because the arrangement of nucleotides is not exactly the same in any two polymers.

Sucrose $C_{12}H_{22}O_{11}$

Glucose $C_6H_{12}O_6$

Carbohydrates

Figure 13-18

Sucrose and glucose are sugars found in foods. Fruits contain glucose and another simple sugar called fructose. *Why are sugars carbohydrates?*

If you hear the word *carbohydrate*, you may think of a sweet fruit or sugary treat. Do you also think of carbohydrate loading by athletes? Runners, for example, often prepare in advance for a long-distance race by eating, or "loading," carbohydrates in starchy foods such as vegetables and pasta. Starches provide high-energy, long-lasting fuel for the body.

Carbohydrates are organic compounds in which there are twice as many hydrogen atoms as oxygen atoms. One group of carbohydrates is the sugars, as shown in **Figure 13-18.** The sugar glucose is found in your blood and also in many sweet foods such as grapes and honey. The sugar sucrose is common table sugar.

Figure 13-19 shows a part of a starch molecule. Starch is a carbohydrate that is also a polymer. During digestion, sucrose and starch are broken down into smaller molecules of glucose and other similar sugars.

Figure 13-19

Starch is the major component of pasta.

Figure 13-20

At room temperature, fats are normally solids, and oils are usually liquids.

Lipids

Fats, oils, and related compounds make up a group of organic compounds known as **lipids.** Lipids, examples of which are shown in **Figure 13-20,** include animal fats, such as butter, and vegetable oils, such as corn oil. Lipids contain the same elements as carbohydrates, but in different proportions and arrangements.

USING TECHNOLOGY

DNA Fingerprinting ▽ △

Fingerprints! When crime investigators find a print left by the oil of someone's skin, they know that an identifying piece of evidence has been found. Could other complex molecules at a crime scene be just as important? Each of us carries a unique arrangement of several billion nucleotide monomers. Within the DNA of our cells, nucleotides are arranged in groups called genes. These structures make the synthesis of proteins possible.

With the possible exception of identical twins, each person's DNA is unique. Therefore, the fragment break-up pattern can be used to identify someone. From a tissue sample, such as blood, chemists extract DNA, break it up, separate the fragments, obtain a radioactive image that emits X rays, and develop a film picture of the nucleotide pattern.

Think Critically:

It is currently estimated that the odds of two unrelated people having the same DNA "fingerprint" are approximately one in 10 billion. How can simple monomers—made up of only a sugar, a nitrogen base, and a phosphate group—provide so many different nucleotide combinations?

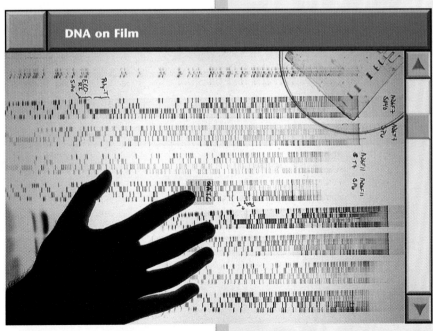

DNA on Film

CONNECT TO
LIFE SCIENCE

Check the label on any available carton of milk. What percentage of fat is in the milk? *Infer* the advantages of drinking low-fat milk.

INTEGRATION
Life Science

Figure 13-21

Pheromones enable bees to communicate information such as the location of a food source or the invasion of the hive by an enemy.

Fats and oils are similar in structure to hydrocarbons, so they can be classified as saturated and unsaturated, according to the types of bonds in their carbon chains. Saturated fats contain only single bonds between carbon atoms, and unsaturated fats contain at least one double bond. Most animal fats contain a great deal of saturated fats. Oils from plants are mainly unsaturated.

Have you heard that eating too much fat can be unhealthy? There is evidence that too much saturated fat and cholesterol in the diet contributes to heart disease and that unsaturated fats may help to prevent heart disease. A balanced diet includes some fats, just as it includes proteins and carbohydrates.

Cholesterol

Another lipid found in meat and fish is cholesterol. Even if you never ate foods containing cholesterol, your body would make its own supply. Cholesterol is used by the body to build cell membranes and is also found in bile, a digestive fluid. Although cholesterol is a lipid, it is not a fat.

Pheromones

In other species of the animal kingdom, cholesterol plays an unusual role. Female ticks combine cholesterol, which they have obtained from blood, with another compound to form an attractant for male ticks. This chemical attractant coats the outside of their bodies and is an example of a pheromone.

The term *pheromone* is used to describe a chemical used in communication among individuals within the same species. Ants from a nest are able to follow an individual food trail by detecting organic compounds left by the first ant. In beehives, as shown in **Figure 13-21,** the queen emits controlling chemicals to other members of the colony. Pheromones have dramatic effects even when present in extremely small amounts.

One way to trap insects for study or pest control is to use the attracting pheromone from a species as bait in traps, as shown in **Figure 13-22.** Chemicals that indicate a warning alarm to a species may be used in a repellent in place of using a more harsh chemical treatment.

Are there human pheromones? Human behavior is complex, and we react in many ways to outside stimuli. Aromas, both natural and those added from fragrances, do have perceived effects. Research is still being done on human pheromones. From insects to larger animals, communication of many important feeding, fighting, mating, and migration activities is regulated by organic molecules, including cholesterol.

Figure 13-22

Traps for certain insect pests, such as the Japanese beetle, use bait consisting of pheromones that attract the pest to the trap.

Section Wrap-up

Review

1. What is a polymer? Why are polymers important organic compounds?

2. Compare and contrast proteins and nucleic acids.

3. **Think Critically:** Is ethanol a carbohydrate? Explain.

Skill Builder
Comparing and Contrasting
In terms of DNA, compare and contrast identical twins and two people who are not identical twins. If you need help, refer to Comparing and Contrasting in the **Skill Handbook.**

USING MATH

By changing just one amino acid in a chain, the function of the entire protein changes. If the letters *G, L, C,* and *I* represent four amino acids, how many different four-amino acid protein chains could be made?

Design Your Own Experiment
Mixing Many Monomers

A common expression about food is, "You are what you eat." This statement is true because your digestive system changes food into useful compounds in your body, such as glucose and amino acids.

PREPARATION

Problem
How can you demonstrate the bonding in the basic components of food?

Form a Hypothesis
From what you know about polymers, state a hypothesis about how models of glucose monomers and amino acid monomers can be shown to bond into starch and protein, respectively.

Objectives
- Make a model of glucose and amino acids that can be used to demonstrate linkage of monomers into biological polymers.
- Observe that certain areas of molecules have structures that can be used for attachments to other molecules.

Possible Materials
- note cards of 2 different colors
- paper clips
- fine-line markers

PLAN THE EXPERIMENT

1. As a group, agree upon and write out the hypothesis statement about your model.
2. As a group, list the steps that you need to take to produce your models. Be specific, describing exactly what you will do at each step.
3. Make a list of the materials that you will need to complete your model.

Check the Plan

1. Have you shown the structure of glucose on a note card so that it can hook on either end to another glucose model?
2. What have you used to show linkage between monomers of glucose?

3. Have you found amino acid structures to make a model protein?
4. *Make sure your teacher approves your plan and that you have included any changes suggested in the plan.*

DO THE EXPERIMENT

1. Prepare your monomer models as planned and approved.
2. How many monomers can you hook together?

Analyze and Apply

1. **Compare** your note card models to those of your classmates.
2. **Contrast** the glucose and amino acid monomer models.
3. How can you use the same amino acid models to make a different protein?

Go Further

What small molecule is also produced in the actual formation of biological polymers such as starch and protein?

People and Science

NORMA MARTINEZ, *Food Scientist*

On the Job

Q What are your job responsibilities?

A I monitor the manufacturing process of a very popular sports drink. I analyze the formulations to make sure the salt, sugar, and water are in the right proportions. That involves measuring such properties as the amount of detectable acidity and the acid-base balance.

Q How do sports drinks differ from soft drinks?

A Sports drinks are formulated so that the electrolytes they contain "hook up" with the electrolytes in the body and speed the absorption of liquid. It's rather like tricking your body into thinking it's the same fluid so your body will absorb the water faster. Sports drinks have been scientifically proven to do that.

Q Did your training require education in food science?

A Yes. I took courses in areas such as microbiology, food engineering, and dairy science, in which we learned to make ice cream. That was my favorite class.

Personal Insights

Q Do you prefer practical application of science over doing research or lab work?

A Yes. I enjoy real-world application of science. The area of food science is constantly changing. Although people will always need to eat and drink, they seek novelty along with nutrition.

Q How does your job affect your outlook on life?

A As a Hispanic in a managerial position, I try to set a positive example for the people who actually work on the line making our product. When I was in high school, I was encouraged by a group that provided support for minorities in engineering. I'd like to help in a similar way.

Career Connection

Write to the consumer information division of the manufacturer of your favorite packaged food. (You can get the address from the label.) Ask for product information and data about nutrition. Prepare a poster display showing what you learned.

- Caterer
- Dietician
- Nutritionist

Summary

13-1: Simple Organic Compounds

1. Carbon is an element with a structure that enables it to form a large number of compounds, known as organic compounds.
2. Saturated hydrocarbons contain only single bonds between carbon atoms, and unsaturated hydrocarbons contain double or triple bonds.
3. Isomers of organic compounds have identical formulas but different molecular shapes.

13-2: Other Organic Compounds

1. Aromatic compounds, many of which have odors, contain the benzene ring structure.
2. A substituted hydrocarbon contains one or more atoms of other elements that have replaced hydrogen atoms.

13-3: Science and Society: Growing Energy on the Farm

1. Biomass is the source of biogas and gasohol, two fuels that can be used to increase our energy supply.
2. Ethanol and gasohol are useful as substitutes for gasoline, but their production may damage the environment.

13-4: Biological Compounds

1. Many important biological compounds are polymers—huge organic molecules made of many smaller units, or monomers.
2. Proteins, nucleic acids, carbohydrates, and lipids are major groups of biological compounds.

Key Science Words

a. alcohol
b. aromatic compound
c. biogas
d. biomass
e. carbohydrate
f. energy farming
g. gasohol
h. hydrocarbon
i. isomers
j. lipid
k. nucleic acid
l. organic compound
m. polymer
n. protein
o. saturated hydrocarbon
p. substituted hydrocarbon
q. unsaturated hydrocarbon

Reviewing Vocabulary

Match each phrase with the correct term from the list of Key Science Words.

1. a combination of ethanol and gasoline
2. a hydrocarbon containing only single bonds
3. all animal and plant material
4. specific type of compound formed when an –OH group replaces one or more hydrogen atoms in a hydrocarbon
5. compounds with identical chemical formulas but different molecular structures
6. a hydrocarbon containing at least one double or triple bond between carbons
7. contains the benzene ring structure
8. a fat, oil, or related compound
9. formed from plant and animal waste
10. growing plants for use as fuel

Checking Concepts

Choose the word or phrase that completes the sentence or answers the question.

1. A benzene ring is _____.
   a. rare   c. unstable
   b. stable   d. saturated
2. Alcohols and organic acids are both _____ hydrocarbons.
   a. aromatic   c. substituted
   b. saturated   d. unsaturated
3. Two examples of _____ are cow manure and a tree.
   a. biogas   c. energy farming
   b. biomass   d. hydrocarbons
4. The units of polymers are _____.
   a. monomers   c. plastics
   b. isomers   d. carbohydrates
5. Some examples of _____ are enzymes and hemoglobin.
   a. carbohydrates   c. nucleic acids
   b. lipids   d. proteins
6. DNA codes and stores _____.
   a. genetic information   c. proteins
   b. nucleic acids   d. lipids
7. DNA is made up of _____.
   a. amino acids   c. polymers
   b. nucleotides   d. carbohydrates
8. Glucose and fructose, both $C_6H_{12}O_6$, are _____.
   a. amino acids   c. isomers
   b. alcohols   d. polymers
9. If a carbohydrate has 16 oxygen atoms, how many hydrogen atoms does it have?
   a. 4   c. 16
   b. 8   d. 32
10. Cholesterol is a type of _____.
    a. sugar   c. protein
    b. starch   d. lipid

Understanding Concepts

Answer the following questions in your Science Journal using complete sentences.

11. Too much saturated or unsaturated fat in the diet is unhealthful. What is the difference in the composition of saturated fat and unsaturated fat?
12. Rubbing alcohol is isopropyl alcohol. How does this differ from propyl alcohol?
13. Carbon tetrachloride, a former dry cleaning fluid, is formed when all the hydrogen in methane is replaced by chlorine. Write the formula for carbon tetrachloride.
14. Explain how biomass has been used as an energy source throughout history.
15. Luminol, found in light sticks, is an example of an organic compound. How many different elements are bonded to carbon in a molecule of luminol, shown below?

Thinking Critically

16. Why are more than 90 percent of all compounds organic compounds?
17. Use a diagram to explain single, double, · and triple bonds in hydrocarbons. Draw a chain of carbon atoms that shows each type of bond.
18. Explain why a marsh provides an environment that produces biogas.
19. Show how the structure of an amino acid explains the term *amino acid.*
20. Some fats are polyunsaturated. Draw a chain of polyunsaturated carbon atoms.

Developing Skills

If you need help, refer to the **Skill Handbook.**

21. **Making and Using Graphs:** Using the following table, plot the number of carbon atoms on one axis and the boiling point on the other axis on a graph. Use the graph to predict the boiling points of butane, octane, and dodecane ($C_{12}H_{26}$).

Graph Data

Name	Formula	Boiling Point (°C)
Methane	CH_4	−162
Ethane	C_2H_6	−89
Propane	C_3H_8	−42

22. **Interpreting Scientific Illustrations:** Which of the following terms apply to the illustration below? *alcohol, aromatic, carbohydrate, hydrocarbon, lipid, organic compound, polymer, saturated, substituted hydrocarbon, unsaturated*

23. **Concept Mapping:** Use a network tree to describe types of fats. Include the terms *saturated fats, unsaturated fats, single bonds,* and *double bonds.*
24. **Recognizing Cause and Effect:** Our society has a definite need for more energy farming. List several causes and several effects of this need.
25. **Hypothesizing:** Sarah decided to go on a weight-reduction diet. She is eating only lettuce and fruit. What do you predict will happen to Sarah as a result?

Performance Assessment

1. **Scientific Drawing:** Research hydrocarbons containing five carbon atoms. Draw diagrams of their structures, name them, and tell their uses.
2. **Conducting a Survey and Graphing the Results:** Survey local gasoline stations to find out whether they sell gasohol or only gasoline. Find out how much of each fuel is sold per month. Display results in a graph.
3. **Oral Presentation:** Research ways crops are used as energy resources. Make an oral presentation of your findings. Suggest how these ways could be implemented locally.

Previewing the Chapter

Useful Materials

Many products are redesigned to take advantage of special properties of new materials such as alloys, plastics, and composites. These new materials add strength to a product, cut production time, reduce weight, and protect against corrosion. The airplane shown here is made up of a graphite-carbon composite material that makes it stronger, lighter-weight, and keeps it free from corrosion. In the Explore Activity below, you will investigate another type of useful material.

EXPLORE ACTIVITY

Ceramic Smiles

A ceramic material called dental porcelain is used to restore damaged teeth to their original appearance.
1. Predict the properties porcelain needs to replace tooth enamel.
2. The substances commonly used in dental porcelain are alumina and silica. What chemical elements do you think make up alumina and silica?
3. How are ceramic materials made?

Observe: Survey the members of your class to determine whether they, or members of their families, have made dental visits during which dental porcelain has been used. In your Science Journal, record different reasons people have for having extensive dental work. Analyze these reasons.

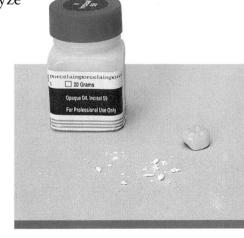

Previewing Science Skills

▶ In the Skill Builders, you will **map concepts, observe,** and **infer.**

▶ In the Activities, you will **observe, infer,** and **predict.**

▶ In the MiniLABs, you will **observe, compare,** and **contrast.**

14•1 Materials with a Past

Science Words

alloy
amalgam
ceramic
glass
cermet

Objectives

- Identify common alloys and ceramics.
- Compare and contrast alloys and ceramics.

Alloys

Imagine interstate highways without steel bridges, cities without brick buildings, and rooms without glass windows. It's almost impossible to imagine such things because materials such as steel, brick, and glass are part of your everyday life. As you will see, the characteristics that make these and many more familiar materials useful are rooted in discoveries made thousands of years ago.

When a marching band goes by, you can easily recognize the brass section. The instruments are brilliant in both sound and color. Trumpets, trombones, and tubas are made of an alloy called brass. An **alloy** is a mixture of a metal and one or more other elements. An alloy retains the properties common to metals, but it is not a pure metal. Brass is a mixture of copper and zinc. The brass used in musical instruments and in some hardware is composed of about 80 percent copper and 20 percent zinc. Brass of this quality is a solid solution of the two metals. As you recall from Chapter 9, a solution is a homogeneous mixture. Any brass that contains more than 40 percent zinc is a heterogeneous mixture. This means that the mixture of atoms of the two metals is not completely uniform.

Award-Winning Alloy

Have you ever been awarded a plaque or trophy? Chances are it is made of bronze, an alloy similar to brass. **Figure 14-1** shows several bronze-covered objects. About 5000 years ago, people discovered that a new material could be made by mixing melted copper and tin. The new material—bronze—was

Figure 14-1

These bronze objects show two of the many uses of bronze. *Why is bronze more expensive than brass?*

stronger and more durable than either copper or tin. This first known alloy became so popular and so widely used that a 2000-year span of history is known as the Bronze Age. The Bronze Age ended with the discovery of iron.

Bronze is more expensive than brass because tin is more expensive than zinc. However, bronze is especially useful in plumbing fixtures and in hardware that will be exposed to salt water. Brass is not suitable for such items as boat propellers because the zinc reacts with minerals in salt water, leaving porous copper behind. The tin in bronze does not react with saltwater minerals.

Metals can be combined with other elements in different amounts to produce many different mixtures. **Table 14-1** lists some common alloys, and several are shown in **Figure 14-2.** Thousands of alloys have been created since the time bronze was first made.

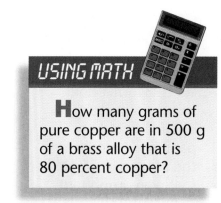

USING MATH

How many grams of pure copper are in 500 g of a brass alloy that is 80 percent copper?

Figure 14-2

Alloys are in use all around us.

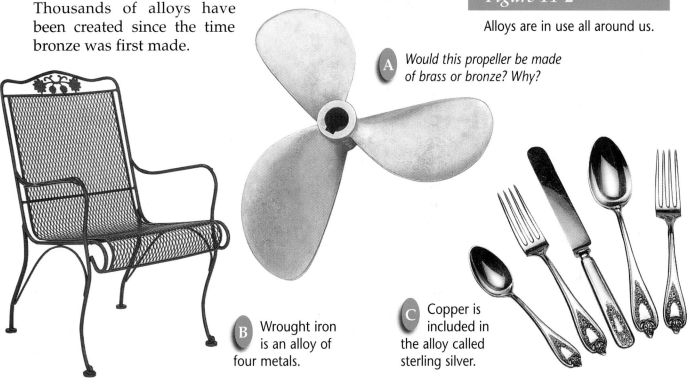

A Would this propeller be made of brass or bronze? Why?

B Wrought iron is an alloy of four metals.

C Copper is included in the alloy called sterling silver.

Table 14-1

Common Alloys		
Name	**Composition**	**Use**
Bronze	copper, tin	jewelry, marine hardware
Brass	copper, zinc	hardware
Sterling silver	silver, copper	tableware
Pewter	tin, copper, antimony	tableware
Solder	lead, tin	plumbing
Wrought iron	iron, lead, copper, magnesium	porch railings, fences

CONNECT TO

EARTH SCIENCE

During the California gold rush, prospectors obtained gold by panning. *Describe* the properties of gold that were important in making this technique useful.

An alloy has properties that are different from and more useful than the properties of the elements in it. Look at any gold jewelry. It appears to be made of pure gold. It is actually made of an alloy. As you know, gold is a bright, expensive metal that is soft and bends easily. Copper, on the other hand, is a somewhat dull, inexpensive metal that is harder than gold. When melted gold and copper are mixed and then allowed to cool, an alloy forms. It has most of the brilliance of gold and most of the sturdiness of copper. By varying the amounts of gold and copper, alloys with properties designed for different purposes are produced. **Figure 14-3** shows several gold alloys.

The alloys shown in **Figure 14-3** contain only two metals. Not all alloys are that simple. Do you or someone you know wear dental braces? Some of the wire used in the braces is an alloy of gold, silver, platinum, palladium, zinc, and copper.

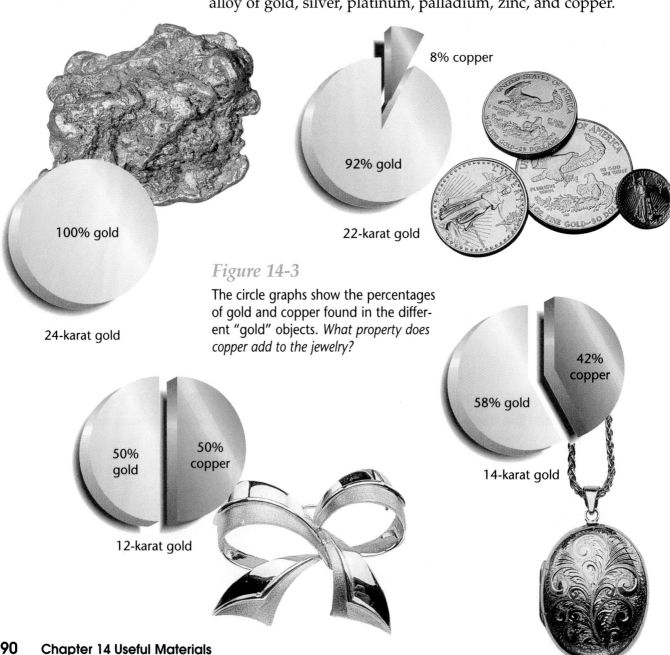

Figure 14-3

The circle graphs show the percentages of gold and copper found in the different "gold" objects. *What property does copper add to the jewelry?*

24-karat gold — 100% gold

22-karat gold — 92% gold, 8% copper

14-karat gold — 58% gold, 42% copper

12-karat gold — 50% gold, 50% copper

Some other alloys used by dentists are called amalgams. An **amalgam** is an alloy that contains mercury. Dental amalgams consist of mercury, silver, and zinc. You may have one in your mouth right now. Amalgams are used as fillings for cavities.

Uses of Alloys

Various types of steel make up an important group of alloys. **Figure 14-4** shows a medical use of a steel alloy. Steel production is greater than that of any other alloy. All types of steel are alloys of iron and carbon. You may have seen advertisements for carving knives with blades made of high-carbon steel. The carbon content of this alloy ranges from 1.0 percent to 1.7 percent. Because this steel is hard, the knife blades will be sharp. As you can see from **Table 14-2,** steels of different compositions are made for different uses.

Aluminum alloys are the second largest group of alloys produced. Aluminum alloys are used to manufacture products ranging from foils used for food wraps to automobile bodies.

In the last decade, aluminum-lithium alloys have become important. Because lithium is the lightest metal, these alloys are lightweight, yet exceedingly strong. Unlike other alloys, aluminum-lithium alloys maintain their strength at very high temperatures. In the future, these alloys may be used to make the bodies of aircraft that will travel near the outer limits of Earth's atmosphere.

Figure 14-4

Surgical steel can be used to join bones together. *What properties of this type of steel are most important?*

Table 14-2

Some Steel Alloys			
Name	**Composition**	**Properties**	**Uses**
Manganese	10-18% Mn	very hard	railroads, armor plate, conveyors
Duriron	12-15% Si	acid resistant	pipes, condensers, containers
Nickel	2-5% Ni	elastic, corrosion resistant	gears, drive shafts, cables
Invar	36% Ni	does not expand or contract	measuring tapes, pendulums
Permalloy	78% Ni	magnetic	cables
Stainless	14-19% Cr 7-9% Ni	strong, corrosion resistant	surgical instruments, knives, flatware
High speed	14-20% W, 4% Cr or 6-12% Mo, 4% Cr	keeps hardness at high temperatures	cutting tools, drill bits, saw blades

Problem Solving

Ceramic Decoys

How does our immune system tell the difference between disease-causing organisms and healthy, necessary cells? You may remember receiving vaccinations against certain diseases. The vaccine probably contained some protein from a virus. That noninfectious part could trigger your body's production of chemicals that would be ready to fight an actual virus invasion.

Finding a noninfectious portion of some viruses has proven difficult. Most viruses consist of an outer protein layer and a core of genetic material. Typically, the outer protein layer of a virus is the part that will begin the immune process without causing a major infection. Can the infectious core of a virus be replaced while retaining the outer protein layer? Researchers are looking to ceramics for a possible answer.

Solve the Problem:

1. Describe the part of a typical virus organism that causes our immune system to begin producing disease-fighting compounds.
2. Ceramic structure can be made strong and small. Ceramics can also be made to attach to some proteins. How could ceramic beads be used to make imitation virus particles?

Think Critically:

If other attachments can be made to small ceramic beads, there may be additional medical applications. What other attachments might there be for these ceramic messengers?

Ceramics

Have you ever watched a potter making a bowl? If you have, you know that the potter spins wet clay on a wheel while shaping it into a bowl by hand. The bowl is then heated in a hot oven, or kiln, to dry it and bring about important chemical changes that harden the material. Pottery like this is made of a material called ceramic. A **ceramic** is a material made from dried clay or claylike mixtures. People began making ceramic containers like the ones in **Figure 14-5** thousands of years ago to store food and carry water.

Figure 14-5

This ancient ceramic pottery is made of a mixture of clay and water.

As with alloys, there are thousands of different ceramics. Is your school building made of bricks? Does it have tiled hallways? Bricks and tiles are examples of structural ceramics. The construction industry uses structural ceramics because of their rigidity and strength. These ceramics contain silicon or aluminum, which can form small, rigid structures that bond together when water is removed. These bonds make the ceramics strong and chemically stable. The porcelain ceramics used on sinks and bathtubs are called whitewares. **Figure 14-6** shows examples of several types of ceramics.

Fragile: Handle with Care

Look at some bricks or bathroom tiles, or at the porcelain enamel around the burner plates of a stove. You'll probably see small breaks in their surfaces. These breaks are evidence of one disadvantage of some ceramics: they are so rigid that they crack. If you've ever had to pick up the pieces of a broken dinner plate, you are well aware of this.

Figure 14-6

Ceramics are used in a variety of ways.

A These structural ceramics are used in construction. *What property of ceramics makes them useful for this?*

B Porcelain enamel is a durable coating for surfaces that are subject to a lot of wear.

C This ceramic piece is an example of the delicate, breakable nature of ceramics.

MiniLAB

How do properties of ceramics change?

Procedure
1. Mix 100 mL each of flour, salt, and water in a microwave-safe bowl. Add 5 mL each of cream of tartar and a light cooking oil.
2. Heat for one minute in the microwave.
3. Cool the material and observe its properties.

Analysis
1. Did any physical properties of this material change? If so, explain what differences you notice.
2. In the formation of actual ceramics, high temperatures are used to drive off the water. Explain why the finished product could withstand extreme heat.

Almost half of the ceramics produced today are classified as glasses. A **glass** is a ceramic without a regular crystal structure. Glasses come in thousands of varieties. You are probably most familiar with the type of glass that you see in windows. This glass contains mostly oxygen and silicon, with smaller amounts of sodium and calcium and a trace of aluminum. The major ingredient that is used to make glass is silicon dioxide, SiO_2—sand.

Elemental Additions

Glasses can be made to have desired properties by changing the kinds and proportions of elements that make them up. Crystal pendants and vases are made from glass that contains lead as well as silicon and oxygen. Food-storage dishes, like the ones in **Figure 14-7** that you can pull from a freezer and place in an oven to heat, are made of glass that contains boron and magnesium or lithium.

Figure 14-7

Glass can be made to suit different purposes. This dish can be taken directly from the freezer (A) and placed in a hot oven (B). *Why can't all glass products handle the drastic temperature changes shown in these pictures?*

Do you have magnets stuck to your refrigerator door? If so, chances are that the magnet itself is a ceramic magnet. These magnets are examples of cermets. **Cermets,** or ceramic-metals, are materials that have properties of both ceramics and alloys. Cermets are tough and heat resistant and are used in gas turbines and rocket motors.

Section Wrap-up

Review

1. What is an alloy?

2. What is a ceramic?

3. **Think Critically:** Why are alloys often preferred to a pure element or metal?

Skill Builder
Concept Mapping
Make a network tree to describe the composition of common alloys using the alloys and elements mentioned in this section. If you need help, refer to Concept Mapping in the **Skill Handbook.**

USING MATH

Use the information from **Figure 14-3** to calculate the grams of actual gold in a 65-g, 14-karat gold necklace.

Activity 14-1

Preparing an Alloy

You have learned that brass is a mixture of copper and zinc. Brass looks very much like gold. In ancient times, people called alchemists attempted to change other elements into gold. They never succeeded, but they did produce some alloys.

Problem

How can you produce an alloy that gives the same appearance as gold?

Materials

- copper penny
- zinc, 30-mesh
- hot plate
- nitric acid, HNO_3, dilute
- sodium hydroxide solution, NaOH, dilute
- evaporating dishes (2)
- tongs

CAUTION: *Acids and bases can cause burns. Rinse spills immediately. Use nitric acid where there is adequate ventilation.*

Procedure

1. Carefully pour enough dilute HNO_3 into one evaporating dish to fill the dish halfway. Using tongs, grasp the penny and hold it in the acid for about 20 seconds.
2. Still using tongs, remove the penny from the acid and rinse it with cold tap water.

3. Place one teaspoon of 30-mesh zinc in the second evaporating dish. Carefully add dilute NaOH to the dish to a depth of about 2 cm above the zinc.
4. Using tongs, carefully place the penny on top of the zinc. Gently heat the contents of the dish and observe the color of the penny.
5. Set the control of the hot plate on medium high. Using tongs, carefully remove the penny from the dish and rinse it in cold tap water. Dry the penny and place it on the preheated hot plate until the penny has a golden color. **CAUTION:** *Do not touch the hot penny.*

Analyze

1. Observe and describe the appearance of the penny after it was immersed in the nitric acid. Why did its appearance change?
2. In step 4, the penny turned a silver color. Was it actually becoming silver? Was it, at this point, an alloy?

Conclude and Apply

3. Do alloys require specific amounts of ingredients to form?
4. What alloy has this procedure produced?
5. **Infer** why heat is usually necessary for two metals to combine to form an alloy.

14•2 New Materials

Science Words

plastic
synthetic fiber
composite

Objectives

* Compare and contrast plastics and synthetic fibers.
* Describe a composite.

Plastics

Think how often you and your family use the telephone. How often have you accidentally dropped the receiver or knocked a telephone over? Did the phone still work? Phones last because most of their parts are made of durable plastics. A **plastic** is a polymer-based material that can be easily molded into various shapes. **Figure 14-8** illustrates a sturdy plastic telephone. The first synthetic plastic was made only about a century ago. You may be thinking that one hundred years is a long time. However, if you remember that alloys and ceramics have been around for thousands of years, you'll realize that plastics are really modern materials.

Gigantic Molecules

Recall from the last chapter that a polymer is a gigantic molecule formed from thousands of smaller organic molecules, such as hydrocarbons. Molecules that form polymers are called monomers. You are made up of natural polymers, such as proteins and nucleic acids. Polymers that do not form naturally can be manufactured from organic compounds. These polymers are synthetic polymers.

You are probably familiar with the rolls of plastic bags that you find in the produce section of supermarkets. These bags are made of polyethylene, one of the world's most widely produced and used plastics. Among other things, polyethylene is used to make food-storage containers, bottles, and the bands used around beverage six-packs. This synthetic polymer is made of monomers of ethene, an unsaturated hydrocarbon. **Figure 14-9** shows how polyethylene is formed.

Many different organic compounds can be used as monomers, so there are many different plastics, as shown in **Table 14-3.**

Figure 14-8

The versatility and ruggedness of plastics make them ideal for use in objects that receive a lot of rough handling. *Can you think of objects you use that are plastic and sustain rough treatment?*

Figure 14-9

Polymers are formed through a series of repeating steps.

A An initiating molecule is attracted to the double bond in the monomer.

Initiator

B The double bond in the monomer breaks, causing one electron to be available for bonding to another molecule.

1st monomer

C This monomer is now active and will bond to another monomer, breaking its double bond.

D Eventually, long chains called polymers are formed.

Table 14-3

Common Plastics		
Name	**Polymer Structure**	**Uses**
Polypropylene	$\cdots C-CH_2-C-CH_2-C-CH_2 \cdots$ with H above and CH_3 below each C	Rope, protective clothing, textiles, carpet
Polystyrene	$\cdots CH-CH_2-CH-CH_2-CH-CH_2 \cdots$ with benzene rings below	Containers, boats, coolers, insulation, furniture, models
Polyvinyl chloride (PVC)	$\cdots CH_2-CH-CH_2-CH-CH_2-CH \cdots$ with Cl below	Rubber substitute, cable covering, tubing, rainwear, gaskets
Teflon (polytetrafluoroethane)	$\cdots C-C-C-C-C-C \cdots$ with F above and below each C	Nonstick cookware surfaces
Saran (polyvinylidene chloride)	$\cdots C-C-C-C-C-C \cdots$ with H, Cl, H, Cl, H, Cl above and H, Cl, H, Cl, H, Cl below	Clinging food wraps

Do you know that making plastic soft-drink bottles is similar to blowing up a balloon? Refer to **Figure 14-10** as you read how polyethylene bottles are manufactured. First, a tube of warm polyethylene is placed inside a bottle-shaped mold. Then the mold is closed, sealing the bottom of the tube. Next, compressed air is blown into the polyethylene tube; the tube expands and takes the shape of the mold. The mold is then opened and the bottle is removed.

Mold

Compressed air

Blow-molded bottle

Polyethylene tube

Figure 14-10

The major use of high-density polyethylene (HDPE) is to make blow-molded products. *How does this process illustrate Boyle's law?*

Table 14-4

Name	Structural Formula	Uses
Common Polymers		
Dacron (a polyester)	···C—⬡—C—OCH₂CH₂O—C—⬡—C—OCH₂CH₂O···	Textiles, arterial grafts
Nylon 66	···C(CH₂)₄—CN(CH₂)₆N—C(CH₂)₄C—N(CH₂)₆N···	Tire cord, textiles, brush bristles, netting, carpet, athletic turf, sutures
Polyethylene	···CH₂—CH₂—CH₂—CH₂—CH₂—CH₂···	Tubing, prosthetic devices, packaging materials, kitchen utensils, paper coating
Orlon (polyacrylonitrile)	···C—C—C—C—C—C···	Textiles

Polymers in Fabrics

The clothing you are wearing may be made of fabrics that have been woven from synthetic fibers. A **synthetic fiber** is a strand of a synthetic polymer. A strand of a synthetic fiber called Kevlar is five times stronger than a similar strand of steel. It is so strong it is used to make bulletproof vests. Synthetic fibers are used to weave both indoor and indoor-outdoor carpeting, upholstery coverings, and other textiles. Today, the use of synthetic fibers is greater than that of natural fibers. **Table 14-4** lists the names and polymer structures of several familiar synthetic fibers. Fabrics with new properties are made by weaving natural fibers, such as cotton and silk, with synthetic fibers. If you look at the label of the permanent-press shirt in **Figure 14-11,** on page 400, you will see that the fabric is a mixture of natural and synthetic fibers.

Model for new polymer

USING TECHNOLOGY

A Sticky Lesson

In the 1940s, a walk in the woods led to the discovery of a popular method of fastening objects. Today, scientists are using the same idea to improve the manufacturing of composite materials.

Instead of merely complaining about the way some burrs from pesky plants hooked to his trousers, Swiss engineer George de Mestral studied the persistent clinging seeds and saw a possible improvement on the traditional zipper. A few years later, he patented his idea for a fastener called Velcro.

When scientists want to experiment with blending two polymers to make a composite, they must find a way for the polymers to remain connected. Compounds known as compatibilizers can be added to bring the two polymers together. Scientists are studying a new type of polymer that may hold materials together in new composites. Like Velcro, this polymer has two important structural features. It has a rigid framework with long, branched parts that stick out in loops and curves.

Think Critically:

Look at the structures of the polymers on pages 397 and 398. Explain in your Science Journal why this new connecting polymer might prove to be rather effective.

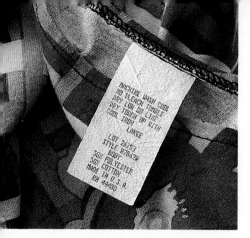

Figure 14-11

Wrinkle-resistant materials can be produced by combining synthetic and natural fibers. *What synthetic fibers can you identify in this label?*

One synthetic fiber that is widely used today is nylon. **Figure 14-12** shows how nylon fibers are manufactured. Nylon chips are heated until they melt. The melted nylon is pumped into a high-pressure chamber. It is then forced through tiny openings of a nozzle called a spinneret. As it cools, the nylon forms long strands.

You may wonder where the raw materials—the hydrocarbons and organic compounds—used to produce plastics and synthetic fibers come from. Most of them are found in petroleum—crude oil—and in natural gas. Can you explain why plastics and synthetic fibers are sometimes called petrochemical products? As the production of plastics and synthetic fibers continues to increase, so will the demand for crude oil.

Figure 14-12

Nylon production results in long strands just as silk production does.

Nitrogen gas

Nylon chips

Pressure

285°C

Spinneret

Pump

Nylon fibers

INTEGRATION
Life Science

A Natural Polymer

Silk is a natural polymer. It is made when silkworms stop eating and begin to make a cocoon in which to live as they change into moths. The worm secretes a protein polymer and gumlike material from its mouth. The protein dries and stiffens as the worm swings its head from side to side, weaving a continuous string of silk. Eventually, the worm seals itself inside of the lightweight but strong cocoon.

Today, silk farmers harvest this natural polymer by pulling off the long continuous fiber to later weave it into fabrics. One thin silk strand from a cocoon may be from 500 to 800 m long. Natural silk is lower in density than rayon and stronger than nylon. It has excellent dying properties and is warmer than cotton.

When synthetic polymers such as nylon became cheaper to produce and exhibited many of the same properties as silk, they replaced silk in many uses.

Composites

Many high school seniors take college entrance exams. Their score is called a composite score. It is a rating that depends on several subtest scores in different subjects. The word *composite* means "made of two or more parts."

A bridge built of concrete has long steel rods running through it. These rods reinforce the concrete, giving it additional strength and support. Reinforced concrete is an example of a composite. A **composite** is a mixture of two materials, one embedded in the other.

Have you ever heard of cars with fiberglass bodies? These bodies are made of a glass-fiber composite that is a mixture of small threads, or fibers, of glass embedded in a plastic. The structures of the fiberglass reinforce the plastic, making a strong, lightweight composite. A glass-fiber composite, like the one shown in **Figure 14-13,** is an example of a ceramic embedded in a plastic. How would you describe reinforced concrete? Many different composites can be made using various metals, plastics, and ceramics. In the future, you may be driving a car or living in a house that is made almost entirely of composites.

Figure 14-13

This fiberglass piece shows clearly the glass fibers embedded in the plastic. *What advantage is gained by using composites?*

Section Wrap-up

Review

1. Compare and contrast plastics and synthetic fibers.

2. Describe a composite.

3. **Think Critically:** Many athletes now play on nylon-based artificial playing surfaces. What properties of plastic make this surface an advantage for the athletes?

Skill Builder

Observing and Inferring
Look at the figures in this section. Describe a way to manufacture a roll of polyethylene bags. If you need help, refer to Observing and Inferring in the **Skill Handbook.**

Science Journal

In the future, many objects will be made of plastic that are not today. In your Science Journal, write a paragraph about one of those objects, including new properties it might have.

Design Your Own Experiment
Compose Your Own Composite

When designing composites, engineers carefully consider the properties of the individual materials that they want to blend. The resulting composite utilizes the most desirable properties of each component to make new materials.

PREPARATION

Problem
How do various embedded materials give new properties to plaster of paris?

Form a Hypothesis
Based on the properties of the embedding materials and the brittleness of plaster of paris, form a hypothesis about the properties of the new composite.

Objectives
- Observe the effects of blending various materials on changing the properties of plaster of paris.
- Infer the relationship between the characteristics of individual components and the final properties of a new composite.

Possible Materials
- plaster of paris
- water
- measuring cup
- heavy-duty aluminum foil
- hammer
- paper towels
- beaker
- miscellaneous possible embedding materials; i.e., paper clips, plastic soda straws, pipe cleaners, crayons, etc.

Safety Precautions

Be sure to use protective eyeware.

PLAN THE EXPERIMENT

1. As a group, agree upon and write out the hypothesis statement.
2. As a group, list the exact activity you need for each step in testing the hypothesis.
3. Decide what type of material you want to embed in the plaster of paris. Think about the properties of the embedding material and its possible effect on the resulting composite.
4. Decide how you will compare the properties of the composite with those of the original plaster of paris.

Check the Plan
1. Make sure that your plan makes sense as you have stated it.

2. Have you included the directions for making your aluminum foil compartments and for making the plaster of paris?
3. Will you need to repeat any of your steps?
4. How will you report your findings?
5. *Make sure that your teacher approves all embedding components and comparative tests.*

DO THE EXPERIMENT

1. Carry out the experiment, being sure to record in your Science Journal the placement of the embedding materials.
2. Write down any new properties your composite exhibits.

Analyze and Apply
1. **Compare** the materials and results other groups had with their new composites.

2. How do you think the density of the composite **compares** to the density of plaster of paris?
3. **Hypothesize** what would happen if you doubled the amount of embedding material while holding the amount of plaster of paris constant.

Go Further

Think about a few familiar concrete structures you have seen. In what way is your composite similar to these concrete structures?

ISSUE:

14•3 Record Breaking with Sports Technology

Objectives
- Compare and contrast the advantages of new materials used in sports with older materials.
- Identify chemical elements and materials of technology used in sports.
- Determine whether sports should alter rules about the use of technology.

Records: Made to be broken?

Can you think of any sports record in your school, or are you aware of a recent professional accomplishment in sports? It seems that when each record or "best-ever" achievement is set, someone quickly makes plans to break it. Many top competitors have come to realize that record performances can be helped by technology.

Making Every Second Count

In the Olympic sport of speed skating, races are won and records are set by less than a tenth of a second. How can technology give skaters that tiny time advantage? Composite materials such as steel and carbon for the blade and other carbon composites for the shoe cut the overall mass and air drag on a skate. Silicon-based polymers in the skating suit shown in **Figure 14-14** can help direct the wind current around a fast-moving skater for a slight air pressure advantage. In other winter sports, new plastic materials are used to stabilize skis during jumping and to aid bobsled racers.

Carbon and boron fibers are used to build lightweight, streamlined auto racing-car bodies. Reducing the weight of an Indianapolis racing car could increase the gas mileage, alter the friction, and result in a faster race time.

Figure 14-14

The use of composite materials has benefits for many sports.

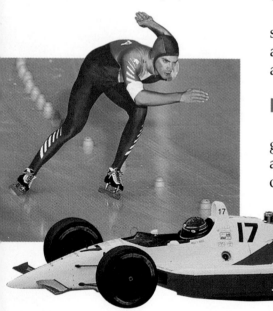

Performance Advantages

Not every sports record or win depends on time. Tennis and golf are examples. One of the premier tennis events is the annual Wimbledon grass court tournament. How has technology affected this traditional contest? In tennis, an accurate and fast serve gives a player a tremendous advantage. Strong rackets, such as the one in **Figure 14-15,** made from carbon and boron composites, are now being used to improve the speeds of some serves. These improvements give the receiving player little time to react. New boron-composite golf clubs are also giving golfers more powerful swings than ever.

2 Points of View

If It Works, Use It

Many improvements in sports performance have been brought about by using scientific analysis to change training methods, athlete nutrition, and coaching techniques. Why not use technology when designing the equipment? A running shoe with new lightweight, but supportive materials will still require a talented runner to win the race.

Winning Isn't Everything

Setting a record or winning the game is not the only reason we enjoy sports. Many fans and participants enjoy the strategy and efforts in a contest based on the present restrictions. Changes in some equipment could cause drastic changes in the basic aspects of the game. For example, would baseball sluggers have such an advantage with special composite bats that home runs would become as common as singles?

Figure 14-15

These athletes are using materials made with new technology. *How might the properties of a new tennis racket or golf club compare with the older wooden models?*

Section Wrap-up

Review

1. What are two chemical elements that are finding new uses in the world of sports?

2. What advantages do composite-based materials offer players?

Explore the Issue

Some critics at tennis tournaments have claimed that the matches are turning into serving contests. They prefer a full range of tennis ability to still be the determining factor in the sport. If you were on the rules committee, would you favor restricting the racket material? Would you suggest making it more difficult by raising the net? Would you favor no restrictions on the equipment? Explain your choice.

SCIENCE & SOCIETY

People and Science

MARTIN CAVEZA, *Industrial Designer*

On the Job

Q How do the designers at your toy company come up with new product ideas?

A We regularly hold brainstorming sessions in which the major guideline is "There's no such thing as a bad idea." Even a really silly idea can snowball into something great. Other times, we might go to the people in the chemistry lab and say, "What have you guys found that might be fun for us to look at?" Some classic toys have had their starts in this somewhat accidental fashion.

Q What determines the kind of plastic you use in a particular toy?

A For the durability most of our toys demand, we use a super-high-impact styrene. For an even more impact-resistant, scratch-resistant version, we use a plastic called ABS, acrylic butyl styrene. However, some toys need bendable parts. For those we use a polypropylene, which has a property we call a living hinge. Think of the lid on a plastic box, for example. Its hinge must be flexible enough to bend back and forth many times without breaking.

Personal Insights

Q How did you get into the business of designing toys?

A After beginning in engineering and intending to be an architect, I found out about the field of industrial design, designing products. Industrial designers design everything from cars, to blenders, to drills, to almost anything the consumer touches. Then I was a winner in a design contest held by a toy company. My entry was a clear plastic space vehicle with rubber-band power. The company liked my concept and offered me a job.

Career Connection

The manufacturers of toys are interested in feedback from their customers. Think of a toy that you have enjoyed, or even one that you found disappointing. Write a letter to the manufacturer. Outline what you consider to be the best (or worst) features of the toy. Investigate the following related careers.

• Architect   • Manufacturing Engineering

Summary

14-1: Materials with a Past

1. People have been making and using alloys and ceramics for thousands of years. Some common alloys include bronze, brass, amalgams, and various alloys of iron. Some common ceramics include structural ceramics, such as brick and tile, and various kinds of glass.
2. An alloy is a mixture of a metal with one or more other elements. Alloys exhibit metallic properties. Ceramics are composed of clay or claylike mixtures. Except for cermets—ceramic metals—ceramics generally have nonmetallic properties.

14-2: New Materials

1. Plastics and synthetic fibers are materials made from synthetic polymers. Plastics can be produced in many forms, ranging from thin films to thick slabs or blocks. Synthetic fibers are produced in thin strands that can be woven into fabrics.
2. A composite is a mixture of two materials, one embedded in the other. Reinforced concrete is an example of a composite.

14-3: Science and Society: Record Breaking with Sports Technology

1. New composite materials used in sporting events allow top-level athletes to challenge records. Examples in speed events such as auto racing, bobsledding, and skating point out the advantages of strong, lightweight materials.
2. Some people feel that either equipment updates should not be permitted, or some game rules must be changed to preserve traditions and skills in games such as tennis and baseball.

Key Science Words

a. alloy
b. amalgam
c. ceramic
d. cermet
e. composite
f. glass
g. plastic
h. synthetic fiber

Reviewing Vocabulary

Match each phrase with the correct term from the list of Key Science Words.

1. a strand of a synthetic polymer
2. ceramic with no regular crystal structure
3. mixture consisting of a metal and one or more other elements
4. made from dried clay or claylike mixtures
5. material made from polymers; can be easily molded
6. mixture of one material embedded in another
7. has properties of ceramics and alloys
8. alloy containing mercury

Checking Concepts

Choose the word or phrase that completes the sentence.

1. The production of _____ is greater than that of any other alloy.
   a. amalgam   c. bronze
   b. brass   d. steel
2. Steel is an alloy of iron and _____.
   a. carbon   c. tin
   b. mercury   d. zinc
3. Structural ceramics contain silicon or _____.
   a. aluminum   c. copper
   b. carbon   d. lithium
4. A source of the materials used to make plastics is _____.
   a. clay   c. petroleum
   b. ore   d. synthetic fiber
5. _____ is an element used in fibers to build lightweight car bodies.
   a. Sodium   c. Lithium
   b. Chlorine   d. Boron
6. Brass and bronze both contain _____.
   a. mercury   c. tin
   b. copper   d. zinc
7. _____ alloys are lightweight and strong.
   a. Aluminum-lithium   c. Copper-tin
   b. Copper-zinc   d. Iron-carbon
8. _____ is a natural protein polymer.
   a. Nylon   c. Teflon
   b. Polyethylene   d. Silk
9. Clay is used to make _____.
   a. alloys   c. ores
   b. ceramics   d. plastics
10. _____ is not a recent use of technology that has improved speed-skating performance.
    a. New fiber in suits
    b. Colder ice
    c. Composite blades
    d. Lighter shoes

Understanding Concepts

Answer the following questions in your Science Journal using complete sentences.

11. Explain why most glass products are relatively inexpensive.
12. One reason to use new materials in sports technology is to decrease the mass of objects. Explain how this can be an advantage in a sport.
13. Explain why the rigidity of ceramics can be an advantage as well as a disadvantage.
14. Iron bonds more readily with other elements than does copper. Why do you think copper was discovered so much earlier than iron was?
15. In what way is steel different from such alloys as brass, bronze, and most aluminum alloys?

Thinking Critically

16. Describe two benefits carbon and boron fibers give to race cars.
17. List three ways silk is better than other natural or synthetic fibers.
18. A lower karat gold has less gold in it than a higher karat gold. Why might you prefer a ring that is 10-karat gold over a ring that is 20-karat gold?
19. Explain why the use of composites can be considered as a problem in the world of sports.
20. A synthetic fiber might be preferred over a natural fiber for use outdoors because it will not rot. Why might this property become a negative feature in the environment?

Developing Skills

If you need help, refer to the **Skill Handbook.**

21. Comparing and Contrasting: Compare and contrast alloys and ceramics.

22. Measuring in SI: A bronze trophy has a mass of 952 g. If the bronze is 85 percent copper, how many grams of tin are contained in the trophy?

23. Interpreting Scientific Illustrations: Look at the polymer below. Draw the monomer upon which the polymer is based.

$$\cdots -\overset{\overset{\displaystyle H}{|}}{\underset{\underset{\displaystyle H}{|}}{C}} - \overset{\overset{\displaystyle H}{|}}{\underset{\underset{\displaystyle CN}{|}}{C}} - \overset{\overset{\displaystyle H}{|}}{\underset{\underset{\displaystyle H}{|}}{C}} - \overset{\overset{\displaystyle H}{|}}{\underset{\underset{\displaystyle CN}{|}}{C}} - \overset{\overset{\displaystyle H}{|}}{\underset{\underset{\displaystyle H}{|}}{C}} - \overset{\overset{\displaystyle H}{|}}{\underset{\underset{\displaystyle CN}{|}}{C}} - \cdots$$

24. Recognizing Cause and Effect: A student performing Activity 14-1 finished with step 5, but did not see any change. What are some possible causes of this effect?

25. Concept Mapping: Draw a network tree classifying matter, moving from the most general term to the most specific. Use the terms *compounds, elements, heterogeneous, heterogeneous mixtures, homogeneous, homogeneous mixtures, materials, solutions, substances.* Check (✓) the most specific term that describes an alloy and underline the most specific term that describes a composite.

Performance Assessment

1. Data Table: Research gold, its alloys, and karats. Find out several uses for gold and its alloys and what karat gold is used for each. Show your findings in a table.

2. Poster: Make a poster of the floor plan of your school or an area of the school. On the floor plan, list locations where ceramics are used and the types of ceramics used there.

3. Project: Research the production of silk fabric and compare it with production of synthetic fabrics such as nylon. Display samples of each.

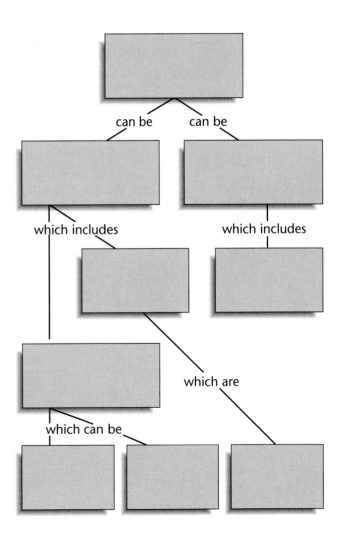

Plastic Polymers

As you got ready for school today, you may have poured the milk for your breakfast cereal from a plastic milk jug. You probably brushed your teeth using a toothbrush that has plastic bristles and a plastic handle. As you left your home, you may have grabbed your plastic-coated binder on your way out the door. Think of all the objects around you that are made of plastic. The chemicals that compose plastics typically share one common property. They can hook together to form long molecules called polymers. Polymers, including plastics, require a lot of energy to produce, and after they are formed, they can be difficult to break down. Because of these energy and disposal problems, people are now finding ways to reuse plastics by saving and recycling them.

Recycling: As Easy as 1, 2, 3

Many industries have begun to imprint a code number on their plastic products. This number refers to a code that allows consumers to sort their plastic products based on chemical makeup. For example, if you looked on the bottom of a plastic milk container, you may likely see the number 2 in a triangle formed from three arrows, perhaps followed by the letters *HDPE*. By examining several types of containers and using the classifying codes, you will learn more about polymer chemistry and possibly help improve our environment.

Purpose

Use Section 14-2 of your textbook and other references to determine the general formula for the materials named in the plastic code table. Then, use the following directions to explore plastics and to make a sample polymer.

Procedure

1. Find examples of plastic products that are marked examples of each number.

2. Prepare a display for the class that shows each number and examples of plastic products that illustrate that number.

3. Make a list of all the objects in the classroom that are made from plastics.

4. Prepare your own polymer with common white school glue and a saturated solution of borax and water. Squeeze some of the glue into a cup containing the saturated borax solution. As the product forms, use your hands to pinch it together and form it into a ball. Dry the formed ball with a paper towel.

Using Your Research

Start a plastics awareness week in your class. Have students bring clean plastics from home and sort them into boxes pre-marked with the recycling number. At the end of a week decide what type is the most common.

Contact your local landfill to determine the availability of plastic recycling operations.

Use your polymer glue ball to illustrate some of the properties of polymers. Does the glue ball bounce? Does it stretch? What caused the glue to go from a liquid to a flexible solid? Many everyday types of polymers also have a flexible nature. Some, however are more rigid.

Plastic Coding System

 PETE (polyethylene terephthalate)

 HDPE (high density polyethylene)

 V (Vinyl)

 LDPE (low density polyethylene)

 PP (polypropylene)

 PS (polystyrene)

 Other

Go Further

The use of plastic in many of our everyday objects is a relatively new development. Ask parents or older family members or friends to describe objects that are now made of plastics but were formerly made of other materials.

Contact a local recycling center to ask about how recycled plastics are used.

Interactions of Matter

What's Happening Here?

Some chemical reactions may take years before an effect is noticed. Acids in air and water that eventually form caves from what was once solid rock can also damage buildings and statues that are exposed to them.

But other chemical reactions can be over in an instant. The chemical changes that enable you to see the images on these pages take place in fractions of a second. What do all these chemical reactions have in common? They all depend on atoms in action.

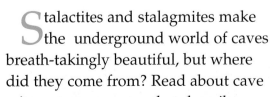

Science Journal

Stalactites and stalagmites make the underground world of caves breath-takingly beautiful, but where did they come from? Read about cave formation and write a story or poem that describes cave formation.

Previewing the Chapter

Chapter

15

Solutions

Do you know that people in the United States consume about 1.5 trillion liters of water daily from sources such as the Colorado River, shown in the photo? Almost all of this drinking water has been filtered before it reaches you. Filtering water removes some contaminants, but not all. In the following activity, find out about contaminants that can be removed by a simple filter. Then, in the chapter that follows, learn why not everything can be filtered from water.

EXPLORE ACTIVITY

Make a model filtration system.

1. Use a sharp pencil point to poke ten holes in the bottom of a foam cup.
2. Put 1 cm of fine gravel in the cup, add 3 cm of clean sand, then 1 cm of powdered charcoal, and finally, another layer of fine gravel.
3. Put a clear container under the filter, and slowly pour 100 mL of dirty water through the model filtration system.

Observe: In your Science Journal, compare the filtered water and the original water.

Previewing Science Skills

▶ In the Skill Builders, you will **compare and contrast, make and use a graph,** and **map concepts.**

▶ In the Activities, you will **measure, graph, calculate,** and **infer.**

▶ In the MiniLABS, you will **observe** and **infer.**

15•1 How Solutions Form

Objectives

- Classify solutions into three types, and identify their solutes and solvents.
- Explain the dissolving process.
- Describe the factors that affect the rates at which solids and gases dissolve in liquids.

Types of Solutions

When you hear the word *solution*, you may think of a liquid mixture, such as salt water or soda. Both of these liquids are examples of solutions. But did you know that the air you breathe is also a solution? So is the sterling silver used to make fine jewelry. Solutions, then, can be gaseous or solid as well as liquid, as the examples show in **Figure 15-1**. What makes all these mixtures solutions? You may recall from Chapter 9 that a solution is a homogeneous mixture, in which the particles of the mixing substances are evenly distributed throughout.

Figure 15-1

There are three classes of solutions: gaseous solutions, liquid solutions, and solid solutions. The type of solution is based on the state of the final mixture.

 A gaseous solution is a mixture of two or more gases. A gaseous solution is used in scuba tanks.

 Solid solutions form when a solid dissolves in a solid, such as when tin dissolves in copper to form bronze.

Solutes and Solvents

To describe a solution, you may say that one substance is dissolved in another. The substance being dissolved is the **solute.** The substance that dissolves the solute is the **solvent.** When a solid dissolves in a liquid, the solid is the solute and the liquid is the solvent. Thus, in salt water, sodium chloride is the solute, and water is the solvent. In a liquid-gas solution, the gas is the solute. In soda, carbon dioxide is the solute and water is the solvent.

Generally, the substance present in the largest amount is considered to be the solvent. Air is 78 percent nitrogen, 21 percent oxygen, and one percent argon. Thus, nitrogen is the solvent. In the alloy sterling silver, made of 92.5 percent silver and 7.5 percent copper, silver is the solvent and copper is the solute.

USING MATH

Make a circle graph that shows the composition of air.

Dissolving

Think about lemonade for a minute. A good way to make lemonade is to prepare a solution of sugar in water before you add the lemon juice and ice. By what process do a solid and a liquid, such as sugar and water, form a solution?

The Process

The dissolving of a solid in a liquid occurs at the surface of the solid. For water solutions, keep in mind two things you have learned about water. Like the particles of any liquid, water molecules are constantly moving. A water molecule is polar, which means it has a positive area and a negative area. Molecules of sugar are also polar. Study **Figure 15-2** on page 418 to see how a sugar crystal dissolves in water.

C A liquid solution results when a gas, liquid, or solid is dissolved in a liquid. A fish uses oxygen that is dissolved in water. Vinegar is a solution of two liquids—water and acetic acid. Many solids, such as salt, dissolve easily in liquids.

Figure 15-2

The dissolving of sugar in water can be thought of as a three-step process.

A The moving water molecules cluster around the sugar molecules. The negative ends of the water molecules are attracted to the positive ends of the sugar molecules.

Water molecule

Sugar molecule

B The water molecules pull the sugar molecules into solution.

C The moving water molecules spread the sugar molecules out equally throughout the solution.

USING MATH

Suppose the length of each edge of a cube is 1 cm. Find the surface area of the cube. Now imagine cutting the cube in half vertically. What is the total new surface area of the two shapes?

The process described in **Figure 15-2** repeats itself as layer after layer of sugar molecules moves away from the crystal, until all the molecules are evenly spread out. The same three steps occur when any polar or ionic compound dissolves in a polar liquid. A similar, but more difficult, process also occurs when a gas dissolves in a liquid.

You know from your study of fluids in Chapter 8 that particles of liquids and gases move much more freely than do the particles of solids. When gases dissolve in gases, or when liquids dissolve in liquids, this movement results in uniform distribution. Alloys are made by first melting the individual components and then mixing them together, which causes the particles in an alloy to be evenly spread out.

Rate of Dissolving

Think again about making a sugar solution for lemonade. When you add the sugar to the water, you stir it. Stirring a solution speeds up dissolving because it brings more fresh solvent into contact with more solute. The fresh solvent attracts the particles in the solute, causing the solid solute to move into solution faster.

A second way to speed the dissolving of a solid in a liquid is to grind large crystals into smaller ones. Suppose you had to use a 5-g crystal of rock candy, which is made of sugar, to sweeten your lemonade. If you put the crystal into a glassful of water, it might take 2 minutes to dissolve, even with stirring. However, 5 g of rock candy ground into a powder would dissolve in the same amount of water in a few seconds with stirring.

Why does powdering a crystal cause it to dissolve faster? Breaking the crystal into smaller pieces greatly increases its surface area, as you can see in **Figure 15-3.** Because dissolving takes place at the surface of the solid, increasing the surface area allows more solvent to come into contact with more solid solute. Thus, the speed of the solution process increases.

Other Methods

A third way to increase the rate at which most solids dissolve is to increase the temperature of a solvent. Think again of making a sugar solution for lemonade. You can make the sugar dissolve faster by putting it in hot water instead of cold water. Increasing the temperature of a solvent speeds up the movement of its particles. This increase causes more solvent particles to bump into the solute. As a result, solute particles break loose faster.

MiniLAB

How does solute surface area affect dissolving?

Find out what happens when you increase the surface area of sugar.

Procedure

1. Grind up two sugar cubes.
2. Place the granules and two other cubes into separate 100-mL beakers with equal amounts of water.

Analysis

1. Compare the times required to dissolve each.
2. What do you conclude about the dissolving rate and surface area?

Total surface area 864 cm²

6 cm
6 cm
6 cm
1728 cm²

Figure 15-3

As a crystal is broken down into smaller pieces, the total surface area of the crystal increases.

Total surface area 6 cm²
1 cm 1 cm
1 cm

10 368 cm²

10 368 cm²

Problem Solving

Solubility and Surface Area

If surface area is related to the rate of dissolving of a crystal, then it makes sense that granulated sugar dissolves faster than a sugar cube. But does a third form, powdered sugar, dissolve even faster? To test this, try an experiment in which you stir the same amount of each of the three types of sugar in equal volumes of water at the same temperature.

Solve the Problem:

1. **Describe what happens to the powdered sugar.**
2. **Explain the results.**
3. **How could you revise the experiment to see if surface area is indeed related to solubility?**

Think Critically:

Reading the ingredients label on the powdered sugar package reveals that there's more than just sugar in powdered sugar.

1. What variables were controlled in the experiment described above?
2. What important variable was not controlled?
3. How can you explain why all of the powdered sugar does not dissolve?

Gases and Stirring

How do you think these same factors will affect a gas-liquid solution? When you shake or stir an opened bottle of soda, it bubbles up and usually spills over or squirts out. Did you ever wonder why? Stirring or shaking a solution of a gas in a liquid causes the gas to come out of solution faster. This change occurs because as you shake or stir the solution, more gas molecules are exposed to the surface. These molecules escape more freely. Shaking and stirring also increases the temperature of the solution slightly.

Temperature and Pressure

What might you do if you wanted the gas to dissolve faster in the liquid? The answer is simple: cool the liquid solvent and increase the pressure of the gas. In a soda-bottling plant, both of these things are done. The machinery cools the solution and keeps it under pressure.

In **Figure 15-4A,** an unopened bottle of soda has no bubbles. In the sealed bottle, pressure keeps all of the gas dissolved. When the bottle is opened, the pressure of the carbon dioxide is greatly reduced. Then the carbon dioxide comes out of solution quickly. Maybe you have noticed the difference between opening a bottle of cold soda and a bottle of warm soda, **Figure 15-4B.** All gases are more soluble in cooler solvents.

Figure 15-4

A Reduced pressure inside an opened bottle of soda causes the gas to come out of solution.

B When bottles of soda are opened, more gas comes out of solution from the warm bottle than from the cold one.

Section Wrap-up

Review

1. What are the three types of solutions? Give an example of each type.

2. What are three ways to increase the rate of dissolving a solid in a liquid?

3. **Think Critically:** Amalgams, sometimes used in tooth fillings, are alloys of mercury with other metals. Is an amalgam a solution? Explain.

Skill Builder
Comparing and Contrasting
Compare and contrast the effects on the rate of dissolving (1) a solid in a liquid and (2) a gas in a liquid, when (a) the solution is cooled, (b) it is stirred, and (c) the pressure on it is lowered. If you need help, refer to Comparing and Contrasting in the **Skill Handbook.**

Science Journal

Write a paragraph in your Science Journal explaining why many fish aquariums have a device that bubbles air into the water. Explain why it is necessary to constantly bring air into the water.

ISSUE:

15•2 Regulating Organic Solvents

Science Words

organic solvent

Objectives

- Compare and contrast the effects of organic solvents.
- Determine whether government agencies should regulate all usage of known organic solvents.

Figure 15-5

Potentially hazardous organic solvents are found in many common materials.

Organic Solvents

Think about home and you probably think about a place that is safe. However, scientists warn that the buildings in which people live may be hazardous to their health because of the number of potentially harmful chemicals found in materials used in construction and remodeling.

Many health problems could be caused by organic solvents present in almost all materials used in building or remodeling. **Organic solvents,** such as those shown in **Figure 15-5,** are found in glues, paints, paint remover, paint and varnish thinners, and in some caulking compounds and carpeting. Organic solvents often give a new house that new smell.

But there are some drawbacks. Organic solvents vaporize easily. They enter the body by being absorbed through the skin or when fumes are inhaled. Many organic solvents are substances that are known to affect the nervous system and to cause growth and development problems. In some instances, a few have been shown to cause cancer.

Those most at risk are professional painters and do-it-yourselfers who work with these substances over long periods of time. What is being done to protect people from these hazardous substances?

Existing Regulations

The United States Occupational Safety and Health Administration (OSHA) has established time limits beyond which a worker cannot be exposed to health-threatening solvents. Another government agency, the Consumer Products Safety Commission (CPSC), requires labels on all corrosive or flammable chemicals. Some labels list harmful ingredients and itemize the dangers to health.

2 Points of View

Regulating Products and Professionals

The OSHA regulations have been established to protect employees of large building contractors. Fines may be incurred if workers are found to be exposed to solvents for extended periods of time. The cost of labeling alone has caused some manufacturers to switch to other materials that may not be as effective. Also, large professional contractors ask who will regulate the do-it-yourselfer. Some professionals feel that these people should have to obtain permits from the local building code inspector before using dangerous solvents.

Regulating the Home Remodeler

Home remodelers or do-it-yourselfers balk at the idea that they should obtain permits to use certain products with organic solvents. They claim that their projects are much smaller and that they probably control ventilation better for their own home projects than professional builders working on large new buildings, **Figure 15-6.**

Figure 15-6

Good ventilation is required when working with materials that contain organic solvents.

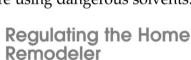

Section Wrap-up

Review

1. In what types of products are organic solvents found?

2. What problems occur when organic solvent vapors are inhaled or absorbed by the body?

Explore the Issue

Should OSHA require local building inspectors to regulate small home-remodeling projects, thereby bringing all people under regulation? If yes, how would OSHA enforce these regulations? If no, then how can the public be informed effectively about the potential danger of these chemicals?

SCIENCE & SOCIETY

Science Words

solubility
saturated solution
unsaturated solution
supersaturated solution

Objectives

- Discuss how solubility varies among different solutes and for the same solute at different temperatures.
- Demonstrate an understanding of solution concentrations.
- Compare and contrast a saturated, an unsaturated, and a super-saturated solution.

Solubility

Sugar, as you know, dissolves easily in water. Suppose you want to make super-sweet lemonade. You stir two, three, four—or more—teaspoons of sugar into a cup of water, and it all dissolves. But eventually, as shown in **Figure 15-7,** you add one more teaspoon of sugar and it no longer dissolves.

Change the scene from your kitchen to a laboratory. Suppose now you measure out 1.3 g of lithium carbonate and add it to 100 g of water at 20°C. You observe that all of the lithium carbonate dissolves. But if you add more lithium carbonate to the same solution, none of it dissolves. However, you could add 34 g of potassium chloride to 100 g of water before no more will dissolve. You would have shown that the amount of these two substances that dissolves in 100 g of water at 20°C varies greatly.

Generally, the **solubility** of a substance is expressed as the maximum number of grams of the substance that will dissolve in 100 g of solvent at a certain temperature. **Table 15-1** shows how the solubility of several substances varies at 20°C. For solutes that are gases, the pressure must also be given, for a reason you will learn soon.

Figure 15-7

The amount of sugar that can dissolve in a glass of water is limited.

Concentration

Suppose you added one spoonful of lemon juice to a glass of water to make lemonade. Your friend decided to add four spoonfuls of lemon juice to another glass of water. You could say that your glass of lemonade is dilute. Your friend's glass of lemonade is concentrated. It would have more lemon flavor than yours. A concentrated solution is one in which there is a large amount of solute in the solvent. A dilute solution is one in which there is a small amount of solute in the solvent.

Table 15-1

Solubility of Substances in Water at 20°C	
Substance	**Solubility in g/100 g of Water**
Solid Substances	
Barium sulfate	0.00025
Lithium carbonate	1.3
Potassium chloride	34.0
Sodium nitrate	87.6
Lithium bromide	166.0
Sucrose (sugar)	203.9
Gaseous Substances*	
Hydrogen	0.00017
Oxygen	0.005
Carbon dioxide	0.16
*when pressure = 1 atmosphere	

CONNECT TO

EARTH SCIENCE

Bronze is stronger and more durable than copper or tin. Bronze is an alloy that can be 90 percent copper and 10 percent tin. *Determine* which metal is the solvent. *Conclude* which metal is the solute.

Precise Concentrations

Concentrated and *dilute* are not precise terms. However, solution concentrations can be described precisely. One way is to state the percentage by volume of the solute. Do you ever have a fruit juice drink with your lunch or for a snack? The next time you do, read the label to see how much actual juice you are getting. The percentage by volume of the juice in the drink shown in **Figure 15-8** is 100 percent. Commonly, fruit-flavored drinks contain ten percent juice and about 90 percent water. Adding 10 mL of juice to 90 mL of water makes 100 mL of drink. Generally, if two or more liquids are being mixed, the concentration is given in percentage by volume, stated in number of milliliters of solute plus enough solvent to make 100 mL of solution.

You can express concentration of a solid dissolved in a liquid as percentage by mass. This percentage is the mass in grams of solute plus enough solvent to make 100 g of solution. Because 1 mL of water has a mass of 1 g, you would mix 10 g of sodium chloride with 90 mL of water to make a ten percent solution of sodium chloride.

Figure 15-8

The concentrations of fruit juices are often given in percent by volume.

425

You can also express concentration as mass of solute in a liter of solution. When a certain volume of solution is measured out, the number of grams of solute it contains can be calculated easily.

USING MATH

Calculating the Mass of Solute Per Liter of Solution

Example Problem:

A potassium chloride solution contains 88 g of KCl in 1.0 L of solution. How many grams of solute are in 50 mL of solution?

Problem-Solving Steps:

1. Change 1.0 L to mL.
   1.0 L = 1000 mL
2. Determine the number of grams of solute in 1 mL of solution.
   88 g/1000 mL = 0.088 g/mL
3. Use the equation: Mass of solute = concentration of 1 mL solution × volume of solution.
4. **Solution:** Mass = 0.088 g/mL × 50 mL = 4.4 g

 Calculator Hint: Steps 2 and 3 can be combined into one calculator operation.
Enter: **88 ÷ 1000 × 50 =** and your calculator will read **4.4.**

Practice Problem

Forty grams of lye (NaOH) were dissolved in enough water to make 1.0 L of solution. How many grams of lye would be in 20 mL of the solution?
Strategy Hint: Divide 40.0 g by 1000 to find the mass of solute in 1 mL of solution.

Limits of Solubility

How much solute can dissolve in a given amount of solvent? That depends on a number of factors. Examine the types of solutions based on the amount of solute dissolved.

Saturated Solutions

If you add 30.0 g of potassium chloride, KCl, to 100 g of water at 0°C, only 28 g will dissolve. You have a saturated solution because no more KCl can dissolve. A **saturated solution** is a solution that has dissolved all the solute it normally can hold at a given temperature. But if you heat the mixture to a higher temperature, more KCl can dissolve. As the temperature of the liquid solvent increases, the amount of solute that can dissolve in it usually increases. **Table 15-2** gives the amounts of a few

Table 15-2

Solubility of Compounds in Water at Various Temperatures

Solubility in g/100 g of Water at the Temperature Indicated

Compound	Formula	0°C	20°C	60°C	100°C
Ammonium chloride	NH_4Cl	29.4	37.2	55.3	77.3
Barium hydroxide	$Ba(OH)_2$	1.67	3.89	20.94	101.4
Copper(II) sulfate	$CuSO_4$	23.1	32.0	61.8	114
Lead(II) chloride	$PbCl_2$	0.67	1.00	1.94	3.20
Potassium bromide	KBr	53.6	65.3	85.5	104
Potassium chloride	KCl	28.0	34.0	45.8	56.3
Potassium nitrate	KNO_3	13.9	31.6	109	245
Sodium acetate	$NaC_2H_3O_2$	36.2	46.4	139	170.15
Sodium chlorate	$NaClO_3$	79.6	95.9	137	204
Sodium chloride	NaCl	35.7	35.9	37.1	39.2
Sodium nitrate	$NaNO_3$	73.0	87.6	122	180
Sucrose (sugar)	$C_{12}H_{22}O_{11}$	179.2	203.9	287.3	487.2

solutes that can dissolve in water at different temperatures, forming saturated solutions.

Another way to picture the effect of higher temperatures on solubility is with a line graph, as shown in **Figure 15-9.** Each line is called a solubility curve for a particular substance. You can use a curve to figure out the amount of solute that will dissolve at any temperature given on the graph. For example, at 47°C, about 82 g of both KBr and KNO_3 form saturated solutions with 100 g of water. How much NaCl will form a saturated solution with 100 g of water at the same temperature?

Unsaturated Solutions

An **unsaturated solution** is any solution that can dissolve more solute at a given temperature. Each time a saturated solution is heated to a higher temperature, it may become unsaturated. The term *unsaturated* isn't precise. If you look at **Table 15-2,** you'll see that at 20°C, 37.2 g of NH_4Cl dissolved in 100 g of water is a saturated solution. However, an unsaturated solution of NH_4Cl could be any amount less than 37.2 g in 100 g of water at 20°C.

Figure 15-9

The solubility of a substance changes with water temperature. *For which substance does solubility increase the least?*

IV Solution

▼ ▲

"**S**tart an IV with 0.9 percent normal saline." You've no doubt heard a doctor use this phrase or something similar on a medical television show. What exactly is an IV, and why is it important? An IV is an apparatus used to administer medication or fluids directly into the blood through a vein. An IV is used in a sick or injured person to restore the fluid and electrolyte balance to the body. In a healthy person, blood is in equilibrium; there are enough of the various types of blood cells and plasma in the solution in which cells are transported. Plasma is a solution made mostly of water. It also contains proteins, food substances, enzymes, oxygen, carbon dioxide, and electrolytes.

Out of Balance

When a person is sick or has been injured, the blood may be out of equilibrium. By using an IV, needed fluids, electrolytes, and sugars flow directly into the person's blood, and balance can be restored quickly. If the person has lost a lot of blood, an IV can replace lost blood volume quickly using a saline solution that is similar to plasma.

Think Critically:

Why is it important to replace lost blood and fluids quickly in a sick or injured person?

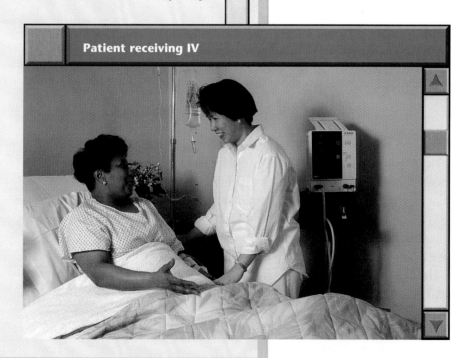

Patient receiving IV

Supersaturated Solutions

If you make a saturated solution of potassium nitrate at 100°C and then let it cool to 20°C, part of the solute comes out of solution. At the lower temperature, a saturated solution is formed with less solute. Most other saturated solutions behave in a similar way when cooled. But if you cool a saturated solution of sodium acetate from 100°C to 20°C, with proper precautions, no solute comes out. This solution is supersaturated. A **supersaturated solution** contains more solute than a saturated one has at that temperature. This kind of solution is unstable. When a small crystal of the solute is added to a supersaturated solution, the excess solute quickly crystallizes out, as is shown in **Figure 15-10**.

How can you determine whether a solution is saturated, unsaturated, or supersaturated? Suppose you add a solute crystal

Figure 15-10
A solution of sodium acetate (left) crystallizes out when a crystal of sodium acetate is added (right).

to a solution. If the crystal dissolves, the solution is unsaturated. If the crystal does not dissolve, the solution is saturated. And if excess solute comes out, the solution is supersaturated.

Section Wrap-up

Review

1. Do all solutes dissolve to the same extent in the same solvent? How do you know?

2. Using **Table 15-2** on page 427, state the following: the mass of $NaNO_3$ that would have to be dissolved in 100 g of water to form a saturated, an unsaturated, and a supersaturated solution of $NaNO_3$ at 20°C.

3. **Think Critically:** By volume, orange drink is ten percent orange juice and ten percent corn syrup. A 1500-mL can of the drink costs $0.95. A 1500-mL can of orange juice is $1.49, and 1500 mL of corn syrup is $1.69. How could you make orange drink? Is it cheaper to make or to buy?

Skill Builder
Making and Using Graphs
Using **Table 15-2** on page 427, make a graph showing the solubility curves for $CuSO_4$ and $NaNO_3$. How would you make a saturated water solution of each substance at 80°C? If you need help, refer to Making and Using Graphs in the **Skill Handbook**.

Using Computers

Spreadsheet You work in the lab stockroom, making solutions for teachers to use in their classes. Use **Table 15-2** on page 427 to prepare a spreadsheet showing the number of grams of solute needed to make 10 mL, 50 mL, 100 mL, 500 mL, and 1000 mL of a saturated solution at 20°C of the following compounds: ammonium chloride, lead(II) chloride, sodium chlorate, and sucrose.

Design Your Own Experiment
Saturation Situation

Two major factors to consider when you are dissolving a solute in water are temperature and the ratio of solute to solvent. What happens to a solution as the temperature changes? Can you learn to predict when a solution will become saturated at a particular temperature?

PREPARATION

Problem
How does solubility change with a change in temperature or amount of solvent?

Form a Hypothesis
Based on observations you previously made, state a hypothesis about how the dissolving rate of table sugar is affected by temperature.

Objectives
- Observe the effects of temperature on the rate at which a solute dissolves.
- Design an experiment that tests the effects of a variable, such as change in temperature or amount of solvent, on the rate at which a solute dissolves.

Possible Materials
- ice
- distilled water

- large test tubes
- thermometer inserted in a two-hole rubber stopper
- table sugar
- copper wire stirrer
- test-tube holder
- 10-mL graduated cylinder
- apron
- safety goggles
- electric hot plate
- oven mitt
- test-tube rack

Safety Precautions

Protect clothing and eyes, and be careful if using a hot plate and heated solutions.

PLAN THE EXPERIMENT

1. As a group, agree upon and write out the hypothesis statement.
2. As a group, list the steps you need to take to test your hypothesis. Be specific; describe exactly what you will do at each step.
3. Make a list of the materials that you will need to complete your experiment.
4. If you need a data table, design one in your Science Journal so that it is ready to use as your group collects data.

Check the Plan

1. Read over your entire experiment to make sure that all steps are in logical order.
2. Identify any constants and the variables of the experiment.

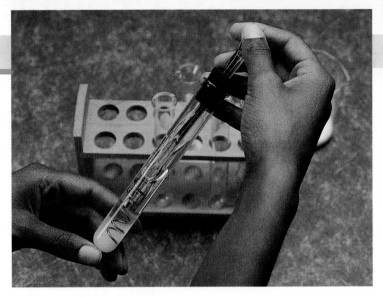

3. Have you allowed for a control? How will the control be treated?
4. Do you have to run any tests more than one time?
5. Will the data be summarized in a graph?
6. *Make sure your teacher approves your plan and that you have included any changes suggested in the plan.*

DO THE EXPERIMENT

1. Carry out the approved experiment as planned.
2. While the experiment is going on, write down any observations that you make, and complete the data table in your Science Journal.

Analyze and Apply

1. **Compare** your results with those of other groups.
2. How did the saturation change as the temperature was changed?

3. **Graph** your results using a line graph. Place grams of solute per 100 g of water on the *y*-axis and temperature on the *x*-axis.
4. Using your graph, **estimate** the solubility of sugar at 100°C, the boiling point of water.

Go Further

Compare the effects of temperature on dissolving cane sugar versus beet sugar.

15•4 Particles in Solution

Science Words

dissociation
ionization
electrolyte
nonelectrolyte

Objectives

- Compare and contrast the behavior of polar and nonpolar substances in forming solutions.
- Relate the processes of dissociation and ionization to solutions that conduct electricity.
- Explain how the addition of solutes to solvents affects the freezing and boiling points of solutions.

The Nature of Solvents and Solutes

Why do you have to shake an oil-and-vinegar salad dressing, such as shown in **Figure 15-11,** immediately before you use it? Oil and vinegar do not form a solution. Oil does not dissolve in vinegar, which is approximately 95 percent water.

What dissolves what?

Why does a substance dissolve in one solvent but not in another? Solvents with nonpolar molecules dissolve solutes with nonpolar molecules. A solvent such as hexane dissolves grease because both the solvent and the solute have nonpolar molecules. Similarly, polar solvents dissolve polar solutes. Water is a polar solvent, and it dissolves sucrose, a polar solute. Polar solvents also dissolve ionic solutes, such as sodium chloride. A polar solvent won't normally dissolve a nonpolar solute. That's why oil, which is nonpolar, won't dissolve in vinegar, which is polar. In general, when predicting which solutes will dissolve in which solvents, remember the phrase, "like dissolves like."

Some substances form solutions with both polar and nonpolar solutes because their molecules have a polar and a nonpolar end. Ethanol, shown in **Figure 15-12,** is such a molecule. The polar end dissolves polar substances, and the nonpolar end dissolves nonpolar substances. Thus, ethanol dissolves iodine, which is nonpolar, and water, which is polar. How important are polar and nonpolar solvents and solutes in nature?

Figure 15-12

Ethanol, C$_2$H$_5$OH, has a polar –OH group at one end and a nonpolar –CH$_3$ group at the other end.

Figure 15-11

Vinegar and oil don't form a solution.

Sodium ion

Chloride ion

Water molecule

Figure 15-13

When sodium chloride dissolves in water, H_2O molecules surround, pull apart, and separate the Na^+ and Cl^- ions.

Particles in Solution

Ions in solution determine the fate of a coral reef, but they also may affect other situations. Why should you never use a hair dryer when standing on a wet floor? You take such precautions because you are an excellent conductor of electricity. Your body is about 70 percent water, with many ionic compounds dissolved in it. Water solutions of ionic compounds and of some polar compounds conduct electricity.

Breaking Up

As an ionic solid dissolves in water, the positive and negative ions separate from one another. This separation process is called **dissociation.** For example, sodium chloride dissociates when it dissolves in water, as shown in **Figure 15-13.** When certain polar substances dissolve in water, the water pulls their molecules apart. This process is called **ionization.** Hydrogen chloride ionizes in water, as shown in **Figure 15-14** below. A substance that separates into ions or forms ions in a water solution is called an **electrolyte.** Thus, both NaCl and HCl are examples of electrolytes.

Pure water is a **nonelectrolyte,** which means it does not conduct electricity. If a water solution is a conductor, the solute must be an electrolyte.

HCl $+$ H_2O $\longrightarrow$ H_3O^+ $+$ Cl^-

Figure 15-14

When hydrogen chloride dissolves in water, H_2O molecules surround and pull apart HCl molecules.

Effects of Solute Particles

Antifreeze that you may add to water in a car radiator makes freezing more difficult. Adding a solute to a solvent lowers the freezing point of the solvent. How much the freezing point goes down depends upon how many solute particles you add.

How does antifreeze work? As a substance freezes, its particles organize themselves into an orderly pattern. The solute particles interfere with the formation of this orderly pattern. This prevents the solvent from freezing at its normal freezing point. To overcome this interference, a lower temperature is required to freeze the solvent. The same principle applies to certain animals that live in extremely cold climates. Caribou, for example, contain substances in the lower section of their legs that prevent their freezing in subzero temperatures. The caribou can stand for long periods of time in snow and ice with no harm to their legs.

You may also know that antifreeze raises the boiling point of the water in a car radiator. What causes this effect? The amount that the boiling point is raised depends upon the number of solute molecules present. Solute particles interfere with the evaporation of solvent particles. Thus, more energy is needed to allow the solvent particles to evaporate, and the solution boils at a higher temperature.

INTEGRATION
Life Science

Section Wrap-up

Review

1. Explain why (a) water dissolves sugar, (b) water does not dissolve oil, and (c) benzene does dissolve oil.

2. What kinds of solute particles are present in water solutions of (a) electrolytes and (b) nonelectrolytes?

3. **Think Critically:** In cold weather, people often put salt on ice that forms on sidewalks and driveways. The salt helps melt the ice, forming a saltwater solution. Explain why this solution may not refreeze.

Skill Builder
Concept Mapping

Draw a concept map to show the relationship among the following terms: *electrolytes, nonelectrolytes, dissociation, ionization, ionic compounds, certain polar compounds, other polar compounds.* If you need help, refer to Concept Mapping in the **Skill Handbook.**

Science Journal

Many insect eggs can survive extremely cold temperatures. What can you conclude about the fluids in these eggs? Summarize your conclusions in your Science Journal.

Science & Literature

Native American Ocean Lore

In this chapter, you've seen that various types of solutions play important and useful roles in the everyday lives of people. However, no solution is more important to living things on Earth than the ocean. The ocean is the world's largest solution, made up of dissolved sodium chloride and many other salts. Three-fourths of Earth's surface is water, and about 97 percent of this total is ocean water. Thus, it's not surprising that the oceans are home to millions of different living things, and that countless other species depend on oceans indirectly.

Historically, oceans have also occupied a special place in human life. For many indigenous peoples who live by or near shore, the importance of oceans is often deeply woven into the fabric of the culture. Consider this folktale entitled "Octopus and Raven" from the Nootka people, a Native American culture from the Pacific Northwest. This story, about a raven who asks a silly question of an octopus looking for food, demonstrates the Nootka culture's knowledge about oceans and ocean life. In this excerpt, Raven is having an argument with Octopus as the tide is coming in.

Science Journal

At your local library, find a children's story, myth, or folktale to read. In your Science Journal, write a summary of the story. Are there any images or characters in the story that might give you clues about the type of environment or animal life in the native country?

. . . The water was now over their waists. Raven saw that it would soon be even deeper. "Octopus, can you please let me go?" But Octopus did not let go. "Raven," she said, "I was digging clams!"

Again Raven begged, but the water continued to get deeper and Octopus held tight. The water came up to their necks and then it was over their heads.

Up on the beach, above the tide line, the old people watched.

"Octopus can hold her breath longer than Raven," one person said.

They watched and finally, after a very long time, Raven could hold his breath no longer and he drowned. Octopus let go and Raven floated up to the surface.

As you can see from this excerpt, the Nootka people show knowledge of ocean tides, as well as about some organisms that live there. The appearance of ocean creatures and information about tides in a children's story illustrates just how important the ocean is in Nootka culture.

Activity 15-2

Boiling Points of Solutions

Adding small amounts of salt to water being boiled to cook pasta and adding antifreeze to a car's radiator have a common result. In each case, the boiling point of the water is now higher than that of pure water.

Problem

How much can the boiling point of a solution be changed?

Materials

- 400 mL distilled water
- thermometer
- ring stand
- 72 g table salt, NaCl
- hot plate
- 250-mL beaker

Procedure

1. Copy the data table and use it to record your observations.
2. Bring 100 mL of distilled water in a 250-mL beaker to a gentle boil. Record the temperature.
3. Dissolve 12 g of NaCl in 100 mL of distilled water. Bring this solution to a gentle boil and record its boiling point. **CAUTION:** *Always keep the thermometer away from the flame.*

4. Repeat step 3, using 24 g of NaCl.
5. Repeat step 3 again, using 36 g of NaCl.
6. Plot your results on a graph that shows boiling point on the *y*-axis and grams of NaCl on the *x*-axis.

Analyze

1. What difference is there between the boiling point of a pure solvent and that of a solution?
2. Instead of doubling the amount of NaCl in step 4, what would have been the effect of doubling the amount of water?
3. What would be the result of using tap water instead of distilled water?

Conclude and Apply

4. In cooking, why would adding salt to water cause some foods to cook faster?
5. If you continued to add more salt, would you **predict** that your graph would continue in the same pattern or level off? Explain your prediction.

Data and Observations

Grams of NaCl Solute	Boiling Point(°C)
0	
12	
24	
36	

Summary

15-1: How Solutions Form
1. Solutions are classified into three types according to their final state: gaseous, liquid, and solid.
2. Dissolving occurs when constantly moving solvent molecules attract particles of solute and surround them with solvent.
3. Stirring, surface area, temperature, and pressure affect the rate of dissolving.

15-2: Science and Society: Regulating Organic Solvents
1. Many materials used for building or furnishing homes contain potentially harmful chemicals.
2. OSHA and the CPSC protect people by controlling use of these materials.

15-3: Solubility and Concentration
1. Solubility of substances varies among different solutes and for the same solute at different temperatures.
2. Two precise ways to express solution concentrations are (1) percentage by volume and (2) percentage by mass.
3. A solution may be saturated, unsaturated, or supersaturated.

15-4: Particles in Solution
1. Usually, among polar and nonpolar solvents and solutes, like dissolves like.
2. Ionic compounds dissociate when dissolved in water, and some polar compounds ionize when dissolved in water.
3. Adding a solute to a solvent lowers its freezing point and raises its boiling point.

Key Science Words

a. dissociation
b. electrolyte
c. ionization
d. nonelectrolyte
e. organic solvent
f. saturated solution
g. solubility
h. solute
i. solvent
j. supersaturated solution
k. unsaturated solution

Reviewing Vocabulary

Match each phrase with the correct term from the list of Key Science Words.

1. a solution that can dissolve more solute at a given temperature
2. the substance being dissolved
3. has more solute than a saturated solution has at that temperature
4. exists as ions in a water solution
5. molecules are pulled apart into ions in solution
6. separation of negative and positive ions
7. the most solute, in grams, that will dissolve in 100 g of solvent at a certain temperature
8. a solution that has dissolved all the solute it can hold at a given temperature
9. the substance that dissolves a solute
10. liquid often found in building materials

Checking Concepts

Choose the word or phrase that completes the sentence or answers the question.

1. Which of the following is not a solution?
   a. a glass of soda
   b. air in a SCUBA tank
   c. bronze (an alloy)
   d. muddy water

2. Solutions may not be _____.
   a. colloidal
   b. gaseous
   c. liquid
   d. solid

3. When iodine is dissolved in alcohol, the alcohol is the _____.
   a. alloy
   b. solvent
   c. solution
   d. solute

4. If a bronze alloy is 85 percent copper and 15 percent tin, tin is the _____.
   a. alloy
   b. solvent
   c. solution
   d. solute

5. Forty-nine mL of water at room temperature have a mass of _____.
   a. 49 g
   b. 51 g
   c. 100 g
   d. 4900 g

6. A polar solvent will dissolve _____.
   a. any solute
   b. a polar solute
   c. a nonpolar solute
   d. no solute

7. If a water solution conducts electricity, the solute must be a(n) _____.
   a. gas
   b. electrolyte
   c. liquid
   d. nonelectrolyte

8. In a water solution, an ionic compound undergoes _____.
   a. dissociation
   b. electrolysis
   c. ionization
   d. no change

9. A gas becomes more soluble in a liquid when you increase _____.
   a. particle size
   b. pressure
   c. stirring
   d. temperature

10. Solute may come out of a solution that is _____.
    a. unsaturated
    b. saturated
    c. supersaturated
    d. miscible

Understanding Concepts

Answer the following questions in your Science Journal using complete sentences.

11. How do the health effects of an organic solvent differ from another solvent such as water?

12. Explain what happens when copper(II) sulfate, $CuSO_4$, an ionic compound, dissolves in water.

13. Why are *concentrated* and *dilute* not exact terms?

14. Explain how you would make a 25 percent solution of apple juice.

15. Why is the statement "Water is the solvent in a solution" not always true?

Thinking Critically

16. Explain why tetrachloroethene, a dry-cleaning fluid, will dissolve grease and water will not.

17. Explain why salt will melt ice on a sidewalk.

18. Why might potatoes cook more quickly in salt water than in unsalted water?

19. Explain why an unrefrigerated glass of soda will go flat more quickly in hot weather.

20. Why might a tropical lake have more minerals dissolved in it than a lake in Minnesota?

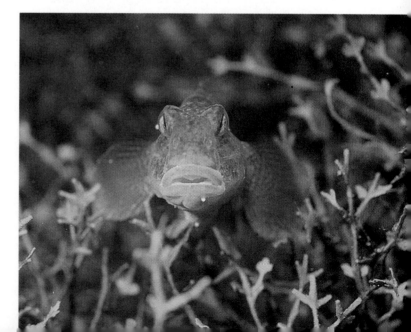

Developing Skills

If you need help, refer to the **Skill Handbook.**

21. **Comparing and Contrasting:** Compare and contrast the processes of ionization and dissociation.

22. **Hypothesizing:** You are stocking a pond in a tropical climate and a pond in a temperate climate with fish. Both ponds contain about the same amount of water. Based on the amount of oxygen dissolved in the water, to which pond would you be able to add more fish? Explain why.

23. **Interpreting Data:** The label on a bottle of rubbing alcohol might read "70 percent isopropanol by volume." Assuming the rest of the solution is water, what does this label tell you about the contents and preparation of the solution in the bottle?

24. **Measuring in SI:** 153 g of potassium nitrate have been dissolved in enough water to make 1.00 L of solution. You use a graduated cylinder to measure 80.0 mL of solution. What mass of potassium nitrate is in the 80.0-mL sample?

25. **Making and Using Tables:** Using the data in **Table 15-2** on page 427, fill in the following table. Use the terms *saturated, unsaturated,* and *supersaturated* to describe the type of solution.

Performance Assessment

1. **Poster:** Visit a SCUBA shop. Find out about the composition of the gas used in diving tanks. In terms of solution, report your findings on a poster.

2. **Making and Using a Classification System:** Based upon information about composition of solutions in **Figure 15-1,** classify 20 different solutions in a grocery store. Explain your classification system to the class.

3. **Display:** Research crystal growing using saturated and supersaturated solutions. Grow several crystals and display them. Accompany the display with a report explaining what you did and your results.

Limits of Solubility

Compound	Type of Solution	g Dissolved in 100 g Water at 20°C
$Ba(OH)_2$	_____	2.96
$CuSO_4$	_____	32.0
KCl	_____	45.8
KNO_3	_____	31.6
$NaClO_3$	_____	79.6

Previewing the Chapter

Chemical Reactions

You know that metals can be made into a variety of shapes. The Statue of Liberty, given to the United States by France, is made primarily of copper. However, the green color of the statue is different from the color of a typical copper penny in your pocket. What causes copper items to lose their shiny surfaces and turn green?

EXPLORE ACTIVITY

Find out why copper surfaces often turn green.

1. Sprinkle some table salt on the tops of two dark pennies.
2. Carefully place five or six drops of vinegar on each of the pennies.
3. After 20 minutes, rinse the pennies with water.
4. Wrap one of the pennies tightly in plastic wrap.
5. Place the other penny in water in a saucer so that the penny is not completely covered.
6. Let both pennies remain undisturbed for one day.

Observe: Record your observations in your Science Journal. From your observations, what can you suggest as the cause of the color changes in the pennies?

Previewing Science Skills

► In the Skill Builders, you will recognize **cause and effect, observe and infer, hypothesize,** and **map concepts.**

► In the Activities, you will **observe, infer,** and **classify.**

► In the MiniLABs, you will **observe and infer.**

16•1 Chemical Changes in Matter

Science Words

chemical reaction
reactant
product
coefficient

Objectives

- Identify reactants and products in a chemical reaction.
- Explain how a chemical reaction satisfies the law of conservation of mass.
- Interpret chemical equations.

CONNECT TO

EARTH SCIENCE

Some darkening of the Statue of Liberty occurs over time. **Infer** what environmental factor may cause this problem to increase.

Describing Chemical Reactions

In Chapter 9, you learned about chemical changes. These changes are taking place all around you and even inside your body. One of the most important chemical changes on Earth is photosynthesis. During photosynthesis, plants use sunlight, carbon dioxide, and water to make sugar and oxygen. Another important chemical change takes place in cells in your body during respiration. This change combines sugar and oxygen to produce energy, carbon dioxide, and water.

A **chemical reaction** is a well-defined example of a chemical change. In a chemical reaction, one or more substances are changed to new substances. The substances that are about to react are called **reactants.** The new substances produced are called **products.** This relationship can be written as follows.

produce
reactants → products

What are the reactants and products in the photosynthesis reaction described in the first paragraph?

Conservation of Mass

In the early 1700s, scientists wondered what happened to the masses of reactants and products in chemical reactions. The French chemist Antoine Lavoisier, shown in **Figure 16-1,** performed many experiments to find out. In one experiment, Lavoisier placed a carefully measured amount of solid mercury(II) oxide into a sealed flask. When he heated this flask, oxygen gas and liquid mercury were produced.

Figure 16-1

Antoine Lavoisier used precise balances to perform experiments that led to the law of conservation of mass.

Lavoisier found that the total mass of the oxygen gas and the mercury produced was equal to the mass of the mercury(II) oxide that he started with.

mercury(II) oxide produces oxygen plus mercury
10.0 g = 0.7 g + 9.3 g

This and other experiments allowed Lavoisier to state the law of conservation of mass: in a chemical reaction, matter is not created or destroyed but is conserved. In Chapter 9, you learned how this law applies to chemical changes. For a chemical reaction in which all of the reactants change to products, this law means that the starting mass of the reactants equals the final mass of the products. The law of conservation of mass must be satisfied when describing a chemical reaction.

Writing Equations

If you wanted to write a description of the chemical reaction shown in **Figure 16-2,** it might look like this.

solid lead(II) nitrate, dissolved in water, plus
solid potassium iodide, dissolved in water, produces
solid lead(II) iodide plus potassium nitrate,
dissolved in water

This series of words is rather long and cumbersome. However, all of the information in this expression is important. The same is true of descriptions of most chemical reactions—many words are needed to state all the important information. As a result, scientists have developed a shorthand method to describe chemical reactions. A chemical equation is an expression that describes a chemical reaction using chemical formulas and other symbols. In Chapter 11, you learned

MiniLAB

Does mass change in a reaction?

Procedure
1. Add NaOH solution to a dropper bottle until the bottle is approximately half full. Fill the dropper with a solution of $FeCl_3$. Stop up the dropper with a soap plug. Screw the dropper onto the bottle. Find and record the mass of the bottle, dropper, and their contents.
2. Gently squeeze the dropper so that the soap plug is forced out of the dropper.
3. Again, determine the mass of the bottle, dropper, and products.

Analysis
1. What changes did you observe to indicate that a chemical reaction has taken place?
2. How did the mass before the reaction compare to the mass after the reaction?
3. What scientific law does this experiment demonstrate?

Figure 16-2

When solutions of lead(II) nitrate and potassium iodide are mixed, a bright yellow solid forms. The yellow solid, lead(II) iodide, settles to the bottom of the beaker. The liquid in the beaker is a potassium nitrate solution.

Problem Solving

Metals and the Atmosphere

When metals are exposed to air, they often corrode. Rusting is one type of corrosion. Rust is hydrated iron(III) oxide.

Aluminum also reacts with oxygen in the air to form aluminum oxide. Unlike rust, which crumbles and exposes more iron to the air, aluminum oxide adheres to the aluminum surface on which it forms, protecting the aluminum underneath.

Copper is another metal that corrodes when exposed to air. When copper corrodes, a green coating called basic copper carbonate is formed. You may have seen this type of corrosion on the Statue of Liberty.

Think Critically:

Identify the reactants and products in the corrosion of iron. When the Statue of Liberty was restored, the green coating was not removed. Why?

how to use chemical symbols and formulas. Some of the other symbols used in chemical equations are listed in **Table 16-1**.

What would the chemical equation for the reaction in **Figure 16-2** look like?

$$Pb(NO_3)_2(aq) + 2KI(aq) \rightarrow$$
$$PbI_2(cr) + 2KNO_3(aq)$$

The symbols to the right of the formulas are (*cr*), for *crystalline solid*, and (*aq*) for *aqueous*, which means "dissolved in water."

Coefficients— Unit Managers

What do the numbers to the left of the formulas for reactants and products mean? Remember that the law of conservation of

Table 16-1

Symbols Used in Chemical Equations	
Symbol	**Meaning**
$\longrightarrow$	produces or forms
+	plus
(*cr*)	crystalline solid
(*l*)	liquid
(*g*)	gas
(*aq*)	aqueous, a solid is dissolved in water
heat $\longrightarrow$	the reactants are heated
light $\longrightarrow$	the reactants are exposed to light
elec. $\longrightarrow$	an electric current is applied to the reactants

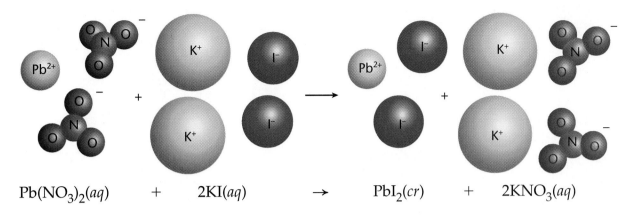

$$Pb(NO_3)_2(aq) \quad + \quad 2KI(aq) \quad \rightarrow \quad PbI_2(cr) \quad + \quad 2KNO_3(aq)$$

mass states that matter is neither created nor destroyed during chemical reactions. Atoms are rearranged but never lost or destroyed. These numbers, called **coefficients,** represent the number of units of each substance taking part in a reaction. For example, in the above reaction, one unit of $Pb(NO_3)_2$ reacts with two units of KI to produce one unit of PbI_2 and two units of KNO_3. **Figure 16-3** will help you visualize this reaction.

You don't always have to analyze the reaction mixture to find out what the coefficients in a chemical reaction are. In the next section, you will find out how to choose coefficients for a chemical equation.

Figure 16-3

Each coefficient in the equation represents the number of units of each type in this reaction.

Section Wrap-up

Review

1. Identify the reactants and the products in the following chemical equation.

$$2B(cr) + 3I_2(g) \rightarrow 2BI_3(cr)$$

2. What is the name and state of matter of each substance in the following reaction?

$$4Al(cr) + 3O_2(g) \rightarrow 2Al_2O_3(cr)$$

3. **Think Critically:** Identify the reactants and the products in the body cell reaction described on page 442.

Skill Builder

Recognizing Cause and Effect
Lavoisier heated mercury(II) oxide in a sealed flask. Explain the effect on Lavoisier's conclusions about the law of conservation of mass if he had used an open flask. If you need help, refer to Recognizing Cause and Effect in the **Skill Handbook.**

USING MATH

When making soap, if 890 g of fat react totally with 120 g of sodium hydroxide, 92 g of glycerin and some soap are formed. Calculate the mass of soap formed to satisfy the law of conservation of mass.

ISSUE:

16•2 Chemical Reactions —Up in the Air

Science Words

chlorofluorocarbon (CFC)

Objectives

- Explain the effect of CFCs on ozone in the atmosphere.
- Compare possible alternatives to CFCs.

The Ozone Layer: Protecting Earth

You may have noticed labels on many sunglasses claiming 100 percent UV protection. *UV* stands for "ultraviolet radiation." Exposure to this type of radiation can lead to many problems for living cells. In some cases, the cells may become cancerous. Other cell mutations associated with UV radiation can mean death to plants and animals.

How are people protected from this potentially harmful radiation? A gas called ozone, O_3, found in Earth's upper atmosphere, helps keep some harmful UV radiation from reaching Earth's surface, shown in **Figure 16-4.** Ozone molecules are formed from three oxygen atoms. Ozone isn't always helpful. Near the ground, ozone is a pollutant found in automobile exhaust. It can be a major irritant in areas with large amounts of air pollution.

So, what's the problem?

With ozone in the stratosphere giving us this protection, why is there any concern? Satellite photos, such as the one shown in **Figure 16-5,** allow scientists to measure the amount of ozone in a layer around Earth. Unmistakable decreases in the level of ozone, particularly around the poles, are now being detected. This is often referred to as the "hole in the ozone layer." Less ozone in the stratosphere means more UV radiation can reach Earth.

O_3

O_2 O

Ultraviolet rays

Stratosphere

Beneficial ozone

Troposphere

1   CFC molecule

2

3

O_3 Cl

O_2 O O_2

4

5

ClO

Figure 16-4

Ozone in the stratosphere absorbs ultraviolet rays, breaking O_3 into O_2 and O. O_2 and O react, forming more ozone.

2 Points of View

A Global Plan

Most scientists now believe that a group of compounds called **chlorofluorocarbons (CFCs)** migrate through Earth's atmosphere and decompose. This decomposition releases chlorine atoms that destroy ozone. CFCs are used in air-conditioning systems and in making some types of polymer foams. If CFC use were banned and substitute compounds found, more protective ozone could be conserved.

Don't Overreact

The decrease of the ozone levels in the atmosphere does appear to be related to chlorine concentrations in the stratosphere. But mounting evidence suggests that human activity is not the only source of chlorine. Scientists have found approximately 2000 chlorine and related compounds that are released into the air from natural phenomena—plants, ocean life, fungi, forest fires, and volcanoes. Blaming CFCs for all the ozone damage will cause economic problems as we try to switch millions of cooling systems to some other coolant.

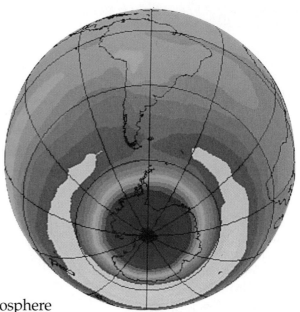

Figure 16-5

The colors in this satellite photo indicate how much ozone is present in the atmosphere. Yellow indicates greater amounts of ozone. Purple shows the least amount.

Section Wrap-up

Review

1. Why is the amount of ozone in Earth's atmosphere important to us?

2. The following equations show chlorine reacting with ozone and what happens to the ClO formed.
   $$Cl(g) + O_3(g) \rightarrow ClO(g) + O_2(g)$$
   $$ClO(g) + O(g) \rightarrow Cl(g) + O_2(g)$$
   Taking these two reactions together, what can you conclude about the potential problem of controlling the amount of Cl in the atmosphere?

Explore the Issue

Would you be willing to pay more for air-conditioning services in order to regulate and recycle CFCs to help keep them out of the environment? Explain.

Science Journal

Many environmental groups are calling for CFC recycling programs to prevent CFCs from entering the atmosphere. In your Science Journal, write a paragraph summarizing your thoughts about whether recycling will solve the problem.

SCIENCE & SOCIETY

Checking for Balance

As you read in Chapter 11, silver tarnish, shown in **Figure 16-6,** is silver sulfide, Ag_2S. It forms when sulfur-containing compounds in the air or food react with silver. Suppose you write this chemical equation for tarnishing.

$$Ag(cr) + H_2S(g) \rightarrow Ag_2S(cr) + H_2(g)$$

Now, examine the equation. Remember that matter is never created or destroyed in a chemical reaction. Notice that one silver atom appears in the reactants, $Ag + H_2S$. However, two silver atoms appear in the products, $Ag_2S + H_2$. As you know, one silver atom can't just become two. The equation must be balanced so it shows a true picture of what takes place in the reaction. A **balanced chemical equation** has the same number of atoms of each element on both sides of the equation. To find out if this equation is balanced, make a chart like that shown in **Table 16-3.**

The number of hydrogen atoms and the number of sulfur atoms are balanced. However, two silver atoms are on the right side of the equation and only one is on the left side. This equation isn't balanced. To balance an equation, never change subscripts of a correct formula. Instead, place whole number coefficients to the left of the formulas of the reactants and products so that equal numbers of silver atoms are on both sides of the equation. If no number is written, the coefficient is 1.

Science Words

balanced chemical equation

Objectives

• Explain what is meant by a balanced chemical equation.
• Demonstrate how to write balanced chemical equations.

Figure 16-6

Tarnish is a type of corrosion that occurs on silver.

Table 16-2

Diatomic Molecules			
Name	**Formula**	**Name**	**Formula**
Hydrogen	H_2	Chlorine	Cl_2
Oxygen	O_2	Bromine	Br_2
Nitrogen	N_2	Iodine	I_2
Fluorine	F_2		

Choosing Coefficients

How do you find out which coefficients to use to balance an equation? This decision is usually a trial-and-error process. With practice, the process becomes simple to perform.

In the chemical equation for tarnishing, the sulfur atoms and the hydrogen atoms are already balanced. Putting a coefficient before formulas that contain these atoms is not necessary at this time. So, look at the formulas containing silver atoms: Ag and Ag_2S. Two atoms of silver are on the right side and only one is on the left side. If you put a coefficient of 2 before Ag, the equation is balanced, as shown in **Table 16-4.**

$$2Ag(cr) + H_2S(g) \rightarrow Ag_2S(cr) + H_2(g)$$

Writing Balanced Chemical Equations

When a piece of magnesium ribbon burns in a flask of oxygen, a white powder called magnesium oxide is formed. To write a balanced chemical equation for this and most other reactions, follow these four steps.

Step 1 Describe the reaction in words, putting the reactants on the left side and the products on the right side.

   magnesium plus oxygen produces magnesium oxide

Step 2 Write a chemical equation for the reaction using formulas and symbols. Review how to write formulas for compounds in Section 11-4. The formulas for elements are generally just their symbols. However, as you read in Chapter 12, some elements ordinarily exist as diatomic molecules, as shown in **Table 16-2.** Oxygen is a diatomic molecule.

$$Mg(cr) + O_2(g) \rightarrow MgO(cr)$$

Step 3 Check the equation for atom balance. Set up a chart similar to **Table 16-5** to help you. The magnesium atoms are balanced, but the oxygen atoms are not. Therefore, this equation isn't balanced.

Step 4 Choose coefficients that balance the equation. Remember, never change subscripts of a correct formula to balance an equation. Try putting a coefficient of 2 before MgO to balance the oxygen.

$$Mg(cr) + O_2(g) \rightarrow 2MgO(cr)$$

Now, there are two Mg atoms on the right side and only one is on the left side. So, a coefficient of 2 is needed before Mg also.

$$2Mg(cr) + O_2(g) \rightarrow 2MgO(cr)$$

Table 16-6 indicates that the equation is now balanced.

Table 16-3

Atoms in Unbalanced Equation		
Kind of Atom	Number of Atoms $Ag + H_2S \rightarrow Ag_2S + H_2$	
Ag	1	2
H	2	2
S	1	1

Table 16-4

Atoms in Balanced Equation		
Kind of Atom	Number of Atoms $2Ag + H_2S \rightarrow Ag_2S + H_2$	
Ag	2	2
H	2	2
S	1	1

Table 16-5

Atoms in Unbalanced Equation		
Kind of Atom	Number of Atoms $Mg + O_2 \rightarrow MgO$	
Mg	1	1
O	2	1

Table 16-6

Atoms in Balanced Equation		
Kind of Atom	Number of Atoms $2Mg + O_2 \rightarrow 2MgO$	
Mg	2	2
O	2	2

Table 16-7

Kind of Atoms	Number of Atoms $AgNO_3 + NaCl \rightarrow AgCl + NaNO_3$	
Ag	1	1
N	1	1
O	3	3
Na	1	1
Cl	1	1

Atoms in AgCl Formation

Work through the following example.

When a silver nitrate solution is mixed with a sodium chloride solution, insoluble silver chloride and sodium nitrate solution form. Write a balanced equation for this reaction. Refer to **Table 16-7** as needed.

Step 1 Describe the reaction in words.
aqueous silver nitrate plus aqueous sodium chloride produces solid silver chloride plus aqueous sodium nitrate

Step 2 Write the chemical equation.

$$AgNO_3(aq) + NaCl(aq) \rightarrow AgCl(cr) + NaNO_3(aq)$$

Step 3 Check the equation for balance.
The equation already has equal numbers of each element on both sides. This equation is balanced.

Step 4 Choose coefficients.
This equation is balanced, so no coefficients other than 1 are needed.

Section Wrap-up

Review

1. What are two reasons for balancing equations for chemical reactions?

2. Write balanced chemical equations for the following reactions: (a) copper metal plus sulfur produces solid copper(I) sulfide, (b) sodium metal plus water produces aqueous sodium hydroxide plus hydrogen gas.

3. **Think Critically:** Explain why the sum of the coefficients on the reactant side of a balanced equation does not have to equal the sum of the coefficients on the product side of the equation.

Using Computers

Spreadsheet Use a spreadsheet to produce your own balance table for the reaction of $CaCO_3$ with HCl to form CO_2, $CaCl_2$, and water.

Skill Builder

Observing and Inferring

Hard water contains ions of calcium, magnesium, and/or iron. When Na_2CO_3 is added to hard water, water is softened because these ions are removed as a white solid. For Mg, this reaction may occur.

$$MgCl_2(aq) + Na_2CO_3(aq) \rightarrow MgCO_3(cr) + 2NaCl(aq)$$

Write a balanced equation showing how water containing $Ca(NO_3)_2$ could be softened. If you need help, refer to Observing and Inferring in the **Skill Handbook.**

Types of Chemical Reactions

Classifying Chemical Reactions

There are hundreds of kinds of chemical reactions. Rather than try to memorize them, it is easier to group reactions by their similarities. You can learn a great deal about a reaction by comparing it to others in its group.

One system of classification is based upon the way the atoms rearrange themselves in a chemical reaction. Most reactions are either synthesis, decomposition, single-displacement, or double-displacement reactions.

Synthesis Reactions

One of the easiest reaction types to recognize is a synthesis reaction. In a **synthesis reaction,** two or more substances combine to form another substance. The generalized formula for this reaction type is as follows.

$$A + B \rightarrow AB$$

The reaction in which hydrogen burns in oxygen to form water is an example of a synthesis reaction.

$$2H_2(g) + O_2(g) \rightarrow 2H_2O(g)$$

This reaction between hydrogen and oxygen occurs between two elements. One type of rocket fuel is hydrogen, which burns explosively in oxygen when the rocket is fired, as shown in **Figure 16-7.**

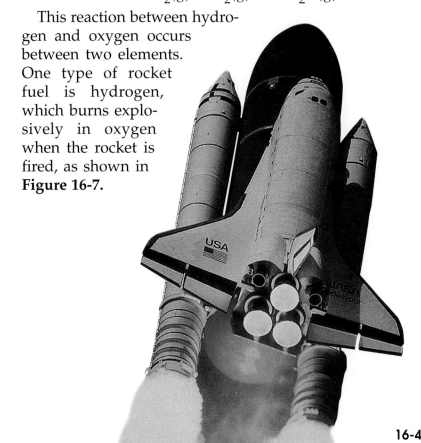

Science Words

synthesis reaction
decomposition reaction
single-displacement reaction
double-displacement reaction
precipitate

Objectives

- Describe four types of chemical reactions using their generalized formulas.
- Classify various chemical reactions by type.

Figure 16-7

The synthesis reaction between hydrogen and oxygen fuels the main stage of the space shuttle.

CONNECT TO

LIFE SCIENCE

Substances in both plants and animals react to form proteins. *Research* the compounds that are the basic units in proteins.

MiniLAB

Must the sums of reactant and product coefficients be equal?

A basketball team is made up of individuals acting as a unit. A chemical compound also consists of individual atoms in one unit.

Procedure

1. Obtain a card marked with one of five basketball team positions.
2. Group together with others in the class to form one basketball team. Assume that a team needs two guards, two forwards, and one center.

Analysis

1. Write the formation of the basketball team in the form of an equation. Use coefficients in front of each type of player needed to make one team.
2. What are two ways this equation is like a chemical equation?
3. Suppose, after the formation of as many complete teams as possible, there were one guard and two centers remaining. Why couldn't these players be added to existing teams? How does this compare to restrictions on the use of subscripts when balancing equations?

Figure 16-8

Copper in a wire replaces silver in silver nitrate, forming a blue solution of a copper nitrate.

Decomposition Reactions

The opposite of a synthesis reaction is a decomposition reaction. The equation below illustrates this relationship.

In a **decomposition reaction,** one substance breaks down, or decomposes, into two or more simpler substances. The generalized formula for this type of reaction is as follows.

$$AB \rightarrow A + B$$

Most decomposition reactions require the use of heat, light, or electricity. The decomposition of water by an electric current produces hydrogen and oxygen.

$$2H_2O(l) \xrightarrow{elec.} 2H_2(g) + O_2(g)$$

Displacement Reactions

A **single-displacement reaction** occurs when one element replaces another in a compound. There are two generalized equations for this type of reaction.

In the first case, A replaces B as follows.

$$A + BC \rightarrow AC + B$$

In the second case, D replaces C as follows.

$$D + BC \rightarrow BD + C$$

In **Figure 16-8,** a copper wire is put into a solution of silver nitrate. Because copper is a more active metal than silver, it replaces the silver, forming a blue copper(II) nitrate solution. The silver forms as an insoluble solid.

Table 16-8 lists metals according to how active they are. A metal will replace any metal beneath it in the table. Notice that copper, silver, and gold are near the bottom of the list. Their inactivity is why these elements often occur in Earth as veins of relatively pure element. Most other metals are more active and occur as compounds.

A **double-displacement reaction** takes place if a precipitate, water, or a gas forms when two ionic compounds in solution are combined. A **precipitate** is an insoluble compound formed during this type of reaction. In a double-displacement reaction, the positive ion of one compound replaces the positive ion of the other compound to form two new compounds. The generalized formula for this type of reaction is as follows.

$$AB + CD \rightarrow AD + CB$$

The reaction of silver nitrate with sodium chloride is an example of this type of reaction. A precipitate—silver chloride—is formed. The chemical equation is as follows.

$$AgNO_3(aq) + NaCl(aq) \rightarrow AgCl(cr) + NaNO_3(aq)$$

You have seen just a few examples of chemical reactions classified into types. Many more reactions of each type occur around you.

Table 16-8

Activity Series of Metals

Lithium	**Most active**
Potassium	
Barium	
Calcium	
Sodium	
Magnesium	
Aluminum	
Zinc	
Iron	
Nickel	
Tin	
Lead	
(Hydrogen)	
Copper	
Mercury	
Silver	
Gold	**Least active**

Section Wrap-up

Review

1. Classify the following reactions by type.
   (a) $2KClO_3(cr) \rightarrow 2KCl(cr) + 3O_2(g)$
   (b) $CaBr_2(aq) + Na_2CO_3(aq) \rightarrow CaCO_3(cr) + 2NaBr(aq)$
   (c) $Zn(cr) + S(cr) \rightarrow ZnS(cr)$
   (d) $Ba(cr) + FeBr_2(aq) \rightarrow BaBr_2(aq) + Fe(cr)$

2. The copper bottoms of some cooking pans turn black after being used. The copper reacts with oxygen, forming black copper(II) oxide. Write a balanced chemical equation for this reaction.

3. **Think Critically:** One method used to obtain gold from its ore involves forming a gold compound, then recovering the gold by using zinc. Balance the following equation and identify the reaction type.
   $$Au(CN)_2^-(aq) + Zn(cr) \rightarrow Au(cr) + Zn(CN)_4^{2-}$$

USING MATH

Most balanced equations use the smallest coefficients possible. Rewrite the following equation, calculating the smallest coefficients that still indicate a balanced equation.

$$9Fe(cr) + 12H_2O(g) \rightarrow 3Fe_3O_4(cr) + 12H_2(g)$$

Skill Builder
Hypothesizing
Group 1 metals replace hydrogen in water in reactions that are often violent. A sample equation for one reaction is as follows.

$$2K(cr) + 2HOH(l) \rightarrow 2KOH(aq) + H_2(g).$$

Use **Table 16-8** to help you hypothesize why these metals are often stored in kerosene. If you need help, refer to Hypothesizing in the **Skill Handbook.**

Activity 16-1

Design Your Own Experiment
Metal Activity

How can you compare the chemical activity of two substances? One test that can be applied is to allow each substance to react with a third substance. Then the results can be compared and ranked.

PREPARATION

Problem
How can the chemical activity of metals be compared?

Form a Hypothesis
Using a dilute acid for comparison, state a hypothesis concerning a way to rank the metals.

Objectives
- Observe the chemical reactions between metals and a dilute acid.
- Design an experiment that compares the degree of chemical reactions among selected metals.

Possible Materials
- test tubes, all the same size
- test-tube rack

- dilute hydrochloric acid, HCl
- 10-mL graduated cylinder
- tongs
- wooden splint
- small pieces of metals

Safety Precautions

Handle hydrochloric acid with care. Report any spills immediately. Wear safety goggles at all times during the experiment. Use only pieces of metal that are less than the size of a pea.

PLAN THE EXPERIMENT

1. As a group, agree upon and write out the hypothesis statement.
2. As a group, list your procedure steps in a logical sequence.
3. Make a list of the materials that you will need to complete your experiment.
4. In your Science Journal, design a data table to make comparisons of your tested metals.

Check the Plan
1. After testing the small pieces of metals, how will you compare your test results?
2. What will be held constant? What will you allow to vary?
3. Should you run any tests more than once?
4. *Make sure your teacher approves of your plan and that you have included any changes suggested in the plan.*

DO THE EXPERIMENT

1. Carry out the experiment as planned.
2. Testing the gas production of a metal and acid reaction will require igniting the gas. Your teacher will carry out this part of the experiment.
3. In the data table in your Science Journal, write down your observations of the chemical reaction between the metals and the acid.

Analyze and Apply
1. **Compare** the results of each metal's reaction with the acid.
2. **Compare** your results with those of other class members.
3. **Sequence** all the metals tested in the order of most reactive first, down to least reactive.

Go Further

Write balanced chemical equations for all of the chemical reactions that took place during the experiment.

Energy and Chemical Reactions

Science Words

exothermic reaction
catalyst
inhibitor
endothermic reaction

Objectives

• Differentiate between an exothermic reaction and an endothermic reaction.
• Describe the effects of catalysts and inhibitors on the speed of chemical reactions.

Energy Changes in Chemical Reactions

Did you ever watch the explosion of dynamite? An explosion results from a rapid chemical reaction. In all chemical reactions, energy is either released or absorbed. This energy can take many forms. It might be in the form of heat, light, sound, or even electricity.

When most chemical reactions take place, some chemical bonds in the reactants must be broken. To break chemical bonds, energy must be provided. In order for products to be produced, new bonds must be formed. Bond formation releases energy.

Exothermic Reactions

In many chemical reactions, less energy is required to break original bonds than is released when new bonds form. In these reactions, called **exothermic reactions,** some form of energy is given off by the reaction. In many instances, the heat given off may cause the reaction mixture to feel hot, as shown in **Figure 16-9.**

The burning of wood and the explosion of dynamite are exothermic reactions. They are exothermic reactions because they give off energy as the reaction proceeds. Rusting is also exothermic, but the reaction proceeds so slowly that it is difficult to detect any temperature change.

INTEGRATION
Life Science

Catalysts and Inhibitors

Some reactions are too slow to be useful. To speed up these reactions, you can add a catalyst. A **catalyst** is a substance that

Figure 16-9

The burning of wood is an example of an exothermic reaction.

speeds up a chemical reaction without itself being permanently changed. When you add a catalyst to a reaction, you end up with the same amount of the catalyst that you started with.

Certain proteins known as enzymes act as catalysts in living organisms. Enzymes allow reactions to occur at faster rates and lower temperatures than would otherwise be possible. Without these enzymes, life as we know it would not be possible.

At times, it is worthwhile to prevent certain reactions from occurring. Substances called **inhibitors** are used to combine with one of the reactants. The reactant is tied up and cannot undergo the original reaction. The food preservatives BHT and BHA are inhibitors. They prevent spoilage of certain foods.

Using catalysts and inhibitors are just a few of the ways scientists control chemical reactions.

Catalytic Converters

The exhaust systems of cars today are equipped with catalytic converters that use rhodium and platinum as the catalysts. These catalysts speed up reactions of three types of toxic compounds given off by cars. The rhodium and platinum don't enter into a chemical reaction, but the rough surface of the catalyst provides a high-surface-area place for reactions to occur. As pollutants adhere to the surface of the catalyst, chemical bonds in the compounds are weakened, so another reactant can more easily break the bond. Catalytic converters change unburned hydrocarbons, carbon monoxide, and nitrogen oxides into harmless compounds.

Two types of reactions are catalyzed. In one type of reaction, oxygen is added. Adding oxygen converts carbon monoxide to carbon dioxide, and unburned hydrocarbons to carbon dioxide and water. In the other type of reaction, oxygen is removed. Removing oxygen converts nitrogen oxides to nitrogen.

Think Critically:

Why is it not necessary to add more rhodium and platinum to a catalytic converter as these substances are used?

Catalytic Converter

Wire-mesh

Platinum-coated beads

Figure 16-10

Figure 16-10

The refining of ores to produce useful metals frequently involves an endothermic reaction.

Endothermic Reactions

Sometimes, more energy is required to break bonds than to form new ones in a chemical reaction. In these reactions, called **endothermic reactions,** energy must be provided for the reaction to take place.

When some endothermic reactions proceed, so much heat is absorbed that their containers feel cold to the touch. In other endothermic reactions, so little heat is absorbed that you would need a thermometer to determine that a temperature change has occurred.

An endothermic reaction is frequently used to obtain a metal from its ore. For example, aluminum metal is obtained by passing an electric current through molten aluminum ore, as shown in **Figure 16-10.**

$$2Al_2O_3 \xrightarrow{elec.} 4Al + 3O_2$$

In this case, electrical energy, not thermal energy, provides the energy needed to keep the reaction going.

Section Wrap-up

Review

1. What is the difference between exothermic and endothermic reactions?

2. Oxygen is produced when potassium chlorate is heated. What is true about manganese dioxide if it is a catalyst for this reaction?

3. **Think Critically:** Suppose you wanted to develop a product for warming people's hands at outdoor winter events. Would you choose an exothermic reaction or an endothermic reaction to use in your device? Why?

Skill Builder
Concept Mapping
Construct a concept map to show the relationship between energy and bond formation and bond breakage. If you need help, refer to Concept Mapping in the **Skill Handbook.**

Science Journal

In your Science Journal, discuss how the profit or loss in an investment or business deal is like the loss or gain of energy in a chemical reaction.

Activity 16-2

Catalyzed Reaction

A balanced chemical equation provides much information about a chemical reaction, but it doesn't tell you about the rate of the reaction. Temperature, concentration, and physical state of reactants and products may all affect the rate of reaction.

Problem
How does the presence of a catalyst affect the rate of a chemical reaction?

Materials

- 3 medium-sized test tubes
- test-tube stand
- 15 mL 3% hydrogen peroxide, H_2O_2
- graduated cylinder
- small plastic spoon
- sand
- manganese dioxide, MnO_2
- wooden splint
- hot plate
- beaker of hot water

CAUTION: *Hydrogen peroxide can irritate skin and eyes. Wear goggles and an apron.*

Procedure

1. Set three test tubes in a test-tube stand. Pour 5 mL of hydrogen peroxide into each tube.
2. Place about 1/4 spoonful of sand in tube 2 and the same amount of manganese dioxide in tube 3.
3. In the presence of some substances that act as catalysts, H_2O_2 decomposes rapidly, producing oxygen gas, O_2. A glowing splint placed in O_2 will relight. Test the gas produced in any of the tubes as follows. Light a wooden splint, blow out the flame, and insert the glowing splint into the tube.
4. Place all three tubes in a beaker of hot water. Heat on a hot plate until all the remaining H_2O_2 is driven away and no liquid is left in the tubes.

Analyze

1. What changes did you observe when the solids were added to the tubes?
2. In which tube was oxygen produced rapidly, and how do you know?
3. Which substance, sand or manganese dioxide, caused the rapid production of gas from the hydrogen peroxide?
4. How did you identify the gas produced?
5. What remained in each tube after the hydrogen peroxide was driven away?

Conclude and Apply

6. What are two characteristics common to catalysts? Which substance in this activity has both characteristics?
7. The word *catalyst* has uses beyond chemistry. If a person who is added to a basketball team acts as a catalyst, **infer** what effect that person is likely to have on the team.

Science & ART

What would you paint if you were going to paint a fresco? In your Science Journal, describe and sketch the large fresco you would paint. Be as detailed as possible. Remember that frescoes are large, wall-sized paintings.

Fresco Painting

A fresco is a kind of painting made on a plaster wall. The word *fresco* is Italian for "fresh." Why would a painting be called fresh? Possibly because only as much plaster as can be painted in a day may be applied each day. Fresco painting makes use of chemical reactions that cause color pigments to crystallize within the plaster as it dries.

The Process

To paint a fresco, a full-scale drawing showing exactly what will be painted that day is prepared. A section of the wall is covered with plaster made of sand and lime, which is calcium hydroxide. The drawing is traced onto the plaster wall, which is then painted. The paint itself is made from natural pigments diluted with water. As the plaster dries, carbon dioxide in the air turns the lime to calcium carbonate, crystallizing the pigments. The color then becomes part of the plaster itself. Any plaster that has not been painted by the end of the day must be cut away. New, wet plaster must be applied the next day.

The lime in plaster bleaches many pigments. Only pigments that resist the action of lime can be used. These pigments are usually earth colors.

Frescoes have been painted for hundreds and hundreds of years. The fresco shown here was painted by Mexican artist Diego Rivera. He is well-known for the magnificent frescoes he painted of Mexican history and politics. Notice the natural golden earth tones Rivera used.

Chapter 16 Review

Summary

16-1: Chemical Changes in Matter

1. In a chemical reaction, the reactants are changed into the products, which are different substances.
2. According to the law of conservation of mass, the mass of the reactants in a chemical reaction equals the mass of the products.
3. A chemical equation is a shorthand way of describing a chemical reaction using symbols, coefficients, and formulas.

16-2: Science and Society: Chemical Reactions—Up in the Air

1. The ozone layer helps protect Earth by absorbing ultraviolet radiation from the sun.
2. In the upper atmosphere, CFCs release atoms of chlorine that destroy ozone molecules.
3. Replacing CFCs and regulating their use may slow down the loss of ozone.

16-3: Chemical Equations

1. A balanced chemical equation has the same number of atoms of each element on both sides of the equation.
2. The final step in the process of balancing a chemical equation is the choice of the correct coefficients.

16-4: Types of Chemical Reactions

1. Many specific chemical reactions can be classified as one of four reaction types—synthesis, decomposition, single-displacement, and double-displacement.

16-5: Energy and Chemical Reactions

1. In an exothermic reaction, energy is released; in an endothermic reaction, energy is absorbed.

2. A catalyst increases the speed of a chemical reaction; an inhibitor prevents a chemical reaction.

Key Science Words

a. balanced chemical equation
b. catalyst
c. chemical reaction
d. chlorofluoro-carbon (CFC)
e. coefficient
f. decomposition reaction
g. double-displacement reaction
h. endothermic reaction
i. exothermic reaction
j. inhibitor
k. precipitate
l. product
m. reactant
n. single-displacement reaction
o. synthesis reaction

Reviewing Vocabulary

Match each phrase with the correct term from the list of Key Science Words.

1. energy is given off
2. has same number of atoms on both sides
3. energy is absorbed
4. an element replaces another in a compound
5. prevents a reaction
6. substance breaks down into simpler substances
7. two ionic compounds react to form a precipitate, water, or a gas
8. two or more substances combine
9. compound that contains chlorine, fluorine, and carbon
10. well-defined example of chemical change

Checking Concepts

Choose the word or phrase that completes the sentence.

1. An example of a chemical reaction is
   _____.
   a. bending   c. melting
   b. evaporation   d. photosynthesis
2. Lavoisier's experiments gave examples of the law of _____.
   a. chemical reaction
   b. conservation of mass
   c. coefficients
   d. gravity
3. An element that is more _____ will replace another element in a compound.
   a. active   c. inhibiting
   b. catalytic   d. soluble
4. In the expression $4Ca(NO_3)_2$, the 4 is a
   _____.
   a. coefficient   c. subscript
   b. formula   d. symbol
5. BHA is an example of a(n) _____.
   a. catalyst   c. inhibitor
   b. formula   d. CFC
6. If a substance is dissolved in water, _____ follows its formula in an equation.
   a. (aq) b. (cr) c. (g) d. (l)
7. In the tarnishing of silver, Ag_2S is a(n)
   _____.
   a. catalyst   c. product
   b. inhibitor   d. reactant
8. In the burning of hydrogen, O_2 is a(n)
   _____.
   a. catalyst   c. product
   b. inhibitor   d. reactant
9. _____ is an allotrope of oxygen, O_2, that absorbs UV radiation.
   a. H_2 b. O_3 c. Cl d. Cl_2
10. If a substance is a solid, _____ follows its formula in an equation.
    a. (l) b. (g) c. (cr) d. (aq)

Understanding Concepts

Answer the following questions in your Science Journal using complete sentences.

11. Chromium is produced by reacting its oxide with aluminum. If 76 g of Cr_2O_3 and 27 g of Al react to form 51 g of Al_2O_3, how many grams of Cr are formed?
12. Propane, $C_3H_8(g)$, burns in oxygen to form carbon dioxide and water vapor. Write a balanced equation for burning propane.
13. $Cl(g) + O_3(g) \rightarrow ClO(g) + O_2(g)$ plays a role in ozone destruction. What is the source of the monatomic chlorine, Cl, in this reaction?
14. In one reaction of a catalytic converter, nitrogen(II) oxide reacts with hydrogen to form ammonia and water vapor. Write a balanced equation for this reaction.
15. If lye, NaOH, is put in water, the solution gets hot. What kind of energy process is this?

Thinking Critically

16. Write a balanced chemical equation and use it to explain the law of conservation of mass.
17. If Zn is placed in a solution of $Cu(NO_3)_2$, and Cu is placed in a $Zn(NO_3)_2$ solution, what reaction takes place? Explain.
18. $PbCl_2$ and Li_2SO_4 react to form LiCl and what other substance?
19. Why should subscripts not be changed to balance an equation?
20. Write a balanced equation for the decomposition of copper(II) oxide.

Developing Skills

If you need help, refer to the **Skill Handbook.**

21. **Concept Mapping:** The arrow in a chemical equation tells the reaction direction. Some reactions are reversible because they don't go in only one direction. Sometimes, the bond formed is weak, and a product breaks apart as it's formed. Double arrows are used in the equation to indicate this reaction. Fill in the cycle map, using the words *product(s)* and *reactant(s)*. In the blanks in the center, fill in the formulas for the substances appearing in the reversible reaction.

$$H_2(g) + I_2(g) \rightleftarrows 2HI(g)$$

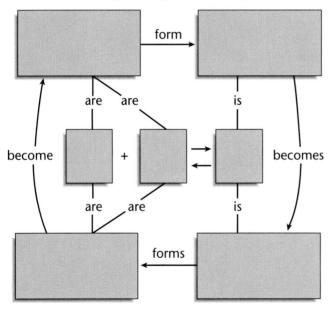

22. **Recognizing Cause and Effect:** Sucrose, table sugar, is a disaccharide. This means that sucrose is composed of two simple sugars chemically bonded together. Sucrose can be separated by digestion or by heating it in an aqueous sulfuric acid solution. Find out what products are formed by breaking up sucrose. What role does the acid play?

23. **Observing and Inferring:** What belongs in the parentheses in the following double-displacement reaction?

$$BaCl_2(aq) + K_2CO_3(aq) \rightarrow$$
$$BaCO_3(\ ) + 2KCl(aq)$$

24. **Interpreting Data:** When 46 g of sodium were exposed to dry air, 62 g of sodium oxide formed over a period of time. How many grams of oxygen from the air were used?

25. **Classifying:** Make an outline with the general heading "Chemical Reactions." Include the four types of reactions, with a description and example of each.

Performance Assessment

1. **Asking Questions:** Investigate the label on a package of cold cuts. Research as many of the substances added as possible. Is anything added as an inhibitor? Report on your findings.

2. **Oral Presentation:** Research common chemical reactions that occur safely in your home. Demonstrate one of these reactions. Tell what type of reaction it is and how it is used. Include in your report a balanced equation for the reaction.

3. **Model:** Use toothpicks and Styrofoam balls of different sizes or colors to balance each of the following chemical reactions and demonstrate the law of conservation of mass.
   a. $Cl_2O(g) + H_2O(l) \rightarrow HClO(aq)$
   b. $Fe_2O_3(cr) + CO(g) \rightarrow Fe(cr) + CO_2(g)$
   c. $H_2(g) + N_2(g) \rightarrow NH_3(g)$
   d. $ZnO(cr) + HCl(aq) \rightarrow ZnCl_2(aq) + H_2O(l)$

Previewing the Chapter

Acids, Bases, and Salts

Imagine the tremendous amount of work that must have gone into this impressive structure. Unfortunately, repair work is needed. What do you think is causing the deterioration of the marble of this ancient structure?

Durable marble structures can resist rain and many weathering factors, but not all. Marble is made mostly of calcium carbonate, $CaCO_3$, also called calcite. In the following activity, you will use a solution that is similar to polluted rainwater. In the chapter that follows, you will find out what kinds of solutions can cause these changes.

EXPLORE ACTIVITY

Explore how marble reacts with some rainwater.

1. Mass approximately 5.0 g of marble chips and place them in a beaker.
2. Add 50.0 mL of soda water, which represents acid rain.
3. After several minutes, stir the mixture and allow it to settle.
4. When the mixture stops reacting, pour the mixture through filter paper.
5. Dry the trapped marble chip residue and determine its mass.

Observe: What was the change in mass of the marble chips? In your Science Journal, write your conclusions about the effect that acid rain may have on marble.

Previewing Science Skills

▶ In the Skill Builders, you will **observe** and **infer, map concepts**, and **interpret data**.

▶ In the Activities, you will **use models, hypothesize, measure, observe**, and **infer**.

▶ In the MiniLABs, you will **observe** and **infer**.

17•1 Acids and Bases

Science Words

acid
indicator
dehydrating agent
pickling
base
hydronium ion

Objectives

- Define *acid* and *base*.
- Describe the characteristic properties of acids and bases.
- List the names, formulas, and uses of some common acids and bases.
- Relate the processes of ionization and dissociation to the formation of acids and bases.

Figure 17-1

These fruits contain citric acid. *What other foods have a sour taste that may be due to the presence of acids?*

Acids

What comes to mind when you hear the word *acid*? Do you think about something that has a sour taste? Do you think of a substance that can burn your skin, or even burn a hole through a piece of metal? Although many acids are not strong enough to burn through metal, or burn skin, these characteristics are, indeed, properties of some acids.

Acids make up an important group of compounds that contain hydrogen. When an acid dissolves in water, some of the hydrogen is released as hydrogen ions, H^+. Thus, an **acid** is a substance that produces hydrogen ions, H^+, in solution. It is the ability to produce H^+ ions that gives acids their characteristic properties.

Properties of Acids

Acids taste sour. The familiar sour taste of the foods shown in **Figure 17-1** is due to the presence of acids. *However, taste should NEVER be used to test for the presence of acids.* Some acids can produce painful burns and damage to tissues.

Acids are electrolytes. Because they always contain some ions, acid solutions conduct electricity.

Acids are corrosive. Some acids react strongly with certain metals, seeming to eat away the metals as metallic compounds and hydrogen gas are produced.

Acids react with certain compounds, called indicators, to produce predictable changes in color. An **indicator** is an organic compound that changes color in an acid or a base. **Figure 17-2** shows this interesting property. Some indicators are soaked into paper strips, such as litmus paper. Litmus paper is red in the presence of an acid and blue in the presence of a base.

Common Acids

Many familiar items that you use every day contain acids. Acids are components of many foods. The gastric juice in your stomach contains an acid that helps to break down food during digestion. Car batteries, some flashlight batteries, and some household cleaners also contain acids. **Table 17-1** gives the names and formulas of a few common acids and tells where they are found.

In addition to these acids that you come in contact with every day, certain acids are vital to industry. The four most important industrial acids are sulfuric acid, phosphoric acid, nitric acid, and hydrochloric acid.

Figure 17-2

Litmus paper is a common acid-base indicator. *Which of these solutions is an acid?*

Sulfuric Acid

Sulfuric acid, H_2SO_4, is the most widely used chemical in the world. The Using Technology feature on page 469 discusses the uses of sulfuric acid in detail. Because of its use in automobile storage batteries, sulfuric acid is sometimes called battery acid. However, most sulfuric acid produced is used in the manufacture of fertilizer.

Table 17-1

Some Common Acids

Name	Formula	Where Found
Acetic acid	CH_3COOH	Vinegar
Acetylsalicylic acid	$HOOC-C_6H_4-OOCCH_3$	Aspirin
Ascorbic acid (vitamin C)	$H_2C_6H_6O_6$	Citrus fruits, tomatoes, vegetables
Boric acid	H_3BO_3	Eyewash solutions
Carbonic acid	H_2CO_3	Carbonated drinks
Hydrochloric acid	HCl	Gastric juice in stomach
Nitric acid	HNO_3	Making fertilizers, explosives (TNT)
Phosphoric acid	H_3PO_4	Making detergents, fertilizers
Sulfuric acid	H_2SO_4	Car batteries, making fertilizers

Figure 17-3

Sulfuric acid reacts with the hydrogen and oxygen in sugar, removing them as water and leaving only carbon.

Sulfuric acid is also an important dehydrating agent. A **dehydrating agent** is a substance that can remove water from materials. As **Figure 17-3** illustrates, organic compounds can be dehydrated by removing hydrogen and oxygen in the form of water from the compounds, leaving only carbon. When sulfuric acid comes in contact with human tissue, this dehydrating action produces painful burns.

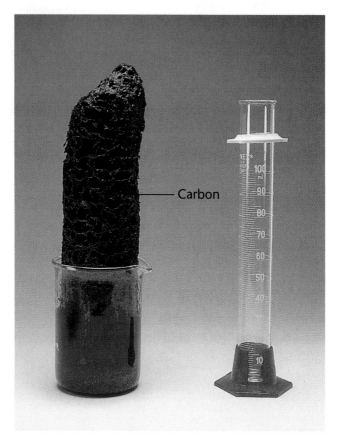

Phosphoric Acid

Phosphoric acid, H_3PO_4, is another acid important to industry worldwide. Eighty percent of phosphoric acid produced is used to make fertilizers.

Dilute phosphoric acid has a slightly sour but pleasant taste and is used in soft drinks. It is also used to make phosphates, which may be added to detergents to enhance their cleaning power. Unfortunately, phosphates cause pollution problems in lakes and streams.

Nitric Acid

Nitric acid, HNO_3, is best known for its use in making explosives. However, as with sulfuric and phosphoric acids, most nitric acid is used in the manufacture of fertilizers. Concentrated nitric acid is a colorless liquid. When exposed to light, the acid slowly changes to yellow. This change in color occurs because some of the nitric acid decomposes into nitrogen dioxide, NO_2, which is a brownish gas. Nitric acid can cause serious burns on human skin. It can even cause burns if it is inhaled or if the vapor comes into contact with skin.

Hydrochloric Acid

Hydrogen chloride, HCl, is a colorless gas. When this gas is dissolved in water, hydrochloric acid forms. Both HCl fumes and the ions that form in solution can harm human tissue.

Hydrochloric acid, when used in industry to clean surfaces of materials, is commonly called muriatic acid. Large quantities of the acid are used by the steel industry for pickling. **Pickling** is a process in which oxides and other impurities are removed from metal surfaces by dipping the metals in hydrochloric acid.

Several methods can be used to make phosphoric, nitric, and

USING TECHNOLOGY

Sulfuric Acid

Each year, more than 35 billion kg of sulfuric acid is produced in the United States by burning bright yellow sulfur and combining the residue with water. This results in the most widely produced chemical in the world. Why is sulfuric acid number one on the all-time chemical charts?

Have you eaten cereal or bread lately? Grain foods come from crops that need phosphates in order to grow. Often, the phosphate in soil is not in a usable form. Sulfuric acid (H_2SO_4) is used to break down phosphate rock into an inexpensive fertilizer.

$$Ca_3(PO_4)_2(cr) + 3H_2SO_4(aq) \rightarrow$$
$$3CaSO_4(cr) + 2H_3PO_4(aq)$$

Sulfuric acid is also used to make clothing, dyes, and synthetic materials like rayon. In addition, it is used in car batteries and to process paper. The widespread use of sulfuric acid reveals many applications of the science of acid reactions.

Think Critically:

The amount of sulfuric acid used by a country has been proposed as a measure of its level of industrialization. In your Science Journal, explain why this might be an accurate measure.

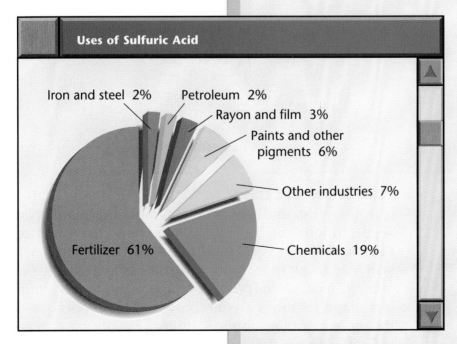

Uses of Sulfuric Acid

Iron and steel 2%
Petroleum 2%
Rayon and film 3%
Paints and other pigments 6%
Other industries 7%
Chemicals 19%
Fertilizer 61%

Find out whether acids and bases conduct an electric current.

Procedure

1. Carefully place the electrodes of a conductivity tester into a glass of orange juice. **CAUTION:** *Do not taste any substance being tested in this lab.*
2. Perform the same test with a solution of ammonia-based household cleaner. **CAUTION:** *Avoid direct contact with these fumes.*

Analysis

1. Identify an acid present in orange juice. What important ion is found in acids?
2. Identify a base present in the cleaner. What important ion is found in bases?

Figure 17-4

Many household materials contain bases. *What property of bases is evident in soaps?*

hydrochloric acids. But one general method can be used to make all three acids. This method involves reacting concentrated sulfuric acid with a compound containing the negative ion of the desired acid.

$$Ca_3(PO_4)_2(cr) + 3H_2SO_4(aq) \rightarrow 2H_3PO_4(aq) + 3CaSO_4(cr)$$

$$NaNO_3(cr) + H_2SO_4(aq) \rightarrow HNO_3(g) + NaHSO_4(aq)$$

$$NaCl(cr) + H_2SO_4(aq) \rightarrow HCl(g) + NaHSO_4(aq)$$

Bases

Like acids, bases are an important group of chemical compounds. Although acids and bases seem to have some features in common, the two groups are surprisingly different.

A **base** is a substance that produces hydroxide ions, OH^-, in solution. Does this OH combination look familiar? You may recall from Chapter 13 that an alcohol has a hydroxyl group, –OH, as part of its molecule. This hydroxyl group is not an ion and should not be confused with the OH^- ions that are produced by all bases. Because alcohols do not produce OH^- ions, alcohols are not classified as bases.

The hydroxide ions present in all basic solutions are negative ions, whereas the hydrogen ions present in acidic solutions are positive ions. This difference in charge accounts for some of the differences between acids and bases.

Properties of Bases

In the pure, undissolved state, most bases are crystalline solids. In solution, bases feel slippery and have a bitter taste. Like acids, strong bases are corrosive, and contact with the skin may result in severe burns and tissue damage. *Therefore, taste and touch should **NEVER** be used to test for the presence of a base.* Basic solutions are electrolytes. This property is due to the presence of ions in the solutions. Finally, bases react with indicators to produce predictable changes in color.

Table 17-2

Common Bases and Their Uses		
Name	Formula	Uses
Aluminum hydroxide	$Al(OH)_3$	Deodorant, antacid
Calcium hydroxide	$Ca(OH)_2$	Leather production, manufacture of mortar and plaster
Magnesium hydroxide	$Mg(OH)_2$	Laxative, antacid
Sodium hydroxide	NaOH	Drain cleaner, soap making
Ammonia	NH_3	Household cleaners, fertilizer, production of rayon and nylon

Common Bases

Many household products contain bases. **Figure 17-4** shows several of these products. Most soaps, for example, contain bases, which explains their bitter taste and slippery feel. **Table 17-2** contains the names and formulas of some common bases and tells how each base is used.

The most widely used base is ammonia, NH_3. Pure ammonia is a colorless gas with a distinctive, irritating odor. It can be extremely irritating to nasal passages and lungs if inhaled. When ammonia gas dissolves in water, some of its molecules react with water molecules, forming ammonium ions (NH_4^+) and hydroxide ions.

$$NH_3(g) + H_2O(l) \rightarrow NH_4^+(aq) + OH^-(aq)$$

The solution containing ammonium ions and hydroxide ions is called ammonia water. Dilute ammonia water is an excellent household cleaning agent. Ammonia is also used as a fertilizer, as shown in **Figure 17-5**.

Metallic Hydroxides

Another widely used base is calcium hydroxide, $Ca(OH)_2$, commonly called caustic lime. Calcium hydroxide is used in the production of mortar and plaster and to "sweeten" acidic soils.

Sodium hydroxide, NaOH, is a strong, corrosive base. This compound, commonly called lye, dissolves readily in water in an extremely exothermic process. Sodium hydroxide reacts with organic materials such as oils and fats to produce soap and glycerine. This property also enables it to be an effective oven cleaner and drain cleaner.

Figure 17-5

Ammonia is an important base in many products.

Solutions of Acids and Bases

You have learned that substances such as HCl, HNO_3, and H_2SO_4 are acids because of their ability to produce H^+ ions. This ionization process is shown in **Figure 17-6,** using HCl as an example. When a polar molecule, such as HCl, is dissolved in water, the negatively charged area of nearby water molecules attracts the positively charged area of the polar molecule. The H^+ is removed from the polar molecule and a **hydronium ion,** H_3O^+, is formed. Thus, *acid* describes any compound that can be ionized in water to form hydronium ions.

When an organic acid ionizes, the H at the end of the —COOH group combines with water to form the hydronium ion.

Figure 17-6

These equations demonstrate what happens to acids in solution.

$$HCl \quad + \quad H_2O \longrightarrow H_3O^+ \quad + \quad Cl^-$$

A When hydrogen chloride gas dissolves in water, it ionizes to produce hydronium ions and chloride ions. *What is the name of this common acid?*

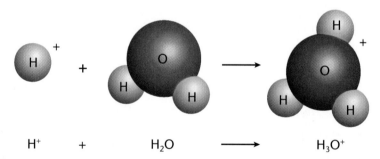

$$H^+ \quad + \quad H_2O \longrightarrow H_3O^+$$

B When an acid dissolves in water, hydrogen ions from the acid combine with water molecules to produce hydronium ions. *What is the overall charge on a hydronium ion?*

Compounds that can form hydroxide ions, OH^-, in solution are classified as bases. If you look back at **Table 17-2,** you will find that most substances listed contain OH within their formulas. Except for ammonia, inorganic compounds that produce bases in aqueous solution are ionic compounds. That is, they are already made up of ions. As the equation at the top of page 473 shows, when such a compound dissolves, the ions dissociate, or pull apart, and exist as individual ions in solution. These substances release OH^- ions in water. If a solution contains more OH^- ions than H_3O^+ ions, it is referred to as a basic solution.

$$NaOH(cr) \xrightarrow{H_2O} Na^+(aq) + OH^-(aq)$$

Ammonia is a polar compound. In solution, ionization takes place when the ammonia molecule attracts a hydrogen atom from a water molecule, as shown in **Figure 17-7.**

The next time you use any of the products described in this section, think about the properties the product has and why it has them.

CONNECT TO
LIFE SCIENCE

Amino acid molecules have properties of both acids and bases. Copy the following structure of glycine, and *classify* the parts that give the molecule its acidic and basic properties.

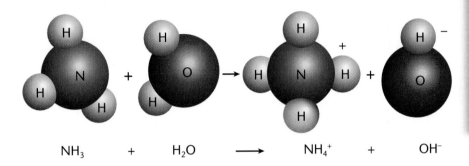

$NH_3 \quad + \quad H_2O \quad \longrightarrow \quad NH_4^+ \quad + \quad OH^-$

Figure 17-7

Even though ammonia is not a hydroxide, it reacts with water to produce some hydroxide ions; therefore, it is a base.

Section Wrap-up

Review

1. Why are acids and bases electrolytes?

2. Name three important acids and three important bases and describe some uses of each.

3. **Think Critically:** When you are stung by an ant, the insect injects formic acid, HCOOH, into your body. What kind of acid is formic acid—organic or inorganic? How do you know? Write an equation showing how formic acid ionizes.

Using Computers

Spreadsheet Make a spreadsheet that compares acids and bases.

Skill Builder

Observing and Inferring

You have observed that alcohols are not classified as bases, even though they have OH in their formulas. What do you infer about the bonding between OH and carbon in alcohols? If you need help, refer to Observing and Inferring in the **Skill Handbook.**

17•2 Strength of Acids and Bases

Science Words

strong acid
weak acid
strong base
weak base
pH

Objectives

- Explain what determines the strength of an acid or a base.
- Differentiate between strength and concentration.
- Define *pH*.
- Describe the relationship between pH and the strength of an acid or a base.

Strong and Weak Acids and Bases

You have learned that all acids have certain properties in common. Yet, some acids are safe enough to swallow or put in your eyes, whereas other acids destroy human tissue and corrode metal. Obviously, all acids are not alike. Some acids are stronger than others. The same is true of bases. **Table 17-3** lists some strong and weak acids and bases.

The strength of an acid or base depends on how completely a compound is pulled apart to form ions when dissolved in water. An acid that ionizes almost completely in solution is a **strong acid.** Conversely, an acid that only partly ionizes in solution is a **weak acid. Figure 17-8** shows how the amount of ions in solution can be compared using a measure of conductivity.

Ionization Evidence

$$HCl(g) + H_2O(l) \rightarrow H_3O^+(aq) + Cl^-(aq)$$

$$CH_3COOH(l) + H_2O(l) \rightleftarrows H_3O^+(aq) + CH_3COO^-(aq)$$

The first equation, with only a forward arrow, indicates that ions are formed when HCl is dissolved in water. All of the HCl ionizes. The second equation illustrates a characteristic of weak acids. Only some of the CH_3COOH ionizes; thus the reaction is incomplete, as indicated by the arrows pointing in opposite directions. In an acetic acid solution, mostly CH_3COOH is present. There are only a few ions in solution. These equations represent the general ionization properties of strong and weak acids.

Remember that many bases are ionic compounds that dissociate to produce individual ions when they dissolve. A **strong base** dissociates completely in solution. The following equations show the dissociation of sodium hydroxide, a strong base, and the ionization of ammonia, a weak base.

$$NaOH(cr) \rightarrow Na^+(aq) + OH^-(aq)$$

$$NH_3(aq) + H_2O(l) \rightleftarrows NH_4^+(aq) + OH^-(aq)$$

Whereas all of the NaOH has broken up into ions, most of the ammonia remains in the form of NH_3. Because ammonia produces few ions, ammonia is a **weak base.**

Figure 17-8

This simple conductivity test indicates the presence of ions in solution. *Which beaker contains the stronger acid?*

Table 17-3

Strengths of Some Acids and Bases		
Acid	**Strength**	**Base**
Hydrochloric, HCl Sulfuric, H_2SO_4 Nitric, HNO_3	Strong	Sodium hydroxide, NaOH Potassium hydroxide, KOH
Acetic, CH_3COOH Carbonic, H_2CO_3 Boric, H_3BO_3	Weak	Ammonia, NH_3 Aluminum hydroxide, $Al(OH)_3$ Iron(III) hydroxide, $Fe(OH)_3$

Strength and Concentration

Often, the *strength* of an acid or base is confused with its *concentration*. As you learned in Chapter 15, *dilute* and *concentrated* are terms used to indicate the concentration of a solution. The concentration of an acid or base refers to the amount of acid or base dissolved in solution. It is possible to have dilute concentrations of strong acids or bases and concentrated solutions of weak acids or bases. *Strong* or *weak* refers to the ease with which an acid or base forms ions in solution.

pH of a Solution

If you have a pool or keep tropical fish, you know that the pH of the water must be controlled. **pH** is a measure of the concentration of hydronium ions in a solution. To determine pH, a scale typically ranging from 0 to 14 has been devised, as shown in **Figure 17-9.**

As the scale shows, solutions with a pH lower than 7 are acidic. The lower the value, the more acidic the solution. Solutions with pH greater than 7 are basic, and the higher the pH, the more basic the solution. A solution with a pH of exactly 7 is neutral—neither acidic nor basic. Pure water has a pH of 7.

A pH meter can be used to determine the pH of a solution. This meter is operated by immersing the electrodes in the solution to be tested and reading the dial. Small, battery-

CONNECT TO

LIFE SCIENCE

The aromas of many fish are caused by compounds called amines. If the pH of a dilute solution of an amine is 11.4, *infer* whether the amine is an acid or a base.

Figure 17-9

The pH scale helps us classify solutions as acidic or basic.

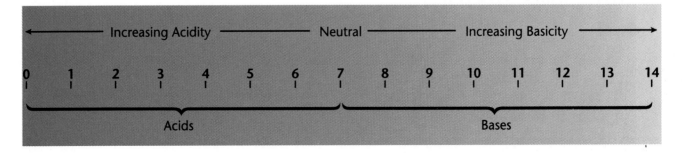

| ← Increasing Acidity ———— Neutral ———— Increasing Basicity → |

0 1 2 3 4 5 6 7 8 9 10 11 12 13 14

Acids   Bases

Figure 17-10

By moistening this treated paper and comparing the resulting color to the chart, the pH of the solution can be approximated. *What would you conclude about the pH of the rainwater being tested in this photo?*

operated pH meters with digital readouts make measuring the pH of materials convenient.

If a pH meter is not available, a universal indicator or pH paper can be used. Both of these undergo a color change in the presence of H_3O^+ ions and OH^- ions in solution. The final color of the solution or the pH paper is matched with colors in a chart to find the pH, as shown in **Figure 17-10.**

INTEGRATION
Life Science

pH of Your Blood

Your blood circulates throughout your body carrying oxygen, removing carbon dioxide, and absorbing nutrients from food that you have eaten. In order to carry out its many functions properly, the pH of blood cannot be allowed to change significantly. Why is the pH of blood affected so little by most foods? Some compounds in blood, called buffers, enable small amounts of acids or bases to be absorbed without harmful effects. Buffers are acids, bases, and salts that react with additional acids or bases to minimize their effects. Buffers help keep your blood close to a nearly constant pH of 7.4.

Section Wrap-up

Review

1. What determines the strength of an acid? A base?

2. How can you make a dilute solution of a strong acid? Include an example as part of your explanation.

3. **Think Critically:** What does the pH of each of the solutions indicate about the solution? Rainwater, 5.8; soda water, 3.0; drain cleaner, 14.0; seawater, 8.9; pure water, 7.0.

Science Journal

In your Science Journal, explain why a weak acid in solution has a higher pH than a strong acid of the same concentration.

Skill Builder
Concept Mapping

Make a concept map of pH values. Start with three boxes labeled *acidic, neutral,* and *basic* and indicate the pH range of each box. Below each box, give some examples of solutions that belong in each pH range. If you need help, refer to Concept Mapping in the **Skill Handbook.**

Activity 17-1

Strong and Weak Acids

When you read about the behavior of things as small as molecules, it is difficult to visualize what causes the behavior.

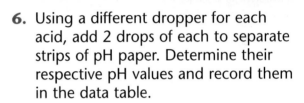

Problem

How can a model be made that represents the relative ionization abilities of weak and strong acids?

Materials

- typing paper (22 cm × 28 cm) marked with rectangles
- thick cardboard (22 cm × 28 cm) marked with rectangles
- scissors
- test tubes (2)
- droppers (2)
- graduated cylinder
- dilute hydrochloric acid (HCl)
- dilute acetic acid (CH₃COOH)
- pH paper
- timer, with second hand

Procedure

1. Prepare a data table like the one shown.
2. Mark your paper and cardboard with equal numbers of rectangles. Mark every other rectangle with a plus sign (+) to represent hydronium ions. Then mark the blank rectangles with a minus sign (−) to represent negative ions.
3. Cut the typing paper into as many rectangles as possible in 10 seconds.
4. Repeat step 3 with the piece of cardboard.
5. Obtain 2 mL each of dilute HCl and dilute CH₃COOH in test tubes. **CAUTION:** *Handle these acids with care. Avoid direct contact. Report any spills immediately.*

6. Using a different dropper for each acid, add 2 drops of each to separate strips of pH paper. Determine their respective pH values and record them in the data table.

Analyze

1. Which was easier to separate into ions, the typing paper or the cardboard?
2. Which acid separated into ions most easily? How do you know?

Conclude and Apply

3. Which acid is stronger, HCl or CH₃COOH? How do you know?
4. Which represents the stronger acid, the typing paper or the cardboard? Explain.
5. **Infer** which has the stronger bonds between fibers, the typing paper or the cardboard. Explain.
6. **Predict** which acids have stronger bonds within their molecules, strong acids or weak acids. Explain.

Data and Observations

____ ions removed from typing paper	____ pH of HCl solution
____ ions removed from cardboard	____ pH of acetic acid solution

ISSUE:

17•3 Acid Rain

Science Words

acid rain
plankton

Objectives

- Use pH units to define *acid rain*.
- Describe the factors contributing to the formation of acid rain.
- Discuss the effects of acid rain, and evaluate methods of controlling this problem.

Figure 17-11

Many industrialized countries use coal as their main source of energy. As coal burns, so does the sulfur that it contains.

A The sulfur dioxide oxidizes and combines with moisture in the air to form sulfuric acid droplets. In addition, nitrogen oxide from automobile exhaust combines with moisture in the air to make dilute solutions of nitric acid.

How can rain be an acid?

Popping up umbrellas, grabbing raincoats, and running for shelter are all common occurrences when a rainstorm approaches. We all seek protection from an uncomfortable drenching. However, rain may be causing more problems for us than getting damp. Unpolluted rain typically has a pH value of 5.6, which is slightly acidic, but not harmful. However, what happens if the pH drops below that level?

If rain in your location has a pH of 4.6, just one unit lower than normal rain, that may not sound like a problem. However, the math used in the pH scale reveals that 4.6 is ten times more acidic than 5.6. Any rain that is below 5.6 is considered **acid rain.** Although acid rain has been documented since the 1870s near large cities in England, only since the 1970s have people in North America become concerned about the causes. **Figure 17-11** illustrates the process that makes acid rain.

Come in Out of the Rain

What could be some of the effects of rain that is more than 100 times more acidic than normal rain? As seen in the chapter opening photograph, acid rain can dissolve marble buildings and statues. Some of the effects are not as easy to notice. Among the first organisms to suffer are plankton. **Plankton** are aquatic plants and animals that form the base of the food chain for small fish. As plankton die, the fish that feed on them eventually feel the effects. If soil near a polluted area becomes more acidic, nutrients and metals may dissolve away. These become unavailable for proper plant growth. These effects are now being noticed in some forest areas.

2 Points of View

No Easy Solutions

Preventing sulfur oxides and nitrogen oxides from reaching the atmosphere is expensive. Chemical attachments, called scrubbers, on smokestacks reduce the amount of these gases. However, power companies would pass the cost to consumers. Using nuclear fuel also would result in less sulfur oxides. However, do we want a nuclear waste problem? Exhaust from automobiles contributes to the formation of acid rain. Are we willing to give up the convenience of personal automobiles to lower acid rain levels?

Pay Now or Pay Later

Reversing the effects of acid rain is already costing nations tens of millions of dollars. Developing cleaner fuel technology must be a research priority in order to save soils, lakes, and crops for the future. Air pollutants released in one country drift to distant environments. International agreements about emissions would help reduce the overall level of pollutants that later contribute to acid rain.

C The acid rain then falls and begins to deteriorate buildings and pollute water.

B This sequence of reactions shows one process by which acid rain forms.

$$S(cr) + O_2(g) \longrightarrow SO_2(g)$$
from burning coal containing sulfur

$$2SO_2(g) + O_2(g) \longrightarrow 2SO_3(g)$$
converting to sulfur trioxide

$$SO_3(g) + H_2O(l) \longrightarrow H_2SO_4(aq)$$
dissolving sulfur trioxide to form sulfuric acid

Section Wrap-up

Review

1. How low must the pH level of rain drop before most scientists classify it as acid rain?

2. What are the steps in burning coal that can lead to the formation of acid rain?

Explore the Issue

If your community passed a law to reduce sulfur emissions, which method would you prefer? Would you pay to install a scrubber? Or, would you reduce the use of electricity, thereby reducing the need to burn as much sulfur-containing coal?

SCIENCE & SOCIETY

17•4 Acids, Bases, and Salts

Objectives

- Describe a neutralization reaction.
- Explain what a salt is and how salts form.
- Differentiate between soaps and detergents.
- Explain how esters are made and what they are used for.

Neutralization

You have probably seen television commercials for antacids that describe how effectively these products neutralize excess stomach acid. Would the pH of such a product be higher or lower than 7? If you answered higher, you are correct. Only a base can neutralize an acid.

Neutralization is a chemical reaction between an acid and a base. During a neutralization reaction, hydronium ions from the acid combine with hydroxide ions from the base to produce water.

$$H_3O^+(aq) + OH^-(aq) \rightarrow 2H_2O(l)$$

As the reactive hydronium and hydroxide ions combine to form water, the acidic and basic properties of the reactants are canceled, or neutralized.

The equation above accounts for only half of the ions present in the solution. What happens to the remaining ions? They react to form a salt. A **salt** is a compound formed when the negative ions from an acid combine with the positive ions from a base.

Neutralization reactions are ionic. The following equations show what happens to all of the ions during a neutralization reaction.

$$H_2O(l) + HCl(aq) + NaOH(aq) \rightarrow$$

$$H_3O^+(aq) + Cl^-(aq) + Na^+(aq) + OH^-(aq)$$

Water Formation: $H_3O^+(aq) + OH^-(aq) \rightarrow 2H_2O(l)$

Salt Formation: $Na^+(aq) + Cl^-(aq) \rightarrow NaCl(cr)^*$

*Note: The formation of crystalline NaCl occurs only if the water is removed by boiling or evaporation.

Salts

Many substances that you come in contact with every day are salts. Of course, the most familiar salt is sodium chloride—common table salt. **Table 17-4** on page 482 contains information about some common salts. As the table shows, most salts are composed of a metal and a nonmetal other than oxygen, or a metal and a polyatomic ion. Ammonium salts contain the polyatomic ammonium ion, NH_4^+, rather than a metal. Salts also form when acids react with metals. Hydrogen gas is released during such reactions.

Acid + Metal →
              Salt + Hydrogen

$$H_2SO_4(aq) + Zn(cr) \rightarrow$$
$$ZnSO_4(aq) + H_2(g)$$

$$6HCl(aq) + 2Fe(cr) \rightarrow$$
$$2FeCl_3(aq) + 3H_2(g)$$

Reactions between metals and acids are single-displacement reactions in which the metal displaces hydrogen from the acid.

Titration

It is sometimes necessary to find the concentration of an acidic or basic solution. This can be accomplished by titration. **Titration** is the process in which a solution of known concentration is used to determine the concentration of another solution. **Figure 17-12** on page 482 shows a titration experiment.

In a titration, a solution of known concentration, called the standard solution, is added to a solution of unknown concentration to which an indicator has been added. If the solution of

Problem Solving

An Upsetting Situation

Most of us have, at some time, experienced an upset stomach. Often, the cause is the presence of excess acid within our stomach. For digestive purposes, our stomachs contain dilute hydrochloric acid. A doctor might recommend an antacid treatment for an upset stomach. What type of compound would be "anti acid"?

You have learned that neutralization reactions change acids and bases into salts. The ingredients of antacids typically contain small amounts of $Ca(OH)_2$, $Al(OH)_3$, or $NaHCO_3$, which are bases. While an excess acid condition lowers the pH of your stomach contents, these compounds raise the pH.

Solve the Problem:
1. **What compounds would be produced from a reaction of HCl and $Ca(OH)_2$?**
2. **Why is it important for there to be some acid in your stomach?**

Think Critically:
If you wanted to know which antacid could neutralize the most acid, you could ask your teacher to help you set up a test. How would you know when the acid in a sample was neutralized? What could you do to make your comparison a fair test?

Stomach Acid	Common Antacid Bases	
HCl +	$Ca(OH)_2$ $Al(OH)_3$ $NaHCO_3$	→ NEUTRALIZATION

Table 17-4

Some Common Salts			
Name	**Formula**	**Common Name**	**Uses**
Sodium chloride	$NaCl$	Salt	Food preparation; manufacture of chemicals
Sodium hydrogen carbonate	$NaHCO_3$	Sodium hydrogen carbonate (baking soda)	Food preparation
Calcium carbonate	$CaCO_3$	Calcite (chalk)	Manufacture of paint and rubber tires
Potassium nitrate	KNO_3	Saltpeter	In fertilizers; manufacture of explosives
Potassium carbonate	K_2CO_3	Potash	Manufacture of soap and glass
Sodium phosphate	Na_3PO_4	TSP	In detergents
Ammonium chloride	NH_4Cl	Sal ammoniac	In dry cells

unknown concentration is a base, a standard acid solution is used. If the unknown is an acid, a standard base solution is used.

The Endpoint Has a Color

As an example, assume that you need to find the concentration of an acid solution. First, you would add a few drops of phenolphthalein indicator to a carefully measured amount of this solution. Phenolphthalein is colorless in an acid, but is pink in a base.

A standard base solution is added to this acid. At some point, one drop of the base just begins to turn the acid solution pink. This is known as the endpoint of the titration. The volume of the base used to neutralize the known volume of acid is determined, and the concentration of the acid can be calculated.

Figure 17-12

This apparatus is used for titration experiments. *How would you calculate how much standard solution you had added?*

Soaps and Detergents

Soaps are organic salts. Soaps are made by reacting fats or oils with sodium hydroxide or potassium hydroxide. One formula for soap made using sodium hydroxide is $C_{17}H_{35}COONa$. The structural formula for this soap is provided below.

$$H-\underset{\overset{|}{H}}{\overset{\overset{H}{|}}{C}}-\underset{\overset{|}{H}}{\overset{\overset{H}{|}}{C}}-\underset{\overset{|}{H}}{\overset{\overset{H}{|}}{C}}-\underset{\overset{|}{H}}{\overset{\overset{H}{|}}{C}}-\underset{\overset{|}{H}}{\overset{\overset{H}{|}}{C}}-\underset{\overset{|}{H}}{\overset{\overset{H}{|}}{C}}-\underset{\overset{|}{H}}{\overset{\overset{H}{|}}{C}}-\underset{\overset{|}{H}}{\overset{\overset{H}{|}}{C}}-\underset{\overset{|}{H}}{\overset{\overset{H}{|}}{C}}-\underset{\overset{|}{H}}{\overset{\overset{H}{|}}{C}}-\underset{\overset{|}{H}}{\overset{\overset{H}{|}}{C}}-\underset{\overset{|}{H}}{\overset{\overset{H}{|}}{C}}-\underset{\overset{|}{H}}{\overset{\overset{H}{|}}{C}}-\underset{\overset{|}{H}}{\overset{\overset{H}{|}}{C}}-\underset{\overset{|}{H}}{\overset{\overset{H}{|}}{C}}-\underset{\overset{|}{H}}{\overset{\overset{H}{|}}{C}}-\underset{\overset{|}{H}}{\overset{\overset{H}{|}}{C}}-COONa$$

A soap made using potassium hydroxide might have the formula $C_{15}H_{31}COOK$. Below is the structural formula for this soap.

$$H-\underset{\overset{|}{H}}{\overset{\overset{H}{|}}{C}}-\underset{\overset{|}{H}}{\overset{\overset{H}{|}}{C}}-\underset{\overset{|}{H}}{\overset{\overset{H}{|}}{C}}-\underset{\overset{|}{H}}{\overset{\overset{H}{|}}{C}}-\underset{\overset{|}{H}}{\overset{\overset{H}{|}}{C}}-\underset{\overset{|}{H}}{\overset{\overset{H}{|}}{C}}-\underset{\overset{|}{H}}{\overset{\overset{H}{|}}{C}}-\underset{\overset{|}{H}}{\overset{\overset{H}{|}}{C}}-\underset{\overset{|}{H}}{\overset{\overset{H}{|}}{C}}-\underset{\overset{|}{H}}{\overset{\overset{H}{|}}{C}}-\underset{\overset{|}{H}}{\overset{\overset{H}{|}}{C}}-\underset{\overset{|}{H}}{\overset{\overset{H}{|}}{C}}-\underset{\overset{|}{H}}{\overset{\overset{H}{|}}{C}}-\underset{\overset{|}{H}}{\overset{\overset{H}{|}}{C}}-\underset{\overset{|}{H}}{\overset{\overset{H}{|}}{C}}-COOK$$

Sodium hydroxide produces solid soaps. Potassium hydroxide makes liquid soaps. Another product of this reaction is glycerin, a softening agent in hand creams.

The process of making soap is called **saponification.** **Figure 17-13** shows how soap works to clean your hands.

Detergents are organic salts having structures similar to those of soaps. The most common detergent in use today has the structural formula shown on page 484.

Figure 17-13

Soap helps the grease and oil on your hands mix with water so they can be carried away when you rinse your hands.

A Soaps have a long, nonpolar hydrocarbon structure like a tail, and an ionic head.

nonpolar hydrocarbon tail   ionic head

water molecules

oil molecules

B Grease and oil on your skin are nonpolar hydrocarbons that do not easily mix with polar water.

C The nonpolar tail of soap molecules can easily mix with the nonpolar grease and oil molecules, while the ionic head interacts with water.

Like soap, the negative ions of detergents have a nonpolar hydrocarbon tail and an ionic head. Detergents enhance the cleaning action of water.

When soap is used in hard water, it forms soap scum. Hard water contains ions of calcium, magnesium, and iron that react with the soap to form a precipitate. Detergents do not form this scum. Therefore, most laundry products are detergents, not soaps.

Organic Acids and Esters

An **ester** is an organic compound formed by the reaction of an organic acid with an alcohol. The reaction requires a compound that will catalyze the formation of a molecule of water from the organic acid and alcohol. Concentrated sulfuric acid, a powerful dehydrating agent, is often present for the organic reaction to take place. **Figure 17-14** shows the reaction of acetic acid and methyl alcohol to produce an ester—methyl acetate—and water.

Esters are responsible for the many wonderful odors and flavors of flowers, fruits, and other foods. Sometimes, esters are added to gelatin desserts or candy to give the characteristic flavors of strawberry, banana, or apple.

acetic acid   methanol

Figure 17-14

This structural equation shows the formation of an ester.

methyl acetate
(an ester)

MiniLAB

How can fruit juices be tested for ascorbic acid, vitamin C?

Procedure
1. Measure 10 mL of each juice sample.
2. Add a pea-sized sample of cornstarch to each sample.
3. Using a pipet or dropper, carefully add 1 drop of iodine solution to each sample and stir. Add one more drop and stir. **CAUTION:** *Do not allow any contact with iodine.*

Analysis
1. Iodine reacts with both cornstarch and ascorbic acid. Iodine will react first with ascorbic acid. When iodine and cornstarch react, a dark color appears. How can you tell which of your samples contains the most ascorbic acid?
2. What common arrangement of carbon, oxygen, and hydrogen atoms would you expect to find in ascorbic acid?

Synthetic fibers known as polyesters are made from an organic acid that has two –COOH groups and an alcohol that has two –OH groups. Because the two compounds form long chains with the ester linkage, a polymer results. This is shown in **Figure 17-15.**

organic acid   alcohol

polymer (1 unit)   water

Figure 17-15

Polymers of this type are important to the textile industry today. Check a label on a piece of clothing you are wearing. *What percent of the garment is polyester?*

Section Wrap-up

Review

1. What is a neutralization reaction? What are the products of such reactions?

2. When doing laundry, what advantage does using a detergent have over using a soap?

3. **Think Critically:** Give the names and formulas of the salt that will form in these neutralizations:

   a. hydrochloric acid and calcium hydroxide

   b. nitric acid and potassium hydroxide

   c. carbonic acid and aluminum hydroxide

Skill Builder
Interpreting Data

Three salts—calcium sulfate, sodium chloride, and potassium nitrate—were obtained in reactions of the acid-base pairs shown here. Match each salt with the acid-base pair that produced it. If you need help, refer to Interpreting Data in the **Skill Handbook.**

$HCl + NaOH$ $HNO_3 + KOH$ $H_2SO_4 + Ca(OH)_2$

Science Journal

In political and labor disputes, a mediator is often called in to bring opposing sides together. In your Science Journal, explain how soap could be thought of as a mediator for cleaning grease.

Activity 17-2

Design Your Own Experiment
Be a Soda Scientist

Carbonated soft drinks contain carbonic acid and sometimes phosphoric acid. You have learned that bases can neutralize acids. Using a proper indicator and a base solution, how could you compare the acidity levels in soft drinks?

PREPARATION

Problem
How can the acidity level of soft drinks be effectively compared?

Form a Hypothesis
Based on observations about acids and bases, develop a hypothesis about how neutralization reactions can be used to rank the acidity of soft drinks.

Objectives
- Observe evidence of a neutralization reaction using an indicator.
- Compare the acidity levels in soft drinks.
- Design an experiment that uses the independent variable of acid content of soft drinks, and the dependent variable of amount of base added to the soft drinks, to determine the acidity of the drinks.

Possible Materials
- 2 different colorless soft drinks
- 2 test tubes
- graduated cylinder
- 2 droppers
- 1% phenolphthalein indicator solution
- dilute NaOH solution

Safety Precautions

Sodium hydroxide is caustic. Wear safety eye protection and avoid any skin contact with the solution.

PLAN THE EXPERIMENT

1. As a group, agree upon and write out the hypothesis statement.
2. As a group, in a logical manner, list the specific steps that you will use to test your hypothesis.
3. Make a list of all the materials that you will need to test your hypothesis.
4. Design a data table in your Science Journal that will allow you to record the amount of NaOH required to neutralize each soda sample.

Check the Plan
1. Did you control the amount of soda to be tested in each trial?
2. Is it important to repeat each trial?

3. Will you be able to test only colorless solutions with this procedure?
4. *Make sure your teacher approves your plan and that you have included any suggested changes.*

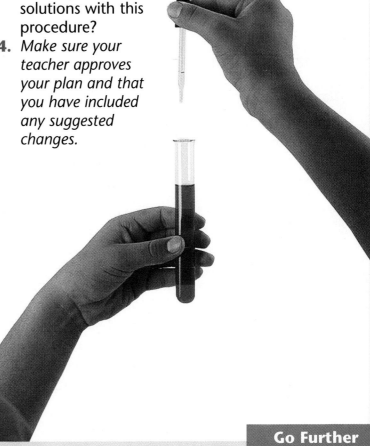

DO THE EXPERIMENT

1. What color change does phenolphthalein undergo in a solution that changes from an acid pH to a basic pH?
2. While the experiment is going on, write down any observations that you make and complete the data table in your Science Journal.

Analyze and Apply
1. **Compare** your soda acid rankings with other class groups.
2. Can your rankings be compared if other groups used a different amount of soda from your group?

Go Further

Dissolving CO_2 in water causes the formation of carbonic acid in soda. At warmer temperatures, less CO_2 dissolves. How would comparing the acidity of two sodas stored at different temperatures affect the validity of the comparison?

People and Science

DENNIS ABRAHAMSON, *Paper Mill Technical Director*

On the Job

Q What is your job at the paper mill?

A I'm responsible for environmental compliance, which includes testing for pH, conductivity, and total dissolved solids in the wastewater produced in papermaking.

Q How does pH affect paper?

A Neutral or slightly alkaline paper can last for hundreds of years. Traditionally, paper is manufactured under acid conditions, with a pH of 4.5 to 5.0. It's the residual acid in the sheet that eventually causes it to break down. Of course, many kinds of paper, like newsprint, don't need to last a long time.

Q How has paper manufacturing changed during your career?

A Today, most paper is made from recycled materials because of state and federal mandates. The only nonrecycled paper is for uses that require very white paper, such as art books, and may have a brightness reflectance of up to 96. Newly fallen snow probably registers at 100. Paper mills make white paper that is anywhere from 78 to 96 on the scale.

Personal Insights

Q Are there new materials for paper?

A I've seen some samples made from kenaf, a type of hibiscus plant. Our company also consults with artists who make handmade artistic and ornate paper. The Japanese make paper out of rice.

Q How did you get interested in the paper business?

A My college major was forest science, and we took a field trip to a paper mill. I guess I was impressed by the immensity of the equipment. Our company's paper machine is comparatively small, at about 10 feet wide and 300-400 feet long, but it turns out over 100 tons of paper each day.

Career Connection

Contact your state's department of natural resources and ask about careers having to do with paper production or environmental management. Make a poster detailing the career options and the education requirements for each career. Start with:

- **Environmental Engineer**
- **Forest Scientist**

Summary

17-1: Acids and Bases

1. An acid is a substance that produces hydrogen ions, H^+, in solution. A base produces hydroxide ions, OH^-, in solution.
2. Properties of acids and bases are due, in part, to the presence of the H^+ and OH^- ions.
3. Common acids include hydrochloric acid, sulfuric acid, nitric acid, and phosphoric acid. Common bases include sodium hydroxide, calcium hydroxide, and ammonia.
4. Acidic solutions form when certain polar compounds ionize as they dissolve in water. Except for ammonia, basic solutions form when certain ionic compounds dissociate upon dissolving in water.

17-2: Strength of Acids and Bases

1. The strength of an acid or base is determined by how easily it forms ions when in solution.
2. Strength and concentration are not the same thing. Concentration involves the relative amounts of solvent and solute in a solution.
3. pH is a measure of the hydronium ion concentration of a solution.
4. For acidic solutions of equal concentration, the stronger the acid, the lower its pH; for basic solutions of equal concentration, the stronger the base, the higher the pH.

17-3: Science and Society: Acid Rain

1. Acid rain is produced by substances in the air reacting with rainwater to make it acidic. Acid rain production is increased by the release of certain oxides into the air when fossil fuels are burned.

2. Acid rain is harmful to plants and animals and increases the rate of weathering.

17-4: Acids, Bases, and Salts

1. In a neutralization reaction, the H_3O^+ ions from an acid react with the OH^- ions from a base to produce water molecules. The products of neutralization are a salt plus water.
2. Salts form by negative ions from an acid combining with the positive ions from a base.
3. Soaps and detergents are organic salts. Unlike soaps, detergents do not react with compounds in hard water to form scum deposits.
4. Esters are organic compounds formed by the reaction of an organic acid and an alcohol.

Key Science Words

a. acid
b. acid rain
c. base
d. dehydrating agent
e. detergent
f. ester
g. hydronium ion
h. indicator
i. neutralization
j. pH
k. pickling
l. plankton
m. salt
n. saponification
o. soap
p. strong acid
q. strong base
r. titration
s. weak acid
t. weak base

Chapter 17 Review

Reviewing Vocabulary

Match each phrase with the correct term from the list of Key Science Words.

1. a hydrogen ion bonded to a water molecule
2. a reaction between an acid and a base
3. acid that ionizes completely in solution
4. base that partly dissociates in solution
5. can remove water from materials
6. formed by negative ions from an acid combining with positive ions from a base
7. process that removes impurities from metal surfaces
8. measures the concentration of H_3O^+ ions
9. any solution that has a pH less than 7
10. the process of making soap

Checking Concepts

Choose the word or phrase that completes the sentence.

1. Solutions of equal concentrations of HCl and CH_3COOH _____.
   a. will not have the same pH
   b. will react the same with metals
   c. will make the same salts
   d. will have the same amount of ionization
2. Sulfuric acid is also known as _____.
   a. battery acid   c. stomach acid
   b. citric acid   d. vinegar
3. Most sulfuric acid is used to produce _____.
   a. batteries   c. petroleum products
   b. fertilizer   d. plastics
4. _____ is used to make phosphoric, nitric, and hydrochloric acids.
   a. Dehydration   c. Pickling
   b. A base   d. Sulfuric acid
5. The most widely used base is _____.
   a. ammonia   c. lye
   b. caustic lime   d. milk of magnesia
6. Carrots have a pH of 5.0, so carrots are _____.
   a. acidic   c. neutral
   b. basic   d. an indicator

7. Pure water has a pH of _____.
   a. 0   b. 5.2   c. 7   d. 14
8. Certain materials can act as indicators because they change _____.
   a. acidity   c. concentration
   b. color   d. taste
9. KBr is an example of a(n) _____.
   a. acid   c. indicator
   b. base   d. salt
10. You might use a solution of _____ to titrate an oxalic acid solution.
    a. HBr   c. NaOH
    b. $Ca(NO_3)_2$ d. NH_4Cl

Understanding Concepts

Answer the following questions in your Science Journal using complete sentences.

11. When hydrogen chloride, HCl, is dissolved in water to form hydrochloric acid, what happens to the HCl?
12. Explain how the hydroxide ion differs from the –OH group in an alcohol.
13. Why is ammonia considered a base, even though it contains no hydroxide ions?
14. Explain why a concentrated acid is not necessarily a strong acid.
15. Ashes from a wood fire are basic. Explain how early settlers used this fact when making soap.

Thinking Critically

16. Explain why you should never use taste to test for an acid, even though acetic, citric, and dilute phosphoric acids are in things you eat and drink.
17. How would the pH of a dilute solution of HCl compare with the pH of a concentrated solution of the same acid? Explain.
18. Acid rain containing sulfuric acid, H_2SO_4, will react with iron objects. What products will result from this reaction?

19. Chalk, $CaCO_3$, is a salt. What acid and what base react to form this salt?

20. Suppose you have hard water in your home. Would you use a soap or a detergent for washing your clothes and dishes? Explain your answer.

Developing Skills

If you need help, refer to the **Skill Handbook.**

21. Making and Using Tables: Make a table that lists the chemical and physical properties of acids and bases.

22. Recognizing Cause and Effect: Complete the table below by describing the cause and effect of each change listed in the left-hand column.

23. Comparing and Contrasting: Compare and contrast the reactions that would be produced by pouring sulfuric acid on a piece of paper and burning a marshmallow.

24. Observing and Inferring: You have equal amounts of three colorless liquids: A, B, and C. You add several drops of phenolphthalein to each liquid. A and B remain colorless, but C turns pink. Next, you add some of liquid C to liquid A and the pink color disappears. You add the rest of C to liquid B and the mixture remains pink. What can you infer about each of these liquids? Which liquid probably has a pH of 7?

25. Interpreting Data: A soil test indicates that the pH of the soil in a field is 4.8. To neutralize the soil, would you add a substance containing H_3PO_4 or one containing $Ca(OH)_2$? Explain your answer.

Performance Assessment

1. Display: Make a display and write a report about common household acids and bases, how they are used, and cautions to be taken.

2. Lab Report: Do research to find out how acids are used in making fertilizer. Name several acids and tell why each is needed and how their proportions may vary from fertilizer to fertilizer. Conduct an investigation by growing seedlings using different fertilizers. Describe your results in a report.

3. Analyzing the Data: In Activity 17-2 on pages 486 and 487, you neutralized an unknown acid solution with a basic solution. If you found that 1 mL of the NaOH would neutralize 5 mL of the carbonated beverage, which is more concentrated, the acid or the base? Explain in your Science Journal.

Chemical Changes

Process	Cause	Effect
Saponification		
Esterification		
Acid rain		
Neutralization		
Corrosion		

Enzymes: Your Body's Catalysts

As you read this, think of the last meal that you ate. The meal may have included some foods that are similar in makeup, such as bread and potatoes. It may have included some foods that are quite different, such as meat and vegetables. How is your body able to break down such different, complex food materials into simple, useful products that your body can use? The chemicals responsible for this relatively quick process are produced by your body and are called enzymes. Enzymes are part of a broader classification of chemicals called catalysts.

A Catalyzed Reaction

Enzymes are typically named after a specific reaction and given an *-ase* ending. For example, *protease* refers to enzymes that break down proteins. Proteases are found in some fresh fruits. Meat-tenderizing products also contain proteases.

Purpose
In this project, investigate the ways in which catalysts change reaction rates. You will find out more about the importance of these interesting chemicals that bring about change without being permanently changed themselves.

Procedure

1. Using the printed instructions on the box, prepare a gelatin dessert and divide it into five samples.

2. Place a piece of freshly cut kiwi fruit on the first sample, freshly cut pineapple on the second, canned pineapple on the third, some meat tenderizer on the fourth, and use the other sample as a control.

3. After one hour, examine the gelatin to note any changes near the fruits and tenderizer areas.

4. As the protein in the gelatin breaks down, water from the gelatin is released. Make a chart showing the degree of protein breakdown in each sample.

5. Which of your samples showed the most protein breakdown in one hour? What could cause canned and fresh pineapple to have different results? What are the general breakdown products of proteins?

Using Your Research

Do other fruits contain protease enzymes? Design a testing procedure to determine the relative levels of protease in fruits supplied by classmates.

Go Further

Just as opening a lock is most effectively done with a specific key, enzymes are able to effectively change the rate of specific reactions. In fact, the fit between a lock and key is often used as a model to explain enzyme activity.

Model Molecule

You can illustrate an enzyme model by cutting the shapes shown below from a piece of poster board.

A and B represent two molecules that will react when the two dotted areas are close. That particular positioning takes place more quickly when the enzyme molecule is present. The enzyme enables A and B to fit together. Once A and B are attached to the enzyme, the dots are aligned and A attaches to B. The enzyme then releases and is free to attach to other A and B molecules.

UNIT
6

494

Waves, Light, and Sound

What's Happening Here?

Perhaps you have been to a concert or play that used light for unusual effects. The combination of special sound and lighting is often used to enhance entertainment. In fact, most human communication makes use of light or sound in some way. How does a spoken comment actually reach another person? What happens to light when it shines through a prism? Light and sound both travel in the form of waves. In addition to communication and entertainment, waves are used for many other purposes. How do you think light is being used in the small photo above?

Science Journal

You are probably most familiar with lasers as part of a light show during a concert or some other entertainment, but lasers have many other uses. Research the different uses for lasers and write a report in your Science Journal.

Previewing the Chapter

Waves and Sound

Music can be made in a variety of different ways: plucking the strings on a guitar, blowing air into a flute or oboe, beating the membrane on a drum, or even pushing air through your own vocal chords. All of these are ways to vibrate air, creating sound waves.

EXPLORE ACTIVITY

Making Music with a Ruler

1. Hold one end of a thin metal, plastic, or wood ruler firmly down on the edge of a desk, allowing the free end to extend beyond the desk.
2. Gently pull up on and release the free end of the ruler. What do you see and hear?
3. Move the ruler to allow more or less length to hang over the edge and repeat the experiment several times. Do you hear different sounds?

Observe: How does the length of ruler extending beyond the table affect the sound you hear? In your Science Journal, write a paragraph about how the ruler could be moved to play a musical scale. Try tuning the ruler to a piano and writing a few measures of music. Then let someone play the tune using the ruler.

Previewing Science Skills

▶ In the Skill Builders, you will **map concepts, recognize cause and effect,** and **compare and contrast.**

▶ In the Activities, you will **observe, measure,** and **define operationally.**

▶ In the MiniLABs, you will **observe, interpret,** and **compare.**

18●1 Characteristics of Waves

Objectives

- Sketch a transverse wave and identify its characteristics.
- Discuss the relationship between the frequency and wavelength in a transverse wave.
- Using the relationship among wavelength, frequency, and velocity, find one variable when two are given.

What are waves?

What examples come to mind when you think of waves? Do water waves, microwaves, sound waves, and radio waves have anything in common with each other? These and all other types of waves transfer energy from one place to another.

Look at **Figure 18-1.** Water waves are probably the easiest type of wave to visualize. If you've been in a boat on a lake, you know that approaching waves bump against the boat but do not carry the boat along with them as they pass. The boat mostly moves up and down as the waves pass by. Only energy carried by the waves moves forward.

Waves are rhythmic disturbances that carry energy through matter or space. Water waves transfer energy through the water. Earthquakes transfer energy in powerful waves that travel through Earth. Both types of waves travel through a **medium,** a material through which a wave transfers energy. This medium may be a solid, a liquid, a gas, or a combination of these. Radio waves and light waves, however, are types of waves that can travel without a medium.

Figure 18-1

Waves transfer energy. The energy of a water wave does work on anything in its path. *What instances have you seen that indicated that waves have done work?*

Transverse Waves

Two types of waves carry energy. These are transverse and compressional waves. In one type, a **transverse wave,** the medium moves at right angles to the direction the wave travels. **Figure 18-2** shows how you can make transverse waves by shaking the end of a rope up and down while your friend holds one end. Compressional waves will be described in the next section.

Measuring Transverse Waves

The transverse wave in **Figure 18-2** can be described by its characteristics. When you snap the rope up and down, you may notice that high points and low points form. The highest points of a wave are called the **crests,** and the lowest points are called the **troughs.** Waves are measured by their wavelength. **Wavelength** is the distance between a point on one wave and the identical point on the next wave, such as from crest to crest or trough to trough. The wavelength between two crests is labeled on **Figure 18-2.**

Ocean or lake waves can be described by how high they appear above the normal water level. **Amplitude** is the distance from the crest (or trough) of a wave to the rest position of the medium, as shown in **Figure 18-2.** The amplitude corresponds to the amount of energy carried by the wave. Waves that carry great amounts of energy have large heights or amplitudes, and waves that carry less energy have smaller amplitudes.

CONNECT TO

EARTH SCIENCE

Earthquakes and volcanic activity under the ocean floor can cause giant tidal waves. *Research* what these waves are called and why they are so dangerous.

Figure 18-2

The parts of a transverse wave are shown on the wave in this rope. *How could you measure the wavelength on other parts of the wave?*

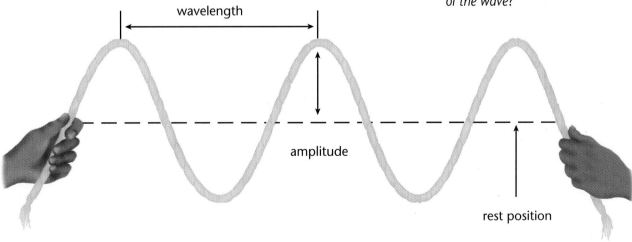

wavelength

amplitude

rest position

Wave Frequency

Do you know the frequency of your favorite radio station? When you tune your radio to a station, you are actually looking for waves of a certain frequency. The **frequency** of a wave

Figure 18-3

How do the waves shown on this drawing compare? Wave **A** has a longer wavelength and a lower frequency than wave **B**. The speed of the wave is the same for both waves because wave speed is determined by the medium.

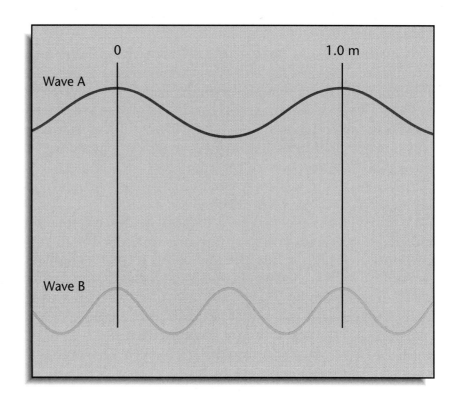

MiniLAB

How do different transverse waves compare?

Procedure
1. On your paper, draw a transverse wave with at least three complete wavelengths.
2. Label one wavelength, the amplitude, a crest, and a trough on your wave. Use a ruler to measure the wavelength and the amplitude to the nearest tenth of a centimeter.
3. In groups of four, compare your wave sketches.
4. In your group, rank your waves from longest to shortest wavelength and then from largest to smallest amplitude.

Analysis
1. How were your waves similar? How did they differ?
2. Assume all of your waves traveled at the same speed of 20 cm/s. Count the number of complete waves in a 20-cm stretch of your wave to determine its frequency.
3. Identify the waves in your group with the highest and lowest frequency.

is the number of wave crests that pass one place each second. Frequency is expressed in hertz (Hz). One hertz is the same as one wave per second.

How do you increase the frequency of a wave? To do this with a rope, simply move the rope up and down faster to create more crests per second. Because the speed of a wave in a given medium is constant and does not depend on the wavelength or frequency, as the frequency increases, the wavelength becomes shorter. In other words, as the frequency increases, the wavelength decreases. Using a rope, you can demonstrate this principle, as shown in **Figure 18-3.**

Wave Velocity

Sometimes you may want to know how fast a wave is traveling. For example, earthquakes below the ocean can produce giant waves. You will want to know how soon such a wave will reach you and whether you need to seek shelter. Wave velocity, v, describes how fast the wave moves forward.

Wave velocity can be determined by multiplying the wavelength and frequency as shown below. Wavelength is represented by the Greek letter *lambda*, λ. If you know any two variables in the following equation, you can find the remaining unknown variable.

$$velocity = wavelength \times frequency$$

$$v = \lambda \times f$$

The following examples show how you can use this equation to solve for the unknown variable. Rewrite the equation to make the desired quantity the unknown.

USING MATH

Calculating the Velocity of a Wave

Example Problem:

A wave is generated in a wave pool at a water amusement park. The wavelength is 3.2 m. The frequency of the wave is 0.60 Hz. What is the velocity of the wave?
1. What is known?   wavelength, λ = 3.2 m
                       frequency, f = 0.60 Hz

Strategy Hint: Another way to express hertz is 1/second, therefore, m × 1/s = m/s.
2. What is unknown?   velocity, v
3. Choose the equation. $v = \lambda \times f$

Solution: 3.2 m × 0.60 Hz = 1.92 m/s

Practice Problems

1. A wave moving along a rope has a wavelength of 1.2 m and a frequency of 4.5 Hz. How fast is the wave traveling along the rope?
2. An ocean wave has a length of 10.0 m. Two waves pass a fixed point every 1.0 s. What is the speed of the wave?

Strategy Hint: Make sure all units correspond.

Calculating the Frequency of a Wave

Example Problem:

Earthquakes can produce three types of waves. One of these is a transverse wave called an S wave. A typical S wave travels at 5000 m/s. Its wavelength is about 417 m. What is its frequency?
1. What is known?   velocity, v = 5000 m/s
                       wavelength, λ = 417 m

Strategy Hint: Remember, Hz = 1/s, so m/s ÷ m = 1/s = 1 Hz.
2. What is unknown?   frequency, f
3. Choose the equation. $v = \lambda \times f$ so $f = v/\lambda$

Solution: f = (5000 m/s)/(417 m) = 12 Hz

Practice Problem

A tuning fork produces a sound wave with a wavelength of 0.20 m and a velocity of 25.6 m/s. What is the frequency of the tuning fork?

Strategy Hint: What formula do you use to find frequency?

Design Your Own Experiment
Making Waves

All waves carry energy from one place to another. How can you make waves in a spiral spring? What happens to these waves when they hit a solid barrier? In this activity, you will create waves in a spiral spring and observe the characteristics of the waves.

PREPARATION

Problem
Which wave quantities can you influence when making transverse waves in a spiral spring? How does a transverse wave in a spring behave when it hits an immovable barrier?

Form a Hypothesis
State a hypothesis concerning the expected behavior of the spring in the situations described above.

Objectives
- Design an experiment to test the behavior of transverse waves in a spiral spring.

- Observe what happens to a transverse wave when it hits a fixed boundary.

Possible Materials
- coiled, spiral spring
- meterstick
- stopwatch

Safety Precautions
Use caution with possible sharp ends of the springs. Do not twist or stretch the spiral springs.

PLAN THE EXPERIMENT

1. As a group, agree upon and write out your hypothesis statements.
2. List the steps you will take to test your hypothesis. Be specific in your directions for each step.
3. Collect all materials you will need. Design a data table in your Science Journal if needed.

Check the Plan

1. Two people in your group should be seated on a smooth floor with the spring stretched between them. Decide who will be the wave maker. The other person will hold his or her end as still as possible.

2. The wave maker should start by quickly shaking the end of the spring horizontally about 30 cm to create a single transverse wave pulse. How else could you make a transverse wave?
3. How will you attempt to change the amplitude of the wave?
4. How will you shake one end to experiment with the relationship between wave frequency and wavelength?
5. *Make sure your teacher approves your plan and that you have included any changes suggested in the plan.*

DO THE EXPERIMENT

1. Carry out the experiment as planned.
2. During the experiment, write down any observations that you make in your Science Journal.

Analyze and Apply

1. How did you change the amplitude of the wave? Did the amplitude stay the same as the pulse traveled along the spring? Explain why or why not.
2. **Predict** what happens when the wave hits the fixed boundary.
3. **Infer** how you can make waves of greater frequency. **Compare** frequency and wavelength.

Go Further

Can you make a different kind of wave by pushing the spring straight forward and back, rather than moving it side to side or up and down? Does this kind of wave seem to have an amplitude or a wavelength? What happens when you push it to compress it with more force and speed? You will learn more about this type of wave in the next section.

Figure 18-4

Earth experiences hundreds of earthquakes in a typical day, but most are too small to be easily noticed. An earthquake measuring 7.1 on the Richter scale shook northern California on October 17, 1989, collapsing this highway in Oakland. Every increase of 1 on the Richter scale represents an increase by a factor of 10 in amplitude.

Section Wrap-up

Review

1. Sketch a transverse wave and label a crest, a trough, a wavelength, and the amplitude.

2. What is the relationship between the frequency and wavelength of a water wave?

3. A wave travels at a velocity of 4.0 m/s and has a frequency of 3.5 Hz. What is the wavelength?

4. **Think Critically:** You learned in Chapter 5 that gravity causes a pendulum to oscillate. How is its motion similar to that of a transverse wave?

Skill Builder
Comparing and Contrasting

Use **Figure 18-2** and information from this section to compare the frequency, amplitude, and wavelength of a wave. Which of these measurements depends on energy? Which is measured in meters? Which depends on the number of waves? If you need help, refer to Comparing and Contrasting in the **Skill Handbook.**

USING MATH

FM radio stations use frequencies in the megahertz (MHz) range. Your favorite radio station is at 104.1 MHz and your friend prefers a station at 101.9 MHz. Calculate whose station uses longer wavelengths. Explain your answer.

The Nature of Sound

What causes sound?

Think of all the sounds you've heard since you awoke this morning. Did you hear a blaring alarm, honking horns, human voices, or lockers slamming? Your ears allow you to recognize these different sounds, but do you know what they all have in common? These sounds are all produced by the vibrations of objects. For example, your voice is produced by the vibrations of your own vocal cords. The energy produced by these vibrations is carried to your friends' ears by sound waves.

Compressional Waves

The waves discussed in the last section were described as transverse waves because the matter moved at right angles to the direction the wave was traveling. You could produce this type of wave in a rope or spring by moving one end from side to side or up and down. Sound waves carry energy by a different type of wave motion. You can model sound waves with a coil spring. If you hold one end of a spring, squeeze the coils together, and then release the coils while holding the end of the spring, you will produce a compressional wave. Matter vibrates in the same direction as the wave travels in a **compressional wave. Figure 18-5** shows how a compressional wave made with a spring should look.

Science Words

Define

compressional wave
pitch
intensity
loudness

Objectives

- Describe the transmission of sound through a medium.
- Recognize the relationships between intensity and loudness and frequency and pitch.
- Illustrate the Doppler effect with a practical example.

Figure 18-5

In compressional waves, the medium is displaced in the same direction as the energy is moving. Practice creating compressional waves with a spring.

How is sound different when it travels through solids?

Procedure
1. Tie a metal object, such as a wire hanger or a spoon, to the center of a piece of string.
2. Wrap each of the two ends of the string around one finger on each hand.
3. Gently place the fingers holding the string in your ears. Let the object swing until it bumps against the edge of a chair or table and listen to the sound.
4. Listen to the sound made by the collisions when your fingers are not in your ears.

Analysis
1. Compare the sounds you hear when your fingers are and are not in your ears. Do sounds travel better through air or through the string?

Describing Compressional Waves

Notice in **Figure 18-5** that as the wave moves, some of the coils are squeezed together, just as you squeezed the ones on the end of the spring. This crowded area is called a *compression*. The compressed area then expands, spreading the coils apart and creating a less dense area. This less dense area of the wave is called a *rarefaction*. Does the whole spring move forward? Tie a piece of string onto one of the coils and observe its motion. The string moves back and forth with the coils. Therefore, the matter in the medium does not move forward with the wave. Instead, the wave carries only the energy forward.

Recall that transverse waves have wavelengths, frequencies, amplitudes, and velocities. Compressional waves also have these characteristics. A wavelength in a compressional wave is made of one compression and one rarefaction, as shown in **Figure 18-6.** Notice that one wavelength is the distance between two compressions or two rarefactions of the same wave. The frequency is the number of compressions that pass a place each second. If you could repeatedly squeeze and release the end of the spring two times each second, you would produce a wave with a frequency of 2 Hz. The amount of compression is like the amplitude of the transverse wave, and it depends on the energy content of the wave. Think about what you would do to increase the amount of compression in the coil spring. You would have to squeeze harder, and you would be putting more energy into the wave.

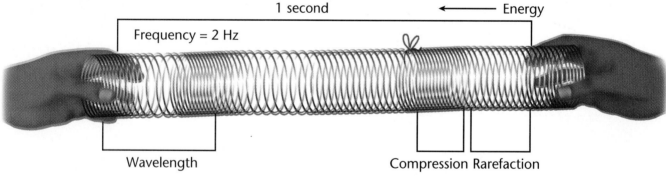

1 second   ← Energy

Frequency = 2 Hz

Wavelength   Compression Rarefaction

Figure 18-6

The spring vibrates back and forth, but the energy of this compressional wave moves forward. *How could you measure the wavelength of a compressional wave?*

Moving Through Media

How does sound travel when you have a conversation with a friend? The vibrations generated by your vocal cords produce compressional waves that travel through the air to your friend. This process is similar to what you saw when you made compressional waves on a spring. Your voice causes compressions and rarefactions among the particles in the air.

Comparing Media: Solids, Liquids, and Gases

The speed of sound waves depends on two things—the medium through which the waves travel and the temperature of the medium. Air is the most common medium through which you hear sound waves, such as the sounds of the porpoise in **Figure 18-7.** Sound waves, however, can be transmitted through any type of matter. Liquids and solids are even better conductors of sound than air is because the individual particles in a liquid or solid have greater influence on each other than the particles in air, making the transmission of energy easier. Can sound be transmitted if there is no matter to form a medium? Astronauts on the moon would find it impossible to talk to each other without the aid of modern electronic communication systems. Because the moon has no atmosphere, there is no air to compress and expand.

The Speed of Sound

The temperature of the medium is also an important factor in determining the speed of sound waves. As the temperature of a substance increases, the molecules move faster and, therefore, collide more frequently. This increase in molecular collisions transfers more energy in a shorter amount of time. This allows the sound waves to be transmitted faster. Sound travels through air at 344 m/s if the temperature is 20°C, but at only 332 m/s when the temperature is 0°C.

Have you seen fireworks explode in the sky before you heard the boom? The speed of sound is much slower than the speed of light. Have you ever tried to guess how far away a lightning bolt is by counting the time interval between when you see a lightning flash and when you hear the thunder? You see the light before you hear the sound because light waves travel through air about 1 million times faster than sound waves do.

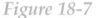

Figure 18-7

Porpoises communicate with each other vocally. *Does the sound of this porpoise's voice travel slower in air or water?*

INTEGRATION
Life Science

Human Hearing

Think of the last conversation you had with a friend. How were you able to understand what your friend was saying? It is amazing that compressional waves caused by speech, music, or other sounds around us can be turned into meaningful sounds by our sense of hearing. Making sense of these waves involves three stages: the gathering and amplification of the compressional waves by the ear mechanism, the conversion of these waves into nerve impulses, and the decoding of these signals in the brain.

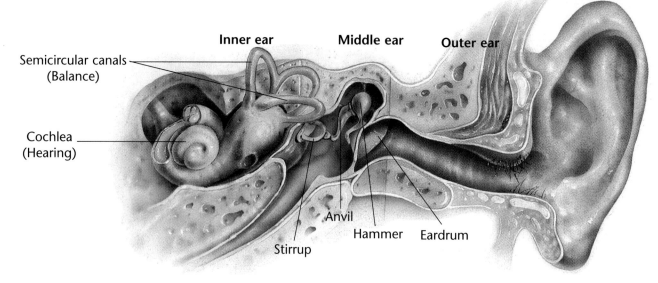

Inner ear   Middle ear   Outer ear

Semicircular canals
(Balance)

Cochlea
(Hearing)

Anvil

Hammer   Eardrum

Stirrup

Figure 18-8

The human ear is made up of the outer ear, the middle ear, and the inner ear. *Which parts vibrate and multiply the force and pressure of the sound waves?*

CONNECT TO

PHYSICS

You have just formed a new company, Ultrasonics Unlimited. **Design** an advertisement for a product that uses ultrasonic energy.

The Ear as a Sound Detector

Sound detectors, such as microphones, collect and convert kinetic energy from the moving particles in sound waves into another form of energy, usually electrical energy. Your ear is a versatile sound detector. It is sensitive to a range of intensities and frequencies. The human ear, seen in **Figure 18-8,** has three sections: the outer ear, the middle ear, and the inner ear.

Although you probably think of your ear as the fleshy, visible outer part, this part contributes little to your hearing abilities. It helps direct sound waves into the ear canal, which is a little narrower than your index finger and is 2-3 cm long. It leads to the eardrum, which is a tough membrane about 0.1 mm thick that is vibrated by incoming sound waves. The eardrum vibrates three tiny bones in the middle ear: the hammer, the anvil, and the stirrup. These bones, which are full adult size at birth, make a lever system that multiplies the force and pressure of the sound wave.

They transmit the sound vibrations to the oval window in the inner ear. The inner ear contains the liquid-filled, spiral-shaped cochlea. Tiny hair cells in the cochlea are vibrated, causing nerve impulses to be sent to the brain through the auditory nerve. Hearing damage inflicted by sudden or ongoing loud sounds is generally the result of destruction of these tiny, hair-like cells. Do you like to listen to your music loud? Remember, intense sounds can result in permanent hearing damage.

Frequency and Pitch

If you have ever taken a music class, you are probably familiar with the scale "do re mi fa so la ti do." As you sing this scale, your voice starts low and becomes higher with each note. You hear a change in pitch. **Pitch** is the highness or lowness of a sound. The pitch you hear depends on the frequency of the sound waves. The higher the frequency is, the higher the pitch is, and the lower the frequency is, the lower the pitch is. A healthy human ear can hear sound frequencies from about 20 Hz to 20 000 Hz. As people age, they often have some trouble hearing high frequencies.

Ultrasonic and Infrasonic Waves

Most people can't hear sound frequencies above 20 000 Hz, which are called ultrasonic waves. Bats, however, can detect frequencies as high as 100 000 Hz. Ultrasonic waves are used in sonar as well as in medical diagnosis and treatment. Sonar, or sound navigation ranging, is a method of using sound waves to estimate the size, shape, and depth of underwater objects. Infrasonic, or subsonic, waves have frequencies below 20 Hz. These are produced by sources such as heavy machinery and thunder. Although you probably can't hear them, you may have sensed these sound waves as a disturbing rumble inside of your body.

USING TECHNOLOGY

Searching with Sound

More than 130 years ago, a ship named the *Central America* disappeared in a hurricane off the coast of South Carolina. In its hold lay three tons of newly minted gold coins and bars worth more than $560 million in the current market. How would you find such a vessel?

The wrecked ship was located under 2800 m of water using advanced sonar technology. In sonar techniques, a sound pulse is emitted toward the bottom of the ocean. The sound travels through the water and is reflected when it encounters solid barriers. When this time interval and the speed of sound in water are both known, the distance to the barrier or object can be calculated. Ultrasound frequencies are typically used because they provide better resolution of small details. Sonar can locate an object as small as a book at a depth of 7000 m!

In addition to locating sunken ships, sonar technology has made it possible to map geologic features on the bottom of the ocean, to locate reefs, and to monitor the location of submarines. Sonar is commonly used in commercial fishing to locate schools of fish.

Think Critically:

How do you think sonar technology might be useful in locating deposits of oil and mineral resources?

Sonar image of a sunken ship

Intensity and Loudness

Have you ever been told to turn down your CD player? If so, you probably adjusted the volume. The music still had the same notes, so the frequencies didn't change, but the amplitude of each sound wave was reduced. The **intensity** of a sound wave depends on the amount of energy in each wave. This, in turn, corresponds to the wave's amplitude. Intensity of a sound wave increases as its amplitude increases.

Sensing Loudness

Loudness is the human perception of sound intensity. The higher the intensity and amplitude, the louder the sound. People vary in sensitivity to different frequencies. What seems loud to one person may not seem loud to you. The intensity level of a sound is measured in units called decibels, abbreviated *dB*. On this scale, the faintest sound that can be heard by most humans is 0 dB. Sounds with intensity levels above 120 dB may cause pain and permanent hearing loss.

Table 18-1

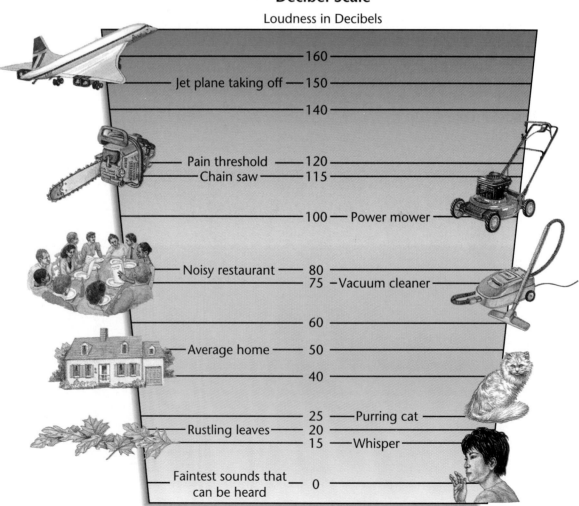

Decibel Scale

Loudness in Decibels

	160
Jet plane taking off	150
	140
Pain threshold	120
Chain saw	115
	100 — Power mower
Noisy restaurant	80
	75 — Vacuum cleaner
	60
Average home	50
	40
	25 — Purring cat
Rustling leaves	20
	15 — Whisper
Faintest sounds that can be heard	0

Figure 18-9

The pitch of the emergency vehicle's siren is higher when the vehicle is approaching because the wave crests are closer together. *Why does the sound have a lower pitch after the vehicle has passed?*

Sounds at this intensity level occur during some rock concerts. **Table 18-1** shows some familiar sounds and their intensity levels in decibels.

The Doppler Effect

Imagine the sound you hear when an emergency vehicle with its siren on rapidly approaches and then passes you. As the truck is moving toward you, the pitch of the siren sounds higher than it would if the truck were not moving. Each wave crest forms an expanding circle around the spot where it started. See crests **A** and **B** in **Figure 18-9.** By the time crest **B** left the siren, the truck has moved forward causing crest **B** to be closer to crest **A** in front of the truck. The result is a higher frequency and pitch in front of the moving truck. This change in wave frequency due to a moving wave source is called the Doppler effect. You can also see from **Figure 18-9** that the frequency is lower in the area behind the moving truck.

What would you expect would happen if you were moving past a stationary sound source? Suppose you were riding a school bus and passed by a building with a ringing alarm bell. The pitch would sound higher as you approached the building and lower as you rode away from it. The Doppler effect is observed when the source of sound is moving relative to the observer.

Look at **Figure 18-10.** Think again of the alarm clock that woke you up this morning. Can you describe how the rhythmic vibrations of the clock produced compressional waves in the air?

The sound waves carried energy to your ears through a series of compressions and rarefactions of air molecules. If your clock gives off high-frequency vibrations, you hear a high pitch. The more intense the waves, or the more energy they carry, the louder your clock sounds.

Figure 18-10

When the alarm clock starts to ring in the morning, it makes compressional waves in the air that are interpreted by your ears as sound.

Section Wrap-up

Review

1. What type of waves are sound waves, and how do they transfer energy?

2. While watching a "Star Trek" rerun, you hear the roaring approach of another ship in space. Is this possible? Explain.

3. While on your way to school, you turn up the volume on the car radio. Which of the following quantities change as a result: velocity of sound, intensity, pitch, amplitude, frequency, wavelength, loudness?

4. **Think Critically:** A bat in a dark cave sends out a high-frequency sound wave and detects an increase in frequency after the sound reflects off the prey. Describe the possible motions of the bat and the prey.

Skill Builder
Concept Mapping
Prepare a concept map that shows the series of events that occur to produce sound. Include the terms *rarefaction*, *vibration*, and *compression*. If you need help, refer to Concept Mapping in the **Skill Handbook.**

Using Computers

Word Processors Use a word processor to make an outline showing the characteristics of transverse and compressional waves.

Activity 18-2

Frequency of Sound Waves

Sounds originate with a vibration. Sometimes this vibration also causes nearby objects to vibrate, or resonate, at the same frequency. Many musical instruments make use of a column of air that vibrates at a certain frequency. How is pitch controlled in instruments such as trumpets? By closing and opening specific valves, the length of the air column, the wavelength, and the frequency are changed.

Problem
Can you find the wavelength and frequency of the sound made in an open-ended pipe?

Materials
- rubber band
- metric ruler
- plastic pipe (open at both ends)

Procedure
1. Measure the length of the pipe and record it on the data table.
2. Stretch a rubber band across one open end of the pipe and hold it firmly in place as shown. **CAUTION:** *Be careful not to release your grip on the ends of the rubber band.*
3. Hold the rubber band close to your ear and pluck it. Listen for a *double* note.
4. Slowly relax the tightness of the rubber band. Listen for one part of the double note to change and the other part to remain the same.
5. Continue to adjust the tightness until you hear only one note.
6. Exchange pipes with another group and repeat the experiment.

Analyze
1. The wavelength you obtained in step 5 is twice the length of the pipe. **Calculate** the wavelength.
2. Assume the velocity of sound to be 34 400 cm/s. Use the equation frequency = velocity/wavelength to **calculate** the frequency of the note.
3. What were the wavelength and frequency of the sound waves in the second pipe?

Conclude and Apply
4. How does the length of a pipe **compare** with the frequency and wavelength of the sound it can make?
5. A pipe organ uses pipes of different lengths to produce various notes. **List** other musical instruments that use lengths of pipe to produce musical notes.

Data and Observations
Sound Frequencies Produced by Open Pipes

Length of pipe	Length of wave	Frequency of sound

TECHNOLOGY:
18●3 Using Sound Advice in Medicine

Science Words

ultrasonic technology

Objectives

• Explain how sound waves can be used to create images of organs inside the body.

• Describe some of the uses of ultrasound technology in medicine.

Ultrasonic Technology

Can you think of ways a doctor could check the function of organs or other tissue inside your body? You might think of stethoscopes, X rays, or even surgical methods, but did you think of using sound waves to create images? In the last section, you learned how sonar techniques can help oceanographers in exploring ocean depths. Sound can also be used to aid medical professionals in "seeing" inside your body without surgery or using the ionizing radiation found in X rays.

Ultrasonic technology is used for a wide variety of purposes. Recall that *ultrasonic* refers to sound waves of frequencies greater than 20 000 Hz, above which most humans cannot hear. Jewelers use ultrasonic sound to remove stubborn deposits from jewelry, and chemists sometimes use ultrasonic baths to clean glassware. Medical professionals use high-frequency sound waves to interact with tissue inside the body, **Figure 18-11.**

Seeing with Sound

How can we see with sound? Medical ultrasound technologists use a special probe to send high-frequency sound waves into a specific part of the body. These sound waves reflect off of the targeted organs or tissues and are used to produce electrical signals. A computer program converts these electrical signals into video images. Trained physicians can use these images to detect potential problems without invasive surgery.

Probably the best-known use of ultrasound in medicine is to monitor the development of a fetus in a woman's uterus. This procedure produces a sonogram. An image of a fetus from a sonogram is shown in **Figure 18-12.** Ultrasound is commonly

Figure 18-11

A technician applies an ultrasonic probe to the surface of a patient's body. The sound waves bounce off of structures inside the body and are converted to images on a monitor.

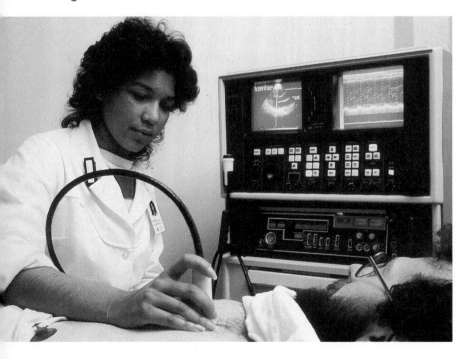

used to examine a variety of abdominal organs, including the liver, pancreas, gallbladder, and spleen. Physicians can also use ultrasound Doppler shifts with cardiac patients to gather information about blood flow.

Preventing Surgery with Ultrasound

Sometimes small, hard deposits of calcium oxalate form in the kidneys. Surgical removal of kidney stones used to be the primary treatment option, but ultrasonic treatments create vibrations that can often break up the stones without surgery. The smaller pieces can then be naturally passed with urine. A similar treatment is available for gallstones. Patients successfully receiving ultrasound treatment make a quicker recovery than those who required surgical treatment.

Figure 18-12

A sonogram of a developing fetus helps doctors check on the progress of the pregnancy. *What are some advantages of ultrasound testing?*

Section Wrap-up

Review

1. Describe at least three uses of ultrasonic technology in medicine.

2. How can images of an organ in your body be created from sound waves?

Explore the Technology

Suppose a family member has been diagnosed with a kidney stone large enough to require treatment. Why should ultrasonic treatment be considered? If possible in this case, why would ultrasonic treatment be a better option than surgery? Try to think of as many factors as possible.

Science Journal

Ultrasound gives doctors and parents a first view of a baby. In your Science Journal, list some things you think might be learned from a sonogram and write a short paragraph about how parents might feel on first seeing their baby.

SCIENCE & SOCIETY

18•4 Music to Your Ears

Science Words

music
noise
resonance
quality
interference
reverberation
acoustics

Objectives

- Distinguish between music and noise.
- Describe why different instruments produce sounds of different quality.
- Explain two types of wave interference.

What is music?

Has anyone ever commented that the music you were listening to sounded like a jumble of noise? Both music and noise are caused by vibrations, but there are some important differences. You can easily make a noise by just speaking a word or tapping a pencil on a desk, but it takes some deliberate actions to create music. Of course, you also may be able to create music with your voice or your pencil if you try. **Music** is created using specific pitches and sound quality and by following a regular pattern. The most common kind of sound is **noise,** which has no set pattern and no definite pitch. If all the frequencies of noise are present in equal amplitude, the result is called white noise. White noise has been found to have a relaxing effect and is sometimes used by dentists or to help people sleep. **Figure 18-13** shows a comparison of noise and music patterns.

Natural Frequencies

A stringed musical instrument, such as a guitar, generates a sound when you pluck a string. Because the ends of the string are fastened, the waves created reflect back and forth between the ends. This causes the string to vibrate at its natural frequency. Most objects have a natural frequency of vibration.

What kind of sound would be produced if you held a guitar string tightly between your hands while a friend plucked it? It would be much quieter than if the string were fixed on a guitar because the guitar frame and the air inside the instrument absorb energy from the vibrating string. The vibration of the guitar and the air inside it is called a forced vibration, and this makes the sound of the string louder.

Figure 18-13

Music and pushing a chair across a floor both generate sound waves. *How do the waveforms representing music and noise differ?*

Musical sound

Noise

If the sound that reaches an object is at the same frequency as the natural frequency of the object, the object will begin to vibrate at this frequency. This type of vibration is called **resonance.**

Musical Sounds

If you were to play a note of the same pitch and loudness on a flute and on a piano, the sound wouldn't be the same. These instruments have a different quality of sound. This quality does not refer to how good or bad the instrument sounds. Sound **quality** describes the differences among sounds of the same pitch and loudness. All sounds are produced by vibrations of matter, but most objects vibrate at more than one frequency. Distinct sounds from musical instruments are produced by different combinations of these wave frequencies. The patterns of frequencies of three different instruments are shown in **Figure 18-14.**

Overtones Cause Unique Quality

Imagine producing a tone by plucking a guitar string. The tone produced when the string vibrates along its entire length is called the fundamental frequency. At the same time, each half-length of the string can vibrate on its own.

Figure 18-14

A violin, clarinet, and piano have a characteristic pattern of frequencies. *Which instrument has more higher-pitched sounds for a given note?*

Problem Solving

The Mysterious Bouncing Bridge

You have learned that resonance is important in amplifying sounds made in musical instruments. Resonance was also blamed in the destruction of this bridge on November 7, 1940, shortly after it was completed.

The Tacoma Narrows Bridge, in the state of Washington, was a large suspension bridge constructed largely of steel and concrete. In a storm with gusty winds, the bridge began to oscillate in a wavelike pattern. Over several hours, the amplitude of the waving bridge increased and it finally collapsed. What do you think caused the bridge to vibrate at its natural frequency?

Solve the Problem:
1. What is resonance?
2. What might have produced the force that caused the bridge to vibrate on this day?

Think Critically:
How do you think engineers could prevent something like this from happening again?

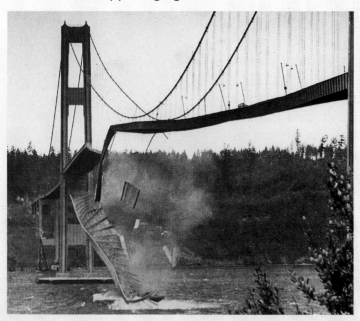

This produces the first overtone. Its frequency is twice the fundamental frequency. Overtones have frequencies that are multiples of the fundamental frequency. The intensity and number of overtones vary with each instrument to form a distinct quality of sound. **Figure 18-15** illustrates the fundamental frequency and the first three overtones of a guitar string.

Music is written and played based on a musical scale of eight notes. Each note has a characteristic frequency, and all eight notes span a frequency range called an octave. The highest note in an octave has exactly twice the frequency of the lowest note in that octave.

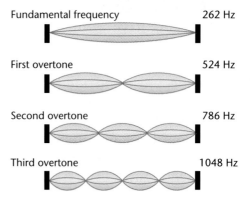

Fundamental frequency	262 Hz
First overtone	524 Hz
Second overtone	786 Hz
Third overtone	1048 Hz

Figure 18-15

A guitar string can vibrate in different ways to produce overtones, giving it a unique sound quality. *How is its sound different from a piano?*

Interference

In a band performance, you may have heard several instruments playing the same notes at the same time. What is the purpose of having more than one instrument creating the same sound? The waves are combining to form a new wave. **Interference** is the ability of two or more waves to combine and form a new wave. Because the musicians are simultaneously playing the same note, their compressions overlap to form a greater compression. As a result, the music sounds much louder. Constructive interference occurs when the compressions of different waves arrive at the same place at the same time.

Figure 18-16

Two or more waves can interfere and add together to produce a new wave.

A In constructive interference, the sound compressions overlap to produce a louder sound.

B In destructive interference, the compressions and rarefactions combine to cancel the sound waves.

C Two slightly different frequencies will result in alternating constructive and destructive interference. This results in a pattern of increases and decreases in sound intensity called beats. *How could beats be used to tune orchestra instruments?*

Sometimes the compression of one wave will arrive with the rarefaction of another wave. They cancel each other, resulting in a decrease in loudness. This is an example of destructive interference.

Destructive Interference

If a tuning fork with a frequency corresponding to A at 440 Hz is used to tune a piano, the piano frequency of A should blend perfectly with the tuning fork. If the piano produces a slightly different frequency from A, the compressions from the fork can't continue to arrive at the same time as the compressions from the piano. The musician will hear variations of sound intensity called beats. The sum of the amplitudes of the waves causes the loudness to regularly rise and fall. Have you ever heard two flutes play the same note when they weren't properly tuned? You could clearly hear the beats until the musicians correctly adjusted their instruments. **Figure 18-16** shows a comparison of the types of sound wave interference.

Mini LAB

How can a hearing loss change the sounds you hear?

Procedure

1. To simulate a hearing loss, tune a radio to a news or talk station. Turn the volume down to the lowest level you can hear and understand.
2. Turn the bass to maximum and the treble to minimum. If the radio does not have these controls, mask out the higher frequency sounds with heavy pads over your ears.
3. Observe which kinds of sounds are most difficult to hear and which are easiest to hear.

Analysis

1. Are high or low pitches harder to hear? Are men's or women's voices harder to understand?
2. Are vowel or consonant sounds more difficult to hear?
3. How could you help a person with a hearing loss understand what you say?

Acoustics

At a concert or school assembly where a speaker sound system is used, someone usually speaks into the microphone to test the system. Sometimes you hear the sound linger for a couple of seconds. Perhaps you hear echoes of the sound. The sound reaches your ears at different times because it has been reflected off different walls and objects around you. This effect produced by many reflections of sound is called **reverberation.**

Concert halls and theaters like the one shown in **Figure 18-17** are designed by scientists and engineers who specialize in **acoustics,** the study of sound. You will often see carpets

Figure 18-17

This auditorium has good acoustic properties. Its shape was carefully designed by acoustical engineers, and it has both hard and soft surfaces.

and draperies lining the walls of concert halls. Soft, porous materials and certain room shapes can reduce excess reverberation. An anechoic chamber, **Figure 18-18,** is designed to deaden all reverberations. Acoustic scientists also work on understanding human hearing and speaking processes.

Figure 18-18

An anechoic chamber is designed to eliminate nearly all reflection of sound. Such rooms are used for testing sound equipment.

Section Wrap-up

Review

1. Compare and contrast music and noise.

2. If you were to close your eyes and listen to middle C played both on a flute and on a cello, what musical property would enable you to distinguish one instrument from the other?

3. Explain the difference between constructive and destructive interference.

4. **Think Critically:** Intense, high-frequency sound can actually cause glass to shatter. What might be happening to the glass that causes it to break?

Skill Builder

Recognizing Cause and Effect

What is the effect when sound waves interact by constructive interference? Describe the cause-and-effect sequence for destructive interference. If you need help, refer to Recognizing Cause and Effect in the **Skill Handbook.**

Science Journal

It can be difficult to converse in a crowded room. In your Science Journal, write a paragraph explaining why it might be hard to distinguish the words from a nearby friend in such a situation.

Science & Literature

The Sound of Poetry

The sound of words is an essential part of literature in general and poetry in particular. All sounds start with an object vibrating. These vibrations cause compressional waves in a medium, usually air, that are interpreted by the ear as sound. It is the human brain that gives special meaning to certain sounds. Skilled poets choose words with sounds that help reinforce the meaning and the feeling of their poetry.

Sound Words

Onomatopoeia is the use of real or made-up words that mimic sounds, such as *buzz*, *hiss*, *rustle*, *sip*, and *snap*. See how poet Vachel Lindsay uses onomatopoeia in this section of "The Congo":

Beat an empty barrel with the handle of a broom
Hard as they were able,
Boom, boom, BOOM,
With the silk umbrella and the handle of a broom
Boomlay, boomlay, boomlay, BOOM.

The rhythm of the lines combined with the use of onomatopoeia gives life to Lindsay's poem.

Letter Power

Words with long vowels, such as *seamless* and *ooze*, take time to pronounce and slow down the pace of a poem. On the other hand, *-att-* in the middle of a word suggests quick, uncontrolled movement, as in *rattle*, *shatter*, *clatter*, and *splatter*. A final *-ck* can suggest movement that stops abruptly, as in *peck*, *hack*, and *flick*.

The sounds of certain letter combinations can foster visual and tactile images. For example, an initial blend *fl-* often suggests a quickly moving light, as in *flicker*, *flare*, and *flash*. The sensation of slippery wetness can enter a poem through words beginning with *sl-*, such as *slick*, *slide*—and *slippery*. The short *i* vowel can add a feeling of smallness, as in *thin*, *inch*, *little*, *chip*, and *sliver*.

While the physical characteristics of sound waves determine their loudness and pitch, carefully chosen combinations of sound help poets share their ideas with readers and listeners.

Science Journal

In your Science Journal, write a poem that uses onomatopoeia and/or the sound of words to reinforce the viewpoint, idea, or feeling you want to share.

Summary

18-1: Characteristics of Waves

1. In a transverse wave, the medium moves at right angles to the direction the wave travels.
2. If the speed of a wave remains constant, as the frequency increases, the wavelength decreases and vice versa.
3. The velocity of a wave is equal to its wavelength multiplied by its frequency.

18-2: The Nature of Sound

1. Sound begins as a vibration that is transferred through a medium in a series of compressions and rarefactions.
2. The pitch of a sound becomes higher as the frequency increases. Both amplitude and intensity increase as energy is added to a wave.
3. The Doppler effect is a change of frequency and pitch of a sound as a result of motion.

18-3: Science and Society: Using Sound Advice in Medicine

1. High-frequency sound waves can be used to generate images of tissue inside the body.
2. Ultrasonic technology has many uses, including sonar, cleaning jewelry and glassware, medical diagnosis, and medical treatment.

18-4: Music to Your Ears

1. Music is created using specific pitches, sound quality, and a pattern.
2. Sound quality describes the differences among sounds of the same pitch and loudness.
3. Interference is the ability of two or more waves to combine and form a new wave.

Key Science Words

a. acoustics
b. amplitude
c. compressional wave
d. crest
e. frequency
f. intensity
g. interference
h. loudness
i. medium
j. music
k. noise
l. pitch
m. quality
n. resonance
o. reverberation
p. transverse wave
q. trough
r. ultrasonic technology
s. wave
t. wavelength

Reviewing Vocabulary

Match each phrase with the correct term from the list of Key Science Words.

1. distance between identical points on two waves
2. using high-frequency sound waves
3. the study of sound
4. matter vibrates in the same direction as the wave travels
5. the highness or lowness of a sound
6. material through which a wave travels
7. expressed in hertz
8. the highest points of a transverse wave
9. distance from the rest position of a medium to the trough or crest of a wave
10. human perception of sound intensity

Chapter 18 Review

Checking Concepts

Choose the word or phrase that completes the sentence.

1. All waves carry _____ forward.
   a. matter   c. matter and energy
   b. energy   d. the medium
2. A wave that carries a large amount of energy will always have a _____.
   a. large amplitude   c. high frequency
   b. small amplitude   d. short wavelength
3. A sound with a low pitch always has a low _____.
   a. amplitude   c. wavelength
   b. frequency   d. wave velocity
4. As _____, sound intensity decreases.
   a. wave velocity decreases
   b. wavelength decreases
   c. quality decreases
   d. amplitude decreases
5. Sounds with the same pitch and loudness traveling in the same medium may differ in _____.
   a. frequency   c. quality
   b. amplitude   d. wavelength
6. Sound cannot travel through _____.
   a. solids   c. gases
   b. liquids   d. empty space
7. Variations in the loudness of sound that are caused by wave interference are called _____.
   a. beats   c. pitch
   b. standing waves d. forced vibrations
8. _____ is shown when a windowpane vibrates at the same frequency as a thunderclap.
   a. The Doppler effect
   b. Resonance
   c. Reverberation
   d. Destructive interference
9. Wave frequency is measured in _____.
   a. hertz   c. meters
   b. decibels   d. meters/second

10. When a sound source moves away from you, the sound's _____.
    a. velocity decreases
    b. loudness increases
    c. pitch decreases
    d. frequency increases

Understanding Concepts

Answer the following questions in your Science Journal using complete sentences.

11. Describe how amplitude, frequency, and wavelength are determined in transverse and compressional waves.
12. What do constructive interference, destructive interference, and the formation of beats have in common? How are they different?
13. Explain how different combinations of wave frequencies make a guitar and a trumpet sound different even when the same note is played.
14. In what ways can ultrasonic technology be used in medicine?
15. Why does the ringing of an alarm clock enclosed in an airtight container become softer as the air is drawn out of the container?

Thinking Critically

16. A wave has a wavelength of 6 m and a wave velocity of 420 m/s. What is its frequency?
17. A bus driver is rounding a curve approaching a railroad crossing. She hears a train's whistle and then hears the whistle's pitch become lower. What assumptions can she make about what she will see when she rounds the curve and looks at the crossing?
18. When a little boy blows a dog whistle, his dog comes, even though the boy can't hear the whistle. Explain why the boy can't hear the whistle, but his dog can.

19. An earthquake beneath the middle of the Pacific Ocean produces a tidal wave that hits a remote island. Is the water that hits the island the same water that was above the earthquake? Explain.

Developing Skills

If you need help, refer to the **Skill Handbook.**

20. Hypothesizing: Sound travels slower in air at high altitudes than at low altitudes. State a hypothesis to explain this observation.

21. Observing and Inferring: Infer the effect of increasing wave velocity on the wavelength of a compressional wave that has a constant frequency.

22. Concept Mapping: Design a concept map that shows the characteristics of compressional waves. Include the terms *pitch, compression, medium, rarefaction, speed, loudness, wavelength, frequency,* and *intensity*. Indicate how pitch and the loudness you hear in sound waves relate to these characteristics.

23. Using Numbers: Study the speed of sound for various materials at 25°C in the table below. Rank the materials from the fastest to slowest transmitter of sound waves. Approximately how many times faster does sound travel in steel compared to in air?

Sound Transmission

Substance	Speed of Sound 25°C
Air	347 m/s
Brick	3650 m/s
Cork	500 m/s
Water	1498 m/s
Steel	5200 m/s

24. Making and Using Tables: You have started a lawn-mowing business during summer vacation. Your family's power lawn mower has a sound level of 100 dB. Using the table below, determine how many hours a day you can safely work mowing lawns. If you want to work longer hours, what can you do to protect your hearing? If your family purchases a new lawn mower with a sound level of 95 dB, how will your business be affected?

Federally Recommended Noise Exposure Limits

Sound Level (decibels)	Time Permitted (hours per day)
90	8
95	4
100	2
105	1
110	0.5

Performance Assessment

1. Poster: In Activity 18-1 on pages 502-503, you observed some of the behaviors of transverse waves on a Slinky. Use the Slinky to create constructive and destructive interference by sending waves toward each other. Make a poster showing the spring before, during, and after the waves overlap.

2. Designing an Experiment: Try to use an empty cardboard paper-towel roll to repeat the procedure used in Activity 18-2 on page 513 to find the tube's natural frequency. Do you hear as clear a sound? Explain why or why not.

3. Project: Using materials you have at home, make a musical instrument. Play your instrument for your classmates and explain how you can change the pitch of your instrument.

Previewing the Chapter

Light

Light passing through a prism can produce exciting patterns of color. Imagine what your surroundings would look like now if humans could see only shades of gray, and not distinct colors. The ability to see color depends on the cells in your eyes that are sensitive to different wavelengths of light. What color is the light produced by a flashlight or the sun?

EXPLORE ACTIVITY

Find out how you can make a rainbow.

1. In a darkened room, shine a flashlight through a glass prism and try to project the resulting colors onto a white wall or ceiling.
2. In a darkened room, shine a flashlight over the surface of some water with dishwashing liquid bubbles in it. What do you see?
3. Aim a flashlight at the surface of a compact disc.

Observe: What did you see while aiming the white light of the flashlight at these three different materials? How did your observations differ? In your Science Journal, explain where you think the colors came from.

Previewing Science Skills

► In the Skill Builders, you will **observe and infer**, and **map concepts**.

► In the Activities, you will **observe, hypothesize, compare,** and **infer**.

► In the MiniLABs, you will **observe, interpret,** and **measure**.

19•1 Electromagnetic Radiation

Science Words

electromagnetic radiation
photon
radio wave
modulation
microwave
infrared radiation
visible radiation
ultraviolet radiation
X ray
gamma ray

Objectives

- Contrast electromagnetic waves with other kinds of waves.
- Describe the arrangement of electromagnetic waves on the electromagnetic spectrum.
- Explain at least one application of each type of electromagnetic wave.

The Electromagnetic Spectrum

Do you listen to the radio, watch television, play video games, or cook with a microwave oven? These devices all make use of different kinds of electromagnetic waves. Light, radio waves, and microwaves are all examples of electromagnetic waves.

Electromagnetic waves are transverse waves produced by the motion of electrically charged particles. We often call these waves **electromagnetic radiation** because they radiate from the particles. The transfer of energy by electromagnetic waves is called radiation. One way these waves differ from those you learned about in Chapter 18 is that electromagnetic waves do not need a medium to transfer energy. They can travel through a vacuum—empty space—at a speed of 300 000 km/s. The light from the stars in **Figure 19-1** is one type of electromagnetic wave. These waves travel slower when they pass through any type of matter, but they still travel much faster than sound or water waves.

Describing Electromagnetic Radiation

All electromagnetic waves travel at the same speed in a vacuum, but their frequencies and wavelengths may vary. The shorter the wavelength of a wave, the higher its frequency. **Figure 19-2** shows how electromagnetic waves are classified from low-frequency, long-wavelength radio waves to high-frequency, short-wavelength gamma rays according to their wavelengths on the *electromagnetic spectrum.*

Figure 19-1

Objects in outer space emit different types of electromagnetic radiation.

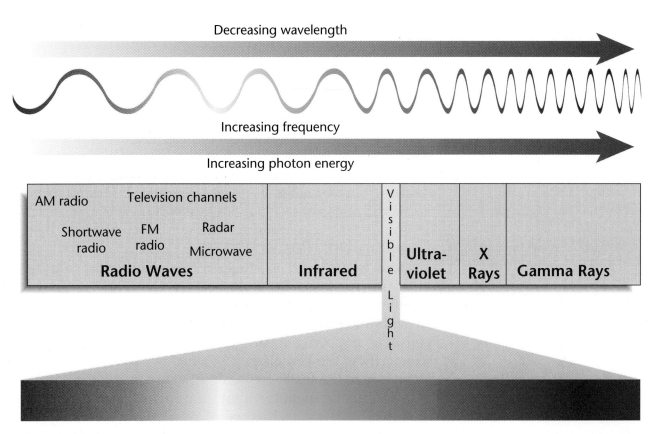

Figure 19-2

All electromagnetic waves are classified by their wavelengths on the electromagnetic spectrum.

Scientists have observed that radiation not only carries energy, but also has momentum. This means that electromagnetic radiation may have particlelike behavior as well as wavelike behavior. In 1905, Albert Einstein hypothesized that light is composed of tiny particles. These tiny, particle-like bundles of radiation are called **photons.** Photons with the highest energy correspond to light with the highest frequency. Very high-energy photons can actually damage matter, such as the cells in your body.

Figure 19-3

You use the tuner to select the station you want to hear. *What characteristic of the radio wave are you selecting?*

Radio Waves

When the listener in **Figure 19-3** tunes his radio to a station, he is actually adjusting it to respond to radio waves of a certain frequency. Even though radio waves are all around you right now, you can't sense them. **Radio waves** have long wavelengths and low frequencies. Thus, radio waves have the lowest photon energy. Locate radio waves on the electromagnetic spectrum in **Figure 19-2.**

In addition to radio communications, radio waves are used in television, cellular telephones, and cordless telephones. How is your voice transmitted by radio waves on a cordless telephone? The sound waves produced by your voice are changed to electrical currents that represent your speech patterns and pitches. These electrical currents are used to vary either the amplitudes or frequencies of radio waves that are transmitted from the handset to the base of the telephone. This process of varying radio waves is called **modulation.** Besides your voice, light images, computer information, and music can also be used to modulate radio waves.

Cooking with Radio Waves

Radio waves with the highest frequency and energy are called **microwaves.** They are used in communications, but, like the person in **Figure 19-4A,** you are probably most familiar with microwaves for their speedy cooking abilities. Have you ever popped popcorn in a microwave oven? Do you wonder how the kernels pop so quickly? Microwaves transfer energy to the water molecules that are inside the popcorn kernels, causing them to vibrate and rotate faster. As a result, the kinetic energy and temperature of the water molecules increase; the water inside the popcorn kernel turns to steam; and the kernel explodes due to the increased pressure built up by the steam. Containers made of glass, paper, and some plastics are used in microwave ovens because the microwaves pass through them easily and little energy is absorbed by the container. **Figure 19-4B** illustrates the operation of a microwave oven.

Figure 19-4

Conventional ovens heat food from the outside in. Microwave ovens heat the food molecules internally.

A The popcorn container absorbs very little energy so it remains cool enough to handle.

Microwaves   Fan   Microwave beam   Magnetron

Food

Turntable

B The spinning fan reflects microwaves onto the food from all directions inside the oven. This heats the food evenly.

Infrared Radiation

Do you like to nap outdoors on a hot summer day? Even with your eyes closed, you feel when clouds move in front of the sun. When the sunlight isn't blocked by the clouds, you feel its warmth on your skin. This warm feeling is caused by the infrared radiation from the sun. **Infrared radiation** has a wavelength slightly longer than visible light, as you can see by its location on the electromagnetic spectrum. Your skin feels warm because it is absorbing some of the infrared radiation from the sun. This causes the molecules in your skin to vibrate more, increasing their kinetic energy as well as your skin's temperature.

How We Use Infrared Radiation

Warm objects, such as your body, give off more infrared radiation than do cool objects. Some parts of your body are warmer than others and, as a result, give off or emit more infrared radiation. Measurement of the body's emission of infrared radiation helps doctors make some medical diagnoses. A thermogram, such as the one shown in **Figure 19-5A,** is produced by measuring the infrared radiation given off by different body parts. Tumors are sometimes detected in a thermogram because they are warmer than the healthy tissue around them.

If you live in a colder climate, an infrared photograph like the one in **Figure 19-5B** can show you where your house or apartment needs insulation. People using infrared-sensitive binoculars can see humans and animals in complete darkness. These binoculars detect infrared waves given off by warm bodies. Some home security systems are designed to detect objects giving off infrared radiation and to respond by activating a light or an alarm.

Figure 19-5

Temperature differences can be detected by devices that are sensitive to infrared radiation. Warmer areas show up as yellow, orange, and red. Cooler areas are green, blue, and black.

A A thermogram of a hand can help detect circulation problems. *Would the problem area show up as warmer or cooler than the other parts of your hand?*

B Heat loss in your home can be detected by infrared radiation.

Figure 19-6
You may have seen infrared lamps like these in restaurants, keeping food warm until it is served.

MiniLAB

Do lightbulbs waste energy?

Procedure

1. Obtain an incandescent bulb and a fluorescent bulb of identical wattage.
2. Make a heat collector by covering the top of a foam cup with a plastic food wrap to make a window. Carefully make a small hole (diameter less than the thermometer's) in the side of the cup. Push a thermometer through the hole while supporting the cup with your hand.
3. Measure the temperature of the air inside the cup. Then, hold the window of the tester 1 cm from one of the lights for 2 minutes and measure the temperature.
4. Cool the heat collector and thermometer. Repeat step 3 using the second type of bulb.

Analysis

1. What was the temperature inside the cup for each bulb?
2. Which bulb appears to give off more heat?

Because infrared radiation raises the temperature of matter, it can be used to warm and dry objects. Infrared lamps, like the ones shown in **Figure 19-6,** are used in some restaurants to keep cooked food hot until it is served. Some auto paint shops use infrared radiation to dry car finishes. Can you think of any other uses of this form of radiant energy?

Visible Radiation

Visible radiation, or light, is the only part of the electromagnetic spectrum you can see. Find visible radiation on the electromagnetic spectrum diagram in **Figure 19-2.** Notice that it covers a small range of the spectrum compared to the other types of radiation.

Hot objects, such as the sun, radiate a great deal of electromagnetic energy. Some of this energy is in the range of the electromagnetic spectrum that is visible to humans.

Light can cause chemical reactions to occur. It provides the energy for the process of photosynthesis in which green plants make their own food through a series of chemical reactions. Light also stimulates chemical reactions in your eyes that allow you to see. As you learned in Chapter 16, light can also stimulate decomposition reactions of materials such as hydrogen peroxide.

Ultraviolet Radiation

Why do you wear sunglasses or use sunscreen when you're in strong sunlight? These two products are designed to protect you from large doses of ultraviolet radiation. **Ultraviolet**

radiation has a higher frequency than visible light, so its photons are more energetic and have greater penetrating power than photons of visible light. Exposure to ultraviolet radiation enables the skin cells to produce vitamin D, which is needed for healthy bones and teeth. Ultraviolet lamps are used in hospitals to kill bacteria and viruses and to sterilize surgical instruments. However, overexposure to ultraviolet radiation kills healthy cells. Prolonged and frequent overexposure can lead to sagging, dry skin and even skin cancer. For this reason, it is important to use a sunscreen regularly if you spend a lot of time outdoors. Sunscreens, such as that being used in **Figure 19-7,** contain chemicals that absorb many of the ultraviolet rays before they penetrate your skin.

Ozone, a gaseous form of oxygen, is found in Earth's upper atmosphere and protects us by blocking most of the sun's ultraviolet radiation, as **Figure 19-8** illustrates. It is produced naturally through photochemical reactions and electric discharge reactions (such as lightning) in the atmosphere.

Figure 19-7

Tanning is the skin's method of trying to protect itself against ultraviolet radiation. Sunscreens provide additional protection.

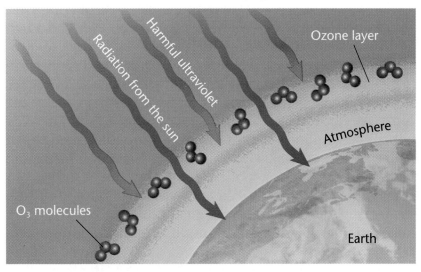

Figure 19-8

A layer of ozone molecules in Earth's atmosphere blocks most of the sun's ultraviolet rays. *Why should we be concerned if this layer gets thinner or develops holes?*

Ozone—Our Protector

Earth's atmosphere has a natural filter, ozone, that blocks most of the sun's ultraviolet rays. Ozone is a form of oxygen where three oxygen atoms combine to make each ozone molecule. A reduction in the amount of ozone in Earth's atmosphere results in an increase in the ultraviolet radiation reaching Earth's surface. Some chemicals break down ozone molecules. Use of some spray-can propellants and refrigerants containing these chemicals may be breaking down the ozone layer, so use of these compounds should be limited.

CONNECT TO

CHEMISTRY

In photosynthesis, chlorophyll in green plants absorbs sunlight to provide energy for chemical reactions that produce carbohydrates. In addition to providing food for plants, this reaction produces a chemical element that is important to humans. *Investigate* to find out what this product is.

Figure 19-9

Irradiated food has been treated with ultra-violet light to kill microorganisms.

On a more positive side, because ultraviolet rays can penetrate cells, they can be used to kill microorganisms in food and on hospital equipment. The label in **Figure 19-9** informs the customer that the food has been irradiated. Some minerals, such as fluorite and scheelite, become fluorescent when exposed to ultraviolet light. Fluorescence occurs when a material absorbs ultraviolet radiation and re-emits visible light.

X Rays and Gamma Rays

Your dentist uses X rays to examine the parts of your teeth that can't be seen in a visual inspection. If you ever had a bad fall, you probably had to have an X ray taken to check for broken bones. **X rays** have a shorter wavelength and higher frequency than ultraviolet radiation. X-ray photons carry higher energy and have a greater penetrating power than any of the forms of electromagnetic radiation discussed so far. This higher energy allows X rays to travel through some types of matter, such as your skin and muscles. When X rays hit a more dense material, such as tooth or bone, they are absorbed. An X-ray photograph of a broken bone is shown in **Figure 19-10.** An X-ray photograph is a negative; thus, the bones appear much brighter than the surrounding tissues because they absorb most of the X rays.

As **Figure 19-11** shows, X rays also help us in other ways. They are used in airports to scan passengers' luggage. Personnel can examine luggage and packages without opening them.

Destroying Cells

Gamma rays have the highest frequency and are the most penetrating of all the electromagnetic waves, so they are located at the opposite end of the electromagnetic spectrum from radio waves. Gamma rays are emitted from the nuclei of radioactive atoms. Earth also receives some gamma radiation from space. Concentrated gamma rays are destructive to human cells and can be used to kill cancerous cells. People who undergo gamma radiation therapy for cancer frequently suffer side effects, such as fatigue, nausea, and hair loss, from the therapy because healthy cells are also damaged.

Figure 19-10

X rays can help locate the break in a bone.

Doctors and technicians who give gamma radiation therapy or take X-ray pictures protect themselves from this penetrating radiation by standing behind lead shields. Patients are protected by aprons lined with lead. These shields and aprons absorb the high-energy photons. Excessive exposure to X rays and gamma radiation is harmful and should be avoided.

Think of all the uses of the waves of the electromagnetic spectrum that you read about in this section. Can you think of some uses that weren't mentioned? In the next section, you will learn more about the visible part of the spectrum, light.

Figure 19-11

X rays assist in providing airport security. An X-ray image shows the contents of the suitcase.

Section Wrap-up

Review

1. Describe at least two ways electromagnetic waves differ from sound waves.

2. Using **Figure 19-2,** rank the six main types of electromagnetic radiation by wavelength, from shortest to longest.

3. **Think Critically:** Describe at least one helpful use for each of the six main types of electromagnetic radiation.

Skill Builder
Observing and Inferring
Observe a colorful object under a regular light-bulb and then under a fluorescent light. Which light has more waves in the red end of the spectrum? If you need more help, refer to Observing and Inferring in the **Skill Handbook.**

Science Journal

After reading this section about radio waves, write a paragraph in your Science Journal explaining whether or not you can hear radio waves. Give evidence for your answer.

19●2 Light and Color

Light and Matter

Have you ever been asleep in a dark room when someone suddenly opened the curtains and bright light came streaming in? You probably squinted because of the brightness of the light. As your eyes adjusted to the light, you could see all the objects in the room and their colors. But when there was little light in the room, your eyes couldn't distinguish those objects or their colors. What you are able to see depends on the amount of light and the color of the objects as they reflect or absorb light. In order for you to see an object, it must reflect some light.

The type of matter in an object determines the amount of light it absorbs and reflects. For example, heavy window curtains that are completely closed may keep a room dark. The curtains are opaque. **Opaque materials** absorb or reflect all light, and you cannot see objects through them. When the curtains are opened, bright sunlight shines through the glass windowpanes. Most glass windows are transparent. **Transparent materials** allow light to pass through and you can clearly see objects through them. Other materials, such as frosted glass, sheer curtains, or waxed paper, allow some light to pass through, but you cannot clearly see objects through them. These materials are **translucent materials.** The use of these different types of materials results in the variety of lighting fixtures and effects shown in **Figure 19-12.**

Objectives

• Describe the differences among opaque, transparent, and translucent materials.
• Explain how you see color.
• Describe the difference between light color and pigment color.

Figure 19-12

A lighting store is a good place to see materials with different light-transmitting properties.

Figure 19-13

You can see many colorful costumes at parades and celebrations. *Do the costumes reflect or absorb the colors that you see?*

Colors

Perhaps you have wondered why your blue jeans look blue or why grass looks green. What makes them reflect color differently from one another? They are both opaque materials, either absorbing or reflecting nearly all of the light that strikes them. But when struck by white light, which is actually a blend of a spectrum of colors, your blue jeans reflect blue light back to your eyes and absorb all of the other colors. Knowing this, explain what happens when white light strikes green grass. White objects appear white because they reflect all colors of light in the visible spectrum. The colors present in white light, arranged in order of decreasing wavelengths, are red, orange, yellow, green, blue, indigo, and violet. The costumes in **Figure 19-13** reflect many different colors. Objects that appear black absorb all colors of light and reflect little or no light back to your eye.

Filtering Light

If you placed a colored, transparent plastic sheet over this white page, what color would the page seem to be? The paper would appear to be the same color as the plastic. The plastic sheet is a filter. A filter is a transparent material that transmits one or more colors of light but absorbs all others. The color of a filter is the same as the color of light it transmits. What happens when you look at colored objects through colored filters? In the white light in **Figure 19-14A**, a green jersey

Figure 19-14

The green jersey is shown in white light (A). The jersey appears green when viewed through a green filter (B) and black when viewed through a red filter (C).

looks green because it reflects only the green light in the white light striking it. It absorbs light of all other colors. If you look at the jersey through the green filter in **Figure 19-14B,** the jersey still looks green because the filter transmits the reflected green light. **Figure 19-14C** shows how the jersey looks when you look at it through a red filter. Why does it appear this way?

Red, green, and blue are the primary colors of light. They can be mixed in different amounts to produce any color of light. **Figure 19-15** shows how all three primary colors form white light.

INTEGRATION
Life Science

Figure 19-15

White light is produced when the three primary colors of light are mixed.

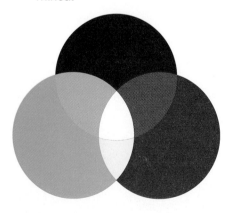

Color—Seeing the Light

As you approach a busy intersection, the color of the traffic light changes from green to yellow to red. On the cross street, the color changes from red to green. In this situation, traffic safety depends on your ability to detect immediate color changes. How do you actually see colors?

Light enters your eye and is focused on the retina, which is made up of two types of nerve cells that act as photo-receptors. When these photoreceptors absorb light, chemical reactions convert light energy into nerve impulses that are transmitted to the brain. One type of photoreceptor, called a cone, allows you to distinguish colors and detailed shapes of objects. Cones are most effective in daytime vision. There are three types of cones, each of which absorbs a different range of wavelengths. Red cones absorb mostly red and yellow, green cones absorb mostly yellow and green, and blue cones absorb mostly blue and violet. The second type of photo-receptor, called a rod, is more sensitive to dim light and is useful for night vision.

Interpreting Color

What happens in your eye when you look at a yellow banana? Both your red and green cones respond by absorbing the yellow light, and your brain interprets the combined signal as yellow. Your brain would get the same signal if a mixture of red light and green light reached your eye. Again, your red and green cones would respond, and you would see yellow light because your brain can't perceive the difference between incoming yellow light and yellow light produced by combining red and green light. What happens when you look at a white T-shirt? You see white light when a mixture of all visible wavelengths of light enters your eye because all of your cones are stimulated.

Color Blindness

What would happen to your vision if one or more of your sets of cones did not function properly? This in an inherited condition that affects a small portion of the population. About eight percent of men and one-half percent of women have a problem with one of their sets of color receptors. This condition is sometimes called *color blindness* because it results in an inability to distinguish between certain colors. Most people who are said to be color blind are not truly blind to color, but they have difficulty distinguishing between a few colors, most commonly red and green. Because these two colors are used in traffic signals, drivers and pedestrians must be able to identify them. The person in **Figure 19-16** is taking a color-blindness test.

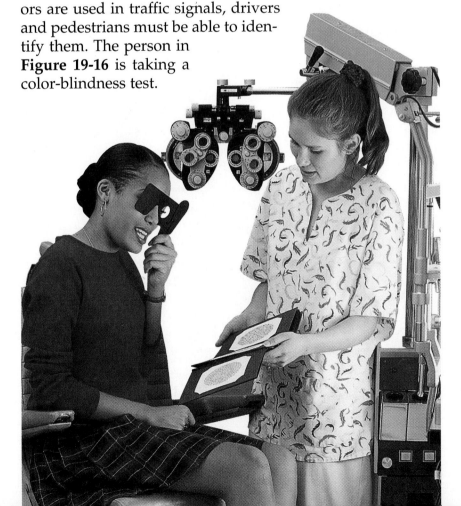

MiniLAB

How do filters affect the colors you see?

Procedure

1. Write the word COLOR on your paper, writing the C, L, and R in red and the two Os in green.
2. View the word *COLOR* by looking through a green plastic filter. How does the color of each letter appear?
3. View the word *COLOR* through a red filter.
4. View the word *COLOR* through the red and green filters stacked together.

Analysis

1. What did you observe through the green filter? The red filter? Both filters together? Explain your observations.
2. If you viewed a multicolored picture or article of clothing through a red filter, what colors would you most likely observe? Try it.

Figure 19-16

Color blindness is a sex-linked condition, more often revealed in males than in females, in which cones for "green" are deficient.

Problem Solving

Color in the Sunday Comics

Where are you most likely to find color in a daily newspaper? More and more, you find color photographs, but most of the color in newspapers is found in the Sunday comics or in the ads. Are you curious about how color gets into comics?

Use a magnifying glass to examine a color comic strip closely. What do you see? If you look closely enough, you will probably see many small, colored dots. The dots are made up of the three pigment colors—magenta (pinkish-purple), cyan (blue-green), and yellow. Red areas are composed of varying amounts of magenta dots and yellow dots. What color of dots do you think would create a blue sky in a comic?

Combinations of these three pigments are used to create the wide variety of colors you see in the comics. For example, an orange shirt would be made of a mixture of varying amounts of magenta and yellow dots, and a purple book would be a mixture of magenta and cyan dots. What other colors could you easily make?

Solve the Problem:

1. **What colors would make it possible to have green grass in a comic?**
2. **Examine one particular comic strip with a magnifying glass. Make a list of all of the colors you observe and what combinations of colored dots create each color.**

Think Critically:

If you had only magenta, cyan, and yellow paints, could you color a dog's ear black on a painting? Explain why this would or would not be possible.

Pigments

A **pigment** is a colored material that absorbs some colors and reflects others. Pigments are used by artists to make various colors of paints. Paint pigments are usually made of powdered insoluble chemicals such as titanium(IV) oxide, a bright white pigment, and lead(II) chromate, used in painting yellow lines on highways.

You can make any pigment color by mixing different amounts of the three primary pigments—magenta, cyan, and yellow. A primary pigment's color depends on the color of light it reflects. For

©1993 Bill Watterson

example, in white light, the yellow pigment appears yellow because it reflects red and green light but absorbs blue light. The color of a mixture of two primary pigments is determined by the primary colors of light that both pigments can reflect.

Look at **Figure 19-17.** Its center appears black because the three blended primary pigments absorb all the primary colors of light. Recall that in **Figure 19-15,** the primary colors of *light* combine to produce white light; they are called additive colors. However, the primary *pigment* colors combine to produce black. Because black results from the absence of reflected light, the primary pigments are called subtractive colors.

Pigmentation is also found in skin. Few people have exactly the same skin color because the amount of pigmentation varies.

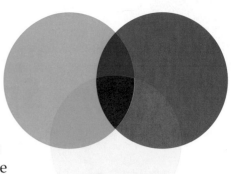

Figure 19-17

The three primary colors of pigment appear black when they are mixed.

Section Wrap-up

Review

1. Contrast opaque, transparent, and translucent materials. Give at least one example of each.

2. If white light shines on a red shirt, what colors are reflected and what colors are absorbed?

3. **Think Critically:** Consider the following parts of your body: the lens of your eye, a fingernail, your skin, and a tooth. Decide whether each of these is opaque, transparent, or translucent. Explain.

Skill Builder
Concept Mapping
Design a concept map to show the chain of events that must happen for you to see a blue object. Work with a partner. If you need help, refer to Concept Mapping in the **Skill Handbook.**

Using Computers

Graphing How are the wavelength and frequency of light related to each other? The table below shows the wavelength and frequency that correspond to colors of visible light. Use a computer and a graphing program to make a graph of these data. Put wavelength on the horizontal axis and frequency on the vertical axis. What does the shape of the graph tell you about the relationship between wavelength and frequency?

Wavelength and Frequency of Colors		
Color	Wavelength (nm) (in vacuum)	Frequency (10^{14} Hz)
Red	700	4.3
Orange-Yellow	600	5.0
Green-Blue	500	6.0
Violet	400	7.5

Activity 19-1

Design Your Own Experiment
Spectrum Inspection

Have you ever used a dimmer switch to control the brightness of the lighting in a room? Are all of the same wavelengths present at all settings of a dimmer switch, or do they vary with brightness? The following experiment will help you find out.

PREPARATION

Problem
How does the brightness of a lightbulb relate to the wavelengths of light produced by the bulb?

Form a Hypothesis
Which colors of the visible spectrum have the highest frequency? The highest energy? Write a hypothesis describing which colors will be produced by the lightbulb and how they will be affected by reducing its brightness.

Objectives
- Design an experiment that tests the relationship between bulb brightness and the colors of light produced by the bulb.
- Observe the color spectrum produced by a variety of bulbs.

Possible Materials
- diffraction grating
- power supply with variable resistor (dimmer switch)
- clear, tubular lightbulb and socket
- colored pencils (at least red, yellow, and blue)

Safety Precautions
Be sure all electrical cords and connections are intact and that you have a dry working area. Do not touch the bulbs, as they may be hot.

PLAN THE EXPERIMENT

1. As a group, agree upon and write out the hypothesis statement.
2. As shown in the photo at the right, you will look toward the light through the diffraction grating to detect the colors of light emitted by the bulb. The color spectrum will appear to the right and left of the bulb. Given this information, list the specific steps you will need to take to test your hypothesis.
3. Make a list of the needed materials and gather them.

Check the Plan
1. Be sure you have identified any constants and variables in your experiment.
2. Will you first test the bulb at a bright or dim setting? How many settings will you test? (Try at least three.)

3. Make sure each person in your group observes each setting. How will you record each person's observations in an organized way?
4. *Make sure your teacher approves your plan and that you have included any changes suggested in the plan.*

DO THE EXPERIMENT

1. Carry out the approved experiment as planned.
2. While doing your experiment, be sure to write down any observations you make in your Science Journal.

Analyze and Apply
1. **Compare** the spectra from the brightest and dimmest settings you tested.

2. What can you **infer** about the connection between color, frequency, and the brightness of the light source?
3. **Hypothesize** how you might make the spectrum easier to see.

Go Further

Recall your original spectrum from your bulb on the highest setting. Would you expect to find the same spectrum if you used a different kind of bulb, such as a colored lightbulb, neon light, or fluorescent bulb? Try it and see.

TECHNOLOGY:
19•3 Battle of the Bulbs

Science Words

incandescent light
fluorescent light

Objectives

- Explain how incandescent and fluorescent bulbs work.
- Analyze the advantages and disadvantages of different light sources.

Two Kinds of Lighting

Are you using light from a lightbulb to illuminate this page as you read it? Do you know what actually produces this light?

Incandescent Lighting

If you touch a lightbulb after it has been on for a while, it may feel hot. **Incandescent light** is produced by a thin wire called a filament. If you look into an unlit incandescent light-bulb, you will see the filament. It is usually made of the element tungsten. When you turn on the light, electricity flows through the filament and causes it to heat up. When it gets hot, tungsten gives off light. However, more than 80 percent of the energy given off by incandescent bulbs is in the form of heat.

Fluorescent Lighting

Fluorescent lighting is an alternative to incandescent lighting. A fluorescent bulb is filled with gas, typically argon, at a low pressure. As **Figure 19-18** shows, the inner side of the bulb is coated with phosphors, which are fluorescent materials that give off light when they absorb ultraviolet radiation. When the electricity is turned on, electrons collide with the gas molecules in the bulb to make them give off ultraviolet radiation. You can't see the ultraviolet radiation, but the phosphors absorb it and give off visible light.

A **fluorescent light** produces light without excessive loss of thermal energy. These bulbs use as little as one-fifth of the electricity as ordinary incandescent bulbs to produce the same amount of light. Fluorescent bulbs also last much longer than incandescent bulbs. This difference in energy usage will save money during the life of the fluorescent bulb. Reduced energy usage could significantly lower the amount of coal burned to generate electricity, which also decreases

Figure 19-18

Fluorescent lightbulbs do not use filaments. *What property of phosphors makes them useful in fluorescent bulbs?*

Lead-in wire
Electrode
Pin
Exhaust tube
Gas
Bulb
Pin
Mercury
Phosphorescent coating

the release of carbon dioxide and other pollutants into Earth's atmosphere.

Some users have observed that fluorescent bulbs can sometimes interfere with their TV remote controls and use of a cable box. Most remote controls transmit pulsed signals of infrared radiation in codes that cause the TVs or VCRs to respond in a desired way. The frequencies at which the fluorescent tubes operate occasionally produce infrared signals that the remote receiver confuses with the remote's infrared signals. Scientists are working to solve this problem.

Lighting enables the student in **Figure 19-19** to study and learn at any time of day. About 20 percent of all electricity consumed in the United States is used for lighting. Advances in developing more efficient lights could save a great deal of energy. What types of lighting are used in your home and school? What products or habits could be changed to save energy and money?

CONNECT TO

CHEMISTRY

Tungsten, used in making the filament in incandescent bulbs, has the highest melting point of all metals. *Research* at least one other property and one other use of tungsten.

Figure 19-19

This student's lamp uses an incandescent lightbulb.

Section Wrap-up

Review

1. Explain how light is produced in an ordinary incandescent bulb.

2. What are the advantages and disadvantages of using a fluorescent bulb instead of an incandescent bulb?

Explore the Technology

You are at the store to purchase a new study lamp. The fluorescent and incandescent lamps cost about the same, but the fluorescent bulb costs about ten times as much as the incandescent bulb. The fluorescent bulb is also guaranteed to last ten times longer than the incandescent bulb. Which would you buy? Explain your reasoning.

SCIENCE & SOCIETY

19•4 Wave Properties of Light

Reflection

Just before you left for school this morning, you might have glanced in a mirror one last time to check your appearance. In order for you to see your reflection in the mirror, light had to reflect off you, hit the mirror, and be reflected off the mirror into your eye. **Reflection** occurs when a wave strikes an object and bounces off. **Figure 19-20A** shows an example of reflection.

Reflection occurs with all types of waves: electromagnetic waves, sound waves, and water waves. Look at the light beam striking a mirror in **Figure 19-20B.** The beam striking the mirror is called the incident beam. The beam that bounces off the mirror is called the reflected beam.

Law of Reflection

Notice that in **Figure 19-20B,** a line is drawn perpendicular to the surface of the mirror. This line is called the *normal.* The angle formed by the incident beam and the normal is the angle of incidence, labeled *i.* The angle formed by the reflected beam and the normal is the angle of reflection, labeled *r.* The law of reflection states that *the angle of incidence is equal to the angle of reflection.* Any reflected light, whether it is reflected from a mirror, a piece of foil, or the moon, follows the law of reflection.

If you took a smooth piece of aluminum foil and looked into it, you would see a slightly distorted image of yourself. What if you crumpled up the foil and then unfolded it again? What would you see? The creases in the foil create an uneven surface. You couldn't see an image of yourself because the reflected light is scattered in different directions. Smooth surfaces reflect light in one direction, but rough surfaces scatter light in many directions.

Objectives

- State and give an example of the law of reflection.
- Explain how refraction is used to separate white light into the colors of the spectrum.
- Describe how diffraction and interference patterns demonstrate the wave behavior of light.

Figure 19-20

Seeing yourself in a mirror (A) is an illustration of the reflection of light, illustrated in B. *How many times is light reflected when you use a mirror?*

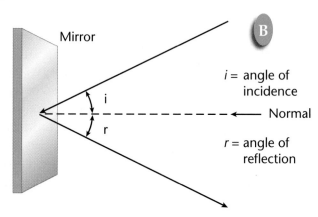

Mirror

i = angle of incidence

Normal

r = angle of reflection

Figure 19-21

The handle of the net looks bent in (A) because the light waves are refracted as they change speed when they pass from the water to the air. Light slows down and refracts toward the normal as it passes into a more dense medium (B). Light speeds up and bends away from the normal as it passes into a less dense medium (C).

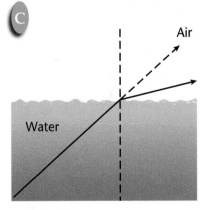

Refraction

Place your finger at an angle halfway into a glass of water and look at it through the side of the glass. Do you notice anything unusual? Your finger appears to be bent or even split into two pieces at the point where it enters the water. This happens because of refraction.

Bending Light

Refraction is the bending of waves caused by a change in their speed when they move from one medium to another. The amount of bending that occurs depends on the speed of light in both materials. The greater the difference between the speeds of light in two media, the more the light is bent as it passes at an angle from one medium to another. The light-refracting properties of certain materials can be especially pleasing to the human eye. When we admire the sparkle in a diamond or other gems, we are seeing refraction in action. Perhaps you have a decorative glass prism hung in a window where you live. When the sun is shining, the prism refracts the sunlight. Have you observed the colorful refraction pattern that the prism projects in the room? **Figure 19-21A** shows an example of refraction.

When light passes into a material that slows it down, **Figure 19-21B** shows that the light is refracted (bent) toward an imaginary line, called the *normal*, drawn perpendicularly through the surface of the medium at the point where the wave strikes the surface. The angle between the normal and the ray entering the medium is called the angle of incidence. The angle between the normal and the ray after it has entered the medium is called the angle of refraction. As **Figure 19-21C** shows, when light passes into a material in which light travels faster, it will be refracted (bent) away from the normal.

The amount of refraction also depends on the wavelength of the light. In the visible spectrum, the wavelengths of light vary from the longer red waves to the shorter violet waves.

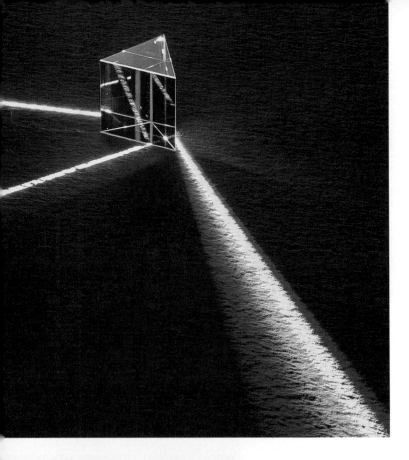

Figure 19-22

White light is refracted into the colors of the visible spectrum as it passes through a prism.

Figure 19-22 shows what happens when white light passes through a prism. The triangular prism refracts the light twice: once when it enters the prism and again when it leaves the prism and reenters the air. Because the shorter wavelengths of light are refracted more than the longer wavelengths, violet light is bent the most. Which color of light would you expect to bend the least? As a result of this varied refraction, the different colors are separated when they emerge from the prism.

Does the light leaving a prism remind you of a rainbow? Like prisms, rain droplets also refract light. The refraction of the different wavelengths can cause white light from the sun to separate into the individual colors of the visible spectrum. Isaac Newton recognized that white light actually includes all of the seven colors of the rainbow. In order of decreasing wavelength, the colors you should see in the rainbow are red, orange, yellow, green, blue, indigo, and violet—the same order as the electromagnetic spectrum.

Diffraction and Interference

One of the sounds of summer is the bells or music played by vendors selling ice cream as they drive their trucks through your neighborhood. Maybe you have heard cars drive by your home with blasting stereos. You can hear these sounds even when buildings separate you from the source. Sound waves can bend around corners to reach you. **Diffraction** is the bending of waves around a barrier. In the 1600s, an Italian physicist, Francesco Grimaldi, observed light and dark areas on the edge of a shadow. If you observe the shadow formed when light passes through an open door, you'll see no clearly defined boundary between light and dark. Instead, you will see a gradual transition. Grimaldi explained this phenomenon by suggesting that light could be bent around the edges of barriers.

Electromagnetic waves, sound waves, and water waves can all be diffracted. Water waves bend around you as you swim. Sandbars form along shorelines when water that

MiniLAB

How does water bend light?

Procedure

1. Place a penny at the bottom of a short, opaque cup. Set it on a table in front of you.
2. Have a partner slowly slide the cup away from you just until you can no longer see the penny.
3. Without disturbing the penny, have your partner slowly pour water into the cup until you can see the penny.
4. Reverse roles and repeat the experiment.

Analysis

1. What did you observe? Explain how this is possible.
2. Sketch the light path from the penny to your eye after the water was added.

carries sand is diffracted by some obstruction in the water. The pattern of the waves changes as the waves are diffracted. Diffraction is important in the transfer of radio waves. Longer wavelengths, such as those used by AM radio stations, are easier to diffract than short FM waves. That is why AM reception is often better than FM reception around tall buildings and natural barriers.

Interference—A Wave Property

Recall from Section 18-4 that sound waves can interfere with each other to form constructive and destructive interference. In the early 1800s, Thomas Young, an English scientist, expanded the diffraction theory Grimaldi had developed. In a famous experiment, he passed light of a uniform wavelength through a narrow slit. The new diffraction pattern of the light waves then passed through a barrier with two slits. You can

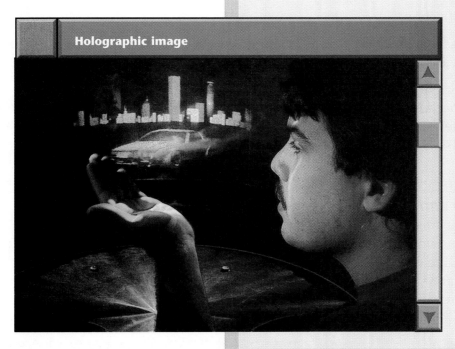
Holographic image

USING TECHNOLOGY

Holograms

A hologram is a vivid, three-dimensional image that appears to float in space. As you walk by a hologram, you see the image from a slightly different angle.

Holograms are produced by illuminating the object you wish to make an image of with light from a laser. Laser light reflected from the object shines on photographic film simultaneously with light from a second laser of the same wavelength. The interference pattern created on the photographic film produces a hologram image when laser light shines through it.

How We Use Holograms

A hologram conveys more information to your eye than a conventional two-dimensional photograph by controlling both the intensity and direction of the light that departs from the image. As a result, these vivid, three-dimensional objects are difficult to copy. For this reason, holographic images are used on credit cards, identification cards, and on the labels of some clothing to help prevent counterfeiting. Scientists are also working on ways to record and display data holographically.

Think Critically:

Why might storing massive amounts of data as tiny holograms in special crystals be a useful technology?

Figure 19-23

Diffraction patterns (A) can be produced by compact discs (B).

A

Double slits

Light source

B

see the results, wave interference, in **Figure 19-23A.** The wave crests are shown by the semicircles. The light from these slits was projected onto a screen. Young observed light bands where two crests or two troughs combined, and dark areas where a crest and a trough crossed paths. This experiment shows how light behaves as a wave. Only waves exhibit interference; particles do not.

You know that white light can be separated into colors by refraction in a prism. Colors can also be separated by diffraction and interference using many slits. A **diffraction grating** is a piece of glass or plastic made up of many parallel slits. Diffraction gratings commonly have as many as 12 000 slits per centimeter. When white light shines through a diffraction grating, the colors separate. Reflective materials can be ruled with closely spaced grooves to produce diffraction patterns. For example, shiny bumper stickers sometimes diffract light into a wide array of colors. You can also see the dazzling results of simple diffraction gratings by looking at the reflection of light from the microscopic recording pits in the compact discs in **Figure 19-23B.**

Section Wrap-up

Review

1. State the law of reflection.

2. When light moves from air into glass at an angle, is the light refracted toward or away from the normal?

3. **Think Critically:** Scientists say that light has both particle and wave properties. Explain why observations of diffraction and interference patterns conflict with the idea that light consists of particles.

Skill Builder
Observing and Inferring
Imagine you are on the shore of a large lake and see waves moving toward you from the center of the lake. However, the waves pass by a boat dock and move toward you at a slightly different angle afterward. What would you infer is happening? If you need help, refer to Observing and Inferring in the **Skill Handbook.**

USING MATH

If you are using a diffraction grating with 12 000 slits per centimeter, how wide is each slit? Express your answer as a decimal in centimeters.

Activity 19-2

Make a Light Bender

Can you recall seeing your reflection in the surface of a lake or other body of water? You can see your image because some of the light that reflects off your face also strikes the water's surface and reflects into your eyes. However, you don't see a clear, color image because much of the light enters the water rather than being reflected.

Problem

How does being underwater affect the viewer's image of an object that is above the water's surface?

Materials

- light source
- pencil
- clear rectangular container
- water
- notebook paper
- clay

Procedure

1. Fill the container with water and place it on a sheet of notebook paper.
2. Outline the container on the paper.
3. Stand the pencil on end in the clay and place it on the paper in front of the container as shown in the figure below.
4. Place the light in an upright position near the paper and turn it on.
5. Adjust the position of the paper and the pencil so the pencil's shadow on the paper goes completely through the container.
6. Draw lines on the shadow where it enters and leaves the container. Draw a line on the shadow that reflects from the surface of the container.
7. Move the container. Connect the lines to show the shadow through the container.

Analyze

1. Draw a reference line (normal) at right angles through the outline of the container at the point where the shadow touches its surface. As the shadow enters the container, does it refract toward the reference line or away from it? What happens when the shadow leaves the other side of the container?
2. Alter the experiment by changing a variable—the angle between the reference line and the shadow. What happens to the reflected and refracted shadows?

Conclude and Apply

3. **Compare** the angles of reflection and refraction for light striking the flat surface of the container.
4. **Predict** how the angles of reflection or refraction would change in question 3 if the surface of the container were curved. **Explain** your answer.

The Art of Lighting

Candles burning in jack-o'-lanterns create an eerie mood at a Halloween party. Light has the ability to cause a special psychological effect in a viewer. The kind of effect depends upon the angle at which the light strikes an object. Artists know this and use light accordingly. They adapt light to convey effect.

Stage Lighting

When the stage in a theater is dimly lighted and dark shadows conceal parts of the faces of the actors, the audience gets an uneasy feeling that something bad has happened or is about to happen. They become edgy, fearing that someone is lurking in the shadows to harm the characters they identify with.

Faces can be distorted by the direction of the light, as seen in the photograph of the girl on this page. Light striking from a low angle, such as from a low fire or a lantern, can transform a pleasant face into a frightening one.

On the other hand, bright lights or front lights alone tend to flatten and wash out an actor. Both top lights and side lights create highlights along the edges of the head and body, but cause deep shadows across the head and the front of the body. However, when side and top lights are combined with front lights, proper lighting can be achieved.

Outdoor Lighting

Downlighting is a lighting technique that imitates nature. Just as the morning sun falls on a patio, downlights placed in tall trees provide pleasant light in a garden at night. Uplighting, which is lighting from below, is more dramatic but rarely occurs in nature. That's why it gives a less natural look. Uplighting can be used to emphasize a statue or a large tree, but should be used less often than downlighting. All in all, there's much more to artistic lighting than turning on a switch.

Science Journal

Think about a video in which your favorite singer performs. What do you recall about the lighting? In your Science Journal, describe the lighting effects used for the performance.

Summary

19-1: Electromagnetic Radiation

1. Electromagnetic waves differ from other types of waves because they do not need a medium to transfer energy.
2. Electromagnetic waves are arranged on the electromagnetic spectrum by their wavelength and frequency.
3. Radio waves are used in communications. Infrared radiation indicates the presence of heat. Visible light is only a small part of the electromagnetic spectrum. Ultraviolet radiation causes fluorescent bulbs to glow. X rays aid medical diagnosis. Gamma rays can be used to destroy cancer cells.

19-2: Light and Color

1. You can't see through opaque materials. You can see clearly through transparent materials and hazily through translucent materials.
2. You see color when light is reflected off objects and into your eyes. Inside your eyes, chemical reactions convert light into nerve impulses.
3. The three primary colors of light can be mixed to form all other colors. The colors of pigments are determined by the colors they reflect.

19-3: Science and Society: Battle of the Bulbs

1. Incandescent bulbs produce light by heating a tungsten filament until it glows brightly. Fluorescent bulbs give off light when ultraviolet radiation produced inside the bulb causes a fluorescent coating inside the bulb to glow.

2. Although expensive to purchase, fluorescent bulbs waste less energy, last longer, and cost much less to use than incandescent bulbs.

19-4: Wave Properties of Light

1. The law of reflection states that the angle of incidence is equal to the angle of reflection.
2. White light can be separated into the colors of the visible spectrum because each wavelength refracts at a different angle as it passes into a medium.
3. Diffraction and interference show wave patterns of light by showing that light waves bend around a barrier and can cancel each other.

Key Science Words

a. diffraction
b. diffraction grating
c. electromagnetic radiation
d. fluorescent light
e. gamma ray
f. incandescent light
g. infrared radiation
h. microwave
i. modulation
j. opaque material
k. photon
l. pigment
m. radio wave
n. reflection
o. refraction
p. translucent material
q. transparent material
r. ultraviolet radiation
s. visible radiation
t. X ray

Chapter 19 Review

Reviewing Vocabulary

Match each phrase with the correct term from the list of Key Science Words.

1. transverse wave produced by the motion of electrically charged particles
2. bundle of radiation with no mass
3. electromagnetic radiation that is felt as heat
4. object that can't be seen through
5. light produced by a heated filament
6. occurs when a wave strikes an object and then bounces off
7. the bending of waves around a barrier
8. contains many parallel slits that can separate white light into colors
9. highest frequency electromagnetic wave
10. radio wave with the greatest energy

Checking Concepts

Choose the word or phrase that completes the sentence.

1. Electromagnetic waves are different from other types of waves in that they do not _____.
   a. have amplitude   c. transfer energy
   b. have frequency   d. need a medium
2. When light enters matter, it ____.
   a. slows down
   b. speeds up
   c. travels at 300 000 km/s
   d. travels at the speed of sound
3. A contact lens is _____.
   a. transparent   c. opaque
   b. translucent   d. square
4. Electromagnetic waves with the longest wavelengths are _____.
   a. radio waves   c. X rays
   b. visible light   d. gamma rays

5. The process of changing the frequency or amplitude of radio waves in order to encode a signal is _____.
   a. diffraction   c. reflection
   b. modulation   d. refraction
6. When food molecules absorb microwaves, they vibrate faster and their _____.
   a. kinetic energy decreases
   b. kinetic energy increases
   c. temperature decreases
   d. temperature remains constant
7. Your body gives off _____.
   a. radio waves   c. infrared radiation
   b. visible light   d. ultraviolet radiation
8. Fluorescent bulbs glow when the phosphors inside absorb _____.
   a. microwaves   c. infrared radiation
   b. gamma rays   d. ultraviolet radiation
9. X rays are best absorbed by _____.
   a. bone   c. muscle
   b. hair   d. skin
10. Objects that partially scatter light that passes through them are called _____.
    a. reflective   c. translucent
    b. opaque   d. transparent

Understanding Concepts

Answer the following questions in your Science Journal using complete sentences.

11. Explain how sound waves are converted to radio waves. Give some examples.
12. What is the difference between light color and pigment color?
13. How is the reflection of light off a white wall similar to the reflection of light off a mirror? How is it different?
14. Explain which property of light helps produce a rainbow.
15. Describe the wave model of light and note one of the scientists who studied it.

Thinking Critically

look for in chp. sec 2 of this chp.

16. Heated objects often give off light of a particular color. Explain why an object that glows blue is hotter than one that glows red. *pg 34*

17. How would a blue shirt appear if a blue filter were placed in front of it? A red filter? A green filter? *pgs 37*

18. Use the law of reflection to explain why you see only a portion of the area behind you when you look into a mirror. *pg 54u*

19. Which color of light changes speed the most when it passes through a prism? Explain. *pg 548*

20. Explain why you can hear a fire engine coming around a street corner before you can see it. *section 1 of this chp.*

Initiating step

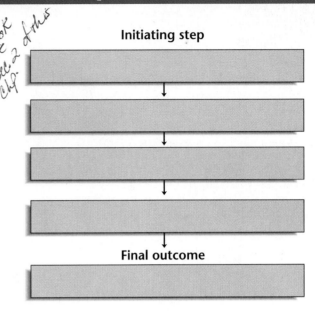

Final outcome

Developing Skills

If you need help, refer to the **Skill Handbook**.

21. Sequencing: List the types of radiation in the electromagnetic spectrum in order of decreasing penetrating power. Use **Figure 19-2,** the electromagnetic spectrum, as a reference.

22. Making and Using Tables: Construct a table to show the applications of each type of electromagnetic wave. Which type would an electronics engineer be most interested in? A doctor?

23. Observing and Inferring: Most mammals, such as dogs and cats, can't see colors. Infer how a cat's eye might be different from your eye.

24. Concept Mapping: Use the blank concept map in the column to the right to show the five steps in the production of fluorescent light.

25. Using Scientific Illustrations: Whales make sounds that can be detected for miles. Make a drawing that shows the wave properties that enable the sound to travel so far.

Performance Assessment

1. Scrapbook: Make a scrapbook of newspaper and magazine articles describing the dangers of ultraviolet radiation and how this harmful radiation is absorbed by Earth's ozone layer. Write a short summary of each article.

2. Poster: Make a poster to show how the three primary pigments are combined to produce common colors such as blue, red, yellow, green, purple, brown, and black.

3. Making Observations and Inferences: Repeat Activity 19-2 on page 551. Measure the angle of incidence and the angle of refraction as the shadow enters and leaves the container. Show the angles on the diagram. What do you notice?

Previewing the Chapter

556

Chapter
20

Mirrors and Lenses

How do mirrors and lenses help the people in this photograph? In the last chapter, you learned about the wave properties of light—reflection, refraction, diffraction, and interference. Which of these are most useful in helping people see images clearly? Mirrors, which reflect light, and lenses, which refract light, are used to change the way you see things. Knowing this, do you still believe everything you see?

EXPLORE ACTIVITY

Find out how familiar surfaces can produce different images.

1. Observe your reflection in a flat mirror. What do you see? Is the reflection the same size as your face? Is it right side up?
2. Look at your image in the back of a large, shiny spoon. Slowly move the spoon close to your face and then far away. How does the image change?
3. Turn the spoon over and look into the inside of the spoon. Slowly move it close to your face and then far away.

Observe: In your Science Journal, compare and contrast the images produced by the three shiny surfaces.

Previewing Science Skills

▶ In the **Skill Builders**, you will **recognize cause and effect, map concepts, hypothesize,** and **sequence.**

▶ In the **Activities**, you will **observe, measure, predict,** and **infer.**

▶ In the **MiniLABs**, you will **hypothesize, infer,** and **measure.**

20•1 The Optics of Mirrors

Science Words

plane mirror
virtual image
concave mirror
focal point
focal length
real image
convex mirror

Objectives

- Explain how an image is formed in three types of mirrors.
- Identify examples and uses of plane, concave, and convex mirrors.

Plane Mirrors

Close your eyes and picture your own face. How do you know what you look like? In what objects have you seen your reflection? The most obvious answer is a mirror, but you probably have also seen your reflection in windows and pieces of aluminum foil. Any smooth object that reflects light to form an image is a mirror.

Virtual Images

You are probably used to seeing your image in a **plane mirror,** one with a flat surface. A plane mirror is a piece of glass with a reflective coating on the front or the back. What do you see when you stand in front of the mirror and look directly into it? Your reflection is upright and appears to be the same size as you. **Figure 20-1** shows how your image is formed by a plane mirror. Light is reflected off you toward the mirror, which reflects the light back to your eyes.

The image appears to be behind the mirror because you perceive the reflected light as coming from somewhere beyond the mirror. However, these light rays do not exist *behind* the mirror; it is opaque. Because the image only *seems* to be behind the plane mirror, it is called a virtual image. A **virtual image** is an image in which no light rays pass through the image. The virtual image formed by a plane mirror is erect and appears as far behind the mirror as the object is in front of it.

Figure 20-1

A plane mirror forms an upright, same-size virtual image.

Mirror

Virtual image

Wall

Concave Mirrors

Mirrors are not always flat. If the surface of a mirror is curved inward, like the inside of a spoon, it is a **concave mirror.** The flower in **Figure 20-2A** is being reflected in a concave mirror. Concave mirrors form images differently from the way plane mirrors do. The way an image is formed depends on the position of the object in front of the mirror. **Figure 20-2B** shows one way an image can be formed in a concave mirror.

The straight line drawn through the center of the mirror is the optical axis. Light rays parallel to the optical axis are all reflected to pass through one point on the optical axis, called the **focal point.** The distance from the center of the mirror to the focal point is called the **focal length.**

Suppose that the distance from the object to the mirror is a little greater than the focal length, as in **Figure 20-2B.** You can locate the top of the image by following the two red rays. One ray is drawn from the top of the flower through the focal point to the mirror. All rays that pass through the focal point on the way to the mirror are reflected parallel to the optical axis. A second ray is drawn from the top of the flower parallel to the optical axis. This ray is reflected through the focal point. The point where the two red rays meet is the top of the reflected image. Using the same method, blue rays from the bottom of the flower locate the bottom of the image. The image is real, enlarged, and upside-down. This is a **real image** because the rays of light actually meet at the image, so you could hold a screen there and see it. Recall that light does not pass through a virtual image.

MiniLAB

What happens when light strikes a concave mirror?

Find out what happens to the image of an object in a concave mirror when the distance from the mirror to the screen is changed.

Procedure

1. Hold a large, shiny spoon near a bright light (such as a flashlight) so the light reflects from the bowl of a spoon or the inner side of a concave mirror toward an index card.
2. Slowly move the card back and forth while looking for the image. When the image is clearest, measure the distance from the card to the mirror in centimeters.
3. Move the card closer to the mirror. What do you observe?
4. Now move the card farther from the mirror than the distance you measured earlier. What do you see?

Analysis

1. What can you infer about the relationship between the distance of the index card from the mirror and the clarity of the image on the index card?
2. What do you think would happen if you used the back of the spoon in this experiment? Try it. How do your observations differ?

Figure 20-2

The image in this concave mirror is enlarged and inverted (A). The diagram in (B) shows how the image is created.

Concave mirror surface

Object

Optical axis

Inverted real image

Focal point

A The lighthouse uses a strong light source placed at the focal point of a concave mirror.

Figure 20-3

Some light beams are used to prevent accidents.

B The mirror produces a beam of parallel light rays that do not converge.

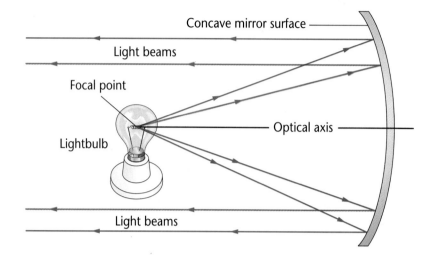

What if you placed an object exactly at the focal point of the concave mirror? The lighthouse in **Figure 20-3A** gives us a hint. **Figure 20-3B** shows that if the object is at the focal point, the mirror reflects all light rays parallel to the optical axis. No image can be seen because the rays do not converge. Therefore, a light placed at the focal point is reflected in a beam. Devices such as car headlights, flashlights, and spotlights use this technique to create a concentrated light beam of nearly parallel rays.

Figure 20-4

The image of the rose is virtual, upright, and enlarged (A) when the rose is placed between the focal point and the surface of a concave mirror (B). *Can you think of places where such a mirror would be helpful?*

Mirrors That Magnify

What if you placed an object between the mirror and the focal point as shown in **Figure 20-4A?** You can find the top of the image using two rays from the top of the flower in **Figure 20-4B.** One ray is drawn as if it comes through the focal point

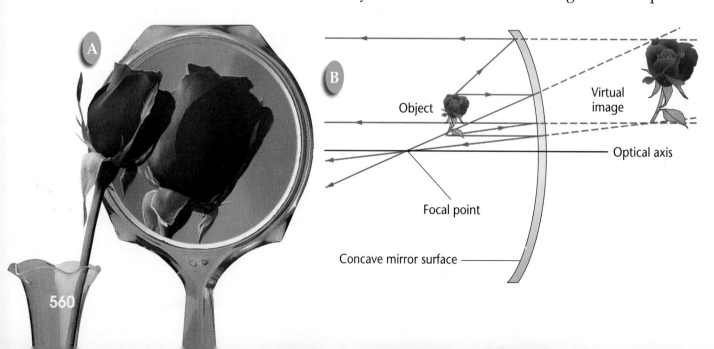

and is reflected parallel to the optical axis. The second ray leaves the flower parallel to the optical axis and reflects through the focal point. These rays never meet to form a real image. Instead, they appear to come from a single point behind the mirror. You can use rays from the bottom of the object to locate the bottom of the upright, enlarged, and virtual image. Hand mirrors that magnify reflections use this technique. The effect can also be seen when the bowl of a shiny spoon is placed close to your face.

Convex Mirrors

Have you noticed a large mirror mounted above the aisles in a store? This type of mirror that curves outward is called a **convex mirror. Figure 20-5** on the next page shows how convex mirrors produce an image. The reflected rays never meet, so the image is always virtual, upright, and smaller than the actual object.

Because convex mirrors spread out the reflected light,

Problem Solving

Looking Back with Car Mirrors

What kinds of mirrors would you find in or on a car? Mirrors that provide a view of the traffic beside or behind a car are necessary for safe, defensive driving. Have you ever noticed any side mirrors on cars and trucks that have a warning stating "OBJECTS IN MIRROR ARE CLOSER THAN THEY APPEAR"? The rearview mirror inside typically does not have these warnings.

If you were to examine the shapes of these mirrors carefully, you would notice that the inside mirror is a plane mirror. However, the mirrors with the warning stated above are convex mirrors because they bulge slightly outward. Can you think of any other places you would expect to find reflective or mirrored surfaces on a car?

Solve the Problem:
1. Describe the images you would see if you looked at your face closely in each type of mirror discussed above.
2. What type of image, real or virtual, is formed in a convex mirror? Explain.

Think Critically:
Explain why convex mirrors are sometimes used as outside rearview mirrors on cars. Why are they stamped with a warning?

Student

Optical axis

Virtual image

Convex mirror surface

Figure 20-5

A convex rearview mirror forms a virtual image that is always upright and smaller than the object (A). The mirror diverges reflected rays (B) to form the image.

they allow large areas to be viewed. In addition to increasing the field of view in places like grocery stores and factories, convex mirrors can widen the view of traffic that can be seen in rear- or sideview mirrors of automobiles. However, your perception of distance can be distorted; objects are always closer than they appear in a convex mirror. Some mirrors that are on automobiles warn the driver that distances and sizes as seen in the mirror are not realistic.

So far, you have read about three ways that light can be reflected to form images. Review the three types of mirrors and describe the images that each mirror produces. In Section 20-2, you will find out the ways in which light can be refracted to form images.

Section Wrap-up

Review

1. What are convex mirrors used for? Explain.

2. Contrast the differences between the surfaces of plane, concave, and convex mirrors.

3. **Think Critically:** What kind of mirror would you use to focus light entering a telescope? Explain.

Skill Builder

Recognizing Cause and Effect

Suppose you drop a flashlight that has a concave mirror in it. When you turn the flashlight on, you notice that the light is less intense than it was before you dropped it. What may have happened? If you need help, refer to Recognizing Cause and Effect in the **Skill Handbook.**

Science Journal

In your Science Journal, make a list of all the mirrors you might see during an average day. Describe what each is used for and try to identify each one as plane, concave, or convex.

Activity 20-1

Reflections of Reflections

You have probably looked at your face in a mirror sometime today, but have you seen a reflected image of the back of your head? If so, you most likely looked into a mirror held at an angle in front of your face into a mirror directly behind you. You actually saw a reflection of the original reflection of the back of your head.

Problem

How can you create multiple reflections of an object?

Materials

- 2 plane mirrors
- cellophane tape
- masking tape
- protractor
- paper clip

Procedure

1. Lay the two mirrors side by side and tape them together so they will open and close. Label them *R* and *L* as shown in the photo to the right.
2. Place the mirrors on a sheet of paper and, using the protractor, close the mirrors to an angle of 72°. Mark the position of the *R* mirror on the paper.
3. Bend one leg of a paper clip up 90° and place it close to the front of the *R* mirror.
4. Count the number of images of the paper clip you see in the *R* and *L* mirrors. Don't move the clip.
5. Count the images as you slowly open the mirrors to 90° and then to 120°, keeping the paper clip close to the *R* mirror.
6. Make a data table to record the number of images you can see in the *R* and *L* mirrors when they are at 72°, 90°, and 120°.

Analyze

1. The mirror arrangement creates an image of a complete circle divided into

wedges by the mirrors. How many wedges did you observe with the 72°, 90°, and 120° angles?

Conclude and Apply

2. What angle would divide a circle into six wedges? **Hypothesize** how many images would be produced.
3. **Analyze** your results to determine which is the better **predictor** of the number of paper clip images that can be seen—the number of mirror images or the number of wedges.

Data and Observations

Angle of Mirrors	Number of Paper Clip Images	
	R	L
72°		
90°		
120°		

20•2 The Optics of Lenses

Science Words

convex lens
concave lens

Objectives

- Describe the types of images formed with convex and concave lenses.
- Cite examples of how these lenses are used.
- Explain how lenses are used to correct vision.

Figure 20-6

A thick convex lens (A) bends light more than a thin convex lens (B). *Which lens has the shorter focal length?*

Convex Lenses

Do you wear glasses or contact lenses? If so, you use lenses to improve your ability to see. Like curved mirrors, lenses are described as convex or concave, depending on their shape.

Convex lenses are thicker in the middle than at the edges. Light rays approaching the lens parallel to the optical axis are refracted toward the center of the lens. They converge at the focal point, so they are capable of forming real images that can be projected onto a screen.

The amount of refraction depends on the change in the speed of light as it passes through a material and the shape of the object. As shown in **Figure 20-6,** thick lenses with highly curved surfaces bend light much more than thin ones with less curved surfaces. The focal length of the thick convex lens in the top diagram in **Figure 20-6** is shorter than that of the thin convex lens below it. Convex lenses can produce many kinds of images, both real and virtual, upright, inverted, enlarged, or reduced. The type of image formed depends on the position of the object and the focal length of the lens. The diagrams in **Figure 20-7** show the images that result from three different locations of the object and focal point.

A

B

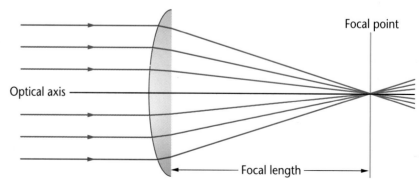

Figure 20-7

The image formed by a convex lens depends upon the location of the object relative to the focal length of the lens.

A If a person is photographing a faraway object, it's likely that the object is more than two focal lengths from the camera lens. If you follow the light paths, you'll notice that the real image is smaller than the object, and inverted. The lens in your eye forms images in the same way that a camera forms images.

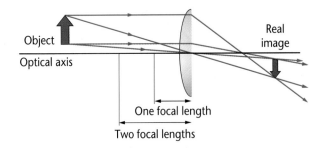

B If an object is between one and two focal lengths from the lens, the real image is inverted and larger than the object. This is the method used to project a movie from a small film to the large screen of a theater or from an overhead projector to a screen in your classroom.

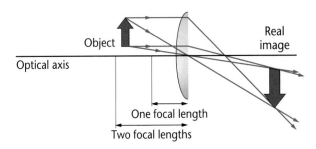

C Have you ever used a magnifying glass to closely examine an object? A magnifying glass is a convex lens, so you must hold it less than one focal length from the object. The light rays can't converge, and an enlarged, upright, and virtual image is formed. Look at the position of the image. Notice that the object seems larger and farther away than it really is.

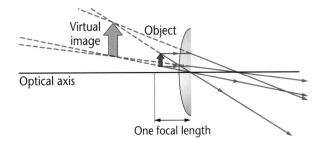

Concave Lenses

Concave lenses are thinner in the middle and thicker at the edges. As is shown in **Figure 20-8,** light passing through a concave lens bends toward the edges. The rays diverge and never form a real image. The image is virtual, upright, and smaller than the actual object. The image formed by a concave lens is similar to the image produced by a convex mirror because they both diverge light to form virtual images.

Concave lenses are usually used in combination with other lenses. They can be used with convex lenses in telescopes and cameras to spread out incoming light and extend the focal length so you can see a clear image of a faraway object. Concave lenses are also used to correct nearsighted vision.

Figure 20-8

Light rays passing through a concave lens diverge and form a virtual image. *Are concave lenses similar to or different from convex mirrors?*

MiniLAB

Can lenses be made of liquid?

Procedure

1. Cut a 10-cm × 10-cm piece of plastic wrap. Set it on a page of printed text.
2. Place a small water drop on the plastic. Look at the text through the drop. What do you observe?
3. Make your water drop larger and observe the text through it again. Did anything change?
4. Use a medicine dropper to drop water onto the head of a penny. How does the penny look? How many drops of water can you fit on the head of a penny?

Analysis

1. What kind of lens does the drop form?
2. How would your image look if you moved the liquid lens farther from the text you are observing? Try it.

Lenses and Eyesight

What determines how well you can see the words on this page? Your ability to focus on these words depends on the way your eye is designed. Light enters your eye through the transparent covering of your eye, the cornea. The light then passes through an opening called the pupil. The colored part of your eye, the iris, adjusts the pupil size to control how much light can pass through a flexible convex lens behind the pupil. The light then converges to form an inverted image on your retina. The lens in your eye is soft, and flexible muscles in your eye can change its shape. When you look at a distant object, you need a longer focal length, so your eye muscles adjust your lens to a less convex shape. When you focus on a nearby object, the eye muscles increase the curvature of the lens.

Improving Your Vision

If you have healthy vision, you should be able to see objects clearly from a distance of about 25 cm or more. Many people need their vision corrected. To have normal vision, the image of an object should focus on the retina inside your eye. If the image is focused in front of or behind the retina, vision problems will result. **Figure 20-9A** illustrates how concave lenses correct nearsightedness by diverging the light rays before they enter the eye. **Figure 20-9B** shows how farsightedness can be corrected with a convex lens.

Another vision problem is blurry vision from astigmatism, which occurs when the surface of the cornea is curved

Figure 20-9

Some vision problems can easily be corrected with concave (A) and convex (B) lenses. *Examine some eyeglasses. Can you tell which type of lens they use?*

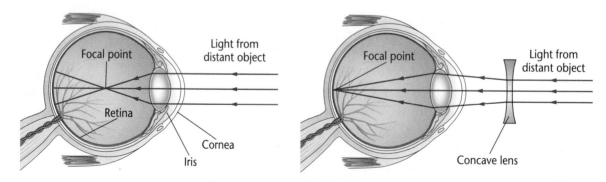

A A nearsighted person has difficulty seeing distant objects clearly. The eyeball is too long or the cornea bulges out, focusing the image in front of the retina.

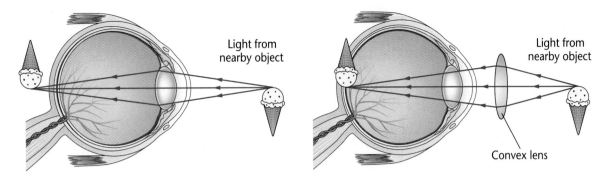

Light from nearby object

Light from nearby object

Convex lens

unevenly. Corrective lenses for this condition have an uneven curvature, as well.

There are currently several ways to correct poor vision caused by lens problems in the eye. Artificial lenses in the form of eyeglasses or contacts can be worn to refract light before it enters the eye, so the light will focus on the retina. As a result, the wearer will see clear images. Contact lenses are actually worn over the cornea. In some cases, vision can be corrected by using surgical lasers to reshape the cornea.

Can you recall what all lenses have in common? They all refract light that passes through them. Convex lenses refract light toward the center of the lens, and concave lenses refract light away from the center of the lens. As you read the next section, you'll see how these two kinds of lenses are used in cameras, microscopes, and telescopes.

B Farsighted people can see faraway objects, but they can't focus clearly on nearby objects. Their eyeballs are either too short or their corneas are too flat to allow the rays to converge on the retina. As a result, the image is focused behind the retina.

Section Wrap-up

Review

1. When using a slide projector, why are the slides inserted in the projector upside down?

2. What type of lens would you use to examine a tiny spider on your desk?

3. **Think Critically:** If you have difficulty reading the chalkboard from the back row, what is most likely your vision problem? How could it be corrected?

Skill Builder
Concept Mapping
Mirrors and lenses are the simplest optical devices. Design a network tree concept map to show some uses for each shape of mirror and lens. If you need help, refer to Concept Mapping in the **Skill Handbook.**

Using Computers

Spreadsheet Prepare a spreadsheet that organizes the information you have acquired about vision problems. For cases of nearsightedness, farsightedness, and astigmatism, display the symptom, the cause, and the method of correction.

20•3 Optical Instruments

Telescopes

Lenses and mirrors are important components of optical instruments—devices that are designed to aid the human eye in making observations. In this section, you'll learn about three common optical instruments—telescopes, microscopes, and cameras.

Have you ever looked at the moon through a telescope? With a good telescope, you should be able to see the craters and other features on the moon's surface clearly. Telescopes are designed to collect light from faraway objects. Much of the information we have today about the moon, the planets, our galaxy, and other galaxies has been gathered by viewing these celestial bodies through telescopes.

Around the year 1600, lens makers in Holland constructed a telescope to view distant objects. In 1609, Galileo built and used his own telescope to discover the moons of Jupiter, the phases of Venus, and some details of the Milky Way galaxy. Today, scientists use several kinds of telescopes with many design improvements. **Figure 20-10** shows how a telescope can improve our view of the moon.

Refracting Telescopes

One common telescope is the **refracting telescope.** A simple refracting telescope uses two convex lenses to gather and focus light from distant objects. **Figure 20-11A** is a diagram of a refracting telescope.

Several problems are associated with refracting telescopes. The objective lens must be large to allow enough light in to form a bright image. These heavy glass lenses are hard to make and costly. Their own weight can cause them to sag and distort the image.

Science Words

refracting telescope
reflecting telescope
microscope
wide-angle lens
telephoto lens

Objectives

- Compare refracting and reflecting telescopes.
- Explain how a camera creates an image.

Figure 20-10

The moon can be seen in greater detail when viewed through a telescope, as in the lower photo.

568 Chapter 20 Mirrors and Lenses

Light from distant object

Objective lens

Real image of distant object

Focal point

Eyepiece lens

Figure 20-11

Refracting and reflecting telescopes collect light to produce images of distant objects.

A Light enters the refracting telescope through a convex lens called the objective lens. The real image formed by this lens is magnified by a second convex lens, called the eyepiece, with a shorter focal length. You see an enlarged, inverted, virtual image of the real image.

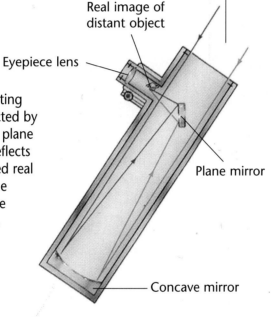

Light from distant object

Real image of distant object

Eyepiece lens

Plane mirror

Concave mirror

B Light enters the reflecting telescope and is reflected by the concave mirror onto a plane mirror. The plane mirror reflects the rays to form an inverted real image in the telescope. The convex lens in the eyepiece then magnifies this image.

MiniLAB

How can the location of a lens affect the observed image?

Procedure
1. Fill a glass test tube with water and seal it with a lid or stopper.
2. Type or print the compound name "SULFUR DIOXIDE" in capital letters on a piece of paper or a note card.
3. Set the test tube horizontally over the words and observe them. What do you notice?
4. Hold the tube 1 cm over the words and observe them again. Record your observations. Repeat, holding the tube at several other heights above the words.

Analysis
1. What were your observations of the words at these distances? Can you explain your observations?
2. Are the images you see at these heights real or virtual?

Reflecting Telescopes

Because of the problems described on the opposite page, most large telescopes are reflecting telescopes. A **reflecting telescope** uses a concave mirror, a plane mirror, and a convex lens to collect and focus light from distant objects. **Figure 20-11B** is a diagram of a reflecting telescope.

Sometimes, you might want to view distant objects so they appear upright. Imagine trying to watch a baseball game through binoculars if the image were upside down. Binoculars work on the same principle as a refracting telescope, except there are two sets of lenses—one for each eye. A third lens or a pair of reflecting prisms has been added to binoculars to invert the upside-down image so it appears upright. Terrestrial telescopes, such as those used for bird-watching, are also designed to produce an upright image.

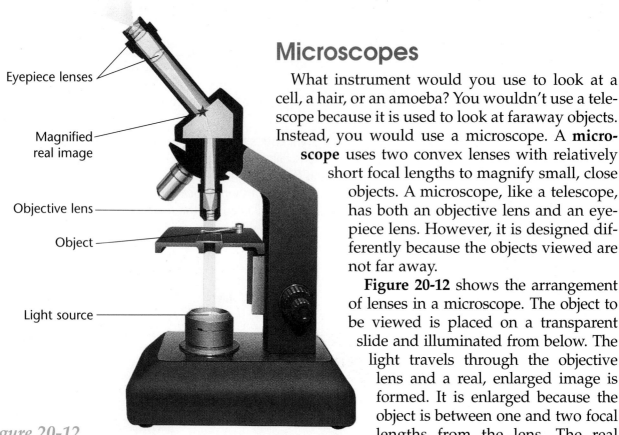

Eyepiece lenses

Magnified real image

Objective lens

Object

Light source

Microscopes

What instrument would you use to look at a cell, a hair, or an amoeba? You wouldn't use a telescope because it is used to look at faraway objects. Instead, you would use a microscope. A **microscope** uses two convex lenses with relatively short focal lengths to magnify small, close objects. A microscope, like a telescope, has both an objective lens and an eyepiece lens. However, it is designed differently because the objects viewed are not far away.

Figure 20-12 shows the arrangement of lenses in a microscope. The object to be viewed is placed on a transparent slide and illuminated from below. The light travels through the objective lens and a real, enlarged image is formed. It is enlarged because the object is between one and two focal lengths from the lens. The real image is magnified again by the eyepiece to create a virtual, enlarged image. This results in an image up to several hundred times larger than the actual object.

Figure 20-12

A microscope contains two convex lenses so it can magnify small objects.

Figure 20-13

This photo was taken with a wide-angle lens; it includes much of the surroundings. Observe how this photo differs from the one of the same scene on the next page.

Cameras

Do you keep a photograph album with your favorite pictures? Have you stopped to think about how a camera transfers an image onto film? A camera gathers light through a lens and projects an image onto light-sensitive film.

When you take a picture with a camera, the light reflected off the subject enters an opening in the camera called the aperture. A shutter on the aperture opens to allow light to enter the camera.

The light passes through the camera lens, which focuses the image on the photographic film. The image is real, inverted, and smaller than the actual object. The size of the image depends upon the focal length of the lens and how close the lens is to the film.

Suppose you and a friend photograph the same object at the same distance. Your picture would look different from that of your friend if the cameras had different lenses. Some lenses have short focal lengths that produce a relatively small image of the object but include much of its surroundings. These lenses are called **wide-angle lenses,** and they must be placed close to the film to focus the image with their short focal length. The photo in **Figure 20-13** was taken with a wide-angle lens. **Tele-photo lenses** have longer focal lengths and are located farther from the film than wide-angle lenses. Telephoto lenses are easy to recognize because they protrude from the camera to increase the distance between the lens and the film. The image seems enlarged and the object seems closer than it actually is, as shown in **Figure 20-14.** These lenses are preferred when photographing people's faces from a distance.

Telescopes, microscopes, and cameras are examples of instruments that contain mirrors and lenses and help you to make observations. How many other types of optical instruments can you name?

Figure 20-14

This photo was taken with a tele-photo lens. It gives a close-up view that omits most of the surroundings.

Section Wrap-up

Review

1. Compare and contrast reflecting and refracting telescopes.

2. If you wanted to photograph a single rose on a rose-bush, what kind of lens would you use? Explain why you chose this lens.

3. **Think Critically:** Which optical instrument—a telescope, a microscope, or a camera—forms images in a way most like your eye? Explain.

Skill Builder
Hypothesizing
You notice that all the objects in a photograph you've taken are blurry. Use your knowledge of lenses and focal lengths to form a hypothesis that could explain why the photo was blurred. If you need help, refer to Hypothesizing in the **Skill Handbook.**

Science Journal

Investigate the latest technologies and designs being used in new telescopes. Write several paragraphs about one of the designs and explain its advantages. Make a drawing that illustrates this design.

TECHNOLOGY:
20●4 The Hubble Space Telescope

Objectives

- Describe the development and repair of the Hubble Space Telescope.
- Discuss the goals and uses of the Hubble Space Telescope.

Seeking a Clear View from Space

Imagine trying to read a sign from the bottom of a swimming pool. The water distorts your view of objects beyond the water's surface. In a similar way, Earth's atmosphere blurs our view of objects in outer space. On April 20, 1990, the National Aeronautics and Space Administration (NASA) used the space shuttle *Discovery* to launch the Hubble Space Telescope into an orbit about 600 km above Earth. The telescope has produced images sharper than powerful telescopes on Earth, and has enabled scientists to detect visible light and infrared and ultraviolet radiation from the planets, stars, and distant galaxies usually blocked by Earth's atmosphere.

Look at the diagram of the Hubble Space Telescope on the opposite page. The solar panels provide electrical power to the system. A 2.4-m primary and a smaller secondary mirror collect and focus light to form an image. Various instruments on the telescope interpret the data and communicate it to scientists on Earth.

Troubleshooting on the Telescope

The Hubble Space Telescope is a complex instrument that at first experienced a major problem. Once in orbit, the telescope sent back blurry images because of a defect in the shape of its primary mirror. In December 1993, a repair mission was launched using the space shuttle. In five space walks, astronauts repaired or replaced several faulty parts and updated the telescope's detectors. As **Figure 20-15** illustrates, this dramatically improved the sharpness of the images sent back to Earth. The diagram in **Figure 20-16** shows the main parts of the telescope.

Figure 20-15

An early Hubble photo is shown at the top. The same view is shown at the bottom, after the Hubble's primary mirror was corrected.

Light from
distant object

Aperture door

Secondary mirror

Solar panel

Primary
mirror

Solar
panel

Computer

Widefield
planetary camera

Pointing
sensor

Scientific
instruments

Secrets from Space

The final cost of the Hubble project is more than $2 billion. What do we hope to gain in return for our investment? Scientists hope for new insight into scientific puzzles such as star formation, the evolution and ages of galaxies, black holes, and whether there are planets circling nearby stars. Information about the chemical makeup of the environments on other planets and moons in our solar system has already been obtained. What mysteries would you like the Hubble to help solve?

Figure 20-16

The Hubble's components include aiming instruments, camera, and power supply.

Section Wrap-up

Review

1. Why can an orbiting telescope form clearer images than one on Earth?

2. What kinds of knowledge do scientists hope to gain from the Hubble Space Telescope?

Explore the Technology

The Hubble Space Telescope has many complex parts that work together to produce images from different kinds of electromagnetic radiation. Study the diagram of the Hubble above. What optical system is used to focus the incoming light? Is this device more like a refracting or reflecting telescope? Explain. What source of energy is used to operate its moving parts?

Science Journal

Several environmental factors need to be considered when deciding where to build a new Earth telescope. Write down at least two of these factors that you think would be important and explain why.

SCIENCE & SOCIETY

20•5 Applications of Light

Science Words

polarized light
laser
coherent light
incoherent light
total internal reflection
optical fiber

Objectives

- Describe polarized light and the uses of polarizing filters.
- Explain how a laser produces coherent light and how it differs from incoherent light.
- Apply the concept of total internal reflection to the uses of optical fibers.

Polarized Light

Have you seen sunglasses with a sticker on them that says *polarized*? What makes them different?

Recall modeling a transverse wave on a rope in Chapter 18. You could make the waves vibrate in any direction—horizontal, vertical, or anywhere in between. Most light sources, such as incandescent lamps and the sun, emit light that vibrates in many directions. If this light passes through a special filter, called a polarizing filter, the light becomes polarized. In **polarized light,** the transverse waves vibrate in only one plane. A polarizing filter contains molecules that act like parallel slits to allow only those light waves vibrating in one direction to pass through. If a second polarizing filter is aligned so its molecules are oriented at right angles to the first filter, no light passes through, as **Figure 20-17** shows.

Figure 20-17

No light passes through two polarized filters that are aligned at right angles to each other (A).

Light waves vibrating in all planes

Polarizing filters

Light waves polarized in horizontal plane

No light waves pass through

B Light that is not polarized can produce glare and unwanted reflections.

C Using a polarizing filter on the camera produces a picture in which glare is blocked.

Figure 20-18

More and more, shoppers want to buy sunglasses that are polarized. *Why might this shopper prefer polarized lenses?*

A The *polarized* label means that these sunglasses can do something that other sunglasses can't. They can reduce glare and reflections.

Light reflected from horizontal surfaces, such as a lake or a car hood, is partially polarized horizontally through natural processes. Polarizing sunglasses are made with vertically polarizing filters to block out most of the glare while allowing vertically polarized light through.

The shopper in **Figure 20-18** knows that some sunglasses are polarized to reduce glare and others are not.

B In addition to style, fit, color, and price, this shopper is also examining the polarization of the sunglasses.

Have you ever watched a three-dimensional (3-D) movie? Did you wear special glasses to see the effects? The characters probably seemed to be right in front of you. One kind of 3-D glasses uses polarizing filters. The filter in front of one eye is aligned vertically, and the other filter is aligned horizontally. The movie is shown through two projectors, one with a horizontally polarizing filter and the other with a vertically polarizing filter. As a result, your right eye sees a slightly different picture from what is seen by your left eye. This creates the impression of depth, or three dimensions. Polarizing filters, such as those in **Figure 20-19,** can also be placed over camera lenses to reduce glare in photographs.

Lasers

The narrow beams of light that zip across the stage and through the auditorium during a rock concert are produced by **lasers.** Beams of laser light do not spread out because laser light is coherent. **Coherent light** is electromagnetic energy of only one wavelength that travels with its crests and troughs aligned. The beam does not spread out because all the waves

Figure 20-19

Polarizing filters are often an important part of a photographer's equipment.

travel in the same direction. Light from an ordinary lightbulb is incoherent. **Incoherent light** may contain more than one wavelength, and its electromagnetic waves do not travel in the same direction, causing the beam to spread out.

High-voltage power supply

Photon

Metal cylinder

Flashtube

Coherent light

Mirror (95% reflective)

Mirror (100% reflective)

Figure 20-20

A laser produces a coherent beam of visible light of the same wavelength.

Creating Laser Light

Photons in a beam of coherent light are identical, travel in the same direction, and can be produced by a laser. A laser's light begins when a photon is spontaneously emitted from an atom. This photon is reflected between two facing mirrors at opposite ends of the laser, one of which is only partially coated to allow some light to pass through. Some emitted photons travel back and forth between the mirrors many times, stimulating other atoms to also emit identical photons. This continual process produces a coherent beam of laser light.

Lasers can be made with many different materials, including gases, liquids, and solids. One of the most common is the helium-neon laser, which produces a beam of red light. A mixture of helium and neon gases sealed in a tube with mirrors at both ends is excited by a flashtube, as shown in **Figure 20-20.** The excited atoms then lose their excess energy by emitting photons.

Using Lasers

Lasers are inefficient. In many types, no more than one percent of the electrical energy that is used by the laser is converted to light energy. Despite this inefficiency, lasers have many unique properties that make them useful. The beam of the laser is narrow and focused. It does not spread out as it travels over long distances.

Laser light has many applications, such as reading the bar codes on packages or maintaining high sound quality from compact discs by not scratching the discs' surfaces. Surgeons

CONNECT TO

CHEMISTRY

A particular helium-neon laser contains a mixture of 15 percent He and 85 percent Ne. Where are these gases located on the periodic table? *Analyze* their chemical characteristics. Would you be concerned about their reacting chemically in the laser? Explain.

use lasers in place of scalpels to cut cleanly through body tissues. The energy from the laser seals off blood vessels in the incision to reduce bleeding. Lasers are routinely used to remove cataracts and repair the retina in the eye. In industry, powerful lasers are used for cutting and welding materials. Surveyors and builders use lasers for measuring and leveling. To measure the moon's orbit with great accuracy, scientists use laser light reflected from instruments on the moon's surface. Lasers also provide a coherent light source for fiber-optic communications. **Figure 20-21** shows a laser being used in an industrial application.

Optical Fibers

Did you ever dangle your legs into the water from the side of a swimming pool, and bending your knees, slowly raise your feet? If so, you saw your feet seem to disappear as you raised them in the water. The disappearance of your feet is an example of total internal reflection. **Total internal reflection** occurs when light striking a surface between two materials reflects totally back into the first material. As you know, to see your feet in the pool, light reflecting from your feet must reach your eyes. As you raise your feet in the pool, the light reflecting from your feet strikes the surface between the water and the air and reflects back into the water. Your feet seem to disappear because light reflecting from your feet never reaches your eyes. Total internal reflection depends on the speed of light in the two materials and the angle at which the light strikes the surface. The speed of light in the first material must be less than it is in the second. Also, the angle at which the light strikes the surface of the first material must be large. The sparkle of the gemstones in **Figure 20-22** is a result of total internal reflection.

Figure 20-21

There are many practical uses for laser light. *How many can you think of?*

Figure 20-22

Total internal reflection causes gems to sparkle.

20-5 Applications of Light   577

The Light Scalpel

Optical fibers transmitting laser energy deep inside the human body are replacing some surgical procedures. The effect of the laser on human tissue depends on the wavelength and intensity of the laser light and the type of the tissue. By varying the wavelength and intensity of a laser, a particular kind of tissue can be targeted.

Low-power lasers are used to seal soft tissue and to treat ulcers in the stomach, intestine, and colon. However, many other surgical applications require high-power lasers. One of the most exciting applications would be in the treatment of cardiovascular diseases. An optical fiber-conducted laser may be used to deliver pulses of laser light to clear a blocked artery.

Surgical Lighting

Lasers are also used to light the way for other surgical tools. Do you know anyone who has had arthroscopic surgery? In this procedure, tubes containing optical fibers are inserted through small incisions to help doctors see inside the body.

Think Critically:

What problems might arise in using a high-power laser to clear an artery of an obstruction?

Light Pipes

Total internal reflection makes light transmission in optical fibers possible. **Optical fibers** are transparent glass fibers that can transmit light from one place to another. As shown in **Figure 20-23,** light entering one end of the fiber is continuously reflected from the sides of the fiber until it emerges from the other end. Little light is lost or absorbed in optical fibers.

Optical fibers are most commonly used in communications. Telephone conversations, television programs, and computer information can be coded in modulated light beams. The signals are transmitted by a laser through the optical fibers with far less loss of signal than if similar electric signals were transmitted through copper wires. Because of total internal reflection, signals can't leak from one fiber to another and interfere with other messages. As a result, the signal is transmitted clearly.

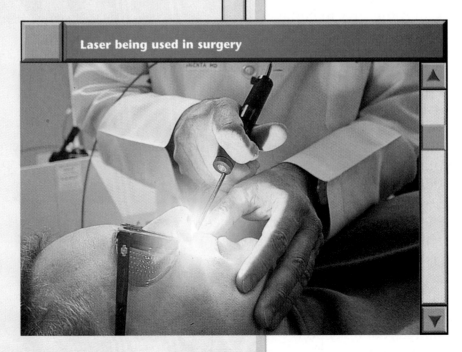

Laser being used in surgery

One optical fiber can carry thousands of phone conversations at the same time because the signals can be produced rapidly and travel at high speed through the fiber. **Figure 20-24** shows the size of typical optical fibers.

Optical fibers are also used to explore the inside of the human body. One bundle of fibers transmits light, while the other carries the reflected light back to the doctor. Plants have also been shown to use the same principles used in optical fibers to transport light to cells that use light energy.

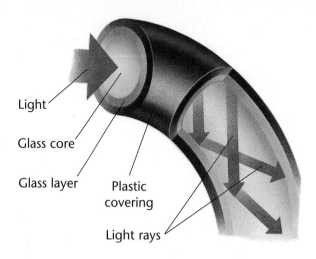

Light
Glass core
Glass layer
Plastic covering
Light rays

Figure 20-23

An optical fiber is designed to reflect light so that it is piped through the fiber without leaving it, except at the ends.

Figure 20-24

Just one of these optical fibers can carry thousands of phone conversations at the same time.

Section Wrap-up

Review

1. What is polarized light?

2. Explain how an optical fiber transmits light.

3. **Think Critically:** Geologists and surveyors often use lasers for aligning equipment, measuring, and mapping. Explain why.

Skill Builder
Sequencing
Sequence the events that occur in a laser in order to produce coherent light. Begin with the emission of a photon from an atom. If you need help, refer to Sequencing in the **Skill Handbook.**

Science Journal

Many people wear polarized sunglasses while they are working. Write a list of jobs or occupations in which wearing polarized sunglasses is helpful and desirable. Explain why.

Design Your Own Experiment
What's behind those shades?

Imagine being near a swimming pool or lake on a bright, sunny day. You would likely be squinting because some sunlight is reflected from the water's surface rather than being absorbed.

PREPARATION

Problem
How do polarizing lenses affect light from the sun and glare?

Form a Hypothesis
In what plane is glare from the ground polarized? How should the polarizing filters in sunglasses be oriented? Write a hypothesis about how polarizing filters affect light and how they affect light reflected off a horizontal surface.

Objectives
- Design an experiment to test the effects of polarizing filters on light from a bulb and on glare from sunlight.
- Relate your observations to some practical uses of these filters.

Possible Materials
- 2 polarizing filters
- masking tape
- light source
- objects with flat, hard surfaces (such as the tabletop)

Safety Precautions
Be sure not to touch the light source. Do not look directly at the sun or the lighted bulb at any time, even with a polarizing filter.

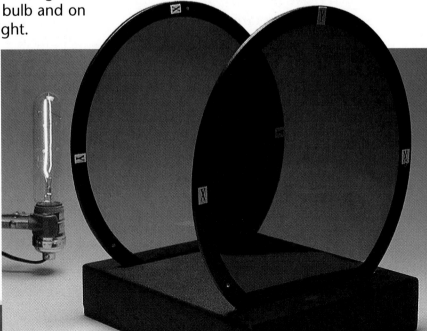

PLAN THE EXPERIMENT

1. As a group, agree upon and write out the hypothesis statement.
2. Develop a procedure to test your hypothesis. Make a detailed list of the steps you will take. Remember that a filter's orientation affects the blocking or transmitting of light.
3. List the materials you will need and gather them.

Check the Plan

1. Before you start the experiment, label the axes of the polarizing filters. To do this, hold both filters still and look through them. Rotate one filter while holding the other still. When maximum light can be seen, use tape labels to mark the top and bottom edges of both filters *X* and the side edges *Y*.
2. How will you find a way to block nearly all light using the two polarizing filters?
3. How will you test the effect of a polarizing filter on glare from both horizontal and vertical surfaces? Be sure to rotate only one filter as you test glare.
4. *Make sure your teacher approves your plan and that you have included any changes suggested in the plan.*

DO THE EXPERIMENT

1. Carry out the approved experiment as planned.
2. Be sure to record any observations that you make during the experiment in your Science Journal.

Analyze and Apply

1. **Estimate** how many degrees you must turn one filter relative to the other to change light passing through from brightest to darkest.
2. When the glare from the horizontal surface nearly disappears, **observe** which edge of the rotated filter is up. Is this also true for glare from the vertical surface?
3. What advantage do polarizing sunglasses have over regular sunglasses? Glare reflected from a horizontal surface is horizontally polarized. **Predict** how polarizing lenses in sunglasses should be oriented to block this glare.

Go Further

Light from the portion of the sky that is 90° from the sun is polarized. Look through the filter at this part of the sky and rotate it to make the sky darken. If there are clouds in the sky, observe their appearance as the filter darkens the sky.

People and Science

JEFF BALDWIN, *Telescope Mirror Maker*

On the Job

Q How do you create a mirror for a telescope?

A I take a piece of borosilicate glass and use abrasives to grind it to a general curve. Then I smooth and polish it so it's accurate to about one-millionth of an inch. All this work is done by hand. Finally, a very thin layer of aluminum is applied to make the glass reflective, creating a mirror.

Q Is a telescope's mirror as important as its lens?

A Mirrors are more important. A lot of people think that the idea of a telescope is to make things look bigger. However, the main interest of astronomers is making distant objects look brighter so they can be observed closely. The larger a telescope's mirror, the more photons it can reflect from an object and the brighter that object will appear.

Q Is astronomy popular with kids and adults?

A Our astronomy club here in Stockton, California, has members ranging from 11 to 93 years old.

Personal Insights

Q Where do you set up your own telescope, and what do you look for?

A Since I live in a light-polluted area, I take my truck and telescope up into the sierra. Right now, I'm studying what are called deep-sky objects—clusters of galaxies that are 4 billion light-years away. Wherever I point my telescope in the sky, I can see galaxies. Each galaxy has about 2 billion stars.

Career Connection

Is there an astronomy club in your area? Find out by inquiring at a museum, a library, a university, or a store that sells telescopes. If you locate a club, invite a member to host a "Star Party" for your class. Then make posters to announce the event. Gather and distribute information about the following careers:

- **Astronomer**
- **Precision Lens Grinder/Polisher**

Chapter 20 Review

Summary

20-1: The Optics of Mirrors

1. Plane mirrors and convex mirrors produce virtual images. Concave mirrors produce real or virtual images.
2. Plane mirrors are used in bathroom mirrors, concave mirrors are used to create flashlight beams and magnify images, and rearview mirrors and shoplifting mirrors are convex.

20-2: The Optics of Lenses

1. Convex lenses form real or virtual images; concave lenses form virtual images.
2. Convex lenses converge light rays and can form images on a screen. Concave lenses diverge light rays and are often used in combination with other lenses.
3. Corrective lenses can be used to focus images on the retina. Farsighted people must wear convex lenses, and nearsighted people must wear concave lenses.

20-3: Optical Instruments

1. A refracting telescope uses convex lenses to magnify distant objects; a reflecting telescope uses concave and plane mirrors and a convex lens to magnify distant objects.
2. Light passing through the lens of a camera is focused on photographic film inside the camera. The image on the film is real, inverted, and smaller than the object being photographed.

20-4: Science and Society: The Hubble Space Telescope

1. By avoiding atmospheric distortion, the Hubble Space Telescope produces sharper images than telescopes on Earth.

In addition, it can detect infrared and ultraviolet radiation.
2. Scientists hope space telescopes will lead to new information about the universe.

20-5: Applications of Light

1. Polarized light consists of transverse waves that vibrate along only one plane. Polarizing filters block light waves that aren't vibrating in the same plane as the filter.
2. A laser produces coherent light by emitting a beam of photons that travel in the same phase and direction. Light that spreads out from its source is incoherent.
3. Optical fibers can pipe light rays because the fibers are made of a material that allows the light rays to reflect totally inside the fibers.

Key Science Words

a. coherent light
b. concave lens
c. concave mirror
d. convex lens
e. convex mirror
f. focal length
g. focal point
h. incoherent light
i. laser
j. microscope
k. optical fiber
l. plane mirror
m. polarized light
n. real image
o. reflecting telescope
p. refracting telescope
q. telephoto lens
r. total internal reflection
s. virtual image
t. wide-angle lens

Reviewing Vocabulary

Match each phrase with the correct term from the list of Key Science Words.

1. mirror with a flat surface
2. image that cannot be projected onto a screen
3. image formed where light rays actually meet
4. curved mirror that diverges reflected light
5. lens that converges light from a distant object at its focal point
6. a telescope that uses two convex lenses
7. an instrument used to study very small objects
8. light waves that vibrate in only one plane
9. light produced by lasers
10. often used to transmit telephone signals

Checking Concepts

Choose the word or phrase that completes the sentence.

1. Images formed by plane mirrors are not _____.

   a. upright   c. enlarged
   b. reversed   d. virtual
2. An object that reflects light and curves inward is called a _____.
   a. plane mirror   c. convex mirror
   b. concave mirror   d. concave lens
3. Mirrors that can magnify a reflection are _____.

   a. convex   c. concave
   b. plane   d. transparent
4. The lightbulb in a headlight, flashlight, or spotlight is placed at the focal point of a _____.

   a. concave lens   c. concave mirror
   b. convex lens   d. convex mirror
5. Lenses form images by _____.
   a. reflecting light   c. diffracting light
   b. refracting light   d. interfering with light

6. A concave lens bends light toward its _____.
   a. optical axis   c. edges
   b. center   d. focal point
7. Farsighted people must wear _____.
   a. flat lenses
   b. convex lenses
   c. concave lenses
   d. unevenly curved lenses
8. Reflecting telescopes don't contain a _____.
   a. plane mirror   c. convex lens
   b. concave mirror   d. concave lens
9. Some sunglasses and 3-D glasses use _____.
   a. concave lenses   c. telephoto lenses
   b. convex lenses   d. polarizing filters
10. Lasers are often used in _____.
    a. cooking food   c. surgery
    b. traffic control   d. headlights

Understanding Concepts

Answer the following questions in your Science Journal using complete sentences.

11. Describe how a concave mirror reflects light rays that approach it parallel to its optical axis. How does such a mirror reflect approaching light rays that pass through its focal point?
12. Why was the Hubble Space Telescope built?
13. Convex lenses are often called converging lenses, while concave lenses are often called diverging lenses. Explain these different names by describing how each type of lens refracts light.
14. Compare and contrast the uses of telescopes and microscopes. Which type of telescope is built most like a microscope?
15. Explain how a laser produces coherent light.

Thinking Critically

16. Magicians often make objects disappear by using trick mirrors. How might a magician seem to make an object disappear by using a concave mirror?

17. What would happen if a movie projector's lens were less than one focal length from the film?

18. If you were an optician, what type of lens would you prescribe for a patient who can't focus clearly on close objects?

19. Would a reflecting telescope work properly if its concave mirror were replaced by a convex mirror? Explain.

20. You have enough money to buy only one lens for your camera. What type of lens would be most useful? Explain.

Developing Skills

If you need help, refer to the **Skill Handbook.**

21. **Classifying:** Classify the different types of images formed by plane, concave, and convex mirrors.

22. **Observing and Inferring:** Infer the effects of a hard, rigid eye lens on human vision. Would this make the eye more or less like a simple camera?

23. **Recognizing Cause and Effect:** Distinguish and describe the causes and effects of the following vision problems: nearsightedness, farsightedness, and astigmatism.

24. **Hypothesizing:** Rough, uncut diamonds lack the sparkle of diamonds that have been cut by a gem cutter. Propose a hypothesis to explain this observation.

25. **Concept Mapping:** Make a concept map summarizing characteristics of coherent and incoherent light. Use the following terms to complete the map (terms may be used more than once): *wavelength(s), frequency(ies), color(s), sun, lasers, coherent light, incoherent light.*

Performance Assessment

1. **Writing in Science:** Write a report tracing the development of the telescope from the time of Galileo to the Hubble Space Telescope. Illustrate your report using diagrams or pictures.

2. **Oral Presentation:** Investigate the types of mirrors used in fun houses. Explain how these mirrors are formed and give distorted images. Demonstrate your findings to the class.

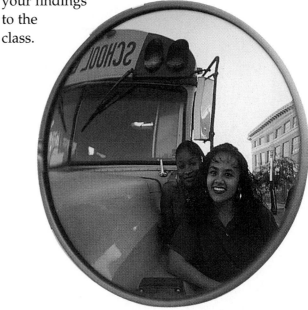

3. **Making Observations and Inferences:** Liquid Crystal Displays (LCDs) in digital watches and calculators have polarizing filters. Observe an LCD through a polarizing filter and rotate the filter while you view the display. Why does it matter which way a digital watch's polarizing filter is oriented?

Vision: More Than Meets the Eye

How are your eyes able to focus on the words on this page? Your eye contains a lens that causes light that is reflected from objects to converge on the retina. But why do so many people wear corrective eyewear? In Chapter 20, you learned that a number of vision problems, such as farsightedness, nearsightedness, and astigmatism, can result when one or more parts of the eye do not function correctly. Eyeglasses and contact lenses are the most common ways to correct these vision problems, although laser surgery is becoming increasingly popular. Perhaps after researching some common vision problems and their methods of correction, you will see the world of vision through new eyes.

Investigating Vision

Have you ever wondered who invented and wore the first eyeglasses? What kinds of materials are used in making corrective eyewear? Who is responsible for testing and treating health of the eyes? With your group, research information in three different categories: eye and vision problems, lenses and correction of eye problems, and careers related to eye care.

Materials
- a selection of convex and concave lenses
- a ruler
- two watch glasses
- grafting wax
- a bowl of water

Procedure
1. Sketch a diagram of the eye and label each part. Find out the role of each part in human vision.

2. Build a convex lens to model the lens in your eye. Do this by placing two watch glasses together under water to trap water inside. Seal them together with grafting wax. How is this model lens similar to and different from the lens in your eye?

3. Find the focal length of several convex lenses, including the one you made. Hold your lens against a piece of white paper across the room from a window in a slightly darkened room. Slowly move the lens away from the paper until you see a clear image of a light source or a brightly lighted outside object on the paper. Measure the distance from the lens to the paper to find the focal length.

4. Identify as many vision or eye health problems as you can. Be sure to investigate near-sightedness, farsightedness, astigmatism, cataracts, glaucoma, and colorblindness. How are each of these problems corrected?

5. What is the difference between an optometrist and an ophthalmologist? Write a list of questions you would like to ask, and interview a person employed in the field of eye care.

Go Further

Think about the advances in diagnosing and treating problems of the eyes that have occurred during your lifetime. What new kinds of contact lenses and eyeglasses are available? What kinds of materials are used in corrective eyewear? What are the advantages of having glass lenses? Plastic lenses? How are lasers currently being used to treat eye problems? Will there be a time when most common eyesight problems are corrected surgically rather than with eyeglasses?

Using Your Research

Design two posters to share your information with other students in the class. One poster should illustrate the human eye, including the parts and their functions. You can also describe on this poster what optometrists and ophthalmologists do. On the second poster, illustrate some of the types of eye problems you learned about. Be sure you can explain how these problems can be corrected. Present your posters to the class and encourage students to identify the problems they or someone they know have been examined or treated for.

UNIT
7

Unit Contents

Electricity and Energy Resources

What's Happening Here?

As the sun sets, electric lights start to go on. Most cities generate electricity for lighting by burning fossil fuel, by harnessing the energy in falling water, or by controlling nuclear reactions. The solar car in the small picture runs on electricity generated when light from the sun falls on solar cells attached to the car's surface. But what does it mean to generate electricity? Why is it an advantage to be able to use different energy sources to generate electricity? How do we safely bring electricity to our homes, businesses, and schools to operate our computers and other appliances? In this power-packed unit, you'll investigate some of these questions.

Science Journal

City skylines are beautiful at night with so many electric lights shining in the dark, but electric lights are only a small part of the use of electricity in an office building. In your Science Journal, write a story about what happened to one person in an electrical blackout.

Previewing the Chapter

Electricity

How many devices can you locate in this office that make use of electricity? Many people in the world have come to depend on electricity to carry out routine daily activities. Electricity provides us with transportation, the ability to control the temperature of indoor environments, entertainment, and many other conveniences. But what is electricity and where does it come from?

EXPLORE ACTIVITY

Can you move matter with electric charges?

1. Blow up a latex balloon and tie it off.
2. Gather small pieces of a variety of different materials, such as a small plate of salt and pepper flakes, shreds of tissue paper, or a pile of small pieces of aluminum foil (less than 1 cm^2).
3. Briskly rub the balloon with a piece of wool or across your clothing to give it an electric charge.
4. Bring the balloon near the different materials you gathered. Record your observations about the behavior of each material.
5. Touch the balloon to a metal surface and then repeat step 4.

Observe: In your Science Journal, write a paragraph describing how the balloon interacted with each material in step 4. Did the results change after you caused the balloon to lose its charge in step 5?

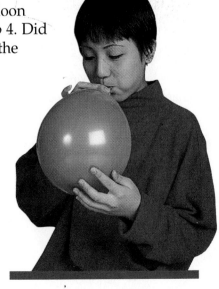

Previewing Science Skills

▶ In the Skill Builders, you will **observe and infer**, **hypothesize**, and **map concepts**.

▶ In the Activities, you will **measure in SI**, **predict**, and **formulate models**.

▶ In the MiniLABs, you will **observe, hypothesize**, and **interpret data**.

21•1 Electric Charge

Static Electricity

Have you ever walked across a carpeted floor and gotten a sharp, painful shock by a spark as you reached out to touch something? If you immediately touched the object a second time, you might have felt a very small spark or none at all. What caused this startling and sometimes painful phenomenon?

When your feet rubbed on the carpet, some of the atoms in the carpet were disturbed. Recall from Chapter 10 that atoms contain protons, neutrons, and electrons. Neutrons have no charge, protons are positively charged, and electrons are negatively charged. An atom is electrically neutral if it has an equal number of protons and electrons. Sometimes, electrons are not held tightly in the atom. As you walked on the carpet, some electrons that were loosely held by the atoms were transferred from the carpet to your shoes. As a result, your shoes gained electrons, and they were no longer neutral but instead had a negative charge. The carpet lost electrons, leaving it positively charged. The excess electrons, stored on your body, gave you an overall negative electric charge. This is an example of static electricity. **Static electricity** is the net accumulation of electric charges on an object. Think of other examples of static electricity.

Opposites Attract

Have you noticed how clothes sometimes cling together when removed from the dryer? Electrons rub off some clothes

Figure 21-1

There are just two kinds of electric charge, positive and negative. *How do charged objects interact with each other?*

Opposite charges attract

Like charges repel

Like charges repel

while they are tumbling around inside the dryer. Clothes that gain electrons become negatively charged, whereas those that lose electrons become positively charged. Clothes with opposite charges cling together, but clothes with the same charge repel each other. As shown in **Figure 21-1,** electrically charged objects obey the following rule: opposite charges attract, and like charges repel.

Figure 21-2

The negatively charged balloon induces a positively charged area in the sleeve by repelling its electrons away from the surface. *What happens if it actually touches the sleeve?*

Because of attractive and repulsive forces, charged objects, when brought near a neutral object, can cause electrons to rearrange their positions on the neutral object. Look at **Figure 21-2.** Suppose you charge a balloon by rubbing it with a cloth. If you bring the negatively charged balloon near your sleeve, the extra electrons on the balloon repel the electrons in the sleeve. The electrons near the surface move away from the balloon, leaving a positively charged area on the surface of the sleeve. As a result, the negatively charged balloon attracts the positively charged area of the sleeve. The rearrangement of electrons on a neutral object caused by a nearby charged object is called charging by induction.

Electric Fields

How does an electron exert a force on another charged particle that is some distance away? It does so by setting up

MiniLAB

How do charged objects interact with each other?

Procedure

1. Fold over about 1 cm on the end of a roll of tape to make a handle that is not sticky. Tear off a strip about 10 cm long.
2. Stick the strip on a clean, dry, smooth surface, such as your desktop. Make another identical strip and tape it directly on top of the first.
3. Quickly pull both pieces off the desk together and pull them apart. Then bring the nonsticky sides of both tapes together. What happens?
4. Now stick the two strips of tape side by side onto the smooth surface. Pull them off with a quick motion and bring the nonsticky sides near each other again. What do you observe?

Analysis

1. What happened when you brought the first pair of tapes close together? Were they charged alike or opposite to each other? What may have caused this?
2. What did you observe when you brought the second pair of tapes together? How were they charged? What did you do differently that may have changed the behavior?

Problem Solving

Take Charge of Pollution

Have you ever noticed a layer of smog in the air over a city? This situation is caused mostly by particulates emitted in combustion processes. Coal-burning power plants, waste incinerators, and other industrial processes contribute to this type of air pollution. How can this pollution be reduced?

A leading method of cleaning up these particulate emissions makes use of static electricity. Electrostatic precipitators are used to trap particles in smoke and ash before they escape into the atmosphere. The ash passes through an electric field to give the particles a charge. They are then trapped as they pass near plates with an opposite electric charge. The collected ash is disposed of in hazardous waste sites or in sanitary landfills.

Solve the Problem:

1. **How do opposite charges interact with each other? Why is such behavior critical to this pollution-control device?**
2. **Would this technique be effective at reducing the emissions of sulfur dioxide gas, which contribute to acid rain formation? Why or why not?**

Think Critically:

Schools, businesses, and even homes also make use of the technology of electrostatic precipitators.

1. Excluding incineration, for what purpose might electrostatic precipitators be used in a shopping mall? Explain.
2. Would there be any kind of waste-disposal problem when using particle precipitators?

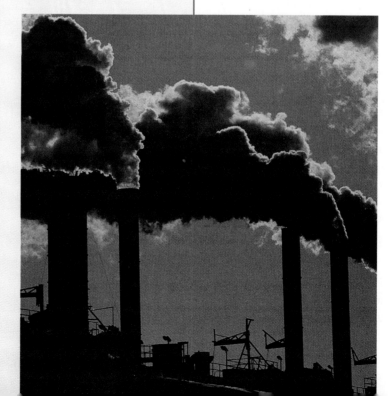

an **electric field** in space. This electric field exerts a force on anything that has an electric charge. The electric field is strongest near the electron and becomes weaker as the distance from the electron increases.

Conductors and Insulators

You now know you can build up a negative charge by walking across a carpet. Suppose you then could touch either a wooden door or a metal doorknob. Which one would you prefer to touch? If your choice was the metal doorknob, be prepared to feel a spark.

Carrying Charges

Look at **Figure 21-3** on page 595. The electrons can move through your body to the metal doorknob because both your body and the metal are conductors. Your skin is not as good a conductor as the metal doorknob. A **conductor** is a material that allows electrons to

Figure 21-3

In the winter, when the dry air indoors is a good insulator, your body builds up a static charge as you walk across a carpeted floor. When you reach for a metal doorknob, the charge flows between your hand and the doorknob and you feel a shock.

move easily through it. Metals such as copper and silver are made of atoms that don't hold their electrons tightly, so electrons move easily through materials made up of these kinds of atoms. For this reason, electric wires are usually made of copper, a good conductor. Silver wire also conducts electricity very well, but silver is much more expensive than copper.

The largest object you are in touch with is Earth. Earth contains a large supply of electrons and functions as a conductor of electricity. It is sometimes desirable to provide a path for the static discharge to reach Earth so that a large static charge doesn't build up on an object and cause damage when it discharges. An object connected to Earth, or the ground, by a good conductor is said to be grounded. Look around you. Do you see anything that might act as a path to the ground? Plumbing fixtures, such as metal faucets, sinks, and pipes, often provide a convenient ground connection.

Insulators—Blocking the Flow

What covers the metal wires in cords attached to telephones and other household appliances? They are usually coated with some type of plastic, an insulating material. An **insulator** is a material that doesn't allow electrons to

Figure 21-4
Pictured here are examples
of conducting and insulating
materials. *Which do you think
are conductors and
which are insulators?*

move through it easily. In addition to plastic, wood, rubber, and glass are good insulators. Would you expect static discharge to occur if you touched the wooden door instead of the metal doorknob? **Figure 21-4** shows some conducting and insulating materials.

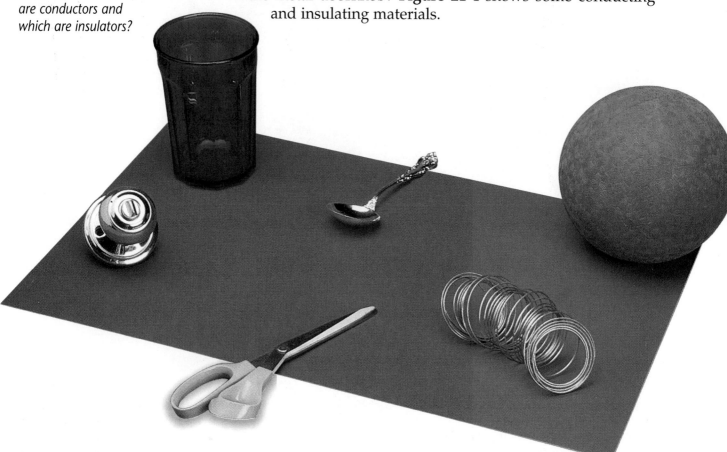

The Electroscope

The presence of electric charges can be detected by an electroscope. An **electroscope** is made of two thin metal leaves attached to a metal rod with a knob at the top. The leaves are allowed to swing freely from the metal rod. When the device is not charged, the leaves hang straight down, as shown in **Figure 21-5A.**

Detecting Positive and Negative Charges

Suppose a negatively charged balloon touches the knob. Because the metal is a good conductor, electrons travel down the rod into the leaves. Both leaves become negatively charged as they gain electrons, **Figure 21-5B.** Now because the leaves have similar charges, they repel each other.

If a glass rod is rubbed with silk, electrons leave the glass rod and build up on the silk. The glass rod becomes positively charged. When the positively charged glass rod is touched to the metal knob, electrons are conducted out of the metal leaves and onto the rod. The leaves repel each other because

A — Knob, Metal rod, Metal leaves

B — Electrons move away from knob

C — Electrons move toward knob

Figure 21-5

Notice the position of the leaves on the electroscope when they are uncharged (A), negatively charged (B), and positively charged (C). *Could you tell whether a charged electroscope was positively or negatively charged by looking at it?*

each leaf becomes positively charged as it loses electrons, **Figure 21-5C.**

Can you think of any other effects of static electricity you have seen? Can you explain them in terms of like or opposite charges? How do objects become charged, and what happens when they discharge?

Section Wrap-up

Review

1. What is static electricity?

2. Distinguish between electrical conductors and insulators and give an example of each.

3. **Think Critically:** Assume you have already charged an electroscope with a positively charged glass rod. Hypothesize what would happen if you touched the knob again with another positively charged object.

Skill Builder
Observing and Inferring

Suppose that you observe the individual hairs on your arm rise up when a balloon is placed near them. Using the concept of induction and the rules of electricity, what could you infer about the cause of this phenomenon? If you need help, refer to Observing and Inferring in the **Skill Handbook.**

Science Journal

Moist air is more of a conductor than dry air. It is more difficult to observe events related to static electricity, such as clothes clinging or hair standing out, on humid days. More water is in the air on humid days. In your Science Journal, explain how humidity affects static electricity.

ISSUE:

21•2 To Burn or Not

Objectives

- Explain the occurrence of lightning in terms of induction and static discharge.
- Evaluate the positive and negative aspects of lightning-induced forest fires.

Lightning—A Natural Fire Starter

Have you ever seen lightning strike Earth? Lightning is a large discharge of static electricity. The friction from the movement of water droplets in a cloud can build up areas of positive and negative charges, just as scuffing your feet on a carpet builds opposite charges on you and the carpet. The bottom portion of a cloud develops a negative charge, causing a positive charge to be induced on Earth's surface. As the difference in charge increases, electrons may be attracted to the positively charged ground. A lightning bolt occurs when many billions of electrons are transferred at the same time. The electricity in lightning can have a potential of up to 100 million volts!

Much of the lightning you see doesn't strike Earth's surface. Lightning bolts also occur between the negative area of one cloud and a positive area of another cloud. The electrical energy in a lightning bolt ionizes atoms in the atmosphere and produces great amounts of heat, warming the surrounding air to temperatures as high as 30 000°C—several times hotter than the sun's surface! The heat causes air in the bolt's path to expand rapidly, producing compressional waves that we hear as thunder.

The sudden discharge of so much electricity can be dangerous. As seen in **Figure 21-6,** lightning strikes Earth many times each day. It can cause power outages, injury or loss of life, and fires. There is some controversy about whether to put out fires started by lightning in regions unpopulated by humans. Because these fires are natural, they can be viewed as part of nature's cycle of growth and renewal. What do you think?

Figure 21-6

Lightning is beautiful to look at but it can be dangerous to property. Many forest fires are started every year by lightning.

2 Points of View

Letting Nature Take Its Course

Natural fires, like the one in **Figure 21-7,** that are started by lightning serve an important function in many environments. Some people point out that without occasional fires, a thick layer of dead debris can accumulate on a forest floor. This prevents sunlight from reaching the soil and reduces the amount of new growth. The accumulated tinder also increases the likelihood of a fast-moving, destructive, hot fire when one inevitably does occur. Some ecologists point out that few animals actually die in fires. Drought and starvation take a much greater toll on animal populations. In the years following a fire, the variety of plant and animal life in the area typically increases. With the National Park Service supporting this view, laws were passed in the 1970s to allow fires started by lightning to burn naturally unless they threaten people or private property.

Preserve and Protect

Many people were upset in 1988 when one-third of Yellowstone National Park burned. The scenery caused by the seemingly lush growth will not be as spectacular for many years to come. Some argue that the loss of plant and animal life due to fires should be reduced whenever possible. They believe that this destruction of public forests should be prevented by fighting all fires, regardless of their origin.

Figure 21-7

Often, fires creep along the ground and don't destroy large, healthy trees. *In what ways might fires help new vegetation grow?*

Section Wrap-up

Review

1. How are lightning and thunder produced?

2. What is the purpose of a lightning rod?

Explore the Issue

Suppose a lightning storm has started a large fire in Yosemite National Park in California. Should it be allowed to burn along its natural course, or should it be put out to preserve areas for human and wildlife use? Would your decision be different if the fire were caused by careless campers?

SCIENCE & SOCIETY

Flowing Electrons

You learned in Section 21-1 that if you touch a conductor after building up a negative charge in your body, electrons will move from you to the conductor. Could you light a bulb in this manner? Probably not, because the bulb needs a continuous flow of electrons to stay lit.

Potential Difference

Recall from Chapter 5 that thermal energy flows from objects with higher temperatures to objects with lower temperatures. This flow ceases when the temperatures of the objects become the same. Similarly, a negatively charged object has electrons with more potential energy to move and do work than those of an uncharged object. This difference in potential energy causes the electrons to flow from places of higher potential energy to those with lower potential energy. In a static discharge, the potentials quickly become equal and electron flow stops.

The potential energy difference per unit of charge is called the electrical potential. The difference in potential between two different places is the **potential difference.** Potential difference

Science Words

potential difference
circuit
current
dry cell
wet cell
resistance
Ohm's law

Objectives

• Describe how static electricity is different from current electricity.
• Explain how a dry cell is a source of electricity.
• Conceptually and mathematically relate potential difference, resistance, and current.

Figure 21-8

Although the systems are not exactly alike, the similarities between how a pump makes water flow and how a battery makes electric charge flow are helpful to examine.

Pump

Reservoir water with potential energy

Water doing work

A The water pump increases the potential energy of the water as it does work by lifting the water against the force of gravity. As the water falls, it does work on the wheel to turn it.

Waterwheel

Water at rest

Direction of flow

is measured in volts (V). Potential difference, often called voltage, is measured by a voltmeter. The voltage doesn't depend on the number of electrons flowing, but on a comparison of the energy carried by electrons at different points.

Circuit Connections

How can you get electrons to flow through a lamp continuously? You must connect it in an electric circuit. A **circuit** is a closed path through which electrons can flow. Because the lamp is part of a circuit, there is a potential difference across it. If the lamp is turned on, electrons will move through it, causing it to produce light. The electrons will continue to flow in the circuit as long as there is a potential difference and the path of the flowing electrons is unbroken.

The flow of electrons through a wire or any conductor is called **current.** The amount of electric current depends on the number of electrons passing a point in a given time. The current in a circuit is measured in amperes (A). **Figure 21-8** shows how an electrical circuit resembles a water-pumping system.

In order to keep the current moving through a circuit, there must be a device that maintains a potential difference. One common source of potential difference is a battery. Unlike a static discharge from your finger to a doorknob, a battery can light a lamp by maintaining a potential difference in the circuit.

Batteries—A Series of Chemical Cells

INTEGRATION
Chemistry

Have you ever noticed that a tape or CD begins to slow down in a portable player after using it for several hours? You may also have noticed that a flashlight becomes dim with prolonged use. Perhaps you decided the batteries were dead and you replaced them. Some devices can be plugged into a wall outlet or can use batteries for the energy they need to operate. How do batteries enable these devices to function?

B A chemical reaction in the battery, or dry cell, adds potential energy to the circuit as it separates charges. Charges move along a conducting wire. The charges do work on the filament atoms, and electrical energy is transformed into light and thermal energy.

← Flow

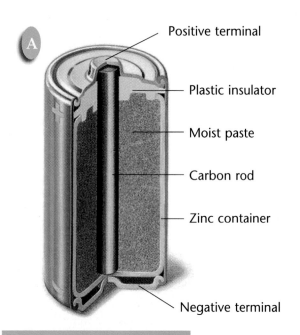

Positive terminal

Plastic insulator

Moist paste

Carbon rod

Zinc container

Negative terminal

Positive terminal

Negative terminal

Partition

Lead dioxide plates

Lead plates

Figure 21-9

The dry cell (A) can be connected with other dry cells to form a battery. A single dry cell is also called a battery. The car battery (B) is a series of wet cells. *How are these devices similar?*

CONNECT TO

CHEMISTRY

In a car battery, also called a lead storage battery, the following chemical reaction occurs: $Pb + PbO_2 + H_2SO_4 \rightarrow PbSO_4 + H_2O$. Use coefficients to *balance* this equation.

Dry Cell Batteries—The Inside Story

The individual batteries you are most familiar with are dry cells. Look at the dry cell shown in **Figure 21-9A.** Notice that the zinc container of the dry cell surrounds a moist chemical paste with a solid carbon rod suspended in the middle. Can you locate the positive and negative terminals of the dry cell in the diagram? A **dry cell** can act as an electron pump because it has a potential difference between the positive and negative terminals. What causes this potential difference?

When the two terminals of a standard D dry cell are connected in a circuit, such as in a flashlight, a chemical reaction involving zinc and several chemicals in the paste (MnO_2, NH_4Cl, and carbon) occurs. The carbon rod does not take part in the reaction; it serves as a conductor to transfer electrons. Electrons are transferred between some materials in this chemical reaction. As a result, the carbon rod becomes positive, forming the positive (+) terminal of the battery. Electrons accumulate on the zinc, making it the negative (−) terminal of the battery.

The potential difference between these two terminals causes current to flow through a closed circuit, such as when you turn on a portable CD player. You make a battery when you connect two or more cells together in series to produce a higher voltage. Can you think of a device in your home or school that requires more than one dry cell to operate?

Wet Cells—Starting Your Engines

Batteries can also be wet cells. A **wet cell, Figure 21-9B,** contains two connected plates made of different metals or metallic compounds in an electrolyte solution. Have you ever examined the battery under the hood of a car? Most car batteries, called lead storage batteries, contain a series of six wet cells made up of lead and lead dioxide plates in a sulfuric acid solution. The chemical reaction in each cell provides a potential difference of about 2 V, giving a total potential of 12 V. As a car is driven, the alternator helps recharge the battery by sending current through the battery in the opposite direction to reverse the chemical reaction.

Plug It In

Most types of household devices are designed to use the potential difference provided by a wall socket. In the United States, the potential difference across the two holes in a wall socket is usually 120 V. The electrical energy is provided by a generator at a power plant. In a later section, you will learn about how this energy is purchased from the electric company.

Resistance

One function of the car battery mentioned earlier is to light various lightbulbs in the car's electric circuits. Do you know what makes a lightbulb glow? Look at the lightbulb in **Figure 21-10.** Part of the circuit through the bulb contains a filament. As a current flows through the filament, electrical energy is converted by the filament into light and heat. The current loses electrical energy as it moves through the filament because the filament resists the flow of electrons, as do most materials.

Resistance is the tendency for a material to oppose the flow of electrons, changing electrical energy into thermal energy and light. With the exception of a few substances that become superconductors at very low temperatures, all conductors have some resistance. The amount of resistance varies with each conductor. Resistance is measured in ohms (Ω).

Figure 21-10

The wire filament of a lightbulb has a high resistance. Electrical energy is converted into light and heat energy.

MiniLAB

Why do some flashlights require more C or D cells than others?

Procedure
1. Make a complete circuit by linking two bulbs and one C or D cell battery in a complete loop. Observe the brightness of the bulbs.
2. Disconnect the D cell. Use a wire to connect the positive terminal of one D cell to the negative terminal of the other D cell.
3. Assemble the new circuit by attaching the wire from one bulb to the remaining negative terminal and attaching the wire from the other bulb to the remaining positive terminal. Observe the brightness of the bulbs.

Analysis
1. What is the potential difference of each D cell? Add them together to find the total potential for the circuit you tested in step 3.
2. Assuming that a brighter bulb indicates a greater current, what can you conclude about the relationship between voltage and current?

USING TECHNOLOGY

Resistive Heating

Is resistance in a circuit a problem or a benefit? If you have ever used a hair dryer or a warm-air hand dryer, you have used a popular technology called *resistive heating*. These appliances contain coils of wire made of materials with high resistances, such as tungsten or nichrome. Some electric energy is converted to heat, along with light, as current passes through these wires. Hot coils are then used to heat the air around them as a fan blows the air toward you.

Resistive heating is also used to warm devices such as clothes irons, electric blankets, toasters, and car window defoggers. Can you think of other appliances in your home or school that use resistive heating?

Think Critically:

Many devices, such as irons and hair dryers, that use resistive heating have several temperature settings. Because the potential difference is the same for all settings, how is the temperature controlled? How do you think the resistance and the current are affected by choosing a hotter setting?

Choosing Resistances for Different Tasks

Copper is an excellent conductor; it has low resistance to the flow of electrons. Copper is used in household wiring because little electrical energy is converted to thermal energy as current passes through the wires. In contrast, tungsten wire glows white-hot as current passes through it. Tungsten's high resistance to current makes it suitable for use as filaments in lightbulbs.

The size of wires also affects their resistance. **Figure 21-11** illustrates how electrons move more efficiently through thick wires

Figure 21-11

The resistance of a short, thick piece of wire is less than the resistance of a long, thin piece of wire.

High-resistance wire makes up the heating element.

than thin wires. In wires of the same length and material, thinner wires have greater resistance to electron flow. Likewise, if the diameters of two wires of a material are the same, the longer wire offers a greater resistance. In most conductors, the resistance also increases as the temperature increases.

Figure 21-12

The amount of current flowing through a circuit is related to the amount of resistance in the circuit.

A By changing the length of the graphite rod the current must pass through, the resistance of the circuit can be changed. Recall that longer wires of a given material have higher resistances than shorter wires.

B Notice that the contact to the graphite has been moved so that the circuit includes only a short portion of the graphite. This decreases the total resistance of the circuit, while the voltage remains the same. *How does the brightness of the bulb compare to the brightness of the bulb in the first photo?*

Ohm's Law

When you try to understand the relationship among voltage, current, and resistance, it is helpful to think of the way water behaves in a pipe. If one end of the pipe is higher than the other, there is a difference in the potential energy of the water due to gravity, and pressure at the nozzle increases. This causes a stream, or current, of water to flow. If the height difference increases, the current increases. In a similar way, a greater potential difference in a circuit also causes the electric current to increase. Also, just as the walls and any obstructions in the pipe resist the flow of water, atoms in a wire resist the flow of electricity. As a result, the current in a circuit depends on both the voltage and the resistance, **Figure 21-12.**

George Simon Ohm, a German physicist, found experimentally that the current in a metal conductor is directly proportional to the potential difference across its ends and inversely proportional to the resistance. This is expressed mathematically in the equation called **Ohm's law:**

Potential difference = current × resistance

V (volts) = I (amperes) × R (ohms)

USING MATH

Calculating Current

Example Problem:

A lightbulb with a resistance of 160 Ω is plugged into a 120-V outlet. What is the current flowing through the bulb?

Problem-Solving Steps:

1. What is known?   resistance, R = 160 Ω
                      voltage, V = 120 V
2. What is unknown?   current, I
3. Choose the equation. $I = V/R$
4. **Solution:** I = 120 V/160 Ω = 0.75 A

Practice Problem

Find the current flowing through a 20-Ω wire connected to a 12-V battery. What if it were connected to a 6-V battery?

Section Wrap-up

Review

1. How does a current traveling through a circuit differ from the static discharge?

2. Briefly describe how a carbon-zinc dry cell supplies electricity for your tape player.

3. **Think Critically:** Calculate the potential difference across a 25-Ω resistor if a 0.3-A current is flowing through it.

Skill Builder

Making and Using Tables

Suppose you individually connect three copper wires of unequal length to a 1.5-V dry cell and an ammeter. The following currents are obtained: wire 1, 1.2 A; wire 2, 1.4 A; wire 3, 1.1 A. Make a table showing current (given) and resistance (use Ohm's law). If you need help, refer to Making and Using Tables in the **Skill Handbook.**

USING MATH

How is the current in a simple series circuit affected by an increase in the resistance of the circuit? Suppose you placed a 60-Ω bulb in a circuit with a 12-V battery. What would be the current through this circuit? Predict how the current would change if you added one more bulb. Two more bulbs?

Modeling Ohm's Law

After several hours of use, batteries may go dead. What has changed in the batteries? For the batteries to cause a current in your stereo, there must be a potential difference across the ends of the batteries. In this activity, you will use gravitational potential energy and water to model potential difference and current in an electric circuit.

Problem

How is a water system like an electric circuit?

Materials

- plastic funnel
- meterstick
- ring stand with ring
- 2 beakers (250-mL)
- rubber tubing (1 m)
- stopwatch or clock

Procedure

1. Create a data table like the one below.
2. Assemble the apparatus as shown. Place the funnel as high as possible.
3. Measure the height from the top of the funnel to the outlet end of the rubber tubing, in meters. Record your data on the table.
4. Pour 200 mL of water into the funnel fast enough to keep it full, but not overflowing.
5. Measure the time for 0.10 L of water to flow into the lower beaker, and record it.
6. Repeat steps 3 through 5 at least three more times, lowering the funnel for each trial.

Analyze

1. Gravity causing water to move can be compared to voltage causing electrons to move. Which trial represents a **model** of a circuit with the highest voltage?
2. The rate (L/sec) of flow of water from the tubing can be compared to current. Which trial represents the highest current?
3. If voltage is increased, **predict** what happens to current.

Conclude and Apply

4. According to Ohm's law, what should happen to the current if the voltage stays the same but the resistance is reduced?
5. If a long tube has more resistance, **predict** what should happen to the rate of flow of water if the tube is shorter.

Data and Observations

Trial	Height (m)	Time (s)	Rate (L/s)
1			
2			
3			

21•4 Electrical Circuits

Objectives

- Sketch a series and a parallel circuit, and list applications of each type of circuit.
- Recognize the function of circuit breakers and fuses.

Finding Familiar Circuits

Look around you. How many electrical devices, such as lights, alarm clocks, stereos, and televisions, do you see that are plugged into wall outlets? These devices all rely on a source of electrical energy and wires to complete an electrical circuit. Most circuits include a voltage source, a conductor, and one or more devices that use the electricity to do work.

Consider, for example, a circuit that includes an electric hair dryer. The dryer must be plugged into a wall outlet to operate. A generator at a power plant produces a potential difference across the outlet, causing the electrons to move when the circuit is complete. The dryer and the circuit in the house both contain conducting wires to carry current. The hair dryer turns the electricity into thermal energy and mechanical energy to do work. When you unplug the hair dryer or turn off its switch, you are opening the circuit and breaking the path of the current.

Series Circuits—Only One Path

There are several kinds of circuits. One kind of circuit is called a series circuit. Some holiday lights are wired together in a series circuit. In a **series circuit,** the current has only one path it can travel along. Look at the diagram of the series circuit in **Figure 21-13.** If you have ever decorated a window or a tree with a string of lights, you may have had the frustrating experience of trying to find one burned out bulb. How can one faulty bulb cause the whole string to be out? Because the parts of a series circuit are wired one after another, the amount of current is the same through every part. When any part of a series

Figure 21-13

A series circuit provides only one path for the current to follow. *What happens to the brightness as more bulbs are added?*

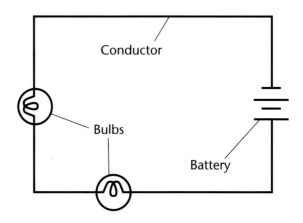

Conductor

Bulbs

Battery

Table 21-1

Circuit Symbols					
Connection	──●──	Resistor	─╲╱╲╱──	Ammeter	─(A)─
No connection	──┼──	Variable resistor	─╲╱╲╱──	Voltmeter	─(V)─
Switch	─○╱	Lightbulb	─(⊗)─	Battery	─┤│├─

circuit is disconnected, no current flows through the circuit. This is called an open circuit. Does this explain how a broken bulb can ruin a whole string of lights?

Table 21-1 shows the symbols used in diagramming electric circuits. Notice that the switch must be closed for the circuit to be continuous.

Parallel Circuits—Branching Out

What would happen if your home were wired in series and you turned off a light? All other lights and appliances in your home would go out, too. Fortunately, houses are wired in parallel. **Parallel circuits** contain separate branches for current to move through. Look at the parallel circuit in **Figure 21-14.** The current splits up to flow through the different branches. More current flows through the paths of lowest resistance. Because all branches connect the same two points of the circuit, the potential difference is the same in each branch.

CONNECT TO

EARTH SCIENCE

Rivers sometimes form different branches that separate and then rejoin, possibly making an island. Write a paragraph *describing* which kind of circuit this is most like and why.

Conductor

Lightbulbs in parallel

Battery

Figure 21-14

In parallel circuits, there is more than one path for the current to follow. *How will the voltage compare in each branch?*

Figure 21-15

What type of circuit is most
common in household wiring?

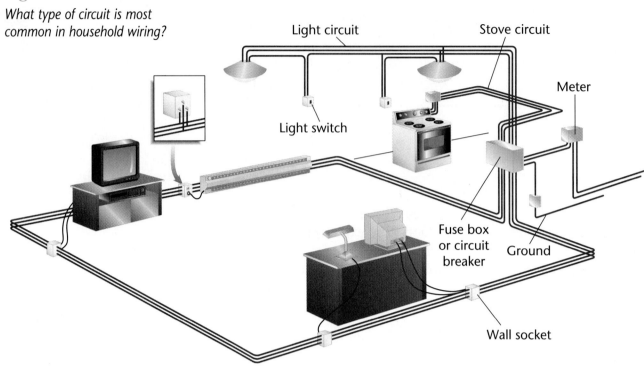

Light circuit   Stove circuit

Meter

Light switch

Fuse box
or circuit   Ground
breaker

Wall socket

Parallel circuits have several advantages. When one branch of the circuit is opened, such as when you turn a light off, the current continues to flow through the other branches. Because each branch of a parallel circuit has the same potential difference across it, lights or appliances on parallel branches receive more current than if they were placed in a series arrangement.

Household Circuits

Try to count how many different things in your home require electricity. You don't see the wires because most of them are hidden behind the walls, ceilings, and floors. This wiring is composed mostly of a combination of parallel circuits connected in an organized and logical network. **Figure 21-15** shows how electrical energy enters your house and is distributed. Each branch receives the standard voltage from the electric company, which is 120 V in the United States. The main switch and circuit breaker box serve as a sort of electrical headquarters for your home. Parallel circuits branch out from the breaker box to wall sockets, major appliances, and lights.

Many appliances can draw current from the same circuit, so protection against overheating must be built in to prevent fires. Either a fuse or a circuit breaker is wired between every parallel circuit and the main switch box as a safety device.

Figure 21-16

The fuses in the fuse box
below prevent circuits from
overheating.

Fuses and Circuit Breakers

What does it mean to say somebody has "blown a fuse"? Usually, it refers to somebody losing his or her temper. This expression comes from the function of an electrical fuse, **Figure 21-16,** which contains a small piece of metal that melts if the current becomes too high and heats the circuit wire too much. When it melts, it causes a break in the circuit and prevents more current from flowing through the overloaded circuit. To fix this, you must replace the damaged fuse with a new one rated for the same amount of current as the original fuse was rated.

A circuit breaker, **Figure 21-17,** is another guard against overheating a wire. A circuit breaker contains a piece of metal that bends when it gets hot. The bending causes a switch to open the circuit, preventing the flow of more current. Circuit breakers can usually be reset by flipping the switch. Before you reset a circuit breaker or replace a blown fuse, you should unplug some of the appliances from the overloaded circuit.

Figure 21-17

A newer device to prevent circuits from overheating is a circuit breaker. *Which device, a fuse or a circuit breaker, seems more convenient to have in the home?*

Section Wrap-up

Review

1. Use circuit diagram symbols to draw a series circuit containing a battery, an open switch, a resistor, and a lightbulb.

2. Use symbols to draw a parallel circuit with a battery and two resistors wired in parallel.

3. Compare and contrast fuses and circuit breakers. Which is easier to use? Why?

4. **Think Critically:** Pennies are made of copper and are excellent conductors of heat and electricity. Explain why you should **never** replace a blown fuse with a penny.

Skill Builder

Hypothesizing

You are walking by a sign made of lighted bulbs. One of the lights begins to flicker and goes out. All other bulbs are still lit. Use your knowledge of circuits to form a hypothesis to explain why only one bulb went out instead of the entire sign. If you need help, refer to Hypothesizing in the **Skill Handbook.**

Science Journal

In your Science Journal, draw a circuit diagram of your bedroom or another room. Show all lights or appliances, and consider whether they behave as if wired in series or parallel. Would you like to have two or more devices controlled by the same switch?

Design Your Own Experiment
Comparing Electric Circuits

Imagine what a bedroom might be like if it were wired in series. In order for an alarm clock to keep time and wake you in the morning, your lights and anything else that uses electricity would have to be on! Fortunately, most outlets in homes are wired on separate branches of the main circuit. Can you design simple circuits that have specific behaviors and uses?

PREPARATION

Problem
How do the behaviors of series and parallel circuits compare?

Form a Hypothesis
Predict what will happen if one bulb is disconnected when connected in series and in parallel. Also, write a hypothesis predicting in which circuit the lights shine the brightest.

Objectives
- Design and construct series and parallel circuits.
- Compare and contrast the behaviors of series and parallel circuits.

Possible Materials
- dry-cell battery (6 V)
- 3 small lights with sockets
- aluminum foil
- cellophane tape
- scissors
- paper clips

Safety Precautions
Some parts of circuits can become hot. Do not leave the battery connected or the circuit completed for more than a few seconds at a time. *Never* connect the positive and negative terminals of the dry-cell battery directly without including at least one bulb in the circuit.

PLAN THE EXPERIMENT

1. As a group, agree upon and write out the hypothesis statement.
2. Work together to determine and write out the steps you will take to test your hypothesis.
3. Make a list of the materials you will need in your experiment and gather them.

Check the Plan

1. How will your circuits be arranged? On a piece of paper, draw a large series circuit of three lights and the dry-cell battery as shown. On the other side, draw another circuit with the three bulbs arranged in parallel.
2. Make conducting wires by taping a 30-cm piece of cellophane tape to a sheet of aluminum foil and folding the foil over twice to cover the tape. Cut these to any length that works in your design.
3. Design several experiments you would like to try with each type of circuit. Be sure you have planned to test your hypothesis.
4. *Make sure your teacher approves your plan and that you have included any changes suggested in the plan.*

DO THE EXPERIMENT

1. Carry out the experiment. Be sure to leave the circuit on for only a few seconds at a time to avoid overheating.
2. As you do the experiment, record your observations in your Science Journal.

Analyze and Apply

1. **Compare** your results with those of other groups.
2. **Predict** what happens in the series circuit when one end of a bulb is left unconnected.

What happens in the parallel circuit? Explain your observations.

3. **Compare** the brightness of the lights in the different circuits. Explain.
4. **Predict** what happens to the brightness of the series circuit if you complete it with two bulbs instead of three bulbs. How does this demonstrate Ohm's law?

Go Further

Hypothesize where in the parallel circuit you would place a switch to control all three lights. To control only one light? Try it.

Electrical Power and Energy

Science Words

electrical power
kilowatt-hour

Objectives

- Explain and calculate electrical power.
- Calculate the amount of electrical energy in kilowatt-hours.

Electrical Power

What do you think of when you hear the word *power?* It has many different meanings. In Chapter 7, you read that power is the rate at which work is done. Electricity can do work for us. Electrical energy is easily converted to other types of energy. For example, the blades of a fan can rotate and cool you as electrical energy is changed into mechanical energy. An iron changes electrical energy into thermal energy. **Electrical power** is the rate at which electrical energy is converted to another form of energy.

The rate at which different appliances use energy varies. Appliances are often advertised with their power rating, which depends on the amount of electrical energy each appliance needs to operate. Electric heating elements in ovens and hair dryers have large power ratings. However, they aren't usually on all the time. Appliances that run a lot of the time, such as refrigerators, usually use more energy. **Table 21-2** shows the power requirements of some appliances, and **Figure 21-18** shows a label with power information.

Table 21-2

Energy Used by Home Appliances			
Appliance	**Time of Usage (hours/day)**	**Power Usage (watts)**	**Energy Usage (kWh/day)**
Hair dryer, blower	0.25	1000	0.25
Microwave oven	0.5	700	0.35
Stereo	2.5	109	0.27
Range (oven)	1	2600	2.60
Refrigerator/freezer (15 cu ft, frostless)	10	615	6.15
Television (color)	3.25	200	0.65
Electric toothbrush	0.08	7	0.0006
100-watt lightbulb	6	100	0.60
40-watt fluorescent lightbulb	1	40	0.04

Calculating Power

Electrical power is expressed in watts (W) or kilowatts (kW). The amount of power used by an appliance can be calculated by multiplying the potential difference by the current.

$$power = current \times voltage$$

$$watts = amperes \times volts$$

$$P = I \times V$$

One watt of power is produced when one ampere of current flows through a circuit with a potential difference of one volt. Look again at **Table 21-2.** Which appliance requires the most electrical power to operate? You can tell by looking at the number of watts listed for that appliance under the power usage column. The example problem below shows you how to calculate the electrical power usage for an appliance. This can be done easily as long as you know the values of the current and voltage.

Work the following problems to practice calculating power.

ENERGUIDE

Energy consumption / Consommation énergétique

724 kWh
per year / par année

▼ This model / Ce modèle

| 724 kWh | 1020 kWh |

| Uses least energy / Consomme le moins d'énergie | | Uses most energy / Consomme le plus d'énergie |

Type 7

| Similar models compared | 24.5 – 26.4 volume in ft³ / volume en pi³ | Modèles similaires compares |
| Model number | 25SIA02 | Numéro de modèle |

Removal of this label before first retail purchase is an offense (S.C. 1992. c.36)
Le retrait de cette étiquette avant le premier achat au détail consititue une violation de la loi (S.C. 1992. c.36)

2173470

Figure 21-18

Most new electrical appliances have labels that show how much power they use.

USING MATH

Calculating Power

Example Problem:

A calculator has a 0.01-A current flowing through it. It operates with a potential difference of 9 V. How much power does it use?

Problem-Solving Steps:

1. What is known?   current, $I = 0.01$ A
   potential difference, $V = 9$ V
2. What is unknown?   power, P
3. Choose the equation. $P = I \times V$
4. **Solution:** $P = 0.01$ A $\times$ 9 V $= 0.09$ W

Practice Problems

1. A lamp operates with a current of 0.625 A and a potential difference of 120 V. How much power does the lamp use?
2. A microwave oven uses 1000 W of power. The voltage source is 120 V. What is the current flowing through the microwave?

MiniLAB

How much power operates an electric toy?

Procedure

1. Remove the battery from an electric toy. Fasten wires to the battery with tape or rubber bands.
2. Attach one wire to the proper battery connection in the toy. Attach the other wire to an ammeter.
3. Use a wire to connect the other pole of the ammeter to the other connection in the toy.
4. Turn on the toy and measure the current on the ammeter.
5. Determine the voltage from the battery size. If two cells were used, be sure to add their voltages together to get the total potential.

Analysis

1. Use the voltage and current to calculate the electric power in watts.
2. Would you expect power usage to change if the toy is allowed to run on different speeds? If possible, try it. When is power usage the highest?

Electrical Energy

Why is it important that you not waste electricity? Most electrical energy is produced from natural resources, which are limited in supply. Electrical energy also costs you money. All the electricity you use in your home is measured by a device called an electric meter. You may have noticed that the meter for your home has a wheel that spins quickly when you are using a great deal of electricity and is stopped when no electricity is being used. The amount of electrical energy you use depends on the power required by appliances in your home and how long they are used. For example, you can calculate the amount of energy a refrigerator uses in a day by multiplying the power required by the amount of time it uses that power.

$$energy = power \times time$$

$$kWh = kW \times h$$

$$E = P \times t$$

The unit of electrical energy is the **kilowatt-hour** (kWh). One kilowatt-hour is 1000 watts of power used for one hour. The electric utility company charges you periodically for each kilowatt-hour you use. You can figure your electric bill by multiplying the energy used by the cost per kilowatt-hour. **Table 21-3** shows some sample costs of running electrical appliances.

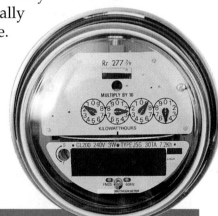

Table 21-3

Energy Used by Home Appliances

	Appliance		
	Hair Dryer	Stereo	Color Television
Average power in watts	1000	109	200
Hours used daily	0.25	2.5	2.5
Hours used monthly	7.5	75.0	75.0
Monthly watt hours	7500	8175	15 000
kWh used a month	7.5	8.175	15.000
Rate charge	$0.09	$0.09	$0.09
Monthly cost	$0.68	$0.74	$1.35

Use the energy equation to calculate the energy used by the refrigerator in the following example problem.

USING MATH

Calculating Electrical Energy

Example Problem:

A refrigerator is one of the major users of electrical power in your home. If it uses 700 W and runs 10 hours each day, how much energy (in kWh) is used in one day?

Problem-Solving Steps:

1. What is known?   power, $P = 700$ W $= 0.7$ kW
                     time, $t = 10$ h
2. What is unknown?   energy, E
3. Choose the equation. $E = P \times t$
4. **Solution:** $E = 0.7$ kW $\times 10$ h $= 7$ kWh

Practice Problem

A 100-W lightbulb is left on for 5.5 hours. How many kilowatt-hours of energy are used?

Section Wrap-up

Review

1. What is electrical power?

2. A television uses a current of 1.5 A at 120 V. The television is used for 2 hours. Calculate the power used in kW and the energy used in kWh.

3. **Think Critically:** How many kWh of energy would be needed for brushing your teeth with an electric toothbrush daily for the month of May? How much would it cost at $0.09 per kWh?

Skill Builder
Concept Mapping
Prepare a concept map that shows the steps in calculating the energy used in operating an electrical device with known voltage and current for a known amount of time. If you need help, refer to Concept Mapping in the **Skill Handbook.**

Using Computers

Spreadsheet On a spreadsheet, list the appliances your family uses daily, the estimated hours per day, and, from **Table 21-2,** the power usage. Multiply the power usage by the hours per day to find the daily energy use for each appliance. Which is responsible for the greatest energy use?

People and Science

GIOVONNAE ANDERSON, Ph.D., *Electrical Engineer*

On the Job

Q Dr. Anderson, what kinds of electronics devices do you design?

A I help design things that test the performance of electronics equipment, such as high-speed telephone lines or satellite communications systems. Right now, I'm working on a device that will test the semiconductor chips used in cellular telephones.

Q What is a semiconductor chip?

A It's a tiny, thin piece of metal with very small electrical circuits printed on it. The chip itself is made of a semiconductor, usually silicon. When you hear people talk about a "computer chip," they're talking about a semiconductor chip that runs a computer. Radios, computers, and virtually all electronics are gradually getting smaller and less expensive.

Q What is a typical workday like for you?

A I spend a lot of time thinking about how electric fields will act under certain conditions, and using a computer to

Personal Insights

model what will happen if I design a circuit a particular way. I also talk to other engineers to find out if we can really make whatever I've come up with. Then technicians build a prototype for me to test. That's when I actually get to sit at a lab bench and play with wires.

Q What advice do you have for students who find physical science interesting but difficult?

A Ask questions. The old saying, "The only dumb question is the one not asked" is really true. People learn in different ways. Often, the person who seems to be struggling is just looking at the information a different way. If you can help that person to understand, he or she will show you something you hadn't noticed before because you've been so busy looking at it your way.

Career Connection

Electrical engineers design and develop electrical equipment, such as household appliances and industrial machinery, and electronics equipment, such as computers and communications equipment. Electronics technicians help build devices designed by engineers. Talk to a career counselor at a local high school or college to find out what kind of education and training these careers require.

- **Electrical Engineer**
- **Electronics Technician**

Summary

21-1: Electric Charge

1. Static electricity is the accumulation of electric charges on an object.
2. An electrical conductor allows electrons to move through it easily. An electrical insulator doesn't allow electrons to move through it easily.
3. An electroscope contains two suspended metal leaves in a jar that move apart when charged.

21-2: Science and Society: To Burn or Not

1. Lightning occurs when excess electrons flow between a cloud and the ground.
2. Some lightning-caused forest fires are allowed to burn as part of the natural processes in the forest.

21-3: Electric Current

1. The potential energy stored in an electron decreases as it moves through a circuit.
2. A dry cell creates a potential difference in a circuit, causing the electrons to flow.
3. Ohm's law states that $V = IR$.

21-4: Electrical Circuits

1. Current has only one path in a series circuit. Parallel circuits provide more than one path for current to follow.
2. Circuit breakers and fuses are safety devices.

21-5: Electrical Power and Energy

1. Electrical power is the rate at which electrical energy can be transformed.
2. A kilowatt-hour is 1000 watts of power used for 1 hour.

Key Science Words

a. circuit
b. conductor
c. current
d. dry cell
e. electric field
f. electrical power
g. electroscope
h. insulator
i. kilowatt-hour
j. Ohm's law
k. parallel circuit
l. potential difference
m. resistance
n. series circuit
o. static electricity
p. wet cell

Reviewing Vocabulary

Match each phrase with the correct term from the list of Key Science Words.

1. buildup of electric charges on an object
2. exerts a force on an electric charge
3. a material through which electrons can move easily
4. a device used to detect electric charges
5. closed path through which electrons flow
6. two plates made of different metals or metallic compounds in an electrolyte solution
7. opposes electron flow in a conductor
8. electric current has at least two separate paths
9. the rate at which electrical energy is converted to a different form of energy
10. relates voltage to resistance and current

Chapter 21 Review

Checking Concepts

Choose the word or phrase that completes the sentence or answers the question.

1. An object becomes positively charged when it _____.
   - a. loses electrons
   - b. loses protons
   - c. gains electrons
   - d. gains neutrons
2. When two negative charges are brought close together, they will _____.
   - a. repel
   - b. attract
   - c. neither attract nor repel
   - d. ground
3. As the distance from a charged particle increases, the strength of the electric field _____.
   - a. can't be determined
   - b. remains the same
   - c. increases
   - d. decreases
4. An example of a good insulator is _____.
   - a. copper
   - b. silver
   - c. wood
   - d. salt water
5. Connecting a charged object to Earth in order to discharge the object into Earth is called _____.
   - a. charging
   - b. grounding
   - c. draining
   - d. induction
6. The difference in potential energy per unit charge between two electrodes is measured in _____.
   - a. amperes
   - b. coulombs
   - c. ohms
   - d. volts
7. The difference in energy carried by electrons at different points in a circuit will determine the _____.
   - a. voltage
   - b. resistance
   - c. current
   - d. power
8. Resistance in an electrical wire causes electrical energy to be converted to _____.
   - a. chemical energy
   - b. nuclear energy
   - c. thermal energy
   - d. sound
9. Which of the following wires would tend to have the least amount of electrical resistance?
   - a. long
   - b. fiberglass
   - c. hot
   - d. thick
10. Electrical energy is measured in _____.
    - a. volts
    - b. newtons
    - c. kilowatts
    - d. kilowatt-hours

Understanding Concepts

Answer the following questions in your Science Journal using complete sentences.

11. Compare and contrast static electricity and current electricity.
12. How are the atoms of conductors different from the atoms of insulators?
13. What causes electrons to move through a circuit? What happens to the electrons' potential energy as they pass through an electrical appliance?
14. How does lightning occur?
15. How are resistance and potential difference related to the amount of current flowing through a circuit?

Thinking Critically

16. Lightning rods are grounded conductors located on roofs of buildings. How do they protect buildings from lightning?
17. Explain how an electroscope could be used to detect a negatively charged object.

18. A toy car has a 1.5-A current, and its internal resistance is 2 ohms. How much voltage does the car require?

19. The current flowing through an appliance connected to a 120-V source is 2 A. How many kilowatt-hours of electrical energy does the appliance use in 4 hours?

20. You are asked to connect a stereo, a television, a VCR, and a lamp in a single, complex circuit. Would you connect these appliances in parallel or in series? How would you prevent an electrical fire? Explain your answers.

Developing Skills

If you need help, refer to the **Skill Handbook**.

21. **Making and Using Graphs:** The resistance in a 1-cm length of copper wire at different temperatures is shown below.

Sample data	
Resistance in Microohms	Temperature in °C
2	50
3	200
5	475

Construct a line graph for the above data. Is copper a better conductor on a cold day or a hot day?

22. **Interpreting Data:** Look at the power usage of the appliances in **Table 21-2** and calculate the current each appliance pulls from a 120-V source. Which appliance draws the most current?

23. **Concept Mapping:** Make a network concept map sequencing the events that occur when an electroscope is brought near a positively charged object and a negatively charged object. Be sure to indicate which way electrons flow and the charge and responses of the leaves.

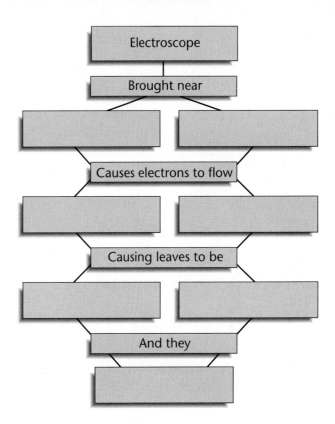

24. **Using Variables, Constants, and Controls:** Design an experiment to test the effect on current and voltage in a circuit when two batteries of equal voltage are connected in series. What is your hypothesis? What are the variables and control?

Performance Assessment

1. **Make a Model:** In Activity 21-1 on page 607, you created a model of Ohm's law with a water system. How would you expect the results of this experiment to differ if you used a tube with a wide diameter?

2. **Design an Experiment:** Review your circuit designs from Activity 21-2 on pages 612-613. How would you design a switch from the materials used in these circuits?

3. **Problem Solving:** You have probably seen warnings about contacting overhead power lines. However, as seen in the photo, birds can safely perch on these power lines. Make a report about how this is possible.

Previewing the Chapter

Chapter 22

Magnetism and Its Uses

What do a speeding train, stereo speakers, TV screens, and floppy disks for storing computer programs and information all have in common? Although they serve different purposes, the technology that makes each of these devices work involves the use of magnets. You can start learning about magnets by doing the following activity. Then, in the chapter that follows, you can continue your study of magnets and their uses.

EXPLORE ACTIVITY

Find out where a bar magnet has its greatest attraction for other magnetizable objects.

1. Suspend a paper clip from the north end of a bar magnet, while holding the bar magnet still. Add a second paper clip to the end of the first one. Continue adding paper clips to the chain until the magnet will hold no more. Record the number of clips held.
2. Repeat step 1, suspending the paper clips about 2 cm from the end of the magnet, and again, suspending the clips near the center of the magnet.

Observe: In your Science Journal, compare the number of clips suspended from each point. Infer where you think the magnetic field is strongest and explain why.

Previewing Science Skills

▶ In the Skill Builders, you will **hypothesize, compare and contrast,** and **map concepts.**

▶ In the Activities, you will **observe, predict, interpret,** and **formulate models.**

▶ In the MiniLABs, you will **hypothesize, observe,** and **interpret data.**

22•1 Characteristics of Magnets

Objectives

- Describe the properties of magnets.
- Define the region of force around a magnet.
- Model magnetic behavior using domains.

Magnets

More than 2000 years ago, the Greeks experimented with a mineral that pulled iron objects toward it. One end of this mineral always pointed north when suspended freely on a string. They described this mineral, shown in **Figure 22-1,** as being magnetic. Today, we know that magnetism is related to electricity. Together, magnetic and electric forces generate electricity and operate electric motors.

Magnetism is a property of matter in which there is a force of attraction or repulsion between unlike or like poles. The magnetic forces are strongest near the ends, or **magnetic poles,** of the magnets. All magnets have two magnetically opposite poles, north (N) and south (S). If a bar magnet is suspended so it turns freely, the north end will point north.

How Magnets Interact with Each Other

When you bring the north ends of two magnets close together, they repel each other. However, the north and south ends will attract. Like magnetic poles repel, and opposite magnetic poles attract. These forces decrease as the distance between the magnets increases.

Only a few materials show strong magnetic properties. Permanent magnets are made from materials such as iron, cobalt, and nickel, which retain their magnetic properties for a long time. Being near or rubbing against a magnet can cause paper clips and nails to become temporary magnets, but they lose their magnetic properties soon after they are separated from the other magnet.

Figure 22-1

Magnetite is a mineral with natural magnetic properties. *What kinds of materials are attracted to magnetite?*

Magnetic Fields

Hold one bar magnet still and move another magnet slowly around it. What happens? Depending on the positions of the magnets, you may feel attractive forces, repulsive forces, or no force at all. As shown in **Figure 22-2,** the **magnetic field** is the region around the magnet where magnetic forces act.

Figure 22-2

You can model the magnetic field by sprinkling iron filings around a bar magnet. The filings line up along the magnetic field lines.

A The magnetic field around this bar magnet can be modeled with iron filings. *Where does the field appear the strongest?*

B Like poles repel.

C Unlike poles attract.

A Giant Bar Magnet

Have you ever used a compass to find out which direction you were traveling? A compass contains a magnetic needle that freely rotates in a circle and always points north. This happens because Earth acts like a giant bar magnet surrounded by a magnetic field that extends beyond the atmosphere. The compass needle aligns with Earth's magnetic field lines. Any other direction can be determined on a compass if the northern direction is known.

Does it seem surprising that the north pole of a compass needle is attracted to Earth's north pole? The place we conveniently call Earth's magnetic north pole is actually a south pole. It follows that Earth's actual magnetic north pole is near the geographic south pole, as shown in **Figure 22-3**.

A Model for Magnetism

What happens if you hold an iron nail close to a refrigerator door and let go? It falls to the floor. Many magnets are made of iron, so why doesn't the nail stick to the refrigerator? You can make the nail behave like a magnet. Because you can't see magnetism, a model, or mental picture, will help you understand how.

INTEGRATION
Earth Science

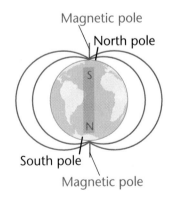

Figure 22-3

The geographic poles are not exactly in the same location as the magnetic poles. What we commonly call the north magnetic pole is actually a south pole.

Problem Solving

Magnet Metal Recycling

Have you ever seen a junkyard for old cars and trucks by the side of a highway? Most of the 10 million cars discarded by Americans each year go through a recycling process to reclaim some of the more than 600 different materials they contain. Magnets play an important role in auto recycling.

An average U.S. passenger car built in the early 1990s contains more than 700 kg of steel (an alloy of iron and other elements), 180 kg of iron, 100 kg of plastics, about 70 kg each of aluminum and fluids, 60 kg of rubber, 20 kg of copper, and more than 50 kg of other materials. After fluids and reusable parts are removed, the car is fed into a huge shredder. Large magnets are then used to separate some of the valuable materials from the shredded car. Inseparable or less valuable materials, commonly called fluff, are usually incinerated or taken to a landfill.

Solve the Problem:

1. **Which materials from the list above would be pulled away from the shredded car by strong magnets?**
2. **Why do some materials behave magnetically and other materials do not?**

Think Critically:

Many recycling centers collect aluminum beverage cans and steel food cans in the same containers. Aluminum and steel cannot be processed together, so why do you think they are collected together if they must later be separated?

In iron, cobalt, nickel, and other magnetic materials, the magnetic field created by each atom exerts force on the other atoms. This causes groups of atoms to align their magnetic poles so all like poles are facing the same direction. These groups of atoms with aligned magnetic poles are called **magnetic domains. Figure 22-4A** shows how the domains are randomly arranged in an ordinary, unmagnetized nail. If a permanent magnet strokes the nail or comes near it, the domains rearrange to orient themselves in the direction of the nearby magnetic field, as in **Figure 22-4B.** The nail now acts as a magnet itself. When the external magnetic field is removed, the magnetic domains in the nail soon return to their random arrangement. For this reason, the nail is a temporary magnet. Even permanent magnets can lose some of their magnetic properties if they are dropped or heated. Their magnetic domains would be jostled out of alignment due to increased motion of the particles.

Can a pole be isolated?

What happens when a magnet is broken in two? Would you expect one piece to be a north pole and one piece to be a south pole? Look again at the domain models in **Figure 22-4.** Because each magnet is actually made of many aligned smaller magnets, even the smallest pieces have both a north and south pole.

Figure 22-4

Groups of atoms are arranged in domains.

and so on

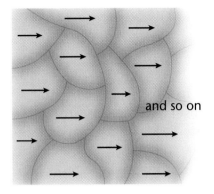

and so on

A The domains are randomly arranged in an unmagnetized object, such as an iron nail.

B In a magnetized object, the domains are aligned.

Although the magnetic domain model explains many observations about magnets, some questions are still unanswered. Scientists have, however, found many uses and applications for magnetism. As you read the next section, you will find out more about these applications.

MiniLAB

What interferes with a magnet?

Procedure

1. Clamp a bar magnet to a ring stand. Tie a thread around one end of a paper clip, and stick the paper clip to one pole of the magnet.
2. Anchor the other end of the thread under a mass on the table. Slowly pull the thread until the paper clip is suspended below the magnet.
3. Without touching the paper clip, slip some paper between the magnet and the paper clip. Does the paper cause the clip to fall?
4. Try other materials.

Analysis

1. What materials interfered with the magnetic field? What materials did not?

Section Wrap-up

Review

1. Describe what happens when you bring two magnetic poles together.
2. What is a magnetic field, and where is it strongest?
3. **Think Critically:** Explain in terms of magnetic domains what happens when another magnet is brought close to a suspended magnet.

Skill Builder
Hypothesizing
Suppose you allowed your younger brother or sister to play with a strong bar magnet. When you got it back, it was barely magnetic. Write a hypothesis to explain what might have happened to your magnet. How could you fix it? If you need help, refer to Hypothesizing in the **Skill Handbook.**

Science Journal

In your Science Journal, make a list of all of the uses you can think of for magnets. Write a paragraph describing what these magnets seem to have in common.

22•2 Uses of Magnetic Fields

Science Words

electromagnet
ammeter
voltmeter
electric motor

Objectives

- Explain the magnetic effects of a current in a wire.
- Compare and contrast ammeters and voltmeters.
- Describe the function of an electric motor.

Electromagnets

In 1820, Hans Christian Oersted, a Danish physics teacher, observed that a current moving through a wire moved the needle on a nearby compass. When the current was reversed, the compass needle was deflected in the opposite direction. These magnetic effects ceased when the current in the wire stopped. Therefore, Oersted hypothesized, the electric current must produce a magnetic field around the wire, the direction of which changes with the direction of the current.

Figure 22-5A shows magnetic field lines around wires with current in them. **Figure 22-5B** shows that adding turns of the wire to make a coil causes more overlapping of the magnetic field lines, and, as a result, the magnetic field grows stronger. When an iron core is inserted into such a coil and a current is passed through the coil, a strong temporary magnet called an **electromagnet** is formed. The iron core becomes a magnet, and its magnetic field is aligned with that of the coil carrying the current. One end of the coil acts as the north pole and the other end as the south pole. The strength of the magnetic field can be increased by adding more turns to the wire coil and by increasing the current passing through the wire.

Music to Your Ears

How does an electrical signal from a CD player become sound you can hear? Electromagnets are used in loudspeakers to change electrical energy to mechanical energy that vibrates the speakers to produce sound. Electromagnets operate doorbells and loudspeakers and lift large metal objects in construction machines. They change electrical energy to mechanical energy to do work and can be turned on and off by controlling the flow of current through the coil. What would happen if the magnetic field in a doorbell were permanent instead of temporary?

Figure 22-5

Magnetic fields form around any wire that is conducting current.

 A The red arrows show the direction of the magnetic field.

 B An electromagnet is made of a coil of wire around a soft iron core.

Battery

Coil of wire

Soft iron core

Figure 22-6

A galvanometer uses an electromagnet to detect electric currents. *What causes the needle to move?*

Meters

Because electromagnets are sensitive to electrical currents, they can detect electric current. An instrument used to detect currents is called a galvanometer, shown in **Figure 22-6.** It is made of a coil of wire connected to a circuit and suspended so it can rotate in the magnetic field of a permanent magnet. When current flows through the coil, the magnetic force causes the coil to rotate against a spring. A needle attached to the coil turns with it to provide a reading on a scale.

USING TECHNOLOGY

MRI—The Inside Story

Did you know you have billions and billions of nuclei in your body that will respond to an applied magnetic field? Doctors can safely use this property to develop clear, three-dimensional images of overlapping structures that can aid in the identification of unhealthy tissue.

In a technique called magnetic resonance imaging, or MRI, a person is placed in the center of a chamber that contains large coils capable of creating a stable magnetic field. This magnetic field causes the nuclei of certain atoms—most notably hydrogen atoms—to align parallel to the magnetic field. A pulse of radio-frequency electromagnetic waves is sent into the region of the body to be examined. If this frequency can be absorbed by atoms in the tissue, the nuclei respond by flipping to an antiparallel alignment.

This change in magnetic alignment of the nuclei provides information a computer can use to create a three-dimensional image of the desired area of the body. MRI can be used to detect such problems as tumors, skeletal injuries, arthritic swelling, and blocked blood vessels.

Think Critically:

How do the advantages and disadvantages of MRI technology compare to those of X-ray technology?

MRI Image of a Human Brain

MiniLAB

How can you observe the relationship between electricity and magnetism?

Procedure

1. Attach an insulated wire to each side of a bulb. Obtain a 6-V dry cell and a compass.
2. Set the compass on top of one of the two connecting wires. Before connecting the dry cell, observe the direction the compass needle is pointing.
3. While watching the compass, complete the circuit. The bulb should light if the circuit is complete. What happened to the compass needle?
4. Slowly rotate the compass, keeping it over the wire. Does the needle change directions or is it still pointing the same way?
5. Gradually move the compass away from the current-carrying wire. What do you notice?
6. While watching the compass, disconnect the circuit. Record your observations.

Analysis

1. What direction does the needle point when the circuit is not connected? What causes it to be oriented in this direction?
2. What can you infer about the relationship between electricity and magnetism from your observations?

Figure 22-7

Ammeters and voltmeters are wired into circuits differently.

A An ammeter measures electric current and should be connected in series with the circuit.

B A voltmeter measures potential difference across part of a circuit. *How is the voltmeter connected in this diagram?*

 Ammeter

 Voltmeter

A galvanometer can be calibrated to measure current or electrical potential, depending on whether it will be used as an ammeter or a voltmeter. **Ammeters** measure the electrical current passing through a circuit in amperes and should be connected in series with the circuit, **Figure 22-7A.**

Voltmeters measure the potential difference of a circuit in volts. Unlike ammeters, voltmeters should be placed in parallel across a part of a circuit, as in **Figure 22-7B.** The reading in volts depends on the potential difference across the voltmeter.

Electric Motors—From Electrical to Mechanical Energy

Do you ever use an electric fan to keep cool? Your fan uses an **electric motor,** a device that changes electrical energy into mechanical energy, to turn the blades. The turning blades push air toward you so your skin feels cooler.

Like galvanometers, electric motors contain an electromagnet that is free to rotate. It rotates between opposite poles of a permanent, fixed magnet. When a current flows through the movable electromagnet, a magnetic field is induced. This causes enough attraction and repulsion with the permanent magnet to force the coil to turn. But the rotation would stop once the magnetic fields aligned. How could you make the coil turn again? Study **Figure 22-8** to see how an electric motor works.

As you will learn in the next section, current supplied by the potential difference in a wall outlet reverses itself at a regular rate, and many devices that operate on household current do not require a commutator.

Figure 22-8

Electric motors use both a permanent magnet and an electromagnet.

Permanent magnet

Brushes

Direction of current flow

A When the battery causes a current to flow through the coil, a magnetic field is induced. Attraction and repulsion between the coil and the permanent magnet cause the coil to rotate.

B To make the coil continue to spin, the direction of the current through the coil must be reversed after each half revolution. A commutator is a reversing switch that rotates with the electromagnet and alternately contacts the positive and negative terminals of the battery. The reversing current causes the poles of the rotating electromagnet to switch and rotate toward the opposite pole of the permanent magnet.

Direction of rotation

Commutator

Shaft

C This process is repeated many times each second.

Coil

Section Wrap-up

Review

1. Does a straight wire or a looped wire have a stronger magnetic field when both carry the same amount of current? Explain your answer.

2. Compare and contrast the wiring of a voltmeter and an ammeter.

3. **Think Critically:** Trace the energy conversion from a coal-burning power plant, through an electric motor, and into a CD player.

Skill Builder
Comparing and Contrasting

Compare and contrast ammeters and voltmeters. Discuss what they measure and how they are connected to the rest of the circuit. If you need help, refer to Comparing and Contrasting in the **Skill Handbook.**

Using Computers

Spreadsheet Take an inventory of all the devices in your home or school that make use of an electric motor. Organize your inventory using a data base or spreadsheet indicating the name of the device, the place you found it, the voltage source used, and which parts the motor causes to move.

Activity 22-1

Electricity and Magnetism

Can you make a magnet by passing a current through a coil of wire? This discovery led to the development of the electric motor. If you can use electricity to make a magnet, do you think it might be possible to use a magnet to help generate an electric current? Try this activity to find out.

Problem
How can a magnet cause electric current?

Materials
- thin, flexible insulated wire
- cardboard tube
- scissors
- galvanometer or milliammeter
- bar magnet

Procedure
1. Leaving about 15 cm for a lead at the end of the wire, make a coil of about 20 turns by wrapping the wire around a cardboard tube. Remove the tube from the coil.
2. Carefully, use the scissors to scrape about 2 cm of insulation off both ends of the wire.
3. Connect the ends of the wire to a galvanometer or milliammeter. Take the reading on your meter.
4. While closely watching the meter, insert one end of the bar magnet into the coil. Then, pull it out of the coil. Repeat this motion and record any observations or measurements you can make.
5. Vary the speed with which you move the magnet. Record your measurements from the meter.
6. Have one partner hold the magnet still while another partner moves the coil over the magnet until it is inside the coil. Record your observations.

7. While watching the meter, move the bar magnet in different directions around the outside of the coil. What do you observe?

Analyze
1. What information does the meter tell you in steps 4-7? Which circumstances that you tested generated the greatest current?
2. How does the speed at which you move the magnet influence the amount of current produced?
3. Does the current you generate by moving the magnet always move in the same direction? What observations help you with this answer?

Conclude and Apply
4. **Predict** what effect using fewer coils would have on the current produced by moving the magnet in and out of the center of the coil. Try it to check your prediction.
5. **Infer** whether a current would have been generated if the cardboard tube were left in the coil. Why or why not? Try it.

Producing Electric Current

Generators—From Mechanical to Electrical Energy

Once scientists knew that magnetism could be produced from electric currents, they tried to produce an electric current using magnets. Working independently in 1831, a British scientist, Michael Faraday, and an American scientist, Joseph Henry, found that moving a wire through a magnetic field induced an electric current in that wire. **Electromagnetic induction** is the process by which moving a wire through a magnetic field produces a current. Moving a magnet in and out of a coil of wire also produces a current. This important discovery led to numerous applications.

Where Household Electricity Comes From

What produces the electricity that comes to your home and school? Most of the electricity you use each day was electromagnetically induced in generators. A **generator** produces electric current by rotating a loop of wire in a magnetic field. The wire loop is connected to a source of mechanical energy and placed between the poles of a magnet, as shown in **Figure 22-9.** The design of the generator is much like that of an electric motor, except the wire loop is rotated by external forces. When it rotates, an electric current is produced. This is the opposite of how a motor acts. In a generator, the wire crosses through the magnetic lines of force as it rotates, causing electrons to move along the wire in one direction. After one-half revolution of the wire loop, each side of the coil passes near the opposite pole of the

Science Words

electromagnetic induction
generator
direct current (DC)
alternating current (AC)
transformer

Objectives

- Describe how a generator produces an electric current using electromagnetic induction.
- Distinguish between alternating current and direct current.
- Explain how a transformer can step up or step down the voltage of an alternating current.

Magnet

Coil

Slip rings

Shaft

Brushes

Figure 22-9

Electric current is produced in a generator when a loop of wire is rotated in a magnetic field. *How does a generator differ from a motor?*

Generator   Electromagnets

Coil

Transformer

Steam from boiler
or water from lake or dam

Turbine

Figure 22-10

The electricity you use in your home is produced
by huge generators at a power plant.

magnet, causing the current to change direction. As a result,
the direction of the current changes twice with each revolution. The rotation speed of generators is regulated so the current always changes direction with the same frequency.

Electricity in Your Home

Do you have a generator in your home that supplies all the
electricity you need to watch television or wash your clothes?
Probably not. You get your electricity from huge generators at
a power plant, like the one in **Figure 22-10.** These generators
are more complex than the ones discussed here. The electromagnets in these generators are made of many loops of wire
wrapped around iron cores. A source of mechanical energy is
needed to rotate the loop in the generator. The loop is usually
connected to a turbine, which is a large wheel that rotates
when pushed by water, wind, or steam. Potential energy
released by the burning of fossil fuels or from nuclear reactions can heat water to produce steam. The thermal energy of
the steam changes to mechanical energy as it pushes the turbine. The generator then changes this mechanical energy into
an electric current that is easily conducted to your home.

CONNECT TO

EARTH SCIENCE

Study the generator
diagrammed above.
What role does water
play in generating
electricity? *Infer* what
might be some advan-
tages and disadvan-
tages of using water
from a dam to push
a turbine.

Direct and Alternating Currents

Do you have a portable stereo like the one in **Figure 22-11** that operates either on batteries or on the electric current in your home? Is the electric current from a generator the same as the current produced by a dry cell? Both devices cause the electrons to move through a wire and can operate appliances. However, the currents produced by these electric sources are not the same.

When you use a dry-cell battery to run your stereo, you are using direct current. **Direct current (DC)** flows only in one direction through a wire. When you plug a CD player or any appliance into the wall outlet, you are using alternating current. **Alternating current (AC)** reverses its direction in a regular pattern. In North America, generators produce alternating current at a frequency of 60 cycles per second (60 Hz). Because current in a generator changes direction twice during each rotation of the shaft, 60-Hz alternating current changes direction 120 times each second.

Figure 22-11

Some electrical devices, such as the portable stereo shown, are designed to operate on AC or DC. *Why wouldn't you want to use dry-cell batteries to operate it all of the time?*

Transformers

The alternating current traveling through power lines is at an extremely high voltage. Before alternating current from the power plant can enter your home, its voltage must be decreased. The current must flow through a device called a transformer to decrease the voltage. A **transformer** can increase or decrease the voltage of an alternating current. The operation of a transformer involves principles of both electromagnetism and electromagnetic induction.

Figure 22-12

Transformers make it possible to transport current to homes at very high voltage.

Iron core

Secondary coil—200 turns of wire

120 volts AC in

240 volts AC out

Primary coil— 100 turns of wire

A A step-up transformer increases voltage.

120 volts AC in

6 volts AC out

Primary coil— 100 turns of wire

Secondary coil—5 turns of wire

B A step-down transformer decreases voltage. *How do the primary and secondary coils compare in each case?*

Stepping Up and Stepping Down

A simple transformer is made of two coils of wire called the primary and secondary coils. These coils are wrapped around an iron core, as shown in **Figure 22-12.** As an alternating current passes through the primary coil, the iron core becomes an electromagnet. Because the current changes direction many times each second, the magnetic field also changes its direction and induces an alternating current in the secondary coil. If the secondary coil has more turns of wire than the primary coil, then it increases, or steps up, voltage.

A transformer reduces the voltage of the alternating current to 120 volts before it enters your home. A transformer that reduces voltage is called a step-down transformer. **Figure 22-12B** shows how the output voltage of a transformer will be decreased if the number of turns in the secondary coil is less than the number of turns in the primary coil. Suppose the secondary coil of a transformer has half as many turns as the primary coil. An input voltage of 120 V will yield an output voltage of 60 V. Step-down transformers, like the one shown in **Figure 22-13,** allow you to operate devices such as CD players, model trains, and doorbells with 120-V household current.

Transmitting Alternating Current

Power plants commonly produce alternating current because its voltage can be increased or decreased with transformers. To transmit alternating current efficiently over long distances, power plants increase their voltages to high values. In a step-up transformer, **Figure 22-12A,** the output voltage is greater than the input voltage because the secondary coil has more turns than the primary coil. For example, the secondary

USING MATH

A step-up transformer has 80 turns on its primary coil and 1200 turns on its secondary coil. The primary coil is supplied with an alternating current at 120 V. Determine what voltage is across the secondary.

coil of a step-up transformer at a generating plant may have 100 times the number of turns as the primary coil. That means that an input voltage of 2000 V would increase to 200 000 V—high voltage indeed!

Think back over this section. Could you describe how electromagnetic induction, generators, alternating current, and transformers all affect your CD player? See if you can recall the series of steps in which AC current is produced, transported, and delivered to your home in a form that you can safely use.

Figure 22-13

Transformers are found in most residential neighborhoods.

Section Wrap-up

Review

1. How does a generator use electromagnetic induction to produce a current?

2. A transformer in a neon sign contains 20 turns in the primary coil and 80 turns in the secondary coil. Which is greater—the output voltage or the input voltage?

3. Compare and contrast alternating current and direct current.

4. **Think Critically:** Explain why a transformer can't be used to step up the voltage in a direct current.

Skill Builder
Concept Mapping

Prepare an events chain concept map to show how electricity is produced by a generator, as discussed on pages 633 and 634. If you need help, refer to Concept Mapping in the **Skill Handbook.**

USING MATH

How would a transformer convert 120-V AC input current into a 6-V output in a portable CD player? Explain the device and use math to determine the ratio of input coils to output coils.

Activity 22-2

Design Your Own Experiment
Trying Transformers

How do transformers illustrate the connection between electricity and magnetism? Review the design of transformers in the previous sections. Build and experiment with the transformer described below to find out how current can pass between unconnected coils of wire.

PREPARATION

Problem
How does a current move between the unconnected coils of wire in a transformer?

Form a Hypothesis
Write a hypothesis about how you can build a simple transformer and what kind of current can pass through a transformer.

Objectives
- Design and build a transformer.
- Observe the effectiveness of a transformer at transferring direct and alternating current.

Possible Materials
- dry-cell battery, 6-V
- AC power supply, low-voltage
- lightbulb, low-voltage, with holder
- insulated wire, 32-gauge
- large nail
- soda straw, cut to length of nail
- scissors
- paper clip

Safety Precautions

Make sure the output voltage of the AC supply does not exceed 7 volts. Do not perform any experiments unless your teacher has approved them.

PLAN THE EXPERIMENT

1. In your group, agree upon and write a hypothesis.
2. Determine and write out the steps you will need to take to test your hypothesis.
3. Make a list of the materials you will need and gather them.

Check the Plan

1. How will you construct your transformer? You can make one version by inserting the nail in the straw. Wrap about 300 turns of insulated wire in a tight coil at one end of the straw. Use another piece of wire to make a similar coil at the other end of the straw. Scrape the insulation off the wire ends with scissors to give you electrical contacts.

2. Be sure you place a light in the circuit so you can detect whether the transformer is working and to provide a resistance in the circuit. Where will you place it?
3. How will you test the transformer with both the dry-cell battery and the AC power supply?
4. Where will you make a switch, or a simple contact point, to easily turn the circuit on and off?
5. *Make sure your teacher approves your plan and that you have included any changes suggested in the plan.*

DO THE EXPERIMENT

1. Carry out the experiment as planned.
2. While the experiment is going on, write down any observations you make in your Science Journal.

Analyze and Apply

1. Did both sources of potential difference allow the transformer to function? In your Science Journal, explain your observations. **Compare and contrast** the magnetism produced by the DC current in battery-driven circuits with

the AC current in circuits with AC generators.
2. The two coils of insulated wire in this circuit are not physically in contact with each other. How does this circuit function?
3. **Make a model** of a step-down transformer using the same materials. Where might you find a step-down transformer in your household?

Go Further

Observe the light as you slide the nail out of the straw. What happens? The nail is similar to a standard part in most transformers. Infer what the role of the nail is in this design.

TECHNOLOGY:
22•4 Superconductivity

Science Words

superconductor

Objectives

• Describe the characteristics of superconductors.
• Consider various applications of superconductivity.

Figure 22-14

The magnetic field of the levitating magnet and the current-carrying superconductor repel each other. *Can you think of any practical use for magnetic levitation?*

In Search of a Perfect Conductor

What do you think about the idea of having train systems that would be levitated, or suspended over magnets, instead of running on rails? How would this be possible?

Recall that conducting materials all have some resistance to electron flow. Some of the electricity moving through the conductor is lost as heat due to this resistance. Likewise, as the temperature of a material increases, the resistance of the material increases. Ideally, the most efficient transfer of electricity would occur if conducting materials had no electrical resistance.

Superconductors are materials that have no electrical resistance. In 1911, a Dutch physicist, Heike Kamerlingh Onnes, discovered that some materials lose all electrical resistance when cooled to temperatures near absolute zero (0 K), –273°C. The temperature at which a material becomes superconducting is called the critical temperature.

One way to cool a material to superconducting temperatures is to submerge it in liquid helium. Helium is normally a gas, but it liquefies at 4.2 K. In 1987, J.G. Bednorz and K.A. Müller received a Nobel prize for making a ceramic material that became a superconductor at 30 K. This opened a new field of research to find "high-temperature" superconductors that become superconducting above the temperature of liquid nitrogen (77 K), which is much cheaper than liquid helium. New materials have been developed that are superconducting at more than 130 K.

Increasing Efficiency

Because superconductors have no electrical resistance, a current can flow indefinitely through them without losing energy. In one experiment, a current traveled through a superconducting loop for more than two years without losing energy. How can we make use of such efficient conductors?

The use of superconductors could eliminate much of the electrical energy waste we experience today. Ten percent of the energy transmitted through electrical power lines is lost as heat. Superconductors could also make electric motors, generators, computer

Figure 22-15

One of the most studied high-temperature superconductors is a compound of yttrium, barium, copper, and oxygen.

parts, and magnetic resonance imaging instruments more efficient, as well. One problem to be resolved is that superconducting materials are often brittle, and therefore hard to shape into wires, although researchers have had some success in developing thin films of superconducting materials.

Magnetic Levitation

Figure 22-14 shows the spectacular levitation effects of magnets over superconductors. Recall that a magnet moving toward a conductor induces a current in the conductor. The current, in turn, produces a magnetic field. If the conductor is a superconductor cooled to its critical temperature, the current will move continuously through it. The magnetic forces induced by these currents repel the magnet and cause the magnet to float, or levitate, above the superconductor. If a train had a powerful magnet beneath it and the rails were made of a superconducting material, the train would move above the rails. The only friction would be with the air. The train would lose little energy to the environment and would not give off pollutants.

Section Wrap-up

Review

1. How do superconductors differ from ordinary conductors?

2. What physical property of superconducting materials currently prevents them from being used in devices such as computers or motors?

Explore the Technology

What would be the advantages and disadvantages of developing superconducting trains? Use information in this section to determine what the difficulties of perfecting this system might be. In what ways might superconducting trains be a part of the solution to energy shortages?

CONNECT TO

CHEMISTRY

In 1987, a new compound of yttrium, barium, copper, and oxygen was discovered to be superconducting at 90 K. Find the symbols and atomic numbers of these four elements and *identify* each as a metal, a nonmetal, or a metalloid.

SCIENCE & SOCIETY

Science & ART

Guitars—Plugged or Unplugged

Strumming Along

Historians have found evidence of a guitar-like instrument dating back to the Renaissance period of history. Since then, the guitar has become the world's most popular music maker. How does an acoustic guitar differ from its electrical counterpart?

Soundboard

Strings

Sound hole

Sound box

The Acoustic Guitar

Acoustic guitars produce sound when the strings are plucked. This transfer of energy from the musician to the instrument causes the strings to vibrate. The energy is then transferred from the strings to the hollow sound box, or body, of the guitar. The sound box then amplifies the sound waves so that they can be heard. The sounds made by this type of guitar are bright and clear, but early guitarists strained to be heard above other instruments. This desire to be heard led to the development of the electric guitar.

Pickups

Output socket

Volume control knob

The Electric Guitar

Electric guitars vary widely. But the one thing these generally solid-bodied guitars have in common is one or more magnetic pickups. A pickup is a device that converts the vibrations of the strings into alternating current. These electrical signals travel to an amplifier that magnifies them. The signals are then converted back into sound waves by the loudspeakers.

The single-coil pickup consists of a small, permanent magnet wrapped with copper wiring. The magnet generates a magnetic field that allows the vibrating steel strings of an electric guitar to interact with the field to generate small pulses of electrical energy in the wire. The twin-coil pickup consists of two coils wired in series that allow electrical currents to flow out of phase. Sound distortion, often referred to as humming, is eliminated in twin-coil pickups.

Science Journal

In your Science Journal, explain why you like or don't like the sounds made with electric guitars. How do they compare to sounds made by acoustic guitars?

Summary

22-1: Characteristics of Magnets

1. Opposite poles of magnets attract; like poles repel.
2. The magnetic field is the region around the magnet where magnetic forces act.
3. Groups of atoms with aligned magnetic poles are called magnetic domains.

22-2: Uses of Magnetic Fields

1. An electric current passing through a coil of wire can produce a magnetic field around the wire. The coil becomes an electromagnet; one end of the coil forms a north pole, and the other end forms a south pole.
2. Ammeters measure electrical current in amperes and should be connected in series. Voltmeters measure the potential difference in volts and should be connected in parallel.
3. An electric motor contains a rotating electromagnet that converts electrical energy to mechanical energy.

22-3: Producing Electric Current

1. A generator produces electric current by rotating a loop of wire in a magnetic field.
2. Direct current flows in one direction through a wire; alternating current reverses its direction in a regular pattern.
3. The number of turns of wire in the primary and secondary coils of a transformer determines whether it increases or decreases voltage.

22-4: Science and Society: Superconductivity

1. Superconductors are materials that have no electrical resistance.
2. The use of superconductors can eliminate electrical energy waste in the form of heat.

Key Science Words

a. alternating current (AC)
b. ammeter
c. direct current (DC)
d. electric motor
e. electromagnet
f. electromagnetic induction
g. generator
h. magnetic domain
i. magnetic field
j. magnetic pole
k. magnetism
l. superconductor
m. transformer
n. voltmeter

Reviewing Vocabulary

Match each phrase with the correct term from the list of Key Science Words.

1. region around a magnet in which a magnetic force acts
2. a property of some materials in which there is a force of repulsion or attraction between like or unlike poles
3. a temporary magnet made of a wire coil through which an electric current passes
4. measures electric current
5. a device that converts electrical energy into mechanical energy
6. the production of an electric current by moving a wire through a magnetic field
7. current that flows in only one direction
8. a device that changes the voltage of an alternating current
9. material with no electrical resistance
10. region of a magnet where magnetic lines of force are most dense

Chapter 22 Review

Checking Concepts

Choose the word or phrase that completes the sentence or answers the question.

1. A magnet's force is strongest at its _____.
   a. north and south poles
   b. south pole
   c. north pole
   d. center
2. As the distance between two magnetic poles decreases, the magnetic force _____.
   a. remains constant
   b. changes unpredictably
   c. increases
   d. decreases
3. Domains at the north pole of a bar magnet have _____.
   a. north magnetic poles only
   b. south magnetic poles only
   c. no magnetic poles
   d. both north and south magnetic poles
4. Which of the following would not change the strength of an electromagnet?
   a. increasing the amount of current
   b. changing the current's direction
   c. inserting an iron core inside the loop
   d. increasing the number of loops
5. Ammeters should be _____.
   a. designed to have high resistance
   b. designed without magnets
   c. connected in parallel
   d. calibrated in amperes
6. A device containing a wire coil suspended in a magnetic field that measures potential difference is called a(n) _____.
   a. transformer
   b. electromagnet
   c. ammeter
   d. voltmeter
7. The direction of the electric current in an AC circuit _____.
   a. remains constant
   b. is direct
   c. changes regularly
   d. changes irregularly
8. Before current in power lines can enter your home, it must pass through a _____.
   a. step-up transformer
   b. step-down transformer
   c. commutator
   d. voltmeter
9. Some materials lose all electrical resistance when they are _____.
   a. at room temperature
   b. at their critical temperature
   c. below absolute zero
   d. heated
10. Superconductors can levitate magnets because the continuous electric current through the superconductor produces _____.
    a. a repulsive magnetic force
    b. an attractive magnetic force
    c. an antigravity force
    d. a mechanical force

Understanding Concepts

Answer the following questions in your Science Journal using complete sentences.

11. Describe the magnetic domain model.
12. Describe the basic device used in both galvanometers and DC electric motors. What additional device does an electric motor have? Why is this device necessary?
13. Explain how a generator produces an electric current.
14. Explain how a transformer works. How do step-up and step-down transformers differ?
15. How might superconductors help conserve energy resources?

Thinking Critically

16. If a magnetic compass needle points north, what is the actual polarity of Earth's northern magnetic pole? Explain.
17. Explain why dropping or heating a permanent magnet causes its magnetic domains to shift out of alignment.
18. Why must an ammeter be connected in series with a circuit? Why must a voltmeter be connected in parallel across a circuit?

19. A step-down transformer reduces a 1200-V current to 120 V. If the primary coil has 100 turns, how many must its secondary coil have?
20. You are developing a superconducting train. On what two problems will you concentrate your research? Why?

Developing Skills

If you need help, refer to the **Skill Handbook.**

21. **Comparing and Contrasting:** Compare and contrast electric and magnetic forces.
22. **Comparing and Contrasting:** Compare and contrast AC generators and DC motors.
23. **Recognizing Cause and Effect:** Earth's magnetic field has reversed itself many times in the past. What would be the likely effect of this switching of Earth's magnetic poles on the alignment of magnetic minerals deposited in Earth?
24. **Hypothesizing:** A compass needle will point north due to the magnetic field of Earth. When a bar magnet is brought near the compass, the needle is attracted or repelled by the bar magnet. Propose a hypothesis about the relative strengths of a bar magnet and Earth's magnetic field.

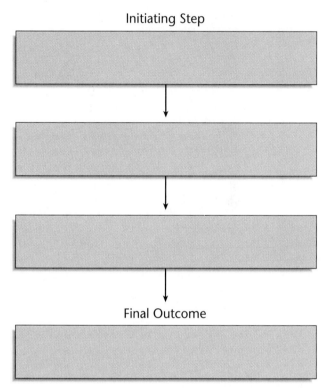

25. **Concept Mapping:** Complete the following events chain map by supplying the name and function of devices used to convert the mechanical energy of a turbine at an electrical power plant into the mechanical energy of an electric fan in your home.

Initiating Step

Final Outcome

Performance Assessment

1. **Writing a Newspaper Article:** Research the most recent developments in superconductors. Write a newspaper editorial stating whether or not the government should spend more money on superconductor research.
2. **Poster:** In Activity 22-2 on pages 638-639, you built and experimented with a simple transformer. Make a poster showing what transformers have in common with AC generators.
3. **Invention:** Invent a new device that uses an electric motor. Demonstrate your device for the class.

Previewing the Chapter

Chapter

23

Electronics and Computers

What ways do people have today of communicating with each other over great distances? The telephone has been around for many years, but advances in electronics and computers have made it possible for people to communicate through methods such as portable cellular phones, and computer networks run games and educational programs on CD-ROM. Have you ever examined the parts inside an electronic device like a calculator or radio?

EXPLORE ACTIVITY

Observe the electronics inside a musical greeting card.
1. Obtain a musical greeting card and listen to the greeting.
2. Remove the electronic device from the card. Examine it with a powerful hand lens, and in your Science Journal, sketch and label the parts you see.
3. Observe the card again. Can you determine what turns the musical card on and off?

Observe: Along with the diagram in your Science Journal, predict the function of any of the parts you see. Which part is the speaker?

Previewing Science Skills

▶ In the Skill Builders, you will interpret scientific illustrations, map concepts, and compare and contrast.

▶ In the Activities, you will observe, infer, classify, and communicate.

▶ In the MiniLABs, you will observe, infer, and interpret.

23 • 1 Semiconductor Devices

Objectives

- Describe how the two types of doped semiconductors conduct a current.
- Explain the device that changes AC into DC.
- Describe the practical benefits of an integrated circuit.

INTEGRATION
Chemistry

Semiconductors

Do you use a calculator when you do your homework, average your grades, or add up the amount of money you've saved? Your calculator is only one of thousands of complex electronic devices made possible by advances in the applications of electricity and magnetism. If you carefully removed the front of your calculator, as shown in **Figure 23-1,** you would see tiny circuits with all sorts of unusual parts inside. You might see several kinds of semiconductor devices: a diode, a rectifier, and a transistor.

Chemistry in Your Calculator

What elements do you think might act as semiconductors? To answer this question, you must first think about the periodic table you studied in Chapter 10. Recall that the elements on the left side and center of the table are metals and conduct electricity. Nonmetals—poor conductors of electricity—are found on the right side of the table. They are electrical insulators. How would you classify the elements found along the staircase-shaped border between the metals and nonmetals? Would you call these conductors or insulators?

The elements located between the metals and nonmetals on the periodic table are metalloids. Some metalloids, such as silicon and germanium, are semiconductors. Semiconductors are less conductive than metals but more conductive than nonmetal insulators. Your calculator and other electronic devices in

Figure 23-1

A calculator contains several different types of semiconductor devices. It contains tiny diodes, rectifiers, and transistors.

Figure 23-2

In the periodic table, the metalloids form a sort of staircase that separates the metals, which are to the left of the metalloids, from the nonmetals, which are on the right. *What are the names of the metalloid elements?*

your home that use semiconductors use less current to operate than similar devices that don't use semiconductors. **Figure 23-2** shows the location of the materials on the periodic table.

Adding Impurities

The conductivity of semiconductor crystals can be increased by adding impurities. This process is called doping. Doped silicon is a commonly used semiconductor. Silicon atoms have four electrons in their outer energy level. This electron arrangement stabilizes the crystal lattice structure. If small amounts of another element with either more or fewer than four outer energy level electrons are added, a few high-energy electrons will be able to move more easily through the material. So, the conductivity of the compound is higher than that of pure silicon.

Silicon is often doped with arsenic or gallium. Locate these elements on the periodic table. How many electrons does each of these elements have in its outer energy level? Even one other type of atom among a million silicon atoms will significantly change the conducting properties of the material. By controlling the type and amount of doping, semiconductors with a variety of conducting properties can be created.

CONNECT TO

CHEMISTRY

Germanium and silicon are commonly used semiconductors. Locate them in the periodic table. Explain why you might *predict* they would have similar electronic properties.

Activity 23-1

Semiconductors

Have you ever passed through a turnstile as you entered a store? You and other people could go through in only one direction. Electrical devices called diodes change AC to DC current by allowing current in a circuit to flow in only one direction.

Problem
How do diodes affect AC and DC circuits?

Materials
- diode
- 2 LEDs, different colors
- hook-up wire
- resistor, 1000 ohms
- battery, 6-volt
- AC power supply, 6 volts

Procedure
1. Attach the resistor to one of the LEDs before connecting it to the battery. Reverse battery connections until the LED lights.
2. Mark the positive side of the LED.
3. Repeat steps 1 and 2 with the second LED.
4. Twist the positive wire of one LED with the negative wire of the other. Attach the resistor to the other two wires.

5. Connect the assembly to the poles of the battery and observe which LED light works. Reverse the battery connections and observe.
6. Connect the assembly to 6 volts AC and observe.
7. Attach the diode in series with the assembly and connect it to 6 volts AC.
8. Reverse the direction of the diode and reconnect to AC. Observe the response of the LEDs.

Analyze
1. A battery sends current in one direction. How does the LED assembly show this?
2. How does the LED assembly detect an alternating current?
3. **Infer** what the addition of a diode does to an alternating current.
4. **Infer** what reversing the direction of the diode accomplishes.

Conclude and Apply
5. In an AC circuit, are the LEDs on all the time? How about in the DC circuit?
6. The resistance of a diode is high in one direction and low in the other. **Discuss** how this experiment shows this to be true.

LANTERN & GENERAL PURPOSE BATTERY

Electronic Gates—Rectifiers and Diodes

Have you noticed that some portable radios can operate on batteries, but they may also have adapters that plug into wall sockets? Why do they need an adapter? Radios operate on low-voltage direct current. For the radio to operate with household alternating current, the voltage of the current must be lowered and the current must be changed to flow in one direction. A radio adapter contains a transformer, which reduces the voltage, and a rectifier. A **rectifier** is a device that changes alternating current into direct current.

Many household devices are built to operate on direct current. Some, such as smoke detectors and clocks, can easily be supplied with direct current from batteries. Other appliances that use large amounts of electricity, such as your television or computer, would not be practical to operate with direct current from batteries. Therefore, transformers and rectifiers are wired into the circuits inside of radios, televisions, computers, and other similar appliances so that they can be supplied with low-voltage direct current from a source of alternating current.

Diodes

A diode is one type of rectifier. A **diode** can be thought of as a type of valve or gate that allows current to flow only in one direction. A diode can be made by doping the ends of a crystal with different elements. Electrons can easily flow through the diode in one direction only. This device, the portable radio's adapter plug, shown in **Figure 23-3,** probably contains a diode rectifier.

Transistors

Have you wondered why radios are sometimes called transistor radios? They contain electrical devices called transistors. A **transistor** is a semiconductor that amplifies or strengthens an electric signal or acts as a tiny electric on-off switch. The signal in an electronic device is the varying electric current that represents a sound, picture, or some other piece of information. Transistors like those shown in **Figure 23-4C** on page 652 amplify a weak electric signal until it is strong enough to be useful. **Amplification** is the process of increasing the strength of an electric signal.

Figure 23-3

Diodes and rectifiers, above, change alternating current into direct current. *Why are these useful in a radio?*

Figure 23-4

Portable stereos (A) contain circuit boards (B), which contain miniaturized transistors (C).

Amplifying Signals

The radio wave that travels many kilometers from a broadcast station to your stereo and television receivers is converted into an electric signal that is too weak to reproduce the information it carries into picture or sound. In other words, it is not strong enough to cause vibration of the loudspeaker and create sound that can be heard. As seen in **Figure 23-4,** a transistor in the electric circuit of the stereo uses a small current from a weak incoming signal to control a large current provided by a power source. Thus, the small input signal supplied to the transistor results in a large, varying output current that can vibrate the speaker.

Your school public address (PA) system contains several transistors. When someone speaks over the system, the sound wave is converted to an electrical signal by a microphone and amplified by transistors within the circuit of the system. The amplified signal is then changed back into sound waves by a speaker. Transistors and their ability to amplify signals make it possible for you to use tape players, bullhorns, hearing aids, and televisions. None of these electronic devices or their applications would be possible without the transistor. It is considered to be the most fundamental part of an electronic circuit.

Integrated Circuits

Look at **Figure 23-5.** Before transistors were invented, devices called vacuum tubes were used to amplify electric signals. These low-pressure glass or metal tubes regulated the electron flow of a circuit's current as it went through each tube. Your grandparents probably owned a television or radio that used these tubes to amplify signals. Televisions and radios today have semiconductor components instead of vacuum tubes. After the development of the transistor, integrated circuits became a reality. As a result of this electronics break-through, today's televisions, radios, calculators, and other electronic devices can be much smaller than the older ones.

An **integrated circuit** can contain thousands of resistors, diodes, and transistors on a thin slice of silicon. These thin silicon slices, called chips, can be smaller than 1 cm on a side. The miniature circuit components in an integrated circuit are made by doping the silicon chip with small amounts of impurities. The conductors between the components are made by using photosensitive chemicals to etch circuits on the silicon chip. Having circuit components so close together reduces the time required for a current to travel through a circuit. As a result, the integrated circuit is an effective design for rapid information processing, which is essential in devices such as microcomputers.

Figure 23-5

Ⓐ Before the invention of transistors, vacuum tubes were used to amplify signals in early electronic devices.

Ⓑ Thousands of resistors, diodes, transistors, and other devices exist in an integrated circuit on a silicon chip a little larger than your thumbnail.

Section Wrap-up

Review

1. Describe how the conductivity of silicon as a semiconductor can be improved.

2. What device can you use to change AC to DC? How does it work?

3. How are integrated circuits made?

4. **Think Critically:** Would carbon atoms be useful in doping a silicon semiconductor? Explain.

Skill Builder
Interpreting Scientific Illustrations
Look at the periodic table of the elements on page 649. List at least four examples each of metals, nonmetals, and metalloids. Classify each of these as a conductor, an insulator, or a semiconductor. If you need help, refer to Interpreting Scientific Illustrations in the **Skill Handbook.**

Science Journal
Radio and television are relatively recent inventions that make use of such devices as diodes and transistors. In your Science Journal, write a paragraph describing how your life would be different without these technologies.

Science Words

cathode-ray tube (CRT)

Objectives

- Describe how radio and television programs are transmitted.
- Explain the operation of a cathode-ray tube.

Radio Transmission

Now that you've studied sound, electromagnetic waves, and electricity, you should be comfortable with most of the concepts needed to explain how a radio works. Radios operate by changing electromagnetic radio waves into vibrations that produce compressional sound waves. Recall that radio waves are the kind of electromagnetic radiation with the longest wavelength and shortest frequency. Like all electromagnetic radiation, radio waves travel at the speed of light. However, the conversion to sound waves is not possible without first converting the radio waves to electrical signals.

Carrier Waves

On a radio dial, a set of numbers on the top of the dial corresponds to the FM frequency range, and a separate set of numbers on the bottom corresponds to the AM frequency range. Every radio station, AM or FM, operates at a specific frequency and wavelength called a carrier wave. FM stations broadcast at carrier frequencies ranging from 88 to 108 megahertz. AM stations broadcast at carrier frequencies between 540 and 1600 kilohertz (sometimes written on a scale labeled from 54 to 160 kHz × 10). Do AM or FM stations operate at a higher frequency?

Sound waves

Figure 23-6

This diagram illustrates the steps that must occur to change music at a radio station into radio waves and back to music. *Why are radio waves used to transmit the signal over long distances rather than sound waves?*

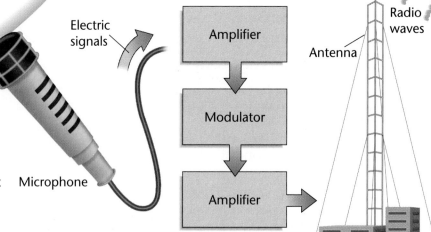

Electric signals

Microphone

Amplifier

Modulator

Amplifier

Antenna

Radio waves

Sending Signals—From Sound Waves to Radio Waves

At the radio station, a microphone collects the compressional waves created by sounds, as shown in **Figure 23-6,** and the microphone changes the sound waves into electrical signals. The electric current vibrations vary according to the sound vibrations. These signals are then amplified and passed through the modulator, as discussed in Chapter 19. The type of modulation varies in AM and FM radio stations. When the electrical signals are used to produce variations in the amplitude of the carrier waves, they are called *amplitude-modulated,* or AM, waves. When the electrical signals are used to produce variations in the frequency of the carrier waves, they are called *frequency-modulated,* or FM, waves. The amplified, modulated electric currents are sent to an antenna, where they are transformed into radio waves.

Receiving Signals—From Radio Waves to Sound Waves

Figure 23-6 shows that your receiving radio has an antenna that collects these radio waves and transforms them into electric currents. If the radio is tuned to the same frequency as the carrier waves, the signal will be amplified again. The carrier wave is then removed, leaving only the electric signal that corresponds to the original sound waves. The radio's loudspeaker vibrates to cause sound waves for you to hear.

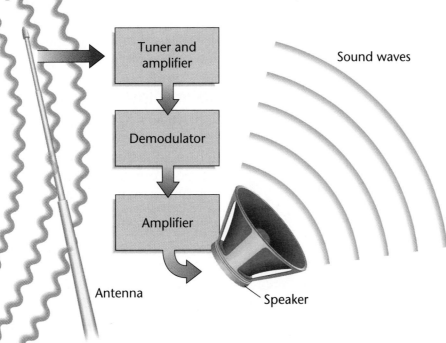

Sound waves

Tuner and amplifier

Demodulator

Amplifier

Antenna

Speaker

MiniLAB

What influences the reception of radio signals?

Procedure
1. Obtain an AM/FM radio with a tall antenna and one without a visible antenna, such as on a clock radio.
2. Using the FM broadcast band of one radio, count the stations you can clearly receive as you slowly scan from the highest to the lowest frequency. Record this information in your Science Journal.
3. Repeat step 2 with the other radio and record your data.
4. Using the radio with the best reception, listen for the locations of the broadcasting stations as you scan both AM and FM bands. Record the locations of stations from each band.

Analysis
1. Which radio clearly received signals from the most radio stations? How does this relate to the antenna system in each radio?
2. Do you have reception from greater distances on AM or FM bands?

Television Transmission

What do radios have in common with television sets? Both have tuners that tune the circuits to the frequency of the carrier waves. Both also have loudspeakers to vibrate and produce sound and an antenna to collect radio signals. The antennas on modern radios and television sets are often hidden in the circuits of these devices. Televisions not only turn the radio waves into sound, but they also use these signals to create a visual image. Television is like a radio with pictures.

Problem Solving

Sending Signals with Remote Control

Do you use a remote control to change a television channel, control a VCR, or change the volume on a stereo? Remote controls are now available that can communicate with up to 16 different electronic devices in a home entertainment system. How do remote controls work?

Most remote controls emit pulses of infrared radiation at a frequency that can be detected by the electronic products designed for remote operation. Pressing different keys causes unique groups of pulses to be produced. Part of the infrared code is used to select which electronic product should respond to the remote command. The other part of each code tells the responding device what to do, such as change a channel, raise the volume, or rewind a tape.

Sometimes, people become frustrated when a remote included with a new television set will not control their VCR or other remote-operated devices. What do you think might cause this problem?

Solve the Problem:

1. **What carries the signal from a remote control to a television set? Do you think it would be possible to block this signal with your hand?**
2. **What kinds of information are included in the signal emitted from a remote control?**

Think Critically:

Suppose you purchased a new television that came with a remote control, but the remote control would not operate your VCR or stereo.

1. What possible explanations for this problem can you suggest?
2. How is it possible for remote controls made by different manufacturers to control other products?

The audio and video signals for television programs are sent and received like an FM radio signal. Just as a microphone is used to change sound waves into varying electric currents, a television camera is used to change light into electric currents that represent the images. This electric video signal then modulates a carrier wave. A television station simultaneously transmits the audio and video signals from its antenna.

Tuning into a television station is much like tuning a radio. When you select a channel, only a certain carrier frequency is picked up and amplified within the set. The audio portion of the television program is changed to sound by a loudspeaker. The picture you see on the screen is created by a more complex process.

Making Images with Cathode-Ray Tubes

You may have heard that if the picture tube inside your television goes out, you are faced with a major repair bill or should probably buy a new television. That's because this picture tube is the most expensive component in your TV set. The picture tube is a type of cathode-ray tube. A **cathode-ray tube (CRT)** uses electrons and fluorescent materials to produce images on a screen.

Look at the CRT in the television set in **Figure 23-7.** A CRT is a sealed glass vacuum tube. When power is applied to the components in the tube, electrons come off a negative cathode and are focused into a beam. They move toward the screen, which is coated on the inside with materials that glow when struck by the electrons. The direction of the beam is changed by electromagnets outside of the CRT. This allows the beam of electrons to sweep the surface of the screen many times each second.

The cathode-ray tube of a color TV contains a screen lined with different materials that give off light in one of the three primary colors: red, blue, or green. The radio waves that carry the picture signal are changed into electrical signals in the television. These electrical signals control the intensity and position of the electron beams, which determine the colors and patterns of the image that forms on the screen. How is this process similar to the way your eye forms color images?

Figure 23-7

The screen of a television set is really the end of a cathode-ray tube that is coated with fluorescent materials.

Section Wrap-up

Review

1. Explain what happens inside your radio when you tune in to a particular radio station.

2. How does a cathode-ray tube produce an image?

3. **Think Critically:** Explain the similarities in how eyes and CRTs in televisions produce color images.

Skill Builder
Concept Mapping

Make a concept map that shows the steps involved in radio broadcasts. Begin with the voice at the microphone and end with the radio waves leaving the transmitter. If you need help, refer to Concept Mapping in the **Skill Handbook.**

USING MATH

Radio waves travel at the speed of light, about 3.0×10^8 m/s. Calculate the wavelength of the radio waves if you are listening to an AM station with a frequency of 1000 kHz. (Hint: Recall that the velocity of a wave = wavelength $\times$ frequency.)

Science Words

microprocessor
RAM
ROM

Objectives

- Identify the basic parts of a microcomputer.
- Describe the role of the microprocessor.
- Distinguish between RAM and ROM.

Figure 23-8

When you think of a computer, you probably picture the input and output devices.

Microcomputer Components

How often do you use microcomputers? You may use them to play computer games, practice math problems, or locate a book in the library. A computer is a device you can program to carry out calculations and make logical decisions. How many simple addition problems can you do in 10 seconds? Computers can perform up to several billion calculations each second. This ability makes them efficient at processing and storing large amounts of information.

Microcomputers must have three main capabilities. First, they must be capable of receiving and storing the data or information needed to solve a problem. Next, microcomputers must be able to follow instructions to perform tasks in a logical way. Finally, microcomputers must communicate their information to the outside world. These requirements can be fulfilled with a combination of hardware and software components. Computer hardware refers to the major permanent components of the microcomputer, as shown in **Figure 23-8.**

A Input devices allow you to enter data in the computer in a variety of forms. These might include keyboards, mice, microphones, joysticks, scanners, and tablets.

Scanner

Mouse

Microphone

Joystick

Tablet

CPU

Keyboard

B Input devices send information to the microprocessor. The main circuit board inside the computer contains the CPU and the main memory. Here, information is processed and sent to the output devices.

Microprocessors

The first computers were very large and slow compared to the computers you are familiar with. The United States built several of the first computers shortly after World War II, between 1946 and 1951. These early computers operated on complex circuits composed of thousands of vacuum tubes. They used a lot of energy and were large enough to fill entire rooms. The invention of the integrated circuit rapidly improved the efficiency of computers. **Figure 23-9** illustrates a computer using vacuum tubes.

A **microprocessor** serves as the brain of the computer. A microprocessor is an integrated circuit on the main circuit board. It receives electrical input from the user and tells other parts of the computer how to respond, just as your brain tells your hand to move when you touch a hot pan. It might store information using a disk drive, change a video display, or make a sound. The microprocessor contains the central processing unit, or CPU, which is the circuitry that actually carries out the arithmetic and logical operations. CPUs are different among various kinds of microcomputers.

Figure 23-9

A modern home video game has more memory and performs more operations than this early computer that used vacuum tubes. *What inventions made this decrease in the size of computers possible?*

C Output devices, such as monitors, speakers, and printers, communicate information to the user.

Monitor

Speaker

Printer

D Some accessories can serve as both input and output devices. Modems allow information to be sent between different computers. Floppy and hard disk drives are used to store and transfer information.

CPU

Modem   Disc drive

Computer Memory

Information is collected and stored in the memory of the computer. The memory contains thousands of tiny circuits that have switches with two positions: open (off) or closed (on). Recall that a switch must be closed for current to flow. All computer information is processed with combinations of just two numbers, zero and one, to represent these situations. This is called a binary number system. Each 0 (off) or 1 (on) represents one binary digit and is called a bit. Numbers, letters, and symbols are represented in your computer by arrangements of eight bits called bytes. **Table 23-1** shows a commonly used binary code for numerical data.

Table 23-1

Binary Code					
Number	Code	Switch	Number	Code	Switch
0	0011 0000	○○●● ○○○○	5	0011 0101	○○●● ○●○●
1	0011 0001	○○●● ○○○●	6	0011 0110	○○●● ○●●○
2	0011 0010	○○●● ○○●○	7	0011 0111	○○●● ○●●●
3	0011 0011	○○●● ○○●●	8	0011 1000	○○●● ●○○○
4	0011 0100	○○●● ○●○○	9	0011 1001	○○●● ●○○●

Random Access Memory

Microcomputers have several kinds of memory. Temporary memory stores documents, programs, and data while they are being used. This temporary memory is called random access memory, or **RAM,** because any bit can be used in storing information. Because information is electronically stored in RAM, the information is lost when the computer is turned off.

Read Only Memory

When you purchase a computer, it comes with some information already stored in permanent memory. This information contains instructions required by the microprocessor to operate the computer. The computer can read this memory, but information can't be added to it. For this reason, it is called read only memory, or **ROM.** Information in ROM is permanently stored inside the computer and, therefore, isn't lost when the computer is turned off. Neither RAM nor ROM is useful in helping you store your work between uses.

Floppy Disks and Hard Drives

One of the main advantages of using computers is that you can save information and then come back later to make changes to it. Most computers have at least one disk drive for storing information on a floppy disk, **Figure 23-10B.** A floppy disk is a thin, round, plastic disk coated with a magnetic material, such as iron oxide. The disk is encased in a thicker plastic case for protection. Information can be saved on the disk, and the disk can be removed from the disk drive for storage. Floppy disks can be used to transfer data or programs from one computer to another computer.

Hard disk drives, **Figure 23-10A,** are found inside the main part of most computers. Hard disks are rigid metal disks that stay inside the computer and spin continuously when the computer is on. Hard drives are useful because they hold many times more information than floppy disks can hold. They also retrieve information much faster.

CD-ROM

Have you listened to music recorded on a compact disk, or CD? If so, you have used an optical disk, on which information is written and read by lasers. You probably know that although you can listen to it, you cannot record music yourself onto a CD. Computers can also read text, sound, and graphics recorded on a similar product called a CD-ROM, **Figure 23-10C.** What do you think *CD-ROM* stands for? This abbreviation represents the term *Compact Disk—Read Only Memory.* Remember that ROM means you cannot save information to the CD. CD-ROMs can hold much greater amounts

Mini LAB

What makes a calculator user friendly?

Procedure

1. Obtain a calculator to test. Write a list of properties you will test to determine whether the calculator is user friendly.
2. Enter a simple mathematical problem. Are the keys large enough for your fingers? Can you tell by the feel of pressing a key when the contact has been made?
3. Is the display large and clear enough to be seen from any practical angle?
4. Does the calculator work by normal rules of arithmetic, or must you push additional buttons to multiply and divide?
5. Can you easily save a number in memory and recall it for use in a later problem?

Analysis

1. What do you think is the most important property that makes a calculator easy to use?
2. How would you change the design of this calculator to make it more user friendly?

Figure 23-10

A A hard disk is a permanent part of microcomputers manufactured today.

C CD-ROMs can store large amounts of information, but a computer cannot write to them.

B Floppy disks come in several sizes, although the 3.5-inch size is the most common today.

Navigating the Net ▼ ▲

Imagine sitting down at a computer in your home or school and being able to access information from computers around the world within seconds! This is possible with use of the Internet, an international system of thousands of smaller networks linked together by wired or wireless connections. Many companies and schools provide Internet access free of charge to employees or students, but you can also pay a monthly fee for access through an Internet service. All you need is a computer, a modem with communications software, and a phone line.

The most popular service on the Internet is electronic mail, or E-mail, which enables users to send and receive messages between computer terminals around the world in just seconds. People can even "talk" over Internet by typing conversation back and forth. Bulletin board discussion groups in a system called Usenet allow people to post messages and read comments from around the world about several thousand different topics of interest.

Because the information available on the Internet changes daily, a directory is not available.

Think Critically:

How might the Internet be helpful if you were assigned to write a paper about the government of Kenya in your social studies class?

of information than floppy disks and even more than some hard disks. They are commonly used to hold reference materials such as encyclopedias, magazines, and digitized video and sound.

Uses for Computers

Computers can't complete a task without instructions for carrying out a series of operations. A program is a group of instructions that tell a computer what to do. Programs are sometimes referred to as software. Computer programmers use special languages that convert your language into instructions the CPU can understand. BASIC, Pascal, Fortran, and COBOL are examples of computer languages. Whenever you play a computer game, use a word processor, or solve mathematical problems, a computer program is instructing the computer to perform in a certain way.

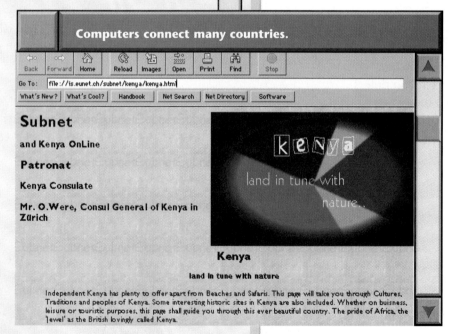

Computers connect many countries.

Go To: file://is.eunet.ch/subnet/kenya/kenya.html

Subnet

and Kenya OnLine

Patronat

Kenya Consulate

Mr. O.Were, Consul General of Kenya in Zürich

Kenya

land in tune with nature

Independent Kenya has plenty to offer apart from Beaches and Safaris. This page will take you through Cultures, Traditions and peoples of Kenya. Some interesting historic sites in Kenya are also included. Whether on buisness, leisure or touristic purposes, this page shall guide you through this ever beautiful country. The pride of Africa, the 'Jewel' as the British lovingly called Kenya.

Hidden Computers

As shown in **Figure 23-11,** microcomputers are becoming useful in more and more applications, such as desktop publishing. You often use them in situations where a computer screen is not visible. For example, computers are regularly used to regulate mechanical processes in cars, to monitor heating and cooling systems in buildings, and to enter inventory bar codes in grocery stores. Many calculators can now be programmed, as well. Even some kitchen appliances contain simple, small computers to enhance their operations. Microcomputers would not exist without advances in electronics, such as the transistor and the integrated circuit. How do you think we'll use microcomputers of the future?

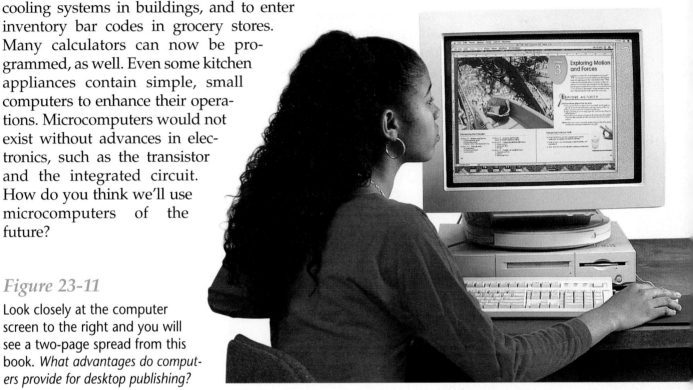

Figure 23-11

Look closely at the computer screen to the right and you will see a two-page spread from this book. *What advantages do computers provide for desktop publishing?*

Section Wrap-up

Review

1. What are the functions of the three main parts of a computer?

2. What is the difference between RAM and ROM?

3. **Think Critically:** How would you transfer a computer program from your computer to a friend's computer?

Skill Builder
Comparing and Contrasting

Compare and contrast the advantages and disadvantages of floppy disk drives and hard disk drives. If you need help, refer to Comparing and Contrasting in the **Skill Handbook.**

Using Computers

Word Processing
Locate a microcomputer in your school. Sketch the system and label any parts you can identify as input, output, or processing devices. Next, examine the software on the machine. Using a word processor, write a report about the hardware and software telling what programs you find and what the purpose of each one is.

Design an Experiment
Magnetic Messages

Computers represent, process, and store information using a binary number system. In this system, coded combinations of the numbers zero and one represent all characters and symbols entered into a computer. Can you design a binary code and store a message magnetically?

PREPARATION

Problem

How can you invent a binary code for the letters of the alphabet and use magnets to write a word in this code?

Form a Hypothesis

Develop a hypothesis about how a binary code could be used to represent all letters of the alphabet. In addition, hypothesize how the attraction and repulsion between magnets could be used to encode a message with your binary code.

Objectives

- Invent a code for each letter of the alphabet using a sequence of five binary digits.

- Use magnets to write and read a message using the binary code.

Possible Materials

- disk magnets, 16
- card stock paper, 2 sheets and a thin strip
- binder-hole reinforcing stickers or other symbols
- transparent tape
- metric ruler

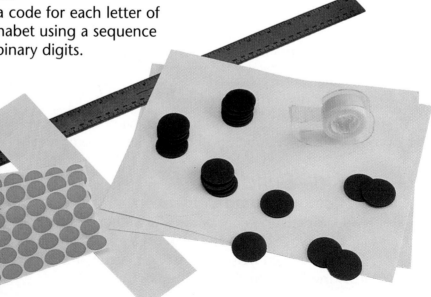

PLAN THE EXPERIMENT

1. As a group, agree upon and write out the hypothesis statement.
2. Invent and record your binary code for each letter of the alphabet. Each letter should be represented by five binary digits, with each digit having the value 0 or 1. For example, the code for *A* might be 00001, *B* might be 00010, and so on.

Check the Plan

1. Put all of the magnets in a single stack. Use small stickers or tape to label the top side of each magnet with the number 1 and the bottom with the number 0.
2. Use a ruler to divide one sheet of the card stock into three rows of five squares as shown. Mark the second sheet in exactly the same way.

3. Choose a three-letter word to write in your magnetic code. Place the code for one letter on each line, and tape the magnets to the cardboard with the appropriate code number right-side up.
4. Cover the magnets with the second sheet marked with the locations of the squares.
5. How will you test and decode the hidden message? Devise a way to use the remaining magnet to test the digit under each square.
6. *Make sure your teacher approves your plan and that you have included any changes suggested in the plan.*

DO THE EXPERIMENT

1. Carry out the magnetic testing of the message as planned, recording in your Science Journal which side of each hidden magnet you believe is facing up.
2. Use the results of your magnetic testing to decode the message.

Analyze and Apply

1. **Explain** how you know which side of the magnet is facing up underneath your testing magnet.

2. Which side, 0 or 1, of your testing magnet was facing the code? If you were to repeat the experiment while holding your test magnet the opposite way, **hypothesize** how your interpretations would differ.
3. **Infer** why there are only two numbers in this magnetic code. Could you think of each digit as being like an off/on switch? Explain.

Go Further

List your operating rules for reading your word. Communicate your rules, letter code, and magnetic message with another team, and see whether they can decode your message.

TECHNOLOGY:
23•4 Computer Crimes

Science Words

computer virus

Objectives

- Discuss the types of crimes that can be committed by computer misuse.
- Predict the possible consequences of computer crimes.

How serious are computer crimes?

What do you think of when you hear the word *crime?* You probably think of stealing, vandalism, or violence. An increasingly common type of crime is being committed by the misuse of computers.

You may have copied a friend's cassette tape onto a blank tape for your own personal use. Computer programs can also be copied from one floppy disk to another. When you purchase a program, the software company usually intends for you to make one backup copy in case the original one becomes damaged. The companies don't intend for you to copy the program to give to your friends. Cassette tapes and many computer programs are protected by copyright laws, as shown in **Figure 23-12.** However, some programs are free and can be legally shared. Sharing of illegal copies of software is probably the most common of computer crimes, as well as the most difficult computer crime to safeguard against.

Figure 23-12

Most purchased computer programs are copyrighted, making it illegal to share copies with other computer owners. You can protect a disk from contracting a virus by keeping the window open when loading files from the disk. This prevents any new material from being written to the disk.

Computer Viruses—A Contagious Problem

In recent years, computer viruses have become a problem. A **computer virus** is a type of program that can multiply inside a computer and use so much memory that it harms the system. Like a virus in your body, it can remain inactive in the computer until something causes it to spread. As a result of the virus attack, data in memory might be lost or a strange message might appear on the screen. The infected computer might even just stop functioning. Viruses can be sent through phone lines linking networked computers or can spread from infected software shared between computers. Sometimes, antivirus programs can find and destroy viruses before they spread or even fix the damage already done. Why do you think it is a crime to purposefully spread a computer virus?

Hacking—Finding Security Flaws

Perhaps the most controversial computer crime is hacking, or entering closed computer or telecommunications systems without permission. Hackers may have several motives. Some hackers claim they try to gain unauthorized access to a system for the intellectual challenge. They argue that breaking into computer systems helps improve security measures by pointing out their flaws.

Hacking is an invasion of privacy. Those who break into systems for malicious purposes are sometimes called crackers. Crackers may be seeking financial information, stealing software, trying to destroy data or computer hardware, or even altering records. This type of crime is so new that until recently law enforcement personnel have been hampered by a lack of laws defining computer crime. Now that the extent and seriousness of the activities of hackers and crackers have been recognized, steps are being taken to pass specific legislation dealing with these crimes. Many believe hacking and cracking are like physically breaking into a home or business and stealing goods or information. They argue that those who enter systems illegally should be prosecuted as criminals. What do you think?

Science Journal

Research computer software laws and write a report in your Science Journal. Distinguish between a felony and a misdemeanor.

Section Wrap-up

Review

1. How does a computer virus interfere with a computer?

2. What is computer cracking?

Explore the Technology

Suppose a computer hacker broke into a secret government computer system. Should this be considered a criminal felony, such as treason, or should it be considered a misdemeanor crime, such as breaking and entering? Do you think the hacker should be punished in the same manner as someone who broke into a building and took secret files? Explain your point of view.

SCIENCE & SOCIETY

People and Science

DR. TRIDIB BANERJEE, *Urban Planner*

On the Job

Personal Insights

Q In what specialized ways are computers used in the Urban Planning Department at your university?

A Geographic Information Systems— GIS for short—are made up of digitalized maps and computer software that allow manipulation of demographic data on the computer screen. This complicated-sounding equipment lets planners play the old game of "What If?" For instance, they might ask themselves, "What if there were a new freeway in this part of the city?" With GIS, planners can look ahead at what could happen and make decisions based on a simulation of reality.

Q Can GIS be helpful to the average citizen?

A Our department is placing computers with GIS capability in community centers and libraries. The aim is to assist in job creation and economic development. Say, for instance, that a person wants to open a laundromat. He or she needs to learn what the potential market is for that business. GIS can show the demographics of the proposed laundromat's location—who lives there and what the income level is. It could also show what similar, competing businesses are already in the area. A person starting a business needs this kind of information to qualify for a bank loan.

Q Why did you choose your career?

A Cities—like Calcutta, where I grew up—are fascinating phenomena. They are becoming the natural habitat of humanity, since 80 percent of Americans now live in cities. Making cities good places to live, work, and play requires careful planning.

Career Connection

Gather some data about your city or town that could be used by urban planners. On a map, mark the areas where young people gather, such as schools, playgrounds, and entertainment centers. Use your data to show where it might be most logical to construct community centers with programs for young people.

Investigate the following careers:

- **Data Analyst**
- **Data Entry Operator**

Summary

23-1: Semiconductor Devices

1. The conductivity of semiconductors can be increased by adding impurities to them.
2. A rectifier changes alternating current into direct current.
3. Electronic devices containing integrated circuits are much smaller than those that don't contain these circuits.

23-2: Radio and Television

1. Radio and television signals are transmitted by changing electrical signals into electro-magnetic radiation.
2. A cathode-ray tube uses electrons and fluorescent materials to produce pictures on a television screen.

23-3: Microcomputers

1. The basic parts of a microcomputer include the input devices, the output devices, disk drives, and the main circuit board.
2. The microprocessor receives input and tells the computer how to respond.
3. RAM is the temporary memory in a computer. ROM is memory that is permanently stored inside the computer.

23-4: Science and Society: Computer Crimes

1. Computer crimes include illegally copying software, planting computer viruses, and hacking.
2. Some computer crimes can involve stealing restricted information or altering records.

Key Science Words

a. amplification
b. cathode-ray tube (CRT)
c. computer virus
d. diode
e. integrated circuit
f. microprocessor
g. RAM
h. rectifier
i. ROM
j. transistor

Reviewing Vocabulary

Match each phrase with the correct term from the list of Key Science Words.

1. miniature components on a slice of silicon
2. any device that converts AC to DC
3. amplifies an electric signal
4. the process of making an electric current stronger
5. a TV picture tube
6. receives input and tells the computer how to respond
7. a computer's temporary memory
8. a computer program that multiplies and affects a computer's memory
9. contains stored information needed by a microprocessor to operate a computer
10. a type of rectifier

Chapter 23 Review

Checking Concepts

Choose the word or phrase that completes the sentence.

1. Elements that are semiconductors are located on the periodic table _____.
   a. between metals and nonmetals
   b. on the right side
   c. at the bottom
   d. on the left side
2. Solid-state electronic devices use _____.
   a. low current   c. no current
   b. high current   d. vacuum tubes
3. Rectifiers are used to _____.
   a. change DC to AC
   b. make sure something is right side up
   c. amplify radio signals
   d. change AC to DC
4. The signal in an electronic device that represents sound and images is a _____.
   a. varying current   c. radio wave
   b. constant current   d. sound wave
5. Transistors are used in all of the following except _____.
   a. compact discs   c. hearing aids
   b. TV vacuum tubes   d. tape players
6. Integrated circuits consist of _____.
   a. doped silicon chips with photographed wires
   b. generators and appliances
   c. televisions and radios
   d. vacuum tubes and transistors
7. The signals from an FM radio station are transmitted to your home as _____.
   a. frequency-modulated radio waves
   b. sound waves
   c. cathode rays
   d. electric current
8. Computer hardware consists of all of the following except _____.
   a. video display terminal   c. disk drives
   b. programs   d. keyboards

9. A computer represents information using _____.
   a. a binary number system
   b. sequences of numbers
   c. arrangements of four bits
   d. the numbers 1 through 10
10. Computer data and programs both can be stored permanently and transferred to other computers using _____.
    a. RAM   c. floppy disks
    b. ROM   d. hard disks

Understanding Concepts

Answer the following questions in your Science Journal using complete sentences.

11. How are semiconductors used in diodes and transistors?
12. Describe the advantages and disadvantages of integrated circuits.
13. Identify three functions of a microcomputer.
14. Describe three types of computer crimes. Which do you think is the most serious? Why?
15. Describe how computers affect you in everyday life.

Thinking Critically

16. What are the advantages and disadvantages of using a CD-ROM as a data-storage method?
17. You have connected your new compact disc player directly to your stereo speakers, but when you turn on the CD, you hear nothing. Should you return the CD player to the store? Why or why not?
18. Which would do more harm to the operation of a computer, the loss of its random access memory or the loss of its read only memory? Explain your answer.

19. You need to store information on your computer that you can retrieve rapidly whenever you use your computer. What is the best way to store this information?

20. Why might your school keep written records even when it has computers that can store these records much more efficiently?

Developing Skills

If you need help, refer to the **Skill Handbook.**

21. Recognizing Cause and Effect: Complete the table below by identifying either the cause or effect of problems associated with cathode-ray tubes.

Cathode-Ray Tubes

Cause	Effect
1. Inside of tube coated with a nonfluorescent material.	1.
2.	2. Electron beam doesn't sweep the entire screen.
3. Incoming electrical signals are garbled.	3.

22. Comparing and Contrasting: Compare and contrast the arrangement of electrons in conductors and insulators. Discuss why the arrangement in conductors makes them suitable to conduct electric currents.

23. Making and Using Tables: Construct a table to organize what you know about the parts of the microcomputer and the function of each.

24. Concept Mapping: Make a concept map showing the transfer of radio waves from the receiving antenna to your ear as sound waves.

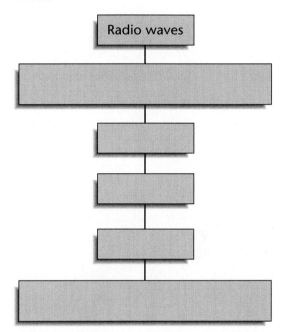

25. Formulating a Hypothesis: While using a word processor to write a paper, suppose you notice smiley faces appearing throughout your text. Suggest a possible explanation for this problem.

Performance Assessment

1. Booklet: If you are computer-wise, help novices by developing a dictionary of computer terms. Start with the terms in computer ads.

2. Formulating a Hypothesis: In Activity 23-2 on pages 664-665, you communicated information magnetically. Hypothesize why your "reading" magnet might no longer interact with your code magnets after being dropped.

3. Poster: Make a poster showing the passage of information through a computer from an input device to an output device.

Previewing the Chapter

Chapter 24

Radioactivity and Nuclear Reactions

Have you ever seen a nuclear power station such as the one in the photo? Inside a reactor in this power station, a change in the nucleus of unstable atoms releases energy that is converted to electrical power. Waste is also produced during the nuclear reaction. How is nuclear waste different from other wastes?

EXPLORE ACTIVITY

Model a nuclear reaction.

1. Put 32 marbles, each with an attached lump of clay, into a large beaker. These marbles with clay represent unstable atoms.
2. During a 45-second period, remove 16 marbles and pull off the clay. Place the clay into a pile and the marbles into another beaker. Marbles without clay represent stable atoms. The clay represents by-products or wastes of the reaction—smaller atoms that may still be capable of giving off additional energy.
3. Repeat this procedure four more times, each time removing half the marbles remaining in the original beaker.

Observe: In your Science Journal, explain how this model points out one of the main problems associated with using nuclear power to make electricity.

Previewing Science Skills

▶ In the Skill Builders, you will **compare and contrast, interpret scientific illustrations, observe and infer,** and **map concepts.**

▶ In the Activities, you will **predict, interpret,** and **formulate models.**

▶ In the MiniLABs, you will **observe and infer.**

24•1 Radioactivity

Science Words

radioactivity
nuclide

Objectives

- Discuss the discovery of radioactivity.
- Contrast properties of radioactive versus stable nuclides.

Radioactive Elements

Do you have a smoke detector, such as the one shown in **Figure 24-1,** in your home to alert you if there's a fire? If it is an ionizing smoke detector, it probably contains a small amount of a radioactive element called americium-241.

Look around the room. Can you detect any evidence of radioactivity? You can't see, hear, taste, touch, or smell radioactivity. Do you realize that there are small amounts of radioactivity all around you? You even have small amounts of radioactive material inside your body.

The discovery of radioactivity about 100 years ago has led to major advances in medical diagnoses and treatments, the use of nuclear energy, and the designing of nuclear weapons. It's certainly easy to see why some uses of radiation and nuclear energy are so controversial.

What is radioactivity?

You know that all elements are made of atoms, and that atoms are made up of protons, neutrons, and electrons. Protons and neutrons are held together in the nucleus by what scientists call the strong force. This force is strong enough to prevent the positive protons from pushing each other out of the nucleus of the atom; however, this force only acts across very small distances. As a result, atoms of elements with high atomic numbers are held together less securely than an oxygen atom, for example, which has relatively few protons and neutrons in its nucleus. Particles or energy can escape from all nuclei with atomic numbers of 84 or higher. This process is called radioactive decay. These nuclei are unstable. **Radioactivity,** therefore, is the emission of high-energy radiation or particles from the nucleus of a radioactive atom.

Figure 24-1

Many smoke detectors, such as this one, contain a small amount of a radioactive element.

Discovery

How was radiation first discovered if it can't be detected by your senses? Henri Becquerel accidentally discovered radioactivity in 1896 when he left uranium salt in a desk drawer with a photographic plate. Later, when he removed the plate and developed it, he found an outline of the uranium salt. He hypothesized that the uranium had given off some invisible energy and exposed the film. This process is called radiation. Two years after Becquerel's discovery, Marie and Pierre Curie discovered the elements polonium and radium. These elements are even more radioactive than uranium.

Notice where these three elements are found on the periodic table. They all have high atomic numbers and, therefore, are located near the bottom of the chart. Each element that has an atomic number greater than 83 is radioactive. Some other elements also have common radioactive isotopes.

Find the elements with atomic numbers 93 to 111 on the periodic table. Elements with these atomic numbers don't exist naturally on Earth. They have been produced only in laboratories and are called synthetic elements. These synthetic elements are unstable. Why might these elements be difficult to study?

Nuclides

Recall from Chapter 10 that most elements have isotopes. Isotopes of an element have the same number of protons but differ in their number of neutrons and in their atomic mass. Some isotopes are radioactive and others are not. Why is this so? The nucleus of an isotope with a certain atomic number and mass is called a **nuclide.** In many nuclides, the strong force is enough to keep the nucleus permanently together, creating a stable nuclide. When the strong force is not sufficient to hold unstable nuclides together permanently, they decay, giving off matter and energy.

Isotopes of elements differ in the ratio of neutrons to protons, shown in **Figure 24-2.** This ratio is related to the stability of the nucleus. An isotope of a less massive element is stable if the ratio is about 1 to 1. Isotopes of the heavier elements are

MiniLAB

How are neutrons and protons related to atomic stability?

Procedure
1. Use **Figure 24-2** or other references to make a list of several stable nuclides and one of several unstable nuclides.
2. By the symbol for each nuclide, write the number of protons and the number of neutrons in the nuclide.

Analysis
1. Compare the neutron-to-proton ratios for stable nuclides to those for unstable nuclides.
2. Count the number of stable nuclides, then the number of unstable nuclides, that have an even number of protons and an even number of neutrons. How do these numbers compare?

Figure 24-2

Elements with low atomic numbers have stable nuclides when the numbers of protons and neutrons are close.

■ **Stable nuclides**

■ **Unstable nuclides**

- - - **Neutrons = Protons**

Irradiated Food ▼ ▲

Even well-planned food storage and preparation do not prevent thousands of food-related deaths and millions of food poisoning cases each year. The battle to control organisms that cause these problems has a weapon in nuclear technology.

Controlled doses of gamma rays can be used to ionize atoms in important molecules in bacteria. When the atoms lose electrons, the way they bond to other atoms changes. These changes in bonding can also change the function of key molecules, which could kill the bacteria. The United Nations has approved irradiation of food. Cobalt-60 and cesium-137 are gamma-producing isotopes used to irradiate potatoes, fruits, pork, poultry, and spices.

Possible Problems

Exposure to radiation does not make the food radioactive, and it reduces the amount of chemicals needed to keep food safe. However, critics are concerned about loss of nutritional value, possible flavor changes, and possible unknown reactions involving newly unbonded atoms.

Think Critically:

Would you support the use of radiation to preserve foods? Justify your answer.

stable when the ratio of neutrons to protons is about 3 to 2. However, the nuclei of isotopes of both lighter and heavier elements that differ much from these ratios are unstable; that is, nuclei with too many or too few neutrons compared to the number of protons are radioactive.

Nuclide Numbers

How can you distinguish one isotope from another of the same element? A nuclide can be represented by a symbol that gives the atomic number, mass number, and element symbol, as shown in **Table 24-1.** You know the atomic number is the same as the number of protons in the element, and the mass number is the total number of protons and neutrons in the nucleus of that atom. The symbol for the nucleus of the stable isotope of potassium is shown as an example. Examine what each number and symbol represents.

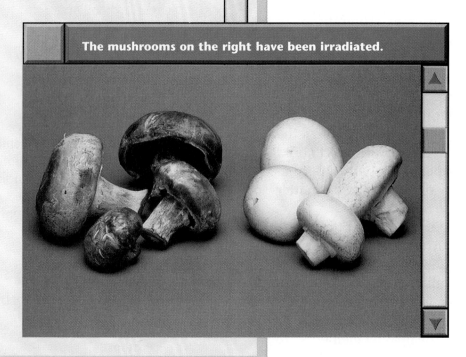

The mushrooms on the right have been irradiated.

Table 24-1

Radioactive Nuclides of Some Elements				
Element	Nuclide	Atomic mass number	Protons (atomic number)	Neutrons
Hydrogen	$_1^3\text{H}$	3	1	2
Helium	$_2^5\text{He}$	5	2	3
Lithium	$_3^8\text{Li}$	8	3	5
Carbon	$_6^{14}\text{C}$	14	6	8
Nitrogen	$_7^{16}\text{N}$	16	7	9
Potassium	$_{19}^{40}\text{K}$	40	19	21

$$\text{mass number} \rightarrow\ _{19}^{39}\text{K} \leftarrow \text{element symbol}$$
$$\text{atomic number} \rightarrow$$

Now, compare the stable isotope of potassium to the radioactive isotope below.

$$\text{mass number} \rightarrow\ _{19}^{40}\text{K} \leftarrow \text{element symbol}$$
$$\text{atomic number} \rightarrow$$

The stable isotope is called potassium-39. This isotope has 19 protons and 20 neutrons. The radioactive isotope is potassium-40. How many neutrons does potassium-40 have?

Section Wrap-up

Review

1. Identify the contributions of the three scientists who discovered the first radioactive elements.

2. What is the range of atomic numbers in which all isotopes are radioactive? Which of these are synthetic?

3. **Think Critically:** What is the ratio of protons to neutrons in lead-214? Explain whether you would expect this isotope to be radioactive or stable.

Skill Builder
Comparing and Contrasting
Compare and contrast stable and unstable isotopes of potassium. What do they have in common? How do they differ? If you need help, refer to Comparing and Contrasting in the **Skill Handbook.**

Science Journal

In your Science Journal, make a list of the first things you think of when you hear the word *radiation.* Write one paragraph describing your positive thoughts about radiation and another describing your negative thoughts.

Science & ART

Is it real or is it fake?

Paintings by great artists are sold for thousands and even millions of dollars. That is why some talented (but dishonest) people paint copies of great works of art and try to pass them off as the real thing. That is also why methods to detect such forgeries have been developed. One method of detecting art forgeries relies on a type of radioactive dating. This method helps date the paint used on the painting.

The chemical makeup of paints has changed over the years. Lead pigments used in oil paints today are not the same as those used hundreds of years ago. Lead that was refined before the year 1650 contains traces of chromium. Lead that was refined after the year 1950 contains traces of zinc and antimony. So the presence or absence of these trace elements in oil paint can show the general time period in which a painting was done. If the paint contains zinc and antimony, it must have been applied within the past few decades and not, for example, by a master artist of the 1700s or 1800s.

Portrait of a Boy, by Sonfonisba Anguissolla

Analysis by Neutron

How can traces of an element in a paint be detected? One way is to bombard the painting with neutrons. Stable atoms within the paint then start to decay. Gamma rays are emitted and are observed with radiation detectors. Because each element produces its own pattern of gamma radiation, studying the patterns can reveal which elements are present in the paint. The age of the paint can then be generally determined. This method of discovering the chemical makeup of an object is called neutron activation analysis.

During the bombardment of the paint with neutrons, beta particles are also released. The trails of these particles can be captured on film, producing a picture called an autoradiograph. An autoradiograph reveals what layers of materials lie under the surface oil paint. Together with X rays, autoradiographs can be used to see the stages of a master artist's work, paintings that were painted over, and parts of a painting that may have been done by students of the artist rather than the artist. Autoradiographs are, therefore, extremely useful to art historians.

Science Journal

What do you think of when you see a great work of art? Do you admire its beauty? Do you try to figure out how and from what it was made? Or do you wonder how much it is worth? In your Science Journal, describe your personal reaction to art.

Nuclear Decay   24•2

Nuclear Radiation

You've heard the terms *radioactivity* and *radioactive* ever since you were a young child. Maybe you didn't know what these words meant then, but now you know that they refer to unstable nuclei that emit radiation composed of small particles or energy called nuclear radiation. There are three common types of nuclear radiation—alpha, beta, and gamma radiation. **Figure 24-3** shows the path that each type of nuclear radiation follows as it moves through a magnetic field. As you can see, each type of radiation is affected differently. Which type of radiation is most affected by a magnetic field?

Radiation in the form of **alpha particles** is given off when a nucleus releases two protons and two neutrons. Notice that the alpha particle is the same as a helium nucleus, as shown in **Table 24-2**. An alpha particle has a charge of 2+ and an atomic mass of 4. It is the largest and slowest form of radiation, so it is also the least penetrating. Alpha particles can be

Science Words

alpha particle
beta particle
transmutation
gamma ray
half-life

Objectives

• Distinguish among alpha, beta, and gamma radiation.
• Calculate the amount of a radioactive substance remaining after a time based on its half-life.
• Relate half-life to the process of radioactive dating.

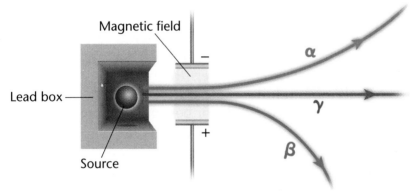

Figure 24-3

Notice how positive alpha and negative beta particles are deflected by a magnetic field. *Why aren't gamma rays deflected?*

Table 24-2

Three Types of Nuclear Radiation				
	Type	**Symbol**	**Charge**	**Mass**
	alpha	$_2^4$He, α	2+	4
	beta	$_{-1}^{0}$e, β	1−	0
	gamma	γ	none	0

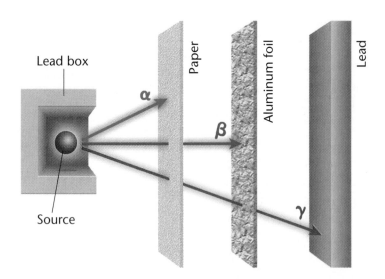

Figure 24-4

Alpha particles can be stopped by paper, beta particles by aluminum foil, and gamma rays by lead.

stopped by a sheet of paper, **Figure 24-4,** but they can be dangerous if they are released by atoms inside your body.

The smoke detector mentioned earlier in this chapter gives off alpha particles that ionize the surrounding air. An electric current flows through the ionized air, but the circuit is broken when smoke particles enter the ionized air. When the circuit is broken, the alarm is set off.

Decaying Neutrons and Protons

Sometimes, a neutron inside a nucleus decays spontaneously into a proton and an electron. The electron is emitted from the nucleus at high speed and is called a **beta particle.** The proton formed by the decaying neutron stays in the nucleus, forming an element with an atomic number one greater than that of the original element. Because the total number of protons and neutrons has not changed, the atomic mass number of the new element is the same as that of the original element. A proton can also decay into a neutron and a positron. A positron is similar to an electron, but has a positive charge. Positrons are also considered to be beta particles. Beta particles are much faster and more penetrating than alpha particles. However, they can be stopped by a sheet of aluminum foil.

Isotopes that give off alpha or beta particles undergo transmutation. **Transmutation** is the process of changing one element to another through nuclear decay. The nuclear equations in **Figure 24-5** show a nuclear transmutation. Because two protons are lost from the nucleus in alpha decay, the new element formed has an atomic number two less than that of the original element. The atomic mass number of the new element is four less than the original element. These two examples of

USING MATH

The most common isotope of uranium, $^{238}_{92}U$, transmutes to thorium by emitting an alpha particle with a mass of 4 and a charge of 2+. What is the symbol for the nucleus of this isotope of thorium?

Figure 24-5

In a transmutation, as in any nuclear reaction, the atomic mass number of the decayed nuclide equals the sum of the mass numbers of the newly formed nuclide and the emitted particles.

$$^{218}_{84}\text{Po} \longrightarrow {}^{214}_{82}\text{Pb} + {}^{4}_{2}\text{He}$$

$$^{214}_{82}\text{Pb} \longrightarrow {}^{214}_{83}\text{Bi} + {}^{0}_{-1}e$$

transmutation confirm that the charge of the original nuclide equals the sum of the charges of the nuclide and particle formed.

The most penetrating form of radiation is not made of particles at all. **Gamma rays** are electromagnetic waves with very high frequency and energy. They have no mass, no charge, and they travel at the speed of light. They are usually released along with alpha or beta particles. Gamma rays are the most penetrating form of radiation, and thick blocks of materials with dense nuclei are required to stop them. Lead and concrete are commonly used barriers for gamma rays. The three kinds of radiation are summarized in **Table 24-2** on page 679.

Half-Life

Safe disposal of some radioisotopes is not a problem because their nuclides decay to stable nuclides in less than a second. However, nuclides of certain radioactive isotopes may require millions of years to decay. A measure of the time required by the nuclides of an isotope to decay is called half-life. The **half-life** of an isotope is the amount of time it takes for half the nuclides in a sample of a given radioactive isotope to decay. Half-lives vary widely among the radioactive isotopes. For example, polonium-214 has a half-life of less than a thousandth of a second, but uranium-238 has a half-life of 4.5 billion years.

Problem Solving

Invisible Invader

In a typical day, everyone comes into contact with many forms of nuclear radiation. Some of the sources are from commercial products or the result of human activity. However, in recent years, there has been increasing awareness of another source of exposure.

Depending on the location, type of soil, and types of building materials, residents may be exposed to unusual amounts of alpha radiation from radon gas. Radon can seep in around building foundations that are not properly sealed. It can also decay into other radioactive elements that accumulate in poorly ventilated areas. Homeowners can purchase kits that can be used to monitor amounts of radon in their homes. Of the total average amount of radiation exposure in the United States, more than 50 percent can be attributed to radon. How can this potentially harmful exposure be reduced?

Think Critically:

1. If you purchased a radon testing kit, where would you most likely place it?
2. If a home tested high in radon levels, why would sealing help solve the problem in some cases and increased ventilation help in other situations?
3. Radon and its by-products emit alpha particles. Because alpha particles are relatively easy to stop, why is radon exposure considered such a risk for humans?

Table 24-3

Sample Half-Lives			
Isotope	Half-Life	Isotope	Half-Life
$^{3}_{1}H$	12.3 years	$^{212}_{82}Pb$	10.6 hours
$^{14}_{6}C$	5730 years	$^{194}_{84}Po$	0.7 second
$^{131}_{53}I$	8.04 days	$^{235}_{92}U$	7.04×10^{8} years

You can determine the amount of a radioactive sample that will remain after a given amount of time if you know the half-life of the sample. The half-lives of some radioactive elements are listed in **Table 24-3.** Look at the problem below to see how to calculate the amount of remaining sodium-24, which has a half-life of 15 hours.

USING MATH

Calculating the Quantity of a Radioactive Element

Example Problem:

How much of a 20-g sample of sodium-24 would remain after decaying for 30 hours?

Problem-Solving Steps:

1. Identify the known information:
   Amount of original sample of sodium-24 = 20 g
   Time elapsed = 30 hours
   Half-life of sodium-24 = 15 hours
2. Identify the unknown information.
   amount of remaining sodium-24
3. Solve for the unknown information.

   $$\text{amount remaining} = \frac{\text{amount of original sample}}{2^{n}}$$

   n = number of half-lives elapsed = 30 hours/15 hours = 2
4. **Solution:**

   $$\frac{20\text{ g}}{2^{2}} = \frac{20\text{ g}}{4} = 5\text{ g}$$

   The sample will contain 5 g of sodium-24 and 15 g of the decay product.

Practice Problem

How much of a 20-g sample of sodium-24 would remain after 45 hours?
Strategy Hint: Determine how many half-lives of sodium-24 elapse in 45 hours.

Radioactive Dating

It was mentioned earlier that you have some radioactive materials inside your body. One of these is a radioactive isotope of carbon, carbon-14. This isotope is in some of the carbon dioxide molecules plants take in as they respire. As a result, you have a small amount of carbon-14 inside of you from the plants and animals you eat. Carbon-14 emits a beta particle and decays into nitrogen-14.

All living things contain a somewhat constant amount of carbon-14. Decaying carbon-14 is constantly replaced by new carbon-14 in a living organism, but when the organism dies, its carbon-14 decays without replacement. The half-life of carbon-14 is 5730 years. It will take 5730 years for half of the carbon-14 atoms in a dead organism to decay to nitrogen-14. In another 5730 years, half of the remaining carbon will decay. By measuring the amount of carbon-14 remaining in a fossil or skeleton, such as those shown in **Figure 24-6,** scientists can determine the approximate age of the material. This process is called carbon-14 dating. Only remains of plants and animals that lived within the last 50 000 years contain enough carbon-14 to measure.

Figure 24-6

Some scientists consider carbon-14 dating to be accurate to only 20 000 years because of the difficulty of detecting lesser amounts of carbon-14. *Do you think carbon-14 dating could be used to determine the age of a dinosaur skeleton? Explain.*

Section Wrap-up

Review

1. Describe each of the three types of radiation, and compare their penetrating power.

2. Write a nuclear equation to show how radon-222 decays to give off an alpha particle and another element. What is the other element?

3. **Think Critically:** Is it possible for an isotope to decay to an element with a higher atomic number? Explain.

Skill Builder
Interpreting Scientific Illustrations
Use **Figure 24-3** on page 679 to explain why the alpha particle curves up, the beta particle curves down, and the gamma particle travels straight through the magnetic field. If you need help, refer to Interpreting Scientific Illustrations in the **Skill Handbook.**

USING MATH

The half-life of iodine-131 is about eight days. Calculate how much of a 40-g sample will be left after eight days. After 16 days? After 32 days?

Activity 24-1

Design Your Own Experiment
Investigating Half-Life

The decay rate of radioactive isotopes can vary from fractions of a second to several billions of years. If the half-life of an isotope is known, can you predict the amount of a radioactive sample that will remain after a known amount of time? Can you predict when a specific atom will decay?

PREPARATION

Problem
How can a model be used to demonstrate the usefulness of half-life in predicting the remaining amounts of a radioactive isotope?

Form a Hypothesis
Based on what you know about half-life, state a hypothesis about how the half-life of a radioactive isotope can be used to calculate the amounts of a radioactive isotope remaining.

Objectives
- Make a model to represent atoms in a radioactive sample.

- Calculate the amount of change in the objects that represent isotopes for each half-life.
- Design an experiment that tests how useful half-life is in predicting the amount of radioactive material remaining after a known amount of time.

Possible Materials
- several pennies
- graph paper

PLAN THE EXPERIMENT

1. As a group, agree upon and write out the hypothesis statement.
2. As a group, list the steps that you need to perform to test your hypothesis. Assume that each penny represents an atom in a radioactive sample and that each coin that lands heads up after flipping has not decayed.
3. Make a list of the materials that you will need to complete your experiment.
4. In your Science Journal, design a data table containing two columns—*Half-Life* and *Atoms Remaining*.

Check the Plan

1. In your model of radioactive decay, what can you do with pennies to represent the radioactive decay of an isotope?

2. What will you consider to be one half-life for your model?
3. How many half-lives do you want to investigate?
4. What are the variables and controls in your model?
5. What will be on each axis of your graph?
6. *Make sure your teacher approves your plan and that you have included any changes suggested in the plan.*

DO THE EXPERIMENT

1. Carry out the approved experiment as planned.
2. Record your results for several half-lives in your data table.

Analyze and Apply

1. **Compare** your results with those of other groups in the class.
2. Make a line **graph** of the data from your model to **compare** the number of half-life intervals with the number

of coins remaining. What common properties does your graph share with others in the class?

3. Can you use your model to **predict** which individual atoms will decay during one half-life? Can you **predict** the total number that will decay in one half-life? Explain.

Go Further

Use the original number of pennies and the method described on page 673 to calculate the expected number of atoms left after three half-lives. Compare this number to your experimental results. Explain any differences.

24●3 Detecting Radioactivity

Science Words

cloud chamber
bubble chamber

Objectives

- Describe how radioactivity can be detected.
- Explain how a Geiger counter can determine the quantity of nuclear radiation present.

Radiation Detectors

Because you can't feel a single particle or gamma ray, you must use instruments to detect their presence. Some methods of detecting radioactivity use the fact that radiation forms ions by removing electrons from matter it passes through. The newly formed ions can be detected in several ways.

A **cloud chamber,** shown in **Figure 24-7A,** can be used to detect charged nuclear particles as they leave cloud tracks. A cloud chamber contains supersaturated water or ethanol vapor. When a charged particle from a radioactive sample moves through the chamber, it leaves a path of ions behind as it knocks electrons off the atoms in the air. The vapor condenses around these ions to provide a visible path of droplets along the track of the particle. Beta particles leave long, thin trails, and alpha particles leave shorter and thicker trails.

Another way to detect and monitor the paths of nuclear particles is by using a bubble chamber. A **bubble chamber** holds a superheated liquid, which doesn't boil because of increased pressure in the system. When a moving particle

Figure 24-7

Several different instruments can be used to detect radiation. *How do you think the trail of a beta particle might differ from the trail of an alpha particle?*

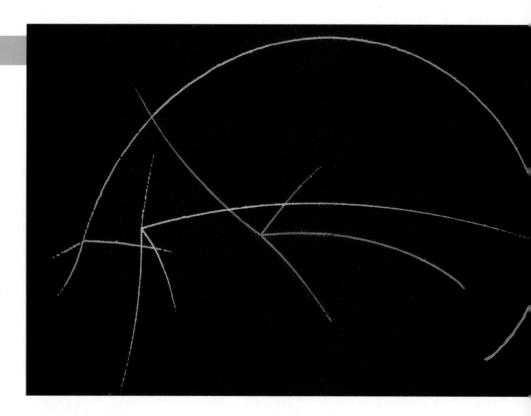

A A cloud chamber is a device used to detect particles of nuclear radiation.

leaves ions behind, the liquid boils along the trail. The path shows up as tracks of bubbles, as you can see in **Figure 24-7B.**

Do you remember how an electroscope was used to detect electric charges in Chapter 21? When an electroscope is given a negative charge, the leaves repel each other and spread apart. They will remain apart until the extra electrons have somewhere to go and discharge the electroscope. A nuclear particle moving through the air will remove electrons from molecules in the air, leaving them positively charged. When this occurs near an electroscope, some positively charged air molecules will come in contact with the electroscope and attract the electrons from the leaves, as shown in **Figure 24-7C.** As these negatively charged leaves lose their charges, they move together.

CONNECT TO

EARTH SCIENCE

Compare the process of forming a visible path of droplets in a cloud chamber with the formation of a cloud in the sky.

Measuring Radiation

You constantly receive small doses of radiation from your environment. It is not known whether this radiation is harmful to your body tissues. However, larger doses of radiation can be harmful to living tissue. If you worked or lived in an environment that had potential for exposure to high levels of radiation—a nuclear testing facility, for example—you might want to know exactly how much radiation you were being exposed to. A simple method of counting radioactivity is to use a Geiger counter. A Geiger counter is a device that produces an electric current when radiation is present.

C As negatively charged leaves lose their charges to positively charged molecules in the air, the leaves no longer repel.

B Particles of nuclear radiation can be detected as they leave trails of bubbles in a bubble chamber.

Figure 24-8

A Geiger counter can be used to measure the intensity of nuclear radiation.

Figure 24-8 shows a Geiger counter. The tube is filled with gas at a low pressure. A positively charged wire runs through the center of a negatively charged copper cylinder. This tube is connected to a voltage source. Radiation enters the tube at one end, stripping electrons from the gaseous atoms. The electrons are attracted to the positive wire. They knock more electrons off the atoms in the gas, and an "electron avalanche" is produced. A large number of electrons reaches the wire, producing a short, intense current in the wire. This current is amplified to produce a clicking sound or flashing light. The intensity of radiation present is determined by the number of clicks in each second.

Geiger counters can be made small and portable. They are often used to test the radioactivity at job sites where workers can be exposed to radioactive materials.

Section Wrap-up

Review
1. What are four ways radioactivity can be detected?
2. Briefly explain how a Geiger counter operates.
3. **Think Critically:** Suppose you needed to check the level of radioactivity in the laboratory of a hospital. Which method would you use? Explain your choice.

Skill Builder
Observing and Inferring

You are observing the presence of nuclear radiation with a bubble chamber and see two kinds of trails. Some trails are short and thick, and others are long and thin. What type of nuclear radiation might have caused each trail? If you need help, refer to Observing and Inferring in the **Skill Handbook.**

Using Computers

Word Processing
Write a short program that allows you to input the mass and the half-life of a radioactive sample and calculate what mass remains after a certain number of half-lives.

Nuclear Reactions 24•4

Nuclear Fission

Have you ever played a game of pool? What happens when you shoot the cue ball into an area of densely packed balls? They spread apart, or "break" the pack. In 1938, physicists Otto Hahn and Fritz Strassmann found that a similar result occurs when a neutron is shot into the large nucleus of a uranium-235 atom. Earlier, physicist Enrico Fermi had tried to bombard large nuclei with neutrons in an effort to make nuclei that would be larger than uranium. Splitting an atomic nucleus wasn't the expected outcome of this process.

Explain the Process

Lise Meitner was the first to offer a theory to explain the splitting of a nucleus. She concluded that the neutron fired into the nucleus disturbs the already unstable nucleus and causes it to split into two nuclei of nearly equal mass. The process of splitting a nucleus into two nuclei with smaller masses is called **nuclear fission.** The term *fission* means "to divide."

Only large nuclei with atomic numbers above 90 can undergo nuclear fission, an example of which is shown in **Figure 24-9.** The products of a fission reaction usually include two or three individual neutrons. The total mass of the products is somewhat less than the mass of the uranium-235 nucleus and the neutron. Some of the mass has been converted to a tremendous amount of energy.

Science Words

nuclear fission
chain reaction
nuclear fusion

Objectives

- Distinguish between nuclear fission and fusion.
- Explain how nuclear fission can begin a chain reaction.
- Discuss how nuclear fusion occurs in the sun.

$$^{1}_{0}n + ^{235}_{92}U \longrightarrow ^{141}_{56}Ba + ^{92}_{36}Kr + 3^{1}_{0}n$$

Figure 24-9

The uranium-235 nucleus is split by bombarding it with a neutron, and there can be many possible fission products. Sometimes, it forms a barium-141 nucleus and a krypton-92 nucleus and releases three neutrons.

Do you think the energy released in the fission of a single nucleus would be significant? Probably not by itself. However, the three neutrons produced in the fission reaction can bombard other nuclei in the sample to split more nuclei.

Figure 24-10

A chain reaction occurs when neutrons produced by nuclear fission bombard other nuclei, releasing more neutrons. Some of these neutrons are absorbed by control rods in the reactor.

$^{141}_{56}$Ba $^{235}_{92}$U

$^{235}_{92}$U

$^{92}_{36}$Kr   Control rod

Neutron $^{235}_{92}$U $^{92}_{36}$Kr $^{235}_{92}$U

$^{141}_{56}$Ba $^{141}_{56}$Ba

$^{235}_{92}$U

$^{235}_{92}$U

$^{92}_{36}$Kr

MiniLAB

How does a chain reaction start?

Find out how a chain reaction starts and then continues.

Procedure
1. Place dominoes close together on their edges in a straight line.
2. When all the dominoes are set up, gently knock over the first domino.

Analysis
1. In what ways is your model similar to the chain reaction that can take place in a sample of uranium-235?
2. What would happen if one domino were not positioned so that it struck the next domino when it fell? How is this situation similar to what could happen in a chain reaction involving uranium?

INTEGRATION
Earth Science

These reactions will each release more neutrons, and so on. If there is not some other material present to absorb these neutrons, an uncontrolled chain reaction can result. A **chain reaction,** shown in **Figure 24-10,** is an ongoing series of fission reactions. This can cause billions of reactions to occur each second, resulting in the release of tremendous amounts of energy. In the next chapter, you will read about ways scientists control nuclear fission and use the energy to produce electricity.

Nuclear Fusion

You read in the last section how tremendous amounts of energy can be released in nuclear fission. In fact, splitting one uranium-235 nucleus produces several million times more energy than chemically reacting one molecule of dynamite. Even more energy can be released in another type of nuclear reaction. This process is caused by the fusing together of nuclei, so it is the opposite of fission. **Nuclear fusion** is the combining of two nuclei with low masses to form one nucleus of larger mass.

Natural Fusion

Controlled nuclear fusion is difficult to induce because extremely high temperatures are required for this process to occur. For this reason, fusion reactions are also known as thermonuclear reactions. However, these extremely high temperatures do exist in the stars, including the sun, shown in **Figure 24-11.** At these high temperatures, atoms have so much kinetic energy that positive nuclei and electrons exist separately. Matter in this state is called plasma.

Scientists hypothesize that when the sun first formed, most of its nuclei were hydrogen nuclei. As thermonuclear fusion occurred, four hydrogen nuclei fused to become a helium nucleus. This process is still occurring, and about one percent of the mass of the sun's original nuclei is changed to energy and released in the form of electromagnetic radiation. As the star ages, the percentage of helium nuclei gradually increases and the number of hydrogen nuclei decreases until they are used up, and the reaction can no longer occur. Scientists estimate that the sun has enough hydrogen to keep this reaction going for another 5 billion years.

Scientists are searching for a way to induce and control nuclear fusion. If they achieve this goal, fusion could provide an almost unlimited supply of energy to produce electricity.

CONNECT TO

CHEMISTRY

Use the periodic table to find the atomic mass of uranium. *Infer* why this value differs from the mass number 235 given for fissionable uranium.

Figure 24-11

The sun is a star of medium internal temperature, averaging about 20 million degrees Celsius.

Section Wrap-up

Review

1. Compare and contrast nuclear fission and fusion.

2. Why does a chain reaction often occur when a uranium-235 nucleus is split?

3. **Think Critically:** Explain why the hydrogen fusion reaction that takes place in the sun can't currently produce energy for electricity on Earth.

Skill Builder
Concept Mapping
Make a concept map to show how a chain reaction occurs when U-235 is bombarded with a neutron. Show how each of the three neutrons given as products begins another fission reaction. If you need help, refer to Concept Mapping in the **Skill Handbook.**

Science Journal

In your Science Journal, explain why finding a practical way to use fusion as an energy source would be an improvement over using fission.

TECHNOLOGY:

24•5 Using Nuclear Reactions in Medicine

Science Words

tracer
PET

Objectives

• Describe how radio-active tracers and PET can be used to diagnose medical problems.

• Discuss how radioactive isotopes can aid in the treatment of cancers.

Tracers—Identified Isotopes

If you were going to meet a friend in a crowded area, it would be easier to find you if you told your friend what you would be wearing. If scientists want to follow where a particular molecule goes in your body or how a particular organ functions, they do some identifying of their own. Just as a bright red hat might set you apart from hundreds of other people, a radioactive atom differs from other surrounding atoms. These radioisotopes that are used inside of a body to monitor body processes are called **tracers.** Examples of tracers include carbon-11, iodine-131, and sodium-24, all of which are used as tracers because of their relatively short half-lives.

Thyroid—The Iodine Connection

The thyroid gland helps regulate several body processes, including growth. Iodine from food is transported to the thyroid, where it is incorporated into hormones that the thyroid produces. If a patient is suspected of having a thyroid problem, he or she may be given a mixture that contains iodine-131, which emits beta particles. The thyroid gland absorbs the iodine-131. The energy from emitted beta particles can be detected and used to evaluate the patient's thyroid, as shown in **Figure 24-12.** If little radiation shows up, the doctor may suspect a tumor.

Figure 24-12

Iodine-131 accumulates in the thyroid gland. The amount of radiation detected is related to how well the thyroid gland functions.

Cancer Treatment

The radiation from nuclear decay is strong enough to ionize nearby atoms. This ionization process can be a way to destroy the advance of some cancerous tumors. Cancerous cells grow quickly, making them more susceptible to absorbing radiation than healthy cells. If a critical molecule, such as the DNA or RNA of a cancerous cell, had an atom that was ionized, then the molecule might no longer function in its intended way. This could cause death or mutation in the cancerous cell. When possible, a radioactive isotope such as gold-198 or iridium-192 is implanted within or near the tumor. If a surgical implant is impractical, a tumor is often treated from outside the body. Typically, an intense gamma ray from cobalt-60 is focused on the tumor for a specific time period. The gamma rays pass through the body and into the tumor.

A Practical Use for Positrons

To study brain functions and disorders, scientists attach radioactive fluorine-18 to molecules that are circulated to the brain. A patient is then placed inside a large tube with an array of detectors. When positrons are emitted from decaying fluorine that is in the blood supply of the brain, they hit electrons from other molecules and form two gamma rays. Analyzing the emitter gamma rays can reveal tumors and various activity levels in the brain. This technological advancement in medicine, shown in **Figure 24-13,** is called Positron Emission Tomography, or **PET.**

Figure 24-13

When detectors are placed around a person's head, PET scans reveal brain function and can reveal brain disorders, such as tumors.

Section Wrap-up

Review

1. What is a radioactive tracer? Give an example of a tracer.

2. Why is it important that tracers have relatively short half-lives?

Explore the Technology

Although many benefits have resulted from nuclear applications in medicine, there are some disadvantages. During cancer treatment, for example, healthy cells are also damaged. In fact, high levels of radiation have been linked with causing cancer. Explain how radiation can both cause and treat cancer.

SCIENCE & SOCIETY

Activity 24-2

Figuring Out Fusion

The energy that warms Earth is produced in thermonuclear reactions in the sun, which is about 1.5×10^8 km away. We can model this process of nuclear fusion.

Problem

How can you model nuclear fusion?

Materials

- 6 balls of green clay
- 6 smaller balls of white clay

Procedure

1. Make six hydrogen nuclei (protons) by sticking one small white positron to each large green neutron.
2. Refer to step 1 of the table and make two particles of $^2_1$H.
3. Refer to step 2 of the table and make two particles of $^3_2$He.
4. Refer to step 3 of the table and make one particle of $^4_2$He.

Analyze

1. Sequence the steps necessary to change $^1_1$H into $^4_2$He.
2. In this process, what is lost and what is left over?
3. How many atoms of hydrogen does it take to make one atom of helium?

Conclude and Apply

4. What can the leftover hydrogen be used for?
5. The mass of a hydrogen-1 nucleus is 1.0078 u, while the mass of a helium-4 nucleus is 4.0026 u. **Compare** the mass of one helium nucleus to the mass of four hydrogen nuclei. If mass changes to energy, where does the energy of the sun come from?

Fusion Reaction

Step 1	$^1_1$H $+$ $^1_1$H $\rightarrow$ $^2_1$H $+$ positron
Step 2	$^1_1$H $+$ $^2_1$H $\rightarrow$ $^3_2$He
Step 3	$^3_2$He $+$ $^3_2$He $\rightarrow$ $^4_2$He $+$ $2\,^1_1$H

Summary

24-1: Radioactivity

1. Radioactivity was accidentally discovered by Henri Becquerel about 100 years ago.
2. Radioactive nuclides are unstable and therefore decay. Stable nuclides don't decay.

24-2: Nuclear Decay

1. The three common types of radiation emitted from a decaying nucleus are alpha particles, beta particles, and gamma rays.
2. The amount of a remaining radioactive substance can be determined if you know the amount of the original sample and the number of half-lives that have elapsed.
3. The age of some previously living materials can be determined by a process called carbon-14 dating.

24-3: Detecting Radioactivity

1. Radioactivity can be detected with a cloud chamber, a bubble chamber, an electroscope, or a Geiger counter.
2. A Geiger counter indicates the intensity of radiation present by producing a clicking sound or a flashing light that increases in frequency as more radiation is present.

24-4: Nuclear Reactions

1. Atomic nuclei are split during fission and combined during fusion.
2. Neutrons released from a nucleus during fission can split other nuclei.

24-5: Science and Society: Using Nuclear Reactions in Medicine

1. Radioactive tracers can go to certain areas of the body to indicate abnormalities.

2. Radiation from some radioactive isotopes can kill cancer cells.

Key Science Words

a. alpha particle
b. beta particle
c. bubble chamber
d. chain reaction
e. cloud chamber
f. gamma ray
g. half-life
h. nuclear fission
i. nuclear fusion
j. nuclide
k. PET
l. radioactivity
m. tracer
n. transmutation

Reviewing Vocabulary

Match each phrase with the correct term from the list of Key Science Words.

1. emission of high-energy particles or radiation from an unstable nucleus
2. a particle of nuclear radiation with a charge of 2+ and an atomic mass of 4
3. nuclear decay that results in the formation of a new element
4. the time for one-half of a sample of a radioactive isotope to decay
5. detects nuclear particles as they leave a trail of condensed water or ethanol vapor
6. splitting a nucleus into two smaller masses
7. radioactive isotopes that are used to monitor human body functions
8. the nucleus of a specific isotope
9. radiation in the form of an electromagnetic wave
10. two nuclei combining into a larger nucleus

Checking Concepts

Choose the word or phrase that completes the sentence.

1. Radioactivity can be _____.
   a. found in your classroom   c. seen
   b. prevented by a tracer   d. smelled
2. Elements that have been produced artificially through nuclear reactions have atomic numbers _____.
   a. greater than 92   c. between 83 and 92
   b. greater than 83   d. between 90 and 111
3. When a neutron decays, the electron produced is called _____.
   a. an alpha particle c. gamma radiation
   b. a beta particle   d. both a and c
4. The time for half the nuclides in a sample of a radioactive isotope to decay _____.
   a. is constant   c. increases with time
   b. varies   d. decreases with time
5. Carbon-14 dating could be used to date _____.
   a. an ancient Roman scroll
   b. an ancient marble column
   c. dinosaur fossils
   d. Earth's oldest rocks
6. Radiation in a nuclear laboratory could best be measured with _____.
   a. a cloud chamber   c. an electroscope
   b. a Geiger counter   d. a bubble chamber
7. A _____ is an ongoing series of fission reactions.
   a. chain reaction
   b. decay reaction
   c. positron emission
   d. fusion reaction

8. The sun is powered by _____.
   a. nuclear decay   c. thermonuclear fusion
   b. nuclear fission   d. combustion
9. A radioisotope that acts as an external source of ionizing radiation in the treatment of cancer is _____.
   a. cobalt-60   c. gold-198
   b. carbon-14   d. technetium-99
10. A major medical use of radiation is to _____.
   a. assist breathing   c. heal broken bones
   b. ease pain   d. treat cancers

Understanding Concepts

Answer the following questions in your Science Journal using complete sentences.

11. Briefly discuss the history of nuclear science.
12. Explain why certain nuclides decay.
13. Describe the basic principles of carbon-14 dating.
14. Discuss the similarities and differences in the devices that detect radioactivity.
15. Discuss the use of radioactive tracers. How do they detect cancer cells?

Thinking Critically

16. Can a radioactive isotope of sodium combine with chlorine to form table salt? If so, would its chemical and physical properties be the same as those of ordinary table salt? Explain your answer.
17. Copper-66 releases a beta particle as it decays, and radium-226 releases an alpha particle. Write a nuclear equation for each of these transmutations.
18. Explain the presence of relatively heavy elements such as carbon, oxygen, magnesium, and iron in stars.
19. Explain how radioisotopes are used to preserve foods and to study how plants take up nutrients from the soil.

20. Nitrogen-13 has a half-life of about 10 minutes. How much of a 320-g sample of nitrogen-13 would remain after decaying for 40 minutes?

Developing Skills

If you need help, refer to the **Skill Handbook.**

21. Concept Mapping: Complete the following concept map summarizing how a Geiger counter works.

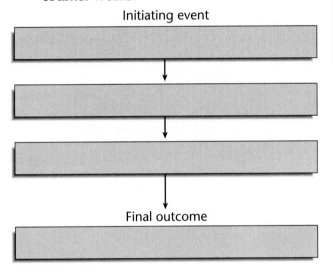

Initiating event

Final outcome

22. Making and Using Tables: Construct a table summarizing the characteristics of each of the three common types of radiation.

23. Observing and Inferring: Another type of particle of nuclear radiation is a positron, which has a charge of 1+ and the same mass as an electron. This particle is given off when a proton spontaneously changes into a neutron. Infer what type of radiation will be emitted from each of the following radioisotopes:

   a. Boron-8, which is unstable due to an extra proton.

   b. Thorium-232, which is unstable due to its large nucleus containing too many protons and neutrons.

   c. Potassium-40, which is unstable due to an extra neutron.

24. Making and Using Graphs: Using the data below, construct a graph plotting the mass numbers vs. the half-lives of radioisotopes. Plot mass numbers to the nearest ten. Is it possible to use your graph to predict the half-life of a radioisotope given its mass number?

Isotope Half-Lives		
Radio-isotope	Mass Number	Half-Life
Radon	222	4 days
Thorium	234	24 days
Iodine	131	8 days
Bismuth	210	5 days
Polonium	210	138 days

25. Interpreting Data: Review your graph of decay from Activity 24-1 on pages 684-685. What would the half-life curve look like if your sample contained twice as many coins? Predict the new data and sketch the corresponding graph. Then try it and see.

Performance Assessment

1. Booklet: Write a biography of a person who made an important contribution to nuclear science. Include sketches or photos of the person and his or her work.

2. Oral Presentation: Research the causes and effects of radon pollution in the home. Report your findings to the class.

3. Model: Use the clay models from Activity 24-2 on page 694 to determine the product of a simple fusion reaction between a proton ($_1^1$H) and a neutron ($_0^1$n). Complete the following nuclear equation.

$$_1^1 H + _0^1 n \rightarrow \underline{\hspace{1cm}} + \text{gamma radiation}$$

Previewing the Chapter

Energy Sources

People need energy daily for almost everything we do. When we need it, where do we get energy? What energy sources and uses do you notice in the photo on the facing page?

In the activity that follows, you will see how straight-line movement of air can be converted into circular motion. Other forces can be used the same way.

Consider some of the alternative ways other forces can be used to generate electricity through moving turbines as you read this chapter.

EXPLORE ACTIVITY

Use the energy from the wind to provide turning power.

1. Cut several different sizes of squares from sheets of paper. Make a cut from each corner of the square toward the center, stopping when you are within 1-2 cm from the center.
2. Fold each point toward the center, running a straight pin through all four tips and the center of the square.
3. Hold the wind catcher by the pointed end of the pin in front of a window fan, and note which size spins fastest.

Observe: In areas of consistent winds, wind power has been the source of energy to generate electricity. In your Science Journal, describe an advantage wind power has over fossil fuels.

Previewing Science Skills

▶ In the Skill Builders, you will **compare and contrast, map concepts,** and **outline.**

▶ In the Activities, you will **diagram, research,** and **make observations.**

▶ In the MiniLABs, you will **measure, observe,** and **draw conclusions.**

25•1 Fossil Fuels

Science Words

petroleum
fractional distillation
nonrenewable resource

Objectives

- Discuss the origin and characteristics of the three main types of fossil fuels.
- Describe the need for and methods of energy conservation.

Petroleum

Do you own a sweater made of synthetic fibers such as polyester or nylon? If so, are you aware that your sweater has something in common with the gasoline used for fuel in cars and buses? Synthetic fibers are made with chemicals that come from crude oil, and gasoline is refined from crude oil.

Crude oil, or **petroleum,** is a liquid source of energy made from the decayed remains of plants and animals. Petroleum, along with natural gas and coal, is called a fossil fuel. When plants and animals died, they were covered with layers of sand, mud, volcanic ash, and other matter that collected on the surface of Earth over many years. Great pressure, heat, and bacterial action acted on these buried organisms, forming fossil fuels.

Petroleum is pumped to the surface from wells drilled deep into the ground, as shown in **Figure 25-1.** The crude oil that comes from these wells contains a variety of chemicals. Because plants and animals contain large amounts of hydrogen and carbon, petroleum is composed mostly of compounds containing these elements, called hydrocarbons.

Figure 25-1

Oil wells are used to find fossil fuels beneath layers of earth. *How might the fossils have ended up under these layers?*

Sorting out Hydrocarbons

These various hydrocarbon compounds must be separated to make use of the chemical energy stored in petroleum. If you have ever seen an oil-refining plant, you may have noticed several tall towers. These towers are called fractionating towers. Fractionating towers use a process called **fractional distillation** to separate hydrocarbon compounds. First, crude oil is pumped into the bottom of the tower and heated. The chemical compounds in the crude oil boil and evaporate according to their individual boiling points. Those materials with the lowest boiling points rise to the top of the column as vapor and are separated and collected. When each vapor cools below its boiling point, it again turns to a liquid. Hydrocarbons with high boiling

< 40°C	Bottled gas
40-180°C	Gasoline and solvents
180-230°C	Solvents, paint thinners, and kerosene
230-300°C	Heating oil and diesel fuel
300-405°C	Lubricating oils and greases
405-515°C	Paraffin, waxes, asphalt

Figure 25-2
Fractional distillation is used to separate the hydrocarbon components in petroleum.

points may remain as liquids and be drained off through the bottom of the tower. Notice the different products made from the petroleum fractions that are shown in **Figure 25-2.**

Oil must travel from the oil fields to the refineries. Oil can be carried through pipelines, by ship, or in tanker trucks. You use petroleum every day for electricity and transportation, but not all the effects of petroleum usage are helpful to you or the environment. When petroleum is burned in cars and at electric power plants, it gives off smoke as well as carbon monoxide and other chemical compounds. These particles and compounds affect the quality of the air you breathe.

Other Fossil Fuels

Do you cook on a gas stove at home? If so, you burn natural gas to get energy to cook your food. Natural gas, like petroleum, is a fossil fuel. It is often found trapped above liquid petroleum reservoirs below Earth's surface; it is extracted with the petroleum.

Natural gas is composed mostly of methane, CH_4, but it also contains smaller amounts of hydrocarbon gases such as propane, C_3H_8, and butane, C_4H_{10}. When natural gas or petroleum is burned, it combines with oxygen, and heat is given off. During this process, carbon dioxide and water are formed as chemical by-products. This is a combustion reaction. Natural gas is burned to provide energy for cooking, heating, and manufacturing. When natural gas is used properly, it doesn't pollute the environment with the compounds that result from burning petroleum. However, the carbon dioxide that it produces can cause Earth's atmospheric temperature to rise.

MiniLAB

How can an updated design improve efficiency?

Procedure
1. Measure and record the mass of a candle.
2. Measure 50 mL of water into a container. Record the temperature of the water.
3. Use the lighted candle to heat the water 10°C. Put out the candle and measure its mass again.
4. Repeat steps 1 to 3 with an aluminum chimney surrounding the candle to help direct the heat upward.

Analysis
1. Compare the mass change in the two trials. Does a smaller or larger mass change in the candle show greater efficiency?
2. Gas burners are used to heat hot-water tanks. What must be considered in the design of these heaters?

USING TECHNOLOGY

No More Gas Tanks? ▼ ▲

Someday, the familiar gasoline pump may be found only in museums. Instead of gasoline, we may be using natural gas, electricity, or hydrogen for our cars. Earth has a limited supply of petroleum to make gasoline. To make existing petroleum supplies last longer, automobile designers are using different technologies to power automobiles.

Natural gas vehicles (NGVs) are designed to run on methane. They produce less air pollution than cars that burn gasoline. Methane can be obtained from naturally decaying plant material. Electrically powered cars produce less exhaust pollution, but the energy used to generate the electricity may offset any savings in petroleum. Solar power could be used to make electricity. This would improve the conservation and pollution advantages of an electrically powered car. Hydrogen is another possible automobile fuel. However, carrying hydrogen in a car would be dangerous. To solve this problem, metal sponges are being made that absorb hydrogen, releasing it only when needed.

Think Critically:

These technologies are not being implemented quickly. How would tripling the current price of gasoline affect the rate of implementation?

Burning Coal for Energy

Coal is a solid fossil fuel made from the remains of plants. It is sometimes mined near the surface but is more commonly mined about one hundred meters underground. The quality of a coal sample depends on its age and on the type of plant life from which it formed.

When used as a fuel, coal is cleaned to remove impurities that would be released into the air when the coal is burned. Sulfur is removed to prevent the formation of compounds that cause acid rain. Harmful nitrogen oxides form when coal is burned at high temperatures. Therefore, it is desirable to find ways to burn coal at lower temperatures.

Because coal is mined, digging coal mines can disturb the environment. Today, laws require that the environment be returned to its original state when a coal mine is closed.

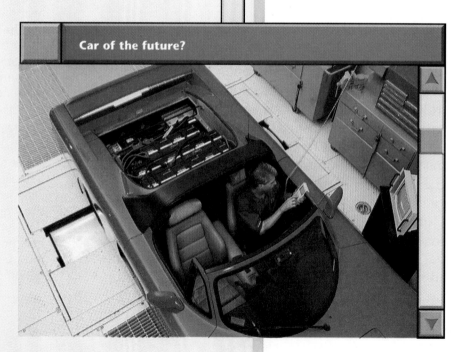

Car of the future?

Fuel Conservation

Think of how many times you ride in a car, turn on a light, or use an electric appliance. Each time you do one of these things, you probably use some type of fossil fuel as a source of energy. Fossil fuel reserves are decreasing as our population and industrial demands are increasing. At our current rate of consumption, the United States may be out of oil in less than one century. Coal is more plentiful, but like petroleum, it is a nonrenewable resource. All fossil fuels are **nonrenewable resources**—they cannot be replaced after they are used.

We must conserve the nonrenewable energy resources we do have. Conservation can be as simple as turning off a light when you leave a room, avoiding excessive speeds when driving a car, or riding a bike instead of driving a car at all. Using energy-efficient appliances can reduce energy use in your home. Trees around your home can keep it cooler in summer and reduce the use of air conditioning. Replacing old windows with new, energy-efficient windows, as shown in **Figure 25-3,** means buildings will use less energy for heating and cooling. We need to develop some alternative energy sources to help us conserve now and to prepare for the time when fossil fuels may not be readily available.

Figure 25-3

Does your school have energy-efficient windows? How could replacing windows save energy?

Section Wrap-up

Review
1. Describe the three main types of fossil fuels.

2. Which type of fossil fuel is the most abundant in the United States? What are the advantages and disadvantages of using this fuel?

3. **Think Critically:** As the plants and animals living on Earth today die, they will decay and be buried to form the fossils of tomorrow. If the formation of fossil fuels is a continuous cycle, why are they considered to be *nonrenewable* resources?

Science Journal

In your Science Journal, make a list of areas in your school where existing energy could be conserved.

Skill Builder
Comparing and Contrasting
Compare and contrast the different fossil fuels. Include the advantages and disadvantages of using each as a source of energy. If you need help, refer to Comparing and Contrasting in the **Skill Handbook.**

25 • 2 Nuclear Energy

Objectives

• Outline the operation of a nuclear reactor.
• Describe the problems and methods associated with nuclear waste disposal.
• Discuss nuclear fusion as a possible energy source.

Nuclear Reactors

In the last chapter, you learned that nuclear fission chain reactions give off a great deal of energy. A **nuclear reactor** uses the energy from a controlled nuclear fission chain reaction to generate electricity. Nuclear reactors can vary in design. Most fission reactors have several parts in common, including fuel, control rods, and cooling systems. The actual fission of the radioactive fuel occurs in a relatively small part of the reactor—the core.

In the reactor core, where the uranium oxide fuel is found, neutrons are being absorbed by U-235. When this happens, U-235 nuclei undergo fission and release more neutrons. These neutrons can strike other U-235 nuclei, causing them to also release two or three neutrons as they undergo fission. This process continues quickly, in the frame of milliseconds, releasing tremendous amounts of energy from the tiny fuel pellets shown in **Figure 25-5.** What keeps the process from continuing out of control, with each millisecond producing more energy than the one before?

To control the reaction, rods containing boron or cadmium are used to absorb some of the neutrons. Moving these control rods deeper into the reactor allows them to capture more neutrons and slow down the chain reaction. Eventually, only one neutron per fission is able to react with a U-235 atom to produce another fission, and energy is released at a constant rate. **Figure 25-4** explains how nuclear fission is used to produce electricity.

Figure 25-4

Nuclear reactors actually use water to turn turbines and generate electricity. The nuclear reaction simply gives the water the energy to move the turbines.

A The core of the reactor uses energy from fission to heat contained water. This water is not released into the main water supply.

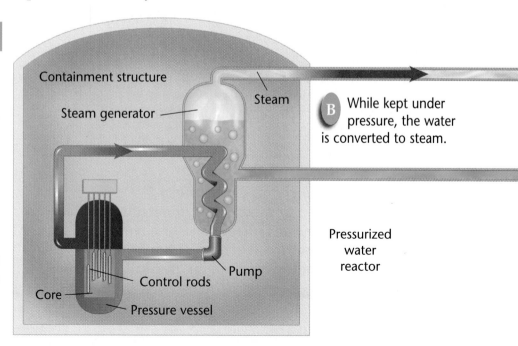

Containment structure

Steam generator

Steam

B While kept under pressure, the water is converted to steam.

Pressurized water reactor

Pump

Control rods

Core

Pressure vessel

Nuclear Generation of Electricity

Nuclear fission reactors currently supply some of our nation's electricity. One advantage of using nuclear energy is that it's less harmful to the environment than the use of fossil fuels. The fission process produces no air pollution, whereas the burning of coal and petroleum creates nearly 20 000 metric tons of pollutants each day. Nuclear fission doesn't produce carbon dioxide that escapes into the atmosphere and contributes to the problem of global warming. On the other hand, the mining of uranium and extraction of U-235 does cause environmental damage.

Using nuclear fission to generate electricity also has other disadvantages. The water that circulates around the core of the reactor must cool before it goes back into streams and rivers. If it is released into those waterways while still warm, the excess heat could harm fish and other animals and plants in the water. **Figure 25-6** on page 706 shows the large, hollow towers used to cool the warm water. The most serious risk of nuclear fission is the escape of harmful radiation from the power plants. Nuclear reactors have elaborate systems of safeguards, strict safety precautions, and highly trained workers who can prevent most accidents.

However, after the chain reaction has occurred, the fuel rods contain fission products that are highly radioactive. These products must be contained in heavily shielded surroundings while they decay so that no radiation escapes

Figure 25-5

Nuclear fuel pellets are assembled into fuel rods. The rods may be up to about 4 m in length.

Turbine

Electric generator

Electrictiy

C The generated steam is then piped into a turbine chamber. The moving steam causes the turbine to turn. The turbine drives an electric generator, which can be used to power electrical devices.

Condenser

D As the steam is condensed, it releases heat through a series of heat exchangers to cooler water. The condensed water can then be recirculated to the core. *Why isn't the cooling water radioactive?*

Pump   Cooling water

To cooling towers

Pump

Figure 25-6

The cooling towers, often the most visible part of a nuclear reactor, help to get rid of extra heat from water that has been heated in the power plant.

USING MATH

In 1945, the sources of energy in the United States were: hydroelectric and other —5%, natural gas—12%, petroleum—32%, and coal—51%. In 1995, the sources were: hydroelectric and other—4% nuclear—7%, coal—23%, natural gas—24%, and petroleum—42%. Use graphs to show how these energy sources have changed.

into the environment. Because these fission products have long half-lives, they must be stored in containers that will last the duration of the period of radioactive decay, which can be as long as tens of thousands of years.

Another problem is the disposal of the reactor itself when it no longer runs as it should. Every nuclear reactor has a limited useful life span of a few decades. After that time, the reactor's efficiency is severely reduced by the presence of large amounts of fission products that can't be cleaned up. The reactor is then shut down or decommissioned.

Nuclear Waste Disposal

Has your watch ever run down because the battery was too old? The battery wasn't able to produce enough energy to allow your watch to keep correct time. Once you replaced the battery, your watch worked. A similar thing happens to the fuel source in a nuclear reactor. After about three years, there is not enough fissionable U-235 left in the fuel pellets to sustain the chain reaction. These used fuel pellets are called *spent fuel*. The spent fuel contains the radioactive fission products in addition to the remaining uranium. This is an example of nuclear waste. **Nuclear wastes** are radioactive by-products that result when radioactive materials are used. They are usually classified as high-level or low-level wastes for disposal.

Radiation is around you all the time. Low-level nuclear waste usually contains a small amount of radioactive material diluted by a large amount of nonradioactive material. Products of some medical and industrial processes are low-level wastes. They may include items of clothing that are used in handling radioactive materials, as shown in **Figure 25-7.**

Low-level wastes are usually buried in sealed containers in locations licensed by the federal government. When dilute enough, they are sometimes released into the air or water.

High-level nuclear waste is generated in nuclear power plants and by defense research. After spent fuel is removed from a reactor, it is stored in a deep, heavily insulated pool of water. Many of the radioactive materials in high-level nuclear waste have short half-lives. But the spent fuel also contains materials that will continue to decay for tens of thousands of years. For this reason, the waste must be disposed of in extremely durable and stable containers.

Figure 25-7

Which type of radiation is most easily shielded against by the clothing and gloves of these workers?

Fusion Power

Imagine the amount of energy the sun must give off to heat Earth from 93 million miles away. In Chapter 24, thermonuclear fusion was explained as the process that releases this energy. Recall that thermonuclear fusion is the joining together of small nuclei at high temperatures. Fusing the nuclei in 1 g of heavy hydrogen gives off about the same amount of energy as burning more than 8 million grams of coal. If we could control thermonuclear fusion in a laboratory, we would likely have the answer to Earth's energy problems.

Let's examine the benefits of nuclear fusion as a source of energy. Hydrogen nuclei are the source of energy for nuclear fusion. Hydrogen is the most abundant element in the universe. Unlike those in nuclear fission, the products of nuclear fusion are not radioactive. Helium is the main product of hydrogen fusion. Someday, nuclear fusion may provide a permanent and economical way to generate electricity.

CONNECT TO

EARTH SCIENCE

In 1987, Congress voted to build the first national permanent nuclear repository site at Yucca Mountain, Nevada. Burial of waste is scheduled to start in 2003, although the plan has changed several times. *Classify* the geological features this location has that make it suitable for a nuclear repository.

The challenge lies in creating and containing nuclear fusion. The temperature needed to carry out a nuclear fusion reaction is more than 1 million degrees Celsius. The plasma containing the hydrogen nuclei can't be contained by any material at this temperature. However, it can be contained for a short time in a magnetic bottle, which uses a magnetic field to keep the particles in a small volume. An experimental fusion reactor is shown in **Figure 25-8.** At the present time, the energy required to maintain the high temperatures needed for the fusion reaction is greater than the energy output from the fusion of the nuclei.

Figure 25-8

This experimental fusion reactor is used to house a nuclear fusion reaction.

Section Wrap-up

Review

1. How is the rate of fission in a nuclear reactor controlled?

2. Explain the major obstacles in controlling nuclear fusion.

3. **Think Critically:** Suppose that in a research project, you have generated a 10-g sample of nuclear waste. Some of the materials have a short half-life and some will decay for thousands of years. How would you classify this waste, and how will it likely be disposed of?

Skill Builder
Concept Mapping
Design an events chain concept map for the generation of electricity in a nuclear fission reactor. Begin with the bombarding neutron and end with electricity in overhead lines. If you need help, refer to Concept Mapping in the **Skill Handbook.**

Using Computers

Word Processing
Create a table with two divisions for the advantages and disadvantages of nuclear power. Type in as many entries under each as you can list.

Activity 25-1

Nuclear Waste Disposal

Because many radioactive wastes will continue to decay for hundreds of years, it is important to test containment procedures that will prevent leakage. What kinds of materials do you think could effectively hold radioactive wastes while they decay?

Problem

How can you build a model to represent the concerns about containment of radioactive waste?

Materials

* sodium hydroxide pellets (4)
* 100-mL beakers (4)
* phenolphthalein solution
* modeling clay
* plastic food wrap
* aluminum foil
* rubber bands (3)
* twist ties (2)
* forceps
* goggles

Procedure

1. Let the sodium hydroxide pellets represent pellets of nuclear waste. Your job is to test materials that may be able to keep unwanted chemicals from leaking into the environment. **CAUTION:** *Do not touch the sodium hydroxide pellets or solution with your hands. Always wear goggles when handling sodium hydroxide. Wipe up all spills.*
2. Fill all four beakers with water and add 3 or 4 drops of phenolphthalein to each.
3. Using the forceps, place one pellet in one of the beakers. Record your observations.
4. Wrap each of the remaining pellets: one in aluminum foil, one in plastic wrap, and one in clay. Secure the plastic with twist ties.

5. Drop the wrapped pellets into the remaining three beakers, and cover them with food wrap.
6. Make observations each day for three days to determine whether there is leakage from the containers. Record your observations in the data table.
7. After the last observations, pour the solutions into a container provided by your teacher.

Data and Observations

Beaker Containing Pellets	Observations		
	Day 1	Day 2	Day 3
Unwrapped			
Wrapped in aluminum foil			
Wrapped in plastic wrap			
Embedded in clay			

Analyze

1. Was red color seen in any of the beakers after the first day?
2. After three days, which, if any, of the beakers show no red color?

Conclude and Apply

3. **Infer** which kind of wrapping is the most leakproof.
4. **Hypothesize** why the storage and disposal of nuclear waste is a major concern of society.

ISSUE:
25•3 Nuclear Waste and NIMBY

Science Words

NIMBY

Objectives

- Discuss problems associated with storing nuclear waste.
- Compare long-term nuclear waste-storage options.

Figure 25-9

This map shows where the different kinds of waste are now being stored.

- Low-level military and commercial waste site
- Temporary high-level military waste site
- Permanent high-level military waste site
- Proposed high-level commercial waste site

NIMBY

Using nuclear fission to generate electrical power offers several advantages. In the United States, a portion of our electrical output can be attributed to this technology. However, you have also read about the problem of nuclear waste disposal. When it comes to trying to find a suitable location for storage of waste or transport of nuclear products, many people support the **NIMBY,** Not in My Backyard, point of view. In other words, nuclear power may be agreeable as long as it is not too close to home.

Classifying Nuclear Waste

In the previous section, you learned that nuclear waste is radioactive and is classified as low level or high level. As you read, low-level waste is disposed of in special landfills licensed by the federal government. However, high-level wastes are not disposed of nearly as easily. **Figure 25-9** shows where nuclear storage sites presently are located in the United States.

The radioactive products of uranium fission pose major problems with storage. What should be done with the radioactive fuel rods? The rods contain high-level waste. High-level waste is made up of such fission products as Sr-90 and Cs-137, with half-lives in the 30-year range. Some I-129 and Tc-99, with half-lives on the order of hundreds of thousands of years, are also in high-level waste. As you have read, a national storage site for this type of waste has been proposed near Yucca Mountain, Nevada. Sealing the waste in ceramic glass, placing the glass globules in protective containers, then storing the containers hundreds of meters below ground in stable rock or salt deposits may keep the material safely away from human activity for hundreds of years.

Exposure to excessive nuclear radiation can cause extreme health problems, and even death. Nuclear waste has already been generated. With approximately

100 active nuclear power plants and many medical applications, we will continue to generate radioactive waste. How can we minimize our exposure to radiation from nuclear waste?

2 Points of View

More Research

At present, temporary storage sites for high-level nuclear wastes, like the one shown in **Figure 25-10,** exist on the west and east coasts. Before making a permanent national storage site, more study should be done about the geology of the site. Will it be safe from underground shifting due to fault lines? Would salt corrode the containers? Would it be better to have a few scattered sites so the waste would not have to be transported long distances to one site?

Safely Below Ground

Research has already shown that deep, stable rock deposits offer the best hope for safely containing radioactive waste. By having one national storage site, federal monitoring of strict design rules and safety standards could be maintained. This would be easier than monitoring several sites. Some of the temporary sites have already shown some leaking. The Nuclear Waste Policy Act of 1982 charges the federal government with establishing a national permanent site by 2010.

Figure 25-10
These temporary sites will be empty when a national site is chosen.

Section Wrap-up

Review

1. What problems are associated with storing nuclear waste?

2. Cite one advantage and one disadvantage to the proposed Yucca Mountain site for permanent nuclear storage.

Explore the Issue

Do you favor sealing away radioactive waste hundreds of meters below ground? Could we be putting these chemicals so far out of reach that they may not be available for future generations? What if technologies of the future could use the buried substances?

SCIENCE & SOCIETY

25•4 Alternative Energy Sources

Objectives

- Analyze the need for alternative energy sources.
- Discuss the methods of generating electricity with several energy sources.
- Describe the advantages and disadvantages of several alternative energy sources.

The Need for Alternatives

Can you name any sources of energy other than fossil fuels and nuclear energy? Although we have enough of these energy sources to fill our energy demands today, there is a great need to develop alternative sources of energy for the future. As you have already discovered, depending on fossil fuels and nuclear fission for our energy needs has many disadvantages.

Nuclear fission and the burning of fossil fuels are both processes used to boil water to produce steam. However, other materials can be burned to give off energy, as well. Biomass is renewable organic matter, such as wood, sugar-cane fibers, rice hulls, and animal manure. It can be burned in the presence of oxygen to convert the stored chemical energy to thermal energy. Burning biomass is probably the oldest use of natural resources for human needs.

You may have seen gasohol advertised at a gas station. How does this fuel differ from normal gasoline? Corn and other plant fibers can be fermented to convert the sugar and starch in the grain to ethanol. The ethanol is combined with gasoline to produce gasohol for use in your car engine.

Biomass and gasohol are just two examples of many energy alternatives that reduce our consumption of nonrenewable fuels. The energy alternatives discussed in this section make use of processes that occur naturally on Earth. What natural processes do you see around you that could be used to generate electricity or provide heat?

Solar Energy

The sun is Earth's only source of new energy. There are now automobiles powered by sunlight. Solar panels on the car collect and use solar energy for power. Methods of collecting and using solar energy are categorized as passive or active.

Passive solar heating is the direct use of the sun's energy in maintaining comfortable indoor temperatures. Passive solar heating was used centuries ago by the Romans to heat their bathhouses. Efforts in energy conservation have renewed interest in this method of heating. Buildings constructed with strategically placed windows can be heated by the sun. On warm days, these windows can be covered with blinds to prevent excessive heating.

In active solar heating, solar panels collect and store solar energy. Solar panels are made of large, dark-colored trays covered with transparent glass or plastic. Large mirrors are sometimes used to focus the sun's radiation into these solar collectors. The panels absorb the sun's energy and use it to heat water. The heated water can be used directly, or it can be stored to give off thermal energy. Solar energy can even be used to drive electric power generators in solar thermal power plants.

Electricity Directly from Light

A device used to convert solar energy into electricity is the **photovoltaic cell,** also called the solar cell. Do you own a solar-powered calculator like the one in **Figure 25-11?** It contains a solar cell. Photovoltaic cells are made of a semiconductor lined on both surfaces with a conducting metal. As light strikes the surface of the cell, electrons flow between the two metal layers, creating a current. Many cells connected in a circuit can provide significant amounts of electricity. In order to be a useful technology, photovoltaic cells must be capable of producing in their lifetime more energy than is used in producing the cells. The cells must also be economical and practical to manufacture.

This method of producing electricity is more expensive on a large scale than the use of non-renewable fuels, but it can be less expensive in isolated areas when the cost of building transmission lines to those areas is considered. Solar energy is a pollution-free resource that is becoming more economical as our solar technology develops.

CONNECT TO

CHEMISTRY

The ethanol used in gasohol has the chemical formula C_2H_5OH.

$$H-\overset{\overset{\displaystyle H}{|}}{\underset{\underset{\displaystyle H}{|}}{C}}-\overset{\overset{\displaystyle H}{|}}{\underset{\underset{\displaystyle H}{|}}{C}}-OH$$

Determine the total atomic mass units of the atoms in this compound.

Figure 25-11

In what way does this solar-powered calculator allow our existing energy resources to last longer?

Hydroelectricity

One way to produce electricity is with water. Water flowing in rivers carries tremendous amounts of kinetic and potential energy. Dams are built to store vast amounts of water. Behind a dam, the water is deep. Near the base of a hydroelectric dam, water is allowed to rush out through tunnels. The rushing water spins a turbine, rotating the shaft of an electric generator to produce electricity.

Hydroelectricity is electricity produced by the energy of moving water. Hydroelectric power plants are an efficient way to produce electricity. They produce almost no pollution. The bodies of water held back by dams can provide lakes for recreational uses and irrigation. The ongoing natural water cycle makes hydroelectric power a permanent resource. After the initial cost of building a dam and power plant, the electricity is relatively cheap. However, artificial dams can disturb the balance of natural ecosystems.

Tidal Energy

The gravitational forces of the moon and the sun cause bulges in Earth's oceans. As Earth rotates, the two bulges of ocean water move westward. Each day, the level of the ocean on a coast rises and falls continually. A kind of hydroelectric power can be generated by these ocean tides. The moving water can be trapped at high tide by building a dam at the opening of a river or bay. **Figure 25-12** shows the forces that can be harnessed in tides and the water level changes associated with them. The flowing water at low tide spins a turbine, which operates an electric generator. Energy generated by tidal motion is called **tidal energy.**

Figure 25-12

Waves caused by the gravitational pull of the sun and moon cause these churning tides in the photograph. Spring tides occur when the sun, moon, and Earth are aligned (at new and full moon). Neap tides occur when the sun, Earth, and moon form a right angle (at the first and third quarters of the moon).
Do you think tidal energy would be a reliable form of energy? Why or why not?

Sun
Moon Earth — Tides
Spring Tide

Sun
Tides
Earth
Neap Tide
Moon

Figure 25-13

This is not a propeller, but a windmill. You don't see many windmills, but in the right place they are powerful producers of energy.

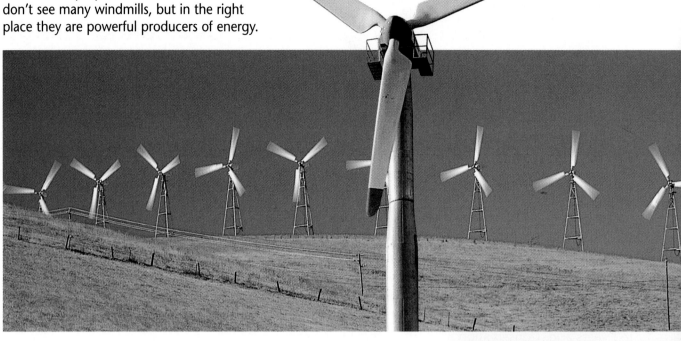

Like producing hydroelectric power, generating electricity from tidal motion is nearly pollution-free. But, there are only a few places on Earth where the difference between high and low tide is large enough to be an efficient source of energy. In the United States, the use of tidal energy is being explored in the Cook Inlet in Alaska and Passamaquoddy Bay in Maine. The ocean environment will possibly make construction and maintenance of these plants difficult. The only functioning tidal power station in North America is at Annapolis Royal, Nova Scotia. Tidal energy probably will be a limited, but useful, source of energy in the future.

Wind Energy

You may have seen a windmill on a farm. Or, in a windy region, you may have seen several hundred windmills like the ones in **Figure 25-13**. A windmill is a turbine that is turned by the wind instead of steam or water. The windmill spins and rotates an electric generator to produce electricity.

Only a few places on Earth consistently have enough wind to rely on wind power to meet energy needs. Improved design of wind generators can increase their efficiency, so new methods of using the wind's energy are being researched. Wind generators do not actually use up any resources. They do not pollute the atmosphere or water. However, they do change the appearance of a landscape.

MiniLAB

How do hydroelectric power plants use water to drive turbines?

Procedure
1. Mold a clay collar around the middle of a pencil.
2. Insert flat wooden sticks into the clay to resemble the spokes of a wheel.
3. Punch a small hole near the bottom of a large plastic container.
4. Fill the container with water, holding your finger over the hole.
5. Release your finger, holding the pencil so that a stream of water strikes the wooden sticks.

Analysis
1. How do you know that the kinetic energy of the water has been transferred to your model turbine?

Problem Solving

Energy Exercises

After reading about several alternative energy sources, you may be thinking that some of them would not easily apply to your community. Certainly, ocean tides will not be much help in states without a coastline. Solar-powered generators may not work in northern areas. However, increased efficiency and better conservation methods can help make our existing energy supplies last longer. *Efficiency* refers to the amount of benefit obtained compared to the amount of energy used. For example, automobiles now obtain more miles per gallon of gasoline used than they did ten years ago. Conservation methods include practices such as recycling. By recycling aluminum cans, coal deposits can be saved. It takes less coal to make a can from recycled aluminum than from mined aluminum.

Solve the Problem:

1. **Compare and contrast the terms** *conservation* **and** *efficiency.*
2. **Is riding a bus to school, rather than riding in a passenger car, an example of a conservation method or an increase in the efficiency of technology?**

Think Critically:

Fluorescent lightbulbs last longer than typical incandescent bulbs. A lower-wattage fluorescent bulb can provide the same light as a higher-wattage incandescent bulb. Discuss the use of each bulb as it relates to efficiency and conservation.

Geothermal Energy

Look down at the ground. What do you see and feel underneath your feet? Although you may think of Earth as a solid sphere, hot gases and molten rock lie far beneath the surface. The inner parts of Earth contain a great deal of thermal energy, called **geothermal energy.** You do not usually notice this energy because most of it is far below Earth's crust.

In some places, Earth's crust has cracks or thin spots in it. These areas allow some of the geothermal energy to rise up near the surface of Earth. Active volcanoes permit hot gases and molten lava from deep within Earth to escape. Perhaps you have seen a geyser shoot steam and hot water from Earth. Have you ever visited or seen pictures of the famous geyser, Old Faithful, in Yellowstone National Park? This water is heated by geothermal energy. Wells can be drilled deep within Earth to pump out this hot water, which ranges in temperature from 150°C to 350°C. The steam can be used to rotate turbines and turn electric generators. Use of geothermal energy can release some sulfur compounds from gases within Earth. This pollution can be controlled by pumping the water and steam back into Earth.

Where on Earth?

Only certain places on Earth have the proper geological characteristics to use geothermal energy. Iceland makes use of geothermal plants, as shown in **Figure 25-14,** because it is located near the boundary of two continental plates. Volcanic activity and hot springs abound in the area. Lardello, Italy, began using geothermal energy in the early 1900s. Geothermal applications are limited because of the geological characteristics needed. However, the United States, particularly in the western areas, has some potential for the use of heat from Earth to make electricity.

Figure 25-14

Geothermal energy may be used in areas like Iceland. *Why isn't this form of energy the answer for other areas on Earth?*

Section Wrap-up

Review

1. Why is there a need for developing and using alternative energy sources?

2. Describe three main ways to use direct solar energy.

3. **Think Critically:** What single resource do most of the energy alternatives discussed in this section depend on, either directly or indirectly?

Skill Builder

Classifying

Classify the following examples of solar heating as passive or active. (A) The interior of an enclosed automobile on a sunny day. (B) Air in a room of a house near a window warms. (C) Hot water in a pipe is pumped from a rooftop to a radiator device in a bedroom.

USING MATH

The sources of energy in the United States are: 42 percent petroleum, 24 percent natural gas, 23 percent coal, 7 percent nuclear, and 4 percent other. If the percent of nuclear energy were represented with a 1-m strip of paper, how long would the other strips be?

Design Your Own Experiment

Energy Alternatives— A Local Plan

Electrical power is a basic need for a community. What power source should be considered when generating electricity? In this activity, you will investigate the main problems associated with building a power plant.

PREPARATION

Problem
Your class has been selected to prepare a recommendation for the construction of a new power plant in your community. What variables should your team consider for your community?

Form a Hypothesis
Based on what you have just read and a knowledge of your community's resources, form a hypothesis about the best type of power plant for your community.

Objectives
- Consider available resources when planning a power plant.
- Consider environmental advantages and disadvantages of your suggested power plant.
- Prepare an oral report with a poster or model of your design for a power plant.

Possible Materials
- large poster board
- colored markers
- miscellaneous construction objects

PLAN THE EXPERIMENT

1. As a group, agree upon and write out your hypothesis statement about your planned power plant.
2. Decide together on the components in your design, such as resources available, possible environmental aspects, and economic factors.
3. Make a list of materials you will need to complete your oral report when you present your findings to the class.

Check the Plan
1. Read over your design to make sure you have considered all variables.
2. Will you have to visit a resource center to obtain more information about the type of power plant you are suggesting?

3. Will your presentation include a scale model, a collage, or a poster?
4. *Make sure your teacher approves your plan.*

POWER STATION

DO THE EXPERIMENT

1. Decide how your team will make its presentation.
2. Obtain the materials for your presentation props.

Analyze and Apply
1. Listen to the reports of other groups. **Compare and contrast** the advantages and disadvantages each power plant design offers.

2. Will the plant designs presented be used primarily as supplements for the existing population, or will they provide for anticipated expanding populations?
3. **Analyze** how economic factors compare to environmental factors when deciding which plant to use.

Go Further

Contact your local power plant authority. Ask what alternatives the community might consider if the present plant were going to be replaced.

People and Science

YVONNE HO CARDINALE,
Hydroelectric Engineer

On the Job

Q Ms. Cardinale, how does a hydro-electric power plant work?

A The power plant is located inside a dam built to hold back the water in a river, creating a reservoir. A large tunnel, called the intake structure, opens into the lowest part of the reservoir. Water flows through the tunnel and across the blades of a turbine. The turbine generates electricity.

Q How is a hydro plant built?

A For a large project here in California several years ago, I was responsible for quality control in the construction of the main tunnel, penstock, and surge chamber. We used a tunnel-boring machine to carve out the main tunnel, and drilling and blasting for smaller access tunnels.

Q What is a surge chamber?

A It's a vertical shaft that serves as a pressure release if a turbine has to be shut down. A huge amount of water—representing a lot of kinetic energy—rushes through the tunnel and penstock, so you have to have somewhere for it to go if it can't move on through the turbine.

Personal Insights

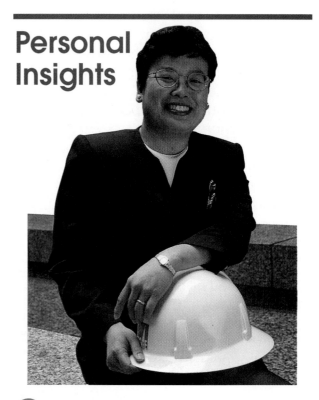

Q What is a typical workday like ?

A I help predict how much electricity some of our hydro plants can generate, based on weather factors. I go out to monitor weather stations and measure snow depth. I use computer models to help decide how much water to save behind the dam to produce power when it's needed.

Career Connection

Civil engineers are involved in the design, planning, and construction of power plants, buildings, roads, and underground cable and pipe systems. Interview a civil engineer who works in your community. Ask about the training needed to become an engineer, as well as for descriptions of a typical workday.

Chapter 25 Review

Summary

25-1: Fossil Fuels

1. The three types of fossil fuels are petroleum, natural gas, and coal. They formed from the buried remains of plants and animals.
2. All fossil fuels are nonrenewable energy resources. Supplies will run out soon if they aren't used wisely.

25-2: Nuclear Energy

1. A nuclear reactor uses the energy from a controlled nuclear chain fission reaction to generate electricity.
2. Nuclear wastes must be carefully contained and disposed of so radiation from nuclear decay will not leak into the environment.
3. Nuclear fusion releases greater amounts of energy than does nuclear fission, but fusion must occur at temperatures that are too high to be contained in a laboratory.

25-3: Science and Society: Nuclear Waste and NIMBY

1. Due to long half-lives and radioactivity levels that can be harmful, storing nuclear waste is an environmental and political problem.
2. A national permanent storage area has been proposed in Nevada.

25-4: Alternative Energy Sources

1. Alternate energy resources are needed to supplement or replace nonrenewable energy resources.
2. Other sources of energy for generating electricity include hydroelectricity and solar, wind, tidal, and geothermal energy.
3. Although some alternative energy sources don't pollute the environment and are renewable, their use is often limited to the regions where the energy source is available.

Key Science Words

a. fractional distillation
b. geothermal energy
c. hydroelectricity
d. NIMBY
e. nonrenewable resource
f. nuclear reactor
g. nuclear waste
h. petroleum
i. photovoltaic cell
j. tidal energy

Reviewing Vocabulary

Match each phrase with the correct term from the list of Key Science Words.

1. separates the hydrocarbons in crude oil
2. liquid remains of dead organisms
3. generates electricity from a controlled fission reaction
4. thermal energy inside Earth
5. source of energy that can't be replaced
6. converts solar energy directly into electricity
7. electricity produced by the energy of moving water
8. energy produced by the rise and fall of ocean levels
9. an attitude that suggests that easy answers to problems can be found as long as the solution is not too close to home
10. by-product of fission reactions

Checking Concepts

Choose the word or phrase that completes the sentence.

1. Plant and animal remains that are buried under sediments are not acted upon by _____ to form fossil fuels.
   a. bacteria   c. heat
   b. pressure   d. radiation

2. Hydrocarbons react with _____ during the combustion of fossil fuels.
   a. carbon dioxide   c. oxygen
   b. carbon monoxide   d. water

3. Fossil fuels are becoming more scarce as industrial demands increase and _____.
   a. the population increases
   b. the population decreases
   c. the number of nuclear reactors increases
   d. fewer plants and animals die

4. Both burning fossil fuels and nuclear fission must first be used to produce _____ in order to produce electricity.
   a. steam   c. plutonium
   b. carbon dioxide   d. water

5. A major disadvantage of using nuclear fusion reactors is that they _____.
   a. use hydrogen from water as fuel
   b. produce less radioactivity
   c. require extremely high temperatures
   d. use only small nuclei

6. Nuclear wastes include _____.
   a. products of fission reactors
   b. materials with short half-lives
   c. products from medical and industrial processes
   d. all of these

7. High-level nuclear wastes are currently disposed of by _____.
   a. releasing them into water
   b. storing them in a deep, insulated pool of water
   c. burying them in unstable areas
   d. releasing them into the air

8. All of Earth's energy resources can ultimately be traced back to _____.
   a. plants   c. geothermal resources
   b. the sun   d. fossil fuels

9. Photovoltaic cells must be made _____ before they can be more widely used to produce electricity.
   a. pollution-free   c. less expensive
   b. nonrenewable   d. larger

10. _____ is an alternate source of energy that uses water heated naturally by Earth's internal heat.
    a. Hydroelectricity   c. Tidal energy
    b. Nuclear fission   d. Geothermal energy

Understanding Concepts

Answer the following questions in your Science Journal using complete sentences.

11. Most of the energy resources discussed in this chapter produce electricity by means of an electric generator. Briefly discuss how each resource is used to do this.

12. Why is energy conservation important? What are some ways to conserve energy?

13. How great is the possibility of a nuclear explosion in a nuclear reactor?

14. Why isn't fusion being used today as a source of energy?

15. What specific problems have created the need for alternative energy resources? Why aren't these resources more widely used today?

Thinking Critically

16. Which fossil fuel do you think we should use to generate electricity? What are the pros and cons of using this fossil fuel?

17. Match each of the energy resources described in the chapter with the proper type of energy conversion listed below.
   a. kinetic energy to electricity
   b. thermal energy to electricity
   c. nuclear energy to electricity
   d. chemical energy to electricity
   e. light energy to electricity

18. Evaluate the following disposal methods of high-level nuclear wastes.
   a. Bury the wastes in an area of high earthquake and volcanic activity.
   b. Place the wastes on the ocean floor.
   c. Rocket the wastes into space.

19. Classify the energy resources discussed in this chapter as renewable or nonrenewable.

20. Suppose that new reserves of petroleum were discovered and that a nonpolluting way to burn them for energy were found. Why would it still be a good idea to decrease our use of petroleum as a source of energy? (HINT: Consider fractional distillation.)

Developing Skills

If you need help, refer to the **Skill Handbook.**

21. Sequencing: The ultimate source of energy for cooking food on an electric stove is the sun. List in order the steps that must occur before you can use the sun's energy in this way.

22. Recognizing Cause and Effect: Complete the following table that describes changes in the normal operation of a nuclear reactor and the possible effects of these changes.

Reactor Problems

Cause	Effect
1. The cooling H_2O is released hot	1.
2. Control rods are removed	2.
3.	3. Reactor core overheats; meltdown

23. Making and Using Tables: Construct a table to summarize the advantages and disadvantages of each of the energy resources discussed in this chapter.

24. Classifying: The following concepts relate to nuclear power as an energy source. Classify each as connected to fission or fusion. (a) Hydrogen nuclei are the main fuel source. (b) Products are not radioactive. (c) Boron and cadmium can be used to help control the process. (d) Magnetic forces can be used to help control the process.

25. Using Numbers: Two radioactive samples have the following half-lives. X has a half-life of 30 years, and Y has a half-life of 10 years. If you have 10.0 g of X and 100 g of Y initially, how much will remain after 90 years?

Performance Assessment

1. Oral Presentation: Research the ways in which scientists are currently trying to contain and control fusion. Write a report and present it to your classmates.

2. Newspaper Article: Write a newspaper article to raise public awareness of current energy problems and solutions.

3. Asking Questions: Review your power plant design from Activity 25-2 as if you were a state representative. What questions would you want answered?

Researching Via the Internet

How do you use resources to find out more about a topic in which you are interested? In the past, you might have gone to the library and used a card catalog or periodical listing to find books, magazine and newspaper articles that were related to your topic. Now, at most libraries, you can find these same book and article listings on a computer. Many libraries have put their holdings in one large database to make research less time consuming and more successful.

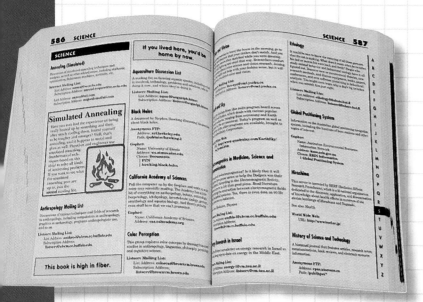

Within the last few years a new, and more powerful source for information retrieval has become widely available. This source of information is called the Internet. If you have a computer or have access to a school computer, you can do research on the Internet without ever leaving your chair.

What is the Internet?

The Internet is made up of millions of computers all around the world that are linked to each other. The information available in these computers is varied and vast. You can find information on almost any imaginable topic. Using electronic mail, or e-mail, you can speak directly to an expert in a particular field or to a person in another country. Some computers store articles or entire books about particular subjects. Others contain thousands of photographs and illustrations.

Getting Started

To use the Internet you must have a way to access it. Many schools have direct access to the Internet or have a connection through a local college or university. A phone line can also give you access by way of a commercial server. Each server differs slightly in the way it works. Time, practice, and perhaps some cooperative work with a few friends will help you locate the information you need. Reference books on using the Internet will be helpful as will consulting with persons already proficient at research using the Internet.

Beginning Your Search

For this project you will choose a new technology that you wish to research and report on to your class. Look at the Using Technology features in this book for an idea. If you have an idea for a topic from another source, check it out with your teacher before beginning. Pick a topic that isn't too broad or narrow.

Internet Yellow Pages

Internet yellow pages contain the Internet addresses for locating information on any imaginable topic. However, because no one is in charge of the Internet, an Internet address may be available for a time, then the people managing it may decide to remove it.

Internet Search Tips

One important method for finding information is a search tool. A search tool allows you to type in a key word or words. The tool then searches thousands of sites on the Internet for those that contain your key words. After a few seconds, the search tool returns many addresses for other links related to your topic. The *Gopher* is one type

of search tool. There are thousands of Gopher servers available on the Internet.

Making Your Presentation

After you've completed your search for information and gathered all of your data, you should be ready to prepare a presentation for your class. Your presentation should be put together using a multimedia computer program. Your presentation should consist of at least five different screens with text, graphics, and perhaps sound and photos. Design each screen so that it is appealing to the audience. Your report should include information from at least five sites on the Internet. Identify your sites and explain to the class how you got to them.

A word of caution. Not everything on the Internet is valid. Much of the information has not been edited, reviewed, or even verified as true. If you have questions about anything you find, ask a parent, teacher or other adult to help you determine if it is useful or not.

Appendices

Appendix A

Appendix B

Appendix C

Appendix A

SI Units of Measurement

Table A-1

SI Base Units

Measurement	Unit	Symbol	Measurement	Unit	Symbol
length	meter	m	temperature	kelvin	K
mass	kilogram	kg	amount of substance	mole	mol
time	second	s	intensity of light	candela	cd
electric current	ampere	A			

Table A-2

Units Derived from SI Base Units

Measurement	Unit	Symbol	Expressed in Base Units
energy	joule	J	$kg \cdot m^2/s^2$ or $N \cdot m$
force	newton	N	$kg \cdot m/s^2$
frequency	hertz	Hz	$1/s$
potential difference	volt	V	$kg \cdot m^2/(A \cdot s^3)$ or W/A
power	watt	W	$kg \cdot m^2/s^3$ or J/s
pressure	pascal	Pa	$kg/(m \cdot s^2)$ or N/m^2
quality of electric charge	coulomb	C	$A \cdot s$

Table A-3

Common SI Prefixes

Prefix	Symbol	Multiplier	Prefix	Symbol	Multiplier
	Greater than 1			Less than 1	
mega-	M	1 000 000	*deci-*	d	0.1
kilo-	k	1 000	*centi-*	c	0.01
hecto-	h	100	*milli-*	m	0.001
deka-	da	10	*micro-*	μ	0.000 001

/Metric to English Conversions

	When you want to convert:	Multiply by:	To find:
Length	inches	2.54	centimeters
	centimeters	0.39	inches
	feet	0.30	meters
	meters	3.28	feet
	yards	0.91	meters
	meters	1.09	yards
	miles	1.61	kilometers
	kilometers	0.62	miles
*Mass and Weight	ounces	28.35	grams
	grams	0.04	ounces
	pounds	0.45	kilograms
	kilograms	2.20	pounds
	tons	0.91	metric tons
	metric tons	1.10	tons
	pounds	4.45	newtons
	newtons	0.23	pounds
Volume	cubic inches	16.39	cubic centimeters
	cubic centimeters	0.06	cubic inches
	cubic feet	0.03	cubic meters
	cubic meters	35.31	cubic feet
	liters	1.06	quarts
	liters	0.26	gallons
	gallons	3.78	liters
Area	square inches	6.45	square centimeters
	square centimeters	0.16	square inches
	square feet	0.09	square meters
	square meters	10.76	square feet
	square miles	2.59	square kilometers
	square kilometers	0.39	square miles

* Weight as measured in standard Earth gravity

SI/Temperature Scale Conversions

Table A-5

SI/Temperature Scale Conversions

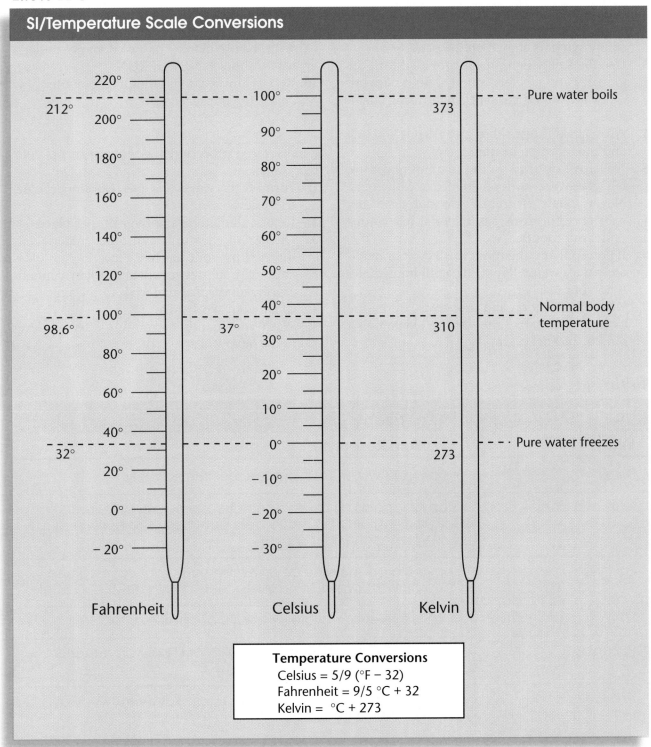

Temperature Conversions
Celsius = 5/9 (°F − 32)
Fahrenheit = 9/5 °C + 32
Kelvin = °C + 273

Safety in the Classroom

1. Always obtain your teacher's permission to begin an investigation.
2. Study the procedure. If you have questions, ask your teacher. Be sure you understand any safety symbols shown on the page.
3. Use the safety equipment provided for you. Goggles and a safety apron should be worn when any investigation calls for using chemicals.
4. Always slant test tubes away from yourself and others when heating them.
5. Never eat or drink in the lab, and never use lab glassware as food or drink containers. Never inhale chemicals. Do not taste any substances or draw any material into a tube with your mouth.
6. If you spill any chemical, wash it off immediately with water. Report the spill immediately to your teacher.
7. Know the location and proper use of the fire extinguisher, safety shower, fire blanket, first aid kit, and fire alarm.
8. Keep all materials away from open flames. Tie back long hair and loose clothing.
9. If a fire should break out in the classroom, or if your clothing should catch fire, smother it with the fire blanket or a coat, or get under a safety shower. NEVER RUN.
10. Report any accident or injury, no matter how small, to your teacher.

Follow these procedures as you clean up your work area.

1. Turn off the water and gas. Disconnect electrical devices.
2. Return all materials to their proper places.
3. Dispose of chemicals and other materials as directed by your teacher. Place broken glass and solid substances in the proper containers. Never discard materials in the sink.
4. Clean your work area.
5. Wash your hands thoroughly after working in the laboratory.

Table B-1

First Aid	
Injury	**Safe Response**
Burns	Apply cold water. Call your teacher immediately.
Cuts and bruises	Stop any bleeding by applying direct pressure. Cover cuts with a clean dressing. Apply cold compresses to bruises. Call your teacher immediately.
Fainting	Leave the person lying down. Loosen any tight clothing and keep crowds away. Call your teacher immediately.
Foreign matter in eye	Flush with plenty of water. Use eyewash bottle or fountain.
Poisoning	Note the suspected poisoning agent and call your teacher immediately.
Any spills on skin	Flush with large amounts of water or use safety shower. Call your teacher immediately.

Safety Symbols

This textbook uses the safety symbols in **Table B-2** below to alert you to possible laboratory dangers.

Table B-2

Safety Symbols

	DISPOSAL ALERT This symbol appears when care must be taken to dispose of materials properly.		**ANIMAL SAFETY** This symbol appears whenever live animals are studied and the safety of the animals and the students must be ensured.
	BIOLOGICAL HAZARD This symbol appears when there is danger involving bacteria, fungi, or protists.		**RADIOACTIVE SAFETY** This symbol appears when radioactive materials are used.
	OPEN FLAME ALERT This symbol appears when use of an open flame could cause a fire or an explosion.		**CLOTHING PROTECTION SAFETY** This symbol appears when substances used could stain or burn clothing.
	THERMAL SAFETY This symbol appears as a reminder to use caution when handling hot objects.		**FIRE SAFETY** This symbol appears when care should be taken around open flames.
	SHARP OBJECT SAFETY This symbol appears when a danger of cuts or punctures caused by the use of sharp objects exists.		**EXPLOSION SAFETY** This symbol appears when the misuse of chemicals could cause an explosion.
	FUME SAFETY This symbol appears when chemicals or chemical reactions could cause dangerous fumes.		**EYE SAFETY** This symbol appears when a danger to the eyes exists. Safety goggles should be worn when this symbol appears.
	ELECTRICAL SAFETY This symbol appears when care should be taken when using electrical equipment.		**POISON SAFETY** This symbol appears when poisonous substances are used.
	PLANT SAFETY This symbol appears when poisonous plants or plants with thorns are handled.		**CHEMICAL SAFETY** This symbol appears when chemicals used can cause burns or are poisonous if absorbed through the skin.

Appendix C

PERIODIC TABLE OF THE ELEMENTS

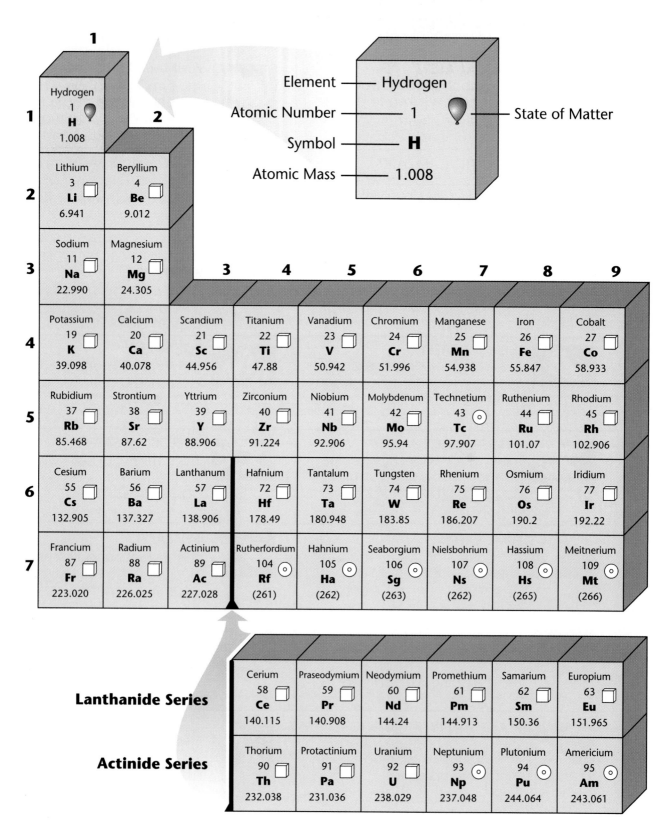

Element — Hydrogen
Atomic Number — 1 — State of Matter
Symbol — H
Atomic Mass — 1.008

Lanthanide Series

Actinide Series

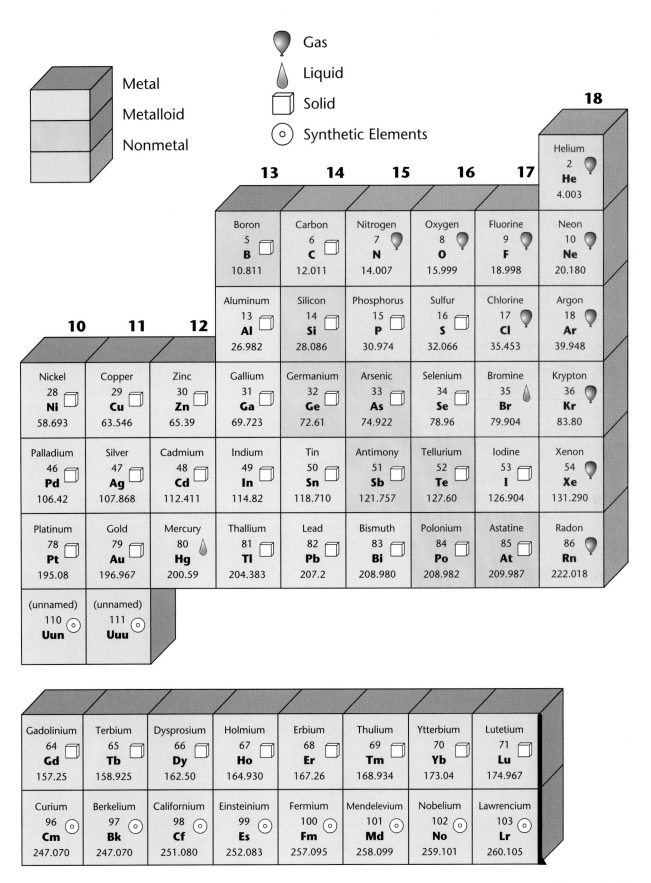

Metal
Metalloid
Nonmetal

Gas
Liquid
Solid
Synthetic Elements

18

Helium
2
He
4.003

13

Boron
5
B
10.811

Aluminum
13
Al
26.982

14

Carbon
6
C
12.011

Silicon
14
Si
28.086

15

Nitrogen
7
N
14.007

Phosphorus
15
P
30.974

16

Oxygen
8
O
15.999

Sulfur
16
S
32.066

17

Fluorine
9
F
18.998

Chlorine
17
Cl
35.453

Neon
10
Ne
20.180

Argon
18
Ar
39.948

10

Nickel
28
Ni
58.693

Palladium
46
Pd
106.42

Platinum
78
Pt
195.08

(unnamed)
110
Uun

11

Copper
29
Cu
63.546

Silver
47
Ag
107.868

Gold
79
Au
196.967

(unnamed)
111
Uuu

12

Zinc
30
Zn
65.39

Cadmium
48
Cd
112.411

Mercury
80
Hg
200.59

Gallium
31
Ga
69.723

Indium
49
In
114.82

Thallium
81
Tl
204.383

Germanium
32
Ge
72.61

Tin
50
Sn
118.710

Lead
82
Pb
207.2

Arsenic
33
As
74.922

Antimony
51
Sb
121.757

Bismuth
83
Bi
208.980

Selenium
34
Se
78.96

Tellurium
52
Te
127.60

Polonium
84
Po
208.982

Bromine
35
Br
79.904

Iodine
53
I
126.904

Astatine
85
At
209.987

Krypton
36
Kr
83.80

Xenon
54
Xe
131.290

Radon
86
Rn
222.018

Gadolinium
64
Gd
157.25

Curium
96
Cm
247.070

Terbium
65
Tb
158.925

Berkelium
97
Bk
247.070

Dysprosium
66
Dy
162.50

Californium
98
Cf
251.080

Holmium
67
Ho
164.930

Einsteinium
99
Es
252.083

Erbium
68
Er
167.26

Fermium
100
Fm
257.095

Thulium
69
Tm
168.934

Mendelevium
101
Md
258.099

Ytterbium
70
Yb
173.04

Nobelium
102
No
259.101

Lutetium
71
Lu
174.967

Lawrencium
103
Lr
260.105

Table of Contents

Organizing Information

Communicating

The communication of ideas is an important part of our everyday lives. Whether reading a book, writing a letter, or watching a television program, people everywhere are expressing opinions and sharing information with one another. Writing in your Science Journal allows you to express your opinions and demonstrate your knowledge of the information presented on a subject. When writing, keep in mind the purpose of the assignment and the audience with which you are communicating.

Examples Science Journal assignments vary greatly. They may ask you to take a viewpoint other than your own; perhaps you will be a scientist, a TV reporter, or a committee member of a local environmental group. Maybe you will be expressing your opinions to a member of Congress, a doctor, or to the editor of your local newspaper, as shown in **Figure 1.** Sometimes, Science Journal writing may allow you to summarize information in the form of an outline, a letter, or in a paragraph.

Figure 1

A Science Journal entry.

Figure 2

Classifying CDs.

Classifying

You may not realize it, but you make things orderly in the world around you. If you hang your shirts together in the closet or if your favorite CDs are stacked together, you have used the skill of classifying.

Classifying is the process of sorting objects or events into groups based on common features. When classifying, first observe the objects or events to be classified. Then, select one feature that is shared by some members in the group but not by all. Place those members that share that feature into a subgroup. You can classify members into smaller and smaller subgroups based on characteristics.

Remember, when you classify, you are grouping objects or events for a purpose. Keep your purpose in mind as you select the features to form groups and subgroups.

Example How would you classify a collection of CDs? As shown in **Figure 2,** you might classify those you like to dance to in one subgroup and CDs you like to listen to in the next column. The CDs you like to dance to could be subdivided into a rap subgroup and a rock subgroup. Note that for each feature selected, each CD fits into only one subgroup. You would keep selecting features until all the CDs are classified. **Figure 2** shows one possible classification.

Figure 3

A recipe for bread contains sequenced instructions.

Sequencing

A sequence is an arrangement of things or events in a particular order. When you are asked to sequence objects or events within a group, figure out what comes first, then think about what should come second. Continue to choose objects or events until all of the objects you started out with are in order. Then, go back over the sequence to make sure each thing or event in your sequence logically leads to the next.

Example A sequence with which you are most familiar is the use of alphabetical order. Another example of sequence would be the steps in a recipe, as shown in **Figure 3.** Think about baking bread. Steps in the recipe have to be followed in order for the bread to turn out right.

Concept Mapping

If you were taking an automobile trip, you would probably take along a road map. The road map shows your location, your destination, and other places along the way. By looking at the map and finding where you are, you can begin to understand where you are in relation to other locations on the map.

A concept map is similar to a road map. But, a concept map shows relationships among ideas (or concepts) rather than places. A concept map is a diagram that visually shows how concepts are related. Because the concept map shows relationships among ideas, it can make the meanings of ideas and terms clear, and help you understand better what you are studying.

There is usually not one correct way to create a concept map. As you construct one type of map, you may discover other

Figure 4

Network tree describing U.S. currency.

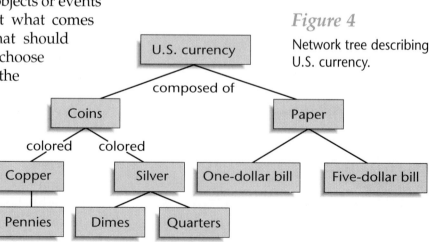

ways to construct the map that show the relationships between concepts in a better way. If you do discover what you think is a better way to create a concept map, go ahead and use the new one. Overall, concept maps are useful for breaking a big concept down into smaller parts, making learning easier.

Examples

Network Tree Look at the concept map about U.S. currency in **Figure 4.** This is called a network tree. Notice how some words are in rectangles while others are written across connecting lines. The words inside the rectangles are science concepts. The lines in the map show related concepts. The words written on the lines describe the relationships between concepts.

When you are asked to construct a network tree, write down the topic and list the major concepts related to that topic on a piece of paper. Then look at your list and begin to put them in order from general to specific. Branch the related concepts from the major concept and describe the relationships on the lines. Continue to write the more specific concepts. Write the relationships between the concepts on the lines until all concepts are mapped. Examine the concept map for relationships that cross branches, and add them to the concept map.

Events Chain An events chain is another type of concept map. An events chain map, such as the one describing a typical morning routine in **Figure 5,** is used to describe ideas in order. In science, an events chain can be used to describe a sequence of events, the steps in a procedure, or the stages of a process.

When making an events chain, first find the one event that starts the chain. This event is called the initiating event. Then,

Initiating event:

Alarm rings

Event 2:

Wake up

Event 3:

Take a shower

Event 4:

Get dressed

Event 5:

Eat breakfast

Event 6:

Leave for school

Figure 5

Events chain of a typical morning routine.

find the next event in the chain and continue until you reach an outcome. Suppose you are asked to describe what happens when your alarm rings. An events chain map describing the steps might look like **Figure 5.** Notice that connecting words are not necessary in an events chain.

Cycle Map A cycle concept map is a special type of events chain map. In a cycle concept map, the series of events does not produce a final outcome. Instead, the last event in the chain relates back to the initiating event.

As in the events chain map, you first decide on an initiating event and then list each event in order. Because there is no outcome and the last event relates back to the initiating event, the cycle repeats itself. Look at the cycle map describing the relationship between day and night in **Figure 6.**

Figure 6

Cycle map of day and night.

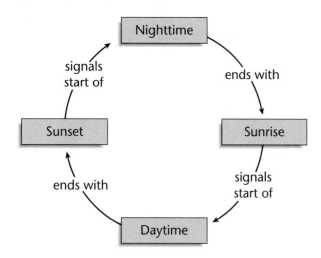

Spider Map A fourth type of concept map is the spider map. This is a map that you can use for brainstorming. Once you have a central idea, you may find you have a jumble of ideas that relate to it, but are not necessarily clearly related to each other. As illustrated by the homework spider map in **Figure 7,** by writing these ideas outside the main concept, you may begin to separate and group unrelated terms so that they become more useful.

Figure 7

Spider map about homework.

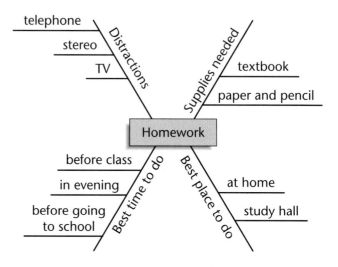

Making and Using Tables

Browse through your textbook and you will notice tables in the text and in the activities. In a table, data or information is arranged in a way that makes it easier for you to understand. Activity tables help organize the data you collect during an activity so that results can be interpreted more easily.

Examples Most tables have a title. At a glance, the title tells you what the table is about. A table is divided into columns and rows. The first column lists items to be compared. In **Figure 8,** the collection of recyclable materials is being compared in a table. The row across the top lists the specific characteristics being compared. Within the grid of the table, the collected data are recorded.

What is the title of the table in **Figure 8?** The title is "Recycled Materials." What is being compared? The different materials being recycled and on which days they are recycled.

Making Tables To make a table, list the items to be compared down in columns

Figure 8

Table of recycled materials.

Recycled Materials			
Day of Week	Paper (kg)	Aluminum (kg)	Plastic (kg)
Mon.	4.0	2.0	0.5
Wed.	3.5	1.5	0.5
Fri.	3.0	1.0	1.5

and the characteristics to be compared across in rows. The table in **Figure 8** compares the mass of recycled materials collected by a class. On Monday, students turned in 4.0 kg of paper, 2.0 kg of aluminum, and 0.5 kg of plastic. On Wednesday, they turned in 3.5 kg of paper, 1.5 kg of aluminum, and 0.5 kg of plastic. On Friday, the totals were 3.0 kg of paper, 1.0 kg of aluminum, and 1.5 kg of plastic.

Using Tables How much plastic, in kilograms, is being recycled on Wednesday? Locate the column labeled "Plastic (kg)" and the row "Wed." The data in the box where the column and row intersect are the answer. Did you answer "0.5"? How much aluminum, in kilograms, is being recycled on Friday? If you answered "1.0," you understand how to use the parts of the table.

Making and Using Graphs

After scientists organize data in tables, they may display the data in a graph. A graph is a diagram that shows the relationship of one variable to another. A graph makes interpretation and analysis of data easier. There are three basic types of graphs used in science—the line graph, the bar graph, and the circle graph.

Examples

Line Graphs A line graph is used to show the relationship between two variables. The variables being compared go on two axes of the graph. The independent variable always goes on the horizontal axis, called the x-axis. The dependent variable always goes on the vertical axis, called the y-axis.

Suppose your class started to record the amount of materials they collected in one week for their school to recycle. The collected information is shown in **Figure 9.**

You could make a graph of the materials collected over the three days of the school week. The three week days are the independent variables and are placed on the x-axis of your graph. The amount of materials collected is the dependent variable and would go on the y-axis.

After drawing your axes, label each with a scale. The x-axis lists the three weekdays. To make a scale of the amount of materials collected on the y-axis, look at the data values. Because the lowest amount collected was 1.0 and the highest

Figure 9

Amount of recyclable materials collected during one week.

Materials Collected During Week		
Day of Week	Paper (kg)	Aluminum (kg)
Mon.	5.0	4.0
Wed.	4.0	1.0
Fri.	2.5	2.0

Material Collected During Week

Figure 10

Graph outline for material collected during week.

Material Collected During Week

Figure 11

Line graph of materials collected during week.

was 5.0, you will have to start numbering at least at 1.0 and go through 5.0. You decide to start numbering at 0 and number by ones through 6.0, as shown in **Figure 10.**

Next, plot the data points for collected paper. The first pair of data you want to plot is Monday and 5.0 kg paper. Locate "Monday" on the *x*-axis and locate "5.0" on the *y*-axis. Where an imaginary vertical line from the *x*-axis and an imaginary horizontal line from the *y*-axis would meet, place the first data point. Place the other data points the same way. After all the points are plotted, connect them with the best smooth curve. Repeat this procedure for the data points for aluminum. Use continuous and dashed lines to distinguish the two line graphs. The resulting graph should look like **Figure 11.**

Bar Graphs Bar graphs are similar to line graphs. They compare data that do not continuously change. In a bar graph, vertical bars show the relationships among data.

To make a bar graph, set up the *x*-axis and *y*-axis as you did for the line graph.

The data are plotted by drawing vertical bars from the *x*-axis up to a point where the *y*-axis would meet the bar if it were extended.

Look at the bar graph in **Figure 12** comparing the mass of aluminum collected over three weekdays. The *x*-axis is the days on which the aluminum was collected. The *y*-axis is the mass of aluminum collected, in kilograms.

Circle Graphs A circle graph uses a circle divided into sections to display data. Each section represents part of the whole. All the sections together equal 100 percent.

Suppose you wanted to make a circle graph to show the number of seeds that germinated in a package. You would count the total number of seeds. You find that there are 143 seeds in the package. This represents 100 percent, the whole circle.

You plant the seeds, and 129 seeds germinate. The seeds that germinated will make up one section of the circle graph, and the seeds that did not germinate will make up the remaining section.

Aluminum Collected During Week

Mass (Kg)

4.0
3.0
2.0
1.0

Monday   Wednesday   Friday

Day of Collection

Figure 12

Bar graph of aluminum collected during week.

To find out how much of the circle each section should take, divide the number of seeds in each section by the total number of seeds. Then multiply your answer by 360, the number of degrees in a circle, and round to the nearest whole number. The section of the circle graph in degrees that represents the seeds germinated is figured below.

$$\frac{129}{143} \times 360 = 324.75 \text{ or } 325 \text{ degrees (or } 325°)$$

Plot this group on the circle graph using a compass and a protractor. Use the compass to draw a circle. It will be easier to measure the part of the circle representing the nongerminating seeds, so subtract 325° from 360° to get 35°. Draw a straight line from the center to the edge of the circle. Place your protractor on this line and use it to mark a point at 35°. Use this point to draw a straight line from the center of the circle to the edge. This is the section for the group of seeds that did not germinate. The other section represents the group of 129 seeds that did germinate. Label the sections of your graph and title the graph as shown in **Figure 13.**

Figure 13

Circle graph of germinated seeds.

Seeds Germinated

Not germinating (35°)

Germinating (325°)

*Thinking Critically*___

Observing and Inferring

Observing Scientists try to make careful and accurate observations. When possible, they use instruments such as microscopes, thermometers, and balances to make observations. Measurements with a balance or thermometer provide numerical data that can be checked and repeated.

When you make observations in science, you'll find it helpful to examine the entire object or situation first. Then, look carefully for details. Write down everything you observe.

Example Imagine that you have just finished a volleyball game. At home, you open the refrigerator and see a jug of orange juice on the back of the top shelf. The jug, shown in **Figure 14,** feels cold as you grasp it. Then you drink the juice, smell the oranges, and enjoy the tart taste in your mouth.

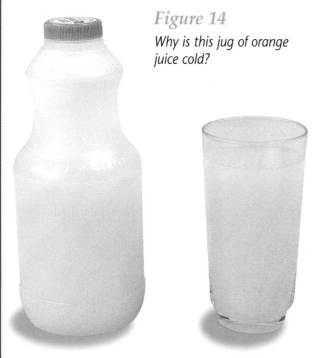

Figure 14

Why is this jug of orange juice cold?

As you imagined yourself in the story, you used your senses to make observations. You used your sense of sight to find the jug in the refrigerator, your sense of touch when you felt the coldness of the jug, your sense of hearing to listen as the liquid filled the glass, and your senses of smell and taste to enjoy the odor and tartness of the juice. The basis of all scientific investigation is observation.

Inferring Scientists often make inferences based on their observations. An inference is an attempt to explain or interpret observations or to say what caused what you observed.

When making an inference, be certain to use accurate data and observations. Analyze all of the data that you've collected. Then, based on everything you know, explain or interpret what you've observed.

Example When you drank a glass of orange juice after the volleyball game, you observed that the orange juice was cold as well as refreshing. You might infer that the juice was cold because it had been made much earlier in the day and had been kept in the refrigerator or you might infer that it had just been made, using both cold water and ice. The only way to be sure which inference is correct is to investigate further.

Comparing and Contrasting

Observations can be analyzed by noting the similarities and differences between two or more objects or events that you observe. When you look at objects or events to see how they are similar, you are comparing them. Contrasting is looking for differences in similar objects or events.

Figure 15

Table comparing the nutritional value of *Candy A* and *Candy B*.

Nutritional Value		
	Candy A	**Candy B**
Serving size	103 g	105 g
Calories	220	160
Total Fat	10 g	10 g
Protein	2.5 g	2.6 g
Total Carbohydrate	30 g	15 g

Example Suppose you were asked to compare and contrast the nutritional value of two candy bars, *Candy A* and *Candy B.* You would start by looking at what is known about these candy bars. Arrange this information in a table, like the one in **Figure 15.**

Similarities you might point out are that both candy bars have similar serving sizes, amounts of total fat, and protein. Differences include *Candy A* having a higher calorie value and containing more total carbohydrates than *Candy B.*

Recognizing Cause and Effect

Have you ever watched something happen and then made suggestions about why it happened? If so, you have observed an effect and inferred a cause. The event is an effect, and the reason for the event is the cause.

Example Suppose that every time your teacher fed the fish in a classroom aquarium, she or he tapped the food container on the edge of the aquarium. Then, one day your teacher just happened to tap the edge of the aquarium with a pencil while making a point. You observed the fish swim to the surface of the aquarium to feed, as shown in **Figure 16.** What is the effect, and what would you infer to be the cause? The effect is the fish swimming to the surface of the aquarium. You might infer the cause to be the teacher tapping on the edge of the aquarium. In determining cause and effect, you have made a logical inference based on your observations.

Perhaps the fish swam to the surface because they reacted to the teacher's waving hand or for some other reason. When scientists are unsure of the cause of a certain event, they design controlled experiments to determine what causes the event. Although you have made a logical conclusion about the behavior of the fish, you would have to perform an experiment to be certain that it was the tapping that caused the effect you observed.

Figure 16

What cause and effect situations are occurring in this aquarium?

Practicing Scientific Processes _____

You might say that the work of a scientist is to solve problems. But when you decide how to dress on a particular day, you are doing problem solving, too. You may observe what the weather looks like through a window. You may go outside and see whether what you are wearing is warm or cool enough.

Scientists use an orderly approach to learn new information and to solve problems. The methods scientists may use include observing to form a hypothesis, designing an experiment to test a hypothesis, separating and controlling variables, and interpreting data.

Forming Operational Definitions

Operational definitions define an object by showing how it functions, works, or behaves. Such definitions are written in terms of how an object works or how it can be used; that is, what is its job or purpose?

Figure 17

What observations can be made about this dog?

Example Some operational definitions explain how an object can be used.
- A ruler is a tool that measures the size of an object.
- An automobile can move things from one place to another.

Or such a definition may explain how an object works.
- A ruler contains a series of marks that can be used as a standard when measuring.
- An automobile is a vehicle that can move from place to place.

Forming a Hypothesis

Observations You observe all the time. Scientists try to observe as much as possible about the things and events they study so they know that what they say about their observations is reliable.

Some observations describe something using only words. These observations are called qualitative observations. Other observations describe how much of something there is. These are quantitative observations and use numbers, as well as words, in the description. Tools or equipment are used to measure the characteristic being described.

Example If you were making qualitative observations of the dog in **Figure 17,** you might use words such as *furry, yellow,* and *short-haired.* Quantitative observations of this dog might include a mass of 14 kg, a height of 46 cm, ear length of 10 cm, and an age of 150 days.

Hypotheses Hypotheses are tested to help explain observations that have been made. They are often stated as *if* and *then* statements.

Examples Suppose you want to make a perfect score on a spelling test. Begin by thinking of several ways to accomplish this. Base these possibilities on past observations. If you put each of these possibilities into sentence form, using the words *if* and *then,* you can form a hypothesis. All of the following are hypotheses you might consider to explain how you could score 100 percent on your test:

If the test is easy, then I will get a perfect score.

If I am intelligent, then I will get a perfect score.

If I study hard, then I will get a perfect score.

Perhaps a scientist has observed that plants that receive fertilizer grow taller than plants that do not. A scientist may form a hypothesis that says: If plants are fertilized, then their growth will increase.

Designing an Experiment to Test a Hypothesis

In order to test a hypothesis, it's best to write out a procedure. A procedure is the plan that you follow in your experiment. A procedure tells you what materials to use and how to use them. After following the procedure, data are generated. From this generated data, you can then draw a conclusion and make a statement about your results.

If the conclusion you draw from the data supports your hypothesis, then you can say that your hypothesis is reliable. *Reliable* means that you can trust your conclusion. If it did not support your hypothesis, then you would have to make new observations and state a new hypothesis—just make sure that it is one that you can test.

Example Super premium gasoline costs more than regular gasoline. Does super premium gasoline increase the efficiency or fuel mileage of your family car? Let's figure out how to conduct an experiment to test the hypothesis, "*if* premium gas is more efficient, *then* it should increase the fuel mileage of our family car." Then a procedure similar to **Figure 18** must be written to generate data presented in **Figure 19** on page 746.

These data show that premium gasoline is less efficient than regular gasoline. It took more gasoline to travel one mile (0.064) using premium gasoline than it does to travel one mile using regular gasoline (0.059). This conclusion does not support the original hypothesis made.

PROCEDURE

1. Use regular gasoline for two weeks.
2. Record the number of miles between fill-ups and the amount of gasoline used.
3. Switch to premium gasoline for two weeks.
4. Record the number of miles between fill-ups and the amount of gasoline used.

Figure 18
Possible procedural steps.

Figure 19

Data generated from procedure steps.

	Miles traveled	Gallons used	Gallons per mile
Regular gasoline	762	45.34	0.059
Premium gasoline	661	42.30	0.064

Separating and Controlling Variables

In any experiment, it is important to keep everything the same except for the item you are testing. The one factor that you change is called the *independent variable*. The factor that changes as a result of the independent variable is called the *dependent variable*. Always make sure that there is only one independent variable. If you allow more than one, you will not know what causes the changes you observe in the independent variable. Many experiments have *controls*—a treatment or an experiment that you can compare with the results of your test groups.

Example In the experiment with the gasoline, you made everything the same except the type of gasoline being used. The driver, the type of automobile, and the weather conditions should remain the same throughout. The gasoline should also be purchased from the same service station. By doing so, you made sure that at the end of the experiment, any differences were the result of the type of fuel being used—regular or premium. The type of gasoline was the *independent factor* and the gas mileage achieved was the *dependent factor*. The use of regular gasoline was the *control*.

Interpreting Data

The word *interpret* means "to explain the meaning of something." Look at the problem originally being explored in the gasoline experiment and find out what the data show. Identify the control group and the test group so you can see whether or not the variable has had an effect. Then you need to check differences between the control and test groups.

Figure 20

Which gasoline type is most efficient?

These differences may be qualitative or quantitative. A qualitative difference would be a difference that you could observe and describe, while a quantitative difference would be a difference you can measure using numbers. If there are differences, the variable being tested may have had an effect. If there is no difference between the control and the test groups, the variable being tested apparently has had no effect.

Example Perhaps you are looking at a table from an experiment designed to test the hypothesis: If premium gas is more efficient, then it should increase the fuel mileage of our family car. Look back at **Figure 19** showing the results of this experiment. In this example, the use of regular gasoline in the family car was the control, while the car being fueled by premium gasoline was the test group.

Data showed a quantitative difference in efficiency for gasoline consumption. It took 0.059 gallons of regular gasoline to travel one mile, while it took 0.064 gallons of the premium gasoline to travel the same distance. The regular gasoline was more efficient; it increased the fuel mileage of the family car.

What are data? In the experiment described on these pages, measurements were taken so that at the end of the experiment, you had something concrete to interpret. You had numbers to work with. Not every experiment that you do will give you data in the form of numbers. Sometimes, data will be in the form of a description. At the end of a chemistry experiment, you might have noted that one solution turned yellow when treated with a particular chemical, and another remained clear, like

Figure 21
Data.

water, when treated with the same chemical. Data, therefore, are stated in different forms for different types of scientific experiments.

Are all experiments alike? Keep in mind as you perform experiments in science that not every experiment makes use of all of the parts that have been described on these pages. For some, it may be difficult to design an experiment that will always have a control. Other experiments are complex enough that it may be hard to have only one dependent variable. Real scientists encounter many variations in the methods that they use when they perform experiments. The skills in this handbook are here for you to use and practice. In real situations, their uses will vary.

Representing and Applying Data

Interpreting Scientific Illustrations

As you read a science textbook, you will see many drawings, diagrams, and photographs. Illustrations help you to understand what you read. Some illustrations are included to help you understand an idea that you can't see easily by yourself. For instance, we can't see atoms, but we can look at a diagram of an atom and that helps us to understand some things about atoms. Seeing something often helps you remember more easily. Illustrations also provide examples that clarify difficult concepts or give additional information about the topic you are studying. Maps, for example, help you to locate places that may be described in the text.

Figure 23

If an inanimate object had dorsal and ventral surfaces, its various sides would be marked for orientation like the one in this drawing.

Examples

Captions and Labels Most illustrations have captions. A caption is a comment that identifies or explains the illustration. Diagrams, such as **Figure 22,** often have labels that identify parts of the organism or the order of steps in a process.

Learning with Illustrations An illustration of an organism shows that organism from a particular view or orientation. In order to understand the illustration, you may need to identify the front (anterior) end, tail (posterior) end, the underside (ventral), and the back (dorsal) side of the object shown in **Figure 23.**

You might also check for symmetry. A shark in **Figure 24** has bilateral symmetry. This means that drawing an imaginary line through the center of the animal from the anterior to posterior end forms two mirror images.

Radial symmetry is the arrangement of similar parts around a central point. An

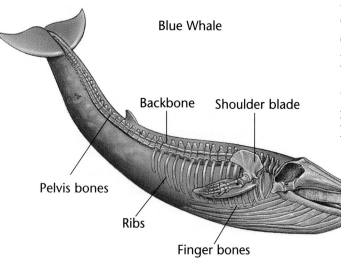

Figure 22

A labeled diagram of a blue whale.

Figure 24

A shark (A) illustrating bilateral symmetry and a pear (B) illustrating a longitudinal section and a cross section.

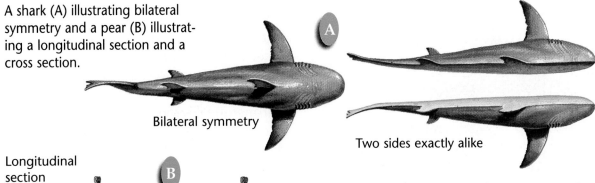

Bilateral symmetry

Two sides exactly alike

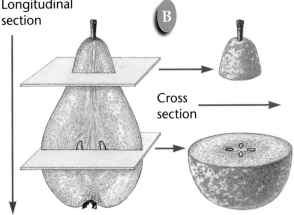

Longitudinal section

Cross section

object or organism such as a hydra can be divided anywhere through the center into similar parts.

Some organisms and objects cannot be divided into two similar parts. If an organism or object cannot be divided, it is asymmetrical. Regardless of how you try to divide a natural sponge, you cannot divide it into two parts that look alike.

Some illustrations enable you to see the inside of an organism or object. These illustrations are called sections. **Figure 24** also illustrates some common sections.

Look at all illustrations carefully. Read captions and labels so that you understand exactly what the illustration is showing you.

Making Models

Have you ever worked on a model car or plane or rocket? These models look, and sometimes work, much like the real thing, but they are often on a different scale than the real thing. In science, models are used to help simplify large or small processes or structures that otherwise would be difficult to see and understand. Your understanding of a structure or process is enhanced when you work with materials to make a model that shows the basic features of the structure or process.

Example In order to make a model, you first have to get a basic idea about the structure or process involved. You decide to make a model to show the differences in size of arteries, veins, and capillaries. First, read about these structures. All three are hollow tubes. Arteries are round and thick. Veins are flat and have thinner walls than arteries. Capillaries are small.

Now, decide what you can use for your model. Common materials are often best and cheapest to work with when making models. As illustrated in **Figure 25** on page 750, different kinds and sizes of pasta might work for these models. Different sizes of rubber tubing might do just as well. Cut and glue the different noodles or tubing onto thick paper so the openings can be seen. Then label each. Now you have a simple, easy-to-understand model showing the differences in size of arteries, veins, and capillaries.

What other scientific ideas might a model help you to understand? A model

Figure 25

Different types of pasta may be used to model blood vessels.

of a molecule can be made from gumdrops (using different colors for the different elements present) and toothpicks (to show different chemical bonds). A working model of a volcano can be made from clay, a small amount of baking soda, vinegar, and a bottle cap. Other models can be devised on a computer. Some models are mathematical and are represented by equations.

Measuring in SI

The metric system is a system of measurement developed by a group of scientists in 1795. It helps scientists avoid problems by providing standard measurements that all scientists around the world can understand. A modern form of the metric system, called the International System, or SI, was adopted for worldwide use in 1960.

The metric system is convenient because unit sizes vary by multiples of 10. When changing from smaller units to larger units, divide by 10. When changing from larger units to smaller, multiply by 10. For example, to convert millimeters to centimeters, divide the millimeters by 10. To convert 30 millimeters to centimeters, divide 30 by 10 (30 millimeters equal 3 centimeters).

Prefixes are used to name units. Look at **Figure 26** for some common metric prefixes and their meanings. Do you see how the prefix *kilo-* attached to the unit *gram* is *kilogram,* or 1000 grams? The prefix *deci-* attached to the unit *meter* is *decimeter,* or one-tenth (0.1) of a meter.

Examples

Length You have probably measured lengths or distances many times. The meter is the SI unit used to measure length. A baseball bat is about one meter long. When measuring smaller lengths, the meter is divided into smaller units called centimeters and millimeters. A centimeter is one-hundredth (0.01) of a meter, which is about the size of the width

Figure 26

Common metric prefixes.

Metric Prefixes			
Prefix	Symbol	Meaning	
kilo-	k	1000	thousand
hecto-	h	100	hundred
deka-	da	10	ten
deci-	d	0.1	tenth
centi-	c	0.01	hundredth
milli-	m	0.001	thousandth

Figure 27

Metric ruler showing centimeter and millimeter divisions.

of the fingernail on your ring finger. A millimeter is one-thousandth of a meter (0.001), about the thickness of a dime.

Most metric rulers have lines indicating centimeters and millimeters, as shown in **Figure 27.** The centimeter lines are the longer, numbered lines; the shorter lines are millimeter lines. When using a metric ruler, line up the 0-centimeter mark with the end of the object being measured, and read the number of the unit where the object ends, in this instance 4.5 cm.

Surface Area Units of length are also used to measure surface area. The standard unit of area is the square meter (m^2). A square that's one meter long on each side has a surface area of one square meter. Similarly, a square centimeter, (cm^2), shown in **Figure 28,** is one centimeter long on each side. The surface area of an object is determined by multiplying the length times the width.

Volume The volume of a rectangular solid is also calculated using units of length. The cubic meter (m^3) is the standard SI unit of volume. A cubic meter is a cube one meter on each side. You can determine the volume of rectangular solids by multiplying length times width times height.

Liquid Volume During science activities, you will measure liquids using beakers and graduated cylinders marked in milliliters, as illustrated in **Figure 29.** A graduated cylinder is a cylindrical container marked with lines from bottom to top.

Liquid volume is measured using a unit called a liter. A liter has the volume of 1000 cubic centimeters. Because the prefix *milli-* means thousandth (0.001), a milliliter equals one cubic centimeter. One

Figure 29

A volume of 79 mL is measured by reading at the lowest point of the curve.

Figure 28

A square centimeter.

milliliter of liquid would completely fill a cube measuring one centimeter on each side.

Mass Scientists use balances to find the mass of objects in grams. You will use a beam balance similar to **Figure 30.** Notice that on one side of the balance is a pan and on the other side is a set of beams. Each beam has an object of a known mass called a *rider* that slides on the beam.

Before you find the mass of an object, set the balance to zero by sliding all the riders back to the zero point. Check the pointer on the right to make sure it swings an equal distance above and below the zero point on the scale. If the swing is unequal, find and turn the adjusting screw until you have an equal swing.

Place an object on the pan. Slide the rider with the largest mass along its beam until the pointer drops below zero. Then move it back one notch. Repeat the process on each beam until the pointer swings an equal distance above and below the zero point. Add the masses on each beam to find the mass of the object.

You should never place a hot object or pour chemicals directly onto the pan. Instead, find the mass of a clean beaker or a glass jar. Place the dry or liquid chemicals in the container. Then find the combined mass of the container and the chemicals. Calculate the mass of the chemicals by subtracting the mass of the empty container from the combined mass.

Predicting

When you apply a hypothesis, or general explanation, to a specific situation, you predict something about that situation. First, you must identify which hypothesis fits the situation you are considering.

Examples People use prediction to make everyday decisions. Based on previous observations and experiences, you may form a hypothesis that if it is wintertime, then temperatures will be lower. From past experience in your area, temperatures are lowest in February. You may then use this hypothesis to predict specific temperatures and weather for the month of February in advance. Someone could use these predictions to plan to set aside more money for heating bills during that month.

Figure 30

A beam balance is used to measure mass.

Using Numbers

When working with large populations of organisms, scientists usually cannot observe or study every organism in the population. Instead, they use a sample or a portion of the population. To sample is to take a small representative portion of organisms of a population for research. By making careful observations or manipulating variables within a portion of a group, information is discovered and conclusions are drawn that might then be applied to the whole population.

Scientific work also involves estimating. To estimate is to make a judgment about the size of something or the number of something without actually measuring or counting every member of a population.

Examples Suppose you are trying to determine the effect of a specific nutrient on the growth of black-eyed Susans. It would be impossible to test the entire population of black-eyed Susans, so you would select part of the population for your experiment. Through careful experimentation and observation on a sample of the population, you could generalize the effect of the chemical on the entire population.

Here is a more familiar example. Have you ever tried to guess how many beans were in a sealed jar? If you did, you were estimating. What if you knew the jar of beans held one liter (1000 mL)? If you knew that 30 beans would fit in a 100-milliliter jar, how many beans would you estimate to be in the one-liter jar? If you said about 300 beans, your estimate would be close to the actual number of beans. Can you estimate how many jelly beans are on the cookie sheet in **Figure 31?**

Scientists use a similar process to estimate populations of organisms from bacteria to buffalo. Scientists count the actual number of organisms in a small sample and then estimate the number of organisms in a larger area. For example, if a scientist wanted to count the number of bacterial colonies in a petri dish, a microscope could be used to count the number of organisms in a one-square-centimeter sample. To determine the total population of the culture, the number of organisms in the square-centimeter sample is multiplied by the total number of square centimeters in the culture.

Figure 31

Sampling a group of jelly beans allows for an estimation of the total number of jelly beans in the group.

English Glossary

This glossary defines each key term that appears in **bold type** in the text. It also shows the page number where you can find the word used. Some additional helpful terms are also provided.

acceleration: The rate of change in velocity (a change in direction or a change in speed). The amount of acceleration depends on velocity change and time interval. (Chap. 3, p. 73)

acid: A substance that produces hydrogen ions (H^+) in solution; acid solutions have a pH less than 7. (Chap. 17, p. 466)

acid rain: Rain with a pH less than 5.6; produced by substances in the air reacting with rainwater to make it acidic. Acid rain is harmful to animals and plants and increases the rate of weathering. (Chap. 17, p. 478)

acoustics: The study of sound. (Chap. 18, p. 520)

actinide: Any of the 14 radioactive elements having atomic numbers 90-103; used in nuclear power generation and nuclear weapons.

active solar heating: Collecting the sun's energy with solar panels, heating water with that energy, and storing the heated water to use the energy later.

aerosol: A liquid sprayed from a pressurized container; for example, a can of insect spray.

air resistance: Frictional force air exerts on a moving object; acts opposite in direction to the object's motion. The amount of air resistance depends on an object's shape, density, speed, and size. (Chap. 4, p. 97)

alchemist: A medieval version of the modern chemist; a practitioner who blended primitive chemistry with magic, seeking to turn ordinary metals into gold.

alcohol: Type of compound formed when −OH groups replace one or more hydrogen atoms in a hydrocarbon. (Chap. 13, p. 368)

allotropes: Different structural forms of the same element; for example, some carbon molecules form soft graphite, whereas others form hard diamonds. (Chap. 12, p. 347)

alloy: A mixture consisting of a metal and one or more elements. (Chap. 14, p. 388)

alpha particle: A particle of nuclear radiation emitted from a decaying atomic nucleus; has a charge of 2+, an atomic mass of 4, and is the largest, slowest, and least penetrating form of radiation. (Chap. 24, p. 679)

alternating current (AC): Electric current that reverses its direction in a regular pattern; the 60-Hz AC in our homes changes direction 120 times each second. (Chap. 22, p. 635)

amalgam: An alloy containing the element mercury; for example, dental fillings are amalgams. (Chap. 14, p. 391)

ammeter: A galvanometer that measures electrical current passing through in amperes; connected in series with the circuit. (Chap. 22, p. 630)

amorphous: Something that has no specific shape; for example, a liquid or gas.

ampere: The unit for measuring current, the rate of flow of electrons in a circuit; abbreviated A; 1 ampere = 1 coulomb of charge flowing past a point in 1 second.

amplification: The process of increasing the strength of an electric signal. (Chap. 23, p. 651)

amplitude: In a wave, the distance from the rest position of the medium to either the crest or trough. (Chap. 18, p. 499)

amplitude-modulated (AM) waves: Radio waves whose amplitude is varied with voice, music, video, or data for transmission over long distances.

angle of incidence: In waves, the angle formed by the incident wave and the normal (perpendicular); labeled i.

angle of reflection: In waves, the angle formed by the reflected wave and the normal (perpendicular); labeled r.

anhydrous: A chemical compound that normally has water molecules attached to its ions but from which the water has been removed.

antacid: An "anti-acid," or a chemical that changes an acid substance to a neutral substance.

antifreeze: A solute added to a solvent to lower the temperature at which the solvent will freeze; for example, the antifreeze added to water in a car's cooling system.

aqueous: Describes a solution made with water; for example, ammonia water is an aqueous solution of ammonia gas.

Archimedes' principle: The Greek mathematician Archimedes stated that the buoyant force on an object in a fluid is equal to the weight of the fluid displaced by the object. (Chap. 8, p. 235)

aromatic compounds: Chemical compounds that contain the benzene ring structure; most have distinctive odors. (Chap. 13, p. 366)

artificial satellite: Human-made device that orbits Earth; used for communication, weather-monitoring, military, and scientific purposes. (Chap. 4, p. 108)

atomic number: The number of protons in an atom's nucleus. (Chap. 10, p. 271)

average atomic mass: The average mass of an element is the average mass of the mixture of its isotopes. (Chap. 10, p. 280)

average speed: A rate of motion determined by dividing the total distance traveled by the total travel time. (Chap. 3, p. 65)

balance: A device used in laboratories to measure mass; it works by balancing a mass to be determined with a standard mass that is known.

balanced chemical equation: A chemical equation that has the same number of atoms of each element on both sides of the equation. (Chap. 16, p. 448)

balanced forces: Forces that are equal in size and opposite in direction; balanced forces acting on a body do not change the motion of the body. (Chap. 3, p. 78)

bar graph: A type of graph used to show information collected by counting; uses vertical or horizontal bars of different lengths to help people compare quantities.

base: A substance that produces hydroxide ions (OH^-) in solution; basic solutions have a pH over 7. (Chap. 17, p. 470)

Bernoulli's principle: The Swiss scientist Daniel Bernoulli stated that as the velocity of a fluid increases, the pressure exerted by the fluid decreases. (Chap. 8, p. 237)

beta particle: A negatively charged electron or positively charged positron emitted from a decaying atomic nucleus; beta particles are faster moving and more penetrating than alpha particles. (Chap. 24, p. 680)

BHA: A food preservative; it is a chemical inhibitor that slows the chemical reactions that spoil food (*Butylated Hydroxy Anisole*).

BHT: A food preservative; it is a chemical inhibitor that slows the chemical reactions that spoil food (*Butylated Hydroxy Toluene*).

binary compound: A chemical compound composed of two elements; for example, sodium chloride. (Chap. 11, p. 315)

biodegradable: Describes a material that can be decomposed into a harmless form by the biological action of organisms such as bacteria.

biogas: Mixture of gases, mostly methane, produced when biomass is allowed to rot in the absence of air. (Chap. 13, p. 370)

biomass: Organic material from such sources as wood, corn, and wastes from animals and crops; biomass is the source of biogas and the ethanol used in gasohol. (Chap. 13, p. 370)

bionics: The science of designing artificial replacements (prostheses) for parts of the human body that are not working properly. (Chap. 7, p. 196)

boiling point: The temperature at which vapor bubbles form in a liquid and rise to the surface, increasing evaporation.

Boyle's law: British scientist Robert Boyle stated that the volume of a gas decreases when the pressure increases, provided the temperature stays the same. (Chap. 8, p. 229)

brittleness: A characteristic of certain materials that makes them break easily when stressed.

bubble chamber: Device filled with superheated liquid; used to detect and monitor the path of charged nuclear particles, which leave a trail of bubbles as they pass through the chamber. (Chap. 24, p. 686)

buoyant force: Ability of a fluid to exert an upward force on an object immersed in the fluid. (Chap. 8, p. 234)

butane: A flammable gas (C_4H_{10}); a part of natural gas.

byte: A basic unit of computer memory that represents a character (number, symbol, or alphabet letter); consists of 8 bits.

calorimeter: An instrument used to measure changes in thermal energy.

carbohydrate: An organic compound having twice as many hydrogen atoms as oxygen atoms. (Chap. 13, p. 376)

carbon-14 dating: Age-determining method for carbon-containing objects up to 50 000 years old; works by calculating the amount of carbon-14 remaining in the object.

catalyst: A substance that speeds a chemical reaction without itself being permanently changed. (Chap. 16, p. 456)

cathode-ray tube (CRT): Sealed glass vacuum tube that uses electrons and fluorescent material to produce images on a screen. (Chap. 23, p. 656)

central processing unit (CPU): The main circuit board inside a computer that performs the calculating and holds the main memory.

centripetal acceleration: Acceleration toward the center of a circle by an object moving along a circular path. (Chap. 4, p. 102)

centripetal force: The force that causes an object moving along a circular path to move toward the center of the path.(Chap. 4, p. 102)

ceramic: A material made from dried clay or claylike mixtures. (Chap. 14, p. 392)

cermet: A tough, heat-resistant material that has the properties of both a ceramic and an alloy; ceramic-metal (*ceramic* + *met*al). (Chap. 14, p. 394)

chain reaction: A continuing series of fission reactions in which neutrons from fissioning nuclei cause other nuclei to split, releasing more neutrons, which split more nuclei, and so on. (Chap. 24, p. 690)

Charles's law: French scientist Jacques Charles stated that the volume of a gas increases when temperature increases, provided the pressure stays the same. (Chap. 8, p. 230)

chemical bond: The force that holds together the atoms in a compound; chemical bonding occurs because atoms of most elements become more stable by losing, gaining, and sharing electrons. (Chap. 11, p. 301)

chemical change: The change of substances to different substances. (Chap. 9, p. 257)

chemical formula: A precise statement that tells which elements are in a compound and their ratios. (Chap. 11, p. 300)

chemical property: A characteristic of a substance that indicates whether it can undergo a specific chemical change. (Chap. 9, p. 259)

chemical reaction: A change in which one or more substances are converted to different substances (the reactants are changed into the products). (Chap. 16, p. 442)

chemical symbol: A shorthand way to write the name of an element; for example: C for carbon, Ag for silver. (Chap. 10, p. 270)

chemically stable: Describes an atom whose outer energy level is completely filled with electrons. (Chap. 11, p. 300)

chemically unstable: Describes an atom whose outermost energy level is not filled with electrons so it seeks electrons from other atoms and thus forms compounds; for example: sodium, chlorine.

chloro-: Prefix that indicates presence of chlorine, as in tetrachloroethylene or chlorofluorocarbon.

chlorofluorocarbon (CFC): A group of compounds whose decomposition releases chlorine atoms that destroy ozone molecules in the upper atmosphere; used, for example, in air-conditioning systems. (Chap. 16, p. 447)

circuit: A closed path through which electrons (electricity) flow. (Chap. 21, p. 601)

circuit breaker: A device that protects an electrical circuit; if too much current flows, the circuit breaker opens the circuit, stopping the current.

cloud chamber: Device filled with water- or ethanol-saturated air; used to detect charged nuclear particles, which leave a trail as they pass through. (Chap. 24, p. 686)

coagulation: Process that destroys colloid structure; can be used to reduce a colloidal form of air pollution. (Chap. 9, p. 253)

coal: A rock formed of ancient decayed plants; burned as a fossil fuel.

coefficient: In a chemical equation, the number that represents the number of units of each substance taking part in a chemical reaction. (Chap. 16, p. 445)

coherent light: A beam of light in which all the electromagnetic waves travel with the crests and troughs aligned; thus, the beam does not spread out. (Chap. 20, p. 575)

colloid: A heterogeneous mixture containing tiny particles that never settle out; for example, milk and gelatin. (Chap. 9, p. 249)

combustion: Rapid burning. (Chap. 6, p. 166)

composite: A mixture of two materials, one of which is embedded in the other. (Chap. 14, p. 401)

compound: Substance made of the combined atoms of two or more elements. (Chap. 9, p. 246)

compound machine: A combination of two or more simple machines. (Chap. 7, p. 198)

compression: In compressional waves, the dense area of the wave.

compressional wave: A type of wave where matter vibrates in the same direction as the wave travels. (Chap. 18, p. 505)

computer: A device you can program to do calculations, make logical decisions, and manipulate data.

computer virus: Type of program designed to infect a computer, erase data, scramble other programs, or fill up so much memory that the system is harmed. (Chap. 23, p. 666)

concave lenses: Lenses that are thinner in the middle and thicker at the edges and thus curve inward; form virtual, upright, smaller images of an object. (Chap. 20, p. 565)

concave mirror: A mirror whose surface curves inward; produces real images. (Chap. 20, p. 558)

concentrated solution: A solution in which the amount of solute is near the maximum the solvent can hold at that temperature.

concentration: Generally, the proportion of a solute dissolved in a solvent.

condensation: The change of a substance from a gas to a liquid, which usually takes place when a gas is cooled to or below its boiling point. (Chap. 8, p. 225)

condense: To go from the gas state to the liquid state, due to a loss of heat.

conduction: The transfer of energy through matter in which energy moves from particle to particle; conduction takes place more easily in solids than in liquids and gases. (Chap. 6, p. 152)

conductor: (electrical) A material that allows electrons to move easily through it. (Chap. 21, p. 594)

constant: In an experiment, a factor that doesn't change. (Chap. 1, p. 21)

constant speed: Speed that does not change. (Chap. 3, p. 65)

contraction: Movement of molecules toward one another, so that they occupy a smaller space.

control: In an experiment, a standard for comparison that is often needed to draw a meaningful conclusion. (Chap. 1, p. 21)

convection: The transfer of energy by the bulk movement of matter in which particles move from place to place in a fluid, carrying the energy with them. (Chap. 6, p. 153)

convex lenses: Lenses that are thicker in the middle than at the edges; can produce both real and virtual images. (Chap. 20, p. 564)

convex mirror: A mirror with a surface that curves outward; produces upright, smaller, virtual images of an object. (Chap. 20, p. 561)

corrosive: Hazardous compound that attacks and alters metals, human tissue, or other materials; for example, oven cleaners and battery acid. (Chap. 11, p. 312)

covalent bond: A type of chemical bond formed by atoms when they share electrons; covalent bonding produces molecules. (Chap. 11, p. 306)

coulomb: The charge carried by 6.24 billion billion electrons.

crest: The highest point of a wave. (Chap. 18, p. 499)

critical temperature: In superconductors, the very low temperature at which a material ceases to have any electrical resistance.

crystals: In most solids, the arrangements of particles in repeating geometric patterns. (Chap. 8, p. 215)

current: The flow of electrons through a wire or any conductor; measured in amperes (A) with an ammeter. (Chap. 21, p. 601)

deceleration: The rate of change in velocity (speed and/or direction) when velocity is decreasing; also called negative acceleration.

decibel: The unit of measure for sound intensity, abbreviated dB. The faintest sound most people can hear = 0 dB.

decomposition reaction: A chemical reaction in which a substance breaks down (decomposes) into two or more simpler substances. (Chap. 16, p. 452)

dehydrating agent: A substance that can remove water from materials. (Chap. 17, p. 468)

density: The mass per unit volume of a material (g/cm^3); describes how tightly packed a substance's molecules are. (Chap. 2, p. 43)

dependent variable: In an experiment, the factor whose value changes because of a change in the independent variable. (Chap. 1, p. 22)

derived unit: Unit of measurement obtained by combining SI units; for example, density is a derived unit formed by dividing an object's mass by its volume. (Chap. 2, p. 42).

detergent: An organic salt similar to soap, except that detergents do not form soap scum in hard water. (Chap. 17, p. 483)

diatomic molecule: A molecule composed of two atoms of the same element; for example, hydrogen (H_2) or oxygen (O_2). (Chap. 12, p. 341)

diesel engine: An internal combustion engine that compresses a fuel-air mixture so much that it ignites from the heat of compression without a spark.

diffraction: The bending of waves around a barrier. (Chap. 19, p. 548)

diffraction grating: A piece of glass or plastic with many parallel slits that acts like a prism, causing white light that passes through it to separate into its component colors (the visible spectrum). (Chap. 19, p. 550)

dilute solution: A solution in which the amount of solute is much less than the maximum the solvent can hold at that temperature.

diode: A type of rectifier that allows electric current to flow in only one direction. (Chap. 23, p. 651)

direct current (DC): Electrical current that flows in only one direction through a wire. (Chap. 22, p. 635)

disinfectant: A chemical that kills bacteria, such as alcohol.

dissociation: The breaking apart of an ionic compound (such as salt) into positive and negative ions when dissolved in water. (Chap. 15, p. 433)

DNA: *DeoxyriboNucleic Acid*; an acid in the nuclei of cells that codes and stores genetic information.

doping: Adding an impurity to a semiconductor to increase its electrical conductivity.

Doppler effect: An increase or decrease in wave frequency, caused by motion of the source and/or motion of the observer; applies to all waves (including light, heat, sound, and so on).

dot diagram: A diagram to represent electrons in the outer energy level of an atom; uses the element symbol and dots. (Chap. 10, p. 288)

double-displacement reaction: A chemical reaction in which two ionic compounds in solution react, forming a precipitate, gas, or water. (Chap. 16, p. 453)

dry cell: A power source that acts as an electron pump and generates electric current by a chemical reaction; "dry" because it uses a thick, pasty electrolyte. (Chap. 21, p. 602)

ductile: Ability of metals to be pulled into wires. (Chap. 12, p. 330)

E

efficiency: The ratio of the useful work put out by a machine to the work put into that machine; efficiency is always less than 100 percent. (Chap. 7, p. 200)

effort arm: The part of a lever on which an effort force (F_e) is applied. (Chap. 7, p. 186)

effort force: The force applied to a machine when a machine is used to do work. (Chap. 7, p. 181)

electric field: An area surrounding an electron that exerts a force on anything nearby with an electric charge; is strongest nearest the electron and weakens with distance. (Chap. 21, p. 594)

electric motor: A device that contains a rotating electromagnet that changes electrical energy to mechanical energy. (Chap. 22, p. 630)

electrical power: The rate at which electrical energy is converted to another form of energy; electrical power is expressed in watts (W) or kilowatts (kW). (Chap. 21, p. 614)

electrolyte: A substance that separates or forms ions in a water solution, making the solution an electrical conductor. (Chap. 15, p. 433)

electromagnet: Strong temporary magnet made by inserting an iron core into a wire coil and passing an electric current through the coil. (Chap. 22, p. 628)

electromagnetic induction: Process by which electrical current is induced in a wire when it is moved through a magnetic field. (Chap. 22, p. 633)

electromagnetic radiation: Transverse waves that transfer energy by radiation; vary in length from very long radio waves to extremely short gamma waves. (Chap. 19, p. 528)

electron arrangement: In an atom, how the electrons are distributed in the atom's various energy levels.

electron cloud: Region where electrons most probably are found surrounding the nucleus of an atom. (Chap. 10, p. 272)

electrons: Negatively charged particles that move around the nucleus of an atom. (Chap. 10, p. 270)

electroscope: A device containing two suspended metal leaves in a jar that move apart when charged; used to detect the presence of electric charges. (Chap. 21, p. 596)

element: Substance in which all the atoms in a sample are alike. (Chap. 9, p. 246)

endothermic reaction: A chemical reaction in which energy is absorbed. (Chap. 16, p. 458)

energy: The ability to cause change. (Chap. 5, p. 124)

energy farming: The growing of plants for use as fuel. (Chap. 13, p. 370)

energy transfer: The movement of energy from one object to another; for example, thermal energy flowing as heat from a heated stove to a skillet.

ester: An organic compound formed by reacting an organic acid with an alcohol; some esters provide scents to flowers and fruits and flavors to gelatin and candy. (Chap. 17, p. 484)

evaporation: The gradual change of a substance from a liquid to a gas at temperatures below the boiling point. (Chap. 8, p. 224)

exothermic reaction: A chemical reaction in which energy is released. (Chap. 16, p. 456)

expansion: Outward movement of molecules away from one another so that they occupy a larger space.

experiment: An organized procedure for testing a hypothesis. An experiment typically has a control and dependent and independent variables. (Chap. 1, p. 20)

external combustion engine: An engine in which the fuel is burned outside the engine; for example, an old-fashioned locomotive steam engine. (Chap. 6, p. 167)

F

factor: A condition that affects the outcome of an event.

farsighted: Describes a person who sees faraway things clearly, but has trouble focusing on nearby objects.

fiberglass: Hairlike strands of glass that make a good insulator when arranged in puffy layers.

filter: In working with light, a device that allows one or more colors to be transmitted while others are absorbed or blocked.

flame test: A laboratory test to identify elements by heating a substance in a flame and observing the flame color.

flammable: A chemical characteristic of a substance that allows it to oxidize rapidly; also called burnable.

flash distillation: A desalination process where seawater is pumped into a vacuum chamber so it boils quickly and at a lower temperature (because the normal air pressure is absent).

fluid: Any material that flows; liquids and gases are fluids. (Chap. 6, p. 153)

fluorescence: Occurs when a material absorbs ultraviolet radiation that stimulates it to radiate visible light.

fluorescent light: Light produced when ultraviolet radiation inside a fluorescent light bulb causes its fluorescent coating to glow; uses less energy than incandescent lights. (Chap. 19, p. 544)

focal length: The distance from the center of a lens or mirror to its focal point. (Chap. 20, p. 559)

focal point: A point on the optical axis of a concave mirror or convex lens where the light rays come together. (Chap. 20, p. 559)

force: A push or a pull one body exerts on another. Unbalanced forces always change the motion of the body. (Chap. 3, p. 78)

fractional distillation: A process based on boiling points used in oil refineries to separate the chemical compounds in crude oil into gasoline, kerosene, and other products. (Chap. 25, p. 700)

fractionating towers: Towers at oil refineries used for fractional distillation of petroleum.

free-fall: How an object moves in space when it is influenced only by gravity.

Freon: A refrigerant gas used in refrigerators and air conditioners.

frequency: The number of wave crests that pass a point during one second; expressed in hertz (Hz). (Chap. 18, p. 499)

frequency-modulated (FM) waves: Radio waves whose frequency is varied with voice, music, video, or data for transmission over long distances.

friction: The force that opposes motion between two surfaces that are touching each other. The amount of friction depends on the types of surfaces and the kinds of force pressing the surfaces together. (Chap. 3, p. 82)

fuel rod: A metal rod filled with uranium pellets, used as the fuel in a nuclear reactor.

fulcrum: The fixed point around which a lever pivots. (Chap. 7, p. 186)

fuse: A device that protects an electrical circuit. If too much current flows, the fuse melts, breaking the circuit to stop current flow.

G

galvanometer: An instrument (meter) used to detect electric currents; most electrical meters are galvanometers.

gamma rays: High-frequency electromagnetic waves that travel at the speed of light, have no mass or charge, and are the most penetrating form of radiation. (Chap. 19, p. 534; Chap. 24, p. 681)

gaseous solution: A homogeneous gas that is composed of two or more gases.

gasohol: A mixture of ethanol and gasoline that is a useful substitute for gasoline, but whose production may be damaging to the environment; a biomass fuel. (Chap. 13, p. 371)

gear: A wheel with teeth around its edge designed to mesh with teeth on another gear so as to transfer force and motion.

gelatin: A substance obtained by boiling animal bones; used in glues and goods.

generator: A device that uses electromagnetic induction to induce electrical current by rotating loops of wire through a magnetic field. (Chap. 22, p. 633)

geothermal energy: Thermal energy source located far below Earth's crust. (Chap. 25, p. 716)

glass: A ceramic mixture with no regular crystal structure. (Chap. 14, p. 394)

graduated cylinder: A cylinder marked with a volume scale, used in laboratories for measuring liquid volumes.

granite: An igneous rock that is a mixture of crystals of several different compounds.

graph: A visual display of information or data—such as line graphs, bar graphs, and circle graphs—organized to help people interpret, understand, or quickly find information. (Chap. 2, p. 48)

graphite: A mineral made of carbon atoms arranged in layers that easily slide past one another, forming a dry lubricant.

gravity: Force exerted by every object in the universe on every other object. The amount of gravitational force depends on the masses of the objects and the distance between them. (Chap. 3, p. 83)

grounded: Electrically connected to Earth (the ground), either directly or through a wire or other metal object.

groundwater: Water in the ground that comes from rain and melting snow. Although often pure enough to drink, it is easily polluted by dumps, sewers, and chemical spills.

group: In the periodic table, each of the 18 vertical columns of elements; each group (family) is made up of elements with similar properties. (Chap. 10, p. 288)

H

hacker: A person who uses a computer to break into other computer systems without permission.

half-life: The amount of time required for one-half of the nuclides in a sample of radioactive isotope to decay. (Chap. 24, p. 681)

halogens: Highly active elements in periodic table Group 17 (fluorine, chlorine, bromine, iodine, astatine); halogens have seven electrons in their outer shells and readily combine with Group 1 elements such as sodium.

heat: Thermal energy that flows from a warmer material to a cooler material. (Chap. 5, p. 136)

heat engine: A device that converts thermal energy that is produced by burning fuel into mechanical energy; for example, an automobile engine. (Chap. 6, p. 166)

heat mover: A device that moves thermal energy from one location and releases it in another location having a different temperature; for example, a refrigerator, air conditioner, or heat pump. (Chap. 6, p. 168)

heat of fusion: The amount of energy needed to change a material from the solid state to the liquid state. (Chap. 8, p. 226)

heat of vaporization: The amount of energy needed to change a material from a liquid to a gas. (Chap. 8, p. 226)

herbicide: A chemical poison that kills undesirable plants.

hertz: The unit of measure for frequency, abbreviated Hz; for example, 440 waves per second = 440 Hz.

heterogeneous mixture: A mixture in which different parts can be easily distinguished. (Chap. 9, p. 248)

high-speed photography: A photographic method that takes clear (not blurred) pictures of fast-moving objects.

homogeneous mixture: A mixture in which different materials are blended evenly so that the mixture is the same throughout; also called a solution. (Chap. 9, p. 248)

horizontal: A direction parallel to Earth's surface.

hydrate: A compound that has water molecules chemically attached to its ions and written into its formula. (Chap. 11, p. 319)

hydraulic: Describes a system operated by applying pressure to a liquid.

hydrocarbon: A compound containing only carbon and hydrogen atoms. (Chap. 13, p. 361)

hydroelectricity: Electricity produced by the energy of moving water. (Chap. 25, p. 714)

hydronium ion: The ion (H_3O^+) that makes a solution acidic; formed when a polar molecule such as HCl is dissolved in water and the H^+ is removed from the polar molecule. (Chap. 17, p. 472)

hypothesis: A testable prediction used to see how something works or to solve a problem. (Chap. 1, p. 16)

ideal machine: A machine in which work input equals work output; such a "perfect" machine would be frictionless and 100 percent efficient. (Chap. 7, p. 181)

incandescent light: Light produced by a thin tungsten wire, or filament, that is heated in an incandescent bulb until it glows. (Chap. 19, p. 544)

inclined plane: A simple machine consisting of a sloping surface (ramp) used to raise objects. (Chap. 7, p. 193)

incoherent light: Light rays that are nearly parallel, but spread out because their electromagnetic waves do not travel in the same direction; crests and troughs do not coincide. (Chap. 20, p. 576)

independent variable: In an experiment, the factor adjusted to a different value by the experimenter to see what effect it will have on the dependent variable. (Chap. 1, p. 22)

indicator: An organic compound that changes color in an acidic solution or a basic solution. (Chap. 17, p. 466)

induction: Electrically charging an object or creating an electrical current in it, without physically touching it.

inertia: The tendency of an object to resist any change in its motion. If motionless, it tends to remain at rest; if moving, it tends to keep moving at the same speed and in the same direction. (Chap. 3, p. 79)

infrared radiation: Electromagnetic waves that have a wavelength slightly longer than visible light; indicates the presence of heat. (Chap. 19, p. 531)

infrasonic waves: Waves at frequencies below the limit of human hearing (below 20 Hz).

inhibitor: A substance that slows or prohibits a chemical reaction. (Chap. 16, p. 457)

instantaneous speed: The rate of motion at a given instant in time, such as that given on a car's speedometer. (Chap. 3, p. 64)

insulator: A material that does not allow heat or electrons to move through it easily. (Chap. 6, p. 155; Chap. 21, p. 595)

integrated circuit: A thin slice of silicon, often less than 1 cm on a side, which can contain thousands of resistors, diodes, and transistors; used in computers and electronic equipment. (Chap. 23, p. 653)

intensity: In sound waves, the amount of energy in each wave; the intensity level of a sound is measured in decibels (dB). (Chap. 18, p. 510)

interference: The ability of two or more waves to combine and form a new wave. (Chap. 18, p. 519)

internal combustion engine: An engine in which fuel is burned inside the engine in chambers (cylinders); for example, an automobile engine. (Chap. 6, p. 166)

ion: A positively or negatively charged atom. (Chap. 11, p. 304)

ionic bond: A type of chemical bond formed by the attraction between opposite charges of the ions in an ionic compound. (Chap. 11, p. 305)

ionization: The breaking apart of certain polar substances to form ions when dissolved in water. (Chap. 15, p. 433)

isomers: Compounds that have identical chemical formulas but different molecular structures and shapes. (Chap. 13, p. 364)

isotopes: Atoms of the same element that have different numbers of neutrons; for example, boron-10 and boron-11. (Chap. 10, p. 279)

joule (JEWL): The basic unit of energy and work, named for English scientist James Prescott Joule; 1 joule (J) = a force of 1 newton moving through 1 meter.

kelvin: The SI unit of temperature; zero K = absolute zero (the coldest possible temperature, −273°C). (Chap. 2, p. 45)

kilogram: The SI unit of mass; 1 kilogram (kg) = 1000 grams (g). (Chap 2, p. 43)

kilowatt-hour: The unit of electrical energy; 1 kilo-watt-hour (kWh) = 1000 watts (W) of power used for 1 hour. (Chap. 21, p. 616)

kinetic energy: Energy in the form of motion, as in a moving car or truck; the greater the mass and velocity of a moving object, the more kinetic energy it has. (Chap. 5, p. 125)

kinetic theory of matter: The idea that all matter is made up of constantly moving, tiny particles. (Chap. 8, p. 215)

lanthanide: Any of the 14 metallic elements having atomic numbers 58-71; used in magnets, ceramics, and television picture tubes.

laser: A device that emits a beam of photons that travel in the same direction and phase, producing a beam of coherent light. (Chap. 20, p. 575)

law of conservation of energy: A law stating that energy can change form but cannot be created or destroyed under ordinary conditions. This law applies to systems in which energy cannot enter or exit the system. (Chap. 5, p. 129)

law of conservation of mass: A law stating that matter is neither created nor destroyed during a chemical change. (Chap. 9, p. 260)

law of conservation of momentum: A law stating that the total momentum of a group of objects is conserved unless a net force acts on the objects. (Chap. 4, p. 115)

lever: A simple machine consisting of a bar that is free to pivot (rotate) around a fixed point (fulcrum). (Chap. 7, p. 186)

line graph: A type of graph used to show trends or continuous change by drawing a line that connects data points.

lipids: Fats, oils, and related organic compounds. (Chap. 13, p. 377)

liquid solution: A liquid solvent that has dissolved in it a gas, liquid, or solid.

liter: The unit of liquid volume (L) that occupies the same volume as a cubic decimeter (dm³) and is slightly larger than a quart. (Chap. 2, p. 42)

loudness: The human perception of sound intensity. (Chap. 18, p. 510)

lubricant: A substance used to reduce the friction between two surfaces that move together; for example, oil, grease, or graphite.

machine: A device that makes work easier by changing the size of the force applied to it and/or the direction of that force. (Chap. 7, p. 180)

magnetic bottle: A powerful magnetic field that creates a container ("bottle") to hold the hydrogen plasma needed for a nuclear fusion reaction.

magnetic domains: Groups of atoms with aligned magnetic poles. (Chap. 22, p. 626)

magnetic field: The region around a magnet where magnetic forces act. (Chap. 22, p. 624)

magnetic poles: The two ends of a piece of magnetic material where the magnetic forces are strongest, labeled north pole (N) and south pole (S). (Chap. 22, p. 624)

magnetism: A property of some materials in which there is a force of repulsion or attraction between certain like and unlike poles. (Chap. 22, p. 624)

magnifier: A device that makes things appear larger so that more detail can be seen; for example, a magnifying glass or microscope.

malleable: Ability of metals to be hammered or rolled into thin sheets. (Chap. 12, p. 330)

mass: A measurement of the amount of matter in a object; its SI unit is the kilogram (kg). (Chap. 2, p. 43)

mass number: Sum of the number of protons and neutrons in an atom's nucleus. (Chap. 10, p. 279)

mechanical advantage: The number of times a machine multiplies the effort force applied to it. (Chap. 7, p. 182)

mechanical energy: The total amount of kinetic energy and potential energy in a system. (Chap. 5, p. 129)

medium: A material (solid, liquid, or gas, or a combination of these) through which a wave travels. (Chap. 18, p. 498)

melt: The changing of a substance from a solid state to a liquid state when heated above the substance's freezing/melting point.

melting point: The temperature at which a solid changes to a liquid.

metallic bonding: The type of chemical bond in which positively charged ions are surrounded by freely moving electrons; metallic bonding holds metals together. (Chap. 12, p. 331)

metalloids: Elements having properties of both metals and nonmetals. In the periodic table, metalloids are found along the stair-step line that separates metals from nonmetals. (Chap. 10, p. 291)

metals: Elements usually having these common properties: shiny, good conductors of heat and electricity, are solids at room temperature. In the periodic table, metals are found at the left of the stair-step line. (Chap. 10, p. 290)

meter: The SI base unit of length (m); 100 cm = 1 m. (Chap. 2, p. 38)

microprocessor: The computer's "brain." It receives input and tells the computer how to respond. (Chap. 23, p. 659)

microscope: An optical instrument that uses two convex lenses with relatively short focal lengths to magnify small, close-up objects. (Chap. 20, p. 570)

microwaves: Radio waves with the highest frequency and energy; used in communications and microwave ovens. (Chap. 19, p. 530)

mixture: A material made of elements or compounds stirred together but not combined chemically.

model: A symbolic representation of an idea, system, or structure to make something understandable. Models help us solve problems and deal with things difficult to see because they are too large or too small. (Chap. 1, p. 12)

modulation: Process of adding voice, music, video, computer information, or other data to radio waves by using electrical currents to vary either amplitude or frequency. (Chap. 19, p. 530)

momentum: A property of any moving object; the momentum *(p)* of an object is the product of its mass and velocity *(p = mv)*. (Chap. 4, p. 112)

monomers: Organic molecules that are strung together to form polymers.

music: Sound created using specific pitches, sound quality, and regular patterns. (Chap. 18, p. 516)

nearsighted: Describes a person who sees nearby things clearly, but has trouble focusing on distant objects.

net force: The sum of the forces on an object when unbalanced forces are applied to it. A net force changes the object's speed or direction or both. (Chap. 3, p. 78)

neutralization: A chemical reaction between an acid and a base; the acid's hydronium ions (H_3O^+) combine with the base's hydroxide ions (OH^-) to produce water (H_2O), and the acid's negative ions combine with the base's positive ions to produce a salt. (Chap. 17, p. 480)

neutralize: To change an acidic solution or a basic solution so that it is neutral.

neutron: Atomic particle with no charge (neutral) that is part of an atom's nucleus. (Chap. 10, p. 271)

Newton's first law of motion: Describes the relationship between velocity and forces. An object moving at a constant velocity keeps moving at that velocity unless a net force acts on it. An object at rest stays at rest unless a net force acts on it. (Chap. 3, p. 81)

Newton's second law of motion: Describes the acceleration of an object in the direction of the net force applied to it. Expressed in equation form as *force = mass × acceleration*, or $F = ma$. (Chap. 4, p. 94)

Newton's third law of motion: Describes action-reaction pairs; for every action force, there is an equal and opposite reaction force. (Chap. 4, p. 110)

NIMBY: *Not in My Backyard*; a point of view that supports an issue such as nuclear generation of electricity as long as it does not take place close to home. (Chap. 25, p. 710)

noise: Sound that has no regular pattern or definite pitch. (Chap. 18, p. 516)

nonelectrolyte: A substance, such as pure water, that does not conduct electricity. (Chap. 15, p. 433)

nonmetals: Elements that usually are gases or brittle solids at room temperature; most do not conduct heat or electricity well. In the periodic table, nonmetals are found at the right of the stair-step line. (Chap. 10, p. 291)

nonpolar molecule: A molecule that does not have oppositely charged ends. (Chap. 11, p. 307)

nonrenewable resources: Resources such as coal, oil, and natural gas, which cannot be replaced after they are used up. (Chap. 25, p. 703)

normal: In the study of light, an imaginary line drawn perpendicular to a reflecting surface or perpendicular to a medium that light is entering.

nuclear fission: Process in which an atom's nucleus is split into two nuclei with smaller masses. (Chap. 24, p. 689)

nuclear fusion: Process in which two atomic nuclei with low masses are fused into a single nucleus of larger mass; also known as a thermonuclear reaction. (Chap. 24, p. 690)

nuclear reactor: A device that generates electricity from a controlled nuclear fission chain reaction. (Chap. 25, p. 704)

nuclear waste: Radioactive by-products from nuclear power generation, nuclear medicine, and so on; storing nuclear waste is a political and environmental problem. (Chap. 25, p. 706)

nucleic acid: An organic polymer that controls the activities and reproduction of cells. (Chap. 13, p. 375)

nucleus: The positively charged center of an atom that contains protons and neutrons. (Chap. 10, p. 270)

nuclide: The nucleus of a specific isotope having a certain specific atomic number and atomic mass. (Chap. 24, p. 675)

observation: Using your senses to gather information; in science we use instruments such as microscopes and balances to carefully gather accurate and detailed observations. (Chap. 1, p. 16)

ocean thermal energy conversion: Process that uses heat engines to convert differences in ocean temperatures into mechanical energy to drive turbines. (Chap. 6, p. 173)

ohm: The unit for measuring resistance.

Ohm's law: States that potential difference = current × resistance, or V (volts) = I (amperes) × R (ohms). (Chap. 21, p. 606)

opaque materials: Materials you can't see through because they absorb or reflect all light. (Chap. 19, p. 536)

optical axis: A line perpendicular to the center of a mirror or lens.

optical fiber: Transparent glass fiber that can transmit light from one place to another. (Chap. 20, p. 578)

organic compounds: Most chemical compounds that contain the element carbon are organic compounds; more than 90 percent of all compounds are organic. (Chap. 13, p. 360)

organic solvent: A type of liquid often found in building materials; contains potentially harmful chemicals. (Chap. 15, p. 422)

oxidation number: A positive or negative number that indicates how many electrons an atom has lost, gained, or shared when bonding with other atoms. (Chap. 11, p. 314)

parallel circuit: An electrical circuit where the current flows through more than one path. If one path is interrupted, current will still flow through the other paths. (Chap. 21, p. 609)

pascal: The SI unit of pressure; 1 pascal (Pa) of pressure = 1 newton/square meter (N/m^2). (Chap. 8, p. 228)

Pascal's principle: French scientist Blaise Pascal stated that pressure applied to the fluid is transmitted unchanged through the fluid. (Chap. 8, p. 236)

passive solar heating: Direct use of the sun's energy to heat something, without using fans or mechanical devices to transfer heat from one area to another.

period: A horizontal row in the periodic table. (Chap. 10, p. 290)

periodic table: A table of the elements arranged according to repeated changes in properties. (Chap. 10, p. 284)

PET: *Positron-Emission Tomography;* PET scans are used in medicine to reveal brain function and certain brain disorders such as tumors. (Chap. 24, p. 693)

petroleum: Crude oil, formed by decayed remains of plants and animals; a fossil fuel that is burned and used to make lubricants and plastics. (Chap. 25, p. 700)

pH: A measure of hydronium ion (H_3O^+) concentration in solution; expressed on the pH scale from 0 to 14. From 7 down to 0, a solution is increasingly acidic; at 7 it is neutral (pure water); from 7 to 14, a solution is increasingly basic (pH = *p*otential of *H*ydrogen). (Chap. 17, p. 475)

phenolphthalein (feen ul THAYL een): A chemical used as a color indicator in titration; colorless in an acidic solution, but turns pink in a basic solution.

photon: A tiny particlelike bundle of radiation. (Chap. 19, p. 529)

photovoltaic cell: A device used to convert solar energy directly into electrical energy; also called a solar cell. (Chap. 25, p. 713)

physical change: A change in the size, shape, color, or state of matter. (Chap. 9, p. 256)

physical property: Any characteristic of a material that can be observed without changing the identity of the material itself. (Chap. 9, p. 254)

physical science: The study of matter and energy; topics for study include chemistry and physics. (Chap. 1, p. 8)

pickling: A process that removes impurities from the surfaces of steel and other metals by dipping them in hydrochloric acid. (Chap. 17, p. 469)

pigment: Colored material that absorbs some colors and reflects others; the colors of pigments are determined by the colors they reflect. (Chap. 19, p. 540)

pitch: The highness or lowness of a sound, which is determined by the frequency of the sound waves. (Chap. 18, p. 508)

plane mirror: A mirror with a flat surface that produces a virtual image. (Chap. 20, p. 558)

plankton: Tiny plants and animals that live in water and are food for small fish; they are easily killed by acid rain. (Chap. 17, p. 478)

plasma: A gaslike mixture of charged particles that

exists at extremely high temperatures. (Chap. 8, p. 218)

plastic: Polymer-based material that can be easily molded. (Chap. 14, p. 396)

polar molecule: A molecule with opposite charges on each end. (Chap. 11, p. 307)

polarized light: Light in which the transverse waves vibrate only along one plane. (Chap. 20, p. 574)

polarizing filter: A filter made of chains of molecules in parallel rows that will transmit only light waves vibrating in the same direction as the molecular chains.

polluted water: Water that contains high levels of unwanted substances that may be harmful to living things. (Chap. 8, p. 222)

polyatomic ion: A group of covalently bonded atoms in which the whole group is positively or negatively charged. (Chap. 11, p. 318)

polymer: A huge molecule made up of many smaller organic molecules, called monomers, that have formed new bonds and are linked together. (Chap. 13, p. 373)

positron: A positively charged particle similar to an electron.

potential difference: The difference in electric potential energy between two different points; measured in volts (V). (Chap. 21, p. 600)

potential energy: Stored energy. The amount of potential energy of an object depends on its position or condition. (Chap. 5, p. 125)

power: The measure of the amount of work done in a specific amount of time; power is measured in watts and equals 1 joule/second. (Chap. 7, p. 202)

precipitate: An insoluble compound formed during a double-displacement reaction. (Chap. 16, p. 453)

pressure: The amount of force exerted per unit of area. (Chap. 8, p. 228)

principle: A basic rule or law describing how something always works in the natural world; for example, "gravity always pulls objects toward each other."

products: In a chemical reaction, the substances produced by the reaction. (Chap. 16, p. 442)

projectile: Any object shot or thrown through the air; all projectiles have both horizontal and vertical velocities. (Chap. 4, p. 100)

propane: A flammable gas (C_3H_8); a part of natural gas.

protein: Organic polymer formed from amino acids. (Chap. 13, p. 373)

proton: Atomic particle with a positive charge that is part of an atom's nucleus. (Chap. 10, p. 271)

pulley: A simple machine consisting of a grooved wheel with a rope or a chain running along the groove. (Chap. 7, p. 190)

quality: In sound, the differences among sounds of the same pitch and loudness. (Chap. 18, p. 517)

quarks: Very small particles of matter that make up protons and neutrons; presently, six different types of quarks are known. (Chap. 10, p. 276)

radiation: The transfer of energy in the form of waves. Radiation is a type of energy transfer that does not require matter. (Chap. 6, p. 154)

radiator: A device with a large surface area that transfers heat to surrounding air by conduction. (Chap. 6, p. 162)

radio waves: Electromagnetic waves that have long wavelengths (low frequencies); radio waves are used in communications. (Chap. 19, p. 529)

radioactive element: An unstable element whose nucleus breaks down and gives off particles, radiation, and energy. (Chap. 12, p. 332)

radioactivity: The emission of high-energy radiation or particles from the nucleus of a radioactive atom. (Chap. 24, p. 674)

RAM: *R*andom-*A*ccess *M*emory in a computer; temporary memory that is lost when the computer is turned off. (Chap. 23, p. 660)

rarefaction: In compressional waves, the less dense area of the wave.

reactants: The starting substances in a chemical reaction. (Chap. 16, p. 442)

real image: An image produced where light rays converge, as with a concave mirror or convex lens; a real image is real, enlarged, upside-down, and can be projected onto a screen. (Chap. 20, p. 559)

rectifier: Any device that converts alternating current (AC) into direct current (DC). (Chap. 23, p. 651)

reflecting telescope: An optical instrument that uses a concave mirror, a plane mirror, and a convex lens to magnify distant objects. (Chap. 20, p. 569)

reflection: Occurs when a wave strikes an object and bounces off. (Chap. 19, p. 546)

refracting telescope: An optical instrument that uses two convex lenses to magnify distant objects. (Chap. 20, p. 568)

refraction: The bending of waves, caused by changing their speed. (Chap. 19, p. 547)

resistance: The opposition to the flow of electrons through a conductor; measured in ohms. (Chap. 21, p. 603)

resistance arm: The part of a lever that exerts the resistance force (F_r). (Chap. 7, p. 186)

resistance force: The force exerted by a machine to overcome resistance to gravity or friction. (Chap. 7, p. 181)

resonance: The tendency of an object to vibrate at the same frequency as another vibrating source. (Chap. 18, p. 517)

reverberation: The echoing effect produced by multiple reflections of sound. (Chap. 18, p. 520)

RNA: *RiboNucleic Acid*; a nucleic acid that controls production of proteins that make new cells.

ROM: *Read-Only Memory* in a computer; it is permanent memory stored inside the computer, even when the power is turned off. (Chap. 23, p. 660)

salt: A compound formed during a neutralization reaction when negative ions from an acid combine with positive ions from a base. (Chap. 17, p. 480)

saponification: The process of making soap. (Chap. 17, p. 483)

saturated hydrocarbon: A hydrocarbon that contains only single-bonded carbon atoms; an example is propane. (Chap. 13, p. 362)

saturated solution: A solution that has dissolved all the solute it can normally hold at a specific temperature. (Chap. 15, p. 426)

scientific law: A rule that describes, but doesn't explain, a pattern in nature and predicts what will happen under specific conditions. (Chap. 1, p. 17)

screw: A simple machine consisting of a special type of inclined plane wrapped in a spiral around a cylindrical post. (Chap. 7, p. 194)

second: The SI unit for time. (Chap. 2, p. 44)

semiconductor: An element that conducts electricity under certain conditions. (Chap. 12, p. 346)

series circuit: An electrical circuit where the current has only one path. If the path is interrupted in any point, it stops current flow in the entire circuit. (Chap. 21, p. 608)

SI: International System of Units; standard, easy to use, worldwide system of measurement based on powers of 10. The SI standards are used by all scientists, and are a modern version of the metric system. (Chap. 2, p. 35)

simple machine: A device that accomplishes work with only one movement. The lever, pulley, wheel and axle, inclined plane, screw, and wedge are all simple machines. (Chap. 7, p. 180)

single-displacement reaction: A chemical reaction in which one element replaces another element in a compound. (Chap. 16, p. 452)

soap: An organic salt made by reacting fats or oils with a strong base such as sodium hydroxide. (Chap. 17, p. 483)

solar collector: A device that absorbs radiant energy from the sun that can be converted to thermal energy and used to heat buildings. (Chap. 6, p. 164)

solar energy: Energy from the sun. Solar energy is free and can be converted into thermal energy to heat homes and other buildings. (Chap. 6, p. 163)

solubility: The amount of a substance (solute) that will dissolve in a solvent; generally expressed as the maximum number of grams of solute that will dissolve in 100 g of a solvent at a specific temperature. (Chap. 15, p. 424)

solute: The substance being dissolved in a solvent. (Chap. 15, p. 417)

solution: A homogeneous mixture containing particles so tiny that they cannot be seen even with a microscope; particles in a solution don't settle and don't scatter light. (Chap. 9, p. 248)

solvent: The substance that dissolves a solute. (Chap. 15, p. 417)

specific heat: The amount of energy needed to raise the temperature of 1 kg of a material 1 K; it is measured in joules per kilogram per kelvin. (Chap. 5, p. 141)

speed: The rate of motion, or the rate at which a body changes position. (Chap. 3, p. 64)

standard: In measurement, an exact quantity that everyone agrees to use as a basis of comparison; for example, a centimeter, meter, kilogram, cubic decimeter, milliliter, liter, kelvin, joule, and so on. (Chap. 2, p. 34)

state of matter: Any of the four conditions in which matter can exist: solid, liquid, gas, or plasma; the state of a sample of matter depends on its temperature. (Chap. 8, p. 214)

static electricity: The net buildup of electric charges on an object. (Chap. 21, p. 592)

step-down transformer: An electrical transformer that decreases (steps down) the voltage of a power line.

step-up transformer: An electrical transformer that increases (steps up) the voltage of a power line.

strong acid: An acid that ionizes almost completely in solution; for example, hydrochloric acid and sulfuric acid. (Chap. 17, p. 474)

strong base: A base that dissociates completely in solution; for example, sodium hydroxide. (Chap. 17, p. 474)

sublimation: The process in which a solid changes directly to a vapor without forming a liquid. (Chap. 12, p. 343)

submerge: to fully immerse (completely cover) something in a fluid.

substance: Matter that is an element or a compound. (Chap. 9, p. 247)

substituted hydrocarbon: A hydrocarbon in which one or more hydrogen atoms have been replaced by atoms of other elements. (Chap. 13, p. 367)

supercollider: A device to make protons collide at high speed so they break apart into quarks.

superconductor: A supercooled material that has no electrical resistance; a current can flow indefinitely through a superconductor without losing energy. (Chap. 22, p. 640)

supersaturated solution: An unstable solution that contains more solute than a saturated solution can at that same specific temperature. (Chap. 15, p. 428)

suspension: A heterogeneous mixture containing a liquid in which larger particles eventually settle out. (Chap. 9, p. 250)

synthesis reaction: A chemical reaction in which two or more substances combine to form a different substance. (Chap. 16, p. 451)

synthetic fiber: A thin strand of synthetic polymer that can be woven into fabrics; examples include nylon and Kevlar fibers. (Chap. 14, p. 399)

technology: The practical use of scientific information to improve the quality of human life. (Chap. 1, p. 8)

telephoto lens: A lens having a long focal length and producing an enlarged, close-up image of an object. (Chap. 20, p. 571)

temperature: A measure of the average kinetic energy of the particles that make up a sample of matter. As an object's particles move faster, its temperature rises, and as an object's particles move slower, its temperature falls. (Chap. 5, p. 134)

terminal velocity: The greatest velocity reached by a falling object. Terminal velocity is achieved when the force of gravity is balanced by air resistance. (Chap. 4, p. 99)

theory: The most logical explanation of why things work the way they do. A theory is a former hypothesis that has been tested with repeated experiments and observations and found always to work. (Chap. 1, p. 17)

thermal energy: Total energy of a material's particles, including both kinetic energy (vibrations and movement within and between particles) and potential energy (resulting from forces that act within or between particles). (Chap. 5, p. 135)

thermal expansion: A characteristic of almost all matter that causes it to expand when heated and contract when cooled. (Chap. 8, p. 219)

thermal pollution: Pollution caused when waste heat raises the temperature of the environment. Thermal pollution in bodies of water can damage or destroy plants and animals that live there. (Chap. 5, p. 138; Chap. 8, p. 223)

thermonuclear fusion: Nuclear fusion that occurs under conditions of enormous heat (millions of degrees), as in a star or our sun.

tidal energy: Energy produced by the rise and fall of ocean levels; used to generate electricity. (Chap. 25, p. 714)

time: The interval between two events; the SI unit for time is the second. (Chap. 2, p. 44)

titration: Process in which a solution of known concentration is used to determine the concentration of an acidic or basic solution. (Chap. 17, p. 481)

total internal reflection: Occurs when all the light striking a surface between two materials is reflected totally back into the first material. (Chap. 20, p. 577)

toxic: Hazardous substance than can injure living tissue; toxic compounds are poisonous. (Chap. 11, p. 312)

tracer: A radioisotope used in medical diagnosis to allow doctors to monitor human body functions, locate tumors, detect fluid movement, and so on. (Chap. 24, p. 692)

transformer: A device that can increase or decrease the voltage of an alternating current. (Chap. 22, p. 635)

transistor: A semiconductor that amplifies or strengthens an electrical signal or acts as a tiny on-off switch. (Chap. 23, p. 651)

transition element: An element in Groups 3-12 of the periodic table; typically, these are metals with one or two electrons in their outer energy level. (Chap. 12, p. 334)

translucent materials: Materials that can be hazily seen through because they allow some light to pass through them, but not enough for a clear image. (Chap. 19, p. 536)

transmutation: Changing one element to another through radioactive decay. (Chap. 24, p. 680)

transparent materials: Materials that can be clearly seen through because they allow light to pass through them. (Chap. 19, p. 536)

transuranium element: Any element having more than 92 protons, the atomic number of uranium. (Chap. 12, p. 338)

transverse wave: A type of wave where the medium moves at right angles to the direction the wave is traveling. (Chap. 18, p. 499)

trough: The lowest point of a wave. (Chap. 18, p. 499)

Tyndall effect: The scattering of light by particles in a mixture; this effect can be seen in all colloids. (Chap. 9, p. 249)

ultrasonic technology: Technology using high-frequency sound waves for many different purposes such as medical diagnoses, sonar, and jewelry cleaning. (Chap. 18, p. 514)

ultraviolet radiation: Electromagnetic waves that have a higher frequency than visible light; abbreviated UV. (Chap. 19, p. 532)

unsaturated hydrocarbons: Hydrocarbons that contain at least one double or triple bond between carbon atoms; an example is ethyne. (Chap. 13, p. 364)

unsaturated solution: A solution that is capable of dissolving more solute at a specific temperature. (Chap. 15, p. 427)

velocity: The speed and direction of a moving body, such as a storm or a basketball thrown across a court. (Chap. 3, p. 72)

Venturi effect: Reduction in pressure of a fluid resulting from the speed increase as fluids are forced to flow faster through narrow spaces. (Chap. 8, p. 238)

virtual image: An image formed of diverging light rays, as in a plane or convex mirror, or seen through a concave lens. A virtual image can't be projected onto a screen. (Chap. 20, p. 558)

visible radiation: Electromagnetic waves in the only part of the electromagnetic spectrum we can see—light. (Chap. 19, p. 532)

volt: The unit for measuring electrical potential energy; abbreviated V.

voltage: A difference in electrical potential, measured in volts with a voltmeter.

voltmeter: A galvanometer that measures potential differences in volts and is placed in parallel across a part of the circuit. (Chap. 22, p. 630)

volume: The amount of space occupied by an object; volume units are found by combining other SI units of length. (Chap. 2, p. 41)

wave: A rhythmic disturbance that carries energy through matter or space. (Chap. 18, p. 498)

wavelength: The distance between identical points on two adjacent waves; for example, the distance between two crests or two troughs. (Chap. 18, p. 499)

weak acid: An acid that partially ionizes in solution; for example, carbonic acid. (Chap. 17, p. 474)

weak base: A base that partially dissociates in solution; for example, magnesium hydroxide. (Chap. 17, p. 474)

wedge: A simple machine consisting of a moving inclined plane with one or two sloping sides; examples are knives and chisels. (Chap. 7, p. 194)

weight: The measure of the force of gravity on an object. Weight changes with changes in gravity and is measured in newtons (N). (Chap. 3, p. 84)

wet cell: A power source that generates electric current by a chemical reaction; "wet" because it uses a liquid electrolyte. (Chap. 21, p. 602)

wheel and axle: A simple machine consisting of two different-sized wheels that rotate together, such as a doorknob or wheel-handled faucet. (Chap. 7, p. 191)

wide-angle lens: A lens with a short focal length that produces a relatively small image of an object, but includes much of the object's surroundings. (Chap. 20, p. 571)

work: The transfer of energy through motion; *work = force × distance.* Work is measured in joules and is accomplished only when force produces motion in the direction of the force. (Chap. 5, p. 126)

X rays: Electromagnetic waves having a wavelength shorter (higher frequency) than ultraviolet radiation; often used in medical diagnosis and photography because they can penetrate human tissue. (Chap. 19, p. 534)

This glossary defines each key term that appears in **bold type** in the text. It also shows the page number where you can find the word used. Some additional helpful terms are also provided.

acceleration/aceleración: índice del cambio en la velocidad (un cambio en la dirección o en la rapidez). La cantidad de aceleración depende del cambio en la velocidad y del intervalo de tiempo. (Cap. 3, pág. 73)

acid/ácido: sustancia que produce iones de hidrógeno H⁺, en solución. La presencia de los iones de H⁺ es lo que les da a los ácidos sus propiedades características. (Cap. 17, pág. 466)

acid rain/lluvia ácida: cualquier lluvia cuyo pH es menor de 5.6. Se produce cuando las sustancias en el aire reaccionan con el agua de lluvia y la vuelven ácida. La lluvia ácida es dañina para los animales y las plantas, además de aumentar el ritmo de la meteorización. (Cap. 17, pág. 478)

acoustics/acústica: estudio del sonido. (Cap. 18, pág. 520)

actinide/actínido: cualquiera de los 14 elementos radiactivos cuyos números atómicos van desde 90 a 103 y los cuales se usan en la producción de potencia nuclear y de armas nucleares.

active solar heating/calefacción solar activa: la recolección de la energía solar con paneles nucleares para calentar agua con esa energía. Esta agua calentada se almacena para ser usada más tarde como fuente energética.

aerosol/aerosol: líquido que se rocía de un recipiente a presión. Por ejemplo, una lata de insecticida.

air resistance/resistencia del aire: fuerza que el aire ejerce sobre un objeto en movimiento. (Cap. 4, pág. 97)

alchemist/alquimista: una versión medieval del químico moderno; un practicante que combinaba la química primitiva con magia, en busca de convertir metales común y corrientes en oro.

alcohol/alcohol: tipo de compuesto que se forma cuando los grupos –OH reemplazan uno o más átomos de hidrógeno en un hidrocarburo. (Cap. 13, pág. 368)

allotrope/alotropo: elemento que exhibe diferentes formas teniendo además estructuras moleculares diferentes. El carbono exhibe alotropía en sus distintas formas cristalinas, como por ejemplo, el grafito y el diamante. (Cap. 12, pág. 347)

alloy/aleación: mezcla de un metal y uno o más elementos. Una aleación conserva las propiedades comunes de los metales, pero no es un metal puro. (Cap. 14, pág. 388)

alpha particle/partícula alfa: tipo de radiación despedido cuando un núcleo libera dos protones y dos neutrones. Es la forma más extensa de radiación y la más lenta, de modo que es la menos penetrante. (Cap. 24, pág. 679)

alternating current (AC)/corriente alterna: corriente que cambia su dirección en un patrón regular. La corriente alterna de 60 Hz de nuestros hogares cambia dirección 120 veces cada segundo. (Cap. 22, pág. 635)

amalgam/amalgama: aleación que contiene mercurio. Las amalgamas dentales consisten de mercurio, plata y cinc. Los dentistas utilizan las amalgamas para rellenar los huecos de las caries dentales. (Cap. 14, pág. 391)

ammeter/amperímetro: instrumento que mide, en amperios, la corriente eléctrica que pasa por un circuito, el cual debe estar conectado en serie. (Cap. 22, pág. 630) amorphous/amorfo: algo que no tiene forma específica; por ejemplo, un líquido o un gas.

ampere/amperio: la unidad para medir la corriente, la razón del flujo de electrones en un circuito; abreviado A; 1 amperio = 1 culombio de carga que pasa por un punto dado en un segundo.

amplification/amplificación: proceso de incrementar la fortaleza de una señal eléctrica. (Cap. 23, pág. 651)

amplitude/amplitud: distancia desde la cresta (o valle) de una onda hasta la posición de descanso del medio. Corresponde a la cantidad de energía transportada por una onda. Las ondas que transportan grandes cantidades de energía tienen alturas o amplitudes altas y las ondas que transportan menos energía tienen amplitudes más bajas. (Cap. 18, pág. 499)

amplitude-modulated (AM) waves/ondas de amplitud modulada: ondas radiales cuya amplitud varía con la voz, la música, el video o los datos al ser transmitidas a través de largas distancias.

angle of incidence/ángulo de incidencia: en ondas, el ángulo formado por la onda de incidencia y la normal (perpendicular); se representa como *i*.

angle of reflection/ángulo de reflexión: en ondas, el ángulo formado por la onda reflejada y la normal (perpendicular); se representa como *r*.

anhydrous/anhidro: un compuesto químico que normalmente contiene moléculas de agua adheridas a sus iones, pero al cual se le ha secado el agua.

antiacid/antiácido: un "anti-ácido" o una sustancia química que cambia una sustancia ácida en una sustancia neutra.

antifreeze/anticongelante: un soluto que se le agrega a un disolvente para reducir la temperatura a la cual se congela el disolvente; por ejemplo, el anticongelante que se le añade al agua del sistema de enfriamiento de un carro.

aqueous/acuoso: describe una solución hecha con agua; por ejemplo, el agua de amoníaco es una solución acuosa de gas amoniacal.

Archimedes' principle/principio de Arquímedes: dice que la fuerza boyante de un objeto en un fluido es igual al peso del fluido desplazado por el objeto. (Cap. 8, pág. 235)

aromatic compound/compuesto aromático: tipo de compuesto que contiene la estructura de anillo bencénico. Un ejemplo de un compuesto aromático es la naftalina. (Cap. 13, pág. 366)

artificial satellites/satélites artificiales: dispositivos hechos por los seres humanos que giran en órbitas alrededor de la Tierra, por lo general, con un propósito específico. (Cap. 4, pág. 108)

atomic number/número atómico: número de protones en el núcleo de un átomo. (Cap. 10, pág. 271)

average atomic mass/masa atómica promedio: masa promedio de la mezcla de isótopos de un elemento. (Cap. 10, pág. 280)

average speed/rapidez promedio: se halla dividiendo el total de la distancia viajada entre el total del tiempo viajado. (Cap. 3, pág. 65)

balance/balanza: un dispositivo que se usa en laboratorios para medir la masa; funciona equilibrando la masa que se está determinando con una masa estándar conocida.

balanced chemical equation/ecuación química equilibrada: ecuación que tiene el mismo número de átomos de cada elemento en ambos lados de la ecuación. (Cap. 16, pág. 448)

balanced forces/fuerzas equilibradas: fuerzas del mismo tamaño pero opuestas en dirección. (Cap. 3, pág. 78)

bar graph/gráfica de barras: un tipo de gráfica que se usa para mostrar información recogida por conteo; utiliza barras horizontales o verticales de diferentes longitudes para ayudarnos en la comparación de cantidades.

base/base: sustancia que produce iones de hidróxido, OH$^-$ en solución. En estado puro y sin disolver, las bases son sólidos cristalinos, pero en solución se sienten resbalosas y tienen sabor amargo. Sin embargo, las bases no se deben nunca tocar ni probar porque pueden causar quemaduras graves. (Cap. 17, pág. 470)

Bernoulli's principle/principio de Bernoulli: dice que a medida que aumenta la velocidad de un fluido, disminuye la presión ejercida por el fluido. (Cap. 8, pág. 237)

beta particle/partícula beta: electrón emitido del núcleo, a alta velocidad. (Cap. 24, pág. 680)

BHA/BHA: una sustancia para preservar alimentos; es un inhibidor químico que demora las reacciones químicas que descomponen los alimentos (*B*util-*h*idroxi*a*nisol).

BHT/BHT: una sustancia para preservar alimentos; es un inhibidor químico que demora las reacciones químicas que descomponen los alimentos (*B*util-*h*idroxi*t*olueno).

binary compound/compuesto binario: compuesto químico formado de dos elementos. Por ejemplo, el cloruro de sodio es un compuesto binario hecho de cloro y sodio. (Cap. 11, pág. 315)

biodegradable/biodegradable: describe un material que se puede descomponer en sustancias no tóxicas mediante la acción biológica de organismos como las bacterias.

biogas/biogas: mezcla de gases, principalmente, metano que se produce de la biomasa. (Cap. 13, pág. 370)

biomass/biomasa: material orgánico proveniente de la madera, la caña de azúcar, el maíz, las cosechas y los desperdicios de los animales. (Cap. 13, pág. 370)

bionics/biónica: ciencia que diseña repuestos artificiales para las partes del cuerpo humano. Los repuestos artificiales a menudo se llaman prótesis. (Cap. 7, pág. 196)

boiling point/punto de ebullición: la temperatura a la cual se forman burbujas de vapor en un líquido y se elevan hasta la superficie, aumentando la evaporación.

Boyle's law/ley de Boyle: dice que si se disminuye el volumen de un recipiente de gas, la presión del gas aumenta, siempre y cuando no se altere la temperatura. Al aumentar el volumen, la presión disminuye. (Cap. 8, pág. 229)

brittleness/quebradizo: una característica de ciertos materiales que hace que se rompan fácilmente bajo estrés.

bubble chamber/cámara de burbuja: cámara llena de un líquido supercalentado, el cual no hierve debido al aumento de presión en el sistema. (Cap. 24, pág. 686)

buoyant force/fuerza boyante: capacidad de un fluido—líquido o gas—de ejercer una fuerza ascendente sobre un objeto sumergido en él. La cantidad de fuerza boyante determina si un objeto se hunde o flota en un fluido. (Cap. 8, pág. 234)

butane/butano: un gas inflamable (C_4H_{10}); una parte del gas natural.

byte/byte: una unidad básica de memoria de computadora que representa un carácter (número, símbolo o letra del alfabeto); consiste de 8 bitios.

calorimeter/calorímetro: un instrumento que se usa para medir cambios en la energía térmica.

carbohydrate/carbohidrato: compuesto orgánico que posee el doble de átomos de hidrógeno que de oxígeno. Un grupo de carbohidratos son los azúcares. (Cap. 13, pág. 376)

carbon-14 dating/datación con carbono 14: método para determinar la edad de objetos que contienen carbono 14 y que datan de hasta 50 000 años atrás; funciona calculando la cantidad de carbono 14 que aún contiene el objeto.

catalyst/catalizador: sustancia que acelera una reacción química, sin cambiar permanentemente la sustancia misma. Cuando se le añade un catalizador a una reacción, se termina con la misma cantidad de catalizador con que se comenzó. (Cap. 16, pág. 456)

cathode–ray tube (CRT)/tubo de rayos catódicos: dispositivo que usa electrones y materiales fluorescentes para producir imágenes sobre una pantalla. (Cap. 23, pág. 656)

central processing unit (CPU)/unidad de procesamiento central: el tablero principal de circuitos dentro de una computadora que ejecuta los cálculos y almacena la memoria principal.

centripetal acceleration/aceleración centrípeta: aceleración que se efectúa hacia el centro de una trayectoria circular o curva. (Cap. 4, pág. 102)

centripetal force/fuerza centrípeta: fuerza que actúa hacia el centro de una trayectoria circular o curva. (Cap. 4, pág. 102)

ceramic/cerámica: material hecho de arcilla seca y de mezclas de arcilla seca. Hace miles de años que los seres humanos comenzaron a fabricar recipientes de cerámica para almacenar alimentos y transportar agua. (Cap. 14, pág. 392)

cermet/cermet: o *cerámica–met*al, es un material que posee propiedades tanto de las cerámicas como de las aleaciones. (Cap. 14, pág. 394)

chain reaction/reacción en cadena: serie de reacciones de fisión en curso. Puede causar billones de reacciones cada segundo, dando como resultado la liberación de tremendas cantidades de energía. (Cap. 24, pág. 690)

Charles's law/ley de Charles: dice que el volumen de un gas aumenta cuando se aumenta la temperatura, siempre y cuando no se altere la presión. Lo contrario también es cierto. (Cap. 8, pág. 230)

chemical bond/enlace químico: fuerza que mantiene unidos los átomos en una sustancia. (Cap. 11, pág. 301)

chemical change/cambio químico: cambio de una sustancia de un material en una sustancia diferente. (Cap. 9, pág. 257)

chemical formula/fórmula química: presentación precisa de los elementos que contiene un compuesto y las proporciones de los átomos de esos elementos. (Cap. 11, pág. 300)

chemical property/propiedad química: característica de una sustancia que indica si puede sufrir cierto cambio químico. (Cap. 9, pág. 259)

chemical reaction/reacción química: un ejemplo de un cambio químico. Cuando ocurre una reacción química, una o más sustancias se convierten en nuevas sustancias. (Cap. 16, pág. 442)

chemical symbol/símbolo químico: forma abreviada de escribir el nombre de un elemento. Por ejemplo,:

C para el carbono, Ag para la plata. (Cap. 10, pág. 270)

chemically stable/estable químicamente: describe un átomo cuyo nivel de energía externo está completamente lleno de electrones. El nivel de energía externo, de la mayoría de los átomos de los elementos, está lleno cuando contiene ocho electrones. (Cap. 11, pág. 300)

chemically unstable/químicamente inestable: describe un átomo cuyo nivel de energía externo no está lleno de electrones de manera que busca electrones de otros átomos y así forma compuestos; por ejemplo, el cloruro sódico.

choloro-/cloro: prefijo que indica la presencia de cloro, como en tetracloroetileno o clorofluorocarbono.

chlorofluorocarbon (CFC)/clorofluorocarbono: grupo de compuestos cuya descomposición libera átomos de cloro que destruyen las moléculas de ozono en la atmósfera superior. Se usan en los sistemas de aire acondicionado y en la fabricación de algunos tipos de espumas de polímeros. (Cap. 16, pág. 447)

circuit/circuito: trayectoria cerrada a través de la cual pueden fluir los electrones. (Cap. 21, pág. 601)

circuit breaker/cortacircuitos: un dispositivo que protege un circuito eléctrico; si fluye demasiada corriente, el cortacircuitos abre el circuito, deteniendo el flujo de corriente.

cloud chamber/cámara de niebla: cámara que contiene agua supersaturada o vapor de etanol y la cual se usa para detectar partículas nucleares cargadas, las cuales dejan rastros de vapor al pasar. (Cap. 24, pág. 686)

coagulation/coagulación: destrucción de la estructura de coloides, debido a la atracción mutua de pequeñas partículas suspendidas. (Cap. 9, pág. 253)

coal/carbón: una roca formada de plantas antiguas descompuestas; se quema como un combustible fósil.

coefficient/coeficiente: representa el número de unidades de cada sustancia que forman parte de una reacción química. (Cap. 16, pág. 445)

coherent light/luz coherente: energía electromagnética de una sola longitud de onda que viaja con sus crestas y valles alineados. El haz no se dispersa porque todas las ondas viajan en la misma dirección. (Cap. 20, pág. 575)

colloid/coloide: mezcla heterogénea que, así como una solución, nunca se asienta. (Cap. 9, pág. 249)

combustion/combustión: quiere decir combustión rápida y es el proceso mediante el cual las máquinas de calor queman combustible. (Cap. 6, pág. 166)

composite/compuesto: mezcla de dos o más materiales, uno de ellos incrustado en el otro. (Cap. 14, pág. 401)

compound/compuesto: material formado de la combinación de átomos de dos o más elementos. La proporción de los diferentes átomos en un compuesto es siempre la misma. Por ejemplo, los elementos hidrógeno y oxígeno se pueden combinar para formar el compuesto agua. Los átomos de los elementos en el agua siempre se encuentran en la proporción de dos átomos de hidrógeno por cada átomo de oxígeno. (Cap. 9, pág. 246)

compound machine/máquina compuesta: combinación de dos o más máquinas simples. (Cap. 7, pág. 198)

compression/compresión: el área densa de la onda, en ondas de compresión.

compressional wave/onda de compresión: onda en la cual la materia vibra en la misma dirección en que viaja la onda. En las ondas de compresión, el medio se desplaza en la misma dirección en que se mueve la energía. (Cap. 18, pág. 505)

computer/computadora: un dispositivo que se programa para ejecutar cálculos, tomar decisiones lógicas y manipular datos.

computer virus/virus de computadora: tipo de programa que se puede multiplicar dentro de una computadora y llegar a usar tanta memoria que perjudica el sistema. (Cap. 23, pág. 666)

concave lenses/lente cóncava: lente más delgada en el centro y más gruesa en las orillas y por consiguiente se curvan hacia adentro, forman una imagen virtual, al derecho y más pequeña que el objeto en sí. (Cap. 20, pág. 565)

concave mirror/espejo cóncavo: espejo cuya superficie se curva hacia adentro, como la parte interior de una cuchara. (Cap. 20, pág. 558)

concentrated solution/solución concentrada: una solución en que la cantidad de soluto está casi al máximo de lo que el disolvente puede retener a una temperatura dada.

concentration/concentración: Por lo general, la proporción de soluto disuelto en un disolvente.

condensation/condensación: sucede cuando un gas se convierte en líquido. Por lo general, un gas se condensa cuando se enfría a su punto de ebullición o por debajo de este. (Cap. 8, pág. 225)

conduction/conducción: transferencia de energía a través de la materia por contacto directo de las partículas. (Cap. 6, pág. 152)

conductor/conductor: material que permite que los electrones se muevan fácilmente a través de él. Los metales como el cobre y la plata están hechos de átomos que no sostienen sus electrones muy apretados, de modo que los electrones pueden moverse fácilmente a través de materiales hechos de estas clases de átomos. (Cap. 21, pág. 594)

constant/constante: factor que no varía en un experimento. (Cap. 1, pág. 21)

constant speed/rapidez constante: rapidez que no varía. (Cap. 3, pág. 65)

contraction/contracción: movimiento en que las moléculas se condensan para ocupar un área más pequeña.

control/control: un estándar para la comparación. (Cap. 1, pág. 21)

convection/convección: transferencia de energía debido al movimiento de materia. (Cap. 6, pág. 153)

convex lenses/lente convexa: lente más gruesa en el centro que en las orillas. Los rayos luminosos que se acercan a la lente paralelos al eje óptico son refractados hacia el centro de la lente. Estos rayos convergen en el centro focal, de modo que pueden formar imágenes reales, las cuales pueden proyectarse sobre una pantalla. (Cap. 20, pág. 564)

convex mirror/espejo convexo: espejo en que los rayos nunca se juntan, de modo que la imagen es siempre virtual, al derecho y más pequeña que el objeto en sí. (Cap. 20, pág. 561)

corrosive/corrosivo: término proveniente de la raíz en latín que quiere decir "desprender, separar". Este tipo de compuesto es útil para destapar cañerías. (Cap. 11, pág. 312)

covalent bond/enlace covalente: atracción que se forma entre los átomos cuando comparten electrones. (Cap. 11, pág. 306)

coulomb/culombio: la carga que transportan 6.24 billones de billones de electrones.

crest/cresta: punto más alto de una onda. (Cap. 18, pág. 499)

crystal/cristal: patrón en que se encuentran arregladas las partículas de la mayoría de los sólidos. (Cap. 8, pág. 215)

current/corriente: flujo de electrones a través de un alambre u otro conductor. La cantidad de corriente eléctrica depende del número de electrones que pasan por un punto en un momento dado. La corriente en un circuito se mide en amperios, (A). (Cap. 21, pág. 601)

deceleration/deceleración: La razón del cambio en velocidad (rapidez o dirección) cuando la velocidad disminuye; también llamada aceleración negativa.

decibel/decibel: la unidad de medida de la intensidad sonora, abreviada dB. El sonido más débil que la mayoría de la gente puede oír es = 0 dB.

decomposition reaction/reacción de descomposición: reacción en la cual una sustancia se descompone en dos o más sustancias más simples. (Cap. 16, pág. 452)

dehydrating agent/agente deshidratador: sustancia que puede extraer agua de los materiales. (Cap. 17, pág. 468)

density/densidad: masa por unidad de volumen de un material. (Cap. 2, pág. 43)

dependent variable/variable dependiente: factor cuyo valor depende del valor de la variable independiente. (Cap. 1, pág. 22)

derived unit/unidad derivada: unidad que se obtiene de la combinación de unidades del SI. (Cap. 2, pág. 42)

detergent/detergente: sal orgánica cuya estructura se parece a la del jabón. (Cap. 17, pág. 483)

diatomic molecule/molécula diatómica: molécula que consiste en dos átomos del mismo elemento. (Cap. 12, pág. 341)

diesel engine/motor diesel: un motor de combustión interna que comprime una mezcla de aire y combustible que se enciende debido al calor de compresión sin necesidad de una chispa.

diffraction/difracción: desviación de las ondas alrededor de una barrera, en la cual las ondas rodean el obstáculo. Todas las ondas electromagnéticas, de sonido y de agua pueden ser difractadas. Por ejemplo, las ondas se desvían alrededor de una persona que nada en el agua. (Cap. 19, pág. 548)

diffraction grating/retícula de difracción: pedazo de vidrio o de plástico hecho de muchas hendiduras paralelas. Cuando se hace brillar una luz blanca a través de una retícula de difracción, los colores de la luz se separan. (Cap. 19, pág. 550)

dilute solution/solución diluida: una solución en que la cantidad de soluto es mucho menor que el máximo que el disolvente puede retener a una temperatura dada.

diode/diodo: parece como un tipo de válvula o de puerta que permite que una corriente fluya en una sola dirección. (Cap. 23, pág. 651)

direct current (DC)/corriente directa: corriente que fluye en una sola dirección a través de un alambre. (Cap. 22, pág. 635)

disinfectant/desinfectante: una sustancia química que mata bacterias. Por ejemplo, el alcohol es un desinfectante.

dissociation/disociación: proceso en que un sólido iónico se disuelve en agua y sus iones positivos y negativos se separan unos de otros. Por ejemplo, el cloruro de sodio se disocia cuando se disuelve en agua. (Cap. 15, pág. 433)

DNA:DNA: *Ácido Desoxirribonucleico*; un ácido en el núcleo de las células que codifica y almacena información genética.

doping/adulteración: la adición de un impureza a un semiconductor con el propósito de aumentar su conductividad eléctrica.

Doppler effect/efecto Dopler: un aumento o disminución en la frecuencia de ondas, causado por movimiento de la fuente o movimiento del observador. Se aplica a todas las ondas (inclusive a las de la luz, de calor, del sonido, etc.).

dot diagram/diagrama de puntos: diagrama que utiliza el símbolo del elemento junto con unos puntos para representar los electrones en el nivel de energía externo. (Cap. 10, pág. 288)

double–displacement reaction/reacción de desplazamiento doble: reacción que ocurre cuando un precipitado, agua o gas se forma de la combinación de dos compuestos iónicos en solución. (Cap. 16, pág. 453)

dry cell/pila seca: es la que puede actuar como una bomba de electrones porque posee una diferencia de potencial entre los terminales positivo y negativo. (Cap. 21, pág. 602)

ductile/ductil: propiedad de los metales que permite que puedan ser enrollados en alambres. (Cap. 12, pág. 330)

efficiency/eficiencia: medida que se usa para calcular la cantidad de trabajo útil que se ha producido, del trabajo inicial aplicado a una máquina. (Cap. 7, pág. 200)

effort arm/brazo de esfuerzo: parte de la palanca donde se aplica la fuerza de esfuerzo. (Cap. 7, pág. 186)

effort force (F_e)/fuerza de esfuerzo: la fuerza que se le aplica a la máquina. (Cap. 7, pág. 181)

electric field/campo eléctrico: espacio que ejerce una fuerza sobre cualquier cosa que tiene una carga eléctrica. El campo eléctrico es más fuerte cerca de un electrón y se debilita al aumentar su distancia del mismo. (Cap. 21, pág. 594)

electric motor/motor eléctrico: dispositivo que cambia la energía eléctrica en energía mecánica, para hacer funcionar un artefacto como por ejemplo, un ventilador. (Cap. 22, pág. 630)

electrical power/potencia eléctrica: proporción a la cual la energía eléctrica se convierte en otra forma de energía. (Cap. 21, pág. 614)

electrolyte/electrolítica: sustancia que se separa en iones o que forma iones en una solución acuosa. (Cap. 15, pág. 433)

electromagnet/electroimán: imán temporal que se forma pasando una corriente por un eje de hierro que ha sido introducido en un espiral. (Cap. 22, pág. 628)

electromagnetic induction/inducción electromagnética: proceso en que al mover un alambre por un campo magnético se produce una corriente. También se produce una corriente moviendo un imán por dentro y por fuera de un espiral de alambre. (Cap. 22, pág. 633)

electromagnetic radiation/radiación electromagnética: ondas electromagnéticas transversales producidas por el movimiento de partículas eléctricamente cargadas. Se llama radiación electromagnética porque las partículas irradian las ondas. (Cap. 19, pág. 528)

electron/electrón: partícula con carga negativa que rodea el núcleo. (Cap. 10, pág. 270)

electron arrangement/disposición de electrones: la manera en que están distribuidos los electrones en los varios niveles de energía de un átomo.

electron cloud/nube de electrones: modelo del átomo que describe la región en donde un electrón se puede encontrar en un momento dado. (Cap. 10, pág. 272)

electroscope/electroscopio: instrumento hecho de dos láminas metálicas delgadas adheridas a una barra metálica que tiene una perilla en la cúspide. Se usa para detectar cargas de electricidad estática. (Cap. 21, pág. 596)

element/elemento: tipo de materia cuyos átomos son todos iguales. (Cap. 9, pág. 246)

endothermic reaction/reacción endotérmica: reacción que requiere energía para llevarse a cabo. Frecuentemente se usa para obtener un metal de su mena. (Cap. 16, pág. 458)

energy/energía: capacidad de causar cambio. Los científicos han tenido problemas definiendo lo que es la energía porque existe en tantas formas diferentes. Algunas de estas formas incluyen la energía radiante, la energía eléctrica, la energía química, la energía térmica y la energía nuclear. (Cap. 5, pág. 124)

energy farming/cultivo de energía: cultivo de plantas con el propósito de usarlas para proporcionar energía. El cultivo y el uso controlados de plantas puede convertir esta fuente energética en una fuente renovable. (Cap. 13, pág. 370)

energy transfer/transferencia de energía: el movimiento de energía de un objeto a otro; por ejemplo, la energía térmica que fluye, en forma de calor, desde una estufa caliente a un sartén.

ester/éster: compuesto orgánico que se forma de la reacción de un ácido orgánico con un alcohol. Los ésteres son los responsables de los maravillosos olores y sabores de flores, frutas y otros alimentos. (Cap. 17, pág. 484)

evaporation/evaporación: cambio gradual de un líquido a un gas, el cual ocurre a temperaturas inferiores al punto de ebullición. (Cap. 8, pág. 224)

exothermic reaction/reacción exotérmica: tipo de reacción en la cual se libera alguna forma de energía. Por ejemplo, la quema de leña o la explosión de la dinamita. (Cap. 16, pág. 456)

expansion/expansión: movimiento hacia afuera de las moléculas alejándose unas de otras, para ocupar un espacio mayor.

experiment/experimento: procedimiento organizado que se hace con el propósito de probar una predicción. (Cap. 1, pág. 20)

external combustion engine/motor de combustión externa: máquina en que el combustible se quema fuera del motor. (Cap. 6, pág. 167)

factor/factor: una condición que afecta el resultado de un evento.

farsighted/présbita: describe a una persona que ve bien los objetos lejanos, pero que tiene problemas para enfocar los objetos cercanos.

fiberglass/vitrofibra: hilos de vidrio que parecen cabellos. Son buenos aisladores cuando se arreglan en capas espumosas.

filter/filtro: un dispositivo que permite que uno o más colores se transmitan mientras que otros son absorbidos o bloqueados, en el trabajo con la luz.

flame test/prueba de la llama: una prueba de laboratorio para identificar elementos mediante el calentamiento de la sustancia en una llama y luego observando el color de la llama.

flammable/inflamable: una característica química de una sustancia que le permite ser oxidada rápidamente; también denominada combustible.

flash distillation/evaporación relámpago: un proceso de desalinización en que el agua de mar se bombea hacia una cámara al vacío, para hierva rápidamente y a una temperatura más baja (debido a la ausencia de presión atmosférica).

fluid/fluido: cualquier material que fluye. El aire y el agua son dos ejemplos de fluidos. (Cap. 6, pág. 153)

fluorescence/fluorescente: cuando un material absorbe radiación ultravioleta, y es estimulado a irradiar luz visible.

fluorescent light/luz fluorescente: tipo de iluminación que produce luz sin pérdida excesiva de energía calórica. Para producir la misma cantidad de luz, este tipo de bombillas usa solo una quinta

parte de la electricidad que la que usa una bombilla común y corriente. (Cap. 19, pág. 544)

focal length/longitud focal: distancia desde el centro de un espejo hasta el punto focal. (Cap. 20, pág. 559)

focal point/punto focal: punto en el eje óptico a través del cual todos los rayos de luz paralelos a dicho eje son reflejados. (Cap. 20, pág. 559)

force/fuerza: empuje o fuerza de atracción que un cuerpo ejerce sobre otro. (Cap. 3, pág. 78)

fractional distillation/destilación fraccional: proceso que se usa en la refinación del petróleo para separar los compuestos hidrocarburos. (Cap. 25, pág. 700)

fractionating towers/torres de fraccionamiento: torres en las refinerías petroleras que se usan para destilar el petróleo por fracciones.

free-fall/caída libre: la manera en que un objeto se mueve por el espacio cuando está bajo la influencia de la gravedad solamente.

Freon/freón: un gas refrigerante que se utiliza en refrigeradores y acondicionadores de aire.

frequency/frecuencia: número de crestas que pasan por un punto fijo cada segundo. Se expresa en hertz (Hz). Un hertz equivale a una onda por segundo. (Cap. 18, pág. 499)

frequency-modulated (FM) waves/ondas de frecuencia modulada: ondas radiales cuya frecuencia varía con la voz, la música, el video o los datos al ser transmitidas a través de largas distancias.

friction/fricción: fuerza que se opone al movimiento entre dos superficies que están en contacto una con otra. (Cap. 3, pág. 82)

fuel rod/barra combustible: una barra metálica llena de perdigones de uranio, la cual se usa como combustible en los reactores nucleares.

fulcrum/fulcro: punto fijo de una palanca. (Cap. 7, pág. 186)

fuse/fusible: un dispositivo que protege un circuito eléctrico. Si fluye mucha corriente, el fusible se derrite interrumpiendo el circuito y detiene así el flujo de corriente.

galvanometer/galvanómetro: un instrumento (medidor) que se usa para detectar corrientes eléctricas; la mayoría de los medidores eléctricos son galvanómetros.

gamma ray/rayo gamma: la más penetrante forma de radiación, la cual no consiste en partículas, sino en ondas electromagnéticas con frecuencia y energía muy altas. Los rayos gamma no tienen ni masa, ni carga y viajan a la velocidad de la luz. (Cap. 24, pág. 681)

gamma ray/rayo gamma: tipo de radiación con la más alta frecuencia y las más penetrantes de todas las ondas electromagnéticas, ubicado en el extremo opuesto al las ondas radiales en el espectro electromagnético. Los núcleos de los átomos radiactivos emiten rayos gamma. (Cap. 19, pág. 534)

gaseous solution/solución gaseosa: un gas homogéneo compuesto de dos o más gases.

gasohol/gasohol: fermentación del maíz para producir alcohol y mezclarlo con gasolina. Este tipo de mezcla permitirá que los abastecimientos actuales de gasolina duren más tiempo. (Cap. 13, pág. 371)

gear/engranaje: una rueda dentada en el borde diseñada para encajar en los dientes de otro engranaje y así transferir la fuerza y el movimiento.

gelatin/gelatina: una sustancia que se obtiene de hervir los huesos de animales. Se usa en las pegas y otros artículos.

generator/generador: dispositivo que produce corriente eléctrica mediante la rotación de una bobina de alambre por un campo magnético. La bobina de alambre se conecta a una fuente de energía mecánica y se coloca en medio de los polos de un imán. (Cap. 22, pág. 633)

geothermal energy/energía geotérmica: tipo de energía que contiene el núcleo terrestre en grandes cantidades. Esta energía se puede utilizar en lugares en donde la corteza terrestre presenta grietas que permiten que parte de la energía geotérmica se escape por ellas. (Cap. 25, pág. 716)

glass/vidrio: cerámica sin la estructura cristalina regular. Existen miles de variedades de vidrios, el más común es el de las ventanas, que está hecho principalmente de oxígeno y silicio, con pequeñas cantidades de sodio y calcio y una pizca de aluminio. (Cap. 14, pág. 394)

graduated cylinder/cilindro graduado: un cilindro marcado con una escala de volumen que se usa en laboratorios para medir volúmenes líquidos.

granite/granito: una roca ígnea que es una mezcla de cristales de diferentes compuestos.

graph/gráfica: despliegue visual de información o datos. (Cap. 2, pág. 48)

graphite/grafito: un mineral hecho de átomos de carbono arreglados en capas que se deslizan fácilmente una sobre otra, formando un lubricante seco.

gravity/gravedad: fuerza que cada objeto en el universo ejerce sobre todos los otros objetos. (Cap. 3, pág. 83)

grounded/soterrado: conectado eléctricamente a tierra, ya sea de forma directa o a través de alambres u otros objetos.

groundwater/agua subterránea: agua que proviene de lluvia y nieve derretida depositada en reservorios bajo tierra. Aunque a menudo es lo suficientemente pura para beber, puede ser contaminada fácilmente por depósitos de basura, cloacas y derrames químicos.

group/grupo: columna vertical en la tabla periódica. (Cap. 10, pág. 288)

hacker/hacker: una persona que usa una computadora para tener acceso ilegalmente a otros sistemas de computadoras.

half–life/período de media vida: cantidad de tiempo que tarda en desintegrarse la mitad de los nucleidos en una muestra de un isótopo radiactivo dado. Los períodos de medias vidas de los isótopos radiactivos varían de un elemento a otro. Por ejemplo, el plutonio–214 tiene un período de media vida de una milésima de segundo, mientras que el período de media vida del uranio–238 es de 4.5 billones de años. (Cap. 24, pág. 681)

halogens/halógenos: elementos altamente activos en el Grupo 17 de la tabla periódica (flúor, cloro, bromo, yodo, astato); los halógenos poseen siete electrones en su exterior y se combinan fácilmente con los elementos del Grupo 1, como el sodio.

heat/calor: energía térmica o interna que fluye desde algo que tiene una temperatura más alta hasta algo con temperatura más baja. El calor siempre fluye de materiales más calientes a materiales más fríos. (Cap. 5, pág. 136)

heat engine/máquina de calor: dispositivo que convierte la energía térmica en energía mecánica. (Cap. 6, pág. 166)

heat mover/movedor de calor: dispositivo que traslada energía térmica de un lugar a otro lugar con una temperatura diferente. (Cap. 6, pág. 168)

heat of fusion/calor de fusión: cantidad de energía necesaria para cambiar un material del estado sólido al líquido. (Cap. 8, pág. 226)

heat of vaporization/calor de evaporación: cantidad de energía necesaria para cambiar un material del estado líquido al gaseoso. (Cap. 8, pág. 226)

herbicide/herbicida: un veneno químico que mata plantas no deseadas.

hertz/hertz: la unidad de medida de la frecuencia, se abrevia Hz. Por ejemplo, 440 ondas por segundo = 440 Hz.

heterogeneous mixture/mezcla heterogénea: mezcla en la que los diferentes materiales que la forman pueden ser distinguidos fácilmente. (Cap. 9, pág. 248)

high-speed photography/fotografía ultrarrápida: un método fotográfico que toma fotografías claras (no borrosas) de objetos que se mueven rápidamente.

homogeneous mixture/mezcla homogénea: mezcla en que dos o más sustancias están esparcidas uniformemente por toda su extensión, como por ejemplo, el agua salada. (Cap. 9, pág. 248)

horizontal/horizontal: una dirección paralela a la superficie terrestre.

hydrate/hidrato: compuesto que tiene agua adherida químicamente a sus iones. Hidrato proviene de la palabra que significa "agua". (Cap. 11, pág. 319)

hydraulic/hidráulico: describe un sistema operado mediante la aplicación de presión a un líquido.

hydrocarbon/hidrocarburo: compuesto formado exclusivamente de átomos de carbono y de hidrógeno. (Cap. 13, pág. 361)

hydroelectricity/hidroelectricidad: electricidad que se produce mediante la utilización del agua en movimiento. Las plantas de energía hidroeléctrica son una manera eficiente de producir electricidad. (Cap. 25, pág. 714)

hydronium ion/ion de hidronio: ion que se forma de la disolución de una molécula polar, como el HCl, en agua. La carga negativa de las moléculas de agua atraen la carga positiva de la molécula polar, extrayendo el H^+ de la molécula polar. (Cap. 17, pág. 472)

hypothesis/hipótesis: predicción científica que se puede medir. (Cap. 1, pág. 16)

ideal machine/máquina ideal: es aquella en que el trabajo de entrada es igual al trabajo de salida. (Cap. 7, pág. 181)

incandescent light/luz incandescente: luz producida por un alambre delgado llamado filamento, el cual por lo general está hecho de tungsteno. (Cap. 19, pág. 544)

inclined plane/plano inclinado: superficie inclinada que se usa para levantar objetos. (Cap. 7, pág. 193)

incoherent light/luz incoherente: luz que puede contener más de una longitud de onda y cuyas ondas electromagnéticas no viajan en la misma dirección, haciendo que el haz se esparza. La luz de una bombilla común y corriente es luz incoherente. (Cap. 20, pág. 576)

independent variable/variable independiente: es el factor que el experimentador modifica. (Cap. 1, pág. 22)

indicator/indicador: compuesto orgánico que cambia de color en un ácido o en una base. (Cap. 17, pág. 466)

induction/inducción: cargar un objeto eléctricamente o crear una corriente eléctrica en el objeto, sin tocarlo físicamente.

inertia/inercia: tendencia de un objeto a resistir cualquier cambio en su movimiento. (Cap. 3, pág. 79)

infrared radiation/radiación infrarroja: radiación con una longitud de onda un poco más larga que la luz visible. La razón por cual la piel se siente más caliente al estar expuesta al sol es porque está absorbiendo parte de la radiación infrarroja proveniente del sol. (Cap. 19, pág. 531)

infrasonic waves/ondas infrasónicas: ondas con frecuencias inferiores a las perceptibles por el oído humano (menos de 20 Hz).

inhibitor/inhibidor: sustancia que impide que ocurra cierta reacción química, como por ejemplo las sustancias preservativas de alimentos BHT y BHA que previenen el deterioro de ciertos alimentos. (Cap. 16, pág. 457)

instantaneous speed/rapidez instantánea: razón de movimiento en cualquier instante dado. (Cap. 3, pág. 64)

insulator/aislador: material que no permite que el calor circule fácilmente a través de él. (Cap. 6, pág. 155)

insulator/aislador: material que no permite que los electrones se muevan fácilmente a través de él. Además del plástico, la madera, el caucho y el vidrio son buenos aisladores. (Cap. 21, pág. 595)

integrated circuit/circuito integrado: circuito que puede contener miles de resistores, diodos y transistores en una lámina delgada de silicio. (Cap. 23, pág. 653)

intensity/intensidad: depende de la cantidad de energía de cada onda sonora. (Cap. 18, pág. 510)

interference/interferencia: capacidad de dos o más ondas de combinarse y formar una nueva onda. (Cap. 18, pág. 519)

internal combustion engine/motor de combustión interna: máquina en que el combustible se quema dentro de unas cámaras llamadas cilindros. (Cap. 6, pág. 166)

ion/ion: átomo con carga negativa o positiva. (Cap. 11, pág. 304)

ionic bond/enlace iónico: fuerza de atracción entre los iones de carga opuesta en un compuesto iónico. (Cap. 11, pág. 305)

ionization/ionización: proceso en que el agua separa las moléculas de ciertas sustancias polares al ser éstas disueltas en agua. (Cap. 15, pág. 433)

isomers/isómeros: compuestos que tienen fórmulas químicas idénticas, pero diferentes estructuras moleculares y formas. (Cap. 13, pág. 364)

isotope/isótopo: átomo del mismo elemento que posee diferentes números de neutrones. (Cap. 10, pág. 279)

joule/julio: la unidad básica de energía y trabajo, nombrada por el científico inglés James Prescott Joule; 1 julio (J) = una fuerza de 1 newton que se mueve a través de una distancia de 1 metro.

kelvin (K)/kelvin (K): es la unidad de temperatura del SI. (Cap. 2, pág. 45)

kilogram/kilogramo: es la unidad de masa del SI. (Cap. 2, pág. 43)

kilowatt-hour/kilovatio-hora: unidad de energía eléctrica. Un kilovatio–hora equivale a 1000 vatios de potencia usada en una hora. (Cap. 21, pág. 616)

kinetic energy/energía cinética: energía en forma de movimiento. (Cap. 5, pág. 125)

kinetic theory of matter/teoría cinética de la materia: ley que dice que toda la materia está compuesta por unas partículas pequeñísimas en constante movimiento. (Cap. 8, pág. 215)

laser/láser: dispositivo que produce rayos de luz coherente. El haz del láser es angosto y enfocado y no se esparce a medida que viaja a través de distancias largas. (Cap. 20, pág. 575)

lanthanide/lantánido: cualquiera de los 14 elementos metálicos con números atómicos del 58 al 71; se usan en imanes, cerámicas e ionoscopios de televisión.

law of conservation of energy/ley de conservación de la energía: enuncia que la energía puede cambiar de forma, pero no puede ser creada ni destrui-

da bajo condiciones común y corrientes. Esta ley se aplica a sistemas cerrados en donde la energía no puede ni entrar ni salir del sistema. (Cap. 5, pág. 129)

law of conservation of mass/ley de conservación de la masa: ley que dice que la materia no puede ser creada ni destruida durante un cambio químico. De acuerdo a esta ley, la masa de todas las sustancias antes de un cambio químico es igual a la masa de todas las sustancias después de dicho cambio químico. (Cap. 9, pág. 260)

law of conservation of momentum/ley de conservación del momento: ley que dice que la cantidad total de momento de un grupo de objetos no cambia a menos que fuerzas exteriores actúen sobre los objetos. (Cap. 4, pág. 115)

lever/palanca: barra que está en libertad de girar, o moverse alrededor de un punto fijo. (Cap. 7, pág. 186)

line graph/gráfica lineal: un tipo de gráfica que se usa para mostrar tendencias haciendo uso de una recta que conecta puntos en la gráfica.

lipid/lípido: compuesto orgánico que contiene los mismos elementos que los carbohidratos, pero en diferentes proporciones y combinaciones, por ejemplo, las grasas y los aceites. (Cap. 13, pág. 377)

liquid solution/solución líquida: un disolvente líquido que ha disuelto un gas, un líquido o un sólido.

liter/litro: ocupa el mismo espacio que un decímetro cúbico. (Cap. 2, pág. 42)

loudness/volumen: percepción humana de la intensidad del sonido. Entre más altas son la intensidad y la amplitud, más alto es el sonido. (Cap. 18, pág. 510)

lubricant/lubricante: sustancia que se usa para disminuir la fricción entre dos superficies que se mueven juntas; por ejemplo, el aceite, la grasa o el grafito.

machine/máquina: dispositivo que facilita el trabajo. (Cap. 7, pág. 180)

magnetic bottle/botella magnética: un poderoso campo magnético que crea un recipiente (botella) para retener el plasma de hidrógeno necesario para causar una reacción de fusión nuclear.

magnetic domain/dominio magnético: grupos de átomos con polos magnéticos alineados en elementos como el cobalto, el níquel y otros materiales magnéticos, en los que el campo magnético creado por cada átomo ejerce una fuerza sobre los otros átomos. (Cap. 22, pág. 626)

magnetic field/campo magnético: región alrededor de un imán en donde actúan las fuerzas magnéticas. (Cap. 22, pág. 624)

magnetic pole/polo magnético: extremo de un imán en donde las fuerzas magnéticas son más fuertes. Todos los imanes tienen dos polos magnéticos opuestos—el norte (N) y el sur (S). Si un imán de barra se suspende de manera que pueda moverse libremente, el extremo norte señalará hacia el norte. (Cap. 22, pág. 624)

magnetism/magnetismo: propiedad de la materia de ejercer una fuerza de atracción entre polos distintos o de repulsión entre polos iguales. Las fuerzas magnéticas son más fuertes cerca de los extremos, o polos magnéticos de un imán. (Cap. 22, pág. 624)

magnifier/amplificador: un dispositivo que hace que las cosas se vean más grandes y con más detalles; por ejemplo, una lupa o un microscopio.

malleable/maleable: propiedad de los metales que hace posible que puedan ser martillados o enrollados en láminas. (Cap. 12, pág. 330)

mass/masa: es una medida de la materia de un objeto. (Cap. 2, pág. 43)

mass number/número de masa: suma del número de protones y de neutrones en el núcleo de un átomo. (Cap. 10, pág. 279)

mechanical advantage (MA)/ventaja mecánica: número de veces en que una máquina multiplica la fuerza de esfuerzo. (Cap. 7, pág. 182)

mechanical energy/energía mecánica: cantidad total de energía cinética y energía potencial en un sistema. (Cap. 5, pág. 129)

medium/medio: material a través del cual una onda transfiere energía. Puede ser sólido, líquido, gas o una combinación de estos. Las ondas radiales y las ondas luminosas son dos tipos de ondas que pueden viajar sin necesidad de un medio. (Cap. 18, pág. 498)

melt/derretir: cambio de una sustancia del estado sólido al líquido cuando se le calienta a más del punto de fusión o de congelación.

melting point/punto de fusión: la temperatura a la cual un sólido se convierte en líquido.

metal/metal: elemento cuyas propiedades comunes son que existe en forma sólida a temperatura ambiental, es brillante y buen conductor de calor y electricidad. (Cap. 10, pág. 290)

metallic bonding/enlace metálico: tipo de enlace en que los iones metálicos positivos están rodeados por un "mar de electrones". (Cap. 12, pág. 331)

metalloid/metaloide: elemento ubicado a los lados de la línea divisoria escalonada de la tabla periódica. (Cap. 10, pág. 291)

meter/metro: es la unidad básica de longitud del SI. La longitud de un bate de béisbol es de más o menos un metro. Las reglas métricas y las varas se usan para medir la longitud. (Cap. 2, pág. 38)

microprocessor/microprocesador: dispositivo que funciona como el cerebro de la computadora. Consiste de un circuito integrado en el tablero principal de circuitos. Recibe datos del usuario y ordena a otras partes de la computadora cómo responder, así como el cerebro de una persona ordena a una mano que se retire de algo caliente. (Cap. 23, pág. 659)

microscope/microscopio: instrumento que usa dos lentes convexas con longitudes focales relativamente cortas para ampliar objetos pequeños y cercanos. (Cap. 20, pág. 570)

microwave/microonda: onda radial con la más altas frecuencia y energía. Algunos usos de las microondas son en la comunicación y en los hornos de microondas. (Cap. 19, pág. 530)

mixture/mezcla: material hecho de elementos o compuestos revueltos, pero que no están combinados químicamente.

model/modelo: idea, sistema o estructura que representa cualquier cosa que uno trate de explicar. Un modelo nunca es exactamente igual a lo que uno trata de explicar, pero se parece lo suficiente para permitir comparaciones. (Cap. 1, pág. 12)

modulation/modulación: proceso de variar las ondas radiales. Además de la voz, otras cosas como las imágenes luminosas, la información de computadoras y la música también se pueden usar para modular las ondas radiales. (Cap. 19, pág. 530)

momentum/momento: una propiedad que posee un objeto en movimiento debido a su masa y a su velocidad. (Cap. 4, pág. 112)

monomers/monómeros: moléculas orgánicas enhebradas para formar polímeros.

music/música: sonido que se crea usando tonos específicos y calidad sonora, siguiendo un patrón regular. (Cap. 18, pág. 516)

nearsighted/miope: describe a una persona que ve claramente los objetos cercanos, pero que tiene dificultad enfocando los objetos lejanos.

net force/fuerza neta: fuerza impuesta sobre un objeto, la cual siempre hace que cambie su velocidad. (Cap. 3, pág. 78)

neutralization/neutralización: reacción química entre un ácido y una base. Durante una reacción de neutralización, los iones de hidronio del ácido se combinan con los iones de hidronio de la base para producir agua. A medida que los iones de hidróxido y de hidronio reactivos son extraídos de la solución, las propiedades ácidas y básicas de los reactantes se cancelan o neutralizan. Las reacciones de neutralización son iónicas. (Cap. 17, pág. 480)

neutralize/neutralizar: proceso de cambiar una solución ácida o una básica, de manera que sea neutra.

neutron/neutrón: uno de dos tipos principales de partículas que componen el núcleo de un átomo. Tiene casi la misma masa que un protón. (Cap. 10, pág. 271)

Newton's first law of motion/primera ley de movimiento de Newton: esta ley enuncia que un objeto que se mueve a una rapidez constante continúa moviéndose a esa rapidez a menos que una fuerza neta actúe sobre él. (Cap. 3, pág. 81)

Newton's second law of motion/segunda ley de movimiento de Newton: ley que dice que una fuerza neta que actúa sobre un objeto hace que el objeto acelere en la dirección de la fuerza. (Cap. 4, pág. 94)

Newton's third law of motion/tercera ley de movimiento de Newton: ley que describe pares de fuerzas de acción–reacción de la siguiente manera: cuando un objeto ejerce una fuerza sobre un segundo objeto, el segundo, ejerce sobre el primero una fuerza igual en tamaño y opuesta en dirección. En otras palabras, por cada fuerza de acción existe una fuerza de reacción igual y opuesta. (Cap. 4, pág. 110)

NIMBY (Not in My Backyard)/NIMBY (No en mi vecindario): punto de vista apoyado por mucha gente que está de acuerdo con el uso de las plantas de energía nuclear, siempre y cuando no se construyan muy cerca a sus vecindarios. (Cap. 25, pág. 710)

noise/ruido: sonido que carece de patrón regular y de tono. (Cap. 18, pág. 516)

nonelectrolyte/no electrolítica: sustancia que no conduce electricidad, como el agua pura. (Cap. 15, pág. 433)

nonmetal/no metal: elemento ubicado a la derecha de la línea divisoria en forma de escalera de la tabla periódica. (Cap. 10, pág. 291)

nonpolar molecule/molécula no polar: molécula que carece de extremos con carga opuesta. (Cap. 11, pág. 307)

nonrenewable resource/recurso no renovable: fuente energética, como los combustibles fósiles, que no se puede reemplazar después de ser usada. (Cap. 25, pág. 703)

normal/normal: una línea imaginaria perpendicular a una superficie reflectora o perpendicular a la superficie de un medio al cual entra la luz.

nuclear fission/fisión nuclear: proceso de romper un núcleo en dos núcleos más pequeños. La palabra fisión quiere decir "dividir". Los núcleos grandes, con números atómicos mayores de 90 pueden ser sometidos a la fisión nuclear. (Cap. 24, pág. 689)

nuclear fusion/fusión nuclear: combinación (o unión) de dos núcleos de masas bajas para formar un núcleo de mayor masa. (Cap. 24, pág. 690)

nuclear reactor/reactor nuclear: dispositivo que usa la energía de una reacción de fisión nuclear en cadena controlada para generar electricidad. (Cap. 25, pág. 704)

nuclear waste/desperdicio nuclear: subproducto radiactivo que resulta del uso de materiales radiactivos. (Cap. 25, pág. 706)

nucleic acid/ácido nucleico: polímero que controla las actividades y la reproducción de las células. Un tipo de ácido nucleico es el ácido desoxirribonucleico, DNA. (Cap. 13, pág. 375)

nucleus/núcleo: centro con carga positiva del átomo. Contiene la mayor parte de la carga de un átomo. (Cap. 10, pág. 270)

nuclide/nucleido: núcleo de un isótopo con cierto número y masa atómicos. En muchos nucleidos, la fuerza nuclear fuerte es suficiente para mantener el núcleo unido permanentemente, creando así un nucleido estable. (Cap. 24, pág. 675)

observation/observación: primer paso en un método científico, en el cual se usan los sentidos para reunir información. En la ciencia, usamos instrumentos como microscopios y balanzas para reunir cuidadosamente observaciones precisas y detalladas. (Cap. 1, pág. 16)

ocean thermal energy conversion (OTEC)/conversión de energía térmica del océano: proceso que utiliza máquinas de calor para convertir las diferencias en temperatura del agua del océano en energía mecánica para accionar turbinas y producir electricidad. (Cap. 6, pág. 173)

ohm/ohmio: la unidad para medir la resistencia.

Ohm's law/ley de Ohm: esta ley enuncia que la diferencia de potencial = corriente × resistencia, o $V = I$ (amperios) × R (ohmios). (Cap. 21, pág. 606)

opaque material/material opaco: material que absorbe o refleja toda la luz y no permite ver ningún objeto a través de él. (Cap. 18, pág. 536)

optical axis/eje óptico: una línea perpendicular al centro de un espejo o una lente.

optical fiber/fibra óptica: fibra de vidrio transparente que puede transmitir la luz de un lugar a otro. (Cap. 20, pág. 578)

organic compound/compuesto orgánico: nombre con que se denominan la mayoría de los compuestos que contienen carbono. Existen algunas excepciones como el monóxido de carbono y los carbonatos. (Cap. 13, pág. 360)

organic solvent/disolvente orgánico: tipo de disolvente que se encuentra en el pegamento, las pinturas, el quitapinturas, el diluyente de pintura o barniz y algunos compuestos de calafateo y alfombrado. Se sabe que muchos disolventes orgánicos afectan el sistema nervioso y ocasionan problemas de crecimiento y desarrollo. En algunos casos, se ha sabido que varios de ellos causan cáncer. (Cap. 15, pág. 422)

oxidation number/número de oxidación: número positivo o negativo asignado a cada elemento para mostrar su capacidad de enlace en un compuesto. (Cap. 11, pág. 314)

parallel circuit/circuito en paralelo: circuito que tiene bifurcaciones a lo largo de las cuales se mueve la corriente. (Cap. 21, pág. 609)

pascal (Pa)/pascal: es la unidad de presión del SI. (Cap. 8, pág. 228)

Pascal's principle/principio de Pascal: el científico francés Blaise Pascal enunció que la presión que se le aplica a un fluido es transmitida sin cambio a través del fluido. (Cap. 8, pág. 236)

passive solar heating/calefacción solar pasiva: uso directo de la energía solar para calentar algo, sin usar ventiladores ni dispositivos mecánicos para transferir el calor de un área a otra.

period/período: hilera horizontal de elementos en la tabla periódica. (Cap. 10, pág. 290)

periodic table/tabla periódica: tabla en que los elementos se clasifican en orden de masa atómica ascendente. Está organizada en hileras y columnas para mostrar las propiedades repetitivas (periódicas) de los elementos. (Cap. 10, pág. 284)

PET/PET: (Positron Emission Tomography o tomografía de emisión de positrones) avance tecnológico en la medicina, en que mediante el análisis de rayos gama emisores se pueden revelar tumores en el encéfalo. (Cap. 24, pág. 693)

petroleum/petróleo: fuente líquida de energía que se formó de la descomposición de plantas y animales hace millones de años. El petróleo, junto con el gas natural y el carbón, se llaman combustibles fósiles. (Cap. 25, pág. 700)

pH/pH: medida de la concentración de iones de hidronio en una solución. (Cap. 17, pág. 475)

phenolphthalein/fenolftaleína: Una sustancia química que se usa como un indicador del color en valoración. Es incolora en una solución ácida, pero se vuelve rosada en una solución básica.

photon/fotón: cuanto diminuto de radiación que se parece a una partícula. Los fotones con la más alta energía corresponden a la luz con la frecuencia más alta. Los fotones con muy alta energía pueden en realidad causar daños a la materia, como por ejemplo, las células del cuerpo humano. (Cap. 19, pág. 529)

photovoltaic cell/pila fotovoltaica: también llamada pila solar, este es un dispositivo que se usa para convertir energía solar en electricidad. (Cap. 25, pág. 713)

physical change/cambio físico: cambio en tamaño, forma o estado de la materia. (Cap. 9, pág. 256)

physical property/propiedad física: cualquier característica que se puede observar en un material sin cambiar las sustancias que lo componen. Por ejemplo: color, forma, tamaño, densidad, punto de ebullición y punto de fusión. (Cap. 9, pág. 254)

physical science/ciencia física: el estudio de la materia y la energía. En el universo, todas las cosas que se pueden medir son materia o energía. Las plantas y los animales, las rocas y las nubes, los huevos y los elefantes son ejemplos de materia. Los relámpagos, los rayos, el movimiento y la luz solar son ejemplos de energía. (Cap. 1, pág. 8)

pickling/decapado: proceso en que se eliminan los óxidos y otras impurezas de las superficies de los metales, mediante la inmersión en ácido clorhídrico. (Cap. 17, pág. 469)

pigment/pigmento: material de color que absorbe algunos colores y refleja otros. Los artistas utilizan los pigmentos para hacer varios colores de pinturas. (Cap. 19, pág. 540)

pitch/tono: la agudeza o gravedad de un sonido, dependiendo de la frecuencia de las ondas sonoras. (Cap. 18, pág. 508)

plane mirror/espejo plano: espejo con una superficie plana. (Cap. 20, pág. 558)

plankton/plancton: plantas y animales acuáticos que forman la base de la cadena alimenticia para los peces pequeños. (Cap. 17, pág. 478)

plasma/plasma: mezcla parecida a un gas de partículas con cargas positivas y negativas. (Cap. 8, pág. 218)

plastic/plástico: material con base de polímeros que puede ser moldeado en diferentes formas. (Cap. 14, pág. 396)

polar molecule/molécula polar: molécula con un extremo positivo y otro negativo. (Cap. 11, pág. 307)

polarized light/luz polarizada: luz en la cual las ondas transversales vibran en un solo plano. (Cap. 20, pág. 574)

polarizing filter/filtro polarizador: un filtro formado de cadenas de moléculas, ubicadas en hileras paralelas que transmiten solo las ondas luminosas que vibran en la misma dirección de las cadenas moleculares.

polluted water/agua contaminada: se refiere al agua que contiene niveles tan altos de materiales residuales que esto la hace inaceptable para beber y otros propósitos específicos. (Cap. 8, pág. 222)

polyatomic ion/ion poliatómico: grupo de átomos unidos covalentemente y cargados positiva o negativamente, de manera que el compuesto en su totalidad contiene tres o más elementos. Muchos compuestos, incluyendo la soda de hornear, están compuestos de dos o más elementos porque contienen iones poliatómicos. El prefijo *poli* significa "-muchos", por consiguiente la palabra poliatómico quiere decir "muchos átomos". (Cap. 11, pág. 318)

polymer/polímero: molécula enorme compuesta de muchas moléculas orgánicas más pequeñas que han formado nuevos enlaces y se han unido unas a otras. (Cap. 13, pág. 373)

positron/positrón: una partícula con carga positiva parecida a un electrón.

potential difference/diferencia de potencial: diferencia en potencial entre dos lugares diferentes. Se mide en voltios, (V). (Cap. 21, pág. 600)

potential energy/energía potencial: es la energía almacenada. (Cap. 5, pág. 125)

power/potencia: proporción a la cual se realiza trabajo. (Cap. 7, pág. 202)

precipitate/precipitado: compuesto insoluble que se forma durante una reacción de desplazamiento doble. (Cap. 16, pág. 453)

pressure/presión: cantidad de fuerza ejercida por unidad de área. (Cap. 8, pág. 228)

principle/principio: una regla o ley básica que describe cómo funciona siempre algo en la naturaleza; por ejemplo, "la gravedad siempre atrae los objetos unos hacia otros".

product/producto: sustancia producida en una reacción química. (Cap. 16, pág. 442)

projectile/proyectil: cualquier cosa que se dispara o se lanza al aire. (Cap. 4, pág. 100)

propane/propano: un gas inflamable (C_3H_8); una parte del gas natural.

protein/proteína: polímero formado de compuestos orgánicos llamados aminoácidos. Existen millones de proteínas, pero solo 20 aminoácidos comunes.

(Cap. 13, pág. 373)

proton/protón: uno de dos tipos principales de partículas que componen el núcleo de un átomo. Tiene casi la misma masa que un neutrón. (Cap. 10, pág. 271)

pulley/polea: rueda que contiene una ranura por donde se puede pasar una cuerda o cadena. (Cap. 7, pág. 190)

quality/calidad: describe las diferencias entre los sonidos del mismo tono y volumen. (Cap. 18, pág. 517)

quark/quark: partícula pequeñísima que compone el protón y el neutrón. (Cap. 10, pág. 276)

radiation/radiación: transferencia de energía en forma de ondas. (Cap. 6, pág. 154)

radiator/radiador: dispositivo que tiene un área de superficie grande, el cual está diseñado para calentar el aire a su alrededor, por medio de la conducción. (Cap. 6, pág. 162)

radio wave/onda radial: onda con longitud de onda larga y frecuencia baja. Las ondas radiales poseen la energía más baja de los fotones. (Cap. 19, pág. 529)

radioactive element/elemento radiactivo: elemento cuyo núcleo se descompone e irradia partículas de energía. (Cap. 12, pág. 332)

radioactivity/radiactividad: emisión de radiación de alta energía o de partículas del núcleo de un átomo radiactivo. (Cap. 24, pág. 674)

RAM/RAM: (*Random Access Memory* o memoria de acceso aleatorio) tipo de memoria temporal de microcomputadora que almacena datos, documentos y programas mientras están en uso. La información almacenada en RAM se pierde cuando se apaga la computadora. (Cap. 23, pág. 660)

rarefaction/rarefacción: el área menos densa de la onda, en ondas de compresión.

reactant/reactante: cualquier sustancia que está a punto de reaccionar en una reacción química. (Cap. 16, pág. 442)

real image/imagen real: imagen verdadera ampliada

y patas arriba en la cual los rayos luminosos se encuentran en la imagen, de modo que uno puede ver una pantalla sostenida allí. (Cap. 20, pág. 559)

rectifier/rectificador: dispositivo que cambia la corriente alterna en corriente directa. (Cap. 23, pág. 651)

reflecting telescope/telescopio reflector: telescopio que usa un espejo cóncavo, un espejo plano y una lente convexa para ampliar objetos distantes. (Cap. 20, pág. 569)

reflection/reflexión: ocurre cuando una onda choca contra un objeto y rebota del mismo. La reflexión ocurre con todo tipo de ondas—electromagnéticas, de sonido y de agua. (Cap. 19, pág. 546)

refracting telescope/telescopio refractor: telescopio que usa dos lentes convexas para recoger y enfocar la luz de objetos distantes. (Cap. 20, pág. 568)

refraction/refracción: cambio en la dirección de propagación de las ondas causado por un cambio en velocidad al moverse de un medio a otro. La cantidad de refracción depende de la velocidad de la luz en ambos materiales. Entre mayor sea la diferencia entre las velocidades en los dos medios, más se dobla o refracta la luz al pasar, haciendo un ángulo de un medio al otro. (Cap. 19, pág. 547)

resistance/resistencia: tendencia de los materiales a oponerse al flujo de electrones, cambiando la energía eléctrica en energía térmica y luz. La resistencia se mide en ohms. (Cap. 21, pág. 603)

resistance arm/brazo de resistencia: parte de la palanca que ejerce la fuerza de resistencia. (Cap. 7, pág. 186)

resistance force (F_r)/fuerza de resistencia: la fuerza aplicada por la máquina para superar la resistencia. (Cap. 7, pág. 181)

resonance/resonancia: tipo de vibración que sucede cuando el sonido que llega hasta un objeto tiene la misma frecuencia natural del objeto, haciendo que el objeto comience a vibrar a esa frecuencia. (Cap. 18, pág. 517)

reverberation/reverberación: efecto producido por múltiples reflexiones del sonido. (Cap. 18, pág. 520)

RNA/RNA: Ácido RiboNucleico; un ácido nucleico que controla la producción de las proteínas que forman nuevas células.

ROM/ROM: (*Read Only Memory* o memoria de solo lectura) tipo de información almacenada permanentemente en una computadora y la cual contiene las instrucciones necesarias para que el microprocesador pueda hacer funcionar la computadora. La computadora puede leer este tipo de información, pero el usuario no puede añadirle más ni cambiar este tipo de información. La información en ROM queda almacenada permanentemente, es decir, no se pierde cuando se apaga la computadora. (Cap. 23, pág. 660)

salt/sal: compuesto que se forma cuando los iones negativos de un ácido se combinan con los iones positivos de una base. (Cap. 17, pág. 480)

saponification/saponificación: proceso de fabricación del jabón. (Cap. 17, pág. 483)

saturated hydrocarbon/hidrocarburo saturado: hidrocarburo que solo contiene átomos de carbono de enlace sencillo. (Cap. 13, pág. 362)

saturated solution/solución saturada: solución que ha disuelto todo el disolvente que era capaz de disolver normalmente, a una temperatura dada. (Cap. 15, pág. 426)

scientific law/ley científica: regla de la naturaleza que resume observaciones relacionadas y resultados experimentales con el propósito de describir patrones en la naturaleza. (Cap. 1, pág. 17)

screw/tornillo: plano inclinado enrollado en forma de espiral alrededor de un poste cilíndrico. (Cap. 7, pág. 194)

second/segundo: es la unidad de tiempo del SI. (Cap. 2, pág. 44)

semiconductor/semiconductor: material que conduce una corriente eléctrica bajo ciertas circunstancias. (Cap. 12, pág. 346)

series circuit/circuito en serie: circuito en el que la corriente solo tiene una ruta a través de la cual puede fluir. (Cap. 21, pág. 608)

SI/SI: o sistema internacional de unidades, es el sistema estándar de medidas que se usa a través del mundo. En el SI, cada tipo de medida tiene una unidad básica, como por ejemplo, el metro, que es la unidad básica de longitud. (Cap. 2, pág. 35)

simple machine/máquina simple: dispositivo que realiza trabajo con un solo movimiento. (Cap. 7, pág. 180)

single–displacement reaction/reacción de desplazamiento simple: ocurre cuando un elemento reemplaza a otro en un compuesto. (Cap. 16, pág. 452)

soap/jabón: sal orgánica. Se forma de la reacción de grasas o aceites con hidróxido de sodio o de potasio. (Cap. 17, pág. 483)

solar collector/colector solar: dispositivo que absorbe la energía radiante del Sol. (Cap. 6, pág. 164)

solar energy/energía solar: energía proveniente del sol. (Cap. 6, pág. 163)

solubility/solubilidad: máximo número de gramos de una sustancia que se pueden disolver en 100 gramos de disolvente a cierta temperatura. (Cap. 15, pág. 424)

solute/soluto: sustancia que se disuelve en el disolvente. (Cap. 15, pág. 417)

solution/solución: es otro nombre para una mezcla homogénea. (Cap. 9, pág. 248)

solvent/disolvente: sustancia que disuelve el soluto. (Cap. 15, pág. 417)

specific heat/calor específico: es la cantidad de energía que se necesita para subir un kelvin, en la temperatura de un kilogramo de material. (Cap. 5, pág. 141)

speed/rapidez: razón de cambio en posición. (Cap. 3, pág. 64)

standard/estándar: una cantidad exacta que la gente acuerda usar para hacer comparaciones. (Cap. 2, pág. 34)

state of matter/estado de la materia: cada una de las cuatro formas en que puede existir la materia: sólido, líquido, gas y plasma. (Cap. 8, pág. 214)

static electricity/electricidad estática: acumulación de cargas eléctricas en un objeto. (Cap. 21, pág. 592)

step-down transformer/transformador rebajador: un transformador eléctrico que disminuye (rebaja) el voltaje de una línea de fuerza eléctrica.

step-up transformer/transformador elevador: un transformador eléctrico que aumenta (eleva) el voltaje de una línea de fuerza eléctrica.

strong acid/ácido fuerte: ácido que se ioniza casi completamente en solución. (Cap. 17, pág. 474)

strong base/base fuerte: es la que se disocia completamente en solución. (Cap. 17, pág. 474)

sublimation/sublimación: proceso en que un sólido cambia directamente a vapor sin pasar por el estado líquido. (Cap. 12, pág. 343)

submerge/sumergir: introducir y cubrir completamente algo en un líquido.

substance/sustancia: puede ser un elemento o un compuesto. (Cap. 9, pág. 247)

substituted hydrocarbon/hidrocarburo de sustitución: hidrocarburo en que uno más de sus átomos de hidrógeno han sido reemplazados por átomos de otros elementos. (Cap. 13, pág. 367)

supercollider/superchocador: un dispositivo que hace que los protones choquen a altas velocidades y se conviertan en quarks.

superconductors/superconductores: materiales que no presentan resistencia eléctrica. Cuando estos materiales se sobreenfrían a una temperatura de casi cero absoluto (0K), –273°C, pierden toda resistencia a la electricidad. (Cap. 22, pág. 640)

supersaturated solution/solución supersaturada: solución que contiene más soluto que una solución saturada a una temperatura dada. (Cap. 15, pág. 428)

suspension/suspensión: mezcla heterogénea que contiene un líquido en el cual se han asentado las partículas visibles. (Cap. 9, pág. 250)

synthesis reaction/reacción de síntesis: reacción en la cual dos o más sustancias se combinan para formar otra sustancia. (Cap. 16, pág. 451)

synthetic fiber/fibra sintética: filamento de un polímero sintético. Un filamento de una fibra sintética llamada Kevlar es cinco veces más fuerte que un filamento similar de acero. (Cap. 14, pág. 399)

technology/tecnología: uso práctico de la información tecnológica. Los descubrimientos científicos pueden conducir a innovaciones tecnológicas, las cuales a su vez, pueden conducir a más descubrimientos. Tanto la ciencia pura, para el avance de los conocimientos, como la ciencia aplicada, o tecnología, son partes importantes de la ciencia. (Cap. 1, pág. 8)

telephoto lens/teleobjetivo: lente con distancia focal más larga y ubicado más lejos de la película que un objetivo granangular. Son fáciles de reconocer porque sobresalen de la cámara para aumentar la distancia entre la lente y la película. La imagen se ve ampliada y el objeto parece estar más cerca de lo que en realidad está. (Cap. 20, pág. 571)

temperature/temperatura: es una medida del promedio de energía cinética de las partículas en una muestra de materia. (Cap. 5, pág. 134)

terminal velocity/velocidad terminal: es la máxima velocidad alcanzada por un objeto que cae. (Cap. 4, pág. 99)

theory/teoría: explicación basada en muchas observaciones, las cuales se basan en resultados experimentales. Es la manera más lógica de explicar el funcionamiento de las cosas. (Cap. 1, pág. 17)

thermal energy/energía térmica: es la energía total de las partículas en un material. Este total incluye tanto energía cinética como potencial. (Cap. 5, pág. 135)

thermal expansion/expansión térmica: cualidad que tiene la materia de expandirse cuando se calienta y de contraerse cuando se enfría. (Cap. 8, pág. 219)

thermal pollution/contaminación térmica: agua calentada excesivamente por las plantas de energía eléctrica o las industrias y que luego se vierte en los ríos o fuentes de agua. (Cap. 8, pág. 223)

thermal pollution/contaminación térmica: ocurre cuando el calor residual cambia la temperatura del ambiente de modo significativo. (Cap. 5, pág. 138)

thermonuclear fusion/fusión termonuclear: fusión nuclear que ocurre bajo condiciones de intenso calor (millones de grados), como en una estrella o en nuestro sol.

tidal energy/energía de las mareas: energía generada por el movimiento de las mareas del océano. (Cap. 25, pág. 714)

time/tiempo: intervalo entre dos eventos. (Cap. 2, pág. 44)

titration/valoración: proceso en que una solución de concentración conocida se usa para determinar la concentración de otra solución. (Cap. 17, pág. 481)

total internal reflection/reflexión interna total: ocurre cuando la luz que choca contra una superficie entre dos materiales se refleja completamente en el primer material. (Cap. 20, pág. 577)

toxic/tóxico: compuestos venenosos. (Cap. 11, pág. 312)

tracer/indicador radiactivo: uso de radioisótopos dentro del cuerpo humano para inspeccionar los procesos corporales. El carbono–11, el yodo–131 y el sodio–123 son indicadores radiactivos porque poseen medias vidas relativamente cortas. (Cap. 24, pág. 692)

transformer/transformador: dispositivo que puede aumentar o disminuir el voltaje de una corriente alterna. Su funcionamiento involucra principios tanto de electromagnetismo como de inducción electromagnética. (Cap. 22, pág. 635)

transistor/transistor: semiconductor que amplifica o fortalece una señal eléctrica o que actúa como un diminuto interruptor eléctrico. (Cap. 23, pág. 651)

transition element/elemento de transición: elementos pertenecientes a los grupos del 3 al 12 de la tabla periódica. (Cap. 12, pág. 334)

translucent material/material translúcido: material que permite que cierta luz lo atraviese, pero no deja ver claramente los objetos a través de él. (Cap. 19, pág. 536)

transmutation/transmutación: proceso de cambiar un elemento en otro mediante la desintegración nuclear. (Cap. 24, pág. 680)

transparent material/material transparente: material que permite que la luz los atraviese y por consiguiente deja ver los objetos a través de él. (Cap. 19, pág. 536)

transuranium elements/elementos transuránicos: elementos que tienen más de 92 protones, que es el número atómico del uranio. Todos estos elementos sintéticos son inestables y se descomponen rápidamente. (Cap. 12, pág. 338)

transverse wave/onda transversal: tipo de onda en el cual el medio se mueve formando ángulos rectos con la dirección en que viaja la onda. (Cap. 18, pág. 499)

trough/valle: punto más bajo de una onda. (Cap. 18, pág. 499)

Tyndall effect/efecto de Tyndall: el esparcimiento de la luz por las partículas de una mezcla. (Cap. 9, pág. 249)

ultrasonic technology/tecnología ultrasónica: tecnología que hace uso del ultrasonido para una variedad de propósitos, como en la joyería, en la medicina y en la industria química. (Cap. 18, pág. 514)

ultraviolet radiation/radiación ultravioleta: radiación con frecuencia más alta que la luz visible, de modo que sus fotones son más energéticos y tienen más potencia de penetración que los fotones de la luz visible. (Cap. 18, pág. 532)

unsaturated hydrocarbon/hidrocarburo no saturado: hidrocarburo, como el etino o el eteno, que contiene por lo menos un enlace doble o triple entre los átomos de carbono. (Cap. 13, pág. 364)

unsaturated solution/solución no saturada: cualquier solución que puede disolver más soluto, a cierta temperatura dada. (Cap. 15, pág. 427)

velocity/velocidad: describe tanto la rapidez como la dirección de un objeto. (Cap. 3, pág. 72)

Venturi effect/efecto de Venturi: aumento en la velocidad de un fluido, que al ser forzado a fluir a través de espacios estrechos, disminuye su presión. Una demostración dramática del efecto de venturi ha ocurrido en ciudades donde el viento es forzado a fluir entre hileras de rascacielos—la reducción en presión fuera del edificio durante vientos fuertes ha hecho que las ventanas se desprendan debido a que la presión dentro del edificio es mayor. (Cap. 8, pág. 238)

virtual image/imagen virtual: imagen en la cual los rayos luminosos no pasan a través de ella. La imagen virtual que forma un espejo plano está erguida y aparece tan atrás del espejo como el objeto esté en frente del mismo. (Cap. 20, pág. 558)

visible radiation/radiación visible: o luz, es la única parte del espectro electromagnético que podemos ver. Cubre solo un pequeño alcance del espectro, comparada con otros tipos de energía. (Cap. 19, pág. 532) volt/voltio: la unidad para medir el potencial de energía eléctrica. Se abrevia V.

voltage/voltaje: una diferencia en potencial eléctrico, medida en voltios con un voltímetro.

voltmeter/voltímetro: instrumento que mide, en voltios, la diferencia de potencial en un circuito. (Cap. 22, pág. 630)

volume/volumen: cantidad de espacio que ocupa un objeto. (Cap. 2, pág. 41)

wave/onda: perturbación rítmica que transporta energía a través de la materia o del espacio. (Cap. 18, pág. 498)

wavelength/longitud de onda: distancia entre un punto de una onda y otro punto idéntico en la siguiente onda, como por ejemplo, de una cresta a la siguiente o de un valle al siguiente. (Cap. 18, pág. 499)

weak acid/ácido débil: ácido que solo se ioniza parcialmente en solución. (Cap. 17, pág. 474)

weak base/base débil: es la que no se disocia completamente en solución. (Cap. 17, pág. 474)

wedge/cuña: plano inclinado con uno o dos lados que se inclinan. (Cap. 7, pág. 194)

weight/peso: medida de la fuerza de gravedad sobre un objeto. (Cap. 3, pág. 84)

wet cell/pila húmeda: es la que tiene dos placas conectadas, las cuales están hechas de diferentes metales o compuestos metálicos, en una solución electrolítica. La mayoría de las baterías de los carros, llamadas baterías de almacenaje de plomo, contienen una serie de seis pilas húmedas hechas de placas de plomo y de dióxido de plomo en una solución de ácido sulfúrico. (Cap. 21, pág. 602)

wheel and axle/rueda y eje: máquina simple que consiste en dos ruedas de diferentes tamaños las cuales rotan juntas. (Cap. 7, pág. 191)

wide-angle lens/objetivo granangular: lente con distancia focal corta que produce una imagen relativamente pequeña del objeto pero que incluye la mayor parte de sus alrededores. Este tipo de lente debe colocarse cerca de la película para enfocar la imagen con su corta longitud focal. (Cap. 20, pág. 571)

work/trabajo: transferencia de energía a través del movimiento. (Cap. 5, pág. 126)

X ray/rayo X: tipo de radiación que posee una longitud de onda más corta y una frecuencia más alta que la radiación ultravioleta. Los fotones de los rayos X transportan energía más alta y poseen una mayor potencia de penetración que cualquier otro tipo de radiación electromagnética, a excepción de los rayos gamma. (Cap. 19, pág. 534)

Index

The Index for *Glencoe Physical Science* will help you locate major topics in the book quickly and easily. Each entry in the Index is followed by the numbers of the pages on which the entry is discussed. A page number given in **boldface type** indicates the page on which that entry is defined. A page number given in *italic type* indicates a page on which the entry is used in an illustration or photograph. The abbreviation *act.* indicates a page on which the entry is used in an activity.

15, 31, 42, 45, 48, Morgan-Cain and Associates; 48, David Ashby; 49, 50, 51, 57, 65, 67, Morgan-Cain and Associates; 68, Bill Singleton/John Edwards; 69, Precision Graphics; 70, 73, 74, Morgan-Cain and Associates; 86, Thomas Gagliano; 91, Morgan-Cain and Associates; 98, Antonio Castro; 101, 108, 109, Morgan-Cain and Associates; 110, Antonio Castro; 112, Jim Shough; 121, Morgan-Cain and Associates; 125, George Bucktell; 128, Dick Smith; 132, 133, 134, 139, Morgan-Cain and Associates; 143, Henry Hill; 149, Morgan-Cain and Associates; 152, Sarah Woodward; 154, 155, Morgan-Cain and Associates; 157, George Bucktell; 158, Jacque Auger; 162, 163, 164, 165, Morgan-Cain and Associates; 166, Thomas Gagliano; 167, Jacque Auger; 168, Morgan-Cain and Associates; 173, Thomas Gagliano; 177, 181, 183, 186, 188, Morgan-Cain and Associates; 189, Thomas Gagliano; 190, 191, Morgan-Cain and Associates; 192, Henry Hill/John Edwards; 197, 199, Thomas Gagliano; 207, (top right) Morgan-Cain and Associates; 207, (bottom left) Dick Smith; 208, Tom Kennedy/Romark Illustration; 215, 216, Morgan-Cain and Associates; 217, Jim Shough; 226, Henry Hill; 226, 228, 231, 235, Morgan-Cain and Associates; 236, Henry Hill/John Edwards; 243, 248, 249, 252 Morgan-Cain and Associates; 272, Henry Hill; 273, 276, 277, 279, Morgan-Cain and Associates; 281, Henry Hill; 285, (t) & (b) Morgan-Cain and Associates; 286-287, Dave Reed; 289 (t) & (b), 295, 299 (t) & (b), 301 (t) & (b), 302, 304, 305 (t) & (b), 306 (t) & (b), 308, 314, 315, 323 (t) & (b), 325, 327, 331-334, 336 (t) & (b), 338-340, 341 (t) & (b), 342, 343, 346, Morgan-Cain and Associates; 347 (t), Tom Kennedy/Romark Illustrations; 347 (b), 348 (t), Morgan-Cain and Associates; 348 (b), George Bucktell; 349, 350, 357, 361 (t) & (b), 362, 363, (t) & (b), 366 (t) & (b), 367, 373, 375, 390, Morgan-Cain and Associates; 398, 400, Jacque Auger; 409, 411, 418, 419, 427, 432, 433 (t) & (b), 445, 446, 463, 469, 472, 473, 475, Morgan-Cain and Associates; 478, 479, Chris Forsey; 481, 483, Morgan-Cain and Associates; 493, Tom Kennedy/Romark Illustration; 499, 500, 505, 506, Morgan-Cain and Associates; 508, Jim Jobst; 510 (t), Morgan-Cain and Associates; 510 (b), Chris Forsey; 517, 518, Morgan-Cain and Associates; 519, Glen Wasserman; 529, 530, 533, 538, Morgan-Cain and Associates; 540, Bill Watterson; 541, 542, 544, 546, 547, 550, 555, Morgan-Cain and Associates; 558, 559, 562, 564, 565, 566, 567, Thomas Gagliano; 569, Jim Shough; 570, David Fischer; 573, Jacque Auger; 574, 576, Thomas Gagliano; 579, Jacque Auger; 556, 592, 593, Morgan-Cain and Associates; 597, Henry Hill/John Edwards; 600, Sarah Woodward; 601, Morgan-Cain and Associates; 602, Jacque Auger; 604, 610, 621, Morgan-Cain and Associates; 634, Jacque Auger; 646, 649, 658-659, 671, 654-655, 675, 679, 680, 689, Morgan-Cain and Associates; 690, Henry Hill; 697, 701, 704-705, 710, Morgan-Cain and Associates; 714, Tom Kennedy/Romark Illustration; 735, 736 (t) & (b), 737, 738 (t) & (b), 740 (t) & (b), 741(t) & (b), 748 (t), Rolin Graphics, 748 (b), Morgan-Cain and Associates; 749 (t), Barbara Hoopes-Ambler, 749 (b), David Ashby; 751, (t) & (b), Morgan-Cain and Associates

Cover Ken Ross/FPG International; **Connect to Chemistry** (flask)K&C Fischer; **vi,** Jeff Smith/Fotosmith; **vii,** (t)Rick Doyle, (b)David W. Hamilton/The Image Bank; **viii,** (t)Timothy Fuller, (b)Peter Skinner/Photo Researchers; **viii-ix,** Jeff Smith/Fotosmith; **ix,** Richard Megna/Fundamental Photographs, (b)Jeff Smith/Fotosmith; **x,** Wayne Sproul/International Stock Photo; **xi,** (t)Jeff Smith/Fotosmith, (b)Dominic Oldershaw; **xii,** (t) Timothy Fuller, (b)Alfred Pasieka/Peter Arnold, Inc.; **xiii,** (t)Timothy Fuller, (c)Yoav Levy/PhotoTake NYC, (b)Richard Megna/Fundamental Photographs; **xiv,** (l)Sean Justice, (r)Doug Martin; **xv,** (t)Michael Tamborrino/FPG International, (b)Gordon Gahar/Lawrence Livermore Laboratory; **xvi,** Russell D. Curtis/Photo Researchers; **xvii, xviii,** Timothy Fuller; **xix,** Dominic Oldershaw; **xx,** Jeff Smith/The Image Bank; **xxi,** Timothy Fuller; **xxii,** (t)GCA/CNRI/PhotoTake NYC, (b)courtesy Insurance Institute for Highway Safety; **xxiii,** Jeff Smith/Fotosmith; **xxiv** David M. Allen; **xxv,** (t)SuperStock, used by permission of the artist's estate, (b)David Sutherland/Tony Stone Images; **2-3,** Jeff Smith/Fotosmith; **3,** Richard T. Nowitz/Photo Researchers; **4-5,** Sean Justice; **6,** Don Smetzer/Tony Stone Images; **7,** Jeff Smith/Fotosmith; **8,** T. Wilfit/The Image Bank; **9,** Timothy Fuller; **10,** Jeff Smith/Fotosmith; **11,** Franklin Over; **12,** Telegraph Colour Library/FPG International; **13,** Dominic Oldershaw; **14,** (tl tr)Franklin Over, (b)Visuals Unlimited/Charlie Heidecker; **16,** Sean Justice; **17,** Telegraph Colour Library/FPG International; **18, 19,** The Kobal Collection; **20,** KS Studios; **21,** Sean Justice; **22,** Thomas Veneklasen; **23,** Sean Justice; **24,** (bc)Thomas Veneklasen, (others)Timothy Fuller; **25,** Timothy Fuller; **26, 27,** Dominic Oldershaw; **28,** Patricia Clancey; **30,** Dominic Oldershaw; **32, 33,** Timothy Fuller; **34,** Jeff Smith/Fotosmith; **35,** National Bureau of Weights and Measures; **37,** Jeff Smith/Fotosmith; **39,** Timothy Fuller; **40,** Jeff Smith/Fotosmith; **41,** NASA; **43,** Jeff Smith/Fotosmith; **44,** (l)courtesy The Children's Museum, (tc)V.A.P Neal/Photo Researchers, (tr bc)Timothy Fuller, (br)Visuals Unlimited/National Bureau of Standards; **46,** Jeff Smith/Fotosmith; **52,** Timothy Fuller; **53,** (t)Dr. E.R. Degginger/Color-Pic, (b)Eunice Harris/Photo Researchers; **54,** SuperStock, used by permission of the artist's estate; **58,** Dr. E.R. Degginger/Color-Pic; **59,** KS Studios; **60-61,** Harold Lee Miller; **61,** Russell D. Curtis/Photo Researchers; **62-63,** Liaison International; **63,** Jeff Smith/Fotosmith; **64,** Yann Guichaoua/Vandystadt/Photo Researchers; **65,** Timothy Fuller; **66,** Jeff Smith/Fotosmith; **70,** StudiOhio; **71,** Timothy Fuller; **72,** Warren Faidley/International Stock Photo; **73,** NHRA Photo; **74,** Bettmann Newsphotos; **76,** courtesy Insurance Institute for Highway Safety; **77,** Bud Fowle; **78,** Tim DeFrisco/Allsport USA; **79,** (t)Timothy Fuller, (b)Harry Skull/Allsport USA; **80,** (t)Ben Rose/The Image Bank, (b)Romilly Lockyer/The Image Bank; **81, 82,** Jeff Smith/Fotosmith; **83,** Jonathan Daniel/Allsport USA; **84, 85,** NASA; **86,** Timothy Fuller; **87,** Doug Martin; **88,** David M. Allen; **92-93,** NASA/Peter Arnold, Inc.; **93,** Jeff Smith/Fotosmith; **94, 95,** Timothy Fuller; **96,** Peticolas-Megna/Fundamental Photographs; **97,** Timothy Fuller; **98,** (l)Bob Firth/International Stock Photo, (r)Warren Faidley/International Stock

Photo Credits

Photo; **99,** Steve Allen/Peter Arnold, Inc.; **100,** Sean Justice; **101,** (t)StudiOhio, (b)Richard Megna/Fundamental Photographs; **102,** David Madison Photography; **103,** Uniphoto; **104,** NASA/Airworks/Tom Stack & Associates; **105,** NASA/Peter Arnold, Inc.; **106, 107,** Dominic Oldershaw; **109,** Francesco Reginato/The Image Bank; **111,** (t)Focus On Sports, (b)StudiOhio; **112,** NASA/SuperStock; **113,** (t c)Timothy Fuller, (b)Rafael Macia/Photo Researchers; **114,** Jeff Smith/Fotosmith; **115,** (l)Jeff Smith/Fotosmith, (r) Dr. E.R. Degginger/Color-Pic; **116,** Phil Degginger/Color-Pic; **117,** Doug Martin; **118,** Stuart Brinin; **120,** The Stock Market; **122, 123, 124,** Dominic Oldershaw; **125,** David Madison Photography; **126,** (t)Timothy Fuller, (b)Dominic Oldershaw; **127, 128,** Dominic Oldershaw; **129,** Rick Doyle; **130,** Dominic Oldershaw; **135,** StudiOhio; **136, 137,** Dominic Oldershaw; **138,** Runk/Schoenberger from Grant Heilman; **140,** David Noble/FPG International; **141,** Dominic Oldershaw; **142,** PhotoTake NYC; **143,** Dominic Oldershaw; **144,** Robert J. Herko/The Image Bank; **146,** Eugene Fisher; **150, 151,** Timothy Fuller; **153,** (t)Timothy Fuller, (b)Steve Satusher/The Image Bank; **155,** Tom Mangelsen/Peter Arnold, Inc.; **156,** H. Abernathy/H. Armstrong Roberts; **157,** Dominic Oldershaw; **159,** Roberto Bruzadin; **160, 161, 162,** Timothy Fuller; **164,** Michael Salas/The Image Bank; **165,** PhotoTake NYC; **166,** Timothy Fuller; **169,** courtesy National Institute of Standards and Technology; **170,** Juan M. Silva/The Image Bank; **171,** Dominic Oldershaw; **172,** David W. Hamilton/The Image Bank; **174,** courtesy Pacific International Center for High Technology Research (PICHTR); **178-179,** Jeff Smith/Fotosmith; **179,** Timothy Fuller; **180,** (t cl cr)Timothy Fuller, (bl)Jeff Smith/Fotosmith,

(br)Sunstar/Photo Researchers; **184,** Timothy Fuller; **185, 186,** Jeff Smith/Fotosmith; **188,** (t)Jeff Smith/Fotosmith, (c)Timothy Fuller, (b)John P. Kelly/The Image Bank; **189,** (t b)Timothy Fuller, (c)Gary S. Chapman/The Image Bank; **190,** Bruno P. Zehnder/Peter Arnold, Inc.; **191, 192,** Hickson & Associates; **193,** (tl)StudiOhio, (tr)Bruce H. Frisch/Photo Researchers, (b)Dominic Oldershaw; **194,** (l)Timothy Fuller, (r)Aaron Haupt; **195,** Doug Martin; **196,** David Madison Photography; **198,** (l)Billy Stickland/Tony Stone Images, (r)Thomas Veneklasen; **201,** (t)Jeff Smith/Fotosmith, (b)Bob Daemmrich; **202,** Manfred Kage/Peter Arnold, Inc.; **204,** David Sutherland/Tony Stone Images; **209,** KS Studios; **210-211,** Lester Lefkowitz/Tony Stone Images; **211,** Skip Comer; **212-213,** Timothy Fuller; **213,** Jeff Smith/Fotosmith; **214,** Visuals Unlimited/John D. Cunningham; **215,** (l)Pat Lynch/Photo Researchers, (r)Jeff Smith/Fotosmith; **216,** (t)Barry Seidman/The Stock Market, (b)Timothy Fuller; **217,** Timothy Fuller; **218,** (t)Phil Degginger/NOAO/Color-Pic, (b)Space Telescope Science Institute/NASA/Science Photo Library/Photo Researchers; **219,** Timothy Fuller; **220,** Jeff Smith/Fotosmith; **221,** Timothy Fuller; **223,** Nicholas Foster/The Image Bank; **224,** Timothy Fuller; **225,** (l)Dominic Oldershaw, (r)Leonard Lessin/Peter Arnold, Inc.; **227,** Timothy Fuller; **228,** Jeff Smith/Fotosmith; **229,** Dominic Oldershaw; **230,** Bob Daemmrich; **231,** (l)Visuals Unlimited/Bill Kamin, (r)Peter Skinner/Photo Researchers; **232, through 236,** Timothy Fuller; **237,** Dominic Oldershaw; **238,** Jeff Smith/Fotosmith; **239,** StudiOhio; **240,** R. Schreiber; **242, 244-245,** Jeff Smith/Fotosmith; **245,** Timothy Fuller; **246,** Jeff Smith/Fotosmith; **247,** (t)Jeff Smith/Fotosmith, (b)Timothy

Photo Credits

Fuller; **249**, (t c)Jeff Smith/Fotosmith, (b)Timothy Fuller; **251**, Doug Martin; **253**, James Stevenson/Science Photo Library/Photo Researchers; **254**, Jeff Smith/Fotosmith; **255**, (t)Jeff Smith/Fotosmith, (bl)Visuals Unlimited/Arthur R. Hill, (br)Doug Martin; **256**, P&G Bowater/The Image Bank; **257**, John Brennels ©1990, DISCOVER Publications; **258**, (t)Visuals Unlimited/Richard Thorn, (b)David W. Hamilton/The Image Bank; **259**, **260**, **261**, Timothy Fuller; **262**, **263**, Jeff Smith/Fotosmith; **264**, David Noble/FPG International; **266**, Jeff Smith/Fotosmith; **267**, Tom McHugh/Photo Researchers; **268**, Mark Marten/NASA/Photo Reserachers; **268-269**, AP/Wide World Photos; **269**, Timothy Fuller; **270**, **272**, Jeff Smith/Fotosmith; **273**, Timothy Fuller; **275**, Doug Martin; **277**, Hank Morgan/Science Source/Photo Researchers; **278**, Timothy Fuller; **279**, **280**, Doug Martin; **283**, Jeff Smith/Fotosmith; **284**, Stamp from the Collection of Prof. C.M. Lang, Photography by Gary Shulfer, University of WI-Steven's Point: Russia 3608; **285**, Dr. E.R. Degginger/Color-Pic; **288**, (t)Jeff Smith/Fotosmith, (b)Timothy Fuller; **290**, Visuals Unlimited/IBMRL; **291**, (t)Manfred Kage/Peter Arnold, Inc., (b)Richard Megna/Fundamental Photographs; **292**, Fermilab Visual Media Services; **295**, Jeff Smith/Fotosmith; **296-297**, Tony Wiles/Tony Stone Images; **297**, **298**, Timothy Fuller; **299**, (l)Charles E. Zirkle, (c)Richard Megna/Fundamental Photographs, (r)Jeff Smith/Fotosmith; **300**, Timothy Fuller; **302**, First Image; **303**, StudiOhio; **304**, Richard Megna/Fundamental Photographs; **307**, Manfred Kage/Peter Arnold, Inc.; **309**, Stuart Brinin; **310**, **311**, **313**, Timothy Fuller; **314**, (l)Mercury Archives/The Image Bank, (r)H.R. Bramaz/Peter Arnold, Inc.; **319**, Jeff Smith/Fotosmith; **320**, Timothy Fuller; **322**, **323**, Jeff Smith/Fotosmith; **324**, (l)FPG International, (tr)Bettmann Archive, (br)UPI/Bettmann Newsphotos; **326-327**, Tim Courlas; **328-329**, SuperStock; **329**, Richard Megna/Fundamental Photographs; **330**, (l)Diane Schiumo/Fundamental Photographs, (r)Visuals Unlimited/Charles Sykes; **331**, Timothy Fuller; **332**, Richard Megna/Fundamental Photographs; **333**, (l)Doug Martin, (c)ZEFA/H. Armstrong Roberts, (r)StudiOhio; **334**, Andy Caulfield/The Image Bank; **335**, Mugshots/The Stock Market; **336**, (t)Jeff Smith/Fotosmith, (b)Timothy Fuller; **338**, EPRI/Science Source/Photo Researchers; **339**, Timothy Fuller; **340**, Mark Burnett/Photo Researchers; **341**, Annie Griffiths/Westlight; **342**, (t)Timothy Fuller, (b)Ben Simmons/The Stock Market; **343**, (t)Jeff Smith/Fotosmith, (b)Dr. E.R. Degginger/Color-Pic; **344**, Charles Steiner/International Stock Photo; **345**, **346**, Timothy Fuller; **347**, (t)Timothy Fuller, (b)Visuals Unlimited/Smithsonian Institution, A.J. Copley; **349**, (l)Timothy Fuller, (r)Doug Martin; **350**, (l)E.R. Degginger/Photo Researchers, (r)Gregory G. Dimijian/Photo Researchers; **351**, Ken Frick; **352**, **through 360**, Timothy Fuller; **362**, Ken Frick; **364**, Timothy Fuller; **365**, (l)Doug Martin, (r)Russell D. Curtis/Photo Researchers; **366**, Timothy Fuller; **367**, Ken Frick; **368**, **369**, Timothy Fuller; **370**, Jean Higgins/Unicorn Stock Photo; **371**, Visuals Unlimited/Link; **372**, Doug Martin; **373**, (l)Visuals Unlimited/David M. Phillips, (r)Ken Frick; **374**, Aaron Haupt; **376**, Timothy Fuller; **377**, (t)Ken Frick, (b)Bill Denison/Uniphoto; **378**, Wayne Sproul/International Stock Photo; **379**, (l)John M. Brunley/Photo Researchers, (r)Visuals Unlimited/William J. Weber; **380**, **381**, Timothy Fuller; **382**, Stuart Brinin; **384**, Aaron Haupt; **386-387**, courtesy Raytheon Aircraft; **387**, Jeff Smith/Fotosmith; **388**, Timothy

Fuller; **389**, (l r)Jeff Smith/Fotosmith, (c)Timothy Fuller; **390**, (tl)Dr. E.R. Degginger/Color-Pic, (others)Doug Martin; **391**, Visuals Unlimited/SIU; **392**, Smithsonian Institution; **393**, (t)Ken Frick, (bl)Brent Turner/BLT Productions, (br)Jeff Smith/Fotosmith; **394**, Timothy Fuller; **395**, Doug Martin; **396**, **399**, **400**, Timothy Fuller; **401**, Jeff Smith/Fotosmith; **402**, Timothy Fuller; **403**, Doug Martin; **404**, (t)David Madison/DUOMO, (b)Marvin E. Newman/The Image Bank; **405**, (t)Mark D. Phillips/Photo Researchers, (b)Timothy Fuller; **406**, Cory Warner; **409**, Dominic Oldershaw; **410**, Timothy Fuller; **412-413**, Laurence Parent; **413**, Simon Fraser/Science Photo Library/Photo Researchers; **414-415**, Wiley & Wales/Adventure Photo; **415**, Thomas Veneklasen; **416**, (l)Tate Gallery, London/Art Resource NY, (r)Norbert Wu; **417**, Mark Burnett; **418**, Sean Justice; **420**, Mark Burnett; **421**, **422**, Matt Meadows; **423**, Ed Taylor/FPG International; **424**, Sean Justice; **425**, Mark Burnett; **428**, Custom Medical Stock Photo; **429**, Richard Megna/Fundamental Photographs; **430**, Thomas Veneklasen; **431**, Matt Meadows; **432**, Jeff Smith/Fotosmith; **433**, Norbert Wu; **435**, Pictor/Uniphoto; **436**, Thomas Veneklasen; **438**, Norbert Wu; **439**, Leonard Lessin/Peter Arnold, Inc.; **440-441**, Visuals Unlimited/Jeff Greenberg; **441**, Timothy Fuller; **442**, Bettmann Archive; **443**, **444**, Timothy Fuller; **447**, NASA; **448**, Timothy Fuller; **451**, TSADO/NASA/Tom Stack & Associates; **452**, Peticolas-Megna/Fundamental Photographs; **454-455**, Timothy Fuller; **456**, Kent & Donna Dennen/Photo Researchers; **457**, AC Delco, General Motors/Peter Arnold, Inc.; **458**, Visuals Unlimited/Bernd Wittich; **459**, Timothy Fuller; **460**, SuperStock; **462**, Jeff Smith/Fotosmith; **463**, Timothy Fuller; **464-465**, Uniphoto; **465**, **466**, **467**, Dominic Oldershaw; **468**, Doug Martin; **470**, Dominic Oldershaw; **471**, Grant Heilman/Grant Heilman Photography; **474**, Dr. E.R. Degginger/Color-Pic; **476**, Dominic Oldershaw; **477**, Doug Martin; **482**, **486**, **487**, Timothy Fuller; **488**, Cory Warner; **492**, **493**, Thomas Veneklasen; **494-495**, Steve Jennings/LGI; **495**, Will & Deni McIntyre/Photo Researchers; **496-497**, Susan McCartney/Photo Researchers; **497**, Timothy Fuller; **498**, Guy Marche/FPG International; **502**, **503**, Timothy Fuller; **504**, **507**, Francois Gohier/Photo Researchers; **509**, NASA/Science Source/Photo Researchers; **511**, Dr. E.R. Degginger/Color-Pic; **512**, Timothy Fuller; **513**, StudiOhio; **514**, Robert Goldstein/Photo Researchers; **515**, PhotoTake NYC; **516**, **517**, Timothy Fuller; **518**, (l)Wide World Photos, (r)Timothy Fuller; **520**, courtesy CAPA, photo by D.R. Goff; **521**, SuperStock; **522**, Runk/Schoenberger from Grant Heilman; **526**, Pete Saloutos/The Stock Market; **527**, Dominic Oldershaw; **528**, Telegraph Colour Library/FPG International; **529**, **530**, Dominic Oldershaw; **531**, (t)Howard Sochurek/The Stock Market, (b)Alfred Pasieka/Peter Arnold, Inc.; **532**, Dominic Oldersahw; **533**, Richard Hutchings/Photo Researchers; **534**, (t)Timothy Fuller, (b)Scott Camazine/Photo Researchers; **535**, Alvis Upitis/The Image Bank; **536**, Thomas Veneklasen; **537**, Gabriel Covian/The Image Bank; **538**, Jeff Smith/Fotosmith; **539**, Timothy Fuller; **540**, CALVIN AND HOBBES ©1993, Bill Watterson./Dist. by UNIVERSAL PRESS SYNDICATE. Reprinted with permission. All rights reserved; **543-547**, Dominic Oldershaw; **548**, David Parker/Science Photo Library/Photo Researchers; **549**, Hank Morgan from Rainbow; **550**, Richard Laird/FPG International; **551**, Doug Martin; **552**, Dominic Oldershaw; **556**, **557**, Timothy Fuller; **559**,

StudiOhio; **560,** (t)John M. Roberts/The Stock Market, (b)Latent Images; **561,** (t)Dominic Oldershaw, (b)Timothy Fuller; **562,** Timothy Fuller; **563,** Matt Meadows; **564,** Dr. E.R. Degginger/Color-Pic; **568,** David Noble/FPG International; **568-569,** Telegraph Colour Library/FPG International; **570, 571,** Timothy Fuller; **572,** NASA photo via Consolidated News Pictures/Archive Photos; **574, 575,** Timothy Fuller; **577,** (t)ZEFA/The Stock Market, (b)Stan Sholik/FPG International; **578,** Will & Deni McIntyre/Photo Researchers; **579,** Bruce Ando/Tony Stone Images; **580,** Doug Martin; **581,** Dominic Oldershaw; **582,** J. Armstrong; **585, 586,** Timothy Fuller; **587,** Dominic Oldershaw; **588-589,** Bill Ross/ Westlight; **589,** Joseph Sohm/Chromosohm/ Photo Researchers; **590-591,** Timothy Fuller; **591,** Thomas Veneklasen; **594,** G. Randall/ FPG International; **595, 596,** Thomas Veneklasen; **598,** Jim Zuckerman/Westlight; **599,** Visuals Unlimited/Joe McDonald; **603,** Yoav Levy/PhotoTake NYC; **604,** Paul Silverman/Fundamental Photographs; **605, 607,** Thomas Veneklasen; **608, 609,** Richard Megna/Fundamental Photographs; **610, through 613,** Thomas Veneklasen; **616,** Sean Justice; **618,** Pat Haley/Hewlett-Packard Co., Sonoma County; **620,** Visuals Unlimited/S. Maslowski; **622-623,** Michael Yamashita; **623,** Thomas Veneklasen; **624,** Doug Martin; **625,** Richard Megna/Fundamental Photographs; **626,** Frank Cezus/Tony Stone Images; **629,** GCA/CNRI/PhotoTake NYC; **630,** Thomas Veneklasen; **632,** Jeff Smith/Fotosmith; **635, through 639,** Thomas Veneklasen; **640,** IBM Research/Peter Arnold, Inc.; **641,** H.R. Bramaz/Peter Arnold, Inc.; **645,** Timothy Fuller; **647,** Dominic Oldershaw; **647-648,** Timothy Fuller; **648,** Sean Justice; **650, 651,** Doug Martin; **652,** Sean Justice; **653,** Timothy Fuller; **656, 657,** Sean Justice; **659,** Moore School of Electrical Engineering, University of

PA; **661,** Dominic Oldershaw; **663,** Timothy Fuller; **664, 665, 666,** Dominic Oldershaw; **668,** courtesy Dr. Tridib Banerjee, photo by Irene Fertik; **673-674,** W. Cody/Westlight; **674,** Dominic Oldershaw; **674,** Timothy Fuller; **676,** Peticolas-Megna/Fundamental Photographs; **678,** courtesy Walters Art Gallery, Baltimore MD; **681,** Timothy Fuller; **683,** Bob Grieser/Uniphoto; **684, 685,** Timothy Fuller; **686,** Lawrence Berkeley Lab/Science Photo Library/Photo Researchers; **687,** (l)CERN, P. Loiez/Science Photo Library/Photo Researchers, (tr br)Richard Megna/Funda-mental Photographs; **688,** Hank Morgan/ Photo Researchers; **691,** NASA/PhotoTake NYC; **692,** SIU/Peter Arnold, Inc.; **693,** Michael Tamborrino/FPG International; **694,** Thomas Veneklasen; **696,** Visuals Unlimited/ Doug Sokell; **698-699,** Jim Wark/Peter Arnold, Inc.; **699,** Sean Justice; **700,** W.A. Logan/The Image Bank; **702, 703,** Jeff Smith/The Image Bank; **705,** Mason Morfit/FPG International; **706,** Edmund Nagele/FPG International; **707,** Jeff Kaufman/FPG International; **708,** Gordon Gahar/Lawrence Livermore Laboratory; **709,** Timothy Fuller; **711,** US DOE; **713,** Sean Justice; **714,** Jeff Divine/FPG International; **715,** (l)Spencer Swanger/Tom Stack & Associates, (r)Phil Degginger/Color-Pic; **716,** Franklin Over; **717,** Barry Griffiths/Photo Researchers; **718, 719,** Timothy Fuller; **720,** David M. Allen; **722,** Alex Bartel/FPG Interntional; **724,** Sean Justice; **725, 734,** Timothy Fuller; **735,** Thomas Veneklasen; **736,** Franklin Over; **737,** Dominic Oldershaw; **740-741,** Jeff Smith/Fotosmith; **742, 743,** Dominic Oldershaw; **744,** Phil Degginger/ Color-Pic; **746,** Timothy Fuller; **747,** Dominic Oldershaw; **750,** Thomas Veneklasen; **751,** Dominic Oldershaw; **752,** Jeff Smith/Foto-smith; **753,** Dominic Oldershaw.